CW00458240

THE

AUTOBIOGRAPHY OF A PHRENOLOGIST.

Geo Combe

Wanted men ʼs 1
3 ...

𝕸𝖞 𝕭𝖆𝖙𝖙𝖑𝖊 𝖋𝖔𝖗 𝕷𝖎𝖋𝖊.

THE AUTOBIOGRAPHY

OF

A PHRENOLOGIST.

EDITED BY

DAVID GEO. GOYDER, F. E. S.,

FORMERLY CURATOR OF THE MUSEUM OF THE GLASGOW PHRENOLOGICAL
SOCIETY, ETC. ETC.

' My rule is deliberately to consider, before I commence, whether the thing is practicable. If it be not practicable I do not attempt it; if it be practicable, I can accomplish it, if I give sufficient pains to it; and, having begun, I never stop till the thing is done.'—DR. HUNTER.

' As Authors are scattered through all ranks of society, among the governors and the governed, and the objects of their pu⋅ ⋅its are usually carried on by their own peculiar idiosyncrasy, we are deeply interested in the secret connection of the incidents of their lives with their intellectual habits, in the development of that predisposition which is ever working in characters of native force. In their felicities and their failures, and the fortunes which such men have shaped for themselves, and oftener for the world, we discover what is not found in Biographical Dictionaries—the history of the mind of the individual, and this constitutes the psychology of genius.'—D'ISRAELI.

' It is a hard and a nice thing for a man to speak of himself; it grates his own heart to say any thing of disparagement, and his readers' ears to hear anything of praise from him. There is no danger of my offending in this matter. Neither my mind, nor my body, nor my fortune allow me any materials for this vanity.'—COWLEY.

LONDON:
SIMPKIN, MARSHALL, AND CO., STATIONERS' HALL COURT.
MDCCCLVII.

IPSWICH :
PRINTED BY J. M. BURTON AND CO.

PREFACE.

In the following pages I present the reader with the story of 'MY BATTLE FOR LIFE.' I have thought it best to detail the vicissitudes in my experience in a plain unvarnished style, and to relate the occurrences as they transpired in the simple language of truth.

Like most persons whose temperaments have a sanguine-nervous predominance, I am, by nature, of a social and cheerful disposition; but since the year 1830 my deafness has so increased as to operate as a bar to social intercourse. A deaf person is always more or less a 'bore' in company. This has been a matter of continual experience with me, and I have often keenly felt that I was indeed solitary in the midst of society. Under these circumstances I have thrown myself almost entirely upon my books. These have been

b

my most constant and dearest companions. Through them, I have studied not only things but mankind. Through them, I have made myself acquainted, not only with literature and science, but also with the characters of their authors. This latter subject has been one of my principal sources of enjoyment, and the reader will find various examples in the following pages. Many of the opinions formed may be erroneous, but I have not set down 'aught in malice.' In single-ness of purpose, I trust, I have expressed my single thought.

With regard to the religious opinions herein advanced, I conceive they require no apology. I have examined most of the creeds of Christendom, and, after a delibe-rate investigation, I have chosen that which I hold to be the Lord's truth, the fundamental principle of which is Love—love to God above all things and charity to my neighbor. Upon this I have staked my salvation. Of others I do not pretend to judge—to their own Master they must stand or fall.

As a minister of the Lord's New Church, I have endeavored to the best of my ability to fulfil the promise made at the altar at my ordination. I have never sought high pecuniary reward for my labor, and have often ministered gratuitously. I can say with pride—and surely this may be pardoned—that during the long period of thirty-six years, I have not been as many days, certainly not as many weeks, off my duty, including periods of sickness. My interest in this matter has probably given a certain coloring to all that I have written, and I do not regret it.

And now, dear reader, before leading you to the threshold of my mortal life, permit me to say that, standing upon the threshold of my immortal life—at sixty-two years of age—I am still strong 'to labor,' and patient 'to wait' for the coming of the hour which shall disclose the mystery of the Present, by unveiling the mystery of the Future.

D. G. G.

Ipswich,
April 1st, 1857.

TO

WM. WEIR, ESQ., M.D.,

YSICIAN AND LECTURER ON CLINICAL MEDICINE TO THE GLASGOW ROYAL
INFIRMARY, FORMERLY PRESIDENT OF THE PHRENOLOGICAL SOCIETY, ETC.;

AND TO

JAMES MACLELLAND, ESQ., F.E.S.,

PRESIDENT OF THE INSTITUTION OF ACCOUNTANTS IN GLASGOW,
MAGISTRATE OF THE COUNTY OF LANARK, AND FORMERLY PRESIDENT OF
THE GLASGOW PHRENOLOGICAL SOCIETY ;

NDER WHOSE UNITED AUSPICES THE AUTHOR PURSUED HIS

PHRENOLOGICAL INVESTIGATIONS, AND TO

WHOSE FOSTERING PATRONAGE HE OWES MUCH OF THE

JCCESS WHICH HAS CROWNED HIS PHRENOLOGICAL LABORS,

THE FOLLOWING

Work is most Respectfully Dedicated,

BY

THE AUTHOR.

IPSWICH,
March, 1857.

ENGRAVINGS.

CONTENTS.

THE

AUTOBIOGRAPHY OF A PHRENOLOGIST.

First Period:

FROM BIRTH TILL NINE YEARS OF AGE.
1796 TO 1805.

'The earthly life is a wondrous maze,
  A labyrinth which all must thread;
Some groping onward through darksome ways,
  Some scorched by the sun o'erhead.
Some amid meadows and quiet streams
  Do a pleasant path pursue:
On craggy mountains, where lightning gleams,
  Some daily their toil renew.

'Some seek a dwelling in murky caves;
  Some lord it in lofty towers;
With storms some wrestle on ocean waves,
  Some nestle in peaceful bowers!
But dark or sunny, in peace or strife,
  As dwelling or path may be,
To each is given a clue of life,
  To lead to the "far countrie."'

MARY C. HUME.

NEAR to the then most aristocratic street in the city of Westminster (termed Great George Street), there stood, sixty years since, a large court, built in the form of a cross, and used in the good old days of Catholicism as a residence for many of the 'holy monks and friars,' whose duty lay so frequently at the noble Abbey Church dedicated to St. Peter. This court terminated

1

at one end in a narrow lane, opening again into a broad space, and termed respectively the 'Narrow' and 'Broad Sanctuary,' used, as the name imports, as a refuge for those whose crimes or misfortunes drove them into the security and protection of 'Holy Mother Church'; and which, at the time I speak of, was the resort of many individuals not of the most estimable character, but who here seemed still to congregate, though the freedom from arrest had long since been abolished. The other end of the court terminated in Princes Street, which still exists and bears its original name, though the court and the sanctuaries have long since been rased to the ground, and numbered among the things that were.

The termination of the court in Princes Street was nearly opposite to another court, handsomely paved, named Princes Court, in which were wont to reside, during the Parliamentary Session, many of the country members. This court led into St. James's Park, towards that part termed Bird-Cage Walk, and in which, at that time, there was going on one uninterrupted drill of recruits. At the corner of Prince's Court was a large Hotel, or Story's Gate Tavern, as it was and is still called, and was the resort of many of the gentlemen members before alluded to, and was besides frequented by some of the most eminent men of the last century and the beginning of the present.

Directly opposite the Abbey Church, which was situated in front of the Broad Sanctuary before mentioned, there stood, and still stands, a very busy, a very dirty, very crowded, and very vile street, called Tothill Street; and if I have described it in the superlative degree, it is no more than it deserves, for it is, in truth, the superlative of wickedness; but as I shall have occasion again to speak about this street, and its purlieus, I shall pass over it now by merely naming it.

In the court before mentioned, and which rejoiced in the name of 'Angel's Court,' probably on account of the angels who were supposed to be on visiting terms with the 'holy monks and friars' who inhabited it,———I was born on the ———. But, stop! there 'is a dispute about the day of my birth, which has never been settled; and as I have no recollection of the precise time myself, I am apprehensive that this important event will always remain in doubt. I was born, then, in the year 1796. There was, so I have been informed, no small stir and commotion in the house at the time, but, whether just before midnight, or just after it, has never been accurately settled. Some contend that it was just before; and if that is the truth, on the 29th of February, 1852, I saw my fifteenth birthday, a ripe youth, with sons and daughters who have seen more birthdays, and, consequently, are older than myself. But some contend that my birthday was after midnight; that I was ushered into the world on the day of the patron saint of Wales, David; that I had brought my name with me, and David was I accordingly named; consequently, that I was born on the 1st of March, 1796, and, therefore, I am now in my sixtieth year; and so my sons and daughters will not have seen more birthdays than myself.

I think it will be advisable for me to settle this matter summarily, and say, I was born March 1st, 1796, in the aforesaid Angel's Court. What passed from this time until I was nearly three years of age, I cannot precisely remember—perhaps I did not cultivate the organ most necessary—perhaps those who had the charge of me were ignorant of its existence, or perhaps it had not developed itself; yet, as long as I can recollect, I have always been celebrated for possessing a good memory. At all events, at or about the age of three years, a circumstance occurred of which I have the most perfect recollection—it was the death of my father. I knew not the loss I had sustained, and I perhaps should not have remembered this event but for the pageant associated with it. My father belonged to the 'Independent Order of Odd Fellows,' an 'order' which at that time enrolled among its members some of the gayest young men of the aristocracy; and I have since been told that some of my relations have sat in the same lodge with the then Prince of Wales (late George IV.) My father was high in favor among this fraternity, and his remains were honored by a public funeral ; and it was this pageant that so forcibly impressed upon my memory my father's death. I saw the whole procession from the window of a neighbor's house in the Court, to which I had been removed, I suppose, to be out of the way. The coffin was preceded by two brothers, as they were called, bearing drawn swords ; then followed a long procession, some before, some after the coffin, with sashes, aprons, and medals of distinction, some of them sparkling with gems, or, as is most probable, with Bristol stones. I thought it a very grand sight, but I have since had my thoughts changed materially. However, this is the first public event which I remember, and the event left me an orphan, and my mother burdened with a heavy family of sons, of whom I was the youngest.

I think the next public event that impressed me was the Peace of 1802, and I remember it on account of the firing of the park guns, and the general illumination. Such demonstrations of joy were then made in colored glass lamps at the public offices, and in small tallow candles from the windows of private houses ! I remember my mother's house was illuminated in the latter way ; and as I rambled up and down the court, I was marvellously pleased with the display of candles in the neighbors' houses. But over the door of the Story's Gate Tavern, the regal star, and the royal initials of 'G. R.,' struck me as inconceivably grand. This grandeur, however, sunk into insignificance by a view of the devices at the Horse Guards and Admiralty. But grand as all this appeared to me, at the period of which I write, and grand as it undoubtedly was to the old people then living, to such as now behold the blaze of light in the splendid shops of our large cities, it would, could they have seen and compared it, have proved a very paltry affair indeed. Still it is deserving of note, if it be but to show the progress we have made in lighting up large towns, by the knowledge of chemistry.

How long this Peace lasted, and upon what a hollow foundation it was based, may be learned from the history of the times. But when it ceased, it introduced a military mania, which has never since, I think, had a parallel in Britain. The first threatened invasion of Napoleon, the great colossus of war, at the commencement of the present century, appeared to call upon all men—aye, and upon all boys, too—to arm. Nor were the woman-kind at all lukewarm in this destructive furor ; such an embroidering of standards by the quality dames of the land, and such a making of regimentals among the humbler class, was, perhaps, never known. Then almost every trade had its company of volunteers, who made a wonderful display of red coats, plumed helmets, and pipe-clay belts, with little drummers and fifers in Grenadier caps almost as large as themselves, and bending beneath the united weight of caps, belts, swords, and drums, looking very fierce, and being the envy and admiration of all the little boys that followed them. And what could the little boys do but imitate the boys of larger growth ?

Accordingly, there sprung up innumerable ragged regiments of boys, armed with wooden swords, having splendid bands of old tin kettles and penny whistles, 'marching to the battle-field,' with old blood-red pocket handkerchiefs tied on the heads of long sticks, which, being shaken out to the breeze, having previously seen good service by the accommodation that had been rendered to their fathers' and mothers' noses, were so well riddled into holes, as to convey an idea of the hard fought fields they had seen, and the honorable scars they had acquired in the battle of the noses. Ah ! the boys were valiant then, and fierce as well as valiant ! It was well the French thought better than to invade ; for had they at that period arrived in Britain, the very infants would have made mincemeat of them.

But to the men this military mania was no child's play. By sea as well as by land, nothing was thought of but reducing the population by violent means. Pressgangs were rife in Westminster, and my poor mother trembled lest I should be seized and made a powder monkey of ; and, truly, numbers of children were kidnapped and conveyed on board ship for this barbarous purpose. This may be denied, but it is a fact nevertheless. But pressing for sea was carried on principally in the neighborhood of Wapping, the London Docks, and other resorts for seamen ; it was recruiting that principally distinguished the neighborhood of Westminster. Children were constantly taken from their parents, and with the consent of parents, too, to become drum boys ; and often have I wished that I could play the fife, and had long hair, that, I might go and offer myself for the band. In short, there was one universal school of soldiers ; war was in every one's mouth ; and while an Englishman made nothing of killing peaceably—that is, by words—his three, or even seven Frenchmen, he was a poor creature of a boy who did not think himself a match for two. I well remember the warlike frenzy that everywhere prevailed, and Government, by its agents, quietly fanned the flame, and secretly heaped on fuel to keep the fire burning. Warlike and patriotic songs were sung in all public thoroughfares, in which young men were stimulated to enter the army, and, rather than become the slaves of the French, die in the field of glory. They were taught to think a victory over the French cheaply bought with life.

Many and curious were the means resorted to by Government to induce young men to enlist—some of them not of the most creditable kind—and, once enlisted, it was difficult indeed to purchase off the recruit, even at the most extravagant price. But there seemed nothing more effectual than the composition of songs to keep this fire or frenzy alive. These songs were set to martial music, but so adapted to the taste of the multitude, as to be the finest specimens of doggrel that can well be conceived.

Military music I have always had a passion for, nor have I lost my zest for it up to the present day ; but now that experience has from history pointed out the horrors of war, I must say that I hate everything connected with it except its music.

When a young man was enlisted, he was immediately turned over to the tender mercies of the corporal or drill sergeant. He was trained by incessant drilling, and when qualified, drafted off, marched to the nearest depôt, shipped, and perhaps never heard of more. Hour after hour have I attended these parties at drill, and watched all their motions, and sighed and wished that I was old enough to take my place among them ; and I do believe that the watching of the men at drill tended to foster that combative feeling of which in youth I had no inconsiderable share.

My memory turns back upon this period with wonderful freshness ; and the military preparations in Bird-Cage Walk, St. James's Park, are still fresh in my recollection. The constant work of drilling drew together whole armies of boys to witness and to admire, as well as to lament they were not yet of age to join the army of heroes. At this time it was a *sine qua non* for the army to wear long hair—ques, or pig-tails, as they were called—and as it was then fashionable to wear hair powder, something as nearly as could possibly resemble it was introduced into the army. Hair powder being too expensive for the common soldiery, they had their heads first well plastered with soap, and then a flour bag was shaken over the head, and the flour adhering to the soap, presented a well whitened crop of hair. The soldiers then wore curious long coats, and huge cocked hats ; and on state occasions they rejoiced in long white jean gaiters, buttoned with numerous bone buttons, dyed black ; and gartered below the knee with a highly polished black leather strap, the gaiter itself being continued half way up the thigh, where it was tightly buttoned. 'Bird-Cage Walk,' so called because originally there were cages of an aviary among

the trees which bordered it, and which led towards the
before-mentioned *Story's Gate,* was the great field of drill.
From daylight in the morning till the twilight of evening,
and sometimes (as a punishment) afterwards, the work of
preparing men as food for gunpowder was carried on.
Marches and counter-marches, advancing and retreating,
and mimic fighting, accompanied by a huge consumption
of bone drivers, showed how often the triggers had been
drawn, and the bone drivers, which were shaped like
flints, snapped by the repeated collision of the steel of
the musket.   In those days percussion caps were unknown, and the musket, when really used in its mur-
derous work, was fired by the spark of a flint falling
into the pan of the musket, which contained a priming
of powder, communicating with the barrel, and so driving
its missile of destruction.

There was nothing heard of but *war — war —
war!* As before hinted, all songs composed for the
common people had a martial bearing; many, perhaps most of them, were doggrel in versification, but
the music to which they were set was enspiriting in
the highest degree; and even those who had been basely
inveigled into the ranks of the army (and there were
many such) caught enthusiasm from the enspiriting
strains; and from the words being well adapted to the
calibre of their understandings, and which made greatness
of soul to consist in being able to destroy the greatest
number of human beings, they soon became contented
with their lot, and went to the field of glory in hope of
returning captains at least.   The song of 'The Awkward
Recruit' was a great favorite, and while it created roars
of laughter at the blunders of the young soldier, it yet
tended to excite the enthusiasm of the very man it
ridiculed. Some of the allusions in this song are still
fresh in my memory, and I have recently visited the scenes
where they were first insinuated into my mind. I will
cite a few of them.

THE AWKWARD RECRUIT.

'Behold poor Will—just come from drill;
  Not long ago I listed;
I sold my cart to pay the smart,
  But money they resisted.
I can't tell what will be my lot,
  But think it mighty odd, sir,
That they should spy a lad like I
  Among their awkward squad, sir.

'I walked and run, with Corporal Gun,
  And wore three pairs of shoes out;
My feet he caned, and almost lamed,
  To make me turn my toes out.
And then the soap and flour too
  Was plastered on my head, sir;
But for my king and country
  I'll fight until I'm dead, sir.

'And now I'm drill'd, and so well filled,
  And padded, that I'm bigger;
Now why mayn't I, in battle try?
  Sure I can pull a trigger.
It is my will the French to kill;
  I'd do it with all my heart, sir;
Perhaps a recruit might chance to shoot
  Great General Buonaparte, sir.

'If I should kill that great Frenchman
  My country'd be befriended,
'Twould be a thunderbolt to France,
  And make the war be ended.
No doubt but I should Captain be;
  Ah! that's a pretty thing, sir;
I'd air my throat from morn till night,
  Shouting, "God save the King!" sir.

'Zounds, now my blood begins to rise;
  It shows that I'm a Briton;
And if the French should dare to land,
  Huzza! my boys! we'll spit 'em.
Each man must to his motto stand
  And that you know's a lion.
England will fight 'em heart and hand,
  And at 'em and defy 'em.'

Such was the character of 'Songs for the Million'—

' *Long, long ago* '—evidence of the animalism of the **age,** and of the lion-like courage which animated the **people** sixty years since.

The songs for the navy were of an equally enspiriting kind; but many of them were much superior in sentiment, in composition, and in tone, to those produced for **the** army.   This was particularly the case with the songs composed by Charles Dibdin.   A captain in the merchant service expressed to a friend of mine his belief that these songs (namely, Dibdin's) made more sailors than any other single cause whatever.

Charles Dibdin was born at Southampton on the 15th of March, 1745.   Being intended for the church, he was placed at Winchester College.   His early love of music recommended him to the notice of the organist of the cathedral, from whom he received some instructions, and these were the whole amount of his education in the art ; such technical knowledge as he possessed having been acquired almost entirely by his own efforts.   His love of music led him to adopt it as a profession.   He was first employed in London as a chorus singer at Covent Garden, where his earliest theatrical work, a little pastoral drama, called ' The Shepherd's Artifice,' was produced in 1762, when he was seventeen.   This was followed by a long series of pieces, among which are ' The Padlock,' ' The Quaker,' ' The Waterman,' ' The Islanders,' and several others, which rank among the standard works of the English Musical Drama.   Notwithstanding the success of these productions, he was always in difficulties, and in 1788, with the view of bettering his fortune, he sailed for India.   Being wind-bound at Torbay, he suddenly thought of giving a sort of lecture, intermixed with songs, which he called ' The Whim of the Moment.' Its reception induced him to give up thoughts of his voyage, and this was the origin of the entertainments which he continued to give for many years in London, and throughout the kingdom, and for which many of his finest songs (his sea songs especially) were written.   In

1803 he received a pension from Government, in consideration of the beneficial effects produced in the navy by these spirit-stirring lyrics, but it was withdrawn a few years afterwards. (See Howe's 'British Songs for the Navy.') As a contrast to the 'Awkward Recruit,' I will cite one of Dibdin's, which, besides being well adapted to inspire nautical heroism, contains many beautiful sentiments; the music, too, has always been admired.

LOVELY NAN.

' Sweet is the ship that's under sail,
Spreads her white bosom to the gale.
   Sweet, oh! sweet's the flowing can!
Sweet to poise the laboring oar,
That tugs us to our native shore,
   When the boatswain pipes the barge to man.
Sweet sailing with a favoring breeze;
But, oh! much sweeter than all these,
   Is Jack's delight with his lovely Nan.

' The needle, faithful to the north,
To show of constancy the worth,
   A curious lesson teaches man:
The needle time may rust, a squall
Capsize the binnacle and all,
   Let seamanship do all it can.
My love in worth shall higher rise!
Nor time shall rust, nor squalls capsize
   My faith and truth to lovely Nan.

' When in the bilboes I was penn'd,
For serving of a worthless friend,
   And every creature from me ran;
No ship performing quarantine
Was ever as deserted seen,
   None hail'd me, woman, child, or man;
But though false friendship's sails were furl'd,
Though cut adrift by all the world,
   I'd all the world in lovely Nan.

' I love my duty, love my friend,
Love truth and merit to defend,
   To moan their loss who hazard ran;

I love to take an honest part,
Love beauty with a spotless heart,
  By manners love to show the man;
To sail through life by honor's breeze;
'Twas all along of loving these,
  First made me doat on lovely Nan.'

But to return to my narrative. I have, when regi
ments were drafted for foreign service, often stood a
Story's Gate aforesaid, and seen the troops defile through,
with martial music playing, and standards floating on the
breeze. I have watched them, and followed them to the
bridge of Westminster, beyond which I was forbidden to
stray; and I have wondered to what unknown country
that bridge led. Then have I again strayed back to the
park—again loitered hours in watching the recruits at
drill, who, in their turn, were drafted off in a similar
manner, when sufficiently instructed.

But in the parks what numerous happy hours have I
spent! All the different walks were to me as familiar as
the court in which was my mother's house. The Green
Park, Constitution Hill, Buckingham House—now a
royal palace—the old Brick Palace of St. James's, the
Malls, the Parade, the before-mentioned Bird-Cage Walk,
the Canal in front of the Horse Guards, the Artillery
House, the Quart Pots, as they were termed (small pieces
of artillery fired on rejoicing days, or on occasion of victories over the French) Spring Gardens, Gwydyr House,
of the proprietor of which I believe I am some hundred-
and-fifty-sixth cousin, *et hoc genus omne.*

A few months since I again visited all these localities,
but many of them were as much changed as myself.
Some of the noble mansions, however, still remain—
Gwydyr House among them—but not a vestige of Carlton
House, the favorite residence of George iv., when Prince
of Wales. I stopped at the Horse Guards, to try if I
could hear the music of the old clock. Yes—I did
hear it! The chimes are still the old familiar sounds.
They fell upon my ears as the voices of old friends,

from whom I had long been separated, and whom I had never anticipated I should hear again. The deep tone of the War Office clock proclaims still, and with a voice seemingly unimpaired by years, the steady flight of Old Time ; and though its tones fell *not* on my ears with the force 'of other days,' it still was the voice of the same dear old clock, and it brought back associations mingled with much pain and many bitter feelings, some of which I may, perhaps, detail at the proper time and place ; but, on the whole, I listened to the chimes of that dear old clock with more of pleasure than of pain. I cannot describe its sound, but my memory assured me there was no change in the music of that old clock.

But I must not so often digress. When sated with the parks, the music of the military bands, the drilling of the recruits, and the departure of the troops for active service, I used to spend much of my time in the old Abbey Church. I delighted in the cloisters; and as I saw the processions of the choristers, the canons, and the prebendaries in their white surplices, I thought how I should like to be a priest, and be constantly engaged in the services of the Abbey Church.

I cannot tell how or when I learned to read. I have not the slightest recollection of any one teaching me my letters—doubtless, this was the work of my good mother —but I do not remember the time when I was unable to read ; and next to the delight which I took in military music, and strolling in the parks, I used to experience intense pleasure in reading the Church Service out of my mother's large Prayer Book, and I well remember that this pleasure was increased, when I was allowed to throw a table-cloth over my shoulders, which gratified me as much as if it were a surplice. Again and again have I heard the deep tones of the noble organ in the Abbey Church, while sitting in my mother's house—this house being a considerable distance from the church— and I have started up and ran off to enjoy the sublime music. Music has ever been my passion. Even now,

when everything else falls upon my ears as though th
tympanum were but so much lead, music lights up m
countenance with joy; its sweet sounds appear to penetrat
my otherwise dull sense ; and if I were closely noticed
while under its soothing influence, my moist eye would
give evidence of the power it has over my affections.   I
am fully of the opinion of our immortal bard, that

'The man that hath not music in his soul,
And is not moved by concord of sweet sounds,
Is fit for treasons, stratagems, and spoils ;
Let no such man be trusted.'

My veneration for the old Abbey was deep, fervent,
and solemn, and that veneration still clings to me.   Its
wonderful extent, its stupendous height, the massy pillars
which support the roof, the sculptured marble monuments
with which it abounds, its gorgeous chapels (that of Henry
VII. I particularly remember);   its   antique wonder-
inspiring waxwork, among which was the maid of honor
who pricked her finger with a needle, and bled to death—
a just punishment, I was told, for working on the Sabbath
day; its cluster of poetic monuments, giving the name of
'Poet's Corner' to the place where the ashes of that
imaginative race rests; and its grand chancel, where
service was performed every day, and where I have so
often heard

'the pealing organ blow
To the full-voiced choir below' ;

all, all steal over my memory at the present day, making
me mourn over the loss of that delightful sense, which
drank in, in early life, such delicious floods of sacred
harmony.   Yes ! the loss of hearing, next to the loss of
sight, must be the most severe privation that man can be
subjected to.   But it will not do to dwell longer on this
privation, or to think what I have lost by it.   It must be
permitted for a wise purpose.

I was now seven years of age, with a growing reputation for tenacity of memory.   I was fond of listening to

the tales that were told in my presence. I would treasure
up the chief incidents, and then invent others, and weave
them into tales, so that at this age I was always welcome
in the evening to the boys of the court. At this time,
and for years previous, the name of Pitt was familiar in
every one's mouth, and his portrait was universally seen
in all the picture shops. He was most unmercifully
caricatured and satirized. Every measure that he
brought forward was sure to call forth a host of satirists,
and he was as easily known for his long nose as the
Duke of Wellington was by his hooked one. He was
universally hated by the poorer people for his tax-
inventing propensities, while those who had the tact to
satirize him, did so without remorse, and doubtless were
well paid for it. A name with so notorious a reputation
could not escape my open ears, and his portrait—always
with his distinguishing nose, however—was presented
under every variety of shape to the public gaze. I
recollect seeing an old caricature (it was old then, inasmuch as it was originally published at the first addition,
by Pitt, to the Salt Tax *), the point of which I could
not then understand, but it was universally admired. A
cook in a gentleman's kitchen was represented as preparing dinner for a large party, and in the midst of her
labor repairs to the salt-box for a handful of salt, which,
upon reaching, up starts the lid of the box, and out pops
the head of Pitt, long nose and all, with the exclamation—' Ah, Cookie, how do you do !' Starting back with
affright, the poor cook exclaims—' The deuce take the
fellow, he's got into the salt-box now.'

Never was there a man so severely lampooned as well
as caricatured as William Pitt. On one occasion, when
he had brought into the House a very obnoxious Budget,
a host of anonymous pamphlets were issued, some of them
exceedingly biting and caustic. I recollect the substance
of one which I have in vain attempted to procure a copy

* The Salt Tax was originally imposed in the reign of Queen Anne,
at 2s. 6d. per cwt. It was increased by Pitt to 5s., and in 1808, to 15s.

.of, and, as perhaps it may have found its way into t᷾
tomb of all the Capulets, I will try to set down as much
it as is still in my memory. It was entitled :

'The Tenth Chapter of the Acts of th᷾ Chancellor of the Exchequer.'

' Now it came to pass after these things, that the᷾
arose up a man out of the tribe of Chatham, whose nan᷾
was Pitt, and in process of time he became Chancellor ᷾
the Exchequer. With respect to his chin he was
Nazarite, for no razor had come thereon. Howbeit, no᷾
withstanding he was but a youth, the princes, and th᷾
nobles, and the knights, and the squires, and they o
whose heads the almond tree did flourish, bowed dow᷾
before him. His voice prevailed mightily in the assembl᷾
of the congregation, and he became a man of renowr᷾
And when his heart was swollen with pride, he sai᷾
within himself—Go to, now ; behold ! I will show th᷾
great power and dominion which I have over this people
and will load them with taxes—obnoxious, partial, an᷾
oppressive. And because by trade this nation prospereth
I will, therefore, tax trade ; and the taxing shall not fal
on the rich and opulent merchant, whose stomach i᷾
crammed with turtle, and who fareth sumptuously ever᷾
day ; because he could easily afford it, verily, he shall no᷾
pay a mite. But it shall fall heavily on the poor indus·
trious shopkeeper, who is driven into the front streets t᷾
expose his wares, who groaneth under burthens too
grievous to be borne, whose house rent is so high that i᷾
keepeth him poor continually ; therefore shall his burthen
be increased by the heavy tax wherewith I will tax him.
And it shall come to pass, that when one asketh me in
time to come, saying, Wherefore dost thou thus oppress
the poor, and drive the needy from their dwelling, and
shut the door of thine ear against their petitions ? that I
will in that day laugh them to scorn ; and because the᷾

leed can by no means be justified, I will say, It is my rumor. Do I not assuredly know that I have power to do all things with this people, by means of the majority which I have in the House, even by means of the men of Belial, who vote against conviction, and sell their country for gold? Then went he straightway into the assembly of the congregation, he and his Secretary Rose,* who is accounted little less than his echo, and he opened his Budget; and the opening of his Budget was as the opening of the box of Pandora, pregnant with plagues. And he spake of one tax, and of another tax, and they answered him to never a word, though the congregation marvelled greatly. At length he cometh to the tax which taxeth the weaker vessel, even the damsel that administereth to the convenience of her master, that getteth up small linen, and putteth her hand to anything. Then the whole congregation rose up as one man, and murmured against the Chancellor of the Exchequer; and they looked on Rose the Secretary, and said, Henceforth thou shalt no more be called the Rose of Sharon, neither shall Pitt be accounted any more the lily of the valley among the daughters of this isle; but ye shall be a bye-word and a reproach among all females whithersoever ye go. And after one had spake on this manner, and another on that, they rose up and departed, many to the gaming table, where they lost the inheritance of their fathers, and some to the harlot, who is subtle of heart, and one or two went unto their own wives. But the Chancellor of the Exchequer cheered his heart with a chapter in the Book of Numbers. And he called unto him his secretary, and said unto him, " Rose ! " and he answered, " Here am I." And he said unto him, " Go to, now ; write me circular letters to each of those whose names I shall give thee ; they shall be even written in letters of gold ; and this is the form of the letters which shall be written : Pensions, and places, and honors, and titles. And thou shalt write below, If ye hope for these, do as I bid ye. And with these will

* The late Right. Hon. G. Rose.

2

I win the hearts of the members of the Lower House for I perceive an opposition arising to my taxes, which, nevertheless, I am determined to carry through." So the Secretary, after having received his instructions, departed to write the letters.

‘And early the next morning, when the barbers, the quidnuncs, and the politicians read the contents of the Budget, they rose up as one man, and murmured against the Chancellor of the Exchequer. And they said one to another, Verily, we are sold for bond servants, both we, and our wives, and also our little ones ; and it shall come to pass in time to come, when any of our sons shall attempt to get into trade, that so many are the taxes thrown in the way, it will be next to madness to attempt it. Go to : let us choose a chairman, and have a committee, and let us draw up a petition, and go to this great man, the Chancellor of the Exchequer. Who knows but he may listen to our prayers, and turn away the fierce anger which he hath devised against us, and spare the remnant that are left : and it seemed good unto them to do so. So they gathered themselves together : many at the tavern called the Paul's Head Tavern, and others at the Judgment Hall at Westminster, as thou goest to the Abbey. And they chose a chairman, who opened the assembly. And one spake on this manner, and another on that manner, and there was a confusion of tongues, and much speechifying. And so it was that finally they drew up the petition, and brake up the assembly. And early the next morning they that bare the petition came into the presence of the Chancellor of the Exchequer, with their faces shaved, their wigs floured, and staves in their hands ; and they bowed down their heads, and did obeisance ; and they delivered the petition to the Chancellor, who delivered it to the Secretary, who delivered it to the Scribe, who delivered it to the Porter, who delivered it to the Devil (query— Printer's Devil ?), who published it in the newspapers. Then these men lifted up their voices with one consent, and said : "O Pitt, live for ever ! We, thy servants, the barbers, the bakers, the butchers, the fishmongers, the cock milliners, the hen milliners, and all kinds of trades-folks, are come before thee. We cannot pay thy taxes, neither can we furnish thee with the golden images which thou requirest at our hands ; wherefore, then, shouldest thou set thy face against us, even the poor shopkeepers of this city, to destroy us ? The occupation of thy servants doth verily oblige us to take up our abode in the front streets of the city, it proceedeth not from choice, neither from pride, nor is our renting a large house proof of our riches : but, contrariwise, it keepeth poor continually ; wherefore spare thy servants, and let our prayer prevail for the remnant that are left." Then the Chancellor of the Exchequer answered and said unto them : " Ye are idle—ye are idle ! Do I not assuredly know that ye will put the tax upon your customers, by raising the price of your commodities ?" And the men answered and said : "We cannot put the tax upon customers ; because, although thy servants are in general very poor, yet there are to be found, thinly scattered up and down among us, men of each profession who have amassed large wealth by the profits of their great returns ; these men will not raise the price of their commodities, and, of course, be able to undersell thy servants. And we do know of a verity, that the fair and delicate women of this isle, who would not put forth their hands for delicacy, even their eyes shall be evil against us, even the poor shopkeepers of this city ; for they will issue forth with their chariots and horses, and an exceeding great train, and pass a whole summer's day in cheapening a pair of gloves." Then the Chancellor of the Exchequer wearied himself for an answer to these men, and found none. So he looked on Rose the Secretary, and he showed them the way to the lobby, and the porter, who waited at the gate, shut the door upon them. And they spake one to another, and said, " Our hope is now crushed for ever." So they departed. And, behold ! they were very sorrowful, and many of them lifted up their voices and wept sore.

'Then I looked forward with my mind's eye to see what should come to pass. And I beheld London, that beautiful city, whereunto all the merchants of the earth were wont to bring their traffic, and lo! where trade once flourished, the grass grew. And all the shops which were aforetime portrayed with scarlet, and purple, and divers colors, the works of the hands of the cunning workmen, were deserted. And all the daughters of music, who aforetime warbled forth their songs of love in St. Paul's Churchyard and Leicester Fields, were laid low. And the hand organ, the pipe, and the tabor, were heard no more. And the shops were shut, and bills were pasted on them; and on one I read—"This shop to let"; and on another I read of that pill, styled "Leake's justly famous pill"; and on another, "This shop will be let to any one who will pay the taxes, in order to prevent it from crumbling to decay." And the curses of the fatherless, and of the widow, and of the poor ruined shopkeeper, ascended up to heaven against the Chancellor of the Exchequer, and on every side there was mourning, and desolation, and woe. Then I said, Verily, shall one man sin, and shall a whole nation perish?

HERE ENDETH THE TENTH CHAPTER OF THE ACTS OF THE CHANCELLOR OF THE EXCHEQUER.'

I think it was about the beginning of the year 1804 that my mother, who was encumbered with a large house, and who was besides in a very delicate state of health, determined upon a removal from Angel Court, and this determination was hastened by the Commissioners of the City of Westminster having determined to pull down the old court, with the broad and narrow sanctuary before mentioned. The removal took me much from my favorite haunts, the parks and the abbey. Our new domicile was in North Street, in the parish of St. John the Evangelist. This removal, however, brought me into neighborhood with the large and handsome church of St. John, where, when able, my mother attended service, and where also I

became a regular attendant, still manifesting the strongest
desire to wear the surplice. The music at this church
was ordinary. It bore no analogy to the cathedral music
I had been accustomed to hear, and I in consequence still
often wandered to Dean's Yard, stole quietly into the
cloisters of the Abbey, and thence got into the church, by a
private door which was often left unfastened by the verger;
and there I would again and again feast my eyes with the
monuments, until the melody of the great organ called me
to the chancel, and the voices of the choristers and canons
filled me with ecstacy. Since those halcyon days, I have
listened to many organs, and have visited most of the
cathedrals in the principal cities of the British Empire,
but no instrument has, in my humble judgment, ever
exceeded, either in power or in brilliancy of tone, that of
the Abbey Church of Westminster.

The house in which my mother had taken up her
abode, and in which she finished her earthly pilgrimage,
was No. 16, in North Street, a very large and respectable
house. She occupied the second floor, which consisted
only of three rooms, in the smallest of which was an
infirm old lady of the name of Greenwood, whom my
mother had to attend upon, and who gave Peggy (such
was the name she called my mother) very little leisure or
rest. I was too noisy, or too inquisitive, or perhaps both,
to be tolerated by this ancient dame. But I did sometimes get into her room, where I was much delighted by a
very fine old screen, adorned with many beautiful water-
color drawings—not such a screen as the ladies hold
in their hands at the present day—but about six feet high,
folding in perhaps half a dozen leaves; and when unfolded and expanded, extending quite across the room,
and keeping out all unwelcome draughts of wind and noise;
but I was never permitted to remain long in this old
lady's sanctum. She was nearly 90 years of age, took an
immoderate quantity of Scotch snuff, and spent her time
between a large print Prayer Book and her Bible. My
poor mother had to submit to many a lecture from this

old lady about my wanderings. I have heard my mother say she was a very good, but a very particular woman. She required the most unremitting attention; and I think the anxiety and labor consequent upon attending her, shortened my mother's existence. I cannot tell how my mother supported me; I know she had some little pittance derived from this lady; and my uncle Lloyd, my mother's brother, who was a barrister, and her constant visitor, allowed her something more; and she besides received some small pension from the Exchequer, in which offices my father had been employed. She, however, always maintained a neat and ladylike appearance, and I considered that I was born a gentleman. My uncle Lloyd always treated her with kindness; and as her health was visibly breaking up fast, he quieted her apprehensions with respect to me, and promised that he would take care of, and bring me up. But as their conversation always was carried on in the Welsh language, which I knew very little of, and that little confined to short tales my mother had taught me, I never could exactly acquire a knowledge of her position or her circumstances. There were some remains of better days in our apartments, and a few articles of old fashioned plate * were occasionally brought out, so that my imagination was satisfied that my mother was a real lady. She was, however, all the world to me, and I know I was her chief anxiety. I was very inquisitive, and pestered her with questions, which she did not seem always willing to answer. I question not that I must often have behaved very undutifully, for her rebukes were frequent, and I particularly remember her once saying to me, ' I feel I shall not be long with you, David: and then you will be sorry that you have not been so dutiful as you ought to be. But, poor child, you are like other children; and duty, and pain, and suffering have small meaning for one of your age.' It may be thought strange, that I should remember these words after the lapse of so many years; but I have already explained

* A few articles have, since my brother's death, been given to me.

that my memory was very tenacious, and anything twice or thrice repeated remains with me, if not in the very words, at least in substance, and I do not think my memory impaired even to this day. Anything that I read three times over remains with me, and I feel that I could acquire any literary knowledge, provided I could only be sufficiently interested as to commence the study.

All this time, though I knew I had many brothers, I could not charge my memory with having often seen them. They were growing up young men, with the single exception of my brother William, who was in a public school, while I was a mere child of eight years of age. I was never much troubled either with their counsel, superintendence, or company. I knew my mother, and that was all; and I sometimes try to recall to my mind the mild and pale face of that dear friend. And when my own children pain me, and I feel grieved at their neglect, I often wonder whether I was not equally disobedient, and this reflection has saved them many a severe lecture.

Among the old-fashioned articles in my mother's room was a picture painted on glass, and rather common in the day of which I write, and it attracted much of my childish attention. It was a tree, very much like a large apple tree, laden with fruit, each apple having written on it its own name and quality. I used to think this the forbidden fruit tree, and I firmly believed it to be an exact representation of that tree which caused the fall of man, of which my good mother had often read me the history. And yet I often wondered how a knowledge of this tree was acquired, so as to represent it so exactly, for I recollected the account of the Fall, and I knew that Adam and Eve were driven out of the garden and could not get in again. I believed the serpent had really spoken to Eve, and I supposed Eve, who was holding the apple in her hand, was considering whether she should eat it or not. But how the tree was so exactly described, was a puzzle to me. At last I supposed that Adam must have

remembered the tree so well as to be able to draw it, and
to keep it as a remembrance of his disobedience, so that
he might be reminded of his sin, and be kept in a state of
continual repentance. And when I had arrived at this
conclusion, I believed it to be really true, and that the
tree was now painted and sold to people that they might
always see Adam's sin, and know what kind of punishment awaited us all from listening to the serpent. Perhaps my mother told me all this in answer to some of my
numerous questions, but this I do not remember ; however, this belief remained with me. I did not for an
instant conceive that the picture was a work of imagination. I had been taught that everything mentioned in the
Bible was literally true, and I believed that this painted
description of the tree was as true as the Bible itself.
On my return to London, in the middle of 1847, I incidentally fell in with a similar picture ; cracked and sadly
mutilated, it is true ; but it immediately attracted my
attention. I made inquiries how the person had become
possessed of it, and found it to be the identical picture I
had so often wondered at in my childish days. I made
proposals for its purchase ; but the possessor, who was the
widow of a deceased brother of mine, very kindly presented me with it. It may be inferred that I value it
highly, as the only relic that has fallen into my hands of
my poor mother's property. But to return to my narrative. Deprived as I was of the glorious harmony of
the Abbey, I now began to love the simpler melody of the
Psalms, and the tunes which then were sung in the parish
churches, many of them eminently beautiful, remain with
me to this day. Among them may be mentioned, St.
David's, Gainsborough, Irish, London New, Peckham,
Rockingham, Sheffield, Wakefield, St. Matthew's, St.
Ann's, Westonfavel, etc. They were all very simple, but
their harmony at this day causes my eyes to swim whenever I hear or sing them. I also was very partial to
Non nobis Domine, Denmark, and some few Anthems in
the Collection of Dr. Miller's Church Music. I never

looked into the collections of Dissenters ; I could conceive no music at all equal to that of the Church of England, out of the pale of which, I was taught to believe, there could be no salvation.

Thus passed my time till I was nearly nine years of age. I was very cheerful in my disposition, but I could assume a quiet solemnity in church. I was very timid and shy among such children as were strange to me ; but to those whom I knew well I was always full of fun—could run, jump, and leap as fast or as high as any of them ; and at night there was none among them who could tell a better story. Meantime, my mother's health continued to decline, and she was at length confined to her bed. My uncle took care of her in her illness—that is, he provided a proper nurse, and saw that she wanted for nothing. I was told that my mother would soon be taken from me. I did not know the loss I was likely to sustain, and I dare say I received the news as most children would do, with tears at first, but which tears were soon dried up. I knew that my uncle lived in a large house, and in good style, some little distance from my mother's lodgings, and I supposed, if my mother died, I should be taken into his house ; and thus, with the usual thoughtlessness of children, I did not give myself much trouble about what would become of me. My mother continued to grow weaker, and the nurse was always glad to get me out of the way. I had been strolling one day to my favorite haunt in the Abbey, and admiring the sculptures in Poet's Corner, when the bell announced the time for closing the Abbey gates. I therefore left the venerable edifice, and returning home by way of Abingdon Street, I began singing the 149th Psalm, of Brady and Tate's version :

> ' O praise ye the Lord,
> Prepare your glad voice,' etc.

I remember I was singing it to the tune of the 'Dead March in Saul,' that being the tune to which it was sung in St. Margaret's and St. John's Churches, and on my arrival at home, found that I had been singing the funeral dirge of my good mother. She had departed somewhat unexpectedly, in the fifty-fifth year of her age, and on a day never to be forgotten by me—namely, on the 1st day of March, the day that I was nine years of age. And thus, at this early age, was I left, bereft of both parents and thrown upon the charity and tender mercy of others. I cried bitterly, and was completely stupified. My mother was the only being that appeared to live for me : her anxiety was for me only ; and although she depended on the word of her brother, my uncle, it may be concluded this did not altogether lessen her anxiety on my account. I was taken care of previous to the funeral by the people of the house. There were no females, if I recollect right, at my mother's funeral. My uncle, my brothers, and myself, together with a cousin from a distance, named Evan Evans, whom I had never seen before, followed her remains to the Broadway Church in Westminster, and I saw the earth thrown upon the coffin which contained the remains of the dearest friend I ever had. I did not know it then ; but it has been painfully brought home to me since. When I have seen children happy under their parents' roof, protected from danger, carefully trained and educated, and guided by parental experience to meet the troubles of the world, I have thought of my own condition at nine years of age, with scarcely a friend to advise me, and with a disposition so flexible that I might easily have been led either to good or to evil. Yet the wonderful interventions of Providence in my behalf have been so marvellous, as often to remind me of the divine words—'Leave your fatherless children to me.' Yes, the Lord has indeed dealt bountifully with me. He has been to me my mother, my father, my friend ; and has raised up instrumental mediums for my support and guidance, some of which I shall have occasion to notice in a future part of this narrative. Yes, I feel I have cause to be much more grateful than I am ; but I can say truly, what perhaps many more can say, that I only began to estimate my mother's worth when she was lost to me for ever. I do in honest truth wish that I had known her better. And 0, that I could more accurately throw her image on the retina of my mind's eye! Vain wish! I must not longer dwell on this part of my life.

I returned with the other mourners to my desolate home, but not to remain there. I was removed, not to my uncle's house, as I had expected, but to the house of the cousin, who for the first time I saw at my mother's funeral, and a weary journey it was for me. The abbey, the parks, and the associations of my infant home, were exchanged for a small house in a small street, far, far from Westminster. My new home was at Cross Street, Holywell Mount, Finsbury Square. The family of my cousin consisted of himself, his wife, two sons, and a daughter ; the oldest son, nearly my own age ; the others respectively seven and five years ; the daughter, the youngest. They were excellent and worthy people, and I shall have occasion to speak of them in a future part of this narrative. I was soon at home in my new abode, and began to be a favorite with my young cousins, for my habit of telling stories returned to me, and in the evening we used to assemble in our little yard, when I would recount some of my wonderful tales.

There was one incident, however, occurred here, which brought me into disgrace, and which for a time made me very miserable. The houses in Cross Street were all very small, and built in a very fragile manner. At the back of each house was a little scullery or kitchen, where the family cooking, and other matters of a domestic nature, were performed in hot weather. I remember it was the month of June. A strong piece of rope had been fastened to the upper part of the outer door of this scullery, and we—that is, myself and young cousins—were alternately amusing ourselves with swinging. I had had my turn, the two youngest followed, and the oldest then took his turn ; he was in full swing, when, in a moment, down came the principal rafter on which the rope was fastened ; and, a bevy of tiles following it, made such a clatter as to lead to the belief, we were literally pulling the house about our ears.   My cousin extricated himself from the rope, and threw the whole blame upon me, in which the other two joined, and I was very soundly thrashed; thrashed because I had pulled down the rafter and broken the tiles ; and thrashed again, because as they said I had done much worse in telling a lie to hide it.   It was in vain I explained the whole matter; I was punished for a lie, when I had actually spoken the truth, and I was punished because I was so wicked as to persist in the lie.   My old cousin, that is the father of the family, saw nothing to blame us for by the falling, or rather the pulling down, of the rafter and the breaking of the tiles ;   these casualties he readily and justly attributed to the fragile manner in which the little scullery was built, but he punished me for persisting, as he said and believed, in the lie.

I now hated my young cousins, would not speak to them for a long time, and was sullen, and refused my food. This only made bad worse, and I was looked upon by the worthy couple as an incorrigible little vagabond, whom it would be necessary to have a strict watch upon.   Alas ! these worthy people never doubted the word of their own children, and all the odium was thrown upon me.   We were all equally to blame ; this they admitted in one respect, because we had all a share in bringing about our ears the rickety piece of workmanship already alluded to, but it seemed to them that I alone was deserving of the severest reprehension, because I would not acknowledge that I was on the swing when the catastrophe happened.

In the midst of all the misery consequent upon this affair, I was summoned to my uncle's house, at which I was greatly rejoiced.   My uncle lived in good style, in, at that time, one of the principal streets of Westminster, and here I was given to understand I was to remain for a few days, or perhaps a few weeks.   I hoped now no longer to be told of the unfortunate accident at Cross Street, Holywell Mount, but I was mistaken. My cousin had narrated the whole circumstance to my uncle, and thus was the fault of one child fastened upon another, nor was it removed from my shoulders, until myself and cousin, the real one upon whom the blame rested, explained the whole affair, when we had respectively attained the age of eighteen.

I now began to exhibit a good deal of timidity, and from being forward in every kind of athletic exercise, rarely indulged in it, unless with boys much bigger and older than myself. At the time when this accident occurred I was considered as a high-spirited boy, but my disposition seemed afterward to change; I became flexible to a degree. Every fault I committed, instead of confessing, as I had been accustomed to do, I strove to hide for fear of consequences. I had been punished for a crime that I had not committed, and punished for persisting in the truth; so I thought I would evade punishment for the future, by not confessing when I was in the wrong. I have ever had a horror of corporal punishment, which has increased with my years.

To digress a little. The summary modes of punishment adopted by teachers and parents, now appear to me to be utterly unsuited to the end designed, and totally incompetent to remove error and evil from the child. Corporal punishment, solitary confinement, and long tasks, were the only means resorted to, in my day, to cure evil, and in my own case I know they did much more harm than good. I never could see the connexion between the offence I had committed, and the punishment inflicted upon me. I knew I was very wrongfully punished, and a feeling of love of concealment took possession of me, which has never entirely left me. The proper punishment for a fault did not then strike me; but since I have been able to reflect, it appears to me, that the proper punishment for every fault is that which springs from the fault itself. We should, therefore, in the correction of errors, allow the natural consequences of the error itself to fall upon the child, and the child in feeling it will abstain from the evil in future, for no one indulges in evil, abstractedly considered as such ; every fault committed arises from the idea that there is something, at least for the time, pleasant in it. But should this be too remote for the child to perceive, then punishment should always have reference to the offence committed. A child, for instance, may be permitted to play in a garden, on condition that nothing is wilfully damaged. If he trample upon flower beds, or eat unripe fruit, he not only receives a punishment from the fruit itself disagreeing with him,' but, having broken the condition 'on which he was permitted to play in the garden, he must for the future be excluded from the enjoyment of the privilege, at all events until such times as to show he is heartily sorry for his fault, and will not · be likely to fall into the commission of 'it again.

The only effectual prevention of error is to show WHY IT IS ERROR ; but while the usual short and lazy way of punishment by the rod is adopted, error is either perpetuated or rendered worse. I am of opinion that parents generate the fearful propensity of lying by the use of corporal punishment. It has been said, it is right to do battle with an obstinate child, and by gaining the victory make the child aware of the habit, and prevent it for the future. But I know from experience that such victories leave a resentfulness and a soreness about them, which take years of kindness to efface. I am fully convinced that the only way to remedy evil is to overcome it by good ; and when a child is punished wrongfully, as in my case, it is very apt to generate revengeful feelings, and to embitter the mind by a sense of the wrong it has endured. To return from this digression.

The day after my arrival at my uncle's house, I accompanied him, to my great delight, to the Abbey Cloisters, and with him was then ushered into the presence of one of the prebendaries of Westminster, the Rev. Dr.

Fynes, and here, for the first time, I learned that my uncle was using all his influence to get me admitted into the Foundation of King Charles I. at Westminster. My uncle, happily for me, possessed interest sufficient to get me entered, and early in the month of July, 1805, I left my uncle's house, and was admitted within the precincts of the institution, with liberty to range the Abbey, cloisters, and all the crypts and chapels which abounded within its venerable walls, on all holidays and saints' days.

Second Period:

FROM NINE TILL FOURTEEN YEARS OF AGE.
1805 to 1810.

'Come; let's tame the fags!'
SCHOOL PROVERB.

'Among the motives to action by which mankind are governed, there
is none which exercises a wider influence than the love of power. . . . .
One cannot become domesticated in a seminary for youth without
seeing it strongly displayed: even the greatest care on the part of the
master can seldom prevent the exercise of cruel tyranny on the part of
the stronger children over the weaker.'
REV. S. NOBLE.

I THINK, as just stated, it was about the month of July,
1805, when I entered on the Foundation of King Charles I.,
at Westminster, and as I was totally ignorant of the
manner in which public schools were conducted, and of
the way in which the boys acted towards each other ;
being of a quick irritable disposition, although naturally
timid and retiring, I was constantly in scrapes, and often
subjected to physical suffering.

I may here remark, that the Foundation at Westminster, by Charles I., is similar to that of Christ Church,
London, founded by Edward V., the education being the
same, and the dress the same (with the exception of
color, Christ Church Hospital being *blue*, and the color of
the Foundation at Westminster being *green*). The dress
of the boys in the Foundation on which I was placed,
consisted of green trowsers, a green petticoat (which last
has since been laid aside), and a long green garment, with
a single row of brass buttons, from the waist up to the

neck, a college band, and a 'leathern girdle about the loins'; with shoes ornamented with large brass buckles, and a cap about the size of a muffin, and usually carried in the hand, but very rarely on the head. I remember hearing my uncle say that it cost all the influence he possessed (and that was not a little) to get me admitted. The number of boys was limited to twenty-four; and the charter enacted that they should be all orphans. I verily believe, however, that I was the only orphan in the establishment at the time I was admitted, and there were many whose parents were not only living, but wealthy; and, indeed, the children of the wealthy seemed at all times to have the preference in point of admission.

I cannot forbear remarking here on the injustice practised at this and several other charitable institutions. The design of the founder was to provide an asylum for such children as were deprived by death of their natural guardians; thus giving them a home in their tenderest years, and providing them with such an education as should enable them to make their own way in the world after suitable training. How mean, then, must it have been for persons in good circumstances to take advantage of a provision designed for the orphan children of the poor and destitute; and how unjust on the part of the governors of the Institution to sanction it. The parents of one of my most intimate friends in the school, at the period of which I write, kept their carriage, and none of the pupils beside myself were, strictly speaking, orphans. But to return :—

When once admitted, we were all treated equally enough. The situation of the school was isolated at that time, but it is now the centre of a large population. It adjoins the Bridewell at Tothill Fields, and is approached by a gate in the centre of what appears a long dead wall. On entering the gate, which opens into a porch, a door on the right leads to the school room, and on the left to the lobby, leading to the Lusorium; at the end of which is a small room, called the wardrobe, where the dresses

3

of the boys were arranged in order. Over the scho
room, lobby, Lusorium, and wardrobe, reached by a broa
flight of stairs in the lobby, are the dormitories or sleepir
rooms of the boys. Each boy has a bed to himself, whic
he has to keep in perfect order, under the direction of
monitor or superintendent. These several apartmen
are well aired, and rather loftily built, occupying one sid
of a square.

Passing from the porch, you come to the play groun
of the boys, a large open space, of about half an acr
cut off from all communication with the world withoul
On the left of this square, by a flight of steps, you ente
a spacious hall, hung round with ancient paintings, an
furnished after the manner of the time of Charles i., wit
high-backed, richly-carved oak chairs, a long oak tabl
reaching nearly from one end of the hall to the other
with an ample fire place in the centre of one side of th
hall. The hall itself may be about forty feet long and
twenty feet wide. This was called the Governors' Hall
in which all meetings of the Institution were held
and all business transacted; and in which, once a
year, the magnates of Westminster School met and
feasted.

Adjoining the Governors' Hall was the Boys' Hall, a
neat square room, supplied with tables and forms, which
served as the refectory on Sundays and festivals, and also
was used as the church. Divided by a porch, but on the
same level, and on the same side of the square, was the
kitchen, a spacious room, in which the provisions of the
Institution were prepared. Every boy was furnished with
his own utensils of eating and drinking, which were engraved with his name, and were of pewter, and polished
as bright as silver. On ordinary days, however, the boys
ate from trenchers, which were kept in a state of the
greatest cleanliness, being scoured regularly after use, and
nearly as white as the table cloths on which they rested.

On a third side of the square, and to the right of the
school, was situated the house of the master, who, for the

time I was in the Institution, and for many years after, was Mr. Robert Blemell Pollard, a most stern disciplinarian, but a most excellent teacher. The fourth side of the square consisted of the palisades of the garden, which extended to some distance in the neighboring fields, and which was exceedingly well kept and dressed, and that, too, principally by the boys. The master's house adjoined the wall of the Tothill Fields Bridewell, and often have we wondered what were the scenes taking place in that fastness of crime.

On my first entrance I was inspected by the surgeon, and then taken to the wardrobe, where my own clothes were taken from me, and I was invested with the uniform of the Institution. I was exceedingly small in stature ; and it was at one time supposed, that when I left the Institution, I should make a fortune by exhibiting myself as a dwarf. Of course, I was what was called the fag of the school. I was not only the youngest, but the weakest ; at the same time, I was one of the least-easily guided, being, as I have said, very irritable, and standing much upon the position of my uncle, who was a barrister, at that time practising in the Court of Common Pleas ; and, of course, I considered myself a gentleman. But I soon found that the boys all considered themselves in the same light, and I was pummelled on every hand. At length the head boy said I should be his fag, and he would soon tame me. I, however, refused to serve him, and threatened to tell the usher, or even the master.

This was enough. I was seized by about seven of the head boys, who all made common cause against the fags. The door of the Lusorium, or play room, was bolted, and a large trap door lifted from the flooring. They tied my legs ; but before putting me into this dungeon, which was, in fact, the potato hole, I was asked whether I would submit to be the head boy's fag. I said, 'No.' 'In with him, then,' said the head boy. And in I was thrown among the potatoes, and the trap door shut down. I roared and shouted lustily ; but my tormenters danced, and

made all the noise they could, to prevent my voice bein
heard, and I was kept there for an hour.

At the end of that time the trap was lifted a little.
was in a fever of heat. 'Are you tame?' said the hea
boy. 'I'll tell master—that I will,' said I. 'O you will
will you?' said he. 'Hollo!' and he shouted to hi
companions. 'Here! come and help him out, that h
may go and tell master.' They all obeyed. I was take
out. I was begrimed with dirt from the potatoes, and
what with my tears and the dirt, I presented a most ludi
crous appearance, and I was besides in a fever of heat
being nearly suffocated for want of air. A roar o
laughter from the boys greeted my appearance, and I wa
beset by the whole school. The boys, with knotte
handkerchiefs, began to belabor my back, every now an
then shouting, 'Keep the game alive ; he is going to tel
master!' After this punishment I was again thrust dow
into the potato hole. 'Now, are you tame, my fin
fellow?' said my tormentor. No answer. 'I say, are
you tame?' No answer. 'O! sulky, are you
BUNKER'S HILL! BUNKER'S HILL!' With that I wa
again taken out, and the boys began to mount on eacl
other's shoulders ; one each of the seven head boy
selecting his own fag, while I was mounted by the bo
who was determined to make me his fag ; and, thu
mounted, the boys commenced a regular *melée*, buttin
against each other with their heads, and fighting witl
their fists, while the fags kicked each other's legs, and se
up such a howling as quite astounded me.

In the midst of all the uproar, in came the usher t
inquire into the reason of such a tumult, and being told tha
they were *only taming the fags,* he quietly withdrew
ordering them, however, not to make so much noise. The
boys called this game the 'Battle of Bunker's Hill,' and
sorely indeed did it punish the poor fags. For my ow
part, I now cared for nothing, but struggled against m
tyrant, and at length unhorsed him, when the battle wa
brought to a close by the re-entrance of the usher, witl

instructions from the master to bring the head boys before him, and they were punished without my being the informer.

It is impossible to describe the tyranny which the senior boys exercise over the junior in public institutions. The utmost vigilance on the part of the masters cannot entirely prevent it ; and, for my part, I was brought to see that my truest policy was to submit, and become the apparently willing servant of the head boy. My duty was to be his horse in all battles, to assist him in any way I was capable during school hours, to clean his shoes, buckles, knife and fork, and pewter dining and chamber utensils ; to find out his lessons, and mark them in his Bible for Sundays ; and, in short, to do anything and everything he might demand of me. The seven head boys had each his fag, who was selected from the seven youngest, those numbering from eight to seventeen were exempt from being fags, but had other duties to perform.

Having become thoroughly *tame*, as the boys termed submission, I was now indoctrinated into the regular practice of the school. We rose in the morning at six o'clock in the summer, and at seven in the winter. The duties of the day commenced with one of the seven head boys (each boy had his own day) reading prayers. After which we had to arrange our dormitory, make our beds, clean our chamber utensils, then brush our shoes, wash, and get into school for an hour, where we prepared our lessons for the day. At eight o'clock we breakfasted. Our breakfast consisted of bread and butter, with warm milk and water, and a very wholesome breakfast it was. At nine o'clock the business of the day commenced, and was continued, with an hour's intermission, until five. The course of instruction was elementary to a University. The elements of Latin and Greek for those who were designed for the ministry, and all the rest a finished English education. Our diet was of the very best description, and we were regulated both in quantity and

quality ; sickness was very rare during my stay, and I
not think a guinea a year was spent in medicine.

I soon began to take a pleasure in my studies, and m
memory now served me most usefully. I learned all tl
Latin declensions, merely by hearing the different boy
repeat them as tasks. I did the same by Lindley Murray
Grammar, which was our task book, and I soon acquire
a character for a good memory. But there was on
thing which I could not accomplish, and that was a goo
hand writing. I was punished for it day by day ;
hated it, and to comfort me, the master used to tell me
as he punished me, that I should never write as long as
lived, and I believed him then, although I have sinc
proved the contrary. I always dreaded the showing o
my copy-book, and always evaded it whenever I could
because I so dreaded the lash. I think for the two firs
years I was in the Institution, I did not pass a day
without corporal punishment ; frequently have I beer
struck on the head with a heavy ruler, until I wa:
almost stupified, and once I was rendered insensible by
the blow. I cannot help digressing here, to relate an
anecdote, which shows the danger as well as the cruelty
of striking boys on the head. The anecdote is of such
tremendous interest that I do not think it possible to speak
in terms too earnest in the condemnation of corporal
punishment :—

A gentleman engaged in the higher department of
trade—a good man, an enlightened man, and an affectionate parent—had two sons, who, at the time I begin
their history, were respectively of the ages of five and
ten. The attachment between them was so remarkable,
as to be the common topic of conversation among all their
friends and acquaintance. The children were incessantly
together ; and to see them walk round the garden with
the arm of the elder round the neck of the younger,
while the other, who could not reach to his neck, endeavored to clasp his waist—with their long auburn
hair, in the fashion of the day, hanging in ringlets, and

s the elder stooped to kiss his little brother, covering his face——those who had seen them thus occupied, their lovely features beaming with affection, would have said, that nothing on earth could give a more vivid idea of angels. The children when separated, for a few hours only, were miserable ; and when the time arrived for sending the elder to school, it was a subject of serious reflection among the parents and friends, whether so intense an affection should be checked or encouraged. The former was decided on, and the elder was sent to a distance. Both children were so exceedingly unhappy, that sleepless nights, loss of appetite, incessant weeping, and rapid wasting of the body, made everyone fearful of the consequence of prolonging the absence, and they were brought together again. Those who witnessed the tumultuous joy of their meeting, describe it as inexpressibly affecting ; they soon recovered their health and spirits ; and their mutual affection seemed, if possible, to be increased by the temporary separation. The experiment after a while was again made, and with similar results; and it was decided never to risk another.

An arrangement was now entered into with a schoolmaster to receive both boys, although contrary to the regulations of his establishment, which professed to admit none under ten years of age. The two boys kept themselves almost entirely aloof from all the rest. The elder helped the younger in his education—watched over him with a kind of parental solicitude—kept a vigilant eye upon the character of the boys who sought his society, and admitted none to intimacy with his brother of whom he did not entirely approve. The slightest hint of his wish sufficed with the younger, who would almost as soon have contemplated deliberately breaking the commandments, as opposing his wishes in the slightest degree. Both made rapid progress in their education, and their parents' hearts were filled with thankfulness for the blessing.

In the midst of this happiness, news arrived from the schoolmaster, that from some unexplained cause, the elder boy had begun to exercise a very unreasonable and tyrannical authority over the younger; that he had been repeatedly punished for it, but although he always promised amendment, and could assign no cause (reasonable or unreasonable) for his conduct, he soon relapsed into his usual habits, and the schoolmaster requested to know what was to be done. The father immediately sent for both boys, and entered into a lengthened investigation. The little one was almost broken-hearted, exclaiming, ' He might beat me every day, if he would but love me; but he hates me, and I shall never be happy again.' The elder could assign no reason for his animosity and ill-treatment; and the father, after many remonstrances, thought fit to inflict on him very severe CORPOREAL CHASTISEMENT [alas! alas!]: and confined him to his room for some days, with nothing but bread and water.

The lad, on his liberation, gave solemn promises of altered conduct, but showed little affection for his brother, although the latter used a thousand innocent stratagems to inspire him with tenderness. They returned to school. In a few days similar scenes and worse occurred—the boy was again and again punished by the master—again and again promised amendment, and in vain; and he was at last taken from school by his father. A repetition of severe punishment—long incarceration and a rejection by all his relatives—had no effect in changing his disposition—his dislike to his brother became fixed animosity, and from animosity degenerated into the most deadly hatred. He made an attempt on the child's life, and if he saw him pass an open door, would throw any missile at him that came in his way, and on one occasion threw the carving knive at him with all the fury of a maniac. The family now resorted to medical advice, and years passed in hopeless endeavors to remove a disposition obviously depending on a diseased brain. Had

bey taken this step earlier, these floggings and imprison-
ments would have been spared, as well as the heart
ickening remorse of the father. Still the boy was not
asane; on every topic but one he was reasonable, but
torpid. It was only at the sight of his brother, or the
sound of his name, that he was roused to madness.

The youth now advanced towards manhood. When
about the age of fifteen, he was taken with a violent but
Platonic passion for a lady more than forty years of age,
and the mother of five children, the eldest older than
himself. His paroxysms of fury now became frightful;
he made several attempts to destroy himself; but, in the
very torrent and whirlwind of his rage, if this lady would
allow him to sit down at her feet, and lay his head on her
knee, he would burst into tears, go off into a sound sleep,
and wake up perfectly calm and composed, and, looking
up into her face with lack-lustre eye, would say—'*Pity
me—I can't help it!*'

Soon after this he began to squint, and was rapidly
passing on into hopeless idiotcy, when he was once more
taken to *Mr. Cline*, a surgeon long since dead. After
another attentive examination of the scull, which had been
shaved for the purpose—'Here,' said he, 'is an almost
imperceptible depression; it would not justify us in
doing anything but in a case entirely hopeless. Here,
however, we can certainly do no harm; and although
there is scarcely a chance of benefit, let us make the
attempt.' A day was fixed for the operation, a circular
piece of the skull was removed by the *trephine*, and, on
examination, there was found to be a specula of bone,
growing from under its surface, and piercing the brain.
Here was the hatred to his brother at once explained. He
soon recovered, became strongly attached to his brother,
and felt no other sentiment towards Mrs. M. than gratitude for the kindness which she had shown him in
his illness, and of which he retained but a faint remembrance.

Here, now, is matter for reflection for the philosopher,

the psychologist, and the legislator. The thoughts which it gives rise are overwhelming. Had this po wretch, in one of his mad paroxysms (before a medic man had been called in) killed his brother, how would th rabble crowd at the Old Bailey have rejoiced at h execution ; and how cordially would the good, the wis the religious, and the benevolent, have echoed thei sentiment!

But now listen to the explanation, for it is the mos frightful of all the circumstances attendant on this extra ordinary case—the most extraordinary, perhaps, upoi record, and of which I am sorry it is not in my power to give the medical details, for it occurred before I understoo the structure of the brain, ·that mysterious organ, oi rather organs. The disease which led to these horribl results took its rise from the blow of a round ruler, in one of the *gentle* reprimands then so common with school-masters ; so that the boy's schoolmaster was himself the originator of all the suffering and misery that ensued ; the sharp edges of the suture broke through the inner table of the skull and the integuments, and set up the process of ossification under the surface ; and, of course, every time that the point of the specula pressed against the brain, the irritability resulting from the portion of the brain against which it pressed, and which was the organ of Destructiveness, led to the frightful results described.*

This boy, therefore, instead of requiring or deserving .punishment, was all along laboring under physical disease, which, when properly treated by medical and surgical means, at once disappeared, and the healthy mental affections and dispositions were restored to their normal state.

In my own case, though occasionally, as I have stated, struck on the head with a ruler, the instruments of torture were, for the hand, a cube of box, of at least one inch; and for the purpose of flagellation, a stout leather strap

* 'Illuminated Magazine.'

'in Scotland called the tawse, I believe), divided into a number of slender thongs, which were laid on the bare posteriors, with all the force of a man's strong arm, and which more than once drew blood from me.

From what has been now stated, it will be seen how necessary it is to guard the brain from injury, seeing that upon its healthy action depends the whole safety and well being of the system, and I know, from positive observation, that more cases of incurable insanity have resulted from blows on the head than from any other cause. To return to my narrative :—

At length I think I tired the master out, and he ceased to punish me, and astonished me by saying he thought me a tractable boy in everything but my pen, and write I never should. With the cessation of punishment, an ardent attachment to learning took possession of me, and I was successful in arithmetic, in mathematics, in grammar, and in Latin. I was passionately fond of poetry, and my memory enabled me to retain an immense number of pieces. At this time the poetry of Sir Walter Scott was creating a great sensation, and our rhetorical teacher introduced his 'Lay of the Last Minstrel,' a great portion of which I acquired by heart by hearing him read it. Nothing captivated my imagination to the same extent as 'this beautiful poem, and from that time all works of imagination were eagerly sought after by me. We had a considerable number of the works of the higher order of poets in our school library, and to this day the pieces I have learned from their writings retain their places in my memory. Our master used frequently to read to us from a work entitled 'Elegant Extracts.' On one occasion he read a fragment called 'Sir Bertrand,' which revived my taste for story-telling.

I was now in my twelfth year, and had served my time as a fag, that is, there were seven boys below me, and I ascended to the middle rank. I now set on foot a system of story-telling after going to bed, in which I took a prominent position, and I very soon became a favorite

with the boys in consequence of the facility with which I
concocted tales. My plan was to borrow books from the
school library, and to make myself master of any striking
incidents, which my retentive memory enabled me to do,
and then to weave a tale out of what I read. In the
winter evenings, when we retired to bed at seven o'clock,
this system of story-telling was kept up till all the boys
in the ward in which I slept had fallen asleep, leaving
the story-teller sometimes telling his tale to no other ears
than his own. Finding myself thus often left alone with
my tale, I adopted the plan of shouting in the middle of
my tale, 'Who's awake?' If any one answered I went
on ; if all were silent, I discontinued my tale, and went
to sleep myself. On one of these occasions, which
brought my tale-telling to a conclusion, I well remember
calling out, 'Who's awake?' No answer. 'Who's
awake, I say?' 'I am, you dog,' suddenly exclaimed
the master ; 'I'll teach you to tell stories after prayers !'
and with that I was hauled out of bed, and received a
sound flagellation, and so finished my story-telling.
But though I left off this practice, I still had a fondness
for all kinds of literary curiosities. Old books, in which
curious pieces were inserted, sometimes fell into my
hands, out of which I have cut scraps,* many of which I
possess to this day, and some I have in my memory.
In a work published in 1808 by Davidson of Alnwick,
and which I then thought was a very amusing book, the
following was found. I had no idea of men manufacturing
incidents of this kind. I thought them all real, and
believed them as such. Whether the one I am about to
narrate, and that which immediately follows it, belong to
the class of fiction, I know not; I believed them at the
time to be true. The following is the scrap first alluded
to :—

'Part of a SERMON lately delivered in the neighborhood
of Litchfield (1808) † :—You have ears to ear, tongues

* I have by me four large 4to volumes, filled with scraps.
† Published 1808, supposed to have been preached 1806 or 1807.

to taste, eyes to see, and throats to swallow : draw near,
I say, and pick up the crumbs that I shall scatter among
you : the crumbs of comfort wherewith you must be
crammed, until you become chickens of grace, and are
cooped up in the hen-coop of righteousness. If your
hearts are as hard as a Suffolk cheese, or a Norfolk dum-
pling, my discourse shall beat them, as it were, on a
cobbler's lap-stone, until they become as soft as a roasted
apple ; aye, even as soft as custard-meat, and melt in your
bellies like a marrow pudding. Do you know what trade
Adam was ? I say, do you know what trade Adam
was ? If you don't, I'll tell you. Why Adam was a
planter, for he planted the beautiful garden of Eden.
Now do you know what was the first thing Adam set in
his garden ! Ho! ho! you don't, don't you ! Then I'll
tell you. His foot, his foot, I say, was the first thing
Adam set in his garden ; but he could not keep it there :
no, no, no : he could not keep it there, for Lucifer came
behind him, tripped up his heels, and trundled him out
again neck and shoulders.

'I'll tell you a secret ! I say, I'll tell you a secret :
knees were make before elbows : aye, knees were made
before elbows, for the beasts of the field were made
before man, and they have no elbows at all. Therefore,
down on your marrow bones, and pray for mercy, else
you will be turned into Beelzebub's under-ground kitchen
to make bubble and squeak of your souls for the Devil's
supper.'

But this scrap, amusing as it is, is not to be compared
to an entire sermon, which actually purports to have been
preached in the parish church of Burston, a small village,
near Diss, in Norfolk, and it is stated that most of the
names mentioned in this oration, are now standing in the
register books of that parish. It was inserted in an old
number of the 'British Magazine,' for November, 1750.
But whether true or false, it is an amusing illustration of
what sermons were a hundred years since.

'A Sermon,

OCCASIONED BY THE DEATH OF MR. PROCTOR, MINISTER OF GISSING, BY THE REV. MR. MOORE, OF BURSTON, IN NORFOLK.

'1 TIMOTHY vi, 12 : "Fight the good fight."

'Beloved! we are met together to solemnise the funeral of Mr. Proctor. His father's name was Mr. Thomas Proctor, of the second family. His brother's name also was Mr. Thomas Proctor. He lived some time at Burston Hall, in Norfolk, and was high constable of Diss hundred. This man's name was Mr. Robert Proctor, and his wife's was Mrs. Buxton, late wife of Mr. Matthew Buxton. She came from Helsdon Hall, beyond Norwich. He was a good husband, and she a good housewife, and they two got money. She brought a thousand pounds with her for her portion.

'But now, beloved, I shall make it clear to you by demonstrative arguments, first, he was a good man, and that in several respects. He was a loving man to his neighbors, a charitable man to the poor, a favorable man in his tithes, a good landlord to his tenants. There sits one Mr. Spurgeon, who can tell what a great sum of money he forgave him upon his death bed; it was fourscore pounds. Now, beloved, was not this a good man, and a man of God? and his wife a good woman? and she came from Helsdon Hall, beyond Norwich : this is the first argument.

'Secondly, to prove this man to be a good man, and a man of God : in the time of his sickness, which was long and tedious, he sent for Mr. Cole, minister of Shimpling, to pray for him. He was not a self-ended man to be prayed for himself only ; no, beloved, he desired him to pray for all his relations and acquaintances, for Mr. Buxton's worship, and for all Mr. Buxton's children, against it should please God to send him any ; and to Mr. Cole's prayers he devoutly said, "Amen—Amen—Amen."

'Was not this a good man, and a man of God, think you? and his wife a good woman? and she came from Helsdon Hall, beyond Norwich.

'Then he sent for Mr. Gibbs to pray for him; and he came, and prayed for him, and for all his friends, relations, and acquaintances; and for Mr. Buxton's worship, and for all Mr. Buxton's children, against it should please God to send him any; and to Mr. Gibbs's prayers he likewise devoutly said, "Amen—Amen—Amen."

'Was not this a good man, and a man of God, think you? and his wife a good woman? and she came from Helsdon Hall, beyond Norwich.

'Then he sent for me, and I came and prayed for this good man, Mr. Proctor, for all his friends, relations, and acquaintances, for Mr. Buxton's worship, and for Mr. Buxton's children, against it should please God to send him any; and to my prayers he devoutly said, "Amen—Amen—Amen."

'Was not this a good man, and a man of God, think you? and his wife a good woman? and she came from Helsdon Hall, beyond Norwich.

. Thirdly and lastly, beloved, I come to a clear demonstrative argument, to prove this man to be a good man, and a man of God, and that is this: There was one Thomas Proctor, a very poor beggar boy; he came into this country upon the back of a dun cow. It was not a black cow, nor a brindled cow, nor a brown cow; no, beloved, it was a *dun* cow. Well, beloved, this poor boy came a begging to this good man's door. He did not do as some would have done, give him a small alms and send him away, or chide him and make him a pass, and send him into his own country; no, beloved, he took him into his own house, and bound him apprentice to a gunsmith in Norwich. After his time was out he took him home again, and married him to a kinswoman of his wife's, one Mrs. Christian Robertson, here present—there she sits. She was a very good fortune, and to her this good man gave a considerable jointure. By her he had three daughters. This good man took home the eldest, brought her up to woman's estate, married her to a very honorable gentleman, Mr. Buxton, here present—there he sits——who gave him a vast portion with her, and the remainder of his estate he gave his two daughters.

'Now, was not this a good man, and a man of God, think you ? and his wife a good woman ? and she came from Helsdon Hall, beyond Norwich.

'Beloved, you may remember some time since, I preached at the funeral of Mrs. Proctor, at which time I troubled you with many of her transcendent virtues, but your memories, perhaps, may fail you, and therefore, I shall now remind you of one or two of them.

'The first is, she was a good knitter, as any in the the county of Norfolk. When her husband and family were in bed and asleep, she would get a cushion, clap herself down by the fire, and sit and knit. But, beloved, be assured she was no prodigal woman, but a sparing woman ; for to spare candle she would stir up the coals with her knitting pins, and by that light she would sit and knit, and make as good work as many other women by daylight. Beloved, I have a pair of stockings upon my legs that were knit in this manner, and they are the best knit stockings that ever I wore in my life.

'Secondly, she was the best maker of a toast in drink that ever I ate in my life—and they were brown toasts too—for when I used to go in a morning, she would ask me to eat a toast, which I was very willing to do, because she had such an artificial way of toasting it ; no ways slack nor burning it ; besides she had such a pretty way of grating nutmeg, and dipping it in the beer, and such a piece of rare cheese, that I must needs say that they were the best toasts that ever I ate in my life.

'Well, beloved : the days are short, and many of you have a great way to your habitations, and, therefore, I will hasten to a conclusion.

'I think I have sufficiently proved this man to be a good man, and his wife a good woman ; but, fearing your memories should fail you, I shall repeat the particulars, namely : 1. His love to his neighbor. 2. His charity to the poor. 3. His favorableness in his tithes. 4. His goodness to his tenants. 5. His devotion in his prayers in saying, Amen, Amen, Amen, to the prayers of Mr. Cole, Mr. Gibbs, and myself. Beloved, go home. Amen.'

I was, as I have said, in my twelfth year, and had made considerable progress in my studies. I rarely saw the outside of the college walls, as they were termed, except on Sundays and *Saint's-days;* for though there were many holidays, I, who had no home, rarely participated in them. Sometimes a schoolfellow would petition for me to accompany and spend a day with him, a favor which the master rarely refused ; but, in general, my home was the college ; my recreation, the play ground ; my amusement, the school library.

About this time it was found I had a good voice, and I obtained admission into the school choir, an addition to my studies which I did not at first like, but of which I grew more enamored as I mastered the notes. I recollect my first essay in singing was at the school festival, when I had to sing a solo before the assembled 'Apprentices,' as they were called, although many of them were old men of sixty and seventy years of age. This festival was held on the anniversary of St. Luke (October 18), and was observed in the following manner : At eleven o'clock the boys were assembled in the school room, and examined in religious exercises by the minister of St. Margaret's church, Westminster. They had to go through the whole 'Exposition of the Church Catechism,' after which they repeated the 'Lord's Sermon on the Mount,' each boy taking a portion. This examination usually lasted *three hours.* The boys then had a slight refection. At five o'clock, three separate dinner tables were spread.

In the Governor's Hall, the Magnates of Westminster

4

School, the Governors of the Hospital, and the minister who had examined us were feasted with all the delicacies the season could produce. In the Lusorium (boy's play-room) were assembled all such persons as had received their education in the school. These varied in age, from the newly emancipated lad of fourteen, to the grey-headed veteran of seventy; and one, I recollect, who was named '*Chip*,' an old man of seventy-five, who was the 'oldest Apprentice,' and took his place at the head of the table. In their own hall, the boys assembled. The tables of the 'Apprentices' and the boys were furnished with the same viands—*roast beef, plum pudding*, and *Windsor ale*, which last beverage was considered *Royal*. Dinner ended, the 'Apprentices' and boys were ordered into the Governor's Hall, where a short.lecture was given by one of the Magnates, and health to the 'Apprentices,' and '*Knowledge*' to the boys, was drunk in good wine by the Magnates, for which *Old Father Chip* returned thanks, and then 'Apprentices' and boys returned to the Lusorium; a psalm was sung by the 'Apprentices,' and an anthem or some piece of sacred music by the boys; and so terminated the Festival within the walls of the college.

But the 'Apprentices' only adjourned from the college to a neighboring tavern, called the '*Green Coat Boy*,' where they continued to enjoy themselves till a late hour. This Festival was to both 'Apprentices' and boys the most joyous of festivals; and I recollect some of the 'Apprentices' were able to come in their carriages. It was on one of these occasions that I was appointed to sing the solo. I went through it tremblingly, but I was encouraged by Mr. Pollard himself, who reminded me that I was only singing before my schoolfellows, for all who were before me were once as I was; so as I said before, though tremblingly, I went through it to the satis-faction of all. And after the Festival, I was appointed the leader of the choir.

To maintain this post, I had to receive instructions

from Mr. William Pollard, who set me to copy music
for him at my leisure hours, and he turned me over for
instructions to his sister, Miss Louisa Pollard, a young
lady about fourteen years of age, who perfected me so
far by the aid of the pianoforte, that I could sing almost
any psalm tune, after once or twice practising. I might
have made good progress in music, had I paid more
attention to the instructions of this young lady; but the
boys jeered me, and called me 'Miss Loo's beau,' and as
I was very shy, and blushed whenever her name was
mentioned, it made the boys enjoy the fun all the more,
until I almost dreaded to hear her call for me to my
lesson.

Meantime, Mr. William Pollard kept me to the drudgery
of rough copying music, which I confess was very
clumsily executed, and for which I often got cuffed by
that gentleman. I was also appointed 'Figure Questioner,'
an office which I dreaded would bring back my punishments for bad writing. The 'Figure Questioner,' had
to enter into the boys' arithmetical books, those sums of
figures, in the Compound Addition and Subtraction rules
of money, weights, and measures. The boys, copying
out the sums from the ciphering books to the slate, and
casting them up, brought them to the 'Questioner' for
examination. If he found them correct, he appended
his initials, and they then entered the answer under the
sum in their respective books : so that, while the 'Figure
Questioner' entered the whole sum except the answer,
the boy who wrought the sum had but the small labor
of a line. The working of arithmetical calculations I
delighted in, but it was the dread of entering the figures
that alarmed me. I had a dozen boys in the compound
rules, for Mr. Pollard had many boarders, beside the
Foundation boys, and for their books, as well as for their
correctness, I was responsible, so that much of my time
for recreation was spent over these books. I had been
for two hours engaged on one occasion setting these
questions, when Mr. Pollard entered the school room, and

seeing my occupation, he stepped up to examine the books.
I expected nothing less than a flogging. The books were
clean, but I feared they would be called execrable.

'So,' said Mr. Pollard, 'you have become "Questioner,"
who appointed you?'

'Mr. Elmy, sir.' *

'Mr. Elmy has more confidence in your pen than I
have; but are these your figures?'

'Yes sir, the figures in the compound rules.'

'And they are good figures, too; come there is promise
for figures, but little I fear for letters; however, the
figures are good.'

I was immeasurably astonished at praise from Mr.
Pollard in the use of my pen, but it encouraged me in
my work, and I took more and more pains.† I was
proud of Mr. Elmy's good opinion of me, and I often
wished I could write as well as I could figure.

Mr. Elmy was very kind to me, and altogether a
different man from Mr. Pollard. He cultivated my taste
for poetry, and was himself, so I then thought, a very
good poet. He got up a kind of recitation meeting, in
which different boys sustained the character of different
poets; and as the poets were ever considered a simple
race, and stood in great awe of the critics, who were
ever looked upon as a race of bears, who would growl,
let the articles be good or bad which were produced—
at our first exhibition, that is the first exhibition at which
I figured, and figured in no less a character than the
representative of Dean Swift, (to recite his poem of
'Baucis and Philemon'), Mr. Elmy put into my hand a
prologue to open the proceedings. I cannot tell whether
the poem was his or not, but I think it was. I have,
however, since seen in print the simile of the 'jaundiced
eye.' However, such as the prologue is, I present it,
minus a few lines. I remember it took very well.

* Mr. Elmy was then under-master or usher.

† This was stimulating love of approbation, a much better mode than
exercising combativeness and destructiveness by flogging.

A PROLOGUE.

BY RICHARD ELMY.

I'm hither sent by way of prologue to you,
Yet mean not in a servile way to sue you.
Let sordid courtiers versed in little arts,
By mean submission strive to gain your hearts;
But truth to say, and surely that's no sin,
Who are thus gained 'tis not my aim to win.
If, like myself, to candor you're inclin'd,
I dare with honest freedom speak my mind.
First, then, if any growling critic's here,
Who comes to daunt us with his brow severe,
I must expect that such a one withdraw,
Nor try our inexperience by law.
I'm told these wretches, with malignant joy,
Like demons triumph where their arts destroy;
Since mercy never prompts their heart to spare,
Learning and ignorance equal sentence share.
Condemn they always will, if wrong or right,
Since censure only yields their breasts delight.
Let those who doubt this listen to my tale,
' For truth is powerful and will prevail:'
It chanc'd a painter who with toil and skill
Had brought the colors subject to his will,
Produced a mimic bunch of flowers to view,
Which nature seem'd, his pencil wrought so true.
The colors all their gorgeous tints disclose:—
A fly alights upon a seeming rose.
A critic now his haughty head erects,
And bent on censure, he the piece inspects.
His opera glass advancing to his eye,
He closely looks and sees th' attracted fly.
' What daub is this?' says he, ' devoid of spirit—
That wretched fly would blast a painter's merit.'
The fly, disturb'd, forsakes its painted seat,
And shows the critic's malice and conceit.
Thus, then, if I conceive aright,
All seems infected to the infected sight;
All seems discolor'd to th' infected spy;
As all looks yellow to the jaundic'd eye.
A fable's worth is like a nut's internal,
The tale's mere shell, the moral is the kernal,
And if you find the moral good and true,
' Applause, in spite of trivial faults, is due.'

After the prologue, a variety of pieces were recited by different boys, and a very pleasant entertainment it was, at which there were a few visitors. It was got up for the purpose of giving the boys a correct taste in reading, Mr. Elmy declaring, that no one could be called a good reader who was incapable of reading poetry, and the best way to read well was to learn and recite poetry.

My time now was fully occupied. What with my *Figure Questions*, my *music writing*, and my *practisings* in the *choir*, together with the general routine of school business, I had no time to be miserable, and I think this was the happiest period of my existence. I was now thirteen years of age, very small, and very fragile apparently, but enjoying most excellent health, and I was at the head of the school. In going to church, the head boy always took the lead; the others followed according to size; and I was followed by a boy who might be considered as a giant when compared to myself. He was a little younger than I was, and was upwards of five feet in height. His name was Edward Fugion. Besides being remarkable for his height, he was remarkable for 'a very large nose; he was intended for the army, and was actually gazetted as ensign when he was thirteen-and-a-half years of age. Though of such huge stature, he was feeble and ungainly; and the boys used to teaze him by saying: 'Fugion, it will be bad for you if you go to battle, for the French will hardly miss your nose.' What became of him after he left school I know not; he doffed the petticoat and donned the scarlet coat, and almost immediately after was draughted off on active service: this was towards the middle of 1809.

About this period Mr. R. B. Pollard, jun., who had been studying at Oxford, returned for a short time to his father's house. I believe he was originally intended for the church, but he settled by marrying, and opened a school at Cadogan Place, Chelsea, in which I believe he has been successful, and must now be an elderly gentleman. He was exceedingly kind to me, and the first pocket money I enjoyed was from his bounty. He was a fine handsome man, though of middle size, and a first-rate scholar.

Towards the conclusion of 1809, Robert Bloomfield, the poet, paid a visit to Mr. Pollard ; and to do him honor several of the boys had pieces from his poems to learn, with the view of reciting them before him. I acquired by heart his 'Highland Drover returning from England,' and was delighted when I was told it was to be recited before him ; and I did recite it before him. I have since thought how much more effective I could have delivered it, had I then the Scottish idiom I have since acquired. But it was a bold stroke for an English agricultural laborer and poor shoemaker to attempt a description of Scottish scenery and manners, and one part I remember amused Mr. Pollard amazingly, and on my reciting the poem to him (Mr. P.) before I was ushered into the poet's presence, he smilingly exclaimed as I uttered,

> ' Perhaps some huge rock in the dusk she may see,
> And will say in her fondness, " *That*, surely is he !" '

' Rather gigantic, that ; don't you think so ? '
I did think so, when Mr. P. pointed it out, but I had not noticed it before.

The Poet was a small man, about five feet five inches in height, and exceedingly modest in his demeanor. When I had finished the poem, he advanced towards me purse in hand, but I caught the eye of Mr. Pollard, and refused the proffered gratuity ; and after his departure I found I had done right, for Mr. Pollard observed, ' You would see I did not wish you to accept any present from Mr. Bloomfield. Poets are a generous, but a poor race; and Bloomfield is one of the poorest of them, and I am sure has nothing to spare out of his slender purse.'

About this time an incident occurred of a most painful nature, which has made a serious impression upon me, and convinced me not only of the cruelty, but impolicy of making boys confess crime under the smartings of the lash.

A boy of wealthy parents had received a present of a rich cake, which he had carefully deposited in his box, and which he indulged himself in eating, when, as he thought, none of the boys were near. But he was mistaken. There were others as cunning as himself, and on one occasion he had been enjoying his cake by himself, and was suddenly called away without locking his box ! the result was, his cake was pounced upon and devoured, so that on his return the remains of the cake had vanished. He set up a howl, and then went to the master and laid his grievance before him.

It chanced that one of the youngest boys in the school was in the Lusorium on his return, and he was immediately charged with the theft. He denied it ; declared that he knew not that the boy had a cake, and if he had known it he would not have touched it. He protested his innocence of the crime. However, after Mr. Pollard had been informed, he said he would soon discover the thief. We were all assembled in the play room, and the poor boy (innocent as he was afterwards proved to be) was first submitted to the lash. He bore it for some time, crying bitterly while smarting under the lash, but protesting his innocence. But as Mr. Pollard continued to flog on, his fortitude gave way under the pain, and, at length, he acknowledged he had eaten the cake, upon which Mr. Pollard first gave him half-a-dozen additional lashes for his lies, and then made him pay out of his own pocket-money for the damage he had done. He was branded both as a liar and a thief.

And yet this boy was innocent ! but this was not discovered until six months after the occurrence ; when another boy was detected in an act similar to the one for which the poor boy had suffered, and during punishment confessed that it was he who had purloined the cake. Mr. Pollard was furious, punished him without mercy, and appeared to me to be even resolved to punish the poor little boy who had previously suffered, because he had not sufficient courage to persist in the truth. Frightened, the poor little fellow, with tears in his eyes, exclaimed, ' O, sir, don't flog me—indeed, indeed, sir, I could not bear the pain. I was obliged to say I took the cake, but I really did not. O, sir, don't flog me ! '

Mr. Pollard was moved, but cautioned him 'never again to tell a falsehood, whatever pain he might suffer.' Alas ! alas ! such advice to a child of ten years of age might be considered good ; but how shall we view it when it proceeds from a man whose powers of reflection ought to have taught him better ? A child accused of a petty theft, protesting his innocence, but his weak sense of truth unable to contend against the unmerciful lash.

I am reminded here of a case of murder on the Continent in days when the rack was in full force. A man had been convicted on circumstantial evidence, and had actually endured the torture of the rack, protesting his innocence. . The authorities, however, were convinced he was guilty, and hit upon a scheme to make him confess. They dressed up an executioner, as nearly as they could devise, in the costume of the devil, surrounding the eyes with a glare of red paint, and covering the whole person with phosphorus, so that a bluish flame appeared to invest him. They then entered the cell of the prisoner at midnight, and one of the conspirators in a hollow voice reproached the prisoner for his obduracy in not confessing. The terrified wretch, who had borne the horrors of the rack, sunk under the terrors of the imaginary visit from hell, and groaned out a confession that he was guilty. This was enough. He was executed. In twelve months, the real murderer was detected in another crime, made confession, with such minute particulars of the crime for which the other had suffered, as left no doubt of the innocence of the poor wretch who had been terrified into confession of a lie. What becomes of extorted confessions with these cases before us ? Alas ! how many an

innocent person may have suffered—how many a guilty
one been screened !

I never liked Mr. Pollard after the manner in which he
treated that poor boy. I thought him a cruel and unjust
man, and imagined no boy safe whom he might charge
with crime. I thought that however innocent a boy might
be, it would avail him nothing, since Mr. Pollard might
continue to flog on, and torture him with the lash, till the
very pain would induce him to tell a lie merely to escape
for the time. I have since had opportunity of knowing
that the first disposition to inveterate lying has originated
in circumstances analogous to this case. It is an example
of the very improper manner in which this school was
conducted.

I was now between thirteen and fourteen years of age ;
as just stated, very small and fragile in person, but enjoying
excellent health, when an event occurred which put an end
to my education, and deprived me of the only friend I had
ever known (except my cousin Evans), namely, my uncle.
He died suddenly, and without a will. He had one son
by a former wife, and all his property of course reverted
to him. No provision had been made for me. Still I
had a home in the institution till I should be fourteen.
Hitherto I have mentioned little of my brothers ; and I had
seen as little of them. Once or twice I remembered they
had called at the school, and I spent a few hours with
them, but as they were engaged in business they had very
little opportunity to attend to me. Now, I found that
they were to be appealed to, to remove me when my time
expired at the Institution, which was in March, 1810.
I had at this time four brothers living, but only two of
them were in London ; a third was in the army, at the East
Indies ; and a step brother took no interest at all in me.
I soon got information that it was determined to put me to
learn a trade. One of my brothers had then himself but
lately concluded his apprenticeship as a printer, and
another brother had also concluded his as a bookbinder.

At the time of which I am speaking (1810), my brothers

had become acquainted with a man named Fleming. He was an ivory and bone brush maker, and learning that my brothers had a younger brother to apprentice, he made overtures to them, to receive me into his house as an indoor apprentice. He was told there would be a small premium of ten or twenty pounds, and at the expiration of the term an additional five pounds ; but he would have to board and lodge me, and my brothers would see to my clothing. He at once agreed to receive me, and I was to be placed in his house in March, 1810, on trial for a month, that I might see how I liked the business.

This was a sad blow to me, for I had been hitherto educated for the ministry, and still hoped to be able to accomplish it ; but there seemed no other prospect. Mr. Pollard did not like the plan at all. He retained me at the Institution three months after my time ; but, nothing else offering, I was, in the month of June, removed to this Mr. Charles Fleming's house, which was in Artillery Place, Westminster. No vestige of this place now remains. Here I remained a month, during which time I was treated kindly, and at the expiration of the month was apprenticed for seven years, my indentures being dated back to March 1st, 1810. And now I turn to a new period of my existence ; and a most eventful and suffering one.

Third Period:

FROM FOURTEEN TILL EIGHTEEN YEARS OF AGE.
1810 TO 1814.

'Observe persons whose heads are very prominent on the sides, and flattened at the top, and you will always find them false, artful, perfidious, venal, vacillating, and hypocritical. . . . . Such persons make you feel at home with them, that they may unexpectedly lay their plots against you, and the more easily work your ruin.'

GALL.

'Artful and hypocritical man constantly endeavors to control the expression of his countenance and motions: he is impenetrable, he dissembles bad offices, smiles upon his enemies, checks his temper, disguises his passions, belies his character, speaks and acts contrary to his sentiments; all these are but refinements of the single vice, falsehood.'

THE COURTIER OF LA BRUYERE.

I HAD not been apprenticed a week to Mr. Fleming before I discovered a vast difference both in him and in the treatment I received. I feel confident my brothers never could have known the real character of this man, or they never would have placed me in such keeping, or under such training. All they could have known of him must have been during seasons of festivity, when the passions were in a comparative state of quietude, and a plausible appearance of good nature predominated. I can truly say he was one of the worst characters I ever knew, and ignorant to a degree that was perfectly amazing to me. He could neither read nor write, was a most profane swearer, and a vile drunkard; but withal he had great plausibility, so that he could and did impose upon almost all with whom

MY MASTER.

(from memory.)

[PAGE 61.

he came in contact. My brothers, I am now persuaded, knew nothing of his tyranny in his own house, nor of his profligacy and infamy out of it, or they would surely have put me somewhere else. But the mischief was done ; and I must now proceed with a description of him and his family, and of the manner in which I was treated.

In person this man, my master, was about five feet six inches high, deeply marked with the small-pox. He had a small head (oh that I had known as much of Phrenology then as I do now), which swelled out above and behind the ears ; his forehead was ' villanously low ' and retreating ; the vertex of the head was very high, but rapidly declined towards the forehead, and also sloped downwards towards the parietal bones ; his eye-brows were thick and bushy ; he had a rather large and prominent eye ; and, while speaking to those who were not members of his house, his face was rarely without a smile, indicative of large secretiveness. His wife was a person about five feet high, of a rather agreeable countenance, but her face also pitted with the small-pox. Like her husband, she could neither read nor write. They had three children at this time—Charles, the eldest, a boy of about 10 years, who gave every promise (which has since been realised) of living his father over again ; Anne, or Nancy, about seven years, a very pretty child indeed ; and Thomas, about five years—all in the same degree of ignorance ; and, so far as I could see, never intended to be instructed. There was also an apprentice in his nineteenth year, named Edwin Rawlinson, who was considered at the time I speak the support of the family. He had a large head, was of a pale countenance, and of a lymphatic constitution —was a slow but regular workman ; when irritated, he would make nothing of returning the master word for word, or blow for blow. Lastly, there was myself, small, weak, and very timid and shy, but also irritable and capable of strong resentment when offended, at the same time never thrusting myself into the quarrels of the master and Edwin, which were very frequent.

I soon found that, as I had my time to serve as fag
school, I had the same to do while in this family as a
prentice—that I was at the call of every one in the hous
from the master and mistress, and the young masters an
mistress down to Mr. Edwin Rawlinson.

I was apprenticed by the College solicitor, a Mr. Drak
who in 1810 lived in Little Charles Street, Parliamer
Street, Westminster. He was a merry little gentlema
usually wore a brown coat, vest, and small-clothes, wit
small silver knee-buckles, and, true to his color, also wor
a brown wig. He was particularly facetious at my bind
ing, calling me his little ivory gentleman, complimentin
me on my marriage with half a glass of wine, and pro
mising me, when I buried my wife, which he hoped h
should live to see, a whole glass. Well, as I said, I wa
bound (married, as the old gentleman termed it) for sevei
years. Indentures were exchanged, the master's bein
held by him, and mine remaining in the hands of Mr
Drake. My two brothers, now both deceased, were pre
sent ; and, after the indentures were signed and sealed
we all adjourned to my new master's house, where a supper was provided, and songs, stories, and witticisms circulated till a late hour, my master telling me to fear nothing,
for he would take care I should become a finished workman, and he would make a man of me. Well, the party
broke up, and I was now the slave of the household. For
a week or two I was treated well enough, compared with
the treatment I afterwards received. I, however, as already
stated, was the fag of the house. My morning's duties
were, first to light the kitchen fire for my mistress, then
to clean my master's boots (top or jockey boots were at
that time worn), the children's shoes, and the knives and
forks. After this I had to repair to the workshop, where
I arranged my master's tool-bench, and swept the shop.
Breakfast was usually ready about nine o'clock, sometimes
earlier, but I never obtained mine till every one else had
finished; and my breakfast never varied, either in quantity
or quality, during my stay. It consisted of a slice of

bread and butter, with a basin full of what was called tea,
but which, in reality, was what was left after six persons
had partaken.

Leaving school, and going directly to my master's house,
I was totally ignorant of the City of London. Twice a
week the elder apprentice always went to some place near
Smithfield, for newly boiled neat's-feet bones. These
were used for an inferior sort of tooth-brush handles,
ivory being used for the finer kinds. This journey, to him,
was never less than two hours, oftener of three, and he
scarcely ever returned without a quarrel, and sometimes
a fight, between him and the master. After I had been
about two months at the business, it was resolved that the
duties of errand boy should devolve upon me. There
were generally two, and sometimes three, dozen of these
bones required. The bone-boiler was a Mr. Stevens,
residing at Castle Street, Great Saffron Hill, a place the
locality of which I was totally ignorant of.

However, I was instructed to cross the park, take
Charing Cross to the right, and the Strand to the left.
Thence I was to proceed straight forward to Shoe Lane,
to go up Shoe Lane, cross the street, Holborn, where
I was to find a narrow lane, called Field Lane ; up
this lane was to lead me to Saffron Hill, once in which
I was to inquire for Castle Street. I was told that two
hours would be allowed me—an hour to go and the same
to return. The bones were given out precisely as the
clock struck eight, so that I left the further part of Westminster by seven. But I did not reach my destination
till half-past eight. I, however, obtained what I was
sent for — at that time they were worth 2s. 6d. per
dozen. If it had taken me an hour and a half to accomplish the journey with an empty bag, there was little
doubt but it would take double that time with a full one;
and it did so, and more, so that when I returned it was
twelve o'clock, and I was in a fever of perspiration with
the weight of my load. I had left home without breakfast,
and I was told I should neither have breakfast nor dinner

for my laziness, and that if I did not manage better the
next time, I should have ' *a good licking* ' into the bargain
I was ordered at once to take off my jacket and get to
work.   At this time my work consisted in what was tech
nically called *shaving* and *polishing* : that is, I received
the stocks or handles of the brushes as they came from
the file, and by the aid of a *hand-plane* or knife, shaved
off all the coarse marks of the file, and with sand, whiting
water, and a piece of coarse cloth, proceeded to put a
polish upon them.   It was an irksome and dirty employ
ment, and this employment was continued during the first
year of my time.   I was kept that day without food til
six o'clock, when I received the usual portion allotted
for what was called tea : namely, a slice of bread and
butter, and a basin of the before mentioned tea.   I certainly might, had I known the way, have done the journey
to Saffron Hill within the hour ; but I was struck with
wonder with many of the shops I saw in the Strand and
Fleet Street; and pictures and books always attracted
me, and of these multitudes were seen in my journey.

I remember I was struck with amazement when I
reached Field Lane.   At that time there was a large
gin shop at one corner, and the groups of horrid looking
men and women, many of the latter in rags, filled me with
amazement and fear.   On the entrance to the lane, perhaps about three doors up on the right hand side, there
was a large shop, devoted to the sale of sheep's heads,
brains, hearts, etc., with a large showy woman behind the
counter ; and my fellow-apprentice informed me that the
proprietor of this shop was worth thousands of pounds,
all made by catering the delicacies above named.   On
each side of the lane, were second-hand clothes and shoe
dealers, most of them of the Jewish persuasion.   From the
shop windows dangled hundreds, perhaps thousands, of
silk handkerchiefs, which I was told were purloined from
the pockets of gentlemen by juvenile thieves ; and on
more than one occasion, it was stated when a person had
bought a silk handkerchief at the beginning of the lane, by

be time of his reaching the end, it was seen dangling
rom another shop window for sale. In truth, it was a
ile place, one that I was obliged to pass up very fre-
[uently, for most of the materials used in the business of
n ivory and bone brush maker were purchased in the
neighborhood of Smithfield, and some of the most expert
hands in the business lived in Field Lane, Shug Lane
now called West Street, and also Chick Lane—I presume
Shug Lane was but a slang name), and Great Saffron Hill.

Well, the second day for fetching the bones came round,
and I was warned that if I was not back by nine o'clock,
. should lose my breakfast, and gain something else. I
had, however, learned my way, and I reached the bone
yard in time; but I was very small and weak, and the
oad was too much for me, and with all my labor it was
near eleven o'clock when I reached home. I knew my
breakfast was forfeited. I deposited my load in the
workshop, took off my jacket, and set to work.

The master was silent; but I had no sooner commenced
my work, than he struck me a tremendous blow with the
back of his hand, which brought me to the ground; the
blow fell on the ear, and for a time I was stunned.
As soon as I recovered I rose, and was going to my work
again, when he struck me on the other side with equal
violence, kicked me out of his way, and swore a fearful
oath that the next time he would half murder me. I
retained the marks of this beating for a long time. I
never could accomplish this journey in the time required.
I could do it very well with the empty bag, but when
filled it was to me a tremendous load. I was very weak,
as I have said, and I was more than half starved. I
therefore bore a severe thrashing twice a week, always
accompanied with the loss of my breakfast, and with a
torrent of harsh and foul language, such as would horrify
any person of moral habits to hear. I was beaten about
the head to a frightful extent; sometimes he would throw
a heavy bone at me, and I recollect his saying to me,
on one occasion, when I had returned late with my load,

5

after he had beaten me with his fist, and with a stick
called the *drill-bow*, that I should have no rest from him
that he would render my life so miserable that I should
be fit to make away with myself each time that he
punished me. In this manner I spent two years of my
apprenticeship. I was little better than a skeleton. I
was lodged in the foul and filthy workshop, where was a
complication of vile odors. I was scarcely allowed time
to wash myself. I ate my food as I stood at my work-
bench, for my tyrant tasked me so many dozen brushes
per day; and when I had served two years, I did the
work of a man upon the food of a child; but to accomplish it, I had to work from four o'clock in the morning
till twelve o'clock at night, and always half the Sunday,
and still I was called a lazy vagabond, not worth the salt
put into my gruel.

On a Saturday evening, after the work of the day,
which on that day terminated at ten o'clock at night, I
had first the knives and forks, and shoes and boots of the
whole family to clean. This done, I had the workshop
to clean up, the tools to arrange, and the floor of the
workshop to scour. I did this from choice as much as
from necessity; for had I neglected it, what with the
refuse from horse and cow hair, and hog's bristles, with
which the brushes were filled, and what with the
medullary substance from the bones, and the bone dust,
etc., we should have been devoured with vermin. On
the Sunday morning all the family indulged themselves
by lying long in bed, and it was often eleven o'clock
before I got my breakfast; but I was up at six, shaving
and polishing to bring up the arrears of my task. When
I had got my breakfast, and washed and cleaned myself,
I then wandered out. I was usually invited to my
brother's to dinner and tea, and these were the only full
meals I had. I also frequently called as I went my
errands, and my kind sister-in-law soon found that I was
more than half starved, and she used to stay my craving
appetite with food. Sunday (after the early part) was

indeed a happy day. I have mentioned that I had a good voice, and my brother introduced me into the choir at York Street Chapel, St. James's Square ; at that time Mr. Proud was minister. I became acquainted with many of the singers, who admired me for my voice, and who treated me with kindness and attention. The music I thought very fine. Some of the tunes by Barthelomon (I think the name was) remain with me to this day ; but the doctrines preached I paid then but little attention to. The Liturgy then in use very nearly resembled that of the Church of England, and with the exception of the omission of the Litanies and Creeds, I did not perceive much difference. I thought Mr. Proud a beautiful preacher, and many more thought so beside me. I used to attend chapel in the evening pretty regularly ; I could not get out in the morning, and in the afternoon I often went to St. Margaret's church. I was always required to be home [alas, such a home !] by nine o'clock, and I never transgressed without punishment. My master was generally intoxicated twice a week. My duty was always to sit up and let him in. This was one of my most miserable duties, and deprived me of what little sleep I ought to have had. I used to sit behind the door, that the first motion of the knocker might be heard. If I failed opening the door on the instant, I was cruelly beaten. And this was frequently the case, for he never returned till two, often three o'clock in the morning, and I was by that time so weary and overpowered with sleep, that I could not always hear the first stroke of the knocker. When he had beaten me, he would stagger to his bed. If there were not a light (and the light that was left burning for him frequently expended itself before he returned), he would make his wife get out of bed and light another candle, and if she demurred, he would immediately beat her most cruelly, and his oaths and imprecations, when intoxicated, were most frightful. Many a time have I dreaded lest he should murder either me or his wife. Both of us have often been left in a state of insensibility; me, he frequently declared he would finish before my time was up, and I believe he would have done so had I stayed my time.

I recollect, on one occasion, when I had finished a heavy day's work, and my mistress wished me to go to bed, she sent me at about half-past eleven o'clock at night with the house-door key to my master, who was at a public house he was in the habit of frequenting. When I arrived he was singing a song, called ' *Will Watch*,' and I waited till it was concluded. He was loudly applauded by the companions by whom he was surrounded. When this applause had subsided, I went up to him and said, ' Please, sir, my mistress has sent the key of the street door, for fear you should be late.'

' —— you,' said he, 'take it back, you lazy young vagabond, and sit up till I come home, and woe be to you if you keep me standing at the door.'

I returned home, afraid to sit in the kitchen, lest I should not hear the knocker. So I sat behind the door, and at half-past two in the morning he returned. I opened the door immediately, but he no sooner entered than he commenced beating me in the most savage manner, knocking me down as frequently as I rose from one blow, until he left me half dead in the passage. Then he ascended to his bed room, and commenced cruelly beating his wife because she had dared to send me with the key of the street door. It was a full month ere I recovered from this dreadful beating, and his wife was even in a worse condition than myself.

I had served in this way nearly three years of my apprenticeship, when, on one of my journeys to the bone yard, who should I meet but my cousin Evan Evans, mentioned in a former part of this narrative. He knew me instantly, and began most kindly to inquire after my situation. Though approaching seventeen years of age, I was still but a child in appearance, and I answered him, crying bitterly all the time, and told him all. He went with me to the bone yard, and when I had got my load, he took me to a breakfast house, and gave me a hearty breakfast, then he accompanied me as far as the park, and gave me his address, which was in Widegate Street, Bishopsgate, and I made an appointment with him for the next Sunday, to call at his house. This appointment I kept, when he made me tell him my story all over again. He was most indignant, and would have gone home with me, and threatened my master. But his wife thought it would be better for me to leave him, and try to get another place. After a while he fell in with this view, and it was arranged that on the next Sunday I should put up my articles of clothing in a bundle, as though it was dirty linen, and should proceed immediately to his house. This I did, and he was to me as a father. I remained with him about three weeks to gain strength. He completely recruited me, and furnished me with clothes, both for the working day and Sunday. He then went out with me to seek for a situation, and, after some time, I was engaged as errand boy to a Mr. Batley, a pocket book, and lady's work-box, and gentleman's dressing-case maker, in High Holborn. This was in the beginning of 1813, somewhere about March. I was then seventeen years of age. I was to receive six shillings a week, and was promised a basin of tea morning and evening. I thought this a fortune, and Mr. and Mrs. Batley were exceedingly kind to me. My cousin told them I was an orphan, which was the truth ; but, of course, we concealed from them that I was a runaway apprentice.

I had been in this gentleman's employ for about four months, when I was sent with a gentleman's dressing case to have a shaving brush fitted in. The person to whom I was sent was an ivory turner of the name of Harris, residing on Great Saffron Hill. Now I had frequently been to this very shop before, on errands for my cruel master Fleming, and I was somewhat afraid I should be recognised ; but there was no help for it. I went accordingly, and, while waiting for the shaving brush to be fitted to the case, as ill luck would have it—so I then thought—

the oldest son of Mr. Fleming came into the shop, for
some turn-backs—shaving brushes similar to the one I
was waiting for. He saw me and recognised me.
'Hollo, Dav.! is that you? Where do you live now?'
'Never you mind,' said I. And, having got my brush,
and paid the money, he asked Mr. Harris, as I was afterwards told, where I lived; and Mr. H., instead of telling
him at Mr. Batley's, Holborn, told him Batcourt, Holborn. He, of course, told his father, but no Batcourt was
to be found in Holborn. Fleming, however, was resolved
to recover me; and one morning, when I was opening
shop, he saw me, collared me, and carried me off. I was
dreadfully afraid, and cried bitterly; but when people
asked what was. the matter, he told them I was a lazy
young rascal, and was his apprentice, and had run away
from him, and he was going to a constable to take me
before a magistrate. And to a constable he brought me.
This man's name was Gilmour; he lived in a court at
Wood Street, Westminster. Mr. Fleming gave him an
account of me as a most depraved and lazy young rascal,
more fond of reading play books, and such like stuff, than
of making brushes, and concluded with requesting Mr.
Gilmour to take me before a magistrate. Mr. Gilmour
eyed me very closely, but seemed not so severe as my
master wished.

'Well,' says the constable, 'I must take you to Queen
Square, and the magistrate will soon tell you what you
must do. Now, have you had your breakfast?' 'No, sir,
not yet.' 'Then you shall get a breakfast before you go,
any way,' said he; and he got me a breakfast, and made
me eat it, too, much to the surprise of my master. When
I had finished, he showed me a pocket pistol, and he
loaded it before my eyes, and then said: 'Now, if you run
away while under my charge, I will shoot you; but
if you will walk quietly to the office, you shall go
without being handcuffed, and nobody will know that
you are in charge.' I told him I would walk quietly,
and I did so. I was very much terrified; I had never

been in a police office before, and I expected to be sent to prison.

Mr. Colquhoun sat on the bench, and the constable introduced me to the magistrate by saying—'A runaway apprentice, your worship.' 'Where is the master?' He was pointed out. 'What was the reason of your running away, boy?' said the magistrate. 'He was always beating me, sir, and swearing at me, and threatening to be the death of me.' 'Hah! where did you get this boy from?' 'From the Green Coat School,' said my master. 'Take the boy into the Inner Office,' said the magistrate. 'And, Gilmour, you go to Mr. Pollard, and with my compliments request his immediate 'attendance.' The officer went on his errand, and in a very little time I was again ordered into the public office.

'Do you know that boy, Mr. Pollard?' said the magistrate.

'Yes, he was educated at our Foundation.'

'And how did he conduct himself?'

'A good boy in everything but one.'

'And what was that?'

'He would not or he could not write well.'

'Is that all?'

'Yes, in everything else he was a good boy—an orphan, without father and mother.'

'Now,' said the magistrate, turning to my master, 'you hear what is said of him. The boy complains of cruel usage—are you willing to use him better if he returns?'

Mr. Fleming replied, 'He has always been used better than he deserved; but this is always the way when a boy gets education; he is saucy and lazy, and thinks he knows more than his master, and can do just as he likes. Now here am I obliged to work hard, and can neither write nor read, obliged to be snubbed by such a young rascal as this. But if he behaves himself he will get no ill usage from me.'

'On that condition he must return,' said the magistrate.

He then told me how wrong I had done in leaving my

master's service, that I ought to have gone to Mr. Polla
or to the college solicitor, or to him ; ' but I hope you w
do better for the future, and if your master again us
you ill, come here *and we'll see you righted.'*

I recollect these last words as if they were spoken b
yesterday, and yet I so hated and dreaded my mast
that I made up my mind to leave him again the very fir
opportunity. But I then left the office. The friendl
officer told me to be a good boy and give him no mo
trouble. I returned to my drudgery.

Great was the rejoicing at my capture. Every one of th
family thought to please the master by sneering at an
abusing me. In particular, one of my master's brothers
who was in the same business with himself, told me, ha
he been my master, he would soon have drill-bowed m
(beat me with a stick) into submission. I told him h
was not my master, and I would not submit to his
abuse.

'Hold your saucy tongue,' said he, 'unless you want
a bone at your head.' At which I was so exasperated
that I snatched up a large bone myself, and placing myself
in an attitude of defence, assured him, if he dared to
touch me, I would retaliate. He thought better of it, and
I threw the bone down again. All this time my master
was present, but he said nothing, and for a week or two
he seemed to have determined upon better usage. But
the bone journeys again began, and with them began my
thrashings, until in a month or two I was used quite as
badly as before. I repaired again to my cousin, and he
again counselled me to abscond ; and at length I took
advantage of another Sunday, and, without going either *to*
Mr. Pollard or the magistrate, went to my cousin, who
received me with his former kindness.

This time I sought quite a different situation. I was,
as I have said, very small and very young looking.
Many people took me for not more than twelve years of
age. I passed for fourteen without question. My cousin
took me to a Register Office and entered me for a lady's

age, with a wish, if it were practicable, to get me a situation in the country. Never shall I forget the kindness with which I was treated by this good man and his wife. All the time that I was out of a situation I remained concealed at his house ; so great was the dread I had of recapture, that I could not sleep at night. I started frequently in my sleep, exclaiming, 'He has got me again, cousin ; O save me ! save me !' Even to this day, when anything seriously affects or agitates me, I dream of him, of his cruel beatings, of his horrid language, of his threats to murder me. But to return :

One morning, after I had been about a month at my cousin's, I was sent for to the Register Office, and told of a situation at Bedford Lodge, Blackheath, where I was immediately to proceed to see the lady. Glad enough was I to go, and glad enough was my cousin, and the hopes of both were raised.

On my arrival at the heath, I soon found the house, and was ushered into the presence of a very stout lady. She asked me, if I had ever been in service before ? I replied, I had not. Where were my parents. I had none. With whom did I live ? A cousin. What was his employment ? He was engaged in the East India Company's tea warehouse. His name ? I told her. My name ? I told her also. What wages did I expect, if she found on inquiry that my cousin's character was good ? I replied, that as I had never been out in service before, I would leave it with her. She then gave me her card to take to my cousin ; on it was engraved, 'The Rt. Hon. the Countess de Byland.' She told me she would make inquiry into the character of my cousin, and if it was good, I should hear from her. To the great joy of myself and of my cousin, in two days I received a communication that his character was satisfactory, and that I was immediately to proceed to Bedford Lodge. I was to receive £10 a year, my clothes, and board and lodging of course. My business was to attend to the lady, to keep her private apartment in order, see to her fire,

and attend her if she went out, and, in short, to be h
page, and do whatever she required. My cousin ferventl
thanked God for this good appointment. To me it ap
peared as rising from the depths of misery to the summ
of happiness. It was at a distance, too, from my perse
cutor — a place he was never likely to reach, and I fe
in my mind, that I should at length be secure from hi
malice and cruelty.

I may here offer my tribute of gratitude to my cousir
who shortly after I had obtained the appointment departe
this life. He was kind to me to the last, and on hi
death bed commended me to the care of his wife, wh
treated me with equal kindness till her death. I cai
truly say of them both, that the blessing of him who wa
ready to perish came from my heart upon them, and thei
affection for a poor orphan boy, though I could neve
repay, is, I am sure, paid by a higher power.

Well, I proceeded to my new place. Accustomed as I
had been to the most wanton cruelty and oppression, my
new position was as Elysium. But I was no sooner
domesticated, than I was told by the other servants that
three months was the utmost time any page could live
with the countess, and indeed that in general no servant
remained a longer time. My previous sufferings, however, had prepared me to endure much, and the prophecies
of the other servants were falsified in my case. But I
must not anticipate.

I had been in my service about a week, when the
count returned from Holland. He was a person of a
tall and spare habit, very poor, and the countess had
married him merely for his title. He was completely
under the control of the lady. Whatever she requested
him to do, he never for a moment hesitated. He was
lampooned sadly in the kitchen, and his broken English
was a never failing source of amusement to the cook and
kitchen maids. The great fault of the countess was
penuriousness, and she exposed the count to many indig-
nities from the servants. I recollect one evening, when

the business of the day was concluded, and the servants were seated round the kitchen fire, previous to retiring for the night, the count suddenly entered the kitchen, and in his usual broken English exclaimed, 'What you all do with this great fire, 'nuf to cook dinner, gi' me de poker, and get to bed! D——, go up to my lady.' He raked out the fire, the servants retired to bed, and I received a lecture from her ladyship for not reporting the extravagance of the servants.

Her ladyship seldom walked out, but it so happened, that the next day I was required to attend her. The count remained at home, and doubtless, at the request of the countess, interfered with the servants in the kitchen, when one of the maids pinned a duster to his coat tail, and so quietly that he did not perceive it. On the return of the countess, he was walking in the drawing room, all unconscious of the appendage to his coat. It caught the eye of her ladyship. 'What's that, count, what's that?' said she, hastily, 'have you been in the kitchen?' He answered in the affirmative. 'Go down instantly, D——, and order all the servants up.' I did so, and they soon appeared. Her ladyship in a fury pointed to the tail of the count's coat, and demanded to know who had been guilty of so foully insulting the count. All were silent, and it was well for me that I had been attending her ladyship. 'I require to know who has dared to insult his lordship in this manner,' said she again. Her face was absolutely livid with passion, and stamping with her feet, she declared they should all leave instantly, and that she would withhold their character unless she was told; but they still continued silent. At length, scarcely able to contain herself, she ordered them out of the room, and then sent me down to them to command them to pack up their boxes, and leave the house. This they seemed at once willing to do, and in a short time all were ready to depart, cook, housemaid, and kitchen-maid. They bade me go to her ladyship, saying, they waited only for their wages. They were

again ordered to the drawing room, and her ladysh
who had now become more calm, but not less determin·
declared, that neither of them should receive a pen
until the culprit was pointed out. Whereupon ·
kitchen-maid, who was a very good-natured girl
the main, but very flippant in her manner, said, that
gentlemen would poke their noses where they had
business, they deserved nor only dusters, but 'dish clout
(those were her very words) pinned to their tails, a·
that she had done it, if possible, to cure him of ·
molly-ooddle habits. Whereupon, her ladyship paid t
other two servants, but told the offender she might g
her wages how she could, and ordered them all off.   B
the kitchen-maid declared that ' unless she was instanti
paid, she would go to every tradesman on the heath a·
let them know for what she was discharged; and sl
would then take out a summons from the Court ·
Requests at Greenwich, and expose both the count an
countess ; and as for her character, she would make the·
give her such a one as should get her another place, ·
the police court should receive a visit from her, and th
papers would soon tell the world all about it.'   Thi
threat had the desired effect ; the countess paid he
wages, and she departed with her fellow-servants.

I was now in a very trying situation, not knowin·
whether I might be retained or discharged.   Fortunatel·
for me I had no hand in these pranks of the females, bu
I was still afraid of losing my place.   I retired to th·
butler's room.   I had the care of the plate, and of th·
china and glass, which I had to keep in order.   About a·
hour after the departure of the servants, her ladyship'·
bell rung.   It must be remembered, that though betwee·
seventeen and eighteen years of age, I did not appear t·
be fourteen, and her ladyship had fortunately not inquire·
my age.

Upon answering her bell, she immediately spoke to m·
as if I had been a child of *twelve years old.*   ' Come
here, D——,' said she, ' you see what a set of evil Turk·

I have had to do with ; what would have become of you, my poor child, had they remained ! They would have made you as evil-minded as themselves. Now, D——, I am determined to have no more servants from London, and so, for a few days, you must do the work of the house, and the house must be shut up in front—the blinds all drawn, and if any one calls—" I'm not at home." '

She had a passion for titles, but during my stay with her there had been but one party, and none of these were titled. Yet she often observed to me, and she now reiterated her orders—' If the Duke of Montrose, or the Duchess, or any of the nobility should call—I'm not at home. I shall order a carriage in a day or two, as soon as ready, and proceed to Brighton, and you must attend me. But, meantime, you must attend to all the duties of the house, and at Brighton I will engage fresh servants.'

For four days I was the factotum, even to the preparing of her ladyship's meals, and I was assisted by the count. Meantime, no noble visitors, or, indeed, visitors of any kind, called. The gardener and his wife were engaged to take charge of the house, and in five days after the discharge of the female servants, I was perched on the dickey of a post chaise, posting on to Brighton as fast as four horses could convey us. I knew nothing of travelling, but his lordship attended to the paying of the post boys, and to the hotel expenses. He had also given me instructions what I was to eat and drink. I was to open the carriage door, follow her ladyship into a private room, receive her instructions, and see them executed, always accompanying the servants to her ladyship's presence, and then leaving the room, waiting outside the door.

I was rather pale at that time, and my complexion was very fair. At one of the inns where we changed horses, I was called into the bar, and interrogated by the landlady, who gave me a glass of wine, at the same time she remarked—' Poor child, you had better be at home with your mother, than at the beck of this would-be fine lady.'

'Ah!' thought I, 'I am very—very grateful that I ha·
to attend her.'   Towards eight o'clock in the evenir
we drove into Brighton, and the carriage proceeded
the 'Ship' hotel.   I attended her ladyship, as usual,
her room, saw her attended by the landlady, and the
had permission to retire, and was told I should be wante
no more that night.

I then descended to the servant's room.   I was totall
ignorant of life at an hotel.   I saw, what appeared   t
me, to be a number of ladies and gentlemen regalin;
themselves at a well-spread table.   I had no idea the·
were servants like myself.   The 'lady' who was pre
siding at the tea table called to me, seeing I was pal
and shy—'Come here, child, and you shall have some
tea.'   I did so, and approached the table very bashfully
She made me sit beside her, gave me a cup of tea, and
requested a gentleman to help me to some ham and
chicken.   'And now, my little beau,' said she, 'pray
who are you travelling with?'

I told her I was page to the Countess de Byland.

'The Countess de—what?' said she.

'No such title in this country,' said a gentleman.

'Come, let me see your crest, little man,' said the lady,
'and your hat.'

My hat was soon produced, but I did not understand
what she meant by my crest.   I was soon enlightened,
however.   It was the crest on my great-coat button she
meant, and my hat, which was ornamented with a black
cockade and an orange rosette of silk in the centre,
called forth from the gentleman who had said there was
no such title as Countess de Byland in England, the
remark—

'There, I told you so, it is a Dutch count, don't you
see the orange rosette?'

I was then told to make myself at home, and the
lady said I should be her little beau, and I should be
called Lord Byland.   'And so, my little lord,' said she,
'I expect your lordship's homage.'   From being pale

I turned crimson. 'There, don't be frightened child,
I shall take care of you.' And while we remained at
the hotel she did take care of me, treating me as
though I was her own child, and considering me *as* a
child. I found that the party I took for ladies and
gentlemen were servants of the gentry then staying
at the hotel, and it astonished me not a little to find
these servants calling one another by their masters' and
mistresses' names, and on this account I was called
Byland.

I was amazed at the style in which they lived.
There was a handsome apartment in which they took
their meals, and they were waited upon by a waiter
with as much deference as if they were really entitled
to the appellations by which they distinguished each
other. The countess had warned me to be upon my
guard against the evil Turks (meaning thereby the
female servants) in the servant's hall. And the count
had ordered me to take nothing but water to my dinner;
but at supper I was to be allowed a pint of porter.
I always waited behind her ladyship's chair at dinner,
and her ladyship always left me her wine glass when
she retired, and seemed pleased that I was so obedient
to the count's orders to avoid drinking at two o'clock,
the servant's general dining hour. I must confess that
I was very kindly treated in the servants' room. I was
as willing to act the page to the servants as to the
countess, and I am sure that my sojourn at Brighton
(although in the menial capacity I was) was one of the
happiest periods in my existence. The servants, both
male and female, were well conducted, and even
polished in their manners. I found none of that coarseness and vulgarity which is attributed to them in the
publications of the present day.

I had very light duties to perform while at Brighton
—an hour's drive in attendance on her ladyship, and half
an hour's attendance at dinner, with an occasional
message. Good living, and regular repose, made a won-

derful alteration in my appearance, so that although
continued dwarfish, I had still the appearance of a well
conditioned lady's page. After a fortnight's sojourn a
the hotel, servants were engaged, and we returned t
Blackheath; where, we had hardly time to domesticat
ourselves, when the count was summoned to Holland, an
the countess resolved to accompany him; so the estab
lishment was broken up. But the countess told me, as
had been a good boy, she would see me in a good situa
tion, and she spoke to a son of hers by a former marriage
who was a captain in the army. His name was N——
He had a cottage on Blackheath, where he resided when
off duty, and he took me on the same terms as her ladyship. But the duties were very different.

I had now for the first time to make myself acquainted
with a horse; but I never went out with the captain,
and did not leave the cottage while in his service. He
was a very passionate man, and used very shocking
language when irritated. But his passion very soon subsided, and a more generous man to his servants and to
the poor I never knew. He had given me strict charge
never to mount his mare, of which he was very fond, and
she was a most beautiful but spirited animal. But after
I had led her several times to the stables, always being
jeered by the grooms for my timidity, I on one occasion
thought I would try to ride her; so I mounted her, and
the mare, doubtless wondering what awkward creature
she had got upon her back, and finding I gave her plenty
of rein, at once galloped off at a furious pace across the
heath, until she suddenly came to a stop at the rails of a
mill, and pitched me clean over. Fortunately, I retained
the reins in my hand, and falling on the soft turf, was
little hurt. I was perfectly ashamed, and had to lead
her—I on one side of the rails, she on the other—till I got
to the gate, where the miller met me, and told me I made
a good jockey. I made an apology, and said I was
not accustomed to horses, but I would lead her to
the stable.

'Lead her to the stable, boy,' said he ; 'why, you little
fool, that will be the ready way to make her serve you so
again ! No, no, that will never do ! Come, give me
a leg ;—now, jump up. Stay !—there, don't give her
a loose rein. There ! cross the bridle—hold tight—
now be off !'—and I went off, she trotting quietly to
the mews.

All this time the Captain had been viewing my
Gilpin-like expedition from the drawing-room window
of the cottage, of which I was in total ignorance. But,
on my return, I was instantly ordered into his presence,
and told, if I ever mounted her again, and escaped with
my life, he would discharge me instantly. I made a
very humble apology, and was forgiven. I remained
with the Captain till he was ordered to India. Had
I been at all acquainted with the management of horses,
it is possible I should have accompanied him. On
leaving him, he made me a handsome present, and
left with a brother of his, a solicitor, a character such
as would obtain me another situation.

I now returned to my cousin's. I had nearly ten
pounds (which to me was a large sum), plenty of good
clothes, and a well-stocked trunk of linen. I did not
immediately seek for another situation, but I was very
desirous of ascertaining whether inquiry had been made
for me by my master ; and I ventured into the neighborhood of Saffron Hill to ascertain whether Mr. Fleming
was still in being. I confess it afforded some satisfaction
to learn that he had ruptured a blood-vessel, and was
believed to have departed this life. This report induced
me to visit Westminster, and upon inquiry I found it true.
His continued fits of drunkenness, and the violence of his
passions while under the influence of liquor, had at length
terminated his existence. I was free ! I might now show
myself anywhere. I returned to my cousin's house, and
she also rejoiced that there was no danger of my being
captured and carried back to the slavery of the brush-
making.

6

I thought I would now visit my brother, who at thi
time resided in Charles Street, Westminster, and who
besides keeping a circulating library, and dealing in
stationery, had commenced business as a printer.
visited him accordingly, told him of my emancipation
from the tyranny of Mr. Fleming—told him how I had
employed myself from the time of my second absconding.
and asked him what he would advise me to do—whether
to seek for another service, or to turn my attention to the
acquisition of a new business; for I hated the brush-
making, and declared I would never follow it. I was
all along conscious that the recent situations I had filled
were what was called menial, and my brother did not
seem pleased with them. I reflected, however, that I
had no friend capable of helping me in my distress, and
that, notwithstanding the menial positions I had filled,
I had been kindly treated, had plenty of good and wholesome food, and had saved money. Then there was no
one who knew me, and what did it matter to me where
or how I was employed so long as it was honest and
respectable, however humble? So I had determined in
my own mind to wait a few days, and, if nothing more
advantageous offered itself, to return to the situation of a
lady's page.

I promised, however, that I would visit my brother
again before I accepted any other place, and then returned
to my cousin's. At the end of a week I again called
upon my brother, when he asked me how I should like
to be a printer. I started: there was nothing I should
like better; it would bring me among books; it might
lead to a means of enabling me to complete my studies;
and, after all, I might obtain the object I so ardently
desired, and become a clergyman. My brother told me I
could not become a printer without serving a seven-years'
apprenticeship, and if I did so, I should be nearly 25 years
of age before I completed my term. But I looked then
so young that I did not mind the length of the servitude,
provided that I could live by my earnings; and I had

what I then conceived something very handsome in hand. So I asked my brother what were the terms; and he told me that I should have to provide for myself, and should receive half my earnings.

I hesitated at this; for I had the business to learn, and I thought it would be some time ere I could earn sufficient to keep myself. My brother told me he could not take me into the house, as he had his wife's brother and sister residing with him, and the brother was learning the business also; he had not, therefore, accommodation for me: but I could, if I pleased, go up into the office for a few days, and see how I should like the business. This I acceded to, and went up into the office.

I watched the proceedings with a careful eye. I was amazed at the simplicity of the process, and I felt satisfied that I should soon be able to accomplish as much as the then apprentice at the case. My great difficulty seemed the press, which was then very cumbrous in its construction, and very laborious to work. My brother's press was then of wood, and the inking apparatus was made of pelt, stuffed with wool—most difficult and most laborious for a small boy like myself. However, my brother told me that I should be principally confined to case for the first year; and if 'called to the bar,' the work should be light, such as cards and bills. So I determined upon venturing, and was again under articles for seven years; and with this agreement I close my Third Period.

Fourth Period:

FROM EIGHTEEN TO TWENTY-FIVE YEARS OF AGE.
1814 to 1821.

'Oh, Albion! still thy gratitude confess
To Caxton, founder of the British press:
Since first thy mountains rose and rivers flow'd,
Who on thine isles so rich a boon bestow'd ?
Yet stands the chapel in yon Gothic shrine
Where wrought the father of our English line.
Our art was hailed from kingdoms far abroad,
And cherish'd in the hallow'd house of God ;
From which we learn the homage it received,
And how our sires its heavenly birth believed.
Each printer hence, howe'er unbless'd his walls,
E'en to this day, his house a CHAPEL calls.'

'THE PRESS.' M'CREERY.

I BEGAN my novitiate as a printer in the beginning of
1814. I was free from all anxiety of my old master, and
anticipated much pleasure from my new profession, which
my brother also seemed pleased with, inasmuch as it
rescued me, according to his view, from menial servitude.

About the end of 1813, the Society of the New Church
(Swedenborgians), under Mr. Proud's ministry, having by
the expiration of their lease of York Street Chapel, St.
James's Square, been obliged to leave, fitted up a large
room in Lisle Street, Leicester Square, which was opened
by Mr. Proud, on the 2nd February, 1814. The situation was very obscure when compared with that of the
chapel in York Street, and, in consequence, the congregations rapidly declined in number ; while in York Street

f-
ed

REV. J. PROUD.

[PAGE 84.

the chapel was always respectably filled, and sometimes, especially in the evening, crowded, in Lisle Street Chapel, which was not more than two-thirds the size of that in York Street, there was a sad display of empty pews.

I now regularly attended chapel, and my voice, which was still equal to a woman's, brought me into notice, and I sat (as a boy) with the ladies in their pew. Here I became acquainted with a Mrs. Peacock, and her family, and for musical ability a delightful family they were. Mrs. P., in particular, was, although an elderly woman, a most charming singer. And the choir in Lisle Street was equally efficient with that of York Street. There was also a Mr. J—— (now living in Birmingham, and I have recently learned, blind), who had a very beautiful voice, and was a universal favorite in the choir.

I have heard nearly all the preachers in the Swedenborgian Connexion, and to my view, not one of them ever equalled (as an orator) Mr. Proud. His temperament had a nervous predominance, but there was enough of the bilious to render his activity enduring. In person he was of the middle height. He had a large and brilliant eye. His head was very finely formed ; his forehead was broad and moderately deep ; he had a beautifully arched eyebrow, and in the course of the temporal ridge of the frontal bone the brain projected to a considerable extent, giving great breadth above the temples ; that portion of the brain assigned by Phrenologists to Ideality was essentially large. His head was very finely rounded at the vertex, rendering Firmness, Conscientiousness, and Cautiousness in equally fair proportion, and rather large. The posterior part of the vertex was somewhat elevated, giving prominence to both Self-esteem and Love of Approbation. The coronal surface of the brain, both before and behind the anterior fontanel, was well rounded. He was at the time I first saw him somewhat stately, it is true, and with much of the natural language of self-esteem in his manner, but this I have since thought added to the dignity of his appearance.

His portrait, which was taken in the 72nd year of his age, was published in 1818, at which time, however, the brain seemed to me to have receded, and the tables of the skull had followed it, so that it had much less fulness than when I first saw him in 1810.

He was then (1810) engaged in the delivery of 'Six Lectures to Young Men and Women on the most Important and Interesting Subjects of Life and Practice.' The chapel was crowded each evening, and the Discourses were afterwards published.

He was fond of amplification, and used frequently the rhetorical figure called climax, making his sentences to go on increasingly in their importance one above another. His action was graceful, and his head, during the delivery of his sermons, was raised obliquely upwards, as though holding intercourse, through the medium of his expressive eye, with heaven and its troops of angels. His discourses were intelligent, feelingly delivered, and of moderate length. He carried his congregation with him to the end—they never wearied.

Mr. Proud was the compiler and part author of a Hymn Book, which for a time was used nearly by the whole body of the Swedenborgians. Many of the hymns of his own composition possessed great poetic beauty. His prose works were numerous, and were freely circulated among the Swedenborgians, but as literary compositions they were not much admired. His forte lay in preaching; and as a pulpit orator, it is my opinion he has never been equalled in the New Church.*

'We sometimes hear a sermon that fills our thoughts as we listen, and yet we forget it all as we turn away from the church door, for it went no deeper than our thoughts. At another time what we hear goes with us to our homes, haunts us through the week, and perhaps is made a standard whereby to measure the virtues or the vices of

* A Memoir of Mr. Proud, prefixed to his last work, the 'Aged Minister's Last Legacy,' has recently been written by Mr. Madeley of Birmingham.—Hodson, Portugal Street, London.

our neighbors; possibly even we try ourselves by its rule, and our consciences are roused to pierce us with the sharp pangs of remorse. All this, however, brings no change over our lives. Here thought has passed into imagination, has become a reality to the mind; but as yet the affections do not warm towards it, and so it dies in the second stage of existence. Yet again we listen to the voice of the preacher, and his words abide in the soul, until they quicken our affections, and as we muse, the fire burns. Then are our eyes lightened to perceive how all that we have heard may become realised in life; and warmed by the heavenly flame that has descended upon our altar, our souls kindle with charity, and we go forth to realise the hope that is within us in works of angelic use.'

Mr. Proud's preaching realised the above description. He united intellect, affection, and earnestness. At one period of his discourse he appealed to the reflecting faculties. He constituted his hearers into judges. He himself acted the part of counsel, pleading a cause earnestly before those whom he exhorted to judge righteously. He then excited the affections. He dwelt upon the love of the Lord; upon the manner in which his love was exercised; and threw the whole power of his eloquence with intense earnestness into the application. He made his hearers *feel* every word he uttered, for they saw that he himself felt. He was no dry, formal, intellectual preacher, but, as already stated, affection and use were the staples of his sermons. An amiable writer* once observed : 'Some preachers lighten, but do not thunder; others thunder, but do not lighten : the true preacher does both; the pretended, neither.' Mr. Proud was a true preacher, and did both. He never failed in his applications to insist upon the utility of trials for the regeneration of man. He showed the love of God in all his providential visitations; and then he made even ' the valley of Achor into a door of hope' for the sufferers, and drew them affectionately to his own warm heart, and ' spake comfortably unto them.'

* Rev. J. Clowes.

Hence, the crowds that attended on his ministry, **three** fourths of whom differed from him in doctrine, yet **loved** him for the efforts he made for their amendment of **heart** and for the candor with which he stated their faults.   **I** believe, however, that more members were added to **the** Swedenborgian church by Mr. Proud than by any **other** minister either before or since his time.

I have said that the Hymn Book compiled and **partly** written by Mr. Proud, was, at one time, used by **nearly** the whole body of the Swedenborgians.   To **many of** these hymns the celebrated Barthelomon, at that **time** conductor of the Orchestra at the Royal Opera, **had** composed tunes.   There were many exceptions taken **to** these hymns, but I always admired them, and **committed** several of them to memory, which, with the tunes **to** which they are set, remain with me to this day.   **The** following hymn I much admired :

' But O, how peaceful is the soul
   Where angry billows never roll ;
   Where all is calm, serene, at rest,
   As in the smiling infant's breast.

   No storms or tempests here intrude ;
   Pride, lust, and evil are subdued ;
   'The heart is ruled by love alone ;
   And peace sits smiling on the throne.

   Infernals try their utmost power,
   And all around the tempests lour ;
   But truth secures the righteous mind,
   Nor storms, nor devils entrance find.

   O, happy state ! devoutly blessed
   The soul that feels this peaceful rest ;
   If worlds in dread convulsions rise,
   He calmly views the angry skies.

   No awful tempests can alarm,
   He stands secure from fear or harm ;
   A wall of fire protects him round,
   In Jesu's hands his soul is found.

   Oh, thou divinest—mighty Friend !
   Before thy throne I humbly bend ;
   This calm and peaceful state I'd prove,
   This heaven within of peace and love.'

The music, which was Barthelomon's, was, to my view, truly charming. I have never seen it in print, and I have no copy of it in manuscript. I recollect a Mr. Gregory wrote out several books of Barthelomon's music which were used in the choir, but I was not rich enough to purchase a copy. I will, however, try to write the tune set to the hymn above-mentioned from memory :—

There are many others of Mr. Proud's hymns that deeply affect me, and 'with all their faults I love them still.'

The diminution of the congregation seemed to depreciate Mr. Proud in the estimation of several of the Society, and discontent gradually expressed itself orally. There were

several, however, who held that Mr. Proud could do n
wrong, and my brother was among the number. A
length the discontent and unpleasantness increased s
much that Mr. Proud resigned, and accepted a call t
Birmingham, to which town he removed.

Dr. Churchill, who was then officiating as the successo
of Dr. Hodson, in Dudley Court, Soho Square, was invite
to become the minister, to which he acceded; and th
whole of the Society in Dudley Court following him,
union was formed between the two societies somewher
about the month of August, 1814.

Although I was not acquainted with Dr. Hodson, i
may be proper, in order to keep my narrative connected
to say a few words respecting him. My knowledge o
him was from his successor, the Rev. Dr. Churchill.

Dr. Hodson's reception of the doctrines of the New
Church was of a particularly providential kind. From
his youth he had been a diligent student of the Sacred
Scriptures, and, from reflection upon them, he was led to
the conviction that Jesus Christ alone was the true God.
So convinced was he of this great truth, that he had
written a work, entitled, 'Jesus Christ the True God and
Sole Object of Supreme Adoration,' for the publication
of which he had issued proposals, never having seen a line
of Swedenborg's Theological Writings. This prospectus
having fallen into the hands of some of the early Swedenborgians, they waited upon the Doctor, and introduced to
his notice the writings of Emanuel Swedenborg. He at
once, and with the greatest enthusiasm, received them.
He ministered to an affectionate flock gratuitously, and on
his death, which took place on the 16th of April, 1812, in
the fifty-ninth year of his age, he was succeeded by Dr.
T. F. Churchill, who wrote the following lines to his
memory :—

'Sweet are the contemplations which attend
The placid moments of the good man's end ;
Sweet is the hope that bids the Christian rise
In bless'd, extatic vision to the skies ;

And sweet the thoughts that soothe the troubled breast,
And lull our sorrows and our cares to rest.
Suppress the sigh! profane no more with grief
The welcome hour which gave his soul relief!
As, like a shock of corn, full ripe, he goes
To the pure haven of secure repose,
Enraptur'd seraphs greet him, " Brother, come!"
And, lingering, wait to waft his spirit home.
Wisdom, who filled thy breast with heav'nly lore,
And taught, with upward wing, thy thoughts to soar;
Virtue, whose deathless image lived enshrined
Within the sacred temple of thy mind;
And Charity, soft smiling through her tears,
And meek Religion, tenant of the spheres,
Thy pious labors and thy love approve,
And bear thee, HODSON, to the realms above:
There shalt thou live, with joys celestial crown'd,
Where Honor, Peace, and Happiness abound.'

Besides his standard work on the ' Sole Divinity of the Lord,' which has served as a model for most of the subsequent works on that subject, he was the author of a valuable volume of sermons on the ' Israelitish Bondage and Deliverance'; and his nephew, Mr. J. S. Hodson, publisher, has recently published a sermon of his on ' Jeremiah in the Dungeon,' which is deserving of an attentive perusal.

It was the congregation who had sat under Dr. Hodson that united with the congregation in Lisle Street, under the pastorate, as just stated, of the Rev. Dr. Churchill.

Meantime, about twenty persons belonging to Lisle Street Society seceded, and formed themselves into a distinct and separate society, still acknowledging Mr. Proud as their minister; and he, on his part, supplied them with manuscript sermons to read at their meetings. They took a large room near the Obelisk, St. George's Fields, which they fitted up very neatly, and it was capable of accommodating about 500 persons. It was opened by Mr. Proud, who came from Birmingham for the purpose, on the 26th of March, 1815.

For a time, a Mr. Thomas Vaughan performed the ministerial duties; but soon it was found that he was

unable to fulfil the entire labor, and several of t
members agreed to officiate alternately. My brothe
the late Rev. Thomas Goyder, took an active part
these services, first reading Mr. Proud's sermons, b
soon relinquishing them for compositions of his own.

I now began to take notice of the difference in doctrir
preached by my brother to that which was preached i
the Church of England, but I was afraid to controve
him openly; for, although in my nineteenth year, I w
so small, and had withal such an infantine look, the
every one regarded me as a child. I taught in th
Sunday school, it is true; but I was put to the lowe
classes.

I determined that I would address the preacher b
letter. So, after each doctrinal lecture, I used to retai
the heads; and, from my previous study of some of th
most eminent of the divines of the Church of England, I
always replied to the allegations made on the previous
Sunday evening, or brought forward objections to some of
the more prominent points of doctrine; and thus I continued objecting and receiving replies from the pulpit
during a period of two years. No one suspected me; I
was too small for notice. I have sat in the Sunday school,
after the dismissal of the children, and heard my brother
and some of the members express wonder at the per-
tinacity of his anonymous correspondent, and devise
means for detecting him. But I kept my own counsel.
I used to obtain a sheet of demy paper, fill it, and send
it to him through the post.

On one occasion, I thought I would notice an irregularity which I had observed in several of the Swedenborgians—of leaving the church before the benediction
was pronounced. I considered it as an indignity offered
to the Lord. I took my ground on what I had heard
stated in a sermon, ' On the Priesthood-of Aaron';—
that the minister, while performing his duty, was representative of the Lord; and asked if the members really
believed this? and if they did, what had they to urge in

excuse for leaving the church before the representative
of the Lord had pronounced the benediction? Was it
not insulting the Lord to his face? This part of my
letter was read from the pulpit, and had the happiest
effect; and I heard Mr. Granger say, 'Who can this
close observer be? What a useful man he would make
among us could we but convince him of the Truth!'

But the Swedenborgian doctrines now really began to
take some hold of me. I was a regular attendant on my
brother's ministry, and began greatly to admire him,
although I still kept my secret.

Meantime my little hoard of money had melted away,
and the business of my brother was not at all sufficient to
find me constant employment, and as my income was only
half of what I did earn, I was sadly pinched for food. My
clothes, too, were growing very shabby, and I was beginning to be ashamed of going to church. I rarely made
more than 12s. a-week, so that my net income did not
exceed 6s. Out of this I had 2s. 6d. per week to pay for
lodging, leaving 3s. 6d. for clothes and food, and bread at
that time was 1s. 6d. the quartern loaf.

In July, 1817, my brother was ordained a minister of
the New Church by the Rev. M. Sibley and the Rev. Dr.
Churchill, and entered upon his duties as a minister with
much activity and energy.

The first sermon after his ordination I have reprinted
and introduced as the leading discourse in the volume of
his sermons edited by me, immediately after his death.
In my own case I began now to believe that *there was
salvation* OUT of the pale of the English Church, and after
a most patient investigation of the doctrines, reading the
writings of Swedenborg, and comparing them with the
Scriptures, I was satisfied that either the doctrines of
the Swedenborgians were true, or there was no truth.
Though now 21 years of age, I was still a child in appearance, but I resolved to join the Church if my brother
would admit me; so I made application and was received,
being baptised in public.

I continued to teach in the Sunday school, and spe
my leisure time, of which I had far too much, in readi
every book—good, bad, or indifferent—novels, romanc
poems, etc., etc., I could lay my hands upon. My broth
kept a circulating library, and I believe I read almo
every book in it. I was always fond of poetry, and
thought, having so much leisure time, I would try my ha
at a long poem, so I took for my subject, ' The Destru
tion of the Great Harlot, and Marriage of the Lamb.'
was merely a paraphrase on this great subject from th
Book of Revelation. I also wrote ' A Vision of
Week,' and a most complete rhapsody it was. I hav
dismissed both from my memory, and I hope no vestiges o
them remain. On the 5th November, 1817, the Princes
Charlotte died. I wrote a *Monody on her death.* I thin
it was the best of my poetical productions. It wa
printed, and a copy sent to Prince Leopold, which wa
acknowledged in a handsome letter, and I think a coupl
of pounds. This was my last poetic effusion of any length
I have since written several songs and hymns for children
a few of my poetical effusions have been inserted in th
' Intellectual Repository,' some in the ' Friend of Youth,'
and some in the ' Juvenile Magazine,' but they possess
very little merit, and I rather think were inserted more out
of respect to my person than my talent. Still I have a
devoted love for poetry. I have all the poets from Milton
to Kirke White, besides Scott, Byron, and very many
others. I do not read them, however, much now, for they
have the singular property of affecting me to tears, and
create a kind of suffocating sensation. The humorous
poets I am very fond of, and have many long pieces in my
memory. I have lectured on poetry more than once, and
am considered a good reader of it.* But I must now
leave my poetic effusions.

Though attached to my brother's congregation, and a
member of his church, I still went occasionally to Lisle
Street. The Society had much of the furniture of York

* Self-esteem, and love of approbation, perhaps.

Street chapel, and I remember a magnificent glass chandelier in the centre of the chapel had a very imposing appearance. Gas had not then been introduced into the chapel at Lisle Street. There was a good organ, and at St. George's Fields there was none. I was passionately fond of the organ, and greatly enjoyed the music of Bartholomon. On this account I often went to Lisle Street, to which, a short time after, a more potent reason was added.

In the beginning of the year 1818, a most melancholy occurrence took place in connection with a female member of the Society at Lisle Street—this was no other than the murder of Mary Minting by a ruffian of the name of Hetch. His addresses had been rejected by the young woman, and he, maddened by her refusal, sought an opportunity, and murdered her, by nearly severing her head from her body with a razor. This took place on the 14th February, 1818, and on the 22nd Dr. Churchill delivered a discourse on the occasion of her death, which produced a great sensation, and was afterwards published. The murderer was tried and convicted, but he escaped hanging by self-destruction. I have tried several times to get a copy of the sermon (which contains an account of an interview between Dr. Churchill and the delinquent in prison, besides copies of several letters between Hetch and his victim, previous to the murder), but I have been unsuccessful, though I doubt not there are copies still in existence.

It may, however, be expedient to give a brief extract from the sermon preached on the occasion of this tragical occurrence,* which created a most intense sensation at the time, and threatened the dissolution of the Swedenborgian Society in Lisle Street. The newspapers, among which the talented Editor of the ' Examiner ' took the lead, fulminated the most bitter invectives against the Swedenborgian doctrines, although, as the sequel will prove, they were ignorant of them in a most remarkable degree.

In the sermon alluded to, Dr. Churchill, having first

* This extract, and those which follow, are taken from the ' Intellectual Repository ' for 1818, p. 122—128.

shewn what was the true nature of the doctrines set forth
in the writings of Swedenborg, and confirmed by every
page in the Sacred Scriptures, proceeded in the following
manner :—

'I have been thus explicit on general principles, that no one
who hears me may rush into the New Church indiscriminately,
without having first counted the cost, that is, unaccompanied with a
fixed and fervent desire and disposition to resist every sin, to
struggle hard with his headstrong passions, for I again repeat it,
that to deliberate murderers and adulterers she has very little
consolation to offer.   We know and believe that such a character is
in the hands of a good and gracious God, who alone is competent
to explore and decide on the most secret motives and intents of the
heart, and who will communicate every good he is capable of
receiving and appropriating.   But we should at all times consider
it as a most dangerous delusion to trust to an imaginary conversion, *instantaneously* wrought, or to a compulsory death-bed
repentance, extorted, most probably, under an impression of
fear, which, if removed, might prove the signal for a repetition
of all evils.

'With such an awful instance of determined depravity before us,
carried on under the alluring disguise of religion, before we
separate, suffer me in the most awful and impressive manner, to
exhort you, my Christian hearers, to take warning, to be " sober
and vigilant, and watch unto prayer," and "let him who thinketh
he standeth, take heed lest he fall."   Above all things, beloved,
and in particular, my young friends, shrink appalled at the sin
of *adultery;* a sin, which though sanctioned by its prevalence
among the licentious part of the world, most assuredly closes
heaven to the soul; and, as with the unhappy wretch in question,
prepares the mind for the perpetration of murder, and crimes of the
deepest dye.   Our Lord hath told us that offences must needs
come; that his Church, his Word, and Kingdom, will be occasionally scandalized by the misconduct of false professors; but he
adds, "Woe to the man by whom they *do* come."   Would we,
then, seriously desire to be Jews of such a pure quality, as that
our fellow-men may experience an increasing disposition to take
hold of our "skirt," expressing a desire "to go with us;" * or to
drop the metaphor, would we earnestly endeavor to manifest to the
world around us that we are in deed and in truth the humble and
sincere followers of the meek and lowly Jesus; oh! on our bended
knees let us fervently implore his Divine assistance to keep us
"from the evil of the world," that God may be and continue with
us for ever; guiding, directing, protecting, and consoling us in

* This is an allusion to the text, which was from Zech. viii. 23.

our progress through this chequered transitory scene of sin and sorrow, to a glorious immortality.'

The 'Examiner' Newspaper of Sunday, March 1st, contained, in reference to the murderer, the following extraordinary paragraph:

'The miserable wretch, Hetch, in the letter he wrote to his murdered wife's mother, spoke of the deed he had committed, and the one he was just going to commit, with great coolness. He thus concludes: "I am anxious to die and be with the dear object of my soul; for I am still persuaded that I shall have that unbounded pleasure of enjoying her company in a far superior way than ever it could be done in this transitory world; and as for what man does with this body—a mere lump of vile clay—it is of no consequence to me; therefore men may do with it as they please. So God Almighty bless you, and the remainder of your unfortunate family, is the last prayer of a satisfied man."

'This ruffian, it seems, attended the New Jerusalem Chapel, and his talk about this "transitory world," and his "vile clay," shows how deeply he had imbibed the gloomy notions of certain sectarians, who daily libel their CREATOR by false and disgusting pictures of the works of his hand. This man, who had just perpetrated one of the foulest acts that a human being can commit; upon a female, too, whom he had already sufficiently injured; writes as if he was quite certain of possessing the joys of heaven! Is it not likely that the notions inculcated at such chapels about the "*rottenness of works*," and the importance of a "*saving faith*," may have had some effect in confounding this man's ideas of right and wrong? It is a pity that those who take upon themselves to instruct the ignorant, will not talk to them about things they could comprehend; but it is much easier to prate darkly about mysteries and spiritual matters, and of another world, than to dilate sensibly on our social duties, and show people the right way to be useful and happy in this.'

The ignorance of the 'Examiner' of the real doctrines of the Swedenborgians, was fully refuted in the following letter, a part only of which the Editor permitted to appear in his paper.

'THE DOCTRINES OF THE NEW JERUSALEM CHURCH, WHOLLY UNCONNECTED WITH THE CONDUCT OF HETCH THE MURDERER.

'TO THE EDITOR OF THE "EXAMINER."

'*Camden Town, March 2nd*, 1818.

'SIR—In your paper of yesterday (p. 138), when making some remarks respecting Hetch the murderer, you insinuate that his

atrocious conduct might have been in some measure the resul
of the doctrines he had been accustomed to hear at the Nev
Jerusalem Chapel in Lisle Street.   The surprise which this insinua
tion excited in some of your readers, was extreme; and, witl
respect to myself, was enhanced by the recollection that I hac
formerly read in your paper some remarks, under the signature,
think, of ",W. H.," in which the purity and grandeur of senti
ment which pervade the writings of Swedenborg were spoken of ii
terms of admiration.   Is, then, the insinuation alluded to, to b
attributed to your not being aware that these once commended
sentiments are those which are maintained by the members of the
New Jerusalem Church, and preached at the above named Chapel i
Or are we to conclude that you have forgotten the remarks of you
correspondent, and are yourself wholly unacquainted with the
subject?   In either case, as a misrepresentation has gone forth,
it is but just that it should be corrected.   Permit me then to say,
that it is impossible for you or any man to regard as more mischievous than we do, the notions that are sometimes " inculcated about
the rottenness of works, and the importance of a saving faith " ;
when such faith is supposed capable of existence independently of
charity and a life of usefulness.   According to the doctrines of the
New Jerusalem Church, Charity and Faith are regarded as the
two essentials of religion;. charity being considered as holding
the first place, and faith the second; and they teach, further, that
neither charity nor faith have any real existence in the mind, unless
they become operative, when opportunity is afforded, in good works.
Where such sentiments are cherished in the heart, how can the
hands be guilty of acts of enormity?

'You suggest further, that such doctrines as represent "the
world" as "transitory," and the body as "vile clay"—language
which means no more than that human life is short, and the body
of little account compared with the soul—are gloomy notions, to
utter which is "to libel the Creator."   But allow me to ask which
sentiment is most truly to be characterised as gloomy; that which
would represent the body as everything, and would lead us to
suppose that when this dies, all dies: or that which represents the
body but as a kind of matrix for the formation of the spirit, which
latter will live eternally after its earthly shell is separated by
death?   This is the doctrine of the New Jerusalem Church; and
can any feelings but cheerful ones be inspired by such a doctrine?
especially when it is affirmed in addition, that man is at full
liberty, whilst he lives here, by the reception or rejection of the
divine influences, to acquire for his spirit such a quality as he
pleases, and is, consequently, the master of his own final destiny.
I make these observations because I am convinced, that "to
dilate," as you recommend, however "sensibly on our social
duties, and to show people the right way to be useful and happy in

this world," if it be done without any reference to another, will be utterly unproductive of any beneficial effect : but whenever people shall be generally instructed, from the nature of God and the nature of man, from the constant tenor of the Scripture (rightly understood), and the clearest suggestions of reason, that there is an eternal world before them, and that the qualification for happiness in that world is solely to be acquired by a life of benevolence, innocence, and usefulness in this; then there may be hopes of the amelioration of mankind; for stony indeed must be the heart, and dull the understanding, which can be altogether unaffected by sentiments so rational, by motives so cogent, by invitations so accordant with the best feelings of human nature, not of corrupt human nature, but of that nature truly human with which the Great Author and Prototype would re-invest us.

'When, therefore, the wretched assassin, in his last letter, speaks slightingly of his body, it must be acknowledged that he speaks in agreement with the doctrine of the New Jerusalem Church (though the sentiment is so very general, that he need not have gone there to learn it); yet allow me to say, that the disgust you express of such sentiments, *as proceeding from him*, is also felt, quite as deeply, by the members of this religious society. The mention of sacred names and things, in connection with deeds so atrocious, is regarded by them as horrible in . the extreme. Indeed, that hideous composition in general, exhibits, in their estimation, a striking picture of the false persuasions which spring, as naturally as a stream from its fountain, from such diabolical lusts as its author had cherished in his breast; which, when once they are permitted to reign without control, soon blind and subjugate the intellectual faculty, and compel it to find reasons to excuse and justify the most outrageous acts of violence and cruelty.

'But it is needless to trespass much further on your patience, as a pamphlet will have been published before this can meet the eye of your readers, in which the doctrines of the New Jerusalem Church are explicitly stated, and the history of the wretched culprit, as far as it is connected with his flagitious deeds, is correctly detailed. It will there be seen that he only intruded himself for a year or two past, into the congregation meeting at the chapel in Lisle Street, for the purpose of prosecuting his design on his deluded victim, who had long been a regular attendant. But had even his attendance been of longer duration, and commenced under less questionable circumstances, where would be the justice of censuring the religious sentiments he exteriorly professed, merely because they were flagrantly violated in his conduct ? Would it not be just as reasonable to impute the atrocities of Nero to the lessons of Socrates, or to libel the great Author of Christianity, because one of his disciples was a Judas ?

'Permit me to conclude with a general remark. Many extravagant misrepresentations have been in circulation respecting Swedenborg and his writings, which, though they must have been originally invented by malignity, are frequently propagated by well-meaning ignorance. The prejudices thus infused into the minds of the majority are very strong; yet the cases are numerous in which they have been compelled to yield to the force of truth that reigns in the pages of this author; and of which the individual who now addresses you affords one instance among many. Let, then, those who have too much probity wilfully to deal in misplaced ridicule, or to disseminate unfounded calumny, *read before they judge,* and they who have already made the experiment can entertain no apprehension as to the general result.

'I am, Sir, yours respectfully,
'AN ADMIRER OF THE DOCTRINES OF THE
'NEW JERUSALEM CHURCH.'

This letter tranquillised the public mind, and, besides, had the effect of increasing the attendance at the chapel in Lisle Street. To return to my narrative.

Dr. Churchill, who was always of a very delicate constitution, now found that the arduous duties of his profession, increased as they were by the labors of the Sabbath, were so great, that he could no longer accomplish them, and was at length induced to resign. This took place about the beginning of the year 1819, and Mr. Noble succeeded him.

At this time I had formed an intimacy with a young lady, a member of Dr. Churchill's congregation, and was, as already hinted, very frequently an attendant at Lisle Street chapel, though I did not relinquish my membership at St. George's Fields. I found, however, that it was now absolutely necessary that I should obtain higher wages than 6s. or 7s. per week. I knew that my brother could not afford to give me any advance, for his business was very limited, and he had heavy expenses. He had besides sustained some severe losses from bad debts. He received no emolument whatever from his labor, as minister of the congregation just alluded to. Indeed, I believe he was one of its principal supporters, in a pecuniary point of view. I at length summoned up courage to tell him that my little hoard of money was exhausted, and I found myself incapable, with what I earned, to support myself—would he allow me to seek for another situation, and did he think I could obtain a situation in an office where regular employment would furnish me with a better income ?

He replied, he should have no objection whatever to transfer me, and he had little doubt I should succeed if I set about it with activity. So I immediately began a canvass, and was soon after enabled to obtain an appointment in the office of Mr. Frederic Thorogood, in Addle Street, Aldermanbury. He was at that time one of the printers to the King's Stationery Office. I was to have 14s. a week for the first year, 16s. for the second year, and 18s. for the third year. This to me was a marvellous rise.

On the first evening of my attendance at Mr. Thorogood's office, after the labors of the day, I was told by the oldest compositor in the office, that I would have to attend a 'Chapel,' in order to be properly introduced to my brethren of both case and press. The 'Father of the Chapel,' as the oldest compositor was styled, was a Mr. Hodson. At this meeting, where a deputation of the hands employed by Mr. Thorogood were assembled, I was informed that I should have to pay 10s. 6d. as an entrance fee, and all the members of the 'Chapel' would also pay a stipulated sum, and we were to spend an evening together at the end of the week. The 'Father of the Chapel' advised me to comply with this rule without demur. 'There were,' he said, 'a good many *devils* in the office, who created a great deal of mischief upon the composition of those who neglected to accede to the "Chapel laws." At the same time, as I was but an apprentice, I should not have to pay the whole sum at once ; it should extend over three weeks.'

In my brother's office, I had not been much indoctrinated into the technicalities used by printers. I knew what *pie* was, namely, loose letters of various sizes or founts, that had accidentally got mixed up together ;

but why the meeting of the men to receive a new apprentice was called a 'Chapel,' I knew not.

Mr. Hodson, as the 'Father of the Chapel,' informed me, that printing in this country was first executed in a chapel, and from that time, printers called their office a chapel, and whenever any business relative to the internal arrangements of the office had to be transacted, or the making of rules, or the reception of apprentices, the compositors and pressmen (or a deputation of them, if the office was large) were always convened together under the designation of a 'Chapel.'

Well, I of course attended the 'Chapel,' and at once agreed to all that was required of me. I had but to consider that for my first week's services I should receive only 10s. 6d. per week, and even this to me was a great advance upon what I had formerly received. So I consoled myself with the old maxim, that 'Contentment silvers the pewter spoon'; and my ready compliance at once ensured me a cordial welcome from my fellow-workmen.

With the view of explaining a few of the technicalities of a printing office, I subjoin the following paragraph (with the necessary illustrations) which went the round of the papers, just previous to the accession of her present Majesty, under the title of 'MYSTERIOUS PROFESSION.'

'"Now Tom," said the printer of a country newspaper to one of his apprentices, in giving him certain directions, "put the foreign leader into the *galleys, and lock 'em up.** Let Napoleon's Remains have a larger head.† *Distribute* the army in the East. ‡ Take up a line, and

---

* That is, put the 'leading article' on Foreign Affairs into temporary frames, and so secure the types, that proofs may be taken of them.

† That is, let the article entitled 'Napoleon's Remains,' have a title or heading in more conspicuous type.

‡ That is, return the types relative to the article of the 'Army in the East,' to the cases.

finish the British Ministers. * Make the young Princess to *run on* with the Duchess of Kent. † Move the Kerry hunt out of the *chase*. ‡ Get your *stick*, and conclude the horrid murder that Joe began last night.§ Wash your hands, and come down to dinner, and then see that all the *pie* is cleared up." ' ‖

I entered upon my duties with much spirit.

My business was the Lottery Office department ; and one part of it was horribly filthy, insomuch that it was termed by the men 'MUCK RAKING.' There were vast numbers of agents in the provincial towns for the sale of lottery tickets, and each agent's name had to be inserted both in the hand and posting bills ; so, as soon as the requisite number for one agent was wrought off, I was called to insert the name of another, and removing the name of the former agent, covered with ink, and inserting the new agent, was required by the pressmen to be executed in. a few seconds. Many a time have I been dabbed with the *ink ball* (no rollers then) in my face for being so slow ; for the pressmen worked by the piece, and posting-bill work was very amply paid, and therefore they took care no time should be lost on my part. I believe I was the dirtiest boy in the office (man, perhaps, I ought to say, for I was between twenty-two and twenty-three years of age). I had first to wash the ink off the agent's name I had taken out, then to hurry up stairs to the composing room, set a new agent's name

---

* Take a line from the bottom of the column, and place it at the head of the next column, so that the article on the ' British Ministers may be in one column.

† This also conveys a similar idea to that of the previous note.

‡ The *chase* is an iron frame, in which the types are firmly wedged. The taking them out of the chase. is their removal, either to make room for some other article, or to return the types, by distribution, to their respective cases.

§ 'Get your *stick*,' means the composing stick, in which the types are set or arranged to a uniform measure, and ' conclude the horrid murder,' of course relates to an article of that crime.

‖ Pie relates to the confused masses of letters that lie about an office, as before explained.

and address, and by this time, and often sooner, I was
again called to alter the form.　But I got on very well
with all the men but one, who was a conceited coxcomb,
but a first-rate pressman.　He was disliked by most of
the men, who described him as the '*descendant of a
roasted bishop*'—his name was Latimer.　He was very
fond of showing off in the presence of Mr. Thorogood,
and of jeering me, and I was too timid to reply in the
master's presence.

Having so much to do with the pressmen, I was frequently invited by them after the closing of the office.
They were a very thirsty set.　Many of them, the bill
pressmen in particular, earned four and five pounds per
week, and yet, when Saturday came, they had less than
half that to receive ; for the overseer became responsible
for their public-house accounts, and he never failed to pay
the landlord before he paid them.　They did not, indeed,
spend the whole in drink.　They resorted to a house in
Wood Street, Cheapside, where was a bagatelle board, and
spent sometimes four and five hours at this table.　They
had also a glee club, at which the aforesaid Latimer, who
was a beautiful singer, presided.　I was, as I said above,
invited to this club very frequently, and, I must say,
enjoyed the singing.　I was looked upon by the men as a
child, and used to be jeeringly asked every Monday
morning what was the text, and when I intended to hold
forth myself to be sure and let them know, for the whole
strength of the office would come (there were about one
hundred men employed) and hear me, and they would not
fail to have some first-rate singing.

The 'Father of the Chapel,' before alluded to, who was
an elderly man, a compositor, and was also '*the Lottery
Poet,*' and whom we used to call 'The Doctor,' was very
kind to me, and watched over me as if I had been his son.
He used to write most of the poetic lottery puffs, some of
them very amusing, and he was besides no indifferent poet
on other subjects.　I subjoin one of his lottery puffs as a
specimen.

'SUNSHINE AFTER RAIN.'

'Sweet Mary had long been the pride of the dale,
And Edward the lord of her heart;
She artlessly heard his affectionate tale,
Till cruelty forced them to part.
A miser the guardian of Mary was left,
Who spurn'd the fond youth from his door;
And thus of felicity both were bereft,
Alas! because Edward was poor!

'He pack'd up his all, of his Mary took leave,
Bade adieu to his cottage so dear;
And Mary knew Edward too true to deceive,
Though she could not suppress the sad tear.
"Believe me," said he, "the fond flame shall still burn,
Wherever I'm destined to roam;
But hope fondly whispers I soon shall return,
To my Mary—my cot—and my home."

'So to London he came, Sivewright's* Offices sought,
For a Lottery Ticket applies;
And the very next day the glad tidings were brought,
It was drawn, and a CAPITAL PRIZE!
With a heart overflowing to Mary he wrote,
The change in his fate to express;
The news made the miser soon alter his note,
And the merits of Edward confess.

'On Edward's return to the altar he led
Sweet Mary, and made her his wife;
On poverty now they can look without dread,
Since plenty has crown'd them for life.
But to Sivewright's again for a ticket they've sent,
Determin'd their friends to remember,
On a share of the *six twenty thousands* intent,
On Thursday, the ninth of December.'

Mr. Hodson had read some of the writings of Sweden-borg, and had been an occasional attendant at Dudley Court Chapel, during the ministry of his uncle, Dr. Hodson, from whom the office had nick-named him 'The Doctor.' This Mr. Hodson was a very kind friend to me and I owe him much for preserving me from the dissipations of the office. He was my champion with the pressmen, and saved me many a beating. He also stood up

* Sivewright was a celebrated Lottery Contractor.

for me against the witty egotist, Latimer, and wo[...]
defend me even in the presence of Mr. Thorogood. [...]
great crime being a Swedenborgian; this rendered me [...]
butt of the office; I was the only religious person, and[...]
believe, but for the countenance Mr. Hodson bestowed up[...]
me, I should have been sneered out of my religious impr[...]
sions. He advised me, by little and little, to avoid the g[...]
club, pleading an engagement with him, which I d[...]
and so escaped the danger which threatened me.

After office hours I spent frequently an hour in M[...]
Tegg's Auction Room, Cheapside, and sometimes bought [...]
book. He was then just commencing his career, a[...]
resorted to the system of puffing. He called his sh[...]
(the back part of which was devoted to the sale of book[...]
every evening, the books being principally the clearings [...]
the other publishers) *The Temple of Apollo.* At tha[...]
time there was an Irish song, called ' Paddy Carey,' ver[...]
much in vogue, and Mr. Tegg had a parody written upo[...]
it, which I thought very amusing. It was to the followin[...]
effect :—

'THE TEMPLE OF APOLLO.

' As I was walking down Cheapside
  I saw a crowd of staring people,
And all their mouths were opened wide,
  As if to swallow Bow Church steeple.*
I hastened on with eager looks,
  To learn what all the folks would swallow,
And there I saw such piles of books,
  At Tegg's rich temple of Apollo.
High they stand—all smiling round—
Tempt the hand—all gilt and bound—
      History, travels,
      Dramas, novels—
   Grave and gay, all follow.
    The poor bending porter,
     The rich city knight,
    With wonder stand
     To admire the sight.

* Mr. Tegg's shop was then opposite Bow Church.

The bright display—
  The pleasing view,
Moroccos lay,
  Both red and blue.
Large and small books, and all cheap books,
  At the Temple of great Apollo.
Oh, sweet reading! beautiful reading!
  Come to the Temple of great Apollo.'

I have said my memory was good. I feel perfectly
e I have not seen this song for thirty-six years, and
; it remains with me. Any event or anecdote impresses
, but I find a difficulty in recollecting names. Persons
d forms I never forget.

In the month of August, 1819, the hands employed by
r. Thorogood, to the number of 150, had what was
lled *a way-goose* at Highbury Barn. This was a grand
nner, and my friend Hodson undertook the care of me.
was held on a Saturday, and the dinner was the most
mptuous that I had ever been present at. The evening
as spent in singing and recitations, and many of the
en, at the conclusion of the banquet, were ' *o'er all the
ls of life victorious.*' I got some credit at this banquet
y a short speech on the advantages of printing, which I
ncluded by proposing the memory of the immortal
axton. It was drank in full glasses, and with solemn
lence. I was able to resume my work on the Monday,
ut the office was very thinly attended by the *Barristers
pressmen*).

Meantime, the Society at St. George's Fields continued
o increase, and a proposal was seriously made for the
rection of a new place of worship. A piece of ground
vas taken on a lease, and on the 19th of October, 1818,
he foundation-stone of a new temple was laid in the
Waterloo Road, Lambeth Marsh, by Mr. Sibly, assisted
by my brother. Mr. John Isaac Hawkins was the
architect, and the building was proceeded with rapidly,
and on Whitsunday following (May 30, 1819) it was
opened by Mr. Sibly preaching in the morning, and Mr.
Goyder in the evening. It was numerously attended, and

there was a promise of many being added to the church I
its erection.

At the back of the church a small house was erect
for the verger, and over this was a moderate sized roo
designed as a Committee Room and Sunday School.
this room I proposed instructing those who were willi
in reading, writing, and arithmetic, on three evenings
the week; and from this small beginning originated tl
day school, which afterwards was erected in Charl
Street, Westminster Road.   But I still continued
attend occasionally at Lisle Street Chapel.   The del
cate health of Dr. Churchill having, as before stated, led t
his resignation, Mr. Noble, who had officiated for som
time, now entirely assumed the pastoral office, bein
ordained on the 21st May, 1820, Messrs. Sibly an
Churchill performing the ceremony, the former gentle
man delivering an appropriate discourse.   Dr. Churchill'
delicate health now required him to relinquish his practic
as a physician.

Meantime, my second apprenticeship was now drawin
towards a close, and I was in receipt of 18s. per wee
permanent wages, which, by overtime, I sometimes in
creased to double that amount.   Mr. Thorogood ha
purchased the business of Messrs. Bryan and Son, o
Grocers' Hall Court, in the Poultry.   Here the books o
the East India Company's tea sale were printed every si
weeks, and I was drafted from Addle Street to Grocers
Hall Court, and continued there till my term expired
The composition of the Tea Catalogues was a most profit
able employment, and I often made 18s., and some
times 20s. above my regular wages, so that I began t
assume an appearance, in externals, of considerabl
respectability.

Towards the close of 1820, I became acquainted with
Mr. James Buchanan, who had been engaged by Mr. H
Brougham to organize, in Westminster, an Infants' Schoo
among the poorest class of people.   He urged me to mak
myself acquainted with the system of Pestalozzi, statin

that he had an application for a master and mistress for a new school, intended to be erected at Bristol, and as I was then contemplating marriage, he assured me he could procure me the appointment. It needed, he said, but one day's attendance in a week, and a careful study of Pestalozzi's works. I considered the matter, and at length determined to follow his advice. The school at Westminster was first supported entirely by Mr. Brougham, but after a while, and during my attendance, there was associated with him Mr. Benjamin Smith, M.P., Mr. Macaulay, Lord Dacre, and the Marquis of Lansdowne. While I was thus preparing myself, I heard glowing accounts of the success of a Mr. Samuel Wilderspin, at Spitalfields. This person was my brother's clerk at the chapel in Saint George's Fields, and through his interest with Mr. James Buchanan, who was a member of my brother's congregation, he had been sent to Mr. Buchanan, instructed by that gentleman in all his plans, and obtained an appointment under Mr. Wilson, at Spitalfields. I thought I would visit his school, and I did so ; but there was nothing to be seen there that I had not seen at the school of Mr. Buchanan, at Westminster. After making myself fully acquainted with the system of Pestalozzi, I was in a condition to accept of the situation at Bristol, so soon as it should be ready ; so on the 11th February, 1821, I was married at St. John's Church, Westminster, to my present wife, and after the legal ceremony we proceeded to our own church in the Waterloo Road, and were married before the congregation, Mr. William Sturgeon acting as father to my bride. My brother married us, and afterwards preached a discourse on the conjugial covenant. We received the congratulations of the congregation. We had neither of us time for an excursion. I returned to my office on Monday morning, and my wife went to school to qualify herself for her new duties.

I do not stop to give a description of the person of my wife. I thought her the most beautiful little woman in

London. Dr. Churchill declared I had made a most eligil
connection.   Mrs. Churchill told me I had got a treasu
indeed.   And so indeed she has proved.   My admiratic
of her now is even greater than when she bestowed h
hand upon me.   It is impossible to speak in terms t
high of her many admirable qualities.   Her tact, h
prudence, her economy in the management of a vel
limited income, her truthfulness, her devoted attachmel
to the doctrines of the New Church, all speak her :
the crown of her husband.   What ! is she faultless
No, no.   But those who want to know her faults wi
not learn them from me.   I will only say, that when sl
thinks herself right, she is very determined.   She is firn
even to obstinacy.

Although, as I have said, I had become a member (
the Swedenborgian Church, and had been married in il
I had not yet wholly given up my attendance at th
Established Church.   I still had a fondness for its forms
its ritual, and its beautiful music ; and having beel
originally designed for the ministry, I had formed acquaintances (I cannot, of course, call them friends) who respectec
me and wished to do me good.   I was known to many of the
clergy connected with the Abbey, as well as to Dr. Fynes
the incumbent of St. Margaret's Church, Westminster
Mr. Groves, the curate, and some others ; and I found
means to visit Mr. Pollard, and to exhibit a gratefu
deference for all he had done for me, though I did no
forget his floggings.

Every Easter Monday, there was bestowed upon a
certain number of newly married couples (married within
the year), by the will of a maiden lady, the sum of
twenty pounds to three couples in the parish of St.
Margaret's, three of St. John's, and three of the parish
of Hackney.   The parties were required to have served
an apprenticeship in their respective parishes, and to
have borne good characters, to be known to the clergy,
and to be residents in the respective parishes.   I applied,
never doubting that I should be successful ; and I was so

well known that I was successful and received the twenty
pounds. I continued at Mr. Thorogood's till May, 1821,
when my appointment to Bristol came, and after taking a
kind farewell of Mr. Hodson, and of all in Mr. Thorogood's
office, I left to commence my career as a teacher, on the
plan of Pestalozzi.

Fifth Period:

FROM TWENTY-FIVE TILL TWENTY-NINE YEARS OF AGE.
1821 TO 1825.

'Pestalozzi may be termed the founder of "*Ragged Schools*." At the age of twenty-two, when he had purchased a little estate at Neuhoff, in Switzerland, and determined to lead a simple country life, he became aware of the wretchedness and ignorance of the peasantry. It was then that he determined to devote his life to the benefit of the poor, and, assisted by his wife, whom he married the year after he settled at Neuhoff, he began to collect poor children, and even mendicant children and outcasts, into his house, and instruct them. His efforts were treated by his neighbors and the world as all such efforts are. They were ridiculed, and pronounced to be actual folly and insanity. Every well-informed reader knows through what opposition, misfortune, and trouble, arising from the exhaustion of his own means, revolutionary disturbances of the times, and the wranglings of those who even came forward to assist in his plans for elevating the people, Pestalozzi passed his life. His plans, however, succeeded, and have spread all over the civilised world : they have been introduced, more or less, into all popular systems of education, and TO HIM THE TUITION OF THE PEOPLE OWES MORE THAN TO ANY MAN WHO EVER LIVED. He was born on the 12th of January, 1746, and on the 12th of January, 1846, the centenary of his birth was celebrated all over Germany and Switzerland with great festivity, and many people's schools were founded in honor of his memory. So it is : the benefactors of mankind go through the world with sorrow and misrepresentation—ruin clogs them—and the worldly wise shake their heads at them—but the seed they sow grows in spite of frost and drought, and after-ages reap the harvest which was watered with their tears. Be strong, hearts of humanity! and the blessing which Heaven sends, though it seems to come late, shall last long.'

NEWSPAPER PARAGRAPH.

'If you would be benefited by what you read, learn to read critically. Look at the characters and see if they be natural and well drawn. Observe the morality, and see if it be true or false ; examine the style, and see if it be good or bad, graceful or awkward, distinct, or vague.'

MARY CHANDLER'S Elements of Character.

ON my arrival in Bristol, and going before the committee, I found it consisted of ladies of various denominations, of whom many were Unitarians, and several others of the Society of Friends.

I laid before them the plans requisite to be pursued, and they gave me full licence to fit up the school according to my own judgment; this took about a month, and in the beginning of June, 1821, I commenced my duties as a teacher.

On leaving London, I had received from my brother a note of introduction to the minister of the Swedenborgian Society at Bristol, whose name was Enoch, and he received me very kindly, and introduced me to the members generally. In my capacity as schoolmaster, it was thought I might occasionally deliver a discourse, and as my desire still was to become a minister, I felt no disinclination to accede to the request. Mr. Enoch, it appeared, was never appreciated in Bristol; so that, having frequently officiated for him, I was at length solicited to take the whole duties upon myself, which I did somewhere about November, 1821. Mr. Enoch, however, still continued to preach occasionally. The place of worship was situated in the lowest part of the city, and no hope was entertained by me of adding respectable persons to the Society.

During the year 1821, my duties at the school were comparatively light, and I had plenty of time for study; but I was assisted in my Sunday duties by a few manuscript sermons from my brother, and I thought I would attempt the delivery of a course of lectures on the Doctrines of the New Church. I applied to my brother for a programme, which he gave me, and I delivered, with some success, a course of six Sunday Evening Lectures, the first of which, on the Divinity of the Lord, was published, and was so very favorably received by the public that it was sold in a few months.*

In these duties passed the first six months of my

* I shall have occasion, in a future part of my narrative, to say something further respecting this discourse.

8

residence in Bristol, and I think this was one of the happiest periods of my existence. I had a very intelligent lady-committee, whose periodical visits to the school were very agreeable. My income was ninety pounds a year, and my labor, comparatively speaking, as I have said, light.

It may be here expedient to say a few words upon the plans of Pestalozzi, on whose system I modelled my school. It was the aim of Pestalozzi to combine the powers of the understanding with the will—of thought with affection—and to bring them both into actual existence in the life. Hence, his system is one of faith and love, or, in other words, he united the cultivation of heart and understanding with the labor of the hand. His motto in education was—*Heart, Head,* and *Hand.* Science he called in as an auxiliary. He contended that what was done for the head alone destroyed the heart; but what was done for the head, *through the instrumentality of the heart, preserved both.* Thus he laid the foundation of his system on the apostolic plan of *Love,* the greatest of all Christian principles. He first gained the affections of his pupils, and then he had the power to direct them without difficulty. I attempted to follow him in this.

Pestalozzi, in his writings and in his conversation, strongly condemned the neglect with which children in their infant state have been treated. From the commencement of his career as an educationist, he maintained that children must no longer be considered as a burden, and their education neglected, but be rather considered as beings holding a high rank in the creation, being endowed with the 'vital spark of heavenly' reason; it must be watched over, fostered, and nourished, until it becomes a bright and glorious flame, diffusing light and warmth on all around. But I will let Pestalozzi speak for himself. He says :—

'After a life spent in the most minute researches, and in the most careful examination of elementary principles, I am convinced that the system of faith and love will no where so perfectly succeed, or be so well executed, as among the members of a private family; the domestic circle containing elements essentially and admirably calculated to produce the necessary development of the innate faculties.

'The mutual dependence, the wants, the sympathies, the relations of the domestic union, are the sacred elements of all the moral, intellectual, and physical activity of man, and thus become the basis of all that he ought to learn, to understand, and to execute.

'The reciprocal LOVE, FAITH, and CONFIDENCE, which unite the members of a family—father, mother, and children—are the divine means by which the development of the faculties are made to advance in the harmony and equilibrium which are necessary to give children those religious and moral feelings which can alone ensure to them the true and durable blessings of intellectual enjoyment.

'According to these views I feel convinced that the whole success of education depends on the good state of the family circle. I am, at the same time, aware, that the spirit and manners of the age have so perverted the condition of private society, that the generality of parents and other members of the family are nearly destitute of those moral qualities and mental acquirements, of that manual dexterity, of that knowledge, and that aptitude to apply their knowledge, which is indispensably requisite to enable them to profit by the advantages which the domestic circle presents for the cultivation and instruction of their children.

' I therefore consider it of the utmost consequence that we search attentively, investigate profoundly, and bring into active operation, every means likely to inspire parents with a sense of their duty, and of its importance to the whole human race; and that we endeavor to excite in them the wish, and bestow upon them the ability, to take advantage of the well-adapted, powerful, and precious aid which their united circle offers, for the development of the powers of their children, and by these means render themselves capable of exercising over them that enlightened, solid, and permanent influence, so indispensable to their cultivation.

' It becomes, therefore, essential to render all elementary means of spiritual, intellectual, and mechanical cultivation, in their whole extent, and in all their branches, so simple and easy, as to make them applicable even in the domestic circle of the poorest classes; and to introduce them into the sanctuary of FAITH AND LOVE; which, in the narrow circle of father, mother, and children, has been assigned and secured to all mankind, from the beginning, by God himself.

'I perceive that it is impossible to attain this end without founding the means of popular culture and instruction upon a basis which cannot be laid otherwise than in a profound examination of man—without such an investigation, and such a basis, all is dark-ness.

'I am convinced that it is only by such study that we can hope to succeed in arriving at the true means of instruction; it is the only way by which we shall discover how to conduct a child to such a point of interior moral and intellectual perfection; that he shall become not only capable of teaching his brothers, sisters, and companions, but also of communicating to them his knowledge, in the same degree of perfection in which he acquired it. This is the true and only method of arriving at complete development; the only means calculated to afford hopes of directing the powers bestowed upon man to their true end; it is the only possible means of rendering KNOWLEDGE UNIVERSAL, of *making man acquainted with himself*, and of placing him in permanent peace, happiness, and prosperity.'

With these principles of Pestalozzi before me, I deter-mined to make my school as nearly resemble a family circle as it was possible, and, by the aid of my wife, to enter upon the training of the children in the school, as if they were all my own. The study of Pestalozzi's works led me to perceive that it was needful to attend to the physical culture of my pupils in the first instance; to secure to them a sound and healthy body, if I would be successful in laying the foundation for a healthy and vigorous mind. I saw, in all other systems of education, 'too much time devoted to the cultivation of the mind, and too little to that of the body. What was the consequence? The intellect, from such premature exertion, and the body from an opposite cause—a want of exertion—were both injured. The mind should never be forced on, but allowed to acquire strength with the growth of the body; and the invigora-tion of the latter, above all, ought to be encouraged, as upon it depends most materially the future health of the individual. Education should be made a pastime with children, and not a task. The young mind, when forcibly exerted, becomes weakened, and a premature decay of its energies takes place. With health comes strength of body, and with strength of body strength of mind.'

The first thing I found neecssary was imitation of Pes-talozzi himself, by becoming as a child among children, and I strove to gain their affection and confidence. It was my desire to convince my pupils that I took an interest in all their affairs. Were any in trouble, I endeavored to soothe and alleviate their little distresses. I was ready to listen to all their grievances, and, on my part, to appear attentive to every device, by the aid of which I could secure their affection and regard. I mingled with them in all their amusements; I related to them short but interesting narratives of various useful animals. I pointed out to them the great necessity of tenderness and kindness to all the creatures whom God had made. In all things I strove to act in such a manner that they might imitate me. 'Children,' says Mr. Locke, 'do most by example,' and that example I endeavored to render harmless and safe. I allowed nothing of magisterial authority or rule to appear in my conduct towards them, but I gained their affection by affection, and thus laid a foundation for solid obedience. As it was desirable to establish strict attention, I introduced signals into all my exercises. I drilled the children every day in marching. I commenced first with simply walking round the room, next with beating time with the feet, and regular clapping of the hands, always accompanying the children with some lively tune on the flute. Then succeeded the single and double file, the circular, semi-circular, square, and zigzag courses; and, lastly, I introduced short, lively airs, which the children sung during the marches, in simple songs which I had composed for them, of the uses of plants, kindness to animals, etc., and in which was introduced a manœuvre of meeting, mingling, and separating into different companies.

The school was not designed to show off the pupils in book learning, which at that time I thought of no use; nay, injurious to infants of three and seven years of age; but the instruction was principally imparted by the aid of objects, and in this way was communicated (without a knowledge of letters) the elements of history, natural history, geography, astronomy, and music. The children were

made acquainted with every object of domestic use, and
with every article of diet, so that questions put at random
by visitors were often answered with an accuracy which
created astonishment. As I have said, I paid great attention to the physical culture of the children, and practised
gymnastics with them ; they were encouraged to run,
jump, swing, as well as to march, and to sing while they
marched. I encouraged them to inflate the lungs, throw
back the arms, and expand the chest. I would not allow
them to speak in a whisper, but to exercise their lungs
freely, and to pronounce distinctly, and accurately, and
forcibly. And what I encouraged them to do I did myself ;
I was at the same time teacher and pupil. I would often
sit on the form myself, and get one of the children to act
as master in the way of teaching, and when the hour of
unrestrained play came, I was just one among them, and
running, shouting, and jumping with them. I recollect
one of the visiting ladies once saying, ironically : ' Well,
if the children learn nothing else, they learn to make a
glorious noise.' Book learning was not entirely neglected,
but was made subservient to every other exercise, and one
hour daily was all that was devoted to it.

I cannot help digressing a little on this part of my
narrative, to protest against the practice which prevails
among many teachers, and even many parents, of forcing
the infant brain to a premature maturity. Committees of
infant schools are much in the habit of influencing teachers
in this respect ; and a spirit of rivalry exists among
teachers themselves, as to which shall exhibit the greatest
progress among the pupils. Their public examinations, as
they are called, tend much to convince the reflecting part
of the community, that however much these institutions
are to be valued, as aids to the poor, and tending to
develope the physical powers of the pupils, they are most
strongly to be reprobated where forcing the brain to a
premature maturity is resorted to. I cannot do better than
quote some valuable hints on this subject from Dr. Caldwell's ' Thoughts on Physical Education ':

'Children ought not to be too soon dismissed from an education exclusively domestic. They ought not, I mean, to be sent to school at too early an age. A practice the contrary of this threatens to be productive of serious, not to say irreparable, mischief. Parents are often too anxious that their children should have a knowledge of the alphabet, of spelling, reading, and other branches of school learning, at a very early age. This is worse than tempting them to walk too early, because the organ likely to be injured by it is much more important than the muscles and bones of the lower extremities. It may do irremediable mischief to the brain. That viscus is yet too immature and feeble to sustain fatigue. Until from the sixth to the eighth year of life, the seventh being perhaps the proper medium, all the energies are necessary for its own healthy development, and that of the other portions of the system. Nor ought they to be diverted, by serious study, to any other purpose. True—exercise is as essential to the health and vigor of the brain at that time of life as at any other; but it should be the general and pleasurable exercise of observation and action. It ought not to be the compulsory exercise of tasks. Early prodigies of mind rarely attain mature distinction. The reason is plain: their brains are injured by premature toil, and their general health impaired. From an unwise attempt to convert at once their flowery spring into a luxuriant summer, that summer, too often, never arrives. The blossom withers ere the fruit is formed. For these reasons, I have never been an advocate of "Infant Schools." Unless they are conducted with great discretion, they cannot fail to eventuate in mischief. They should be nothing but schools of pleasurable exercise, having little to do with books.

'As these institutions are now administered, they are serious evils. The passion in favor of them becoming more extensive in its prevalence, and acquiring daily greater intensity, is among the alarming portents of the time. It is founded on the want of a correct knowledge of the human constitution, and of the amount of labor its different organs can sustain with safety at the different periods of life. Perhaps I should rather say it is founded on the fallacious belief that it is the infant's mind alone that labors in acquiring school learning, and not any organised portion of his body. This is an error which, if not corrected, will prove fatal to hundreds of thousands of the human race. It is not the mind, but the brain—the master organ of the system, essential to the well-being and efficiency of every other part of it—that toils, and is oppressed in the studies of the school. Nor, tender and feeble as it is, is it possible for it to endure the labor often imposed on it, without sustaining irreparable injury—an injury no less subversive of mental than of corporeal soundness and vigor.

'Instead of seeing infants confined to inaction in crowded

school-rooms, with saddened looks, moist eyes, and aching heads, we should then meet them in gardens and lawns, groves and pleasure grounds, breathing wholesome air, leaping, laughing, shouting, cropping flowers, pursuing butterflies, collecting and looking at curious and beautiful insects and stones, listening to bird songs, singing themselves, admiring the bright blue arch of the heavens, and doing all other things fitted to promote health, develope and strengthen their frames, and prepare them for the graver business of after life. And instead of pale faces, flaccid flesh, and wasted bodies, we should find them with ruddy cheeks, firm muscles, and full and well rounded limbs.

'Exercises and pastimes such as these constitute the only "Infant School" that deserves to be encouraged; nor will any other sort receive encouragement, when the business of education shall be thoroughly understood. The brain of infants will be then no longer neglected, as a mass of matter of little importance; skin, muscle, and bone being thought preferable to it. On the contrary, it will be viewed in its true character, as the ruling organ of the body, and the apparatus of the mind. I repeat— and the repetition should be persevered in until its truth be acknowledged and reduced to practice, that most of the evils of education under which the world has so long suffered, and is still suffering, arise from the mistaken belief, that in what is called moral and intellectual education, it is the mind that is exercised, and not the brain, nor will the evils cease, and education be made perfect, until the error shall be exploded.'

Although I was wholly ignorant of phrenology at the commencement of my school exercises, in 1821, I yet saw, from the writings of Pestalozzi, who was my great model, the importance of letting the body acquire strength before I began to work the mind or the brain. Now that I have so long studied and applied its principles, when I read of very precocious or learned children, I invariably turn a few pages forward, and almost invariably find a premature death. I will give one anecdote of this, and then return to my narrative.

'Christian Henry Heinsken was born at Lubeck, February 6th, 1721. He had completed his *first year*, when he already knew and recited the principal facts contained in the five books of Moses, with a number of verses on the creation. In his *fourteenth month* he knew all the history of the Bible; in his *thirtieth month*, the history of the nations of antiquity, geography, anatomy, the use of maps, and nearly eight thousand Latin words.

Before the end of his *third year*, the history of Denmark, and the genealogy of the crowned heads of Europe. In his *fourth year*, he acquired the doctrines of divinity, with the proofs from the Bible; ecclesiastical history; the institutions; two hundred hymns, with their tunes; eighty psalms; entire chapters of the Old and New Testaments; fifteen hundred verses and sentences from the ancient Latin classics; almost the whole Orbis Pictus of Comenius, from which he had derived all his knowledge of the Latin tongue; arithmetic; and history of the European emperors and kingdoms. He could point out in the maps whatever place he was asked for, or had passed through in his journeys, and relate all the ancient and modern historical anecdotes relating to it. His stupendous memory caught and retained every word he was told; his ever active imagination used, at whatever he saw and heard, instantly to apply, according to the laws of association of ideas, some examples or sentences from the Bible, geography, profane or ecclesiastical history, the Orbis Pictus, or from the ancient classics. At the court of Denmark he delivered twelve speeches, and underwent public examination, on a variety of subjects, especially the history of Denmark. He spoke German, Latin, French, and Low Dutch; and he was exceedingly good-natured and well behaved, BUT OF A MOST TENDER AND DELICATE CONSTITUTION, never ate any solid food, but chiefly subsisted on nurse's milk. He was celebrated all over Europe, under the name of the "Learned Child of Lubeck," and died June 27th, 1725, aged FOUR YEARS, FOUR MONTHS, TWENTY DAYS, and TWENTY-ONE HOURS.'

At the time of the birth of this child, the knowledge of the structure of the brain was *nil*, else the parties who had the care and training of him would have been guilty of sacrificing his life. To think of permitting an infant to exercise the brain in the same manner as a man of mature age, counting months as years, nay, to acquire in the tenderest periods of existence what few men in a long life achieve, is, in my estimation, little short of murder. True, the parents and friends of this child were doubtless ignorant of the natural laws, and in that ignorance lies their excuse; but, to return to my narrative.

It must be remembered, that none of my pupils exceeded seven years of age, and many of them were not more than three. A very few were, in the strict sense of the word, infants, and to all under four years I scarcely taught a letter.

The methods I pursued, however, spread the fame of

the school far and near. Persons came many **miles t** spend a day with us, and I received many very **flatterin** testimonials. At a large public meeting and **exhibition** the various exercises of the children in marching, **singing** and lessons on objects, a vote of approval was passed **o** my efforts, which was to this effect :—

'That this meeting has viewed with delight and astonishment th evolutions of the children, and desire to record their testimon that the Superintendent has discharged the important duties of hi situation with the utmost kindness and ability.'

After this I was frequently called upon to assist **in th** organisation of other schools, and soon had an **extensiv** correspondence with the friends of education all over **th** country.

It was at the beginning of the year 1822, that **Dr** Crook, a celebrated professor of mnemonics, called **upo** me at Bristol. He first lectured upon mnemonics, **to a large** and fashionable audience, in the Bristol Athenæum. **This** system to me was entirely new, but, at the same time, **very** attractive, and I was very anxious to learn it ; **but his** terms were too high, and his hours of lecturing **interfered** with my school engagements ; so I was, at that time, **obliged** to forego his instructions. He, however, gave one **evening** lecture, which I attended, and was filled with astonishment at the extent of memory displayed by his pupils in the recollection of dates, facts of history, and in botany. **I** have since completely learned his system, which, **however,** I have not found of any great benefit to myself. **Having** finished his course of mnemonics, he entered upon an **evening** course of phrenology. This was also, then, quite a **new** science. I believe the doctor was the first who **introduced** it into Bristol, and it attracted immense attention, **and** excited much interest in the city. I was among the **most** enthusiastic of its admirers. Dr. Crook presented me **with** his Compendium of the science, but it was a mere **chart.** It gave no idea of the history and discovery of the **science ;** it simply laid down the position of the organs, and **stated** their respective functions, so that I did not learn **much** from him, and he had but very few illustrations. Still it took a firm hold of my mind, and I determined to observe for myself, and to note down my observations.

Dr. Crook was himself a subject well worth study. He had a large head, and, consequently, great power of brain; but his organisation has appeared to me, since I first commenced the study of phrenology, by no means a happy one. His temperament was bilious-nervous, his activity great, but he appeared to me to lack the power of concentration. Of his intellectual faculties, the perceptives were very freely drawn out, and his eye was large and sparkling. The reflecting faculties were not so good as the observing, but the upper and lateral parts of the forehead were prominent. Benevolence was fully developed, and Imitation, Marvellousness, and Ideality, essentially large. His Veneration was also very good, and Firmness very striking; but, from the anterior part of the vertex, the head sloped towards the centre of ossification (parietal bones), and then swelled out, giving great prominence over the opening of the upper part of the ear, and increasing in size towards the temples. His Self-Esteem was large, and his Love of Approbation preternaturally so; and, at the posterior-inferior angle of the parietal bones, the cranium presented a striking eminence. These peculiarities rendered him very irritable, while intense Self-Esteem and Love of Approbation rendered him exacting, and, at the same time, gave him a high opinion of his own abilities, which he expected every one to acknowledge and speak well of. He was also sarcastic, and sneered at the abilities of such persons as he deemed his inferiors, while he covered with applause those who flattered him.

I have known the doctor for many years, and have observed him most carefully, and his organisation was one of the most perfect illustrations of the truth of phrenology I have ever seen. His leading powers were Language, Individuality, Wit, Imitation, Marvellousness, Firmness, Self-Esteem, Love of Approbation, Secretiveness, Combativeness, and Destructiveness. He was a brilliant and

showy, but rather rambling lecturer; but people we
generally disappointed at the conclusion of his lecture
His subjects were Mnemonics and Phrenology. He w:
very skilful in the selection of his pupils, whom he invar
ably chose according to their organisation. He has passe
from this natural state of being, and the conclusion of h:
existence was, I believe, embittered by poverty and neglec:

But, to return to myself. It was from Dr. Crook tha
I received my first phrenological impressions, and so firr
did his instructions take hold of me, that from the time o
his visit to Bristol, I noted the peculiarities of all I cam
in contact with, and then turned to their organisation t
see if those peculiarities harmonised therewith. I wa:
often at fault, mistaking prominent bones for eminences o
brain; and as I had no one to consult, I made many
mistakes.

With a very superficial knowledge of osteology, and
great dread of ridicule, I kept my opinions to myself; but,
from the time of my first hearing Dr. Crook, I became a
portrait collector. I never found a person with a low and
contracted forehead possessed of high intellectual ability;
and eminence of intellect I ever found associated with
depth and breadth of forehead. My portrait collecting
has continued; and, at the present time, a period of thirty-
six years from my first impression of phrenology, I think
I possess the best collection of portraits of any phrenologist in Great Britain.

I continued to take notice of the formation of the head
of the different persons I came in contact with. In other
words, I began to reduce to practice my small amount of
phrenological knowledge.* I did this both with regard to
children as well as adults, and my situation afforded me
abundant opportunities for the study of character. I had
a deaf and dumb pupil, who was largely endowed with
the qualities of imitation and music. I wondered whether
music could be considered as a primitive and independent

* I fell in with two volumes of portraits, magnificently executed, and
dedicated to his Majesty Geo. IV., and I studied them attentively.

power. Here was a child who could neither hear nor speak, and yet, according to phrenology, had the organ of Tune freely and prominently developed. I determined to try whether or no I could by imitation teach him to sing. I therefore always had him near me during the exercise, made him imitate the motion of my mouth, and utter sounds, and at last succeeded perfectly in teaching him several tunes. He became quite a prodigy among us, and many were the persons who came to hear the dumb boy hum a tune. Still, as he could not hear, I was at a loss whether even then I could set this organ down as a primitive power, although it is certain Tune was in this child very largely developed.

But from this child I turned my attention to others, and I drew my monitors from the ranks of my pupils for different duties according to their organisation, and was always successful. I had a music master, an arithmetician, a writing master, a reading master, a teacher of geography, all from my pupils, and all turned out good teachers. Phrenology, therefore, I thought must be true. But I kept all this to myself, for, as I have said, I was exceedingly sensitive and susceptible, and dreaded ridicule above all things ; but no one came near me without being noticed, and if he had peculiarities, they were stored in my memory. As before stated, I had no books but Dr. Crook's Compendium, a little book of about twenty-four pages (which the doctor had presented me), so I could learn but little from that.

In the beginning of the year 1822, the school began to excite so much interest in the public mind, that persons from distant parts of the country came to visit it, with the view of establishing similar schools, and I was now frequently called upon to give explanatory lectures in different parts of Somersetshire, Gloucestershire, and Shropshire, so that, after five days' arduous labor, I often had to travel on the outside of the mail all night, give a lecture, organise a school, and return in the space of a fortnight, the whole duties of my own school devolving upon my wife in my

absence. I still had a very juvenile appearance, though
twenty-six years of age, and people wondered to see a
mere lad stand up before a large audience and address
them in favor of Pestalozzi's plan, explaining his system
at night before parties of ladies and gentlemen, and illustrating it by day upon children who were totally ignorant
of every kind of knowledge.

As long as I can remember, I have ever been a little
deaf, and my repeated exposure and travelling by night,
assisted, I have no doubt, by the harsh treatment I had
received from my cruel master, at length began to affect
my hearing seriously, but it seemed always to leave me in
school. I found no difficulty among my pupils. People
with the most acute hearing could not detect an error in
the children so readily as I could; but when the labors
of the day were concluded, and conversation in private
was entered upon, I sensibly perceived the difference. But
my committee did not seem to notice the defect, and my
popularity as a teacher continued to increase.

Meantime, I continued to officiate for the Society of
Swedenborgians at Bristol, and entirely, so far as I could
learn, to their satisfaction. I began to notice the peculiarities of the members from their organisation ; and though
I never gave an opinion, I still saw many striking proofs
of the truth of phrenological science.

About this time I became personally acquainted with
gentleman named Sanders, of Clifton, near Bristol. H
was a regular attendant every week upon the morning
worship at the place of meeting where I officiated, and
visited him at his residence in Hot Well Square, Clifto
every week. He was an eminent artist ; a member,
believe, of the Academy of Arts, and a highly scienti
gentleman. He frequently operated upon me for n
hearing, and by electricity I think I was much benefit
Among his visitors was a Mr. John Fitchew Fitzhu
who was also an occasional attendant at my chapel, but
was exceedingly eccentric. He would have deligh
some of our would-be ancients of this day, for he w

MR. J. FITCHEW FITZHUGH.

[PAGE 126.

his beard, dressed in purple velvet, white stockings, yellow shoes, and a white hat. He could not be induced to put on anything black. He called it 'the devil's livery.' He constantly labored to induce me to alter my costume, and adopt his. His head was very large, and, from the upper part of the forehead to the anterior part of the vertex, quite bald. The brain spread over the fontanel in a very prominent manner, giving to that part which phrenologists assign to the organ of Marvellousness a very elevated appearance, and this was one of the first observations I made; it was comparatively forced upon me by the eccentricities of the individual. He followed the injunctions given to the apostles of saluting every house he entered by the utterance of the words, ' Peace be to this house,' and the same on leaving it. -

He would not eat or drink at any person's expense, but carried his provisions with him wherever he went, which he stowed away in different parts of his coat; and which, as it respected pockets, was a truly marvellously constructed garment. Each article had its own pocket: tea, sugar, coffee, bread, and cheese. But although he always brought his provisions with him, he never took anything away; the fragments he left were the perquisites of the servant. He frequently visited at my house, but I first became intimate with him at the house of Mr. Sanders. He had a most brilliant and penetrating eye, and one of his peculiarities was gazing up at the sun. He has often directed me to lift my eye to the sun when it was shining with intense brilliancy; and upon my declaring that it was impossible for me to do so without injury, he has remarked—' *Ah! your spiritual sight is not yet opened, or you would experience no difficulty.*' Then he has gazed · upwards himself, and without blinking has looked at the glorious luminary so long and so steadily, as led me to wonder that he was not struck blind.

Whenever he was about to utter any of his spiritual communications, he would always direct his eyes upward, gaze steadily at the sun if shining, then declare what spirits were present, and what their communications. Mr. Sanders executed a portrait in crayon, which bears a striking resemblance to him, which on his death he bequeathed to me, and which I now have by me. It is one of the most magnificently formed heads that I have in my collection, and as I have had it for upwards of thirty years, it must now be very valuable.

Another of Mr. Fitzhugh's peculiarities was, the carrying about his person a black leather pocket book, containing a specific sum of money, and if he had occasion to disburse any portion, he always replenished the book on his return, so that he was never without a large sum of money on his person. He never slept in a bed, but stretched himself on a large table, and, although in the house of his friends he tolerated carpets, in his own house he would not allow them. I have heard him say, 'While so many poor fellow creatures stand in need of clothing, it is sinful to tread under feet that which would clothe them.' He gave to the poor, yearly, what he thought it would cost him yearly for carpets.

In the Society of Swedenborgians, at Bristol, on account of his eccentricities, he was not much respected; but I always found him a worthy and upright character, though at times wildly enthusiastic.

About this time I was thrown much into the society of both Unitarians and members of the Society of Friends, and I must say I ever found them a kind and strictly moral people, and of the most cultivated intellect. I made myself conversant, while at Bristol, with 'Clarkson's Portraiture of Quakerism,' and 'Barclay's Apology.' I was much struck with the discipline of the Quakers, though I observed that it was not strictly conformed to. One of the rules of discipline was, that no member of the Society should cultivate music, it being a science which, in their opinion, tended rather to the gratification of the creature than of praise to the Creator. As I have said, this rule was violated more than once. I knew a young lady of the Society of Friends, who was a very skilful performer on the guitar, and an elderly lady, with whom I was brought in frequent contact, in consequence of her visiting the school, was not only a very sweet singer, but often assisted in teaching it. Here was an anomaly that puzzled me, and I thought that, as the human voice had been so constructed by the Creator to be the most melodious of all instruments, it was a sad mistake on the part of any religious body to prohibit its use. I was also struck with the fact, that although the elder 'Friends' did not encourage music among their own people, they took a particular pleasure in listening to the children sing, and even at times solicited that a hymn might be sung. I thought if it was sinful to sing themselves, it was sinful to encourage it in others. But for all this I continued to sing myself, and to teach it to the children as far as I was able, and found it one of the most efficient aids in moral training.

So much was I impressed in favor of the Quaker discipline, that I made it a model from which I drew up a form of discipline for the government of the small society over which I presided. It was approved, inserted in the journal of the Society, and there I believe it is to this day.

It was in the year 1822, that my friend, the Rev. Dr. Churchill, having, through infirmity and ill health, entirely relinquished practice as a physician, came to reside in Bristol, and, for some time, he sat under me. I received from him much good advice and instruction. He directed me in my studies, and recommended me such books as were most profitable to prepare me for becoming a useful minister.

At that time it was a rule in the Swedenborgian Church, that no person should be admitted by ordination as a minister until he had preached twelve months to some Society recognised by the Swedenborgian Conference as belonging to the church ; and having so ministered, and being called by the Society to become its pastor, it was further necessary that he should have the sanction of two

9

other officiating ministers. The mode of electing ministers is somewhat different now.

The Society at Bristol having expressed a wish for my regular ordination, I consulted with Dr. Churchill on the subject. He concurred with the Society, but recommended me to apply to the Rev. Manoah Sibly, of London, who was then the oldest acting minister in the Connection. I accordingly waited upon him, and preached before him, when he immediately recommended Dr. Churchill to proceed with my ordination. Accordingly, on the 3rd of November, 1822, I was regularly inducted into the ministry by the Rev. Dr. Churchill. Thus far, although not in the Church of England, my desire was accomplished, and I became a minister among the Swedenborgians.

In person, Dr. Churchill was somewhat spare and debilitated by ill health. He was rather above the middle height. His countenance was pale, his eye languid, and he appeared to be constantly suffering pain. His head was of average size, and rose to considerable altitude in the coronal region. His forehead was moderately broad and deep. He was a man of strict integrity, amiable disposition, and good intellectual ability. Beside the sermon on the death of Mary Minting, before alluded to, he was the author of a 'Domestic Medical Guide,' and of a highly useful, but moderately controversial volume, explanatory of the chief doctrine of the New Church, entitled 'Jesus Christ, the True God and Eternal Life.'

In his charge to me, he particularly dwelt on the necessity of simplicity in preaching; advised me to avoid controversy; to take, as nearly as I could, the Rev. J. Proud for my model; and, in every discourse, to bring the subject practically home to the life. He thus proceeded:

A CHARGE.

'Do not expect that you will now be at ease in your mind, or that, having attained to the ministry, you will be free from trial. Be assured your trials as well as your labors, as a minister, are but in commencement. You will be in perils among your brethren as well as among strangers. If you are successful, you will be

REV. T. F. CHURCHILL, M. D.

[PAGE 133.

envied, perhaps misrepresented; and if your ministry is not crowned with an accession of hearers, your own brethren will be most likely to set it down as want of ability.

'You are, however, to follow your Divine Master, and in all things to learn of him; and first imitate him in humility—and this will give you peace of mind amidst all the trials to which you may be subjected. "Learn of me," says he, "for I am meek and lowly, and ye shall find rest to your souls." I recommend you to study most attentively and prayerfully the Word of God. This is the mouth of God, uttering its voice to the children of men; and you are now one of the servants—the professed servants of God—you are to watch over the spiritual interests of the people, you must hear the Word at the mouth of the Lord, and as a faithful watchman, give the people warning from what you hear.

'There are three especial portions of Scripture which I would recommend you to fix permanently in your memory. The 18th chapter of Ezekiel proves plainly that the Divine Being is willing to receive all that repent. It is an antidote to the cruel doctrine of predestination; and, while it describes and particularises almost every crime in which man has indulged; it at the same time offers forgiveness on repentance. Conditional are all heaven's covenants, and the vilest, on repentance, are not only forgiven, but their sins are not to be even mentioned to them again. Never fail to preach repentance in the name of the Lord among all nations—that is, among all classes of people—keep this chapter constantly before you. The thirty-third chapter of the same prophet places before you your own duty as a spiritual watchman. Read it attentively, grave it in your memory, be instant in prayer to God that you may be faithful to its requirements. There are three especial duties devolving upon you from the consideration of this chapter. 1. You are to hear the Word at the mouth of the Lord, and give the people warning from him. This requires you, therefore, to read and meditate frequently on the Word of the Lord. 2. You are to qualify yourself for defending the church, and the members of the church who wait upon your instructions, and this is a further reason for you reading frequently, and incorporating into your understanding the great truths of the Word of the Lord; for these truths alone are to be the weapons wherewith you are to combat. Yours is not to be a carnal warfare—but a spiritual. You are to use the sword of the spirit, and the sword of the spirit is the Word of God. Your third especial duty is practically to apply every word proceeding out of the mouth of the Lord. This is to be done *individually* as well as collectively. You are to remember that " the Divine Word is of no private interpretation "; but the whole is " profitable for doctrine, for reproof, for instruction, that the man of God may be thoroughly furnished unto all good works." These duties are imperative upon you as a watchman set upon the walls of Jerusalem, and upon the faithful performance of them depends the salvation of your own soul: for, "if the watchman see the sword come, and blow not the trumpet, and the people be not warned; if the sword come and take any person from among them, he is taken away in his iniquity, but his blood will I require at the watchman's hand." "Nevertheless, if thou warn the wicked of his way to turn from it, if he do not turn from his way, he shall die in his iniquity; but thou hast delivered thy soul." The other portion of Scripture which I recommend to your especial attention, is contained in the fifth, sixth, and seventh chapters of St. Matthew, it embodies the whole of the Lord's Sermon on the Mount, of which it is not too much to say, that, were there no other portion of the Word of Divine Truth in existence, that alone would be sufficient to guide the soul safely to heaven.

'The writings of the apostles you will find useful—read them, and apply them. But the gospels, being the especial words of the Lord, and the Sermon on the Mount, being an embodiment of the law and the gospel, let these be your especial study, and let your exhortations be drawn principally from them.

'THE WORD, *then*—THE WORD must be your study; and as auxiliaries to the explanation of the Word, take the writings of Emanuel Swedenborg. I admire a wise and temperate use of these writings in the Pulpit, delivered in a familiar and popular style, and practically illustrated and enforced; and you cannot, I repeat, do better than take Mr. Proud for your model in this respect.

'Now as to doctrine. Let the great and glorious doctrine, that "Jesus Christ is over all, God blessed for evermore," be your constant theme: and let the life after death, and the glories of the heavenly state, be your animating appeal to the people for performing the work of repentance. Always unite charity with faith; they are the two heavenly witnesses which you must constantly cite to support your testimony—neither faith alone, nor charity alone, nor works alone will save; but the three united are sure to conduct to heaven. "I was an hungred, and ye gave me meat; thirsty, and ye gave me drink; naked, and ye clothed me; sick, and in prison, and ye came unto me—inasmuch as ye did this unto one of the least of these my brethren, ye did it unto me."

'Cultivate the acquaintance of all good men. Avoid controversy; but when called upon to defend the doctrines, do it in a kindly spirit, and as much as possible, in the words of Scripture. With the Bible as your chief book, your lawgiver, your counsellor, your sure light, your armory of spiritual weapons, your captain to lead you and instruct you in the use of your weapons, you have all that you require. But you may take the writings of all good men, to stimulate you and to assist you; and especially take the writings of Emanuel Swedenborg, as your best instructor in unfolding the spiritual sense of God's most Holy Word.

'And now may the blessing of God be with you, and give you abundant success. May you, through good report and evil report, pursue your way. May you be instant in season and out of season, to reprove, exhort, and correct in all long suffering and doctrine.'

Such was the charge of my excellent friend. I do not, pretend to give it as the precise words of that good man ; but the substance was his ; but I remember as he laid his trembling hand on my head, that he made use of the words, 'I have performed this office upon others of my brethren in the church, but never with more real satisfaction than upon you. May the Lord Jesus Christ bless, and keep, and strengthen you to do your office faithfully, and to give him all the glory.'

I believe that a better man than Dr. Churchill never ascended a pulpit in the New Church. He was charitable in the true sense of the word. He might have been wealthy, for, at one time, he had an extensive practice; but much that he acquired he bestowed upon the humbler class of his patients. His time and his medicines were among the least of his free gifts. His money (many said to an imprudent amount) was freely disbursed to the poor. He was a physician, too, for the soul, and ministered as well to the mind diseased as to the body afflicted with pain. I will conclude the character of my very dear friend, Dr. Churchill, in the words of an anonymous writer.*

'Dr. Churchill, like many other excellent men, had his weak side—his light and his shade. He had infirmities, but these arose more from the debility of his physical powers than from any other cause. Whatever these might have been, let death draw the mantle of love over his remains ; and let the memory of such a man be blessed. Especially let the members of the New Church cherish his memory with affection, because he was an honest man, one who possessed real goodness—STRICTLY CONSCIENTIOUS AND UPRIGHT, of UNSULLIED CHARACTER, and of GENUINE PIETY !'

He died on the 1st of August, 1852, aged about sixty-seven years.

* 'Aleph' in the 'Intellectual Repository,' 1834, p. 111.

I pursued my joint duties both at the chapel and in the school, sometimes being absent from Bristol for a fortnight or three weeks at a time, to establish other schools in different parts of the counties already mentioned. At the same time I continued my phrenological observations.

At the beginning of the year 1823, the newspapers of the day teemed with a singular incident relative to Swedenborg's skull, which had been, some years previous, secretly abstracted from the coffin in which the remains of that distinguished individual had been interred, at the Swedish Church, Ratcliffe Highway, London. It was thought, so the rumor ran, that the Swedenborgians would give to the abstractor a large sum of money for so precious a relic. And the Editor of the 'London Courier,' who warmly took up the subject, put forth some condemnatory articles on the Swedenborgian love of relics.

Of all the different classes of Christians, the Swedenborgians are the least accessible to relics of any kind, but more especially relics of the dead. They believe that the body, once dead, will never be re-assumed. They contend that 'it is the spirit which quickeneth—the flesh profiteth nothing'; and therefore, when the body has fulfilled its use in this world, which use is principally to prepare the soul for heaven, it will be consigned 'to the earth as it was, while the spirit will return to God who gave it.'

The gentleman, therefore, who abstracted the skull with the view of making money of it, if such was his object, would meet with no encouragement, but contrariwise with reprobation. It turned out, however, that the real object of obtaining the skull was to see if it corroborated the doctrines of Gall ; but as the letters which passed on the occasion are exceedingly interesting and worthy of preservation, as showing what ideas the Swedenborgians entertain of relics, I herewith present them.

'EMANUEL SWEDENBORG.

'TO THE EDITOR OF THE "COURIER."

'SIR—In your paper of to-day is an anecdote headed as above, which contains some mistakes, and which I trust you will allow me to correct.

'*It is true* that the skull of Swedenborg was *a few years ago (not soon after his interment),* taken from his coffin in the vault of the Swedish Church, near Ratcliffe Highway, by a Swedish gentleman then, and *now,* living in England; but *it is not true* that the person who executed this singular robbery was or is *one of his disciples.* I understand that the motive which led him to obtain possession of this "relic," was the same as led Drs. Gall and Spurzheim to possess themselves of similar relics of other eminent men. The fact having been heard of by the Countess ——, of Sweden, she requested an English gentleman of rank to wait upon the possessor, and request that he would allow the skull to be restored to its former situation; to which he readily assented. *It is true,* then, that its re-interment took place; but *it is not true* that this was attended with any solemnity, or, "excited unbounded (or any) interest among his numerous followers." Some of them knew that the skull had been taken away; but I believe that none of them (or not more than one), knew when it was restored; and I am sure that none of them cared anything about the matter.

'The sole motive of the lady above alluded to for procuring the re-interment, was, that the admirers of the writings of Swedenborg might not be charged with such stupidity as that of venerating the mortal remains of any man, which, Swedenborg maintains, are entirely unnecessary to the future existence of the soul, and will never be resumed; for she was aware, that if at any future period it should be discovered that the skull was gone, the robbery would be imputed to the admirers of his doctrines, and that misrepresentations of their sentiments, such as your anecdote contains, would be the result. Nothing, I assure you, can be more abhorrent to their principles, or to the doctrines of the New Jerusalem Church, than anything that can tend to the revival of saint-craft.

'I am, Sir, yours respectfully,
'S. NOBLE,
'Minister of Hanover Street Chapel, Long Acre.

'*March* 31, 1823.'

'EMANUEL SWEDENBORG'S SKULL.

'TO THE EDITOR.

'Sir—In the wish of screening the poor sexton or grave-digger, whoever he may be, from the infamous charge of having been bribed to aid in purloining the above-mentioned skull from its coffin, I feel it my duty to state the following circumstance:—

'Captain Ludvig Granholm, of the Royal Navy of Sweden, called on me, near the end of the year 1817, invited me to his lodgings and showed me a skull, which he said was the skull of

Swedenborg. He informed me, that a few days before that time, he had attended the funeral of one of his countrymen, into the vault under the Swedish Ambassador's Chapel, in Prince's Square, Ratcliffe Highway, and that he remained there a short time, with others, looking at the inscriptions on various coffins. That, on reading the name of the Honourable Emanuel Swedenborg, and observing that the coffin lid was loose, he was seized with the idea of making a large sum of money, by taking the skull, and selling it to one of Swedenborg's followers, who, he had heard, amounted to many thousands in this country, and amongst whom, he imagined, there would be much competition for the possession of so valuable a relic. He watched his opportunity, lifted the lid of the coffin, took out the skull, wrapped it in his pocket handkerchief, and carried it out of the chapel unnoticed.

'I informed Captain Granholm, to his great disappointment, that the members of the New Jerusalem Church reprobated the possession of any religious relic, and more particularly a part of a dead body, which, they believe, will never more come into use, the soul remaining, after death, a complete and active man in a spiritual body, not to be again fettered with material flesh, blood, and bones.

'Captain Granholm died a few months afterwards in London, without having disposed of the skull, and without having left this country, so that several particulars of the account in your paper of the 31st ult. are erroneous.

'A very curious circumstance occasioned the coffin lid to be loose. About the year 1790, a Swedish philosopher, then in London, who was a great admirer of Swedenborg's philosophical writings, but had no relish for his theological, became acquainted with some of the members of the New Church, and warmly opposed Swedenborg's tenet—that the soul takes a final leave of the material body at death, and enters on its new scene of superior activity in a spiritual body, more suited to obey its energies. The learned Swede endeavored to persuade them, that all great philosophers had, by virtue of their profound wisdom, the power of taking with them, into the world of spirits, their natural bodies; and he asserted his full conviction, that Swedenborg, whom he considered one of the first philosophers, had taken away his body out of the coffin.

'In order to convince the Swede of his error, leave was obtained to have the coffin opened; when, to the utter confusion of the philosopher, the body of Swedenborg was presented to view. The lid was merely laid on, without being re-fastened; and thus was afforded the facility of which Captain Granholm availed himself twenty-seven years afterwards.

'J. I. HAWKINS.

'*Pentonville, April 3.*'

'TO THE EDITOR.

'SIR—Two different statements having lately appeared in your journal, concerning the re-interment of the skull of this extraordinary individual, neither of which is exactly correct, I take the liberty of presenting the following to your notice :—

'E. Swedenborg died in London in the year 1772, and was interred in the vault of the Swedish church, in Princes Square, Ratcliffe Highway. His death having excited considerable sensation among his numerous followers, one of them, a native of . America, came over to England for the purpose of ascertaining the truth of the fact, being convinced, it is said, that such a *spiritual* man (if, indeed, he had left this lower world) must at least have gone alive to heaven. The parish clerk was bribed, the vault opened, and the coffin pointed out to him. The admirer of Swedenborg could not, however, even then persuade himself that the mortal remains of the venerated man were deposited there, till the coffins were opened, and the mephitic vapours did at the same time expel the sceptic and his doubts upon the subject. Thus the fact is related in Mr. Broling's 'Travels in England,' edited in Stockholm, 1816 or 1817. Be this, however, how it may, it is a well ascertained fact that Emanuel Swedenborg's coffin had been opened before (1816), when the skull was taken out. *It is true*, that this violation of the tomb was not perpetrated by a follower or admirer of Swedenborg, the number of whom among his countrymen is very small indeed. (No prophet is honored in his own country.) It was committed by a person who did not admire Swedenborg, but Gall, and who expected to fix the *organ of imagination* beyond any doubt; but it is *incorrectly* stated by the Rev. Mr. Noble, that "the person who committed this singular (infamous, if you please) robbery, is now residing in London." No, Sir, this violater of the grave having (no doubt greatly against his expectation) been obliged to lay his own head to rest a few years after, the above skull was found among his property by a gentleman who prevented its being carried away, though claimed by the friends of the deceased abroad, and in whose possession it since remained. *It is true*, that a noble Countess much interested herself in this affair, and that the skull, agreeably to her desire, was lately restored to its former abode, (a cast having previously been taken;) but *it is equally certain*, that such a measure had been agreed upon, long ere the interference of the noble Lady alluded to.

'I am, Sir, yours respectfully,
'*April* 4.'   'TERTIUS INTERVENIENS.

I give the letters as they successively appeared, without any comment. I may, however, here observe, that at the time of Gall's residence in Vienna, a perfect panic seized upon the more respectable part of the community against his researches. Every one considered his skull to be in danger, and clauses were inserted in wills to protect the skull from the craniological doctor. In Gall's letter to Baron Retzer, he says, 'Men, unhappily, have such an opinion of themselves, that each one believes that I am watching for his head, as one of the most important objects of my collection. Nevertheless, I have not been able to collect more than twenty in the space of three years, if I except those that I have taken in the hospitals, or in the asylum for idiots.'

This incident, however, of Swedenborg's skull, furnishes me with the opportunity of giving some account of Gall's discovery, together with an outline of his life. My account is compiled from the 'Transactions of the Edinburgh Phrenological Society,' 1824, from the 'Edinburgh Phrenological Journal,' from the 'Journal de la Societé Phrénologique de Paris,' and from the Biography prefixed to the American edition of Gall's Works, 1835.

Francis Joseph Gall was born in a village of the Grand Duchy of Baden, on March 9, 1758. His father was a merchant, and Mayor of Trefenburn, a village two leagues distant from Pforzheim, in Swabia. His parents, professing the Roman Catholic religion, had intended him for the church, but his natural dispositions were opposed to it. His studies were pursued at Baden, afterwards at Burcksal, and then were continued at Strasburg. Having selected the healing art for his profession, he went in 1781 to Vienna, the medical school of which university had obtained great reputation, particularly since the times of Van Swietan and Stahl.

From an early age Gall was given to observation, and was struck·with the fact, that each of his brothers and sisters, companions in play, and school-fellows, possessed some peculiarity of talent or disposition which distinguished him from others. Some of his school-mates were distinguished by the beauty of their penmanship, some by their success in arithmetic, and others by their talent for

upon th————————————table part of the community against

...

... their ...

... success in arithmetic, and others by their ...

GALL.

acquiring a knowledge of natural history or of languages. The compositions of one were remarkable for elegance, while the style of another was stiff and dry ; and a third connected his reasonings in the closest manner, and clothed his argument in the most forcible language. Their dispositions were equally different, and this diversity appeared also to determine the direction of their partialities and aversions. Not a few of them manifested a capacity for employments which they were not taught. Some cut figures in wood, or delineated them on paper. Some devoted their leisure to drawing or painting, others to music, others to arithmetic, the cultivation of a garden, etc., etc. In this manner each individual presented a character peculiar to himself.

The scholars with whom young Gall had the greatest difficulty of competing were those who learned by heart with the greatest facility ; and such individuals frequently gained from him by their repetitions the places which he had obtained by the merit of his original compositions.

Some years afterwards, having changed his place of residence, he still met individuals endowed with an equally great talent of learning to repeat. He then observed that his school-fellows, so gifted, possessed prominent eyes, and he recollected that his rivals in the first school had been distinguished by the same peculiarity. When he entered the university he directed his attention from the first to the students whose eyes were of this description, and he soon found that they all excelled in verbal memory, though many of them were not at all distinguished in point of general talent. This observation was recognised also by the other students in the classes ; and although the connection between the talent and the external sign was not at this time established upon such complete evidence as is requisite for a philosophical conclusion, yet Gall could not believe that the coincidence of the two circumstances thus observed was entirely accidental. He suspected, therefore, from this period, that they stood in an important relation to each other. After much reflection, he conceived that if MEMORY FOR WORDS was indicated by an external sign, the same might be the case with the other intellectual powers, and from that moment all individuals distinguished by any remarkable faculty became the objects of his atten- tion. By degrees he conceived himself to have found external characteristics, which indicated a decided disposi- tion for MECHANISM, PAINTING, and MUSIC. He became acquainted also with some individuals remarkable for the determination of their character, and he observed a par- ticular part of their heads to be very remarkably developed. This fact first suggested to him the idea of looking to the head for signs of the MORAL SENTIMENTS. But in making these observations, he never conceived for a moment that the *skull* was the cause of the different talents, as has been erroneously represented. He referred the influence, whatever it was, to the brain.*

* Dr. Wilkinson, in his truly original and magnificent work, 'The Human Body and its Connection with Man' (pp. 22, 23), has the fol- lowing remarkable observations, with which, however, we do not entirely coincide, though they are deserving the attention of physiologists in general:—'As we understand phrenology, it is a science of independent observation, which is completed in tracing the correspondence between the surface of the living head and the character of the individual. It was as such that its edifice arose, stone by stone, in the hands of the illustrious Gall. He noticed that portions of the surface of the head stood out in those who were prominent in certain faculties, and putting the bodily and mental prominences together (for which may he be hon- ored), he arrived, by repeated instances, at the signs of the character as they are written upon the head. He completed the dark half of the globe of physiognomy, and letting his observation shine upon it, he found the rest of the head representative of the whole character, as the face is expressive of the mind. Expression, we may remark, is living representation, and representation is dead expression. The representa- tion of the man by his head had always been vaguely felt, and the best sculptors and poets had imaged their gods and heroes with phrenological truth. But Gall made their high functions so current that all could buy them. Now this department of physiognomy might be carried to the perfection peculiar to itself, without the head being opened. Nay, it would be best learned without breaking the surface; for the beauty of expression and representation lies in their bringing what they signify to the surface, and depositing it there. But, for this purpose, the surface must be whole. There is no interval between life and its hieroglyphics, but the one is within the other, as a wheel within a wheel. The thing signified by the organ of FORM is FORM, and not a piece of Cerebrum.

In following out by observation the principle which accident had thus suggested, he for some time encountered difficulties of the greatest magnitude. Hitherto, he had been altogether ignorant of the opinions of physiologists touching the brain, and of metaphysicians respecting the mental faculties, and had simply observed nature. When, however, he began to enlarge his knowledge of books, he found the most extraordinary conflict of opinions everywhere prevailing, and this, for the moment, made him hesitate about the correctness of his own observations. He found that the MORAL SENTIMENTS had, by an almost general consent, been consigned to the thoracic and abdominal viscera; and that, while Pythagoras, Plato, Galen, Haller, and other physiologists placed the sentient soul or intellectual faculties in the brain, Aristotle placed it in the heart, Van Helmont in the stomach, Des Cartes and his followers in the pineal gland, and Drelincourt and others in the cerebellum.

He observed also that a greater number of philosophers and physiologists asserted that all men are born with equal mental faculties, and that the differences observable among them are owing either to education or to the accidental circumstances in which they are placed. If all differences are accidental, he inferred that there could be no natural signs of predominating faculties, and, consequently, that

Love is meant by the protuberance of *Amativeness*, and not the Cerebellum, and so forth. It is superficiality and not depth that is excellence here. The deep ones had dug for ages in the brain, and found nothing but abstract truth. Gall came out of the cerebral well, and looking upon the surface, found that it was a landscape, inhabited by human natures in a thousand tents, all dwelling according to passions, faculties, and powers. So much was gained by the first man who came to the surface, where nature speaks by representation; but it is lost again at the point where cerebral anatomy begins. Gall himself was an instance of this. HE WAS ONE OF THE GREATEST AND MOST SUCCESSFUL OF THE ANATOMISTS OF THE BRAIN. But when the skull is off, his phrenology deserts him, the human interest ceases, and his descriptions of the fibres and the grey matter are as purely physical as if they were the ropes and pulleys of a ship.' [With deference to Dr. W., we think otherwise, but we recommend to his attentive perusal the late Dr. Spurzheim's 'Anatomy of the Brain.' Boston, U. S., Edition.]

the project of learning by observation to distinguish the functions of the different portions of the brain must be hopeless. This difficulty he combatted by the reflection that his brothers, sisters, and school-fellows had all received very nearly the same education, but that he had still observed each of them unfolding a distinct character, over which circumstances appeared to exert only a limited control. He observed also that not unfrequently they whose education had been conducted with the greatest care, and on whom the labors of teachers had been most freely lavished, remained far behind their companions in attainments.

Being convinced by these facts that there is a natural and constitutional diversity of talents and dispositions, he encountered in books still another obstacle to his success, in determining the external signs of the mental powers. He found that, instead of faculties, for acquiring languages, drawing, distinguishing places, music, and mechanical arts, corresponding to the different talents which he had observed in his school-fellows, the metaphysicians spoke only of general powers, such as perception, conception, memory, imagination, and judgment ; and when he endeavored to discover external signs in the head corresponding to these general faculties, or to determine the correctness of the physiological doctrines regarding the seat of the mind, as taught by the authors already mentioned, he found perplexities without end, and difficulties insurmountable.

Abandoning every theory and pre-conceived opinion, therefore, Gall gave himself up entirely to the observation of nature. Being physician to a lunatic asylum in Vienna, he had opportunities of which he availed himself of making observations on the insane. He visited prisons, and resorted to schools ; he was introduced to the courts of princes, to colleges, and the seats of justice ; and wherever he heard of an individual distinguished in any particular way, either by remarkable endowment or deficiency, he observed and studied the development of the head. In this manner, by an almost imperceptible induction, he conceived himself warranted in believing that particular mental powers are indicated by particular configurations of the head. The successive steps, by which Dr. Gall proceeded in his discoveries are particularly deserving of attention. He did not, as many have imagined, first dissect the brain, and pretend, by that means, to have discovered the seats of the mental powers; neither did he, as others have conceived, first map out the skull into various compartments, and assign a faculty to each, according as his imagination led him to conceive the place appropriate to the power; on the contrary, he first observed a concomitance betwixt particular talents and dispositions, and particular forms of the head; he next ascertained, by removal of the skull, that the figure and size of the brain are indicated by these external forms, and it was only after these facts were determined that the brain was minutely dissected, and light thrown upon its structure.

The first written notice of Gall's inquiries concerning the head, appeared in a familiar letter to Baron Retzer, which was inserted in the German Periodical Journal ['Deutschen Mercur'] in December, 1798. In this letter he announced the publication of a work upon his views concerning the brain. The following is the letter alluded to, which clearly defines the object of his researches :

'LETTER FROM DR. F. J. GALL, TO JOSEPH FR. DE RETZER, UPON THE FUNCTIONS OF THE BRAIN, IN MAN AND ANIMALS.*

' I have at last the pleasure, my dear Retzer, of presenting you a sketch of my Treatise upon the Functions of the Brain; and upon the possibility of distinguishing some of the dispositions and propensities by the shape of the head and the skull. I have observed that many men of talent and learning awaited with confidence the result of my labors, while others set me down as a visionary, or a dangerous innovator.

'But, to the subject: my purpose is to ascertain the functions of the brain in general, and those of its different parts in particular; to show that it is possible to ascertain different dispositions and

* 'Journal de la Société Phrénologique de Paris.'

inclinations by the elevations and depressions upon the head; and to present in a clear light the most important consequences which result therefrom to medicine, morality, education, and legislation—in a word, to the science of human nature.

'To do this effectually, it is necessary to have a large collection of drawings and plans. Therefore, with regard to particular qualities and their indications only, I shall now submit to my readers so much as is necessary for the establishment and illustration of the fundamental principles.

'The particular design of my work is to mark the historical outline of my researches; to lay down the principles, and to show their application. You will readily conceive, that the study of the real springs of thought and action in man, is an arduous undertaking. Whether I succeed or not, I shall count upon your indulgence and support, if only on account of the hardihood of the enterprise.

'Be so good as to recollect that I mean, by the head or cranium, the bony box which contains the brain; and of this, only those parts which are immediately in contact with it. And do not blame me for not making use of the language of Kant. I have not made progress enough in my researches to discover the particular organ for sagacity, for depth, for imagination, for the different kinds of judgment, etc. I have even been sometimes wanting in precision in the definition of my ideas, my object being to make known to a large number of readers the importance of my subject.

'The whole of the work is divided into two parts, which together makes about ten sheets.

'PART I

contains the principles. I start with my readers from that point to which nature has conducted me. After having collected the result of my *tedious experiments*, I have built up a theory of their laws of relation. I hasten to lay before you the fundamental principles.

'*I. The faculties and the propensities innate in man and animals.*

'You surely are not the man to dispute this ground with me; but, follower of Minerva, you should be armed to defend her cause. Should it appear from my system, that we are rather slaves than masters of our actions, consequently dependent upon our natural impulses, and should it be asked what becomes of liberty? and how can the good or evil we do be attributed to us?—I shall be permitted to give you the answer, by extracting it literally from my preface. You can strengthen the argument by your metaphysical and theological knowledge.

Those who would persuade themselves that our dispositions (or qualities) are not innate, would attribute them to education. But have we not alike acted passively, whether we have been formed by our innate dispositions, or by education ? By this objection, they confound the ideas of faculties, inclinations, and simple disposition, with the mode of action itself. The animals themselves are not altogether subject to their dispositions and propensities. Strong as may be the instinct of the dog to hunt, of the cat to catch mice, repeated punishments will, nevertheless, prevent the action of their instincts ! Birds repair their nests when injured ; and bees cover with wax any carrion which they cannot remove. But man possesses, besides the animal qualities, the faculty of speech, and unlimited *educability*—two inexhaustible sources of knowledge and action. He has the sentiment of truth and error, of right and wrong : he has the consciousness of free-will ; the past and the future may influence his action ; he is endowed with moral feeling, with con- science, etc. Thus armed, man may combat his inclinations : these indeed have always attractions, which lead to temptation ; but they are not so strong, that they cannot be subdued and kept under by other and stronger inclinations which are opposed to them. You have a voluptuous disposition, but, having good morals, conjugal affection,-health, regard for society and of religion as your preserva- tives, you resist it. It is only this struggle against the propensities which gives rise to virtue, to vice, and moral responsibility. What would that self denial, so much recommended, amount to, if it did not suppose a combat with ourselves ? and then, the more we multiply and fortify the preservatives, the more man gains in free agency and moral liberty. The stronger are the internal propensities, the stronger should be the preservatives ; from them result the necessities and the utility of the most intimate knowledge of man, of the theory of the origin of his faculties and inclinations, of education, laws, rewards, punishments, and religion. But the responsibility ceases, even according to the doctrine of the most rigid theologians, if man is either not excited at all, if he is abso- lutely incapable of resistance when violently excited. Can it be that there is any merit in the continence of those who are born eunuchs ? Rush mentions the case of a woman, who, though adorned by every other moral virtue, could not resist her inclination to steal. I know many similar examples, among others, of an irresistible inclination to kill. Although we reserve to ourselves the right to prevent these unhappy beings from injuring us, all punish- ment exercised on them is not less unjust than useless : they merit indeed only our compassion. I hope some day to render the proof of this rare, but sad fact, more familiar to judges and physicians. Now that our opponents are tranquilized, let us take up these questions—In what manner are the faculties and the propensities of man connected with his organisation ? are they the expression of a principle of mind purely spiritual, and acting purely by itself ? or is the mind connected with some particular organisation ? if

10

so, by what organisation?—From the solution of these questions we shall derive the second principle.

' *II. The faculties and propensities of man have their seat in the brain.*

' I adduce the following proofs :—1. The functions of the mind are deranged by the lesion of the brain : they are not immediately deranged by the lesion of other parts of the body.

' 2. The brain is not necessary to life; but as nature creates nothing in vain, it must be that the brain has another distinction ; that is to say—

' 3. The qualities of the mind; or, the faculties and propensities of men and animals, are multiplied and elevated in direct ratio to the increase of the mass of brain, proportionally to that of the body ; and especially in proportion to the nervous mass. Here we find ourselves associated with the boar, the bear, the horse, the ox—with the camel, dolphin, elephant, and the stupid sloth. A man like you possesses more than double the quantity of brain in a stupid bigot; and at least one-sixth more than the wisest or the most sagacious elephant. By this, we are led to admit the second principle here laid down.

' *III. and IV. The faculties are not only distinct and independent of the propensities, but also the faculties among themselves, and the propensities among themselves, are essentially distinct and independent : they ought, consequently, to have their seat in parts of the brain distinct and independent of each other.*

' Proof 1. We can make the qualities of the mind alternately act and repose; so that one, after being fatigued, rests and refreshes itself, while another acts and becomes fatigued in turn.

' 2. The dispositions and propensities exist among themselves, in variable proportions in man, as also in animals of the same kind.

' 3. Different faculties and propensities exist separately in different animals.

' 4. The faculties and propensities develope themselves at different epochs ; some cease, without the other diminishing, and even while the other increases.

' 5. In diseases and wounds of certain parts of the brain, certain qualities are deranged, irritated, or suspended; they return by degrees to their natural state, during the curative process.

' I do not imagine myself a man sufficiently great enough to establish anything by bare assertion : I must endeavor, therefore, to establish each one of these facts by proof. Nevertheless, some timid minds will object thus : If you allow that the functions of the mind are produced by corporeal means, or by certain organs, will you not assail the spiritual nature and the immortality of the soul? Condescend to hear my answer. The naturalist endeavors

to penetrate the laws of the material world only, and supposes that
no natural truth can be in contradiction with an established truth;
he now finds that neither the mind or body can be destroyed
without the immediate order of the Creator; but he can draw
no conclusion as to spiritual life. He contents himself with perceiving and teaching, that the mind is chained in this life to a
corporeal organisation.

'Thus much in general: but for details I answer in the following
manner. In the preceding objection, the being acting is confounded
with the instrument by which he acts. That which I laid down
respecting the lower faculties, that is to say, of the inferior organs
of the functions of the mind, in numbers 1, 2, 3, 4, 5, takes place
also with it in regard to the external senses. For example, while
the fatigued eye reposes, we can listen attentively; the hearing
may be destroyed, without the vision being impaired; some of the
senses may be imperfect, while others are in full force; worms are
entirely destitute of hearing and sight, but they possess a perfect
touch; the new-born puppy is for several days both blind and
deaf, while his taste is perfectly developed; in old age, the hearing
generally diminishes before the sight; while the taste almost
always remains unimpaired. Hence results the proof of the existence of the senses by themselves, and of their independence, which
no one doubts. Has any one ever drawn the conclusion, that the
mind ought to be material or mortal, from the essential difference
of the senses? Is the mind which sees different from the mind
that hears? I extend the comparison a little farther: he is mistaken who thinks that the eye sees, that the ear hears, etc.; — each
external organ of sense is in communication by nerves with the
brain; and at the commencement of the nerves is a proportionable
mass of brain which constitutes the true internal organ of each
sensitive function. Consequently, the eye may be ever so sound,
the optic nerve may be ever so perfect, and yet, if the internal
organ is impaired or destroyed, the eye and the optic nerves are of
no avail. The external instruments of sense have, consequently,
their organs also in the brain, and these external instruments are
only the means by which the internal organs are put in relation
with external objects: it is for these reasons, that it never entered
the head of Boerhaave, nor of Haller, nor of Mayer, nor even of
the pious Lavater, who seeks for the qualities of mind in the head,
and of character in the body, that anything could be inferred
against the doctrine of the immateriality and immortality of the
soul, from the difference and independence of the faculties and
propensities, and of their internal organs. The same mind which
sees through the organ of sight, and which smells through the
olfactory organ, *learns by heart* through the organ of memory,
and does good through the organ of benevolence. It is the
same spring which puts in motion fewer wheels for you and more

for me. In this way the general functions of the brain are established.

'I now proceed to prove, that we can establish the assistance and the relation of many faculties and propensities by the formation of the cerebral development. By which means will be demonstrated, at once, the functions of the different cerebral parts.

'*V. Of the distribution of the different organs and their various development, arising from different forms of the brain.*

'Among the proofs in support of this principle, I point out the differences of conformation between carnivorous, frugivorous, and omnivorous animals. Then I show the cause of the difference between different species of animals, also the cause of accidental differences of species and individuals.

'*VI. From the totality and the development of determinate organs results a determinate form, either of the whole brain, or of its parts as separate regions.*

'Here I take the opportunity to show, that an organ is the more active, the more it is developed, without denying other exciting causes of its activity. But how is all this to lead us to a knowledge of the different faculties and the different propensities, by the formation of the skull? Is, then, the form of the skull moulded upon that of the brain?

'*VII. From the formation of the bones of the head, until the most advanced period of life, the form of the internal surface of the skull is determined by the external form of the brain: we can then be certain of the existence of some faculties and propensities, while the external surface of the skull agrees with its internal surface, or so long as the variation is confined to certain known limits.*

'Here I explain the formation of the bones of the head, and I prove that, from the moment of birth, they receive their form from the brain. I speak afterwards of the influence of other causes upon the conformation of the head; among which causes we may rank continual or repeated violence. I show that the organs develope themselves, from the earliest infancy, until their final completion, in the same proportion, and the same order, as the manifestation of the faculties and natural propensities. I show, besides, that the bones of the head take on their different forms in the same proportion, and in the same order. I show, finally, the gradual diminution of our faculties, by the diminution of the corresponding organs, and how nature deposits in the vacant spaces new portions of bony matter. All these things were heretofore unknown in the doctrine of the bones of the head. By these, is the first step taken for the determination of the particular functions of the different parts of the brain.

'Part II.

'*Application of General Principles.*

'*Establishment and determination of the faculties and propensities existing of themselves.*

'As I suppose a particular organ for each one of our independent qualities, we have only to establish what are the independent qualities, in order to know what are the organs which we may hope to discover. For many years I met great difficulties in this research, and at last I am convinced, that, as in everything else, we take the nearest and surest road if we lay aside our artificial logic, and allow ourselves to be guided by facts. I make known to my readers some of the difficulties which it was necessary to surmount. They may solve them, if they have more penetration than I have, I come at last to the means, which have served me most in the determination of the independence of the natural qualities, and I begin by pointing out more clearly the seat of the organs. It is necessary, first, to show and to examine the means by which we discover the seat of the organs. Among these means I cite,

'1. The discovery of certain elevations or certain depressions, when there are determined qualities. I mark here the course which it is necessary to follow in like researches.

'2. The existence of certain qualities together with the existence of certain protuberances.

'3. A collection of models in plaster.

'4. A collection of skulls.

'We shall find many difficulties with regard to human skulls: you know how every one fears for his own head : how many stories were told about me, when I undertook such researches. Men, unhappily, have such an opinion of themselves, that each one believes that I am watching for his head, as one of the most important objects of my collection. Nevertheless, I have not been able to collect more than twenty in the space of three years, if I except those that I have taken in the hospitals, or in the asylum for idiots. If I had not been supported by a man who knows how to protect science, and to consult prejudices, by a man justly and universally esteemed for his qualities of mind, and for his character, I should not have been able, in spite of all my labors, to collect even a few miserable specimens.

'There are those, indeed, who do not wish that even their dogs and monkeys should be placed in my collection after their death. It would be very agreeable to me, however, if persons would send me the heads of animals, of which they have observed well the characters ; for example, of a dog, who would eat only what he had stolen : one who could find his master at a great

distance; heads of monkeys, parrots, or other rare animals, wit
the histories of their lives, which ought to be written after the
death, lest they should contain too much flattery.   I wish yo
could establish the fashion, for every kind of genius should mak
me the heir of his head.   Then, indeed (I will answer for it wit
mine own), we should see in ten years a splendid edifice, for whic
at present I only collect materials.

'However, in the meantime, my dear Retzer, look a little wit
me into futurity, and see assembled the choice spirits of men c
past ages;—how they will mutually congratulate each other, fo
each minute portion of utility and pleasure, which each one o
them has contributed for the happiness of men.   Why has no on
preserved, for us, the skulls of Homer, Ovid, Virgil, Cicero, Hippo
crates, Boerhaave, Alexander, Frederic, Joseph II., Catharine
Voltaire, Rousseau, Locke, Bacon, and of others?—what orna
ments for the beautiful temples of the muses!

'5. I come now to the fifth means: Phenomena of the disease
and lesions of the brain.   I have also much to say on this subject
The most important, is the entirely new doctrine of the differen
kinds of insanity, and the means of cure, all supported by facts
If all my researches should only conduct me to this result, I shoulc
deem myself sufficiently rewarded for my labors.   If men of sens
will not thank me, I ought, at least, to be sure of the thanks o
fools.

'6. The sixth means for discovering the seat of the organs consists in examining the integral parts of different brains and thei
relations, always comparatively with the different faculties and th
different propensities.

'7. I come at last to one of my favorite subjects, the gradua
scale of perfections.

'Here I imagine that I am a Jupiter, who beholds from the
heavens his animal kingdom crowding upon the earth.   Think a
little of the immense space which I am going to pass through:—
from the zoophyte to the simple polypus, up to the philosopher and
the theosophist?   I shall hazard, like you gentlemen poets, some
perilous leaps.   In setting out I shall create only irritable vessels;
then I add nerves and the hermaphrodite nature;   then beings who
merit something better, who can unite, and look around upon the
world by the organs of sense.   I make an arrangement of powers
and instruments, and divide them according to my pleasure; I
create insects, birds, fishes, mammalia.   I make lap-dogs for your
ladies, and horses for your beaux;   and for myself, men, that is to
say, fools and philosophers, poets and historians, theologians and
naturalists.   I end, then, with man, as Moses told you long before;
but it has cost me more than one reflection before I could elevate
him to the rank of the king of the earth.   I give you the language
of signs, or natural language, that you may amuse yourselves, and

that if any mute should be found, there may be for him one other language besides that of speech. I assure you that, although no one has thought of acknowledging it, I have not been able to effect this but by putting in communication, in a strange manner, your body and your muscles with your cerebral organs.

'Strictly speaking, you only play the part of puppets in a show : when certain cerebral organs are put in action, you are led, according to their seat, to take certain positions, as though you were drawn by a wire, so that one can discover the seat of the acting organs by the motions. I know that you are blind enough to laugh at this ; but if you will take the trouble to examine it, you will be persuaded, that by my discovery I have revealed to you more things than you observe. You will find the explanation of many enigmas : for example, why you defend so valiantly your women; why you become churls at your advanced age; why there is no one so tenacious of his opinion as a theologian—*pourquoi plus l'un taureau doit éterneur lorsqu' une Europe le chatouille entre les ormes, etc.* I return at last to you, my dear Retzer, like a poor author, to satisfy you concerning my work.

'The first section of the second part being here finished, I ought to beg my readers to examine all that I have said, so that they may be more convinced of the truth of my first principles, which I have explained in a superficial manner ; but I think that he who is so blind as not to see by the light of the sun, will not do better by the additional light of a candle.

'The second section contains various subjects.

'1. *Of National Heads.*

'Here I agree, in some measure, with Helvetius, whom I have heretofore contradicted. I shall, perhaps, fall out with Blumenbach, Camper, and Sœmmering, although I gladly confess that I am not certain respecting it. You may, nevertheless, perceive why some of our brethren cannot count more than three—why others cannot conceive the difference between *meum* and *tuum*—why lasting peace among men will be always but a dream.

'2. *Of the difference between the Heads of Men and Women.*

'That which I could say on this subject must remain *entre nous*. We know very well that the heads of the women are difficult to unravel.

'3. *On Physiognomy.*

'I shall show here that I am nothing less than a physiognomist. I rather think that the wise men have baptised the child before it was born ; they call me craniologist, and the science which I discovered, craniology ; but, in the first place, all learned words displease me ; next, this is one not applicable to my profession, nor one which really designates it.

'The object of my researches is the brain. The cranium is only a faithful cast of the external surface of the brain, and is consequently but a minor part of the principal object. This title then is as inapplicable as would be that of a maker of rhymes to a poet.

'Lastly, I cite several examples to give to my readers something to examine, so that they may judge, not by principles alone, but also by facts, how much they can hope from the effect of these discoveries. You know, without doubt, my dear friend, how much strictness I observe in my comparisons.

'If, for example, I do not find in *good* horse, the same signification as in *good* dog, and if I do not find in this the same as in *good* cook, or *good* philosopher, and if it is not in the same relation to each of these individuals—the sign or word is of no value to me ; for I admit no exceptions in the works of nature.

'Finally, I would warn my disciples against a rash use of my doctrine, by pointing out many of its difficulties. On the other hand, I shall get rid of many doubters.

'Allow me, at present, to touch upon two important defects in my work. First, it would have been my duty and my interest to conform more to the spirit of the age ; I ought to have maintained, that we could absolutely ascertain by the form of the skull and the head, all the faculties and all the propensities, without exception ; I ought to have given more isolated experiments, as being a hundred times repeated ; I ought to have made of the whole one speculative study, and not to submit my doctrine, as I have done, to so many investigations and comparisons ; I should not ask of the world so much preparatory knowledge and perseverance ; I ought to have mounted Parnassus upon Pegasus, and not upon a tortoise. Where is the charm or the interest of a science so hard to acquire ? The premature sentences which have been pronounced, the jokes and squibs which have been let off at my expense, even before my intention or my object was known, prove that men do not wait for research, in order to draw their conclusions.

'I remark, in the second place, I have not sufficiently appreciated the *a priori*, that is to say, the philosophy which is to be founded upon the *a priori*. I have had the weakness in this, to judge others by myself ; for that which I have considered as well established by my logic, I have invariably found incomplete or erroneous. It was always difficult for me to reason soundly upon the experiments which I make, as well as upon those made by others, although I am persuaded that I can collect truths only on the highway of experience. It is possible, nevertheless, very possible, that others have a more favorable organisation than I have, to arrive at knowledge *a priori*; but you will do me the justice not to insist upon my entering the lists with other arms than my own.'

In 1796 Dr. Gall commenced giving courses of lectures at Vienna. Several of his hearers, as well as others, who had never heard him lecture, published notices of his doctrines, which were represented with greater or less exactness.

In 1800, Dr. Spurzheim commenced his labors in conjunction with Dr. Gall, and in that year assisted, for the first time, at one of his courses of lectures. He entered with great zeal into the consideration of the new doctrines, and to use his own words, he was simply a hearer of Dr. Gall, till 1804, at which period he was associated with him in his labors, and his character of hearer ceased.

'Dr. Spurzheim' (says Dr. Gall), 'who for a long time had been familiar with the physiological part of my doctrine, and who was particularly expert in anatomical researches, and in the dissection of the brain, formed the design of accompanying, and of pursuing in common with me, the investigations which had for their end the anatomy and physiology of the nervous system.'

Gall and Spurzheim quitted Vienna in 1805, to travel together, and to pursue, in common, their researches. Dr. Gall having expressed a desire to inspect the prisons of Berlin, with the view of making himself acquainted with their arrangements and construction, as well as of observing the heads of the prisoners, it was proposed to him that he should visit not only the prisons of that city, but the House of Correction, and the fortress of Spandau.*

Accordingly, on the 17th of April, 1805, Dr. Gall began with those of Berlin, in presence of the directing commissaries, the superior officers of the establishment, the inquisitors of the criminal deputation, the counsellor Thurnagel, and Schmidt, the assessors Muhlberg, and Wunder, the superior counsellor of the medical inspection,

---

* This account is translated from Nos. 97 and 98 of the 'Freymüthige,' May 1805. It is also given by Demangeon in his 'Physiologie Intellectuelle.' Paris, 1806.

Welper, Dr. Flemming, Professor Wildenow, and several other gentlemen.

As soon as Dr. Gall had satisfied himself in regard to the regulations and general management of the establishment, the party went to the criminal prisons, and to the *salles de travail*, where they found about 200 prisoners whom Dr. Gall was allowed to examine, without a word being said to him, either of their crimes, or of their characters.

It may here be remarked, that the great proportion of those detained in the criminal prisons, are robbers or thieves ; and, therefore it was to be expected that if Dr. Gall's doctrine were true, the organ of Acquisitiveness should, as a general rule, be found to predominate in these individuals. This accordingly soon appeared to be the case. The heads of all the thieves resembled each other more or less in shape. All of them presented a width and prominence at that part of the temple where the organ is situated, with a depression above the eyebrows, a retreating forehead, and the skull flattened towards the top. These peculiarities were perceptible at a single glance ; but the touch rendered still more striking the difference between the form of the skulls of robbers, and that of the skulls of those who were detained for other causes. The peculiar shape of the head, generally characteristic of thieves, astonished the party still more, when several prisoners were ranged in a line ; but it was never so strikingly borne out and illustrated as when, at the request of Dr. Gall, all the youths from 12 to 15 years of age, who were confined for theft, were collected together ; their heads presented so very nearly the same configuration, that they might easily have passed for the offspring of the same stock.

It was with great ease that Dr. Gall distinguished confirmed thieves from those who were less dangerous ; and in every instance his opinion was found to agree with the result of the legal interrogatories. The heads in which Acquisitiveness was most predominant, were that of

Columbus, and, among the children, that of the little H., whom Gall recommended to keep in confinement for life as utterly incorrigible. Judging from the judicial proceedings, both had manifested an extraordinary disposition for thieving.

In entering one of the prisons, where all the women presented a predominance of the same organ, except one, (then busy at the same employment, and in precisely the same dress as the offenders,) Dr. Gall asked, as soon as he perceived her, why that person was there, seeing that her head presented no appearance indicative of any propensity to steal. He was then told that she was not a criminal, but the inspectress of works. In the same way he distinguished other individuals confined for different causes besides theft.

Several opportunities of seeing Acquisitiveness, combined with other largely-developed organs, presented themselves. In one prisoner it was joined with Benevolence, and the organ of Theosophy, the latter particularly large. This individual was put to the proof, and in all his discourses showed great horror at robberies accompanied with violence, and manifested much respect for religion. He was asked which he thought the worse action, to ruin a poor laborer by taking his all, or to steal from a church without harming any one? He replied that it was too revolting to rob a church, and that he could never summon resolution enough to do it.

Dr. Gall was requested to examine particularly the heads of the prisoners implicated in the murder of a Jewess which had taken place the preceding year. In the principal murderer, Marcus Hirsch, he found a head, which, besides indicating very depraved dispositions, presented nothing remarkable, except a very great development of the organ of Perseverance. His accomplice, Jeannette Marcus, had an extremely vicious conformation of brain, the organ which leads to theft being greatly developed, as well as that of Destructiveness. He found in the female servants, Benkendorf and Babette, great want of circum-

spection ; and, in the wife of Marcus Hirsch, a form o
head altogether insignificant. All this was found to be in
strict accordance with the respective characters of the prisoners, as ascertained by the legal proceedings.

The prisoner Fritze, suspected of having killed his
wife, and apparently guilty of that crime, although he still
stoutly denied it, was next shown to Dr. Gall. The latter
found the organs of Cunning, and Firmness, highly developed—qualities which his interrogator had found him
manifest in the very highest degree.

In the tailor Maschke, arrested for counterfeiting the
legal coin, and whose genius for the mechanical arts was
apparent in the execution of his crime, Gall found, without knowing for what he was confined, the organ of Constructiveness much developed, and a head so well organised, that he lamented several times the fate of that man.
The truth is, that this Maschke was well known to possess
great mechanical skill, and at the same time much kindness of heart.

Scarcely had Dr. Gall advanced a few steps into
another prison, when he perceived the organ of Constructiveness equally developed, in a man named Troppe, a
shoemaker, who, without any teaching, applied himself to
the making of watches, and other objects, by which he
now lives. In examining him more nearly Gall found also
the organ of Imitation, generally remarkable in comedians,
considerably developed ; a just observation, since the crime
of Troppe was that of having extorted a considerable
sum of money under the feigned character of an officer of
police. Gall observed to him that he must assuredly have
been fond of playing tricks in his youth, which he
acknowledged. When Gall said to those about him, ' *If
that man had fallen in the way of comedians he would have
become an actor,*' Troppe, astonished at the exactness
and precision with which Gall unveiled his disposition,
told them that he had in fact been some time (six months)
a member of a strolling company—a circumstance which
had not till then been discovered.

In the head of the unhappy Heisig, who, in a state of intoxication, had stabbed his friend, Gall found a generally good conformation, with the exception of a very deficient Cautiousness, or great rashness. He remarked in several other prisoners the organs of Language, Color, and Mathematics, in perfect accordance with the manifestations; some of the first spoke several languages; those with large Color were fond of showy clothes, flowers, paintings, etc.; and those with Mathematics large, calculated easily from memory.

, On Saturday, 20th April, the party went to Spandau. Among those who accompanied Dr. Gall, were the Privy Counsellor Hufeland; the Counsellor of the Chamber of Justice, Albrecht; the Privy Counsellor Kols; the Professor Reich, Dr. Meyer, and some others. At the House of Correction, observations were made upon 270 heads, and at the fortress, upon 200. Most of them were thieves and robbers, who presented more or less exactly the same form of head, of which the prisons of Berlin had exhibited a model. Including the whole, the prisons of Berlin, and of Spandau, had thus subjected to the examination of Dr. Gall a total of about five hundred thieves, most of them guilty of repeated offences; and in all it was easy to verify the form of brain indicated by Gall as denoting this unhappy tendency, and to obtain the conviction, from the discourse of most of them, that they felt no remorse for their crimes, but, on the contrary, spoke of them with a sort of internal satisfaction.

The morning was spent in examining the House of . Correction, and its inmates; the most remarkable of whom were submitted, in the Hall of Conference, to the particular observation of Dr. Gall, sometimes one by one, and sometimes several at once. The combination of other organs, with that of Acquisitiveness, was also noticed.

In Kunisch, an infamous thief and robber, who had established himself as a master carpenter at Berlin, and who, in concert with several accomplices, had committed a great number of thefts with " *effraction* " (burglary,) for

which he had been shut up till he should be pardoned.
Gall found, at the first glance, the organs of Mathematics
and of Constructiveness, with a good form of head in other
respects, except that the organ of Acquisitiveness was
exceedingly developed. Gall said on seeing him, '*Here
is an artist, a mathematician, and a good head: it is a pity
he should be here*'—an observation remarkable for its
accuracy, as Kunisch had shown so much talent for
mechanics, that he was appointed inspector of the spinning
machinery, the repairing of which was confided to him.
Gall asked him if he knew arithmetic, to which he answered with a smile, '*How could I invent or construct a
piece of work without having previously calculated all the
details?*'

The head of an old woman, who was in prison for the
second time for theft, presented a great development of
the organs of Acquisitiveness, Theosophy, and the Love of
Offspring, especially the last. Upon being asked the
cause of her detention, she answered, that she had stolen,
but that she fell upon her knees every day to thank her
Creator for the favor she had received in being brought to
this house ; that she saw in this dispensation one of the
clearest proofs of the wonderful ways of Providence, for
she had nothing so much at heart as her children, whom
it was impossible for her to educate properly ; that since
her imprisonment they had been taken into the Orphan
Hospital, where they were now receiving that education
which she had not had the means of giving them.

Deficiency of Cautiousness was often joined to a
great endowment of Acquisitiveness. This was particularly the case in the woman Muller, whose head presented
also a very remarkable development of the organ of
Love of Approbation, which, according to Gall, degenerates into vanity in narrow-minded and ignorant persons.
She was unwilling to acknowledge that she was fond of
dress, thinking that this was not in harmony with her
present situation ; but her companions insisted that she had
much vanity, and was careful about nothing but her dress.

In the prisoner Albert, the organ of Pride was joined with that of Acquisitiveness. *'Is it not the case,'* said Gall to him, *'that you were always desirous of being the first, and of distinguishing yourself, as you used to do, when still a little boy? I am sure that, in all your sports, you then put yourself at the head.'* Albert confessed that it was so; and it is true that he still distinguishes himself by the command which he assumes over the other prisoners, and by his insubordination, to the degree that, when a soldier, he could not be constrained but by the severest punishments ; and even now he generally escapes one punishment only to incur another.

Here, as at Berlin, Gall distinguished at a glance such prisoners as were not thieves. Among others brought before him, was Régine Dœring, an infanticide, imprisoned for life. This woman, different from the other infanticides, showed no repentance and no remorse for her crime, so that she entered the room with a tranquil and serene air. Gall immediately drew the attention of Dr. Spurzheim to this woman, by asking him if she had not exactly the same form of head, and the same disposition to violence, as his gardener at Vienna, Mariendel, whose chief pleasure consisted in killing animals, and whose skull now serves at his lectures, as an example of the organ of Murder. This organ was found to be very largely developed in Régine Dœring, and the posterior part of the head, in the situation of the organ of Love of Offspring, was absolutely flattened. This was in exact accordance with the character of the culprit, in so far as her examination bore upon it ; for, not only has she had several children, of whom she has always secretly got rid, but she lately exposed and murdered one of them, already four years old, which would have led her to the scaffold, if the proofs had not been, in some respects, vague and incomplete, and her judges on that account had preferred sentencing her to imprisonment for life.

One of the gentlemen present was a distinguished musician, upon whom Gall had incidentally pointed out

one of the forms of development of the organ of Tune
which consists in a projection above the external angle of
the eye.   As soon as the prisoner, Kunow, appeared before him, *'Hold,'* said Gall, *' here is the other form in which
the organ of Music shows itself : it is here, as in the head of
Mozart, of a pyramidal shape, pointed upwards.'*   Kunow
immediately acknowledged that he was passionately fond
of music, that he had acquired it with facility ; and the
production of the gaol register showed that he was an
amateur, that he had spent his fortune, and that latterly
he had had in view to give lessons in music at Berlin
Gall asked what was his crime.   It appeared that he had
spent his youth in debauchery, and had been condemned
to imprisonment for an unnatural crime.   Gall having
examined his head, and found the organ of Propagation
in enormous development, immediately exclaimed, *' C'est
sa nuque qui l' a perdu '*: *' It is the nape of his neck which
has been his ruin.'*   Then, carrying his hand upwards towards Cautiousness, which was exceedingly deficient, he
added, *' Maudite légèreté'*—*' Unhappy instability.'*
   After dinner, the party went to the fortress.   Major de
Beckendorf, the commandant, had the politeness to cause
all the prisoners to be drawn up in line, to be presented to
Dr. Gall.   Here the organs of Cunning and Acquisitiveness predominated, as in the other prisons.   They were
sometimes so strikingly apparent, that at a glance the
thief might be distinguished from the other criminals.
Raps, in whom the organ of Acquisitiveness was very conspicuous, attracted, among others, the notice of Gall, who
discovered at the same time large organs of Murder
and Benevolence.   What makes the justness of these
observations very remarkable is, that Raps strangled a
woman whom he had robbed, and that on going away he
untied the cord from compassion, and thus saved the poor
woman's life after robbing her of her property.   He then
examined the young Brunnert, in whom he found the
organs of Acquisitiveness, Locality, Constructiveness, and
Pride, which were curiously verified in his history ; for

Brunnert had committed several robberies ; had been confined in various prisons, from which he had escaped ; fixed himself nowhere ; deserted as a soldier ; underwent several castigations for insubordination ; and, having again rebelled against his superiors, was once more waiting his sentence. He was, besides, skilful in the mechanical arts, and showed some exquisitely finished works in pasteboard which he had executed in a prison, a place very unfavorable to such talents.

The organ of Mathematics was largely developed in some ; and in each case, the power of calculation was found to correspond.

Two peasants, father and son, mixed with the thieves, attracted notice from having quite different forms of head. Gall having examined them, found an enormous development of the organ of Pride, and said, ' *These two have not wished to be ruled, but to rule themselves, and to withdraw from anything like subordination.*" It was discovered that the cause of their confinement was insolence to superiors.

An old soldier, who was among the prisoners, had a very large organ of Acquisitiveness. It was, however, for insubordination, and not for theft, that he was confined in the fortress ; but, on farther research, it appeared, that he had been punished several times in the regiment for having stolen.

In November, 1807, Dr. Gall (who had now made Paris his permanent residence) assisted by Dr. Spurzheim, delivered his first course of lectures at Paris, which created an immense sensation. ' His assertions,' says Chenerix, 'were supported by a numerous collection of skulls, heads, and casts, and by a multitude of physiological and anatomical facts. Great, indeed, was the ardour excited among the Parisians, by the presence of the men who, as they supposed, could tell their fortunes by their heads. Every one wanted to get a peep at them ; every one was anxious to give them a dinner or a supper ; and the writer of this article actually saw a list on which an eager can-

11

didate was delighted to inscribe himself for a breakfast distant only three months and a half, at which breakfast he sat a wondering guest.' *

In 1808 they presented a Memoir to the French Institute on the 'Anatomy of the Brain,' but it was not favorably reported on.

Dr. Gall continued to reside in Paris, and from 1822 to 1826, published an edition of his work, 'Sur les Fonctions du Cerveau,' in six volumes octavo.

In March 1828, at the conclusion of one of his lectures, Dr. Gall was seized with a paralytic attack, from which he never perfectly recovered, and which ultimately carried him off the 22nd of August, 1828, in the seventy-second year of his age.† His remains were followed to the grave by an immense concourse of friends and admirers, five of whom pronounced discourses over his grave, as is the custom in France on such occasions. His death gave rise to a succession of eulogiums and attacks in the French newspapers that had scarcely ever been paralleled, and public sentiment was warmly and loudly expressed in his favor. In proof of this, I may be allowed to quote a few lines of a letter lately received from a French friend, with whom I was intimate in Paris, but who is no phrenologist, and whose testimony is therefore impartial. After speaking of the political relations of France, he adds, ' You will, I am sure, be more affected by the death of Dr. Gall, than by any political events. In truth, it is an immense loss to science. Whatever opinion we may form of the system of that illustrious man, it must be acknowledged that he has made an immense stride in the sciences of medicine and of man. You must have been satisfied with the homage paid to his memory by the side of his grave, by whatever distinguished men Paris possesses. Nothing was wanting to his glory ; not even the abuse and calumnies of our *devots de gazette*.'

The person of Dr. Gall was well developed ; he was

* Article published in the 'Foreign Quarterly Review.'
† Dr. Combe, 'Phren. Jour.' vol. v.

five feet two inches in height, with a large chest and strong muscles ; his step was firm, and his look vivid and penetrating.* His features, though not handsome, possessed a mild and pleasing expression. Every part of his head was strikingly developed, measuring, above the eyebrows and at the top of the ears, twenty-two inches and two lines in circumference, and fourteen inches and nine lines, from the root of the nose to the occiput.

Dr. Gall acquired an honorable reputation as a physician, writer, and philosopher, and independent of the respect shown him by all parties, he realised the additional reward of a handsome fortune.† His skill as a physician may be inferred from the fact, that, in 1820, a medal was presented to him, executed by M. Barre, an eminent artist in Paris, by order of count Potosky, a rich Polish nobleman, who took this method of expressing his deep gratitude to Dr. Gall, who had cured him of an old and dangerous malady, for which he had in vain consulted the best medical men in Paris. On one side of the medal is the head of Dr. Gall, an admirable likeness ; and on the other is Esculapius standing at the bed-side of the patient, chasing away with one hand the birds of darkness, and crushing a frog, the symbol of ignorance, under his right foot. Behind Esculapius is an altar, with a skull placed upon it, to denote the particular kind of study to which Dr. Gall was addicted. Near the couch are the arms of the count himself.

Taking Gall as a model of a phrenological portrait, it is proper that we should speak of all the cerebral organs, belonging to our nature.‡

The organs of Amativeness, Philoprogenitiveness, Adhesiveness, Combativeness, and Destructiveness were all very well developed in Gall. His Secretiveness was also rather large, but he never made a bad use of it. He was too conscious of his intellectual powers to obtain his ends by cunning or fraud. He was frank and honest, but acute and penetrating.

* Dr. Fossati, 'Paris Phren. Jour.'   † 'Phren. Trans.'   ‡ 'Fossati.'

The Marquis de Moscati gives the following account of an attempt to deceive Gall, with regard to himself, and of some interesting trials of his skill, as a phrenologist:

'Dr. Gottfried, of Heidelberg, with whom I was acquainted, informed me that Dr. Gall wished to have an interview with me, in order to demonstrate to me, on the skulls, *the truth* of what he advanced, and I disbelieved; but I declined, and did everything in my power to ridicule his system in society, with all my military friends, and through the German, French, and Italian periodicals. But when I saw that, notwithstanding my repeated diatribes, and the opposition of the medical faculty, Dr. Gall went on in making converts to his doctrine, I determined to see him, and endeavored to deceive him by presenting myself under the dress of a servant. Colonel Bucher, of the 5th Dragoons, took me with him to the house of Dr. Gall, who was in Paris, and told him that he wished to know his opinion about my head ; that I was an Italian, had lived with him as a servant for seven years, and during that interval had been much attached and very faithful to him ; that it was for those good qualities that he had endeavored to have me instructed, but that although he had given me several masters, *for nearly three years*, I had scarcely learned to read and write *Italian*, but had not yet acquired the French language.

'I remember as it were now, Dr. Gall opened his large eyes, fixed them on my countenance with a look of surprise and doubt, and then began to feel my head. While he was making his observations, he now and then murmured, "*Ce n'est pas vrai! Ce n'est pas possible!*" Shortly after having observed my cranium, he said to Bucher, that an individual with a head so well formed could not be of *the character* he had just mentioned ; that, on the contrary, unless I was blind and deaf, by the conformation of my cranium, he thought I was able to acquire *general knowledge, particularly the languages*, and geographical and astronomical sciences. Moreover, that if I had applied according to the development of my organs, I must be a

listinguished person and a *mad poet*. When I heard this
ast remark, I told Bucher, " *Ce n'est pas bien ; tu as trahi
son secret.*" I do not wonder at the Doctor's accuracy.
Bucher swore that he had not betrayed me. Gall remon-
strated against my suspicion, and assured me of his being
totally unacquainted with my trick ; but I remained doubt-
ful about the sincerity of both of them, and continued to
be an adversary to Gall and his system.

'However, from that day I began to study craniology,
and made use of the skulls of the killed in battle ; but I
studied as one of those who *oculos habent, et non vident,
ures habent et non audiunt*, and my obstinacy rendered me
inaccessible to persuasion. Often when I knew well the
character of some of my soldiers who died, I sent the
skulls to Dr. Gall, and requested his opinion ; and I must
say that more than *once* his remarks were truly astonishing ; but I persisted in my incredulity. In 1810, one of
my lieutenants was killed at the battle of Lintz ; he was
a Pole, of a very violent temper, a bloody duellist, and
much addicted to sensuality. I forwarded his skull to
Dr. Gall, and in answer to my question, he replied, that
it belonged to an individual *very violent, ferocious,* and a
sensualist. This time I was the only depository of my
secret.'

We come now to another quality, on which we should
like to dwell, were we not obliged to confine ourselves
within prescribed limits—we mean the sentiment of property.*

Many people in Paris have reproached Gall with being
selfish. It cannot be denied that he was amply paid for
his public lectures ; that he was unfortunate in soliciting
the sale of his work ; and that he prosecuted some of his
patients who refused to pay their bills. But we should
know his own remarks on this point. 'Do you see, my
friend, how these wealthy people treat us and other physicians ? They spend a hundred times more for their pleasures than the health we give them, and expend enormous

* Fossati.

sums on balls and dinners, while they leave their physi
cians unpaid.   Indeed, while they largely remunerate th
lawyer who gains their cause, they give nothing to th
physician who saves their lives.'   Gall was not generous
in the common understanding of the term ; but it mus
be considered that in his domestic economy he failed ir
method, and consequently was always pressed by unfore-
seen and urgent wants.   If he was selfish, let me ask
what kind of selfishness it was.   He educated and supported his nephews, and young people of talents, and his
table was free to everybody.   It is true, he was not generous to all who surrounded him, but he was so towards
his domestics, and people of low condition, whose services
he had received.   We may say he had a love of property,
but that his intellectual powers placed him above its
control.

Another faculty which Gall possessed in a remarkable
degree, as his organisation shows, was that of Elevation,
Pride, or a high opinion of one's self.   We will here quote
a remarkable passage, where, in speaking of that organ,
he has delineated himself.   'There are certain men,'
says he, 'with minds sufficiently strong, who are so
deeply impressed with a sense of their own value, and so
independent withal, that they know how to repel every
external influence which tends to subject them.   As far
as practicable, they choose the freest countries to live in,
and devote themselves to an employment that renders
them independent, and exempts them from the caprices
and favor of the great.   That domination over their inferiors, which becomes slavery under an absolute master,
would be insupportable to them.   The honors and distinctions that are withheld from merit, while they are
lavished on insignificant men, are but humiliations in their
eyes.   If they prosper, it is only by their own efforts ;
like the oak, they are sustained by their own strength,
and it is to their own resources that they would be indebted for all they possess.'   He was, in fact, proud and
independent.   He never was anxious for titles, and cheer-

fully practised the profession of medicine. As a political man, he loved liberty and good laws.

There is another innate sentiment, Vanity, Ambition, Love of Glory, approaching the preceding in its nature, but still quite distinct from it, which was feeble in Gall. We always observed him to be indifferent to the praise and approbation of the multitude, as he was also to their blame and ridicule. He labored for the love of science, and under the conviction that his ideas would triumph in the end. We could recall a thousand anecdotes to prove that his vanity was not very susceptible. How many times have we seen him laugh at the squibs of the little journals, and unaffectedly despise the gross abuse which they heaped upon him. Let us cite one fact which will answer for many others. Gall had lived for some time at Berlin, with the celebrated poet Kotzebue, who profited by the occasion to learn of him the technical terms of his science, and such ideas and principles as he could best turn to ridicule. He composed his play, Craniomania, which was immediately performed at the theatre in Berlin, and Gall attended the first representation, and laughed as heartily as any of them.

Caution, by means of which the effects of our actions are referred to the future, which sometimes renders us distrustful of the world and indecisive in forming our resolutions, was very strong in Gall. Observe what a fulness the head presents in its superior posterior lateral region. Gall proceeded with extreme prudence in every step ; he was distrustful, and much disposed to give credit to bad insinuations against his friends and acquaintances, and would rather break with any one than live in the disquietude of doubt. He often said, that it is more difficult to sustain a reputation than to create one, and that we must always act as if making the first efforts to render ourselves known.

Let us now pass to the faculties whose organs are situated in the anterior part of the head, beginning with the sense of the memory of things (Individuality). This sense is the source of educability in man and other animals. Gall possessed it in a moderate degree, but it was not one of his most remarkable faculties.

He easily forgot whatever had no connection with his doctrines, or with any of his predominant faculties.

It was the same with the faculty of local memory (Locality). We will once more leave him to speak for himself. ' My taste for natural history,' said he, ' often led me into the woods, for the purpose of ensnaring birds or taking them in their nests. In the latter object I was very fortunate, because I had often observed, towards which of the cardinal points each species were accustomed to build their nests. I should have succeeded equally well by disposing my nets properly, because I was in the habit of ascertaining the district the bird frequented, by his song and his movements ; but when, after a week or fortnight, I went to find what birds had been taken, or to carry off a nest, it was often impossible for me to find the tree I had marked, or the nets I had placed.' He also forgot the residence of his patients whom he had frequently visited in his carriage, and had considerable difficulty in remembering in what story of the building they lived. He was ignorant of geography, and whenever he looked upon a map, he found something new, though he had observed it a thousand times before. So we may be sure, that if he travelled, it was not from taste, but with the sole object of propagating his doctrines.

If it be true, as we believe it is, that there is an organ of Order, Gall was absolutely destitute of it. The arrangement of his house was a curiosity. He said it was order to him. Let one imagine to himself, huddled together in his bureau-drawers, for instance, old journals, quittances, quack advertisements, letters from distinguished men, pamphlets, nuts, pieces of gold, silver, and copper, and packets of seeds. We have seen him take up a bundle of these papers, and shake out from them the money he happened to need. In this manner he kept his records and his desk.

Weaker still was his *memory of persons*. ' This faculty,' said he, ' is too feeble in me, and the defect of it has, all my life-time, caused me a thousand troubles. When I rise from the table, I cannot distinguish either man or woman who sat by my side during the meal.' In *verbal memory*, Gall was also deficient. At school he never could learn his lessons, and when the task was one that exercised the memory, he was always surpassed by his school-fellows, whom he excelled in original composition.

The organ of *the sense of language*, which gives the talent of philology, was a little better developed. He knew, besides his own, the Latin and French languages, which he wrote and spoke with facility, though defective in pronunciation, and had some knowledge of English and Italian. He had a strong dislike, however, for questions about mere words, grammatical discussions, compilations, and works of that kind. *Pour les compilations, et autres travaux du même genre.*

The sense of the relations of colors, which is one of the fundamental qualities indispensable to the painter, was absolutely wanting in Gall. He was obliged to depend upon the opinions of his friends, whenever he treated of painters or painting, and by that means was sometimes led to pronounce an erroneous judgment, which the critics never failed to remind him of. As for his taste, he was fond of those brilliant porcelain-like pictures of modern times ; and when in a gallery, he bestowed his attention on portraits, and especially on those of women, when painted in a classical style.

As he was a poor judge of painting, so was he as poor an amateur in music. He generally got wearied at the opera or concert ; but a woman's voice in conversation, he said, was very agreeable.

He was no more apt in the science of numbers ; every kind of numerical calculation fatigued him, and we believe we never saw him go through a process in simple multiplication or division that was at all complicated. He knew nothing of geometry, nor the problems of mathematics. What a contrast to those philosophers who make this same science the basis of all positive knowledge!

In mechanics, architecture, and the arts, he was no happier than in calculation, music, and painting. We will only remark, that the execution of the plates of his great work, after Spurzheim ceased to overlook them, was detestable, which would not have been the case if Gall had possessed the slightest knowledge of design, or of the arts in general.

Having thus finished our notice of the organs situated in the lower part of the forehead, it remains for us to examine those higher faculties whose organs are placed in the upper part of that region. It is these that gave Gall his eminence over the generality of men.

That *comparative* sagacity, by means of which we promptly discern the relations of agreement and disagreement between the objects of our examination, and are led to search for affinities, comparisons, and similes, was very strong in Gall. Accordingly, you will observe, that not only were all his researches but a continual comparison of organisation with faculties, and of the faculties of man with those of other animals, but that he also employed this method in his familiar conversations and public lectures, whenever he was particularly anxious to impress his ideas on the minds of others.

The following interesting account of an interview with Gall was published in the 'Birmingham Gazette,' and may serve to give the reader some idea of the habits of the philosopher at home :

'Most of us find some satisfaction in tracing on Fancy's tablet the portrait of a person of whom we have heard much, and particularly after we have read many of the works of an author, but with whom we have had no personal acquaintance. It generally happens, however, that our portrait is not correct, when we compare it with the original. Thus it was with myself. I found Dr. Gall (in 1826) to be a man of middle stature, of an outline well proportioned. He was thin, and rather pallid, and possessed a capacious head and chest. The peculiar brilliancy of his penetrating eye left an indelible impression. His

countenance was remarkable, his features strongly marked
and rather large, yet devoid of coarseness. The general
impression that a first glance was calculated to convey
would be, that Dr. Gall was a man of originality and
depth of mind, possessing much urbanity, with some self-
esteem and inflexibility of design.

'After presenting my letters of introduction to him at
seven o'clock, a.m., he showed me into a room, the walls
of which were covered with bird-cages, and the floor with
dogs, cats, etc. Observing that I was surprised at the
number of his companions, he observed, "All you English-
men take me for a bird-catcher ; I am sure you feel surprised that I am not somewhat differently made to any
of you, and that I should employ my time in talking to
birds. Birds, Sir, differ in their dispositions like men ;
and if they were but of more consequence, the peculiarity
of their characters would have been as well delineated.
Do you think," said he, turning his eyes to two beautiful
dogs at his feet, that were endeavoring to gain his attention, "do you think that these little pets possess pride
and vanity like man ?" "Yes," said I, "I have remarked
their vanity frequently." "We will call both feelings
into action," said he. He then caressed the whelp, and
took it into his arms. "Mark his mother's offended
pride," said he, as she was walking quietly across the
chamber to her mat. " Do you think she will come if I
call her ?" "Oh yes," I answered. "No, not at all."
He made the attempt ; but she heeded not the hand she
had so earnestly endeavored to lick but an instant before.
"She will not speak to me to-day," said the doctor. He
then described to me the peculiarity of many of his birds ;
and I was astonished to find that he seemed familiar also
with their dispositions (if I may be allowed the word).
"Do you think a man's time would be wasted thus in
England ? You are a wealthy and a powerful nation,
and as long as the equilibrium exists between the two, so
shall you remain ; but this never has, nor cannot exist
beyond a certain period. Such is your industry, stimulated

by the love of gain, that your whole life is spun out
before you are aware the wheel is turning ; and so highly
do you value commerce, that it stands in the place of
self-knowledge, and an acquaintance with nature and her
immense laboratory."

'I was delighted with this conversation : he seemed to
me to take a wider view in the contemplation of man, than
any other person with whom I had ever conversed. During
breakfast, he frequently fed the little suitors, who approached as near as their iron bars would admit.   "You
see they all know me," said he, "and will feed from my
hand, except this blackbird, who must gain his morsel by
stealth before he eats it ; we will retire an instant, and in
our absence he will take the bread."   On our return, we
found he had secreted it in a corner of his cage.   I mention these otherwise uninteresting anecdotes, to show
how much Dr. Gall had studied the peculiarities of the
smaller animals.   After our breakfast, he showed me his
extensive collection ; and thus ended my first visit to the
greatest moral philosopher that Europe has produced ; to
a man, than whom few were ever more ridiculed, and
few ever pursued their bent more determinately, despite
its effects ; to a man, who alone effected more change in
mental philosophy than perhaps any predecessor ; to a
man, who suffered more persecution, and yet possessed
more philanthropy than most philosophers.'

To that other form of human intelligence, viz., the *metaphysical*, Gall was strongly opposed, when it soars into
the spiritual world, and pushes its inquiries into general
principles and general truths, slighting however, the material world and the relations of cause and effect.   This
way of thinking, and directing one's efforts in the search
after truth, was none of his ; he was for the positive, not
the abstract.

Another remarkable manifestation of mind, *wit*, which
gives a kind of relief to its possessor, Gall was endowed
with in no small degree.   Although he never engaged in
the polemics of the Journals, yet in his works, he replied

to his opponents with a keenness of satire truly astonishing. To be convinced of this, one has only to read the sixth volume of his work. Observe his piquant observations on the Editors of the 'Dictionary of Medical Sciences,' in answer to the wish expressed by them, that somebody would, at last, devote himself to the physiology of the brain. He exclaims, 'Behold, an instance of lethargy, in M.M. Fournier and Begin, which has lasted from the time of my arrival in Paris, 1807, to the year 1819 !' While deriding the principles of the transcendentalists, and at the same time answering his opponents, he observes, 'It may be certainly said, with truth, that the dead kill the living. Some time or other, when I shall take it into my head to be admired, cried up, and to have even my follies sanctioned, I mean to drown, hang, and burn myself, till I am well dead ; and if, notwithstanding these means of getting a reputation, my *moi* is still doomed to be concerned with the *non moi*, with the vanities of the world in *space*, I hope at least to have some titles and places to spare in *time*. *Moi*, *space* and *time*, you know, are the pivots on which the metaphysicians turn much of their reasoning.'

While pointing out the piracies many *savans* had made upon his works, he reasons with them in the following style: 'When nations are at war, pillage becomes a right. Now, savans who are engaged in making discoveries, are constantly at war with one another ; therefore, they are allowed to pillage ; therefore, the little malice of M. Boisseau is eminently rational.'

The result of another manifestation of the intellect, is the *poetical talent*. This is not enough to make one a poet (in the ordinary acceptation of the word) ; for versification depends upon another faculty. Gall could never make verses. He even detested poetry, because he had no ear for harmony ; but he possessed, in a high degree, the poetical power of invention.

A fundamental quality inherent in our nature, and which constitutes the strongest bond of our species, is the

sentiment of *benevolence, compassion, moral sense.* Gall
was exceedingly benevolent ; he succored the unfortunate,
and procured them the assistance of his rich patients; he
encouraged talents, and rendered them all the aid in his
power. If a kind of abruptness, or, more properly speaking, nonchalance, was sometimes observed in his manners,
all thought of it was effaced by his benevolence. In his
conversation, he was not too careful to observe those con-
ventional forms and verbal disguises which civilisation has
introduced to cover, as with a fine mantle, the bad dispositions of the soul; but the more intimately he was
known, the more he was loved.

The faculty of *Imitation,* that which makes the actor
and mimic, and is also of great use to the orator, inasmuch
as it excites him to express by external signs what is
passing within, existed in a very high degree in Gall.
We had but imperfect means of judging of him as an
orator in his public lectures, where, however, notwithstanding the disadvantage of speaking in a foreign tongue,
he left a deep impression on the minds of his hearers.

Let us now see what were Gall's opinions respecting
God and religion. 'Everywhere,' he says, 'and in all
times, man, pressed by the feeling of dependence, by
which he is completely surrounded, is forced to recognise
at every instant, the limits of his power, and avow to
himself that his fate is in the hands of a superior power.
Hence, the unanimous consent of all people to adore a
Supreme Being; hence, the ever-felt necessity of recurring
to him, of honoring him, and rendering homage to his
superiority.' Thus Gall recognised God like a philosopher.
He was indignant only against the abuses that men
practised upon the credulity of the people ; against those
who make of religion a refinement of power, of ignorance,
of slavery and corruption. He was indignant against the
persecutions which sectarians, of different faiths, carry on
against their fellow-men in the name of God and religion.
He was indignant against all these abuses, because he
loved the human race, and desired its happiness.

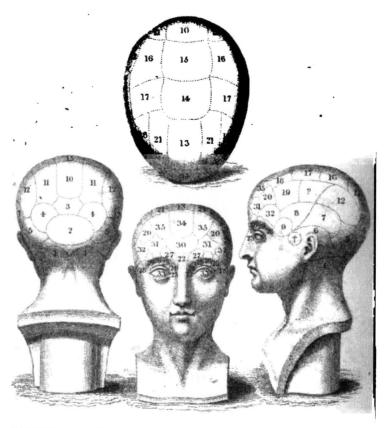

NAMES OF THE PHRENOLOGICAL ORGANS,

REFERRING TO THE FIGURES INDICATING THEIR RELATIVE POSITIONS.

AFFECTIVE		INTELLECTUAL	
I. PROPENSITIES.	*II. SENTIMENTS.*	*I. PERCEPTIVE.*	*II. REFLECTIVE.*
1 Amativeness	10 Self-esteem	22 Individuality	34 Comparison
2 Philoprogenitiveness	11 Love of Approbation	23 Form	35 Causality
3 Concentrativeness	12 Cautiousness	24 Size	
4 Adhesiveness	13 Benevolence	25 Weight	
5 Combativeness	14 Veneration	26 Colouring	
6 Destructiveness	15 Firmness	27 Locality	
7 Alimentiveness	16 Conscientiousness	28 Number	
7 Secretiveness	17 Hope	29 Order	
8 Acquisitiveness	18 Wonder	30 Eventuality	
9 Constructiveness	19 Ideality	31 Time	
	? Unascertained	32 Tune	
	20 Wit or Mirthfulness	33 Language	
	21 Imitation		

16 *Farbensinn*, Perception of Colors } answering to Color.

17 *Tonsin*, Music —answering to Tune.

18 *Zahlensinn*, Number —answering to Number.

19 *Kunstsinn, Bausinn*, Aptitude for the Mechanical Arts } answering to Constructiveness.

20 *Vergleichender, Scharfsinn*, Comparative Sagacity for Drawing Comparisons } answering to Comparison.

21 *Metaphysischer, Tiefsinn*, Metaphysical Depth of Thought, Aptitude for Drawing Conclusions } answering to Causality.

22 *Witz*, Wit —answering to Wit.

23 *Dichtergeist*, Poetry —answering to Ideality.

24 *Gutmüthigkeit, Mitleiden*, Good Nature } answering to Benevolence.

25 *Darstellungsinn*, Mimicry—answering to Imitation.

26 *Theosophy, Theosophie*, Religion } answering to Veneration.

27 *Festigkeit*, Firmness of Character } answering to Firmness.

In the engraved plate the numbers are altered, but the situation of the organs, of course, remains the same. It will be seen that Gall's system extends to twenty-seven organs ; the system now numbers thirty-five ; but it must not be presumed from this that the system is complete. The organ of Gustativeness, or Alimentiveness, is included in the plate, but there is reason to dispute its functions, at least, many Phrenologists contend that there is not a sufficient number of determined facts on record to pronounce it established. There is also a conjectured organ for Love of Life, and the American Phrenologists enumerate many newly discovered organs ; but as I have had no proofs of their actual existence myself, I refrain from enumerating them. The plate, therefore, which accompanies this may be relied upon by the reader as exhibiting a correct delineation of all the organs as yet discovered and established. To return now to my narrative :—

In 1824 there was but one periodical connected with the Swedenborgians, and that was of a learned and highly intellectual character ; it was entitled, the 'Intellectual Repository for the New Church,' a title which it amply sustained. Its circulation, however, was limited to the more wealthy and cultivated members. Books, then, were not, as now, plentiful and cheap. Good treatises were costly ; and none were more expensive than elementary works of science and philosophy, and even of religion and morality. My position soon led me to perceive the want of a magazine for the poorer members of the church, one which should give details of the progress of Swedenborgianism from month to month, written in a plain and popular style, and at the same time give short passages on scientific subjects. So I formed the design of a monthly magazine, and issued a prospectus for its publication. It was entitled the 'New Church Christian's Pocket Magazine.' I communicated with the leading Swedenborgians, and received papers from the Rev: J. Proud, Dr. Churchhill, Rev. S. Noble, Mr. J. W. Salmon, of Nantwich, Mr. Birchwood, of Manchester, and some others. But it was not sufficiently supported, and, after carrying it on for twelve months, I was obliged to discontinue it for want of means.

My perusal of · the discipline of the Quakers made me acquainted with the fact, that that exemplary people supported their own poor, and I thought it a most desirable thing that the Swedenborgians should do the same. I had the greatest reverence for Mr. Proud, who at this time was the patriarch of the New Church ; so I communicated my thoughts to him, and begged him, if he approved the matter, to write a paper on the subject, which I might insert in the 'Pocket Magazine.' He at once responded to my request, and wrote an excellent paper, 'To the Members of the New Church, on the Necessity of Supporting their Own Poor,' which I inserted as the leading article in the May (1824) number of the magazine ; but it did not meet with the encouragement

12

which I anticipated, and the subject dropped.   My
opinion of its utility is still the same, and, did I possess
the means, I would myself commence such an institution
at once.

That my readers, both in the United States and Great
Britain, may form their opinion upon the subject, I subjoin the article of Mr. Proud.

'TO THE MEMBERS OF THE NEW CHURCH ON THE NECES-SITY OF SUPPORTING THEIR OWN POOR.

'Of all the religious professions of churches, so called in the
Christian world, there is not one which knows more, professes
more, or recommends more, the doctrine of true charity, than the
New Church. I may venture to say, *not so much;* but, nevertheless, it is presumed there are religious societies which, in a
general way, exercise their charity *much more* than the New Church.
We consider charity as a fundamental doctrine, without which all
religion is vain, void of true spiritual life. But the manifestation
of this principle in life and conduct is, alas! too little seen ; we
mean, in a *general way.* Worthy individuals there are who are
an exception to this rule. We also profess to believe in Divine
Providence, that in every, the most minute circumstance, he provides for and blesseth those who trust in him, and live in an humble
dependence upon him. And yet we seem fearful of extending our
benevolence and charity to the brethren who stand in need, as
though, in so doing, we should greatly injure ourselves. A church
like ours, which has thousands, yea, perhaps tens of thousands,
within its pale, of almost every class, from the senator, the merchant, the opulent, and the gentleman, down to the poor and indigent, should by this time have attained to that state of real,
spiritual charity, as to provide for, take care of, and comfortably
supply every sincere, faithful, but poor member, in distressed
situations, with whatever is necessary for their relief under such
calamity, that he may not be beholden to a parish, immured in a
workhouse, or pine in want of the real necessaries of life. Can we
be said to be men of charity, while any of our worthy brethren are
known to be in really distressed circumstances, their families half
pined through affliction, age, or want of employment, whether
parents, or those who should labor for their support? Shall we
pass by them, suffer them to implore a hard-hearted overseer for a
scanty pittance, or sustain all the insults, unkind treatment, and
insolence of the master of a workhouse? Nay, shall we know of
one in distress, poverty, or affliction, without affording him prompt
relief and assistance? We have subscriptions, collections, charity

sermons, and funds, for various other objects, and why not a fund established and firmly maintained, by subscriptions from the more opulent, solely for the relief and comfort of our poor brethren under their misfortunes? In vain do we talk of charity, as a principle, if our hearts are steeled, and our hands closed, against the wants and the sufferings of our own worthy and truly Christian friends in the time of need. There is hardly a society of the New Church but contains some one or more in a state which imperatively requires relief, more or less. And can we see a brother in this state, and at the same time love our neighbour as ourselves, wishing others to do to us as we would have them do were we in like situations, and, nevertheless, be regardless of a suffering friend? Shall we content ourselves, "if we see a brother or sister naked, and destitute of daily food, with saying, Be ye warmed and filled, notwithstanding we give them not those things which are needful to the body? what doth it profit?" (Jas. ii, 15, 16.) How often does some severe and long affliction deprive an industrious family of their usual means of support, involve them in debt, both for necessaries and medical aid; and how unexpectedly may some misfortune, accident, or disappointment in temporal concerns, expose others to abject poverty, in which case no blame can be attached to the party. The infirmities and debility of old age, also, render working men incapable of their employment, their wages are withdrawn, their support taken away, and at a time and under circumstances which add greatly to their wants, while the means to provide for them are no more. Now all these distressing circumstances and severe trials may fall to the lot of very sincere and upright Christians of our church. And do they not call upon us, with a voice which can but be heard, to commiserate our poor brethren, and to exert ourselves for their assistance, that they may not pine away in starvation, and sink down to the grave unnoticed, unassisted, the hand of the church never stretched out to bless, relieve, and comfort them? Read Deuteronomy xv, from the seventh to the eleventh verse: "If there be among you a poor man, of one of thy brethren, within any of thy gates in thy land, which the LORD thy GOD giveth thee, thou shalt not harden thy heart, nor shut thine hand from thy poor brother, but thou shalt open thy hand wide unto him, and shalt surely lend him sufficient for his need; in that which he wanteth thou shalt surely give him, and thy heart shall not be *grieved when thou givest* unto him, because, that for *this thing*, the LORD thy GOD shall bless thee in all thy works, and in all that thou puttest thy hand unto." See also Prov. xli, 1, and Isa. lviii, 7, 8. It is not expected that every society can of themselves support and provide for the poor among them; but, at a General Conference, let the subject be taken into serious consideration, and a plan formed to establish a fund, appropriated solely to the relief of poor brethren, in every case where such assistance is required.

'And that so far as this fund should exceed the necessary calls, let the overplus be devoted to some other important use in the Church. By establishing such a fund, and liberally distributing from its store, great good will be done, and a divine blessing attend the benevolence of our community. Such a fund established, a committee appointed, with a treasurer and secretary, entirely devoted to this business, such committee, inquiring into the situation, state, and character of those requiring assistance, that all imposition may be prevented, proper accounts kept, and a clear statement given at every General Conference. Thus the charity bestowed with prudence and judgment, agreeing both with spiritual and moral rules, there cannot be a doubt but that such an institution might easily be supported, and its resources equal its demands. How laudable is the conduct of the people called Quakers in this case! they never suffer a worthy and orderly member to apply to a parish for relief, or to be shut up in a workhouse, under the imperious authority and unfeeling treatment of its governor; their poor never are suffered to want, and their means of assisting them never fail. And, no doubt, if we proceed in a similar manner, from a true spirit of Christian love, we should always have wherewith to comfort our poor, in the time of need our resources would not fail, but, rather, Divine Providence would bless our basket and our store. If it be asked, What plans should be adopted in order to raise a proper fund? let the Conference in its wisdom consult and determine. Perhaps a monthly subscription, if it were only a shilling or sixpence from the more opulent, and three-pence, two-pence, or one penny from the middling classes, if this were done in every society, it is presumed a sufficient sum would be raised for all the purposes required. But as to the method of raising what is necessary, let the Conference determine. The writer of these lines has no *personal interest in the subject*, nor any motive but that of sympathy for the poor, that so far as they are industrious, orderly, and upright members, they may not, at such time, pine away under their sufferings, unheeded and unassisted, but find that relief which shall render them as comfortable as is consistent with their situation.

'Perhaps I may be thought presuming for proposing such an institution to the consideration of the New Church; but if I cannot render it a liberal aid, I shall not require its *assistance*, and, therefore, let no one imagine I have any selfish motive or any reward but the *blessing of the poor*, and the exercise of true charity in that Church, the essential and fundamental principles of which are, PURE LOVE TO GOD, AND TRUE CHARITY TO MAN!

'Most sincerely wishing the subject may be taken into consideration, and abundantly prosper, may the benevolent members of the Church find an increase of their temporal and spiritual wealth, with which to be more and more useful: the writer of these lines subscribes himself the friend of all, and an humble advocate for the indigent, the distressed, and the necessitous poor.

'*Handsworth, February* 24, 1824.' 'J. P.

At the beginning of 1825, a circumstance occurred which terminated my connection with Bristol. The school over which I presided was about one hundred feet in length and about twenty wide. One of my acquaintances, whom, as he is still living, I will call Harrison, waited upon me and inquired if he could have the use of the room in which to hold a fancy dress ball. I replied I could not grant it myself, but if he would call on the Secretary (whose name I gave him), he could gain the necessary information. It appears that he did not obtain permission definitely, but he took it for granted that he had leave, and so, after the dismissal of the children, I gave him the keys of the school, and in the evening the ball was held. In due course, I received from my acquaintance a guinea for the school funds, which, on my taking to the committee, led to the inquiry how the party obtained the room, and I was accused of having let the room for an improper purpose. I contended it was not my fault but the Secretary's; altercation ensued—the money was refused, but given to the funds of the Magdalen Hospital. I would not confess myself in the wrong, and so we separated.

Meantime, I had an engagement to organise a school in Dublin, and in the month of May, after four years' residence in Bristol, and in that time organising schools in Gloucestershire, Somersetshire, Wiltshire, Shropshire, and Warwickshire, I terminated my engagement, and entered upon another field of duty. All this time I had done the duty of the Swedenborgian Society in Bristol gratuitously, and had besides contributed to the general expenses of the meeting. By frequent travelling all night on the top of the mail (there were no railways in those days), and being exposed to great vicissitudes of heat and cold, my hearing had become considerably impaired, but it did not as yet at all interfere with my duties as a teacher; it will be re-

membered that I never permitted the children to speak
to me in an undertone, and I could detect an error in
their exercises sooner than many whose hearing was
quite perfect.   But I sensibly felt the difference in private
company, and though I did not murmur in public, I often
grieved in private, and resorted to every possible expedient
to recover my hearing.

On parting with my friends in Bristol, I received many
tokens of kindness, and among them the portrait of Mr.
Fitzhugh, before alluded to, from my friend Mr.
Sanders' son-in-law.

I think it was about the month of June, 1825, that I
embarked on board the steam packet for Dublin. I had a
most delightful passage. I had never been at sea before,
and everything was novel. I remember Dr. Adam
Clarke was on board, and was requested to deliver a
discourse, to which he kindly acceded, and spoke for
about an hour on the goodness of God and his wonders
in the deep. He was a pleasant looking old gentleman,
with a forehead not very deep but broad, his brow was
finely arched, and he had a large and brilliant eye. Of
his reasoning powers, I did not entertain a high opinion,
but his language was very fluent, and the ladies and
gentlemen in the cabin expressed themselves much pleased
and edified by his discourse.

After a pleasant passage of about thirty hours, I
landed at Dunleary (Kingstown it is now called) and
from thence proceeded in a jaunting car to Dawson's
Hotel, where I spent my first night in Dublin.

Sixth Period:

FROM TWENTY-NINE TO THIRTY-EIGHT YEARS OF AGE.
1825 TO 1834.

'Phrenology is one of a group of sciences, different from anatomy, and its truths are of a larger stature. It belongs to the doctrine not of the human body, but of man, and is one of the lesser departments of Anthropology.

'Considered as a branch of observation, it has never been assailed successfully, because no one has paid so much attention to its facts as the Phrenologists themselves. The word of the phrenological student may be taken, since the oppugners have formed no contrary induction, which in destroying Phrenology, might supplant it by a better practical system. The world will give it a long trial, were it only that it deals with the substances of character, and seems to create a solid play-ground, away from the abstractions of the old metaphysics. Color and life, substance and form, are dear to mankind, as homes against the wind of cold speculation. We cannot give them up for patches of sky a thousand miles from the earth, or for anything, in short, but still more substantial houses.'

DR. WILKINSON.

AFTER passing my first night at Dawson's Hotel, which with a splendid exterior, was one of the dirtiest houses I had ever been in, I began to arrange my letters of introduction, preparatory to my entering on the business of a school in Dublin.

My engagement was with Mr. Thomas Hutton, an eminent coach maker, in Summer Hill, and who afterwards, I believe, was M.P. for Dublin. I had letters to many of the nobility, and to people of the highest standing in Dublin; among others, to Sir M—— S——, of Bushy Park, Lady Powerscourt, of Enniskerry, and to a

Mr. H———, a banker. These letters I first left with my card, and then proceeding to Summer Hill, had an interview with my principal, but I was by him turned over to the care of Mrs. H., and for a few days had apartments at this gentleman's house. The school not being ready for my operations, it was resolved that I should deliver a Lecture on Education, at the Rotunda. I had an audience of about a thousand persons, and though timid at the commencement, as, indeed, I always am even to this day, I soon acquired confidence, and went through an outline of Pestalozzi's plans with apparent satisfaction to the audience. After the lecture, I was closely questioned by several of the Roman Catholic clergy who were present, to whom, as I was afterwards told, I had given entire satisfaction. I had a fortnight at this time at my own disposal, the school not being ready for occupation.

I had a letter of introduction to Lady Powerscourt (as before noted) at Enniskerry ; and I resolved to walk this journey with the view of seeing the country, but by so doing I missed seeing the lady, who had left for the continent about an hour before my arrival. On my return to Dublin, I found a letter inviting me to dine with Mr. H———, the banker ; it was to be what was called a family dinner. I went, and was perfectly dazzled with the assemblage of ladies in the drawing-room, and felt myself grievously embarrassed, and in a fever of perspiration. Mr. H——— himself, however, soon set me at ease, and dinner being served, handed me his youngest daughter to conduct to the dining-room. All went well enough with me till the ladies left the room, and the gentlemen set in for a regular bout of whisky punch. For my part, I believe I had not so much as tasted this potent compound before. But now every one had to drink his wine-glass full at each toast that was given. Mr. H. would not allow me to escape, told me I should have a sample of Irish hospitality, that it would do me good, and that I need not fear, for he would himself see me home ; in short, the party had determined to make me merry, and something more. I sat with them an hour, but I declined returning to the drawing-room, and at last, after much demur, the carriage was ordered, and I was sent home. I think I was not myself again for a week, and I resolved I would go no more to Irish bankers' dinners. I considered this to be a splendid illustration of 'killing by kindness.' I afterwards found that the company had resolved to see what was in me. They started with the view of making me declare myself (*in vino veritas*); and I cannot tell exactly how I conducted myself. I was at Mr. H——'s table several times after this, but I had a strict watch over them, and determined they should no more send me to my lodgings in a carriage.

Besides the parties just named, I had also letters of introduction to Mr. Radley, Mr. Norton, and Mr. O'Connor ; they were Swedenborgians, and I thought I would call upon them previous to entering on my school duties. I did so, and was most hospitably received. At that time there was a meeting of about a dozen Swedenborgians, which was held at Mr. O'Connor's house. I went on the Sunday, and was invited to conduct the service, which I did. I recollect well that I discoursed from 2 Kings iv, 29. The discourse was entirely extempore, and at its conclusion I was overwhelmed with thanks, and in these approvals, no one was more vehement than Mr. O'Connor. I was recommended, nay earnestly requested, to report my visit to the 'Intellectual Repository,' which I did. I mention this so pointedly because I shall have to return to it again shortly. I was now told I could have apartments at the house of a Swedenborgian friend, which would be better for me than being at an hotel, and I at once took them. That friend is now a member of Cross Street Swedenborgian Church.

After a fortnight's residence in Dublin, the school was ready for occupation, and I entered at once upon its duties, remaining for seven weeks, until the school was in such a state of order that it could be left. Having accomplished that for which I came, previous to leaving I was invited to take tea with a small party of Swedenborgian friends, and at this meeting some fourteen shillings odd was contributed to the school funds. Before sailing from Dublin I breakfasted with Mr. H—— and his family, and on the same morning received ten pounds from the Duke of Leinster, which, with the fourteen shillings received from the Swedenborgian friends, I paid into the hands of the Treasurer, but did not deem it necessary to take a receipt for the fourteen shillings, as all benefactions were inscribed in the school room on a black board, where they could be seen. With many presents and thanks from all my friends in Dublin, and leaving the school under the care of a female who had been trained at Bristol, but who afterwards, not suiting, was succeeded by a young lady of Dublin, I returned to England, where I found many letters and more occupation than I could attend to. But I agreed with a lady of the name of T—— to organise two schools for her, one at Wantage in Berkshire, and one at Hackney near London. After which I had engagements at New Lanark, in Scotland, and finally at Liverpool.

I spent six weeks at Wantage, and thought it the pleasantest village I ever was in. The Vicar, whose name was *Shaw*, paid great attention to me. He often visited the school. He was perfectly amazed at the order to which the children were reduced, and astonished at the progress* they had made during the short period I was in the village, and when I left presented me with a testimonial of his approval. From Wantage I proceeded to London, and here I had an interview with Mr. J. P. Greaves; he was then Secretary of the Infant School Society, a most intelligent but very eccentric man. I visited in company with him several of the Infant Schools, and after about eight hours walking from school to school, at the close of the day I invited him to go with me to a chop-house to dine. 'No, no,' said he, 'come home with me. I

* His own words were, 'I am terrified at the progress of these little boors.'

will give you a dinner." So I returned with him to Buck-lesbury, where he then resided, quite spent with hunger and fatigued with walking. I saw no preparations for dinner, but he told me it would soon be ready, and after about a quarter of an hour two covered soup plates appeared. Upon removing the cover, instead of a steak or a chop as I anticipated, lo, there appeared a round of sopped toast, covered with sugar.

'There, my boy,' said he, 'that is a dinner will do you more good then beef-steaks or mutton-chops, besides keeping clear your intellect; don't wait; this is my dinner daily, and a capital dinner it is.'

'No, thank you, Sir,' said I; 'I have left off pap, I am really hungry, and shall go and get something more substantial.' I left him more angry than I ought to have been; but determined I would never spend another day with him, and I kept my word.

I remained at Hackney three months, and then departed for Liverpool; here I embarked on board the Henry Bell steamer for Glasgow. I had a commission to investigate the schools at New Lanark, then under the control of Mr. Robert Owen. I was to note how they were conducted, and to introduce such of the plans as I thought would be useful into the schools at Liverpool. It was in the beginning of the month of October; we set sail from Liverpool about six o'clock on the evening of Saturday, and after a most stormy passage of forty hours, arrived at Greenock. Never shall I forget this passage. I rolled in an agony of sickness on the floor of the cabin. I was perfectly reckless as to what might happen so that I could but escape the sickness. There were only two gentlemen in the cabin beside myself, but very many passengers on deck. It was the night on which the 'Comet' was lost, and, as I have said, we were forty hours on the passage; a passage which now is per-formed in sixteen. But reaching Greenock, after washing and shaving, I had an appetite like an ogre, and in an hour after landing I never remembered to have felt better. We embarked again in a river steamer, and in about four hours arrived at Glasgow, where I waited on a friend of the name of M——, and was kindly received and hospitably entertained by that gentleman.   After recruiting myself for two or three days, and seeing some of the wonders of Glasgow, I proceeded to Lanark, my friend M—— being so kind as to accompany me.   I inspected the schools and took memoranda of every thing connected with them, as well as purchased a large quantity of apparatus.   The rooms were most magnificent for height, width, and length. Before leaving we were invited to be present at an early ball of the children, which was to take place at half-past six on the following morning.   So we adjourned to our inn, where we fell in with a large party of Quakers who had come upon the same errand as ourselves, namely, to inspect the schools ; and with them we spent a very pleasant evening.

We were up betimes in the morning, and enjoyed an hour and a half in the children's ball room.   Every thing was conducted with the most exact order.   The Master of the Ceremonies was a boy of about eleven years of age, the musicians about the same age.   The children, boys and girls, were all bare-foot, but they were all exceedingly clean and neat; in particular, the girls had a most tasty appearance ;   their hair was very beautifully arranged, and they wore a tartan tunic of the clan Mc Gregor. Besides the ball, we were regaled with some very beautiful singing.   One of the Superintendents was present.   But he never interfered in the arrangements ; he was a mere looker on like ourselves.   I was delighted beyond measure with all I saw and heard ; before leaving the premises we visited many of the class rooms and heard the children examined in geography, natural history, and various other exercises, but we were amazed at the extraordinary ability in mental arithmetic which they manifested, and every thing, as we were informed by Mr. Robert Dale Owen (Mr. Owen's son), was according to the plan pursued by Pestalozzi himself, he (Mr. R. D. Owen) having studied at his establishment at Yverdun in Switzerland.

We returned to our inn, enjoyed a regular Scotch breakfast of ham, eggs, fish, tea, coffee, etc., etc. Such a table for breakfast I had before never seen set out.

'Noo, then, Mr. G——,' (said my friend M——) 'ye'll tak a wee drappie by way of a digester, an' I'll shew ye some o' the wunners of the toon ; and then we'll awa' to the fa's and Wallace's Cave, and we'll be back by twal' and then we'll awa' hame to Glasgy.'—So I took a little whisky and water to please my friend, and to be equal with him in the customs of the country, and then we visited the Falls of the Clyde just above New Lanark. They were the first falls I had ever beheld, except as delineated in books, but I was awe-stricken by them, and began to turn dizzy, but my friend suddenly pushed me into a little room, where there were mirrors so arranged as to present all the grandeur of the scene without feeling any danger. I was told this room had been constructed at considerable expense in order to enable the nervous and timid to behold the magnifience of the falls without danger, several tragical occurrences having taken place previously which required the precaution. From the falls we proceeded to roam along the banks of the Clyde. My friend, being intimately acquainted with the localities, conducted me into several of the hiding places of Rob Roy and Wallace.

I had read of Cartland Craigs as being in the vicinity of Lanark, and begged, if we had time, to visit them. My friend said *we wad mak' time,* so we left the banks of the bonnie Clyde, and soon came in sight of the Craigs. We ascended them by some pleasant meadows, and on reaching the top I was in raptures at the magnificence of the view ; we sat and rested some time, when my friend observed, 'We must awa' or we'll be too late for the coach ; so we'll tak' the steppin' stanes, an' ye'll just follow me.' I did not like the descent by the 'steppin' stanes.' It appeared almost perpendicular, with only here and there some loose stones to step on, but as my friend seemed to apprehend no danger, I could do no less than follow him. He proceeded rapidly—I at a more cautious space. I had taken I think about half-a-dozen steps, when, being too cautious, and treading two heavily, I loosened one of the stones, from which I had no sooner raised my foot than down it went from craig to craig, passing Mr. M. on his progress till it reached the bottom. He dared not look back, but expected to see me rolling after it momentarily. I, however, had reached the next step somewhat terrified it is true, and pushing on, at last reached the bottom nearly as soon as my friend ; he grasped me by the hand, and, with considerable emotion, said, 'I'm glad ye're safe, I thought it was a' over wi' ye.' This incident cured me of my climbing, and I did not propose the ascent of any more craigs. We reached the inn at three o'clock instead of twelve, took some refreshment, left by the coach at four, and at seven we were in Glasgow.

On the following Sunday I was invited by the Swedenborgians to address the Society in their place of worship, which I consented to, and delivered three addresses, which were very well attended. They were also well received by the members of the Society, and I was invited to remain among them. This I could not then accede to. When I left them I was presented with a token of approval and friendship. I could not think of again travelling by sea, so I took the coach, travelled part of two nights and a day, and at length arrived in Liverpool, where I at once entered upon the duty of organising anew the Liverpool schools. All the information I had obtained at Lanark was immediately reduced to practice, and I pursued as closely as I could the plans of Pestalozzi, in arithmetic, in natural history, in geography, and in objects. The Committee, however, had a much stronger desire for book-learning than I wished or thought necessary, but I was obliged to succumb to their wishes. I however gained my point in gymnastics, and though the committee was composed of members of the Society of Friends, there was no disinclination to the children being taught singing. I at once pursued the plan I had seen at Lanark, and in the morning had exercises which occupied an hour in marching and singing, so varied, however, that there was no weariness expressed on the part of the children. The school was rapidly brought into notice, and was visited by many eminent personages, and in a short time I had an extensive correspondence in the counties of York and Lancaster, and in Scotland. The present Mr. David Stow (of Glasgow), then but a young man, consulted me on the plans I had adopted. I gave him a full outline, furnished him with many of my lessons, my mode of teaching arithmetic, geography, singing, and marching, gave him also many of my songs. All my information he has embodied in his work, entitled the ' Training System '— a work that he has made a little fortune by, but he has forgotten to state from whom he got a great part of his information. He is now, I am informed, the principal Director of the Glasgow Normal School, in connection with the Free Church of Scotland.

During my residence in Liverpool, the school was twice visited by Dr. Bloomfield, the then Bishop of Chester, and present Bishop of London. On one occasion in company with the Rev. James Hornby, Rector of Winwick, and Rev. Jeoffery Hornby, Rector of Bury (both nephews of the then existing Earl of Derby, grandfather of the present Earl), he was present during a trial of one of the children, for the using of profane words—words, of the meaning of which, the child was of course perfectly ignorant ; but which he had heard his parent make use of. It was my plan always to make the children sensible of crime by appeals to the reflecting faculties. When I speak of appealing to the reflecting faculties of a child, I of course mean the use of such arguments and of such words as are consonant with his capacity. The crime of which my pupil had been guilty was the utterance of the profane words, ' *Go to hell with you and be damned.*' We had a raised platform at one end of the room, which rose by successive seats, similar to the plan now adopted in Mechanics' Institutions. I stood at the lowest seat in the centre, with the faces of the children before me, and the monitors on each side of me, consisting of seven boys and seven girls, also facing the children. The accuser then stood up, and charged James Wilkes with using profane words, the words already stated. I then called npon James Wilkes :—

Myself—Have you used these shocking words ?

James—Silent for some time—[Question repeated and at length replied to] I heard father use them.

Myself—What is Hell ? [Silence.]

Myself—Where is Hell ? [Silence.]

Myself—Has any one read about Heaven ?

Children—Yes, Sir, I have, I have, I have, etc.

Myself—What is Heaven ?

Children—It is the place where good people go to.

Myself—Then what is Hell ?

Children—The place where wicked people go to.

Myself—By good people I suppose you mean such as love God, and try to do good to everybody ?

Children—Yes, yes, that is it.

Myself—Then Hell must be a place opposite to this, a place where people go who do not love God, but love nobody but themselves. Is that a description of Hell ?

Children—[Silent.] At length one said a place of fire where people are always burning.

Myself—O that must be a shocking place. Do you think I could put my hand in the fire, and keep it there, without feeling pain ?

Children—O no, no : it would be shocking ; you would be burned ; you could not hold it in the fire.

Myself—I am sure I could not. Which is the strongest— you or me ?

Children smiled, and said, You.

Myself—Yes, I am the strongest.—Now suppose I was to take James Wilkes by the hand, and hold him fast, and put his hand into the fire, and keep it there.

Children—It would be cruel—no—you could not do it—he will say so no more—O pray do not, do not put it in the fire.

[Children all looked terrified, they seemed to think that I had asked the question about strength that I might show them what I would do to James Wilkes.]

Myself—I am stronger than James Wilkes, I could do it; but it would be wicked, it would be cruel; but still it would be doing to him just what he said to his little school-fellow. [Then calling the weakest child, and placing him by the side of James Wilkes, I said, Which is strongest? and having got the proper answer I proceeded.] Would it be cruel in James Wilkes to hold this little boy's hand in the fire till it was burned?

James Wilkes—O Sir, I would not do.

Myself—But would you like me to do it, or some one stronger than me?

James—O no, no; I did not mean it; I heard father say it.

Myself—But do you think your father would put your hand in the fire, and hold it there?

James—No, Sir, no, father is cross sometimes, but he would not do that, he loves me.

Myself—Yes, I should think he must love you; he could not burn you; he could not wish for anybody stronger than himself to burn you. I believe he spoke without thought, without reflecting upon what he said. Now I have told you, always to think before you speak. You do not want your little school-fellow to go to hell, then?

James—[Crying sadly]—No, no, Sir; I will not use such wicked words again.

Well, said I, turning to the jury of boys and girls, what is to be done to James Wilkes for using those profane words? He would not like me to burn him, and I should be very wicked to do it.

Children—He must ask William Bates to forgive him, and

13

promise to do better and be kind to him, and never use wicked words any more.

So William Bates was called, and James Wilkes went to him and asked him, with tears in his eyes, to forgive him, and William Bates did forgive him, and at my suggestion shook hands ; then I said, ' But can James Wilkes become a better boy by his own efforts ? I think he cannot do it of himself ; he must pray to God to help him to become a better boy, and then God will help him, and he will be sure to succeed, and he ought to tell his father all that he has done, and all that has been said this morning : so now we will say a prayer for James Wilkes, and then we will sing and go to our lessons.'

My visitors were well pleased with the result of the trial, especially Mr. J—— H——, the Rector of Winwick. Not long after this, I was sent for to Orford Hall, near Warrington, by the Hon. G—— H——, with the view of establishing a Pestalozzian School at Warrington in connection with the Established Church. After a long interview with this lady, the establishment of a school was determined upon, and the requisite means were soon obtained, and I was deputed to organise it. This led to my residence at the hall for a month. I was accommodated with a bed room, in which was a library of some two or three hundred volumes, and upon examining them, I found a complete set of Emanuel Swedenborg's works, and also of the works of the late Rev. J. Clowes, A.M., of St. John's Church, Manchester. It was known that I was a Swedenborgian, and I wondered whether I had been placed in this room that I might have the accommodation of the library while at Orford. The next morning I was visited by Miss H——, who inquired whether I had all needful accommodations ; and I then mentioned my gratification at the library. 'Ah !' said the lady, 'that room was my brother Edward's, and the library was his. He and Mr. Clowes, whose portrait we have in the drawing room, were great friends. Select any work from the library that you like, and I will make you a present of it, and you can keep it

for my brother's sake as well as in remembrance of me.'
I selected the 'Apocalypse Explained', in six volumes. This
gentleman, Mr. Edward Thomas Stanley Hornby, was the
elegant writer, who used to contribute to the 'Intellectual
Repository,' under the signature *Seth*, the monogram of his
name. The period that I spent at Orford Hall was one of
the pleasantest in my chequered life. I had many kind
friends while there, and as I was only about four hours a
day at the school, I luxuriated in the library, and read an
immense number of works. It was here that I became
acquainted with ' Clowes' Letters on the Human Soul and
Body,' and I thought I should like to study Medicine, that I
might make myself familiar with the anatomy and physiology of the human frame, and so become more conversant
with Swedenborg's doctrine of correspondence.

On my return to Liverpool, I cultivated the acquaintance of a gentleman who was in business as
an apothecary, chemist, and druggist. I thought this
would be a good opportunity of acquainting myself with
the elements of medical science ; so I made an arrangement with him by indenture, and after the business of
the school, I was a regular and constant attendant at his
establishment, and gradually acquired a competent
knowledge of pharmaceutical chemistry, and of the
properties and qualities of drugs. I was most kindly
treated by this gentleman, and everything conducive to
the future acquisition of medical science was placed in my
way. This gentleman, too, became to me a phrenological
study. He was very benevolent ; he would do any one a
kindness, hoping for nothing again. His head was large,
he had a good eye, large perceptive faculties, and
moderate powers of reflection. His head rose high at
the vertex, and his self-esteem and love of approbation
were both decidedly large. Among his qualities was
one of immense firmness ; nothing daunted him. His
confidence in himself was unbounded, and his perseverance
was equal to his self-esteem. If he thought himself
right, nothing would shake him in his determination. He

would pursue his object even when everybody else thought its attainment hopeless. His temperament had a bilious-nervous predominance, and his activity was uniform and steady.

On one occasion, while visiting at his house, I was introduced by him to a lady of the name of Merton, whom I also began tò notice with a phrenological eye. But she as readily read me; and asked me very unexpectedly if I had ever studied phrenology. I replied that I had gained a smattering of it from the study of Dr. Crook's 'Compendium,' but that I had seen none of the larger works. I said, however, that as soon as my engagement with Mr. —— was completed, I should try and get some further light upon the subject.

She told me that she had Dr. Spurzheim's large work and also a bust, and that, if I would give her my word that I would study the science, master the details, and then engage as a lecturer, she would make me a present of them. I looked at her with surprise, but she only remarked—'Is it a bargain? very well then (without giving time to answer), they shall be at your house to-morrow morning.' She was as good as her word; and, from that time, I began to study Spurzheim most devotedly, though I still kept my own secret. I observed all, but I said very little. I was not yet sufficiently confident to lecture, and if I then had even a more mature knowledge of the science, there was no field in which I could exercise it; so I observed, but held my tongue. I found Dr. Spurzheim's work a wonderful assistance to me; it was so very simple in its illustrations, and was withal so well illustrated by portraits, that I took a pleasure in reading and observing the portraits again and again. In short, Dr. Spurzheim was soon my own in every sense. His arguments, his portraits, his anecdotes were well grounded in my memory. Still, my own experience was very limited, and the facts and illustrations of Dr. Spurzheim were almost all foreign; so I could not hope these would make any very permanent impression on an English audience. But

phrenology was a fresh stimulus to study medicine.
Well, I continued my attendance on my medical friend,
and acquired respectable proficiency. I could, however,
only be present with him in the evening.

My success in teaching introduced me to some wealthy
families, and it was thought a desirable thing to establish
a school for children of the wealthier part of the community, on the principles of Pestalozzi. A lady attended
the Liverpool school for the purpose of being trained,
and a suitable room was obtained and opened, but the
experiment was not successful. The lady, however,
succeeded in establishing a school for children, of from
seven to fourteen years of age. She pursued, though of
course on a more extended scale, my methods ; or, rather,
those of Pestalozzi. She has since realised a competency.
To return to my narrative :—While thus actively
engaged in the duties of my school during the day, and
in the study of medicine during the evening, I was not
unmindful of my promise to Dr. Churchill—to make
myself useful as a minister whenever and wherever I had
the opportunity. My theological studies were usually
in the morning before the duties of the school commenced.

When I first commenced preaching, I wrote my sermons
at full length ; but, by the advice of Mr. Proud, I
discontinued this, and having well studied my subject,
wrote down the leading points, and references to Scripture
for illustration, and then relied upon my memory for
filling up the respective parts. I, however, when any
particular occasion required it, continued to write my
discourse at full length. In 1826, I was solicited to
become the pastor of one of the societies of Swedenborgians in Liverpool, but this I declined, as I still was
occasionally called away to organise other schools, and I
could not pledge myself to be regular in the discharge of
Sunday duties. Still, whenever I was at home, I
officiated. At this time there existed in Manchester a
kind of Home Missionary Society among the Swedenborgians ; it was established as early as 1813, and in

1820 sent preachers to about seven different stations in
the neighborhood of Lancashire, and Cheshire ; but in
1826 these stations had increased to nearly twenty.   I
was solicited to assist in this work, to which I consented,
and generally visited six different stations every quarter.
I recollect I was on one occasion solicited to preach a
sermon on behalf of the Sunday school at a village in
Lancashire, called Westhoughten. It was thought that,
as I was engaged in teaching, I might be able to make a
successful appeal to the public. I consented, and, on this
occasion, wrote the whole of my discourse. At the
conclusion of the afternoon service, I happened to walk
behind two persons who were discussing the merits of the
sermon.

'Well,' said one, 'how did you like the new
praycher ? '

'Oh—middling.'

'Now I thought it was a very good sarmunt, and
much to the purpose.'

'Oh, ah ! so it ought to be ; why he had his sarmunt
book along wi' him.'

I heard no more, but I felt my cheeks burn, and resolved I would for the future write no more sermons for
village congregations. I also determined that I would
practise extemporaneous speaking whenever and · wherever I had the opportunity.

Besides the different societies in connection with the
Manchester Missionary Society, which I periodically
visited, I had been invited to preach at other places,
not in connection with that institution, and on one
occasion was invited by a gentleman farmer residing near
Halsall, to visit him at his hall, and deliver a discourse
or two to his farm servants and tenants. He was a great
admirer of Swedenborg, and had read his writings for
some years. He had frequently invited one of the
ministers in Liverpool to his hall, and on such visits
always called together his friends and his neighbors to
hear the new doctrines preached. I promised to visit

him, and on redeeming my promise was delighted with the simplicity of his character and the warmth of his benevolence. Whenever I was unoccupied on a Saturday, and without a Sunday engagement, I frequently walked over to his house, and remained with him on Saturday and Sunday, always leaving sufficiently early on Monday morning to be in time for my school duties at nine o'clock. The frequency of these visits, and the conversation which the doctrines occasioned, at length reached the village of Halsall, distant about two miles from my friend's residence, and drew together a greater number of hearers than my friend's large drawing-room would accommodate. At length he determined to erect a small chapel adjoining his hall, and to offer free accommodation to all who chose to come and hear. Being an invalid, and at a distance of two miles from the parish church, and at the same time indisposed to sit under a ministry, which, termed Evangelical, still limited the mercy of God to a chosen few, he at once set about the erection of a chapel, which was completed in a few months, and on the 9th September, 1826, it was opened by myself and another Swedenborgian minister from Liverpool. It was numerously attended on the opening, and continued to be well attended during the remainder of my stay at Liverpool, and indeed till the death of its worthy founder. This gentleman's name was Higson. I shall have occasion to speak of him again in a future part of my memoirs.

While thus engaged in the active duty of teaching both on the Sunday and the ordinary days of the week, I was much at a loss for tracts illustrative of the doctrines which I taught. There were, it is true, a few tracts published on the Lord's Divinity, and on the Divinity of the Scriptures, but they were very high priced, and I could not afford to purchase and give them away. At the close of my discourses, I had frequently to remain, and give answers to questions and further illustrations of the doctrines I had preached, occupying me much time and labor, which might have been considerably diminished,

had there been tracts written expressly for the purp
such as we have now in abundance. Add to this, t
was no compiled biography of Swedenborg, and no per
dical which gave any particulars respecting the rise ar
progress of Swedenborgianism in Lancashire, except, indee
the before-mentioned quarterly journal, which was to
learned and too high priced to meet the ability and th
means of those congregations which I visited. I de
termined, therefore, to write a work which should be
divided into sections, and which, besides giving a succinc.
biography of Swedenborg, should also give an abstract o
the doctrines professed by Swedenborg, and notice briefly
in what manner the different congregations in Lancashire
had arisen.

(1.) I wrote a Biography of Swedenborg, which extended to forty pages, post octavo, in very small type. This
biography consisted of about twelve pages of anecdotes,
relative to Swedenborg, including the genealogy of the
noble house of Swedenborg—twelve pages of specimens
of Swedenborg's correspondence, and the remainder of the
principal incidents in his travels and voyages. I then
gave an outline of the rise, progress, and decline successively of the Adamic, Noetic, Jewish, and Israelitish
churches, touched upon the Roman Catholic and Protestant churches, and then proceeded to the [Sweden-
borgian] New Church. In this part of my subject, I gave
a view of the public institutions then in existence among
the Swedenborgians. I then proceeded to give a history
of the rise and progress of the different congregations I
had visited, and concluded the work by a brief abstract of
the doctrines of the Swedenborgians. In this abstract, I
first quoted a paragraph from Swedenborg as a text, and
then proceeded to illustrate by large quotations from the
works of the different ministers then in existence among
the Swedenborgians. The work sold rapidly—a plain
proof that such a work was needed. At the same time
I am free to say that it was not well received by the
principal Swedenborgians, and no word of commendation

estowed upon it. A large work, entitled a 'Com-
m of the Writings of Swedenborg,' with a Biography
edenborg prefixed, has recently been issued by a
r in the United States, who follows my arrangement
e work just named, except indeed that all his extracts
om Swedenborg's writings exclusively, whereas mine,
fore stated, after first quoting a text from Sweden-
g as a motto, was popularly illustrated by the
rent writers and preachers then in existence among
e Swedenborgians. While upon this part of my subject
ay observe, that the compiler of the Compendium of
wedenborg's Works, has, in his Biography, quoted largely
d freely from a recently published Essay of mine, on
e 'Mission of Swedenborg,' without naming the book
om which he has quoted. He has, indeed, marked the
ssages by inverted commas; but while he has freely
iven the names of other authors, he has been quite
lent with regard to the quotations from my Essay. If a
ook is worth quoting at all, its title, or the name of its
athor, ought in justice to be stated.

In 1828, I was requested to give a lecture at Preston,
which I acceded to, and found on my arrival, that no
ess a place had been selected than the theatre. There
was a charge made for the boxes and pit, and the working
lasses were invited to take possession of the gallery free.
This was my first appearance on any stage, and I was a
little astonished on entering to find the house completely
filled. I had a class of pupils with me, and went through
a morning's work.

After the lecture a vote of thanks was given to me and
to my pupils, and I was subsequently invited to undertake the superintendence of the school, which, after some
reflection, I agreed to do, though it would have been much
better for me if I had declined; but I must not anticipate.
In the month of May I left Liverpool, and took up my
abode at Preston. I found there had been an anticipation
at Preston that the school would pay itself; the subscribers
had only guaranteed their subscriptions for one year, and

that had been partly expended in defraying the cost (
fitting up.   However, I entered upon my duties, and i
the course of about three months had an attendance (
nearly a hundred children, and anticipated that I shoul
have a good school in a few months more, when an occur
rence transpired which entirely broke up my prospects i
Preston.

It will be remembered that I had received a fe\
shillings from some Swedenborgian friends at Dubli
(about fourteen and some odd pence), and that I pai
this into the hands of the treasurer at the same time tha
the ten pounds received from the Duke of Leinster ha
been paid.   For these few shillings I had neglected t
take receipts, as already stated.   Well, in the beginning
of the month of July, I received a letter from the Secre
tary of the Swedenborgian Conference, which was to th\
following effect :—'Sir,—As Secretary to the Genera
Conference, I beg to say I conceive it my duty to call th\
attention of that body to your conduct while at Dublin
in 1825.   I am, etc.'   This was a letter fit for an in
quisitor.   A crime or crimes was to be imputed to me
but what they were, I was not to know till the Conferenc\
met, and as it was not likely I could go to the Conference
it being held at a time when the vacation had but jus\
concluded, it was probable that the Conference would a\
once strike off my name from communion.   My absenc\
would have been considered a mark of guilt, be the crim\
what it might.   I, however, by a subsequent post
received a letter from Mr. Thomas Goyder, which was to
this effect :—'There is a report in London, that while
you were in Dublin, in 1825, you received fourteen
pounds, odd, for the Pestalozzian school in that city, which
instead of paying into the funds of the institution, you
appropriated to your own use, etc.'—'So,' said I,
'there are fourteen shillings made into as many pounds,
and I have no receipts to show that I have paid the
money.   This report certainly originates in spite—what
am I to do, however ?'   It immediately occurred to me

I had paid it at the same time as I paid the money
lived from the Duke of Leinster. So I at once wrote
to (Mrs. H.) the Treasurer of the school, called her
lembrance to the several sums, told her the reason of
application, and begged receipts of the respective
ls, which she sent me by return of post, with a very
ldsome letter, which was to the effect, that ' they,
e committee of the Dublin School) would at all times
willing to give their testimony as to the zeal and
lity with which I had assisted in the formation of the
t Pestalozzian school in that city.' So far I had
rned the crime I was to be charged with, and I had
means of rebutting it. The next thing was, how
lld I leave my school at so inconvenient a period. I
l a female assistant, but she was young, and altogether
apable of taking the entire management, even for
week I was to be absent. Then, too, I was without
lds for travelling, and the Conference was to be held
Birmingham, and would require a handsome sum,
there were no railways then, and there would be
mey required for a week's boarding and lodging at
inn, besides the expense of travelling. Yet I was
termined to go some way or other, for I felt
lst exasperated with the Secretary of the Conference,
d I was determined to punish him if it lay in my
wer.

At length I ventured to lay my case before a friend,
ld asked him for the loan of five pounds, for I had but
ree, and my calculation of travelling and living was
ght pounds. My friend begged me to write and explain
e case. I replied I could not do this, for I was not
re that what I was to be charged with was actually
hat I was prepared to meet, since it was not the Secre-
ry that had furnished me with the information, but my
other. My wife begged me to have nothing to do with
further than to write to the Conference and inclose the
ceipts; but I would not listen to her either. I confess
was furious with the Secretary—who seemed to have

contracted a spite against me—and I determined to r
him face to face, if within my power.

'A bad spirit,' you will say ; yes, doubtless it w
it was the spirit of evil against evil ; but so angry we
that I lost for the time all consideration of propriety.
forgot the position I filled.   My combativeness seeme
swallow up all my better feelings, and I was in a stat
comparative insanity. I hide nothing from my readers n
but I have deplored again and again my angry feeli
since.   But to return :—

At last I prevailed with my friend, who gave me
five pounds, and I gave the children ten days' holiday
started for Birmingham, where in due course I arrived,
took up my abode at the Woolpack Inn, in Moor Str
On the first day of the Conference I presented mys
very much to the astonishment, as I thought, of
Secretary, and to the astonishment, also, of two I
gentlemen who were present. No sooner was the C
ference opened than I called upon the Secretary to let
know what he had to say against me, but he said I ma
wait the proper order of business, and the President t
me I must sit down. All eyes were upon me, but I
treated with the most perfect coolness, I thought, conten

I told the Conference that I had come a great distan
and at the risk of losing my situation, to meet an inqui
torial charge of the Secretary, that I was at an inn a
considerable expense, and I wished to get back to Prest
immediately.

'Well, well ; I must wait the regular routine of bus
ness'; and that regular routine would not reach me t
the end of the week. But there was no help. So I w
compelled to sit down, which I did under intensely excit
feelings. However, after a while I calmed down a littl
and I began to take a mental portrait of the Secretary.
carefully noted him. He had well-developed intellectu
faculties, a quick perception, and also good powers
reflection. I saw that there was, also, average power
veneration, but there was a flattening at the anterior pa

he fontanel. The vertex rose high, and declined
rd the parietal bones ; the back part of the head was
d, and the neck was also very broad. I could not
see, however, that I had a shrewd man to deal with.
had large self esteem; the posterior part of the
x of the head rose high, and the adjoining parts
also broad and prominent. My mode of dealing
him was at once determined upon, and I thought
ould first question his right of at all interfering in
business of the Conference.
sat silent during the whole meeting. No one noticed
At the several adjournments, I retired to my inn.
id not attend any of the social tea meetings, but I
very deeply, and I must at the same time acknow-
e that my resentment was intense. I hide nothing
ıy feelings, for it is impossible for me to cloke them
be least. I acknowledge now, after twenty-six years,
they were wrong, very wrong and sinful, but such
bey were then, I detail them.——At length the names
be ministers were called, and that was the time to
g the accusation against me. The Secretary then
ed that he felt it his duty to bring before the Confe-
e a report that I had appropriated certain sums of
ey to my own use which had been given to me for
Dublin Pestalozzian school. I believe this was all he
. I arose and objected to the Secretary having any right
tever to originate an inquiry into my conduct. I said
Secretary of the Conference was the mere servant of
Conference. He was not a representative, but a
l servant, and I objected to him. I demanded, there-
, that the person who had circulated the report should
te his charge, and make it too, specifically.
There was an immediate whispering between two
lemen present, and the countenance of one of them
suffused with a deep tint. I did not hear what was
l, but I immediately set it down in my own mind that
report had originated with these two gentlemen.
re was some little embarrassment. The Secretary then

said : 'I have no antipathy to you, sir; I only · l
this forward as a matter of duty.' 'You have no 1
to speak at all, sir,' said I; 'I repeat, you are the |
servant of the Conference, and have no right to origi
any inquiry; let those two whispering gentlemen say v
they have to say.' This remark created some little se:
tion, but still neither of them seemed at all inclinec
take the matter out of the Secretary's hands, and
Conference saw that I had made a valid objection.

Having brought matters to this state, and quite gai
the ear of the Conference, I addressed myself to
President, and asked whether the Conference was to
turned into an inquisition, in which a member was to
summoned, have a charge. brought against him by
knew not whom, and then either criminate himself,
submit to be criminated by the Secretary. Here wa
person, brought at a considerable expense, at the risk
the loss of his situation, nearly two hundred miles, to m
a vague charge, made by one who had no right to ma
it ; and those who had been at the pains to circulate tl
charge had not now the courage to go on with it, expe
ing, doubtless, that the victim would not dare to me
them (and I then fixed my eyes steadily on one pers
who my brother had told me originated the report |
London) ; but since no one will make the charge—for
will not allow that the Secretary has the right—I w
myself state what I know about it. I then read n
brother's letter, containing the report circulated in Londo
'But for that letter,' said I, 'I should have know
nothing about it. My brother hints that the repo
reached London through some one who has lately been :
a missionary to Dublin. Now, if this be true, it is mo
disgraceful as well as most cruel. Why did not th
person, whoever he was, go to the school and ascertai
from the proper authorities whether the several sum
had been paid or not. Then, again, the charge i
circulated at fourteen pounds odd, whereas the sum
really received were but fourteen shillings odd, and fo

...h trifles I deemed it wholly unnecessary to take ...ipts. But, as through my brother's kindness I was ...t in possession of the real nature of the charge, I ...ote immediately to the Treasurer, stated how I had ...n maligned, and begged immediate receipts to be sent ; ...d,' continued I, taking the letter from my pocket and ...ving it to the Secretary, 'there, sir, read that; or, ...ther, if you please, let the President read it ; let the ...ceipts be read ; and let the testimonial of how I con-...cted myself in Dublin be read ; and let the receipts be ...nded round that the members of Conference may see ...em ; and then, if you please, strike out my name, for ...t is no credit to belong to a body who can use another so ...ruelly and unjustly as I have been used.'

Here I fairly broke down with emotion, and with ...ifficulty refrained from weeping. However, my defence ...ppeared quite satisfactory to the Conference. The receipts ...ere read as well as the letter containing them; and it ...as admitted that I had been most unjustly traduced. A ...roposition was made that my expenses should be paid, ...ut one member objected to this, as it would establish an ...mproper precedent. The Secretary again protested he ...ad no antipathy against me, and this time I said nothing, ...ut taking up my papers, I was about to withdraw, but I ...as now overwhelmed with invitations.

I had previously sat without the notice of a single ...erson ; now I believe I might have stopped a week and been freely entertained, but I told all I must at once return, and I did so. This journey and expenses cost me about seven pounds. I believed, and still do believe, that one of the whisperers was the person who raised the scandalous report, and did so at the instance of a person whom I have since very materially served, and who, indeed, has sent me letters acknowledging that he had spoken disparagingly of me that he might please others.

I returned to Preston, and found that I had given great offence by not first asking for leave of absence before giving the children a holiday, and from that time

the visitors seemed to take but little interest in the scho
Shortly after this there was a slackness at the vario
cotton mills, and from scarcity of money among t
parents, there was a consequent diminution of the s
tendance of the children. However, I continued
struggle on for a year, when I found there was n
sufficient support given me, and I determined to give i
the school.

During my residence in Liverpool, I was, as before state
frequently invited on the Sundays to visit the neighborin
villages and address small societies of Swedenborgian
and I continued to do this while at Preston. The chape
erected by my friend Mr. Higson, was distant abou
eighteen miles from Preston, to which I frequently wen
always meeting with a cordial welcome. My plan was t
start from Preston at about four o'clock in the morning
and walk ; the distance, as I have said, was eighteer
miles. I usually accomplished it in about five hours.]
addressed the people, consisting, besides the gentlemar
and his family, of farm servants and strangers from the
neighboring villages of Halsall and Ormskirk, morning
and afternoon; took tea at about five o'clock, and then
returned to Preston. It took me about six hours to
walk back again, but I did it with tolerable comfort. I
was very active, and my person was light. I usually
walked nine miles, then rested a quarter of an hour ;
taking some refreshment at a roadside inn. Then I
resumed my march, and generally reached Preston about
midnight. I was never molested on any of these
journeys. My kind old friend always gave me seven
shillings for my day's labor. He has long since gone to
the 'better land'; he lived in good style on his own
property in the village of Renacres, near Halsall. He
was a very worthy man, of simple tastes and habits,
and a thorough Swedenborgian. Besides my visits to
this gentleman, I occasionally went to Blackburn and also
to Accrington, at which latter place, I became a great
favorite. I was on one occasion asked by the Committee,

whether it would not be more in accordance with my feelings to keep a school in Accrington, and to unite with the Society there, than to remain in Preston, where there were so few who viewed religious matters as I did. I replied that it mattered not to me where I lived so long as I obtained the means of existence and could make myself useful. So, after a good deal of conversation, I was invited on a special occasion to give my views of education in a lecture. This I did, and had a very large audience, and the result was I was invited to settle at Accrington ; the Swedenborgians offered me sixteen pounds a-year. I removed from Preston accordingly, and entered upon a school at Accrington, but I found my hearing diminish in acuteness, although I continued with great labor to prosecute my scholastic duties, and I had a tolerably good school. The fees were, however, small, and my utmost diligence did not raise me more than about 18s. a-week, including what I received from the Swedenborgians. At this time my family consisted of myself, and wife, and four children ; the oldest only seven years of age, and the youngest an infant. But I became somewhat popular at the Swedenborgian chapel, and the number of hearers increased rapidly. I thought I would now attempt something in the medical way, and I fitted up in my cottage a press in which I stored some of the more useful medicines, and informed my friends that, in case of necessity, persons wanting the usual domestic medicines might obtain them of me, and that I would also perform the minor operations of surgery—as bleeding, tooth-drawing, and cupping. These operations I had made myself conversant with in Liverpool. These additions to my other labors kept me constantly employed, and brought me perhaps an additional two shillings to my weekly income, and every little was a help.

I omitted to notice, in its proper place, an intimacy that I had formed in Liverpool, which I will supply here. While resident in that town, I was in the habit of

14

attending, weekly, a school of theology, and always took part in the debate. The students were of all denominations ; and each student was privileged in turn to frame a question which led to the discussion of the doctrines he professed. One of the questions which I proposed was, 'Which doctrines are most in harmony with Scripture, these propounded by Wesley, or those by Swedenborg ?' I took the Swedenborgian side, and of course, as I proceeded, gave an outline of Swedenborg's views, contrasting them with those of Wesley. The mover always opened and closed the debate. A strong party of Wesleyans mustered to put me down, but I was as combative at that time as any of them, and thought I had the better side of the argument ; so, as I before said, I gave a rapid sketch of Swedenborgian doctrine, and contrasted it with the doctrine of three Divine persons, as held by the Wesleyans, but more especially did I contend against the Methodist doctrine of instantaneous conversion and justification. After speaking my half-hour, I was followed by a young man who commenced with these words : 'Of all the doctrines that ever were palmed upon the credulity of a suffering world, those of my Lord Baron Swedenborg are the most preposterous.' A round of applause followed this opening sentence, and the speaker continued in a vein of humor and sarcasm, meeting my arguments with affirmations, but always contriving to introduce a quotation of Scripture, which appeared at once to refute what I had said. He carried with him the suffrages of the meeting, and my reply made little or no impression.

That speaker was Mr. Joseph Pegg. Though a Methodist, he was the master of the Unitarian school. But he very good humoredly shook me by the hand at the close of the debate, and told me he expected he had completely defeated me. I replied, he would find that a hard matter, for from what he had said, I was convinced he was perfectly ignorant of Swedenborg's writings, and I was sure I could very easily '*seal his lips,*' if I could but

have time to consider, for I confessed I was by no means
a match for him in facility of utterance, and aptitude of
quotation. I contended that what he had uttered was
declamation, not argument. I however invited him to
my house, and as he was a schoolmaster, there were
many points on which we could most cordially unite.
We soon became intimate, and then I put into his hands
Hindmarsh's 'Seal upon the Lips of Unitarians and Trini-
tarians.' He read the book with much attention, and
felt amazed at the force and truth of its author's reasoning,
and at length told me he was a convert to our leading
doctrine of the Divine Unity and Trinity in the person of
the Saviour, but still he could not receive our views of
the atonement. I recommended him to put his objections
in writing, and I would forward them to my brother,
Mr. Thomas Goyder, who would either reply to them himself, or, which would be better, obtain an answer from the
author of the ' Seal.'

Mr. Pegg did so, and, in due time, received the
following letter from Mr. Hindmarsh, which is very
conclusive, as well as interesting, and much to the point.

'*London, Jan.* 18*th,* 1828—72.

' DEAR SIR—I received, through Mr. Thomas Goyder, yours
of the 30th of December last, which afforded me both pleasure and
pain ; *pleasure,* to find that after reading and studying the writings
of Emanuel Swedenborg, you have embraced the first and most
important of all the doctrines of the New Church, " the sole and
entire Divinity of the Redeemer," and *pain,* to understand that
there should be any professors of the truth who act in a manner
unworthy of the characters they have assumed. Your letter
excited in me considerable interest, because it appeared to proceed from a candid and sincere mind, desirous of obtaining the
genuine truth, yet fearful and cautious lest it should be betrayed
into some gross error of doctrine, contrary to the true sense of the
Sacred Scriptures. This state of mind, I have no doubt, is introductory to something more blessed than you have ever yet experienced ; for to all who believe in the Lord, and in the necessity of
living according to his commandments, a voice from heaven is
directed, saying, " Come up hither." (Rev. xi, 12.)

' You have been providentially led to a knowledge of the Lord of his Divine Unity, and his Divine Trinity in one single person. This knowledge is the very gate that opens into the holy city, the New Jerusalem; and it is a pearl of such high price, that we are justified in selling all that we have, that we may be enabled to purchase and secure it for ourselves; that is to say, it is our duty to give up and sacrifice every doctrine, tenet, or opinion, that opposes, either *directly* or *indirectly*, this great truth; that God is one, in essence and in person; that the Divine Trinity in him, consisting of the Essential Divinity, the Divine Humanity, and the Holy Proceeding Influence from both, is like the human trinity in man of soul, body, and operation; and that the Lord and Saviour Jesus Christ is that Triune God. Now, my friend, if you acknowledge and cordially believe this fundamental doctrine of the true Christian religion, how is it that the idea of atonement, or vicarious sacrifice—by which is meant the appeasing of the wrath of one Divine Person by the sufferings and death of another equally Divine Person—can for a moment intrude upon your thoughts, so as to disturb you? If God be only one, and Jesus Christ be that God, to *whom* could he make an atonement? to *what God* could he offer himself a sacrifice for man? or *whose divine wrath* had he to appease, while he himself is the *only God*, the *only Divine Being* in existence? Besides, if there be more Divine Persons than one, which the doctrine of the atonement necessarily implies; and if those persons be all of *equal* divinity, majesty, and glory, why did they not *all* require the same satisfaction that one of them (the Father) demanded? Was not *their* Divinity, *their* Divine Justice, of the *same quality* with that of the Father? Why, then, was not an atonement necessary on *their part*, as well as on the part of the Father? Really the thing will not bear to be looked at in the face; it shrinks from examination, and at length vanishes into the " thin air " of mere imagination.

'Whatever may have been the cause and design of the Lord's sufferings, *this is certain*, that it could not have been to appease Divine wrath—for this odious passion has no place in the Divine bosom—it could not have been to give satisfaction to the offended justice of another Divine Person or Being separate from himself, because there is no other Divine Person or Being in heaven or on earth. And as this is a true and fair statement of the case, it follows that the scriptural doctrine of atonement, or reconciliation of man with God (not of God with man) is quite another thing, differing as much from the notions entertained by professing Christians, as the light of heaven differs from the darkness of this world. But to enter into a minute explanation of the subject is not the purport of this letter. The writings of Baron Swedenborg will give the best and most satisfactory information, and to them I beg leave to refer you, because they clearly demonstrate, from the Scriptures of truth, what was the real nature and process of redemption; and how it consisted with the Divine Unity in the adorable person of Jesus Christ alone.

'With respect to the circumstances of the atonement, as usually understood, being held by so many pious men and considered by them as "the *summum bonum* of Christianity," I think a sincere inquirer after the truth should not suffer himself to be led by mere human opinions, only so far as they are evidently founded on the divine authority of the sacred Scriptures, understood, not according to *appearance*, but according to their *genuine sense*. Neither should he be overawed by the *number* of those who profess doctrines found to be erroneous. This consideration (of number) did not weigh with the primitive Christians, when they emerged from Judaism and Gentilism; nor with the Reformers, when they separated from the Roman Catholics; neither ought it with us of the nineteenth century, on our emerging from the errors and darkness of the Old Christian church, into the truth and heavenly light of the New Jerusalem.

'Who live and die in more confidence of the truth of their religious persuasions than Roman Catholics, nay Jews, Mahomedans, and Pagans? The fact is, that every man is associated in spirit with those *like himself* in the spiritual world, that is, with those who entertain the *same* religious persuasions or sentiments as he himself does; and such spirits infuse into the minds of their associates on earth, whatever their religion may be, a full confidence in its truth, accompanied at times with an air of triumph calculated to deceive the by-standers, and even to impress them with an assurance of their salvation. This is the case, not only with many who have lived uprightly according to the best of their knowledge and judgment, but, as is well known, even with some malefactors, on the eve of their departure from the world, who have been strongly wrought on by the zeal of their religious visitors, and encouraged to hope for that salvation, which is alone the reward of a well-spent life. They are urged to rely on the merits of the Redeemer; and if they can but bring themselves, by an act of faith, as it is called, to depend on those merits, it is too often supposed that the work of repentance is thereby superseded, and that their future happiness is secure. But who cannot see, that a conversion founded in *fear*, on the immediate prospect of death is altogether different from that which arises from the sober conviction of the hatefulness of sin, and a desire to turn from evil, while in health and strength, as a preparation for the reception of the divine mercy?

'These observations are made for the purpose of showing, *First* —That no dependence is to be placed on the mere profession, and apparent confidence of persons dying in any particular tenets of faith: and, *Secondly*—That the only sure ground for hope in the divine mercy is to approach the Lord alone in penitence and prayer; to shun evils as sins against him, while the opportunity of sinning, or refusing to sin, is still granted; that is, while man is in

his usual state of liberty and rationality, free from the immediate
fear of death; and thus to love and do what is just and good for
the sake of justice and goodness, and to seek and practise the truth
for the sake of truth. These are the things taught by the Lord
in his holy Word, and the same are most earnestly recommended in
the writings of the New Church messenger, Emanuel Swedenborg.
Illumination of the understanding, or its elevation even into the
light of heaven, valuable as it is, is not sufficient: for our Lord
says in the gospel, " If ye know these things, happy are ye if
ye do them." (John xiii, 17.)

'I observe with much concern what you state concerning
some professing members of the New Church in Liverpool. I
understand the Society in that place, from causes of which I
am ignorant, has been in a disjointed state for several years
but I can assure you this is not the case with our society
generally. In almost all the societies which I have visited,
spirit of love and harmony prevails—in many of them, to
uncommon degree; and I am sure that this ought to be the happy
experience of the church universally. But where anything of
contrary spirit appears, let us charitably hope that the society itself,
or the individuals of whom it is composed, may be undergoing
states of spiritual temptation, permitted by the Lord for wise
ends, possibly for the sake of humiliation and purification. But
whatever may be the character or states of individuals, we ought
not to look to them, but to the truth; neither is the church to be
judged of by them. When our Lord founded the Primitive Christian
Church, a Judas was found among the disciples; and on one occasion, the chief spokesman and boldest among them denied his
Master; and soon afterwards, when persecution begun, "they all
forsook him and fled." (Mark xiv, 50.) Yet this same church was
the true church of the Lord, and afterwards flourished, and came to
its maturity. So, doubtless, will the present rising New Church
flourish in a still greater degree, and its glory shall be seen over all
the earth; for concerning this very church, the New Jerusalem,
the voice of Divine Truth from heaven hath declared: "Behold,
the tabernacle of God is with man, and he will dwell with them,
and they shall be his people, and God himself shall be with them,
and be their God.' (Rev. xxi, 3.)

'Wishing you may be led by the Divine Providence of the Lord
into the perception of all necessary truth, and that your present
doubts and scruples may, in his good time, be entirely removed, I
have only further to add, that I shall be most happy to hear of
your full entrance into the holy city, the New Jerusalem; because
I shall then know that your name is written in the "Lamb's Book
of Life." (Rev. xxi, 27.)

> 'I remain, dear sir, with great affection,
> 'Yours sincerely,
> 'ROBT. HINDMARSH.'

REV. ROBERT HINDMARSH.

[PAGE 214.

This letter led him to a thorough study of Swedenborg's writings, and to a conviction of their truth, which he afterwards fully avowed; and wrote some admirable Essays in their defence. He was an eccentric genius, a man of marvellous ability, and a very sweet poet. He was, however, of the temperament which may be termed pure nervous. His brain was large and equally balanced. Every region was fully developed, but the excessive nervous predominance of his temperament rendered him erratic in the highest degree. His mind seemed to be the residence of two antithetic genii, which alternately impelled him to good and to evil, and he passed his life in sinning and repenting. At the time I left Liverpool, he was rapidly rising into favor, and he had attracted by his Essays on the 'Improbability of the Destruction of the Earth,' and the 'Eternal Sonship of the Saviour,' the favorable notice of one of the most eminent Swedenborgian ministers, who interested himself warmly in his behalf, and as he was then in great poverty, obtained him considerable pecuniary relief. I shall have occasion to notice him again by and by. But to return to Accrington.

The congregation now had so far increased that there was not a seat to let in the chapel, and always the attendance was such as to inconvenience the hearers from over-crowding. At the same time there were not more than thirty members, and there was a good deal of bickering in consequence, as it was thought, of the high hand which a few of the oldest members manifested, in ruling the society, so that, though there was not an attendant upon worship who was not a cordial Swedenborgian at heart, yet nearly the whole manifested disinclination in joining as members. The person who directed the Society, and who was the most potent man in it, was a Mr. * * *. He was a stern disciplinarian, but I think a very good man upon the whole; certainly he was the most talented member of the church, and he had the whole of the members so entirely under his influence, that whatever he proposed was sure to be acceded to. He had one of the largest and most powerful brains I had yet seen in England. He was very skilful in music, and had written some very beautiful pieces, which were sung in the choir at the chapel; he was, moreover, not an indifferent poet, and a very tolerable linguist, although he would not surrender the Lancashire dialect, which he frequently uttered with a broadness of accent which very much amused, though it surprised me, knowing that he could, if he would, speak with the utmost purity. Add to this, he was a very ingenious mechanic. He had cultivated his mind extensively. He had a broad and deep massy forehead. Was as firm as a rock in his general conduct, and when he once took an antipathy to any one, it was difficult indeed to remove it. I was on intimate terms with him, and he corresponded with me till nearly the time of his death.

Well; I represented to this gentleman that it was indispensible something should be done to enlarge the chapel, for it was exceedingly inconvenient with regard to accommodation. He was an invalid, and towards the conclusion of my stay in Accrington, could not attend worship. In consequence of my representation, a meeting was held at his house, and it was resolved to raise subscriptions and erect a gallery. This was done; a gallery on three sides of the chapel was erected, and in a short time I had the satisfaction of seeing that every seat in this also was let, but still there were no more than thirty members.

It was about the middle of the year 1829 that I became acquainted with a Mr. Cr——n——w, who was an eminent Freemason. He was a member of the Church of England, but occasionally attended at the Swedenborgian chapel, and he invited me to join the fraternity of Freemasons. He said he was quite sure I was a Freemason in principle, for 'many of the discourses he had heard me deliver were beautifully illustrative of their symbols.' I was a little surprised at this, for I certainly had no conception of what constituted the 'mysteries,' or the 'beauties' of Masonry at that time. Moreover, I was somewhat opposed to it. I remembered the misery I had endured under the ODD-FELLOW FLEMING, and I conceived there might be some affinity between the two systems. I mentioned this to my friend C—n—w. He assured me that I was wholly mistaken in my views of the 'sacred craft.' No two systems could be more opposite than Odd Fellowship and Freemasonry. I contended again that I could not tell how my becoming a Freemason would be approved by the Swedenborgians, to which he replied, that he would guarantee there would be no objection, but rather approval, so I at last requested him to propose me for initiation.

When the introductory ceremony had been gone through, I was surprised to find that the majority of the lodge were Swedenborgians, and members of the chapel where I officiated. With this discovery I at once applied myself to the study of the records in the Society's possession, and read all the books I could lay my hands on which were at all illustrative of the Order, and I soon perfected myself in Masonic knowledge, and took my degree in about three months after initiation—was appointed first Secretary, and then Lecturer, to the Lodge, and in the latter capacity was frequently called upon to visit and lecture to other lodges. My lectures were so well approved that, at the beginning of 1830, it was proposed to submit them to the Provincial Grand Master, with the view of selecting such portions as might be communicated to the public; it being a law that no book on Freemasonry should be published without the sanction of the ruler, or master, of the province where the brother resided. They were accordingly submitted to him, and permission was granted in the accompanying letter :—

'*Scaitcliffe, Rochdale, February* 17*th,* 1830,
'*Lancashire—Eastern Division.*

'SIR AND BROTHER—In answer to yours of the 11th of this month, I have to inform you that I have also received and perused

your manuscript copy of a Lecture delivered in your Lodge
which you feel desirous of publishing, and dedicating to myself.

'I have not discovered any improper sentence contained in it
and you have my permission to publish it, and dedicate the same
to me. Would it not be proper to publish all the Lectures
together?

'I am sorry that not one of your Lodge belongs to the Pr. G.
Lodge of this Division, although twice offered; another year I
should be happy to see this altered.

'I am, Sir and Brother,

'Yours faithfully and fraternally,

'JOHN CROSSLEY.'

The publication of the lectures followed as a matter
of course, and a copy having been bound and sent to
that gentlemen, I received a second letter of approval
and congratulation. I also received letters of congratulation from about thirty lodges in the county of Lancaster.
These lectures have gone through three editions, and a
fourth is now called for. For the information of my
readers I subjoin the concluding observations relative to
the brotherly love and charity which are such distinguishing traits of Freemasonry:—

'Brotherly love! most delightful of themes! let us
now dwell upon thy heavenly virtue. Masonry here is
universal; the mason looks upon the whole human race as
one family. This is the first great principle upon which
the order is founded, and the true brother is never so
happy as when in the exercise of it.

'What miseries have sprung from conflicting religious
opinions! What calamities from national antipathies!
What dreadful results from the horrors of civil as well as
foreign wars! But the brotherly love of Masonry unites
every sect, conciliates every nation, heals every breach of
fraternity, unites in perfect harmony those who may have
been in the most hostile states, and in one vast chain of
fraternal affection binds the whole of its votaries. It
knows no distinction of party; the poor is as highly
esteemed as the rich; the lowly as much regarded as the
elevated; the endearing name of brother is on every
tongue, and the purest flame of affection burns in every

heart. "Behold! then, how good and how pleasant it is for brethren to dwell together in unity."

'However the opponents of our art have stigmatised us for our inflexible silence, yet they all unite in commending us for our brotherly affection. May, this, then, be the first principle of our lives, as it is of our profession; may

> "True love,
> Sweet as the precious ointment which bedew'd
> The sacred head of Aaron, and descended
> Upon his hallowed vest,"

reign in every bosom, until the whole human race are closely bound in one fraternal bond of amity.

'When the iron hand of misfortune presses upon some worthy and suffering brother, the true mason immediately stretches forth his hand, raises the sufferer from his abject state, pours into the gaping wounds of his mind the oil and wine * of brotherly love and neighborly consolation, and relieves the necessities of his bodily state, until he is again enabled to pursue his avocations in the world.

---

* 'Mention being here made of oil and wine, an opportunity offers for illustrating the CORN, OIL, and WINE, used in the consecration of a hall or regularly constituted lodge; but, in order to the right understanding of this subject, it will be expedient to transcribe a paragraph from Preston's "Illustrations of Masonry." (Thirteenth Edition.) When a new hall or lodge is about to be set apart for the peculiar uses of the fraternity, "the Grand Secretary informs the Grand Master that it is the design of the fraternity to have the hall dedicated to Masonry; he then orders the Grand Officers to assist in the ceremony, during which the organ continues playing solemn music, excepting only at the intervals of the dedication. The lodge being uncovered, the first procession is made round it, and the Grand Master having reached the east, the organ is silent, and he proclaims the hall duly dedicated to MASONRY, IN THE NAME OF THE GREAT JEHOVAH, TO WHOM BE ALL GLORY AND HONOR; upon which the chaplain strews corn

'And even here he does not forsake his poor brother
for while with his open hand he ministered to his neces
sities at a time when he was sinking for want of assist
ance, with cheerful feet he now engages to place him in

over the lodge.*   The organ plays, and the second proces
sion is made round the lodge ; when on the Grand
Master's arrival at the east, the organ is silent, and he
declares the hall dedicated, as before, to VIRTUE ; on
which the chaplain sprinkles wine.†   The organ plays,
and the third procession is made round the lodge ; when
the Grand Master having reached the east, and the music
being silent, the hall is dedicated to UNIVERSAL BENEVO-
LENCE ; upon which the chaplain dips his fingers in the
oil ‡ and sprinkles it over the lodge ; and at each period
of dedication the grand honors are given.   A solemn
invocation is then made and an anthem sung.'

* 'What can be a more apt emblem of the superior goodness of the
Divine Being than "Corn"?   From it man is endowed with the staff of
life, bread being the principal food which supports his existence; but the
mason knows that "man does not live by bread alone, but by every *word*
[truth] that proceedeth out of the mouth of God"; therefore, when his
servant, in the character of Chaplain, strews the CORN over the Lodge, it
reminds him of "the Bread of Life" of Him who declared, "My meat is
to do the will of Him that sent me"; and, therefore, the true brother
always feels peculiar delight and satisfaction at the consecration of a new
Lodge, because it brings to his mind his ultimate association with the
"Author of Life"—binds him in communion with his Saviour, who is
"the Bread' of Life"—and at one view exemplifies the superior care of
the Divine Goodness, in providing for his spiritual, as well as his natural
support; it is then an extra emblem of the Divine Goodness.

† 'Wine is an expressive emblem of the DIVINE TRUTH of the
WORD of GOD, and therefore it is declared "to cheer both God and
man."   But this is not all; for "TRUTH," being one of the three great
principles of Masonry, is deemed of very considerable importance by the
Society.   Without Truth, the most sacred obligations would be violated,
the inmost secrets of the order betrayed, peace, harmony, and unanimity
destroyed, and the whole fabric of Freemasonry would be sapped at the
very foundation.   Hence, TRUTH is one of the three great principles
which cements the whole fraternity, and for this reason it is expressively
used in the consecration of a new Lodge.   Let the reader contrast
Truth with perjury, and he will speedily discover the importance which
we attach to its most sacred observance.

‡ '"OIL!" "UNIVERSAL BENEVOLENCE!" "BROTHERLY LOVE!"
If mankind could but be induced to practise what they profess, what a

situation where he may recover that which he has lost, nor does he rest until he has accomplished, in the fullest sense of the word, all that can be accomplished.

'All the efforts of man, however, to save or to render assistance to his fellow-man can be of no service, where the blessing of the Almighty does not accompany him ; therefore, when, with humility, he daily offers his petitions at the throne of the Eternal, the wants of his poor brother are brought to his remembrance ; he offers his prayer for him unto that Being who never closes his ears against the petitions of his creatures, and leaves him in the hands of that righteous God, who, while he administers justice, never fails to remember mercy.

'Who has not felt the force of affection exhibited in a confidential intercourse ? Who, on unbosoming himself to his friend, has not experienced relief to his own mind ? happy country would that be in which Christianity was established. "Love is the fulfilling of the Law"; "Love is the end of the commandment." Love is the first great principle upon which the order of Freemasonry is founded.

'"The Chaplain dips his fingers in the OIL, and sprinkles it over the Lodge." Many may consider this as a mere idle ceremony, destitute alike of instruction or edification. Not so the mason; because in the volume of the sacred law he is led to discover the importance of its use. When Aaron was appointed Priest of Israel, previous to his ministry in the tabernacle, the whole of the vessels set apart for sacred use, as well as Aaron himself, were consecrated or anointed with holy oil. This intimates to the intelligent mason *that* pure love of which the sacred oil is the resemblance. It is the principle heaviest in the scale of intellectual excellence; it consecrates the affections to the Grand Architect; it replenishes the heart with the purest evidences of Christianity; it purifies the soul of hereditary as well as actual defilement; and, finally, wheresoever this principle is predominant in the affections, it re-creates the soul in the image and likeness of its Maker. These reflections, and others equally important, recur to the mind of the intelligent mason, when the Chaplain makes use of the oil in the consecrating of a new Lodge :—

> '"Behold! how good a thing it is,
>   And how becoming well,
> For brethren, such as masons are,
>   In unity to dwell.
>
> 'Oh! 'tis like ointment on the head,
>   Or dew on Sion hill !
> For then the Lord of Hosts hath said
>   Peace shall be with you still.' "

While sympathy and commiseration have been **extended** towards him by his friend ; the brotherly love of **a mason** regards the confidence reposed in him by his brother as sacred and inviolable, and he will guard it as safely **and as** effectually as he would the grand secret which unites the whole of the fraternity.

‘Nor will his affection for everything that is **just and** amiable, suffer him to listen to tales of slander **and** detraction. The character of his brother is as **dear to** him as his own, because he views him as his own blood ; he will, therefore, defend him when wrongfully accused ; he will support him when belied or misrepresented ; he **will** uphold his integrity when assailed by the shafts of **malig**nity, and will be as anxious for his honor when absent as when present.*

‘The RELIEF which the true mason is ever ready to bestow, is by no means confined to his own brotherhood :—

> “For every one partakes his store,
> And Want goes smiling from his door ; ”

He delights to whisper peace to the troubled mind. To mourn with those who mourn, as well as to rejoice, is to him the highest of all possible enjoyment. Though he rejoices in the prosperity of his brethren, it is not then that he forms his friendships, or establishes his connections ; but when affliction needs his aid, and the oppressed his interference, then the best feelings of his soul are called forth, the warm effusions of his heart flow genuine and sincere, and the inward satisfaction experienced is more than sufficient to repay all he may expend.

‘Many is the time when the hand of benevolence has opened to the relief of the stranger : I have beheld it among masons, in particular, with secret exultation. Cherish this divine principle ; in nothing does man bring

---

‘* The masonic reader will here recognise the points of fellowship which unite the fraternity. The circumspection with which every writer on Masonry must proceed, prevents me being more explicit.

himself nearer to the likeness of his Maker than in this.

'Brethren! we are citizens of the world; each has some useful employment to fulfil, which tends to the general good of the whole. Be faithful in the discharge of these duties, for it is as great an act of real charity as any with which I am acquainted; look at the COMPASS of SACRED TRUTH and honorable dealing, and let us keep our profits within its points. As far as we are enabled so to do, let our dealings be upon the SQUARE, and when we investigate the state of our minds at the conclusion of our day of labor, we shall find ourselves upon the LEVEL with our conscience.

'A quiet conscience is the greatest of all blessings; it is the surest comfort in affliction; it mitigates the severest anguish, teaches us to bear with fortitude the most bitter reprisals, and even if we be incarcerated within the gloom of a dungeon, it is music at midnight to hear its whispering plaudits.

'Who hath clothed the beauteous fabric we inhabit? Who hath mantled all nature with cheerfulness, and offered abundance of rational pleasures for our innocent gratifications? We reply with gratitude—our dear and heavenly Master; when, therefore, for the purpose of innocent recreation, we relax a little from the cares and anxieties of our several states, let prudence be the governor of our social enjoyments.

'The most innocent of delights may by excess be converted into guilty pleasures! Shall the innocence of the white which we wear, and which is a fair semblance of the truth we profess, be contaminated by foul debauchery? Shall intemperance quench the bright spark of Deity within, and, by its profane babbling, afford the enemy an opportunity to acquire our choicest secrets? Forbid it, every principle of honor and justice! Forbid it, spirit of masonry and of love! Let us enjoy our pleasures, then, with circumspection, that no stain be cast upon the sacred craft.'

FAITH, HOPE, AND CHARITY.

AN ODE.

'The greatest of these is charity (Love.)'—PAUL.

'What power above the rest
Of those that o'er the mind in transport breathe,
When life is past, defies the grave's control—
Bursting the chain of darkness and of death—
O'erleaping with extended sway the goal,
   And dwelling with the bless'd?

'FAITH lifts on high the soul,
And o'er the land of promise speeds the view:
Wide spread the happy vales; and pleasures, new
As coming events in th' Eternal might,
Lie sleeping; and the streams of endless light
Around the vision roll.

'Buoyant the spirit waves;
Glad as the forest dove: her trembling wing
Stands on that mountain top, and far away
Sees night throw back her ebon gates, and day
In glory marching forth; and longs to fling
   Aside the chain that binds her down to clay.

'Alas! the world enslaves—
Vainly she longs! the vision breaks—and still
To earth she's fettered—and on earth must stay
Till death breaks every bond, and from the hill
Of parting nature bids her haste away
   To where no fetters bind, or vision'd joys decay.

'HOPE! o'er the path of years,
Hiding its rugged steeps, thy wild flowers blow!
Dim is the way and rough the scene below:
Yet there they hang, and tempt, with gilded show,
The heart to pluck them: but beset with fears,
As thorns that guard the flower of spring they grow,
   And wake within the soul—the pang of added woe.

'Yet flowers thou hast, that bloom
Unfading and unblighted o'er the tomb:
O'er the dim caverns of dismay they rise;
O'er gloomiest shade their seven-fold beauties wave,
And fix the glazing eye when nature dies;
And sparkle in the midnight of the grave.

Swift as the storm from light-winged summer flies,
So fly the horrors of despair, where these
Shine with the gather'd radiance of the skies,
To cheer the heart when earthly glory flees,
   And bid it smile beneath its utmost agonies.

  ' But lofty Faith and pleasing Hope behind
Must stay—earth is their province: o'er the gloom
Of nature they preside; and while the mind
Tracks the lone vale and closes on the tomb,
These aid the wanderer: but when to his home
He springs in glory, back their treasures flow:
He needs no more the vision'd scenes that come
To cheer with breaks of light the clouds below,
   Nor seeks the buds of hope where flowers of pleasure grow.

  ' LOVE then receives the soul—
Love in its brightness—Love in all its fire!
Where round the throne the streams of glory roll,
Love feeds the flame and fans th' eternal pyre.
High as a seraph's loftiest thoughts aspire—
High as the risings of infinity—
Wide as the widest circle of desire—
Wide as the span of boundless Deity
  Its power and reign extend—eternal, vast, and free!

  ' For GOD himself is LOVE!
And MASONRY is love—and heav'ns first joy:
The rapture of celestial hearts above—
The inmost workings of Divinity
Have here their centre. Love, supreme in all,
Rules in th' Eternal mind, and, like a sea,
Fills every lower deep. This moving vale—
Heaven's countless realms—what hath been—or shall be—
  All rise beneath its rule, and owns its sovereignty.

  ' O mightiest, holiest Love!
Mover of God and comforter of heav'n!
All other graces time or grief may move:
Faith may decay, and Hope to death be driv'n;
But steadfast is thy realm! thy power unriv'n
By all that death can do or sin can dare,
To thee the sceptre and the throne are giv'n—
The rule of things that have been, and that are—
   The spring of MASONRY! "THE BRIGHT, THE MORNING
   STAR!"'

In the meantime I continued to practise a little in
medicine, as a chemist and druggist, and obtained a few
shillings weekly. My Masonic Lectures produced me
15

about twenty pounds, which was a very seasonable help
for business was very bad in Accrington, and my pupil
always fluctuated as business was brisk or dull.   But
with all my economy I could scarcely keep my hea
above water.   I had a family of four children, an incom
from every source not exceeding twenty shillings a-week
and with this I had to keep up the appearance and
manners of a gentleman.   My friend Pegg was also a
constant drain upon me, for he was very importunate
for small loans, which he always forgot to return.   I
obtained assistance for him several times, but he appeared
to have sunk into a confirmed mendicant.   I was continually remonstrating with him against his erratic flights,
and also against the neglect of duties, as one of the local
preachers, or Manchester Missionaries, as they were then
called, and having begged two pounds for him in the
month of April, 1830, I sent it to him and told him
it was the last I could obtain.   I warned him that he
was fast losing his friends, and that he might depend
upon it, unless he was more attentive and orderly, the
New Church friends would discard him altogether.   I,
however, had the editing of a small monthly periodical
in Blackburn, and recommended him to the proprietor
as a very useful auxiliary, and he received some small
remuneration for articles sent to that periodical, which
was entitled the ' Blackburn Mirror.' It was after the plan
of the cheap periodicals of the present day. The proprietor was a printer, and it served to employ much
of the leisure time of his apprentices.   Towards the
close of the year 1830, that which I had anticipated
took place, and my eccentric friend lost the best friend
he had, and he sent me the following poetical letter
describing his feelings :—

' This letter is intended for
" *The Blackburn Mirror's* " *Editor* :
You'll find him, as these doggrels forth state,
In *Thomas Hargrave's* Shop, in *Northgate* :
And lest this letter you should back turn
Remember that the town is——BLACKBURN.'

'*Liverpool, Dec. 20th, 1830.*

' DEAR DAVID,
         I sit down to state
That when thou once foretold me, hate
And envy, and abuse, would follow
('Tis pity promises are hollow,
They sound so sweetly on the ear
And raise such charming visions there)
The smallest, slightest dereliction
From the stern path my friends would fix on,
Oh, thou wert right ; their wish is cross'd,
And I have proved it to my cost.

   *   *   *   *   *

Thus all my hopes to mend my lot
In Manchester, have " gone to pot,"
For long e'er this, I well believe
They think I wrote but to deceive,

   *   *   *   *   *

However, there I wrote to-day,
And when I know the certain way
In which they mean to act towards me,
The information this affords me,
Will lead me to decide the question,
Whether their terms will bear digestion.

I am resolved no class of men
From ten, to threescore years and ten,
Shall ever raise themselves to be
Stern censors of my life or me.
My temper would not brook submission
To such a dateless coalition.
And if they think to make me bend,
They quite mistake thy simple friend.
In such a case I in a trice
Would ask thee for a friend's advice,
That is, if thou wilt condescend,
To write a letter to a friend ;
Though 'tis so long since one came out
Thy wish to do so I much doubt ;
But praying that THE LORD may keep us
I am,
        Thy loving friend,
              JOSEPHUS.'

He had taken to smoke tobacco, chew opium, and drink laudanum. Such an acquaintance, therefore, would no longer suit me, and his poetic letter I never answered.　I did not write him again for two years.

On the close of the year 1830 my wife presented me with another son, and now I seriously turned my attention to some means of increasing my income.　I still received but £16 a year from the society of Swedenborgians, although the number of hearers was doubled, and with all my exertions I could not meet my expenses.　I petitioned for an increase of salary ; it was rudely refused ; and the Secretary contended, that with my various avocations I ought to be able to obtain a good living, and hinted, at the same time, that I was saving money, that the Society never contemplated more than paying the rent of the house of the leader.　So I was obliged to struggle on.

About this time I was invited to give a lecture on the Pestalozzian System of Education, at the ' Hull Mechanics' Institution,' they undertaking to pay my expenses.　I went accordingly, and gave my lecture.　I remained over Sunday, and was invited by the Swedenborgians to occupy their pulpit for that Sunday, with which I complied, and then returned home.　I had not been home more than a week when I received a letter from the Secretary of the Society at Hull, inviting me to become their minister.　I was informed that there was an endowment of forty pounds a year, and that I should also receive the whole of the pew rents, that I might follow my profession as a chemist and druggist, and that it was not doubted I should make a good living.　Still I did not want to leave Accrington, where I had many friends, and where I was much respected.　I, however, wrote to the Society, and stated the invitation I had received ; at the same time I offered to remain in Accrington if they would increase my income, but the Secretary was instructed to say they could get assistance from Manchester, and it would not cost them more than sixteen pounds a year, and this was all they could afford.　I thought this hard.　I had, under Providence, labored most successfully ; the numbers were more than doubled, and there were many who were in good circumstances ; but still they were not members, and, therefore, had no voice. I must not omit here to mention, however, that there were two persons, both long since deceased, who assisted me in my struggles, but as they desired their names not to be mentioned, I refrain from particularising them.

I have refrained hitherto from hinting at the severe privations to which Dissenting ministers are often subject ; but I may here mention, that many a time I have gone with a very scanty meal for my day's support. I have often been considered proud and unwilling to mingle with others who might have advanced my interests, but the truth is, my deafness increased upon me, and I became timid of letting this be known, lest I should lose even the little that I had. In performing journeys, where coach hire was allowed, I would often walk the whole distance of thirty or forty miles. Many a time have I walked from Manchester to Huddersfield, and back again, and in three days thus earned as much by the saving of coach hire as I could earn in a week. I had not yet turned my attention to lecturing as a profession ; I had, it is true, gained some few pounds by lecturing on education, but I perceived that the time was come when I must give up my office as a teacher, because I could not hear sufficiently quick. All things considered, I conceived I could not do better than accept the offered situation at Hull ; so I wrote to the Secretary, whose name was Smith, a schoolmaster, and a very learned man (long since dead), and accepted the offer. I had three months' notice to give. I sold the greater part of my furniture, but retained all my chemical and drug apparatus, as well as my stock of chemicals and drugs, and about the middle of the year 1831 left Accrington for Hull. I travelled by coach from Huddersfield, to which place I had walked, to stay a few days with my dearest and most beneficent friend, the late Mr. George Senior, of Dalton, for whom I had several times preached. I arrived at Hull in due course, and my wife and family followed by the canal packet. My whole amount of money was about thirty pounds, the produce of the sale of a great part of my furniture, and to this sum my kind friend, Mr. Senior, added *ten* more, promising to help me further if I needed it. So closed my engagement at Accrington.*

On my arrival at Hull, I was accommodated in the house of one of the trustees, with whom I remained till my family arrived. The name of this gentleman was Caterson. He was a man of about sixty years of age. He had amassed property, and was living on his means. He was among the least intelligent of the Swedenborgians that I had ever met with. His head was large, and there was a considerable share of back brain. His forehead was but moderately developed, both in height and breadth. He had average Benevolence, and very large Love of Approbation. He was the keenest man after money that I had come in contact with, and was always bargaining for one thing or another, and in general made money by his bargains.

He took a pride in using the broad Yorkshire dialect, and he seemed to pursue this plan as an annoyance to, and in opposition of his wife, who was about his own age, but antipodean to him in almost everything else. She was an elegant, highly accomplished, and intellectual lady. He had met with her at the house of one of his rich friends, where she was in the capacity of governess,

* From the Missionary Report of the Manchester Society for 1831, there is the following confirmation of my statement, which I feel constrained to add as a note. 'The chapel' (says one of the missionaries) 'has been considerably improved since my first visit to that place. A large gallery, capable of holding half as many persons as the body of the church, has been added; it is elegantly finished, beautifully painted, and gives the place a most compact and complete appearance. The zeal of the members, and especially the young ones, is as astonishing as it is delightful to witness; and though at present they are without a minister, as the Rev. D. G. G. has removed to Hull, the attendance is good, all the seats are let.' 'To this it may be added,' says the Editor of the 'Intellectual Repository,' 'that Mr. A. Haworth, brother of the late Mr. G. Haworth, so long the much respected leader of this society, has since gone to settle there in that capacity, which, we trust, will be attended with happy results.'

had proposed and been accepted by her, and they were married. There was no offspring. When first introduced to her by Mr. C. himself, his remark was, 'That's my missis. She can talk to you in your own style, but I care nowght about fine words. Now, Missis, let's have tea !' Of course, I made no observation on this rude speech, but I thought that the lady must have felt his coarseness keenly.

I remained in this gentleman's house about a week, and explained to him what my intentions were. I told him that a portion of my goods were on the way, but that I should want to fit up a small shop in some neighborhood where there was a good population. I found him very useful to me, both in selecting my house, and also in the purchase of such articles as I wanted for my shop. By his keenness in bargaining, he doubtlessly saved me some money ; but I think we went to every broker's shop in the town before he determined what should be purchased, and I was quite passive in his hands. I remember at one shop I saw a set of twelve stone ointment jars, which I was desirous of purchasing, and I asked the price. 'Twelve shillings,' was the reply.

Mr. C.—'They are worth nowght o'th' sort.'

Broker.—'Why, they are stone, and cost not less than double the money.'

Mr. C.—'What dos't matter what they cost, mon? it's what they're worth noo. If you like to send 'em to my house, I'll gi' ye six shillings for 'em, and not a penny more.'

Broker.—'Can't do it, Mr. Caterson.' (The broker seemed to know him well.)

Mr. C.—'O, vera well ! There's plenty o' jars to be had.' [To me—'Come along.']

When we had left the shop Mr. C. said to me, 'He'll send 'em, I ha' no doot.' And, sure enough, on our arrival at Mr. C.'s house, there they were. And in the various purchases he made for me he seldom gave more than one half of the amount that was asked. There was not a place of business that we went to but Mr. Caterson seemed to be well known.

It has since occurred to me that the shop-keepers fought Mr. C. with his own weapons—Secretiveness and Acquisitiveness. They asked double the value of their goods, conscious that he would meet them by proposing one half, and thus they obtained in reality as much as they were honestly worth. The weakness of Mr. Caterson's reflecting faculties prevented him considering this. Although a professor of religion, Mr. Caterson was essentially a man of the world. A keen lover and admirer of himself and his own cleverness, he, nevertheless, appeared to defer to almost every one else ; for he loved to hear himself called a good-natured man, and his subserviency was notorious.

I have somewhere read, that the great secret of knowledge of the world consists in a subserviency to the will of others, and the primary nature of this attention is a mechanical and watchful perception of our own interest. It is not an art that requires a long course of study, the difficulty is in putting oneself apprentice to it. It does not surely imply a very laborious or profound inquiry into the distinctions of truth and falsehood to be able to assent to whatever one hears, nor any great refinement of feeling to approve of whatever has custom, interest, or power on its side. The only question is—WHO IS WILLING TO DO IT ? Those are slow to wear the livery of the world who have any independent resources of their own. It is not that the philosopher, or the man of genius, does not see and know all this—that he is not constantly and forcibly reminded of it, by his own failure, or the success of others—but he cannot stoop to practise it. He has a different scale of excellence and mould of ambition, which have nothing in common with current maxims and time-serving calculations. He cannot bring himself to give up his best grounded convictions to a rich blockhead, or his conscientious principles to a knave, and in doing this consists the chief knowledge of the world.

Mr. Caterson was a man in whom Secretiveness, Acquisitiveness, and Love of Approbation predominated, and the latter feeling prevented, in a great degree, his extreme selfishness from being too glaringly exhibited. But he was a firm believer in the worldly maxim, 'Every man has a right to do the best he can for himself,' and he practised what he believed most industriously.

Secretiveness and Acquisitiveness are perhaps as much, or even more, in the ascendant now, than in the time of which I am writing. That clever and very useful satirist, 'Mr. Punch,' observes : ' The tendency of tradesmen to speak by the card, is made manifest by the enormous extent to which goods in the present day are ticketed. At one establishment articles are being "given away"; whilst at the next door the proprietors are undergoing the daily torment of an "alarming sacrifice"; one would imagine self-immolation was a popular pastime with the tradesmen of London. Nearly every window announces the determination of the proprietor, "to sell considerably under prime cost"; from which it would seem that keeping a shop was a piece of disinterestedness, by which one man determines to victimise himself, and occasionally a few creditors, for the benefit of the public in general. These sacrifices, however, do not seem to be wholly without their reward, for the tradesmen who resort to them very frequently prosper, in spite of their recklessness of their own interests. Thus, while the tickets in the window bespeak a "ruinous sacrifice"; the premises themselves display "a splendid enlargement"; and when sacrifices are to be performed, the temples are often decorated in a style of gorgeous magnificence. That sacrifices are made, there can be no doubt, but it is another question who are the victims.'

I should not so freely have given my opinion upon Mr. Caterson, but he has long since passed from the world, and his person and his money-making was the universal theme, not only of the town of Hull, but of miles around it. But I now return to myself.

My family having arrived, and my little business being arranged, I entered upon the duties of my office, as minister of the Swedenborgian chapel at Hull.

The chapel was a large one, seated for about nine hundred or a thousand people. The congregation did not consist of more than twenty, so that for the time being there was but a small prospect for a man with a family of five children. However, I commenced my duties, and was gathering together a few strangers, when I thought it would be best at once to call a meeting of the trustees, that I might secure the income of £40, and which I had been given to understand belonged to the minister absolutely. I did so, but when the trustees had assembled, I found that there were outstanding debts incurred by processes of law, which the trustees were desirous of liquidating before the minister's salary could be paid, and the payment of these debts would take some years. This was a serious blow to me. I had depended upon the salary, and thought that with attention I might raise enough to pay the rent of my house by pew rents from the chapel, but this at the end of the quarter I found myself incapable of doing, for the whole amount of my pew rents was but two pounds ten shillings. My situation was now in the highest degree painful. I was comparatively a stranger in the town, with a wife and a family of five young children. Although I had commenced business in my profession as a chemist, my entire receipts for the whole quarter had not been more than five pounds, and this was at once absorbed in the payment of rent. I had, when I arrived in Hull, enough money to support my family for three months, but not a shilling more, and I was entering upon a second quarter with but the amount of the before-mentioned pew rents, viz., fifty shillings. My kind friend Mr. George Senior had given me, as already stated, ten pounds, and had expressly enjoined me to write to him at the end of the quarter, and make a statement of my affairs, so I thought I would do so, as I had not another friend in the world to whom I ould apply, and want was absolutely staring me in the face. Previous to doing this, however, I thought it was my duty to make the people who composed the congregation acquainted with my circumstances ; reminding them of the terms of my agreement, namely, that I was to receive £40 a year, besides the pew rents. I did so : but the trustees contended the Society had no right to make such an agreement without first consulting them, and they were determined that no salary should be given until the debts were all paid.

There was one family, of two brothers and a sister, who felt deeply for my situation, and they assured me they would do all in their power to assist me, and they kept their word. Their name was Middlemist. I think they were the most amiable and united family I ever knew. They were at that time all unmarried, and carrying on business as dyers. The elder, Mr. David, has since married, but is now a widower. I cannot speak in terms too high of the kindness I received from them ; they were the means of supporting me in my greatest extremity ; they *were*, and the survivors *are* to this day, my warmest friends. One of this family has gone to the eternal world, and his obituary records that his little property was disposed of for the furtherance of that cause which he had so much at heart. The brother and sister live, and their truly christian conduct is known and admired, not merely among the community of Swedenborgians, but by the whole inhabitants of the town in which they have during their whole lives been residents. 'May they live longer than I have time to tell their years, ever beloved and loving ! '

While my distress in Hull was at its extreme point, when five shillings a week composed the whole of my available means of support—for, as I before said, the whole proceeds of my shop did but afford enough to pay my rent—news arrived of the departure to the spiritual world of the Rev. J. Clowes, M.A., Rector of St. John's Church, Manchester. He was considered, and with justice,

as the most eminent man among the Swedenborgians, and
I was requested to deliver a funeral sermon on the day
of the interment of his mortal remains. I consented conditionally that the Society should make the subject known
to the town; and that the discourse, besides a brief
memoir of Mr. Clowes, should give the Swedenborgian
doctrine of the 'resurrection' and the 'life after death.'
Accordingly the town was placarded, and on the appointed
evening the chapel was, for the first time since my ministry,
filled with an attentive audience.

I first took a view of the life and labors of Mr. Clowes
as a minister of the gospel, and of the catholicity of
spirit in which all his duties were performed. I sum-
med up that part of my discourse, as far as I can
remember, in nearly the following words :—

'I look upon the late Mr. Clowes as an especial
instrument raised up, by the Divine Providence of the
Lord, for the guidance and support of his infant church.
Inflexibly just, his discourses were levelled at every false
doctrine, whether existing in the national church of England, or among the various sects which had separated
from it : but one distinguishing feature in his writings
was the heavenly spirit in which they were expressed.
While he never in the slightest degree compromised the
truth, Christian love, benevolence, meekness, and humility
pervaded everything which passed from his pen. The
reader is insensibly brought into communion with the
author. He had the art of stating the most unpalatable
truths in the most winning language, and the most
determined of his opponents could not refrain from
expressing their admiration at the christian temper with
which he administered his reproofs. I look upon Clowes
in much the same light as Dr. Doddridge viewed Fleet-
wood, "as the silver-tongued champion of Divine truth,"
remarkable amidst the light of his subject for ease and
propriety of expression.'

Besides translations of many of Swedenborg's Works,
Mr. Clowes was a very voluminous author himself. One

REV. J. . . Y . . A. M., OF MAN . . . . .

Mr. Clowes was a very voluminous author himself. One

LATE REV. J. CLOWES, A. M., OF MANCHESTER.

[PAGE 236.

of the most interesting of his works was a 'Treatise on Christian Temper.' He also translated the four gospels, which he illustrated by many original notes, besides a running commentary of extracts from the writings of Swedenborg. The translations were executed with the closest fidelity to the original, and he gave a brief exposition of the spiritual sense throughout.

Like the celebrated Watts, he did not disdain, amidst his more learned avocations, to devote a portion of his time to the guidance and instruction of the young. They have been largely counselled, edified, and amused by his prolific pen. When we behold a man of high literary acquirements and deep erudition, stooping from his eminence to the familiar level of children, we feel assured that he has received the truths of the kingdom of heaven in the spirit of a little child, and we think ourselves justified in affirming that he will assuredly sit down therein.*

· * The following tribute to the memory of Mr. Clowes appeared in 'The Times' of June 4, 1831, and the 'Manchester Courier' of the same date.

TIMES.—'Died on the 29th ult., at Warwick, in his eighty-eighth year, the Rev. John Clowes, formerly Fellow of Trinity College, Cambridge, and Rector of St. John's Church, Manchester, to which he was appointed on its consecration, and which he continued to hold during the long period of *sixty-two* years. Having been incapacited during the latter period of his life, by some of the infirmities attendant upon old age, from the public performance of his professional duties, the powers of his mind, which continued clear and vigorous, were almost to the last devoted to the study and elucidation of the Holy Scriptures ; and his affectionate and anxious thoughts were still peculiarly excited towards those who had constituted his own flock, to whom he had been an indefatigable and beloved pastor, and whom he hoped to recognise again hereafter. His affections, however, were ever alive towards all who came within the sphere of his usefulness ; and it would have been difficult for any one to resist the influence of that goodness which showed itself in all he did, or said, or looked ; and to have been with him, even for a little while, without being impressed with a sense of the loveliness of Christian principle, as it was exemplified in him. He was a scholar—an elegant and a sound one ; but he felt that the highest triumph of human learning or wisdom is, when they are subservient to the establishment of those everlasting truths by which man lives for ever. In simplicity of heart, in unity of purpose, in the abandonment of every selfish consideration, in the unclouded and playful cheerfulness of a pure and benevolent mind, in the ornament of a meek and quiet spirit, in the beauty and happiness of

The style of the late Mr. Clowes was not elegant, but it was simple and dignified ; without meretricious genuine holiness, he truly adorned the doctrine of God his Saviour in all things; and being tried by long suffering, he found that that in which he trusted was sufficient for him in all circumstances, and unto the end. Those who did not know him may believe this tribute to be the offspring of partial friendship and affection; but the many who did, will feel how inefficient must be the attempt rightly to commemorate his admirable and truly Christian excellencies.'

'MANCHESTER COURIER.'—'Died at Warwick, where he had resided some years on account of his health, May 29th, in the eighty-eighth year of his age, the Rev. John Clowes, Rector of St. John's Church, Manchester, and formerly Fellow of Trinity College, Cambridge.

'In zeal, in tenderness, in piety, in wisdom, in activity, in usefulness—as a friend, a counsellor, a pastor, a spiritual father, and an exemplary pattern of holy life—his superior was not to be found; it would be difficult to name his equal. He was a scholar, a philosopher, a finished gentleman, a luminous writer, an impressive preacher, a practical Christian divine. In him the elements of an original happy nature were sweetly blended, tempered, and richly adorned by an abundant portion of the spirit of divine grace; holiness had attained great heights; first principles had gone on to perfection.

'It is not the object of this brief notice to dwell on the details of a combination rich in varied graces; but in recording the excellence of this venerable man, and truly apostolic minister, it may be allowed to mark, as prominent features of a character in which all was lovely, his child-like simplicity, his singleness of heart, the elevation of his devotion, the cheerfulness of his piety, the beauty of his holiness, the charity of his zeal, his bright imagination, his lively fancy, the ease of his seriousness, the innocence of his mirth, the purity of his exuberant joy. He was admirable in all the faculties of an enlightened mind; but the charm by which he won and ruled the hearts of all, was that grace in man which is the nearest image on earth of a holy and merciful God, the boundless benevolence of a truly catholic spirit. Of Mr. Clowes it may be justly said, "his wisdom was a loving spirit"; of his virtue, "the memorial is immortal, because it is known with God and with men ; when it was present, men took example at it, and when it is gone they desire it ; it weareth a crown and triumpheth for ever, having gotten the victory, striving for undefiled rewards."

'This admirable person enjoyed, in a singular degree through life, the respect and affection of all by whom he was known; but in an especial manner the love and veneration of his own flock, over which he was, by God's providence, the shepherd, for the very unusual term of sixty-two years.'

I deem it expedient to add the following brief outline of Mr. Clowes's life, which I extract also from the 'Manchester Courier' of June 11, 1831, and was partly embodied in my sermon.

'The late Rev. John Clowes was born in Manchester, October 20, 1743 (*Old Style*). He was the fourth son of Joseph Clowes, Esq., a barrister (who for many years practised in this town and its neighborhood), ornament, it carries its beauty in its force and the grandeur of his subject. We look in vain for the pas-

and of Katherine, the daughter of a respectable clergyman of the name of Edwards, who was rector of Llanbedar, near Ruthin, in Wales. His excellent mother died when he was about eight years old; but even at that tender age her piety and example had made a deep impression on his mind, and up to a very late period of his life he had a grateful remembrance of the debt which he owed to her constant care and solicitude, in implanting and cultivating every sweet and gentle affection; and to his father, also, for following up, by an admirable course of Christian education, the instruction which she had so happily begun.

'He was educated at the Grammar School of Salford, and at the age of eighteen, his father was persuaded to send him to Cambridge, though not without much entreaty, as he had already an elder son, Richard, at that university. He was entered a pensioner of Trinity College, and there are sufficient reasons for concluding that he pursued his academical studies with the perseverance and ability which distinguished all that he undertook in after life; for in the year 1766, when he took his degree, he was the eighth wrangler of the tripos paper, proving that he was no ordinary proficient in mathematical attainments; and that he was equally distinguished as a classical scholar is shown by his gaining one of the two prizes given by the members of the University to the Middle Bachelors, for the best dissertations in Latin prose; and again the following year, when he was Senior Bachelor, the first prize for a similar dissertation. About this time he was elected a Fellow of his College, had many private pupils, and was, besides, so highly thought of, that it was not surprising that he should have looked forward with ambitious hopes to some station of eminence in the sacred profession which he had chosen. In the midst of this career of worldly distinction, the church of St. John, then building at the sole expense of the late Edward Byrom, Esq., was offered him by the patron; but he actually felt hurt, to use his own words, "at the idea of his being expected to accept an appointment so unequal to his prospects and his wishes." A severe illness, however, which completely broke down his health, and reduced him to the necessity of giving up all study, brought him into what he thought a happy state of humiliation before God; so that upon its being again offered him by Mr. Byrom, when it was nearly ready for consecration, "he accepted it with cheerfulness as a boon of Providence intended for the improvement and security of his eternal good"; and he continued its rector, refusing more than one offer of high preferment in the Church, for the term of sixty-two years. In the spring of the year 1773, he became acquainted with the Theological writings of Emanuel Swedenborg; they were put into his hands by the late Mr. Haughton, of Liverpool, a gentleman of great talents and learning, who was himself an admirer of the pure and elevated system of religion which they embrace. The delight, he said, produced in his mind by the first perusal of the work entitled, "Vera Christiana Religio," no language could fully express. In proceeding from the chapter on the Creator and on Creation, to the succeeding chapter on the Redeemer and on Redemption; on the Divine Trinity, the Sacred Scripture or Word of God, on the Decalogue, on sionate exclamation, or the glowing climax : but we find instead, noble thoughts, plain yet sublime language, beautiful but simple illustrations, and the mild spirit of Christianity.   Such was Mr. Clowes, who passed a long

Faith, Charity, Freewill, on Repentance, Reformation, and Regeneration, on Imputation, on Baptism, the Holy Supper, the Consummation of the Age, and the Advent of the Lord, it seemed as if a continual blaze of new and recreating light had been poured forth on the delighted understanding, opening it to the contemplation of the most sublime mysteries of wisdom in a manner and a degree, and with a force of satisfactory evidence, which it had never known before! From that hour he dedicated all the energies of his powerful mind to the publication of these doctrines, both in the pulpit and by the press. For many years he was employed in translating them from the original Latin; and as eac' volume was translated, it was printed by a society established in this town under his auspices.   But his literary labors were not confined to translations. Besides several volumes of sermons he published at different times many other works on subjects connected with religion and philosophy, and all of them agreeing with the profound and truly catholic views of the author in whose sentiments he, to the last, entirely acquiesced.

'As a minister of religion, no man was ever more profoundly revered, or more affectionately beloved, than he was by his flock. In his public life, they saw and felt that his whole heart, and all his faculties, were devoted to their eternal welfare ; while in his private life they had daily before their eyes a practical illustration of the pure, the heavenly precepts which he taught. His thoughts seemed continually employed in endeavoring to contribute, by the sacrifice of himself, to the happiness and comfort of others. Unwearied in laboring by every possible way for their good, his whole heart seemed enwrapt in this, as if it had been the single object of his life, to which his own ease and comfort were to be at all times cheerfully sacrificed. And in this manner did he cherish the love of God within his heart, by preferring, on every occasion, his neighbor to himself. To commemorate the virtues which adorned his life, and to mark their sense of the signal benefits which they had derived from his ministry, the members of his congregation, when he had been fifty years their pastor, erected in his church a tablet, beautifully sculptured in bas-relief, by Flaxman, in which he is represented as instructing the three generations of one family in those lessons of wisdom which he was accustomed to deliver, with an affectionate earnestness and eloquence peculiarly his own. From the year 1823, his increasing infirmities of body compelled him to give up his public duties; and from that time till within a few months of his decease, he was fully occupied in writing and dictating fresh works explanatory of the pure doctrines of Christianity as they are unfolded in the Holy Scriptures. During the latter years of his life he resided wholly at Warwick; and there, blessing to the last moment of consciousness, those around him, and blessed by all those who came within the circle of his affections, he departed this life on the 29th May, 1831, in the 88th year of his age.'

life in works of charity, piety, and use, and who now reaps his reward in his Father's house.

'"Now! reaps his reward," methinks I hear some of you exclaim—"must he not wait for this till the resurrection of the just at the last day."

'The last day with him has past. "Time with him is now no more." Yes, *he now reaps the reward of his doings*, and to show how this is, I must attempt an explanation of the true apostolic doctrine of the resurrection as it appears to me to be laid down in the writings of the great apostle of the Gentiles. Our friend, being *absent from the body, is present with the Lord.*' I then proceeded to give an illustration of 1 Cor. xv., which I have since embodied in No. 2 of the "Glasgow Series of Christian Tracts," and which has had a large circulation.

This discourse was well received, and the chapel was much better attended, but no more pews were taken ; and I found that I could not exist much longer without help.

While I was hesitating whether I should again avail myself of the proffered aid of my kind friend Mr. Senior, of Dalton, who had before so generously assisted me on my removal from Accrington, I was surprised by a sudden visit from my brother. He had been on a mission to Newcastle-on-Tyne, where a disagreement had arisen between the Minister and the Society of the Swedenborgians in that town, and his object was to ascertain my condition. 'I frankly told him all.' Upon which he stated he was commissioned by the Society at Newcastle-on-Tyne, to offer me a salary of £52 per annum, and with liberty to practise in my profession. Here was a visible interposition of the Divine Providence. At his (my brother's) arrival, I was not only in great straits, but, comparatively speaking, in absolute want, and from this want, a salary of £52 would raise me to comparative affluence. But my great difficulty was—how to remove my family. There were no railways then, and the expense of conveying seven persons by coach, even though five of them were children, was no trifle to me. My brother recommended me at once to proceed to

16

Newcastle, and although far from wealthy himself, he furnished me with the means to pay my own expenses. But previous to my departure, I wrote to my friend, Mr. George Senior, and stated the circumstances in which I was unhappily placed, with the visible interposition of Providence in my behalf; and told him of my determination at once to proceed to Newcastle. I received an almost immediate reply, and a rather severe rebuke for not making my state known to him. He fully concurred in the propriety of my removal, and sent me the means of paying my liabilities, and also enough to defray the travelling charges of my family.

Here was a further visible Providence in my behalf. How wonderfully had I been supported.—In the deepest vicissitudes of my life, there has been always an unseen hand raised to support me. I were the veriest ingrate should I refuse to acknowledge not only a general but a particular Providence, and that Providence, I shall have it further in my power to illustrate as my narrative progresses. 'Trust in the Lord, and do good; so shalt thou dwell in the land, and verily thou shalt be fed.'

Well, I proceeded to Newcastle, and for a time was accommodated in the house of the late Mr. Robert Coulson, where I remained for about a fortnight or three weeks, until my family arrived. This gentleman was collector of excise, and living in good style. He was very benevolent, and paid a large sum annually towards the support of the Swedenborgian church. He was a fine looking man, nearly six feet high, with a person proportionably stout. He had a large head—with a forehead moderately broad and deep, but very high in the coronal region. He was married, but without family. From him I learned the state of the church, which, in consequence of the disagreement with the minister, I found to be very limited in number; and, indeed, the first Sunday that I officiated there were not more than thirty persons present. However, my engagement was confirmed by this gentleman, and from him I was to receive my salary.

It was thought desirable that I should commence my ministry with a course of doctrinal lectures, so I drew up a series of subjects and entered upon their delivery ; and though I still had not more than thirty hearers in the morning (and very frequently less), in the evening the chapel was well filled : it would accommodate between four and five hundred.

My situation was rather delicate and peculiar, for the minister with whom the Society had disagreed was resident in the town, and had engaged a large hall, and secured a congregation quite equal in number to the original Society ; and he also resorted to the plan of Sunday evening lectures, and was very successful. He had one of the most sonorous and beautiful voices (though somewhat monotonous) I had ever heard, and his appearance in the pulpit was dignified and attractive. Of myself I could not perhaps speak with more correctness than by saying, in the words of an apostle—' My bodily presence is weak ' ; and if ' my speech ' was not ' contemptible,' it was certainly not equal to that of the gentleman who had preceded me, and I saw that I should have a hard struggle to maintain my ground. I was emulous, however, and if my Self-esteem was but feebly developed at this time, I had no small share of Love of Approbation, so I determined ' I would push with side and shoulder,' and not interfere, in any sense of the word, with my predecessor, for whom, notwithstanding all that I had heard, I entertained and do still entertain a sincere respect.

Well, my family arrived, and also my chemical and drug fixtures, and there being a small shop in the vicinity to let, I took it, together with apartments, and again entered upon my profession. My rent was low, not more than that of a small house, and as I had a certain but small income from the Swedenborgian Society, and had also an excellent economist in the person of my wife, I did not fear but I should be able to balance my affairs at the end of the year.

Scarcely had I settled in the town, than there arose a

violent controversy between the Roman Catholics and the Protestants, on the subject of Transubstantiation. The Roman Catholics had for their champion a young surgeon of the name of Larkin. It appears that an agent of the Reformation Society had been lecturing in Newcastle against the Romish doctrine of transubstantiation, and in answer to this gentleman, Mr. Larkin had published a very confident reply, maintaining the Romish doctrine, and which reply he concluded by a challenge to the Protestant community in the following words :—' If any Protestant think otherwise, and will pick up the gauntlet of defiance which I here fling down (not in the spirit of bravado, but of calm confidence in the truth of my cause), and will answer me in a candid, open, fair, and manly way, subscribing his name to his production (for to anonymous scurrility I shall not deign to reply), he shall have my thanks and my applause.'

To this challenge my Swedenborgian friends wished me to reply, and my friend Mr. Coulson promised to bear me scatheless with the printer.

So I acceded to their wishes, but was anxious first to have a view of my opponent, or rather of the challenger— for phrenology still was with me a *sine qua non*, though I kept my opinion on this matter to myself, and in desiring to see Mr. Larkin, I thought I should be better able to give an effective answer. At this time the country was agitated through its whole extent with meetings for Reform, and Mr. Larkin was a prominent member of the council of the 'Northern Political Union.' I was acquainted with a member of the council, and by him obtained an introduction to one of their meetings, and there saw and noted Mr. Larkin. His age may have been about twenty-three or twenty-four; he was stoutly built, and about five feet nine inches high, with a large round head—his eyebrows were thick and prominent. The forehead was broad but shallow, he had a very prominent eye, and there was an astonishingly large protuberance both behind and above the ears. There seemed to me to be a great amount of back brain. The posterior part of the vertex was amazingly elevated, and so too were the portions adjoining. Never do I remember to have seen a more complete exhibition of pride, and vanity, and self-conceit than was brought before me in the person of this young man. Here was a noble phrenological study for me. His command of words was amazing, and the bitterness of his invectives fully illustrated his large eye and his well defined Combativeness, Destructiveness, and Wit. He spoke while I was present, and he poured forth his abuse upon Queen Adelaide, whom he considered as the grand obstacle in the way of reform, in language which quite terrified me; I felt assured that what he uttered against that illustrious lady amounted to treason in the eye of the law; from such a council I was glad to effect my escape. I have since read the description which Dr. Gall has given of the man under the influence of intense Self-esteem, and Mr. Larkin might have sat for the portrait, so truly does it delineate him, and sure I am that those who knew Mr. L. in the years' 1831-2, will acknowledge that it would be impossible to describe him more accurately.

'See,' says Dr. Gall, 'the proud man bridle up, straighten himself, and carry his head high. See how he carries his arms forward to the attitude of command; sometimes admiring himself he raises them; then throwing from his high elevation a look of contempt on all that surrounds him, he crosses them on his breast; or, gesticulating with his right, he supports the palm of his left on his side, with the elbow advanced. Ask this man to interest himself in your behalf with the king; he will protect you with a look; he will carry one of his hands on his breast, in testimony of his powerful influence; he will straighten himself on the point of his toes, and a gracious movement of the head directed upward and backward will say to you—" *Leave it to me!* " The more profound the feeling of pride is, the more audaciously does the man swell and erect himself, the more does the look which is thrown about him express **self-sufficiency** and contempt—the more space does he **pass** over in his solemn walk. The man who has a **consciousness** of his own merit, of his own talents, **likewise** raises his head with dignity, straightening the **whole** body.'

Such was the gentleman with whom I had to contend. I saw at once the style in which it was necessary to reply to him. Still I did not make my own friends aware of the fact that I was a student of phrenology, for I was afraid to avow this, and although I had now been a close observer of the form of the head for several years, I did not venture to offer an opinion publicly, but I had, from my study of the works of Dr. Spurzheim, and from numerous portraits which I had collected, stronger and stronger proofs of the truth of the science.

I set to work on my reply, and in the course of a month it was published, and a copy of it sent to Mr. Larkin, and to the President of the Reformation Society, William Chapman, Esq. I also sent a copy to the then Bishop of Durham, from whom I received a letter of thanks and warm approval. Mr. Larkin could not have had time to digest my reply, before he received two others, and the streets of the town were, besides, placarded with replies, printed on broad sheets.

I sent a copy of my reply to the Swedenborgian Reviewer ; he pronounced my letter 'creditable to my talents'; but condemned the style in which it was written. I repeat that I chose the style which, from my phrenological knowledge, I thought would tell most effectively on the challenger ; I answered him ' according to his folly,' and I was informed by a friend who was intimate with him (the same who had introduced me to the Council of the Northern Political Union) that the Swedenborgian's reply was to him the most annoying, and the one which he had the greatest difficulty of meeting.

Although Mr. Larkin had promised his ' thanks and

applause' to such as would answer him in a fair and candid way, yet no sooner did the various replies appear, than he showed the faith to be kept with heretics by insolence and derision.

A writer who assumed the signature of 'Junius' noticed this breach of faith by the publication of a placard, from which I make the following extract: he also addressed his letter to the President of the Reformation Society; W. Chapman, Esq :—' *Ridenda imbecillorum superbiloquentia.*'* 'Mr. Larkin, in concluding his pamphlet on Transubstantiation, says : "If any Protestant," etc. [See the passage quoted just above.] 'This, sir, appears to be very candid, and is another evidence of the easy manner in which Papists keep faith with heretics, if we compare it with a beautiful advertisement of his in the " Newcastle Courant," of Sept. 24th, in which we find that the thanks and applause which were promised, are paid by calling the answers which have appeared, "Literary Abortions," and the writers of them "*Mice.*" He, however, announces his intention to answer Mr. Armstrong's letter, and we may therefore conclude that the others are abortions, because they are beyond the skill of this learned *Accoucheur !*

'If Mr. Larkin's insufferable vanity, or pot-house fervency, has led him to adopt Virgil's description of the ardor of Ascanius in the chase, as his motto, and he really ' desires a boar or a lion to descend from the mountain' as his antagonist, it must be from a fatal miscalculation of his own powers, of which persons in a state of intoxication are sometimes guilty. When he becomes sober, (should such an event ever take place) he may, perhaps, discover that even *mice* have very sharp teeth, and although they are but diminutive animals, they have frequently been very destructive to the labors of literary giants, such as he affects to be ; and often effect what neither "*boar* " or "*lion* " will even attempt. Ascanius warmed by the chase might wish to meet with such game ;

* It is riduculous for mean persons to boast of great things.

but where is the resemblance between him and Mr. Larkin ? Yet had the son of "the pious Æneas" been as destitute of bodily strength and dexterity as Mr. Larkin of mental capacity, the gratification of his desire might have been as fatal to his life as Mr. Larkin's combat with the *Mice* is likely to be to his polemical fame, in the esteem of every one who knows what argument means. The *Mice* have already pierced through all the flimsy wrappings in which he attempted to enclose his idol, and have exposed the object of his idolatry in its pristine nakedness—a mere piece of bread.

'How then has this Popish champion (he has none of the honor of chivalry about him) kept his promise? Has not Mr. GOYDER answered him, in a candid, open, fair, and manly way, subscribing his name? Has not Mr. GRANT done the same? Has not Mr. HALES done so too? Where are the promised thanks and applause? Why, sir, what he cannot answer—and, if he has any understanding, what he *knows* he cannot answer—he calls "*abortions*," and promises to answer him who is at a distance; nothing will serve this valiant polemic for an antagonist, but—

"Spumantimque dari pecori inter inertia votis
Optat aprum aut fulvum des cendere monte leonem."
Æn. iv., 158-9.'*

This letter drew forth some angry comments from Mr. Larkin, and several sneers on me, whom he considered as its author; and he also attacked Swedenborg as a 'POOR DREAMER.' Although I wished to have nothing further to say to such a defamer, whose chief quality appeared to be through the medium of the most foul language to cover his opponents with mud and filth, I was yet urged to write another pamphlet; and, in this,

* 'Impatiently he views the feeble prey,
Wishing some nobler beast to cross his way;
And rather would the tusky boar attend,
Or see the tawny lion downward bend.' DRYDEN.
Althoug---

I drew a parallel between the writings of Swedenborg and the Romish champions whom he adduced.

The controversy ended with this letter, but it brought me into considerable notice, and my congregation became more numerous, and several new members were added. I was also invited to speak occasionally at public meetings, and mingled freely with several of the most respectable inhabitants of the town. I had the pleasure of forming an intimacy with the late Rev. Mr. Turner, by whom I was introduced to the Literary and Philosophical Society of Newcastle, who did me the honor to elect me a member of their body.

There seemed every probability that I should at length find a home in Newcastle.

I still had a fondness for teaching, although my deafness had so far increased that I could not venture upon it as a means of income. But, as I had much time on my hands, and a large room at the back of my shop which was unoccupied, I thought I would collect the children of the members in the evening, and give them religious and scientific instruction, so far as I could, upon the principles of Pestalozzi.

My little business as a chemist occupied me principally from about ten in the morning till six in the evening, after which I was at leisure. The observation of my Westhoughten friend about my 'Sarmunt Book' had not been forgotten; while at Newcastle, I did not write my discourses, but penned a few notes, and with them went into the pulpit; so I did not then spend much time in writing, and though I read extensively, still I could do this without neglecting my business. I had, therefore, always leisure in the evening for the instruction of the children, and I thought I would adopt, as the most efficient and solid, though slow, method of communicating knowledge—the system of Pestalozzi. So I mentioned to the members of the Society my willingness to give gratuitous instruction to the children in the evening. They availed themselves of the offer, and the methods pursued were so attractive to the children, and they advanced so solidly in their various studies, that my pupils often extended to the parents themselves, in consequence of the reports made to them by the children. There was no school of the kind in Newcastle, and it was at length seriously debated by my Swedenborgian friends, whether a day school, conducted upon Pestalozzian principles, would not prove eminently beneficial both to the town at large and to our little community. Of course I could not undertake the conduct of such a school. My daily duties in my profession and in my studies precluded that, and then again my deafness was an insuperable barrier. I did not find my deafness make much against me in my evening tuition; I knew all my pupils, and they knew me, and I always accustomed them to speak in audible and bold tones, but the general public, I conceived, would never tolerate a deaf schoolmaster.

The members of my Society, however, determined to try the system I had introduced. There were funds at the disposal of the Swedenborgian Conference for the education of children, but it was then a rule that no grant could be made until a school had been in existence twelve months, with some probability of its being permanent. The members themselves subscribed liberally, and many parents promised to send their children; so a large school room was taken and a master advertised for, and we fortunately obtained a man every way qualified for the situation. This gentleman's name was *Field*. It is true he was but imperfectly acquainted with the plans pursued by Pestalozzi, but he was willing to adopt them, and I had already trained many of the boys who were to be among his first pupils; so the school was opened, and very soon in a flourishing condition.

Three out of my five children were among its pupils. The school was proceeding very satisfactorily, when my friend Dr. Crook visited the town with the view of giving lectures on the '*Memory, Imagination, and General Powers of the Mind*'; that is, in one word, on *Mnemonics*.

I hailed his arrival with pleasure, anticipating that when he had concluded his course, he would, as he had done at Bristol, give another course on Phrenology. So I introduced him to the Literary and Philosophical Society, and they granted him the use of their large and handsome theatre to deliver his lectures in. He selected his pupils for the introductory lecture from various schools, but chose my daughter from the Pestalozzian school as his botanical pupil. He gave two free lectures, which were attended by the *elite* of the town, and which created the most unbounded astonishment at the powers of memory exhibited by the pupils after only three days' training. He then announced three lectures, the admission to which was *one guinea*, and so great was the excitement which the introductory lecture had produced, that no less than 500 tickets were sold. The charm was dissolved ! The public were offended at the simplicity of the system, and considered themselves over-reached—some said plundered. One of the influential members of the Society, with whom I had interceded for the use of the Philosophical Society's lecture room, observed to me—' Ah, Mr. G——, your friend Dr. Crook, by the aid of your lovely little girl, has cozened us out of *five hundred guineas.*'

And yet I could not see in what the doctor had really offended. He instructed a class of children whom he trained in three days. He exhibited those children—he amazed his audience by their comparatively wonderful powers of memory. He then informed them, that he would impart his art to them for the sum of *one guinea* ; they gave their guineas freely ; he fulfilled his contract—wherein then was he to blame ? He set a high price, it is true, upon his knowledge, but no one was compelled to purchase that knowledge—it was their own act. He profited, and left the town a richer man by five hundred guineas than he entered it. I wanted him to give a course of lectures on Phrenology—' *Not now—not now,*' said he—' *it would not take.*' So he left the town, not, however, without making my little girl a handsome present. In truth, her appearance at the lecture charmed every one who beheld her. She was one of the most lovely children my eyes had ever rested upon, and she grew up an equally lovely woman. Dear dear girl, I fear I shall never again behold her ; she is, alas ! now a widow in a far distant colony ; but my feelings will not allow me to dwell upon this subject. To return to my narrative :—

During my controversy with Mr. Larkin, I found considerable difficulty in replying to his Hebrew quotations, and I was obliged to rely upon a Lexicon. So I resolved to put myself under proper tuition, and as there was a teacher of Hebrew then in the town, a learned Polish Jew, I took lessons of him, and acquired a rudimental knowledge of the 'sacred language,' as my instructor termed it : but alas ! before I could read a chapter, he secured his fee, borrowed from me a cloak under pretence of having to visit another pupil a few miles distant, and I saw him no more. So I furnished myself with Frey's Hebrew Grammar, bought the 'Hebraica Pentateucha,' the 'Psalter,' and a Hebrew New Testament, and pursued the study myself. My chief difficulty lay in the pronunciation. In reading with my Jewish instructor, all the beauties of the language, by the sonorous manner in which he uttered the words, were brought out ; and, so far as I proceeded with him, I imitated him closely, notwithstanding my deafness, for my ear was, and still is, musical. I have never heard any of my friends, even those who profess to have a critical knowledge of the language, give so beautiful an intonation to Hebrew words as did my Jewish instructor ; it was music itself. I had afterwards an opportunity of adding to my small stock of Hebrew, by associating with some of the divinity students at the University of Glasgow during my study of medicine.

I had become now pretty generally known in the town ; among the Swedenborgians I was much respected, and my little business was a source of small emolument ; so that, upon the whole, I was as comfortable as I had ever been in my life.

While Dr. Crook was lecturing, I was waited upon by a person of the name of Martin, who styled himself an astronomer, and who was anxious to deliver some lectures in opposition to the Newtonian system, and he wished for introductions to some of my Swedenborgian friends, who were known to be warm patrons of science. But Anti-Newtonian science! I was puzzled at the request: at last I observed—

Do you really think yourself able to overturn the system of Newton?

Martin.—I am Jehovah's true philosopher, and I am commanded to do it.

Myself.—I am afraid there are none of my friends to whom I could recommend you, who would take tickets.

Martin.—You speak truth; you *are afraid*—I am sure to overturn it. I must overturn it. I am commanded to overturn it. Come, give me their names. I shall soon convince them.

Myself.—No; I cannot take that liberty, but I will mention you to them, and you can call again.

Martin.—Very well; I shall come again in a day or two—Good day!

I was astounded at this coolness and at the confidence displayed by the man; however, I named him to several of my friends, who all knew him well enough, and described him as a man evidently in a state of insanity, and when opposed, very sarcastic and even abusive.

He came again—I took a ticket, but told him my friends had all declined, they being engaged till late at night.

The family of the Martins have been celebrated for their eccentricities; I think the more correct term would be *insanity:* in one or two instances they displayed talents of a very high order, but they were all obviously insane on some points. The painter's name will live as long as art flourishes, and yet he, too, was insane on some points.

Jonathan Martin, who set fire to York Minster in 1829, was obviously insane. After being interrogated by the magistrate who committed him for trial, he was asked if he had anything to say, and he replied in a firm tone of voice—'The reason I set fire to the cathedral was on account of two particular dreams. In the first dream, I dreamed that a man stood by me with a bow and a sheath of arrows. He shot an arrow, and the arrow struck the Minster door. I then wished to shoot, and the man presented me with a bow, and I took an arrow from the sheath, and shot, and it struck on a stone and I lost it. In the second dream, I dreamed that a cloud came down on the cathedral, and came over to the house where I slept, and it made the whole house tremble. Then I awoke, and I thought it was the hand of God pointed out that I was to set fire to the cathedral; and those things which were found on me I took, lest any one should be blamed wrongfully. I cut the hangings from the throne, or cathedra, or whatever you call it, and tore down the curtains.'

William Martin, the person who called on me, was known in Newcastle as an exceedingly ingenious mechanic.

From the time of my purchasing the ticket for his Anti-Newtonian lecture, he frequently visited me. He always designated himself ' *the Natural Philosopher and Anti-Newtonian*,' and the public journalists gave him these titles, taking care, however, to italicise the word *natural* before philosopher, the point of which poor Martin seemed incapable of apprehending, for he always stood much upon the respect paid him by the conductors of the press.

William Martin was a rather handsome and well-built man. There was nothing repulsive in his external appearance. His head was small and presented many inequalities on its surface; in every sense of the word his cranium was peculiar. The vertex of the head was amazingly high, and his self-esteem was enormous, indeed obviously diseased. Towards the lateral parts of the forehead, there was a prominence which attracted universal observation, and which was so striking, as to amount almost to deformity. It was a protuberance in the form of a segment of a sphere developed immediately above, but somewhat behind the external angle of the eye; that is, in phrenological language, behind the organ of Music and just above the organ of Number. This is the part assigned by phrenologists, as the seat of the talent for construction. He sometimes wore, suspended by a ribbon from his vest, a gold medal, which he said he had received as a prize from the *Society of Arts*; and he gave me the following account of the manner by which he obtained it.

'I had made a rough model of a very peculiar wheel,' said he, [but suddenly breaking off—'Do you understand mechanics?' 'Not much;' said I. 'Oh! very well then, I need not stop to describe it,'] and it was to compete for this medal. But I did not get my model finished in Newcastle, for I did not want the Newcastle people to know anything about it, and I put off from time to time having a finished model made, till I could do so no longer with safety to my invention. So I went to London, and waited on an eminent watchmaker [shall I· tell you his name? he was a great scoundrel, but not a match for a philosopher—no; I won't tell you his name, it is no matter] to make me a finished model. I told him I wanted it in twenty-four hours. "Twenty-four hours," says he, "why it will take me a week." He kept looking at my wheel in a way I did not like. "Ah!" says I, "a week won't do"—and still he looked hard at my wheel; and turned it over and over in a way that made me say to myself, "Perhaps he will try to imitate it"; so says I, out loud, "Well, give me the wheel, I must get it done somehow," and away I went. And I found out a journeyman watchmaker, and I said to him, "Now

castle at the time. The nearest public baths were at Tynemouth, about eight miles distant. So I consulted with one of my most intimate friends, who was a cabinet maker, and a very ingenious mechanic besides, and he, as well as myself, thought that a set of baths would be useful to the town. But this involved considerable expense, and I had no capital. My friend, nevertheless, very kindly offered to fit them up, and to receive payment, as I could afford to discharge the debt. I still resolved to continue my shop, but I took a respectable house in Eldon Square, and my kind friend not only had the baths completed for me, but assisted me in the re-furnishing of my house. It was at this time that the dreadful scourge of cholera first visited Britain, and fearful indeed were its ravages at Newcastle-on-Tyne.

During my stay in Hull, I became acquainted with a gentleman of the name of Allenby, who had resided in the East, and who, notwithstanding the alarm which then prevailed of the anticipated visit of this direful disease, treated it very calmly. He informed me that he had seen more cases of cholera cured in the East by simple means, than ever were likely to afflict this country. I told him I thought it was his duty to make his remedy known. 'Let it come! Let it come!' said he, meaning the disease, 'and my remedy is ready for it. But I have no objection to give it to you, and I hope you will use it; for the rest, it is so simple, that were it generally known, it would be certainly rejected by most medical men.'

'But first let me advise you, in case of alarm, to employ as much heat as possible—the vapor bath is an excellent means of inducing perspiration; and if you can produce perspiration, all danger is over. Let the medicine follow. This is the formula for compounding it.

> Take of carbonate of magnesia, 1 ounce.
> Camphorated tincture of opium, 6 drams.
> Russian rhubarb, in fine powder, 30 grains.
> Peppermint water, 16 ounces.
> Take two table spoonfuls every two or three hours.'

I made a memorandum of this, and when the cholera
visited Newcastle, and the services of any one at all
acquainted with medicine were called into requisition,
: used this medicine freely, and with wonderful success.
But the vapor bath was also freely resorted to by me.
: was repeatedly called out, and so indeed was every
chemist in the town, as well as every surgeon ; and I
was several times threatened with the dire destroyer
myself ; but on the first symptoms, I at once got into the
bath, which was always kept ready, and never failed, by
exciting profuse perspiration, to throw off the threatened
disease. I have placed persons in the bath at a tempera-
ure of 70 degrees, and gradually raised it up to 120
degrees. I have at that temperature poured gradually
a stream of cold water over the head, used the friction
of my hand, and thus increased the temperature, until
the perspiration issued profusely from every pore, and
then, throwing a cloak over my patient, rubbed his person
with a coarse towel, until the whole skin, from head to
heel, was in a glow ; then, packing him in a blanket, I
have given him a cup of hot coffee, and stretched him on
a sofa, well packed up, and got him into a comfortable
and refreshing dose, and in two hours placed him in
safety in his own home. I imitated as closely as I could
the Russian vapor bath, and in most cases with the
happiest results. I used also very freely the recipe of
my friend Mr. Allenby, sometimes adding a little more
than the prescribed quantity of the camphorated tincture
of opium, and I can say, with truth, that many of the
worst cases were successfully treated by these simple
remedies. I cannot speak of this fearful visitation without recurring to the dreadful desolation and mourning
which it occasioned. Almost every family was in mourning—sometimes whole families were swept away, but
in the lower parts of the town, where the poorer families
were principally congregated, the mortality was frightful.
I was constantly occupied in the preparation of medicine,
and in assisting to visit the sick. There was no rivalry

among the medical men of the town—no fear that th
druggist could do too much—all labored as they bes
could, and several of the faculty fell victims to the disease
I lost some of my best friends, and among them the wif
of that friend who had so generously assisted me ; an
deeply did I feel for him who had so kindly assisted m
in my struggles. Gloom spread over the whole town—
prayers were offered up in every church—the differen
ministers addressed their respective congregations, and
exhorted them to repentance and holiness of life ; and
meantime, attention was paid to the cleansing and purifying
of the town, and at length the plague was stayed. A day
of solemn thanksgiving was appointed and most devoutly
observed. The following Thanksgiving was drawn up by
me on the occasion for my own little congregation :—

'Most great, most glorious, and adorable Jehovah
Lord, God, and Saviour Almighty ; thou alone art
righteous, thou alone art worthy of praise !

'We adore thy High and Holy name for the great and
abundant mercies wherewith thou hast encircled us ; Oh
God, we magnify thee for thy Divine perfection ; for
perfect thou indeed art, though we too frequently
attribute unto thee that which is abhorrent to thy nature.
Oh, Lord, pardon us if at any time we ascribe unto thee
that which is inimical to thy glorious perfection. Thou art
essential Divine Goodness. "Thy tender mercies are
over all thy works." Thou willest that none should perish.
Surely evil is not in thee. Therefore, though there has
been evil in the city, thou hast not done it. But, O Lord,
thou dost wisely permit us to be assaulted of the powers
of evil, lest in confidence in our strength, we make flesh
our arm, and neglect the arm of the Lord, which alone
bringeth salvation. O Lord ! give us to perceive the
distinction between appointment and permission. We
acknowledge that all temptations are by thy permission ;
but thou wilt not suffer us to be tempted above that
we are able, but wilt with the temptation make a way
for us to escape, so that we may be able to bear it. But

while we acknowledge that our sins have brought upon us the evils with which we have been visited, and that thou hast permitted us to be visited by afflictions in the body, that the soul might escape eternal damnation, never will we dare to pollute thy glorious person, by considering thee as appointing the scourge—never can we behold thee, who art the Author of life and blessedness, the Giver of every good and perfect gift, the unchanging and immutable God, the only perfect Being, the same yesterday, to-day, and for ever ; never can we submit to behold thee degraded as the author of evil, for it is of thy mercy alone that we are not consumed. Thy unchangeable love has followed us all the days of our lives. Thou hast rescued us from the arrow which flieth by night, and from the pestilence which walketh at noon day. Thou hast permitted us to be tried ; but thou hast bound up our wounds ; and pouring into them the oil of thy fatherly love, thou hast healed our souls, and the plague hath been stayed.

'Oh God, we bow before thee in humble gratitude, for thou hast indeed rescued us from great peril. Oh Lord, we adore the infinity of that goodness, which, when we cried unto thee in the day of trouble, delivered us out of distress. Most merciful Saviour, we magnify thee : we join our thanksgiving with our Christian brethren. Thou hast indeed redeemed us from the snares of our infernal enemies ; we are escaped out of their net ; the snare is broken, and we are delivered.

'May the remembrance of these thy gracious mercies, lead us more diligently to walk in the way of thy commandments ; may we turn away from the paths of evil and walk not in the counsel of the ungodly ; may our lives be in accordance with our professions ; may thy Divine goodness purify our wills, and thy Divine truth illuminate our understandings ; and that we may accomplish all that thou hast commanded us, may we look perpetually to thee for assistance ; knowing that thou art a very present help in the time of trouble.

'Creator of the Universe of worlds, Jehovah, God of

Hosts, we magnify thee for the manifestation of thy
glorious perfections.   Redeemer of mankind, Lord Jesus
Christ, we bow in humble gratitude before thee, because
that in thy love and in thy pity thou hast redeemed us, and
so became our Saviour and Regenerator.   We acknowledge
that by thy divine influence, we are freed · from the
infernal and malignant influence which manifested its direful
properties by the late plague.

'Oh Lord Jehovah ; Father, Son, and Holy Ghost ; one
Great, Holy, and Immaculate Being ; we unitedly offer unto
thee our most humble thanksgivings, as the One True God,
and Eternal life, even Jesus Christ our Lord.—Amen.'

It is the belief of the Swedenborgians that all good is
from God, but that all evil is from man.   While many
denominations of Christians declared that the cholera was
a Divine visitation on men for the wickedness of the
world, and God was taking vengeance upon them for their
sins, the Swedenborgians maintained that it was certainly
evil that brought the visitation upon us ; but the punishment arose not from Divine vengeance, but rather from the
evil itself, for every affliction is the result of some violated
law.   But the origin of evil may he seen treated of at
large in Swedenborg's 'Treatise on the Divine Love and
Wisdom,' sections 264 to 270, to which I refer the reader.

Meanwhile, the Pestallozzian school was progressing
satisfactorily ; but its very success cost us our master.
Mr. Field having requested an increase of salary, which
we were at that time unable to grant, resigned his
situation, and for a time the duties of the school devolved
on me.   This brought to my memory my old friend Mr.
Pegg, whose competency as a teacher was well known.
So I wrote to him, told him of the situation, and inquired
if he were willing to undertake its duties. ' He eagerly
offered his services to the committee, and was accepted.
I thought it my duty to acquaint the people of his
eccentricities, but at the same time freely conceded his
abilities as a teacher.   He was, however, elected to

succeed Mr. Field. Of this gentleman, Mr. Field, I cannot speak otherwise than in terms of sincere respect. He was a most indefatigable teacher, and had the art of so interesting his pupils that while he gained their affections their attention never flagged. His head was of average size, his temperament was a compound of sanguine, nervous, and bilious. He was a close and minute observer, rather disputative by reason of large Combativeness. His eyebrows projected, all the observing faculties were fully and freely developed. He was a good arithmetician, an elegant penman, well versed in history, both civil and ecclesiastical, a most ardent Swedenborgian, and is, as I have said, now an accredited minister of the Swedenborgians in the United States. His retirement from the duties of Superintendent of the Pestallozzian school, was a great loss to the Society of the Swedenborgians. But to return to the school :—

I was appointed to visit the school, and soon found that Mr. Pegg was not to be trusted alone. While visitors were present he was active enough, and his wonderful abilities drew down the approval of every one ; but when left to himself, the duties of the school were sadly neglected ; for he still indulged himself in poetic compositions, and to excite the powers of his imagination took frequent doses of opium and laudanum. I often found him from imbibing opium in a state of ecstatic delirium, altogether unfit for the sober duties of teaching.

He had read Swedenborg's work on the 'Earths in the Universe,' and composed a long descriptive poem on the planet Jupiter. He was constantly adding notes and additions to this work, which he expected to bring him a large sum of money. He had also written a very beautiful poem, entitled 'The Spirit's Wandering,' to which he was also adding notes. The spirit was described taking his departure from England, and making a rapid flight through America, Palestine, Persia, India, and China, describing as he proceeded the state of the countries and the quality of its inhabitants. I cannot forbear giving the conclusion

of this poem—which is to my view surpassingly
beautiful :—

> 'I have seen the world—I have crossed the sea ;
> But, alas! 'tis no longer a world for me.
> Though nature is fair in her silent hours,
> And 'tis pleasant to stand in her moon-lit bowers,
> Yet changes have cross'd her like wintry clouds,
> And ages enwrapp'd her in passing shrouds.
> Passion has veil'd her, and folly has thrown
> Over nature's own beauty a garb of her own.

> 'But ages shall rise in their glorious birth
> Upon a renovated earth,
> And the forest scenes and the woodland bowers
> Shall blush in the sunlight of evening showers :
> And time shall turn to youth, and men
> Rise to the life of the bless'd again !
> I shall see—I shall see them—a glorious race—
> Forms fit for Love's own dwelling place ;
> Such as I saw when the world was young,
> Creatures of heavenly light and song.
> Light, that around them on nature was thrown !
> Music, that rivall'd the charms of our own !
> But ages must pass in their headlong flight
> Ere the earth shall again be a mansion of light.
> Now 'tis a dwelling of tumult and care,
> Sin has possess'd it, ambition is there.
> Why should I wander o'er land and sea ?
> This earth is no longer a scene for me.'

This poem he put into my possession, together with the
poem, 'Jupiter,' as security for some money I had advanced
him ; but he obtained them again of me, with the view
of offering them to a publisher, and what became of them
I never learned.   It is certain they were never published.

But the composition or rather the revision of these
works, for they had been written a year or more previous
to my arrival at Newcastle, and the habit of chewing
opium and drinking laudanum to excite the imagination,
rendered him, as I have said, wholly unfit for the business
of the school, and his services were dispensed with.   He
was succeeded by a gentleman who was well acquainted
with Pestallozzi's system, but who, being still living, I
forbear to name.

The school had now been opened a sufficient time to allow of our applying for a grant of money from the Swedenborgian Conference, which was that year held in Bath, and I volunteered to attend the Conference, and use what influence I possessed in obtaining the grant, provided my expenses were paid. This was promised conditionally, that I was successful. The schoolmaster was appointed to conduct the worship in my absence. Well: I attended, and was not only successful in obtaining the grant of money, but also carried a motion by the casting vote of the President, the late Rev. Robert Hindmarsh, that the Conference on the following year should be held in Newcastle. I returned home, and resumed my duties. To my astonishment I found that a party had been formed during my absence with the view of associating the schoolmaster with me in the ministry. I have already stated that my discourses were nearly extemporaneous. The schoolmaster who had officiated for me during my absence at Bath used written discourses, and took exception to my extemporaneous ones. I shall not enter into a description of the scenes which followed, and which for a time estranged from me some of my dearest friends : enough, that I found my usefulness destroyed, and that many withdrew their subscriptions, so that, instead of my usual pound per week, I had nothing whatever for my last six months' services. I resigned, and the schoolmaster was instantly appointed as my successor.

I think my resignation had not been given in a week, when I received two invitations to vacant pulpits—one at Dundee, the other at Glasgow. I chose the latter. I did not, however, break up my little business at once, as I was not certain whether I should be permanently settled at Glasgow. My wife was as good a chemist as myself, and in pharmaceutical chemical manipulation better. She conducted, and successfully too, for a year and a half, my business in Newcastle.

The Missionary Society of the Swedenborgians at London, hearing that I was about to settle at Glasgow, requested me, previous to my settlement in that city, to pay a visit to Scarborough and Pickering in Yorkshire, and to deliver a few lectures in those towns, they undertaking to defray my expenses. I acceded to their request, and found my short sojourn at Scarborough very agreeable. The following report of my labors at Scarborough was communicated to the 'Intellectual Repository' by one of the hearers.

'*Pickering, June* 9, 1834.

'Dear Sir—I write at the request of the Rev. D. G. G., to present you with some account of that gentleman's late missionary visit to Scarborough and Pickering. Mr. G. arrived at Scarborough on May 26th, and was received with great pleasure by our esteemed friend Mr. Bye, and a few warm and zealous receivers of the doctrines, who, having had previous notice of his visit, had obtained permission of the trustees of the Primitive Methodist chapel for him to deliver a course of lectures on the Tuesday, Wednesday, and Thursday evenings, in the said chapel. Notice thereof was accordingly announced by printed bills being posted throughout the town. The subjects were as follows, viz., '1st. On the Doctrine of Election and Predestination, and on the Freewill of Man; 2nd. The Destruction of the world by Fire, and the Resurrection of the Material Body, not doctrines of the Scriptures; 3rd. An investigation of the Objections brought against the Scriptures by Infidels; with Proofs that the Bible is written by Plenary Inspiration.

'The first lecture was well attended; but the chapel was well filled to hear the second. Mr. G. had, however, been informed that the trustees would not permit him to give the lecture that stood on the bill for that evening, but he might give one on any other subject. He accordingly gave the lecture on the Scriptures; on which subject he also gave another the evening following. The disappointment experienced by the congregation at this refusal, and consequent change of subject, was very great, so much so as to induce one of them to call upon Mr. G.

the next morning, and offer him the use of a large room (known by the name of the factory room) to deliver the objectionable lecture in on the Friday evening. This offer Mr. G. accepted, and gave notice of it from the pulpit at the close of his third lecture. Although no other notice had been given of this lecture, so great was the desire to hear it, that the room was completely filled, and it is the opinion of Mr. G. that not less than one thousand people were present. He lectured upwards of an hour and a half on the subject; and although nearly all the assembled multitude were obliged to stand all the while, as very few seats had been procured, yet the most marked attention was observed, and a very general expression of approbation was heard after the lecture was concluded; and many inquiries were afterwards made of our friends, respecting when Mr. G. would come again to Scarborough. I have also the satisfaction further to state, in reference to these lectures, that several highly respectable inhabitants of the town were present, and many expressions of approbation were heard; and from all that we can learn it appears evident that a great impression in favor of the doctrines has been made on the public mind.

'Mr. G. arrived here (at Pickering) on Saturday, May 31st, and preached three times on Sunday, June 1st: the services were well attended and listened to with profound attention. All present seemed to be well satisfied with what they heard, and many expressed their approval of the doctrines delivered. Some disappointment was, however, experienced by our not receiving the tracts promised for the occasion, particularly as we had announced on our bills, that 'tracts illustrative and explanatory of the doctrines of the New Church would be gratuitously distributed at the close of each service.' At Scarborough, the want of tracts will be more felt than at Pickering, as the friends there have no regular meetings for worship or instruction, and we have heard that some very respectable people made inquiry after books or tracts, and were de-

sirous to purchase some.   Altogether, however, the friends
of the Heavenly Doctrines here and at Scarborough, are,
they trust, thankful to the Divine Providence for thus presenting the opportunity of calling public attention more
fully to the sublime truths of the new dispensation of
divine truth, and to the London Missionary and Tract
Society, for the assistance they have afforded them.

' C. Storry.'

'VISIT TO DALTON, ETC.

' *Liverpool, June* 13, 1834.

'Dear Sir—I dare say you have received an account
of my proceedings at Scarborough and Pickering; I trust
they are such as will afford the committee satisfaction ; at
all events, I did not spare labor.

'On Monday, June 2, I left Pickering, and proceeded to
my very worthy friend, Mr. G. Senior's, of Dalton.   I was
not idle while with him.   On Thursday, June 5, I preached
at a village, called Upper Heaton, from the words, " Nevertheless, I have a few things against thee, in that thou suf-
ferest the woman Jezebel, who calleth herself a prophetess,
to teach and to seduce my servants to commit fornication,
and to eat things sacrificed to idols."   There were perhaps
about 80 or 100 persons present.   I did not hear any other
observations but such as were satisfactory.   On Friday,
June 6, at the request of several friends, I preached on the
Resurrection at a place called Mould Green, near Huddersfield.   There were from 200 to 300 present, who, with
the exception of *one person,* were " *much edified by our
views of the eternal world.*"   [An observation of several
strangers.]

'On Sunday, June 8, I preached in Mr. Senior's chapel,
at Dalton.   Morning, " Arise, let us go hence : this is not
our rest," and introduced the apostolic words, " Here we
have no abiding city."   Afternoon, " In my Father's house
are many mansions : if it were not so, I would have told
you."   Evening, " To him that overcometh, I will give to
eat of the tree of life which is in the midst of the Paradise

of God." I had a full chapel at each service, and I bless the assisting Providence of the Lord, who enabled me to labor unweariedly, and to give general pleasure to the hearers. On Monday evening I again preached in the same chapel, on—The true Object of Worship, "One Lord, one faith, one baptism." The chapel was at all the services well filled, and Mr. Senior and his son amply paid my expences.

'On Tuesday I left my kind friends at Dalton, whose unwearied attention to my every want calls forth my sincere gratitude to them and to our dear heavenly Father, whom they endeavor so indefatigably to serve.

'I preached in the evening of the same day (Tuesday) at Liverpool, on Isaiah xxxi, 1 ; and again, on Thursday evening, on Matthew xvii, 1, 2.

This afternoon (Friday) I set sail for Glasgow ; there, if the Lord permit, to commence my labors in Scotland.'

During my stay at Dalton I was requested by my kind friend, Mr. George Senior, to peruse a work which his son had written, in reply to an attack made by the curate of Aldmonbury Church, near Huddersfield, and to make any corrections I might think needful prior to its going to press. I did so, but found very little to alter or amend ; for what I did, however, Mr. Joseph Senior expressed himself most thankful, and presented me with forty copies of his work ; and these corrections, besides laying the foundation of a friendship between us which terminated but with his life, led to very frequent literary employment from him, which I shall name in its proper place.

Seventh Period:

FROM THIRTY-EIGHT TO FIFTY-TWO YEARS OF AGE.
1834 TO 1848.

'If God wills man's happiness, and man's happiness can only be obtained by the exercise of his faculties, then God wills that man should exercise his faculties; that is, it is man's duty to exercise his faculties; for DUTY MEANS THE FULFILMENT OF THE DIVINE WILL. That it is man's duty to exercise his faculties is further proved by the fact, that what we call punishment attaches to the neglect of that exercise. Not only is the normal activity of each faculty productive of pleasure, but the continued suspension of that faculty is productive of pain. As the stomach hungers to digest food, so does every bodily and mental agent hunger to perform its appointed action. And as the refusal to satisfy the cravings of the digestive faculty is productive of suffering, so is the refusal to satisfy the cravings of any other faculty also productive of suffering to an extent proportionate to the importance of that faculty. But as God wills man's happiness, that line of conduct which produces unhappiness is contrary to his will. Therefore the non-exercise of his faculties is contrary to his will. Either way, then, we find that the exercise of the faculties is God's will and man's duty.'

HERBERT SPENCER.—*Social Statics.*

'The qualities and characters of different men may be referred to those of different minerals; so that one man may figuratively be denominated a man of gold, another a man of silver, another of copper or brass, another of lead, another of iron, etc., etc. Some men, also, are combinations of these metals, whilst others outwardly present the aspect of a superior metal, when yet inwardly they have the substance of an inferior one. Perhaps the perfection of the human character results from the combination of all; provided that in the combination, the gold be uppermost, and the other metals have an orderly arrangement beneath it according to their respective value.'

CLOWES.

ON my arrival in Glasgow, my first duty was to present my credentials to the Society of Swedenborgians, who had engaged me as their pastor, and I can with truth say, that from every member, I received a most cordial welcome. Where all were kind and attentive, it would be invidious to particularise any.

The place of worship was exceedingly small, and I think I may say that forty persons would have rendered it inconveniently crowded. The Society, however, was equally limited in number, I think not exceeding twenty-five. They were persons in the middle rank of life, possessed of the ordinary means of subsistence ; but their liberality was great—greater than I have ever found in any other Society of the Swedenborgians, and they subscribed liberally towards the support of the church as well as of myself. They were very orderly in their general conduct ; and punctual and regular in their attendance on the public services of the church, and I may here say, once for all, that during my fourteen years residence in Glasgow, I never found the congregation remiss in their religious duties on the Sabbath. At the appointed time they were found in their places, and neither the minister nor the congregation were annoyed by persons coming in late, except indeed in the case of occasional visits by strangers.

The trials and vicissitudes I had been subjected to induced me to take for my first subject in Glasgow the following text : 'Therefore, behold I will allure her, and bring her into the wilderness, and speak comfortably unto her. And I will give her her vineyards from thence, and the valley of Achor for a door of hope ; and she shall sing there as in the days of her youth, and as in the days when she came up out of the land of Egypt.' (Hosea ii, 14, 15.) This sermon set forth the trials and comforts of the Christian ; it was much approved of, and a request was made from the congregation for its publication ; and the publication of it led to the reception of the doctrines of the New Church, by Mr. Andrew Bain, of the firm of Bell and Bain.

As already noted, my friend Mr. Joseph Senior had presented me with forty copies of his 'Letter to the Rev.

David James '; it was very handsomely printed, and I
was desirous that my sermon should be printed in the
same handsome style ; so I made inquiry for the best
printer in the city, and learned that for accuracy and
elegance of typography no printers were superior to the
firm of Bell and Bain. I therefore took my manuscript
to this firm, and with it a copy of Mr. Senior's letter,
which I left with the printers, expressing a wish that my
sermon might be printed equally well. It was not, however, my sermon that led Mr. Bain to receive the
doctrines, but the perusal by that gentleman of the letter
of Mr. Senior, which I had left as a sample of the style
of printing I wished for my sermon. Shortly after the
printing of this sermon, Mr. Bain began to attend worship
at my little church (the ' wee kirk, ' as it was called) and at
length became a cordial receiver of the doctrines and a
warm friend to me. I afterwards learned that his partner,
Mr. Bell, had long been an admirer of Swedenborg's
writings, but it was not till I had been in Glasgow some
time, that he became a regular attendant at my little church.

I had now to turn my attention to the most efficient
mode of spreading the doctrines of the church with which
I had become connected. There was but one other
minister belonging to the Swedenborgians in the whole
kingdom of Scotland, and he at that time was in a very
delicate state of health, and not able to bear the fatigues
of travelling.

There had been established some few years prior to my
settlement in Glasgow, a Society for the Propagation of
the Doctrines of the New Church as set forth in the
writings of Swedenborg, but with the single exception of
the distribution of tracts, it had languished for want of
an active person able and willing to make rapid journeys.
I proposed to my Glasgow friends that a quarterly visit
should be made to the scattered members of the Church
in Scotland.   There were societies of Swedenborgians in
Paisley and Dundee without a regular minister, and there
were receivers of the New Church views in many other

towns. These societies I proposed to visit once a quarter, remaining one Sabbath with each in its turn, and administering the ordinances of religion, and visiting the scattered members, whenever practicable, on the ordinary days of the week. This proposition I was induced to make at the instance of my friend Mr. Joseph Senior, of Dalton, who earnestly begged me not to let so wide a field remain fallow. He presented me with a copy of Carne's 'Lives of Eminent Missionaries,' and promised further to aid me with any books I might need, if I would but go out and make the doctrines known wherever and whenever I had the opportunity. At the same time, he advised me not to court controversy, but to state the doctrines of the New Church in plain and simple language, and without interfering with the prejudices of others, or placing the Calvinistic doctrines in too strong a contrast. 'Preach the truth,' said he, 'spare no error, but in all things imitate the Great Teacher, and aim at getting the "common people" to hear you; therefore use simple language. Go out wherever you can find a hearer, and be sure that the Lord will prosper you in your efforts, if you look to him for help, and teach the truth in love. What help I can render you pecuniarily, you may depend upon.'

I resolved to follow this advice; and I did so during my stay in Scotland, so that during the latter part of my residence in Glasgow, the principal complaint against me was, not that I labored too little, but that I worked too hard. But I must not anticipate.

My proposition was favorably received, and it was carried into effect before I had been resident in Glasgow three months. My first journey was made to Berwick-on-Tweed, (for, though this town was not absolutely in Scotland, it was yet too remote from the London Society to admit of their visitation), to Alloa, to Dunfermline, and Dundee. At Dundee I delivered a lecture on the Atonement, which was attended by a very large congregation, probably eight hundred persons. This lecture, which

18

was afterwards printed, forms No.
Series of Christian Tracts,' of which
more to say as I proceed. From D
Alloa, a village in Clackmananshire,
house of Mr. Allan Drysdale a few f
them on the subject of the Divine Pro
course forms No. 25 of the 'Glasgo
Tracts.'] After the service I pointe
present the desirability of organising
distinct society, and was successful i
so. Of Mr. Allan Drysdale I canno
speak in terms of admiration. He
unselfish men I ever knew. Follow
calling (a blacksmith), at which
fatigably, he yet finds time to w
discourses, too, of equal ability wit
talented of the Swedenborgians. H
the worship without fee or reward, b
own cost, provided the place in whi
He has a very large and active brai
has a sanguine-nervous predominan
proportion of bilious, which renders
His benevolence is very large, his p
minute, and his reflecting faculties ex
forehead is deep and rather broad,
share of back brain, which gives him
energy. He has well defined Com
conduct an argument with spirit, at t
perfectly free from acrimony. A mor
know in the wide circle of my acquai
of him with perfect confidence, as an
whom is no guile.' I have known hi
of twenty years, and his conduct in
been uniformly upright.

From Alloa I walked to Dunferm
distance I think of about eight miles.
furnished me with a letter of introduc
Paton, then a member of the Society

ɔu wilt have a larger

its to the different places
ɔited Paisley, Greenock,
ɜ in the neighborhood of

procuring rooms to lecture
to hear always contributed
land the old apostolic cus-
ɔn entering the church door
an I adopted in my various
est person would scarcely
worship in Scotland without
ffering plate. With these
ure room, and for publishing
ner, and wherever there was
e up, either by the Sweden-
if sent by them, or by my
or, if engaged in lecturing on
ɔy myself. But for the first
ɔotland, I confined myself ex-
ɔctrines of the Swedenborgians.
four times every week.
ɔblishing a quarterly visitation
Scotland, my next object was,
whole of the church together
ɔat in England a Conference of
ghly beneficial to the church at
brotherly feelings among the
formation of friendships which
ɔes more closely together, and
ergetic exercises of charity and
read, in the discipline of the
ɔuch good had resulted from a
ɔssed to all their members in
ɔom, and I conceived a similar
vitʰ similar advantages. So I
ɔow friends a proposition for

was afterwards printed, forms No. 3 of the 'Glasgow Series of Christian Tracts,' of which series I shall have more to say as I proceed. From Dundee I hastened to Alloa, a village in Clackmananshire, where I met at the house of Mr. Allan Drysdale a few friends, and addressed them on the subject of the Divine Providence. [This discourse forms No. 25 of the 'Glasgow Series of Christian Tracts.'] After the service I pointed out to the persons present the desirability of organising themselves into a distinct society, and was successful in inducing them to do so. Of Mr. Allan Drysdale I cannot do otherwise than speak in terms of admiration. He is one of the most unselfish men I ever knew. Following a most laborious calling (a blacksmith), at which he labors most indefatigably, he yet finds time to write discourses, and discourses, too, of equal ability with some of the most talented of the Swedenborgians. He not only conducts the worship without fee or reward, but has actually at his own cost, provided the place in which the society meets. He has a very large and active brain. His temperament has a sanguine-nervous predominance, but has a small proportion of bilious, which renders his activity, enduring. His benevolence is very large, his powers of observation minute, and his reflecting faculties exceedingly good. His forehead is deep and rather broad, and he has a good share of back brain, which gives him considerable physical energy. He has well defined Combativeness, and can conduct an argument with spirit, at the same time he is perfectly free from acrimony. A more just man I do not know in the wide circle of my acquaintance, and I speak of him with perfect confidence, as an 'Israelite indeed, in whom is no guile.' I have known him now for upwards of twenty years, and his conduct in all that time has been uniformly upright.

From Alloa I walked to Dunfermline in Fifeshire, a distance I think of about eight miles. Mr. Drysdale had furnished me with a letter of introduction to Mr. J. N. Paton, then a member of the Society of Friends, but favorable to the doctrines held by the Swedenborgians. He received me very kindly, and making my purpose known to the workmen of the various table-linen factories, about a hundred and fifty persons assembled, whom I addressed in the open air on the Sanctity and Divinity of the Sacred Scriptures. I spoke for half an hour, and gave notice that I would again address them in the evening, in a hall set apart for the teaching of music; accordingly, in the evening an audience of between two and three hundred persons assembled. I selected for my subject, the Divinity of the Great Redeemer and the Sacred Doctrine of the Divine Trinity. This was the first time the cardinal doctrine of the Swedenborgians had been proclaimed in Dunfermline.

Returning to Mr. Paton's, where I was to pass the night, I had a long conversation with him on the internal or spiritual sense of the Scriptures, and felt happy that my entertainer responded to my opinion in almost every particular.

On retiring to rest I was not a little startled at the furniture and ornaments, perhaps I ought rather to say relics, of my bed chamber. The room itself was small; one end of which was occupied by a massive, but elaborately carved oak bedstead, and had been originally the resting-place of no less a personage than King James VI. of Scotland. The room was lighted at the opposite end by a half-glazed door, which opened into the romantic grounds surrounding the equally romantic cottage of Mr. Paton, and which had been designated the 'Wooer's Alley,' from which Mr. Paton had named his cottage. On one side of the door-window, resting on a small antique table, was a crystal dish (from Holyrood Palace), and in the dish a small bone of King Robert the Bruce, which had been taken from his remains, that were found among the ruins of the Holy Trinity Church, when the foundation was being prepared for the New Church, then about to be erected. On the other side of the window was an ebony cross, and below it a skull and cross bones, a Bible,

and some ancient religious books. Between the bedstead
and the wall of the room there was barely sufficient space
for a small man (like myself) to walk. This room was
contiguous, and opened into a large square apartment,
stored with ancient furniture, which had been originally
the property of royalty, and which consisted principally
of richly-carved oak. The ceiling was divided into compartments, and ornamented with emblematic paintings.
There were also many fine old paintings on the walls,
ponderous two-handled swords were arranged in different
groups; pistols, with ancient matchlocks; instruments of
torture, such as thumb-screws, etc., a number of curious
old books, and an immense variety of other relics and
curiosities, collected by Mr. Paton at considerable expense,
and stored in his romantic cottage. I certainly felt a little
nervous, and could have wished I had been placed in
another apartment; but occupying the position of a
minister of the gospel, I forbore to complain. I retired
to rest, and, after the fatigue of a long walk and twice
preaching, slept soundly; but I may have occasion, in a
future part of my narrative, to speak again of this bed-
chamber.

This visit, which included my attendance at the Swedenborgian Conference, occupied me for three weeks, and I
preached altogether about twelve times in the various
towns to which I had been sent. On my return to Glasgow, I received a letter from Mr. Paton, in which was the
following passage: 'I think I can say, with truth and
great pleasure, that thy visit to Dunfermline, and thy
labors in it, were received with much pleasure by the
people, and thou hast left a favorable impression upon their
minds of the heavenly doctrines of the New Church. I
may just mention one circumstance. An individual
asked one of my workmen, if the doctrines *yon man
preached* were the doctrines his master professed. He
answered, " *Yon's* the real religion, I believe." To
which the person rejoined—" I aye thocht he was wrang,
but if yon be it, I'm sure he's reet." At thy next visit to

Dunfermline, I doubt not, thou wilt have a larger audience.'

I continued my periodical visits to the different places mentioned above, and also visited Paisley, Greenock, Airdrie, and some other towns in the neighborhood of Glasgow.

I rarely had any difficulty in procuring rooms to lecture in, and the people who attended to hear always contributed towards the expense. In Scotland the old apostolic custom of depositing an offering on entering the church door is still continued, and this plan I adopted in my various preachings. The very poorest person would scarcely think of entering a place of worship in Scotland without depositing his mite in the offering plate. With these offerings I paid for the lecture room, and for publishing the lecture by the town drummer, and wherever there was any deficiency, I had it made up, either by the Swedenborgian Missionary Society, if sent by them, or by my friend, Mr. Joseph Senior ; or, if engaged in lecturing on science at the same time, by myself. But for the first year of my residence in Scotland, I confined myself exclusively to preaching the doctrines of the Swedenborgians. I rarely preached less than four times every week.

Having succeeded in establishing a quarterly visitation of the various societies in Scotland, my next object was, if possible, to bring the whole of the church together once a year. I had seen that in England a Conference of the various societies was highly beneficial to the church at large, while it cultivated brotherly feelings among the members, and led to the formation of friendships which linked the different societies more closely together, and stimulated them to the energetic exercises of charity and good works. I had also read, in the discipline of the Society of Friends, how much good had resulted from a yearly epistle being addressed to all their members in various parts of the kingdom, and I conceived a similar plan would be attended with similar advantages. So I brought before my Glasgow friends a proposition for

establishing an annual assembly of all the members of
the New Church in Scotland, or, at least, of a delegation
of members from each society.   The proposition was
favorably received, a circular was addressed to the various
societies and members of the church in Scotland, which
was cordially responded to, and on the 17th of July, 1835,
the first meeting assembled at Glasgow.   There were
members present from Edinburgh, Greenock, Shotts,
Paisley, and Alloa, and letters were received from Dundee,
Dunfermline, Kinross, and Berwick-upon-Tweed.   Resolutions were proposed and adopted, and a spirit of love
seemed to pervade every person present.   Having thus
accomplished the object of bringing the members of the
church in Scotland together, I thought I would conclude
my work with an epistle which should embrace the various
topics embodied in the Resolutions, besides general advices
on the conduct of members, and the education of children.
So I drew up an epistle to the members of the New Church
in Scotland, and presented it to the meeting, who unani-
mously adopted it, and directed their Secretary to sign it.
I was desirous that this plan of addressing the church
should be continued from year to year.   But, although
the meeting has been since regularly held every year, a
second epistle has not appeared.   The following is the
epistle alluded to :—

'Beloved Brethren—The tender mercies of the Lord,
which are over all his works, give us great cause for
spiritual rejoicing in this small corner of his true church
on earth ; for he hath enlarged our steps, and kept us
firm amidst a multitude of attacks.   His truth hath alone
defended us ; his goodness hath followed, and will continue to follow us ; and if we faithfully do his will on
earth, we shall assuredly dwell in the house of the Lord
for ever.   Great and marvellous is the love of our God
towards us, and glorious are the things which are perceived by the true citizens of the New Jerusalem.   For
while almost the whole of professing Christendom is

engaged in strife and warfare, there is peace within the borders of Jerusalem, and they prosper who love her. While there is a constant cry—"Lo ! here is Christ," or, "Lo ; he is there "; and the signs which our Divine Lord predicted are hourly passing before us, there is great cause to rejoice that those who are in Judea are fast fleeing to the mountains, and the pleasant places of Jerusalem are rejoicing in the accession of humble recipients to the true fold of the Redeemer's kingdom. The attacks which we have experienced from without during the past year, have by the divine assistance of our Lord, we humbly trust, been subdued from within, and the Philistines and the Assyrians, those under the predominating influence of *faith alone* and those who are in self-derived intelligence from the abuse of the rational principle, who appear to be in *works alone*, have been silenced by the simple power and energy of divine truth. May the Lord be praised !

'For the first time since the sounding of the trumpet that Babylon the great is fallen, is fallen, the brethren of the New Jerusalem in this ancient kingdom have assembled together, that they might strengthen the weak hands, and confirm the feeble knees of each other, and thus give a more powerful impetus to the opening of the eyes of the blind, and unstopping the ears of the deaf ; using their humble efforts in the propagation of truth, that the lame man might leap as a hart, that the tongue of the dumb might sing, that waters might break out in the wilderness, and streams flow in the desert : and they give grateful thanks to the Lord, that while a spirit of love appeared to watch over their deliberations, a spirit of truth seemed to urge them forward not to be weary in well doing, for in due time they shall reap if they faint not. They cannot but rejoice at the altered prospects which the lapse of a year seems to have placed before them. Throughout our small provinces there is reason to hope that the fields have not been neglected. Some fallow land has been broken up, and some seed attempted to be sown—in one field

with considerable success, and in another not **without**
hopes of fruit, which, no doubt, the Lord will hasten **in**
his time. The stations which have been visited periodically have been Alloa, Dundee, and Dunfermline ; **and**
in those places the state of the church has been such **as**
invariably to afford satisfaction to the Missionary Assembly, and to call forth gratitude to the Lord Almighty.
In Dunfermline, particularly, notwithstanding the recipients have been denominated infidels, and every odious
appellation hath been heaped upon them, a steady and
rapid progress has been made ; and if any serious and
devoted person could attach himself wholly to the ministry
in that town, a Church would very soon be raised. In
Alloa the meetings on the Sabbath are regular, and
attended by all the members, and occasionally by
strangers. In Dundee, though the Church has been
deprived of the labors of our late valuable friend, Mr.
Peter Smith, there is no further diminution. A spirit
of love and zeal pervades them : they continue to meet
regularly ; and of this town it may truly be said, that if
a minister could reside, there would be no want of a good
congregation. The laborers are indeed few. Pray ye
that the Lord of the harvest may send forth laborers
into his harvest. In Paisley there is a regular meeting,
and there have been added three members. In Edinburgh, in consequence of the continued indisposition of
our amiable and excellent friend, the Rev. William
Bruce, there seems to be cause for regret, since there
does not appear that warmth for the spread of divine
truth which ought to characterise the members. They
seem also to neglect assembling themselves together ; and
thus, for lack of mutual assistance, the people languish,
the affections appear torpid, and the thoughts are not
excited to active labor. May the Lord enable the members to arise from their lethargy, and cry aloud for
assistance that Christ may give them *new life*. In Glasgow the cause appears to have made a steady advance,
owing, it is humbly presumed, to there being a stated

minister ; and seventeen members have been added. The Missionary Assembly do therefore most earnestly urge upon their brethren, wherever it is practicable, the engagement of a regular minister ; and where this cannot be accomplished, they entreat their brethren to select from among themselves one or more individuals to attend to the duties of the Sabbath, and to be as deacons for conducting the worship, until the Lord of the vineyard shall send us more laborers.

'To our brethren at large, the Missionary Assembly beg now to address themselves, and this they do in a spirit of love. We beseech you to look upon the mercies which have been showered down upon you by our glorified redeeming Lord. When as yet ye were in Egypt, and the light of science dawned upon you in a land of bondage, the living voice of truth called you forth from your state of servitude. When you were in the land of the Philistines, and the idol Dagon seemed fast winning you to the idolatry of that nation, again the voice of truth awakened you by his providence, and proved that *that* was not your rest. When, at length, by hearing the truth, you became acquainted with the *true God* and *eternal life*, even Jesus Christ our Lord, and the gracious promise to show you plainly of the Father had been fulfilled by the manifestation of the spirit and life of the Holy Word, and your voluntary exclamation of, "Lord, *I will follow thee* whithersoever thou goest," brought you at least in externals under the Divine government *to do his will*, as well as believe the divine truth—he continued his cautions and his warnings, whilst he revealed the arcana of wisdom, with which the Word abounds, so that what has been satirically written by the poet Crabbe, may be considered as sober truth ; viz. :

> " Of Bible mysteries you the keys possess,
>   Assured yourselves where WISER * heads but guess."

* 'The Lord hath hid these things from the *wise* and prudent, and hath revealed them unto babes.'

When you take a retrospect of all these mercies—these astonishing displays of love and wisdom—what springs are opened for devout love and gratitude—for humility of understanding, purity of heart, and gentleness of spirit! "What manner of men ought we to be?" Now, brethren, you will remember the Divine commendation on the woman in the Gospel; you know too its real signification: "Her sins which are many are forgiven, for she loved much." Think often of this passage. Remember too, that love is the fulfilling of the law. The only new commandment given was, that we should love one another: it was to be the badge of true discipleship. "By this shall all men know that ye are my disciples, if ye have love one to another." We most earnestly press it upon you: be diligent in repressing the first appearance of a contentious spirit: good seed has been sown in your field by the Lord—beware how a spirit of carelessness come upon you, and so while you sleep the enemy may sow his tares. Pray much; and pray always for the temper and spirit of Christ. We do not say that man, in early stages of the regenerate life, can at all times be free from anger; but we do say he should be angry and sin not. Let not the sun go down upon your wrath. Ah, beloved brethren! where should we all be now, if God were not a boundless ocean of love? Let, therefore, brotherly love continue. Do not, we entreat you, be estranged from an ardent affection for your brethren by every petty difference of opinion. Be careful of listening to the idle reports of others, which frequently originate in malice: but, oh! be doubly careful how you propagate them, either in writing or verbally. "Behold, how great a matter a little fire kindleth"; so the tongue is a small member, but it hath destroyed more than the sword. Let love then, such as the Lord has for us (as far as the finite can approach the infinite), never sleep in your bosoms; let love universal reign. "He that hateth his brother is a murderer, and we know that no murderer hath eternal life abiding in him." Have a strict watch to keep down the selfish passions and principles. We entreat you, brethren, to consider, that none of us liveth to himself. The doctrine of use is the doctrine of charity. Let members of the New Jerusalem be very careful to fulfil their duties as citizens faithfully and effectually, not with eye service as men pleasers, but as the servants of Christ, doing the will of God from the heart. Every member of the New Church who engages his services to another, should strive not only to be faithful to his employer, and diligent in his employment, but to excel in whatever he does. All excellence is of God. To strive after excellence is, therefore, to place the Lord always before us. Whatever it is right to do, it is right to do well.

'We wish particularly to impress upon our brethren the fact, that though our religious opinions are not popular, such of our members as have regarded the doctrine of uses, have invariably excelled in their different avocations. Flaxman was one of the most amiable of men, as he was also one of the most eminent of sculptors. Crompton was an estimable member of the New Church : though an humble mechanic, yet he rose to eminence by his skill, received the thanks and the remuneration of his country from Parliament, and his talents conduced highly to the improvement of the cotton manufacture. In Manchester, the instances are numerous where members of the New Church are in situations of trust ; and we might easily name individuals in this country who demonstrate the superiority of the doctrine of uses.

'We have lost a master and a prince in Israel, in the removal into eternity of our late father in spiritual instruction, the Rev. Robert Hindmarsh, some instructive memorials of whom will be found in the Sermons of Mr. Noble and Mr. Howarth, which we recommend our brethren to be possessed of. And here we ought rather to rejoice than to be sorrowful ; since every removal into the eternal world increases the influence exercised over this, and advances, rather than retards, the glorious appearing of our great God and Saviour Jesus Christ.

'We beg to address a few words to parents: "Lo, children are an heritage of the Lord," says the Psalmist, "and the fruit of the womb is his reward." We entreat our brethren and sisters who are parents, to watch over their offspring with jealous care. To make them acquainted with the necessity of obedience to the Divine precepts, and diligently set them an example of studying the holy word, and the invaluable writings of our illuminated author. Several essays on domestic education in the "Intellectual Repository" may be studied with great advantage. But whatever parents wish their children to be, they should, on all occasions, endeavor to be themselves. Example is always before precept. Do we wish them to love the holy word ? Let us teach them to prize it by a constant reading of it ourselves. Do we wish them to be useful, active members of society ? Let us ourselves avoid everything like sloth. Is an example of neatness and cleanliness necessary ? Our own persons should be their model. Do we desire them to grow up in the temperate use of worldly gratifications, so that they may use without abusing them ? Let us never be overtaken with excess ourselves, but let the virtues of sobriety, and the pleasures of innocent gratification, prove to them that there are bounds beyond which no Christian, whether parent or child, can pass with impunity or without incurring guilt. Children do most by example, and they will imitate their parents in all things. Parents ! we entreat you to be careful in bringing out the very spirit and life of our doctrines in your children, by training them up in the nurture and admonition of the Lord.

'The Missionary General Assembly now desire to impress upon members the necessity of themselves laboring to advance the cause of the New Church by every effort in their power. Every man should consider himself as a missionary sent forth by the Lord. If he be incapable of speaking in public, he is at least capable of being a living preacher in the excellence of his own life ; but there is no one, however humble his acquirements, or

imited his sphere of action, but that may do good, if
le possess but the will. By the aid of tracts much might
le accomplished; and if members were to obtain a
election of these, and to circulate them in their own
mmediate neighborhood, the good they might effect
rould be incalculable.

'In closing this epistle, the Missionary General Assembly
arnestly pray that the members may be preserved in
leace and unity. Grateful to the Divine Providence of
he Lord for the pleasure they have enjoyed in their
ssembling together this year, they take leave of their
rrethren, with the assurance that, in all they have ad-
lressed to them, they trust no other object has actuated
hem than good, and, with affectionate solicitude for their
velfare, they commit them to the guidance of that
;racious Providence who orders all things well, earnestly
iraying that Jesus Christ our Lord, to whom be glory and
lominion for ever and ever, may be their unfailing portion
ere and hereafter. Amen.'

Although I did not court controversy, for I adhered
:losely to the advice of my dearest friend, Mr. Joseph
Senior, I was yet insensibly drawn into it by a challenge
rom the Unitarian minister then in Glasgow, the Rev.
George Harris. The subject was, 'The Divinity of the
Lord.' I obtained one of the largest halls in Glasgow, and
lelivered a lecture, affirming the supreme Deity of our
Lord and Saviour Jesus Christ. The hall was crowded to
;he door, and I was listened to with breathless attention:
but at the conclusion one of the Unitarians present stepped
forward and stated, if that lecture was published, he would
undertake it should be answered in six weeks. I con-
;ulted with my friend Mr. Senior, who furnished me
with the means of publishing it, and a copy of it was
sent to the Rev. Mr. Harris, but it was never replied to.

This discourse brought me into favorable notice with

the clergy of the Established Church, and was afterwards translated into Gaelic. Subsequently it was reprinted, and it now forms No. 1 of the 'Glasgow Series of Christian Tracts.' It has had a circulation of at least ten thousand copies, and is stereotyped.

From the publication of this sermon originated the idea of publishing a regular series of doctrinal and other tracts, which should embody the views of the Swedenborgians in popular language, and which should be treated on exclusively scriptural grounds, without mentioning the denomination from which they emanated. As usual, I consulted my friend upon this subject, and he so far agreed with me that he promised to assist in the work, but advised that the tracts should be published at long intervals ; he at the same time wished me to undertake the composition of a work which should be suitable for Sunday reading, and be adapted for Sunday Schools as well as simple-minded Christians of adult age, promising that he would secure me from any loss. I shall have to return again to this subject in a future part of my narrative, but I at once proceeded to the composition of the work, which was for the most part original, but there were selections from various authors, as well from Swedenborgians as from other denominations of Christians.

I had been in Glasgow about a year and a-half when I learned that there was a Phrenological Society in the city, and I immediately sought admission into it, and was at length accepted and admitted a member. This gave me access to the highly valuable library of the Society, and I lost no time in the perusal of the works, metaphysical as well as phrenological, which it contained. I was so repeatedly at the library, and spent so much time in the inspection of the different casts and crania in the museum, that I began to attract the attention of the principal members, and was frequently invited to their houses. Most of them were persons moving in the higher circles of society, and all eminent men of science. A few were professors in the medical schools of the University.

At this time an advertisement appeared in most of the London papers offering a prize of a hundred guineas for the best essay, which should illustrate the vice of Covetousness existing in the Christian Church. Although I was much engaged in preaching, I still had much leisure on my hands, for did not write my sermons. It occurred to me that I might profitably occupy my spare time in the composition of an essay which should call into exercise my acquired phrenological knowledge, and enable me to depict the workings of covetousness in the various departments of the non-professing world, as well as in the Christian Church. I resolved, however, that my essay should first do duty as a sermon. I then re-arranged it, and at length sent it to Dr. Conquest. There were upwards of a hundred competitors, and the prize was adjudged to Mr. now Dr. Harris. The title of the prize essay was 'MAMMON, or the Sin of Covetousness in the Christian Church.' Many of the essays were published, and among them mine, which I entitled, 'ACQUISITIVENESS, ITS USES AND ABUSES.' I dedicated my essay to my friends, Messrs. George and Joseph Senior, of Dalton, near Huddersfield. It met with a very favorable reception, and went through two editions.

Meantime, I was unremitting in my attendance at the Phrenological Society's meetings. I took no part in the discussions, but I scarcely missed an essay that was read, or a lecture that was delivered, for nearly two years, and I was a close observer of the casts in the Society's museum. In 1838 I submitted myself for phrenological examination to the President of the Glasgow Phrenological Society, first writing a few preliminary observations on my habits and feelings, and presenting them in a sealed envelope, which was not to be opened until the predication of the character by the persons appointed. I extract this article from the Manuscript Journal of the Glasgow Phrenological Society of 1838 ; the following is a verbatim copy :—

'MEASUREMENT AND MANIPULATION OF THE HEAD OF ——.

'The measurement by Wm. Weir, Esq., M.D., Senior Physician of the Glasgow Infirmary. The inferences deduced from the measurement, by Jonathan Barber, Esq., Member of the Royal College of Surgeons, London. The Preliminary Observations are by ——, and also the notes to Mr. Barber's Inferences.

'From my earliest youth I have been most ardently attached to children, and their company still affords me the highest delight.

I have been, by my friends, strongly censured as being destitute of the homely quality of prudence. This, I am convinced, is an error on their part; I always lay my plans by calculation, but I have such an exuberant share of hope that I imagine such plans are only necessary to be carried into execution to ensure success. I believe my disappointments, in most cases, to have arisen from this exuberant hope.

'I have a passion, almost a mania for books, of which I am very conservative. I am select in my choice. I am fond of works of imagination, (such as Scott and Bulwer) poetry and the higher branches of the drama. I am particularly pleased with such works as reserve the denouement of the plot till the very last moment. I am equally fond of witty and humorous narratives, but prefer reading them when alone.

'I am fond of knowing the opinions of different sects on the important topic of religion. I read works of polemical divinity with intense pleasure.

'I feel very timid on first introduction to a stranger or strange company—I cannot acquire any thing like confidence until I have been assured by kindness. Should I be spoken to with unkindness or asperity, I can scarcely answer without stammering, and my agitation is sometimes so great that I perspire at every pore.

'In matters of religion, I feel the widest tolerance to

...MENT AND MANIPULATION OF THE HEAD OF ——

'The measurement by Wm. Weir, Esq., M.D., Senior ... of the Glasgow Infirmary. The interest ... measurement, by Jonathan Love, ... Member of the Royal College of Surgeons, London. The Preliminary Observations are by ——, and ... the notes to Mr. Barber's Inferences.

'From my earliest youth I have been most ardently attached to children, and their company still affords me ... highest delight.

'I have been, by my friends, strongly censured as being destitute of the homely quality of prudence. This, I am convinced, is an error on their part; I always lay my plans by calculation, but I have such an exuberant share of hope that I imagine such plans are only necessary to be carried into execution to ensure success. I believe my disappointments, in most cases, have arisen from this exuberant hope.

'I have a passion, almost a mania for books, of which I am very conservative. I am select in my choice. I ... works of imagination, (such as Scott and Byron ...) and the higher branches of the drama. I ... especially pleased with such works as reserve the ... of the plot till the very last moment. I am equally fond of witty and humorous narratives, but prefer reading them when alone.

'I am fond of knowing the opinions of different sects on the important topic of religion. I read works of polemical divinity with intense pleasure.

'I feel very timid on first introduction to a stranger or ... company—I cannot admire any thing like ... until I have been assured by kindness. Should I ... ... to with unkindness or asperity, I can scarcely ... without stammering, and my agitation is sometimes ... great that I perspire at every pore.

'In matters of religion, I feel the widest tolerance to

(PAGE 288.

almost all parties. My religious opinions are the result of close investigation of almost every other creed ; I feel, however, considerable antipathy to the doctrines, but not to the persons, of those who limit the mercy of the Divine Being ; if I am in company with persons of this description, and the subject of religion is started, I am impetuous and sometimes passionate. I also feel repugnance to the doctrines of those who deny the divinity of the Saviour, but I never introduce religious topics in private societies unless I am personally solicited.

'Before I knew Phrenology I was frequently hot-tempered and impetuous, but I have learned since to keep a watch over my propensities. I used to be very fond of attending a school of theology in Liverpool, where I was stationed some years since.

'I have a peculiar feeling of what the English call *Comfortableness*. A small snug room, carpeted, with an easy chair, and a well selected library, is the very height of my ambition.

'I feel great pleasure in the possession of drawings, engravings, and paintings ; but I have not the smallest ability in the use of the pencil. I have collected portraits since 1821.*

'I delight in analogies, and am able to reason much better by analogy than induction.

'I am passionately fond of music. In walking the streets, sometimes melodious strains appear to pass through my mind spontaneously, and I have been irresistibly impelled to break forth into a whistle, and sometimes even into the singing of an air. I have composed several moral songs for children.

'I am at times timid, nervous, and subject to palpitations of the heart. I have a most ardent love of life. The smallest illness alarms me. I have tried to conquer this feeling in vain. I know it is wrong, but I cannot, with all my efforts, entirely subdue it. The feeling of love of life absorbs for a time every other. When I

---

* I now possess many hundred portraits of eminent men and women.

19

think exclusively upon spiritual subjects, then I lose this feeling.

'I may add, that I am very quick in my motions, and, if stimulated, can get through almost any labor.

'These remarks are hastily thrown together for the purpose of ascertaining how they harmonise with my organization.'

'MEASUREMENT AND DEVELOPMENT OF THE HEAD OF ——, AGED 42, EDUCATED—TEMPERAMENT, SANGUINE-NERVOUS.

MEASUREMENT OF HEAD, INCLUDING HAIR, WHICH IS THICK.

	Inches.		Inches.
Greatest size round the whole head	22	Ear to Philoprogenitiveness	$4\frac{3}{8}$
From Occipital spine to Individuality, over crown	$14\frac{1}{4}$	From Cautiousness to Cautiousness	$5\frac{3}{4}$
From ear to ear, over crown	$13\frac{5}{8}$	From Secretiveness to Secretiveness	$5\frac{7}{8}$
„ Philoprogenitiveness to Individuality	7	From Destructiveness to Destructiveness	$5\frac{7}{8}$
From Concentrativeness to Comparison	7	From Acquisitiveness to Acquisitiveness	$5\frac{1}{2}$
Ear to Individuality	$4\frac{1}{2}$	From Mastoid process to Mastoid process	$5\frac{1}{4}$
„ Benevolence	$5\frac{1}{2}$	From Constructiveness to Constructiveness	$4\frac{3}{4}$
„ Comparison	$5\frac{1}{4}$	From Ideality to Ideality	$4\frac{1}{4}$
„ Veneration	$5\frac{3}{8}$		
„ Firmness	5		

MEASURED WITH CALLIPERS.

1 Amativeness	16	19 Ideality	17
2 Philoprogenitiveness	18	20 Wit	17
3 Concentrativeness	17	21 Imitation	16
4 Adhesiveness	19	22 Individuality	15
5 Combativeness	17	23 Form	17
6 Destructiveness	17	24 Size	16
7 Secretiveness	19	25 Weight	16
8 Acquisitiveness	18	26 Coloring	17
9 Constructiveness	16	27 Locality	15
10 Self-esteem	15	28 Order	18
11 Love of Approbation	17	29 Number	18
12 Cautiousness	18	30 Eventuality	17
13 Benevolence	20	31 Time	17
14 Veneration	19	32 Tune	17
15 Firmness	16	33 Language	18
16 Conscientiousness	19	34 Comparison	19
17 Hope	18	35 Causality	18
18 Wonder	19		

'Scale of Size: — Full, 14; rather large, 16; large, 18; very large, 20.

'Outer part of eyebrow better developed than inner. Reflective faculties larger than knowing.'

INFERENCES BY JONATHAN BARBER ESQ., M.R.C.S.

'The power of this brain, considered as a whole, is average, with considerable activity. The constitution, *probably*, excitable and delicate. The feelings common to man and animals, will, in their manifestations be subordinated to the intellectual and moral faculties, aided by the caution and regard for character which prevails in the constitution of this brain. They exist, however, in a considerable degree. The domestic affections are strong, especially attachment. Moral would ever be preferred to promiscuous love ; and the amative passion would be prompted by personal regard, and be found in union with it. Pretty and orderly children would be very interesting to this individual. He is exceedingly kind—prompt in rendering assistance, and has pleasure in serving others. I should think a tale of distress would always excite his charity ; but he would inquire into its truth, and be apt to suspect deception ; * and even his benevolence must act in harmony with his reflecting faculties. He values property, and pursues his calling with attention to interest and reputation. His desire of distinction is great, but he is no boaster, nor does he like such as are. His large Caution and Secretiveness, combined with his reflecting faculties, make him modest, particularly as his Self-esteem is not inordinate ; he is consequently free from arrogance, and will be esteemed by his acquaintance. He must have considerable humor and dramatic power †

---

* This is true ; I am certainly suspicious, and have frequently expressed my doubts even to the objects soliciting relief, but with all my caution I have frequently been imposed upon. In truth, in some instances, I have been incapable of withstanding solicitation, even though I have known the objects to be unworthy.

† This is singularly correct, though not mentioned by me in my former observations in so marked a manner. I have said I am fond of works of humor, and of the higher branches of the drama. In my younger days I had a strong predilection for the stage, and few of my companions could excel me in reading a comedy. I have often read to my family, I mean brothers and sisters, with such effect as to hear them observe, it was nearly as good to hear me read, as to witness a performance. With all my love for dramatic literature, I have never witnessed the representation of a tragedy.

—has pleasure in music and the fine arts. In geometry and the mathematics (particularly where number * is concerned), he has superior power. He is more attentive to phenomena than to mere objects ; and natural history is not, in its still departments, his favorite pursuit. He is capable of succeeding in those sciences in which inference and deduction are to be made from phenomena. Phrenology should interest him.† He has a respect for religion, and is no scoffer. If educated in orthodoxy, probably adheres to the kirk. He will require morality, however, as well as doctrine, but will reconcile the myst-ries with the other parts of his faith. When young, tᴌ wonderful‡ attracted him, but his reflective powers lift him above superstition.

'He has temper and spirit, but they never exhibit themselves in ebullitions of passion. § He is honorable in pecuniary transactions, and expects from others the integrity he is disposed to manifest himself.

'He is neat and orderly in his habits—social, and disposed to the pleasures of society. ‖

'In language, and the arts of design, he is not deficient,¶

* This is also very correct. In 1825 I compiled a work on Mental Arithmetic, which went through four editions. The work was an illustration of Pestalozzi's System of Mental Calculation.

† No study more so.

‡ This is true. 'When young,' I devoured fictions by the score, and the more marvellous and intricate they were the better were they suited to my depraved taste. ' Celina,' (a tale of Mystery,) 'The Monk,' Mrs. Radcliffe's works, and the works of the author of 'Bertram,' were among my choicest luxuries of the imagination.

§ This is not so correct. I have frequently, though not of late years, been carried away by passion, but when the ebullition has subsided, I have endured the most bitter suffering from a due sense of the impropriety of my conduct. I attribute my subjugation of this fiery temper to my acquaintance with phrenology, as much as my reflecting faculties. I may add, I am rather touchy, very jealous of my reputation, and sometimes imagine injury or insult where none is intended.

‖ This is correct, and will account for my peculiar feelings of 'comfortableness' mentioned in the preliminary observations.

¶ As observed in the preliminary remarks, I am fond of drawings, engravings, and paintings, and can appreciate their beauties, and point out their defects ; but I am a complete bungler with a pencil. The note of Dr. Weir, that 'the outer part of the eyebrow is better developed than the inner,' will account for this.

but in the former has most ability. He is capable of being a good lecturer on subjects which he understands. A vein of dry humor runs in a continual under-current, and I should think, on the whole, his temper is cheerful.

'I think this head will pass through life employed in intellectual pursuits and lawful occupations, leaving little room for censure; with attention to individual interests, yet respecting those of others, and with the esteem and regard of the great majority of those who know him.'

I now began to study the form of the head, and to occupy myself in drawing analyses of character from measurement and manipulation. I did this for some time without fee or reward, and having been appointed Curator of the Society's Museum, I devoted two hours a day, for three days in the week, to drawing inferences from cerebral development of all persons who came to me. I think in the space of two years I could not have measured less than a thousand heads. I was at length compelled to give up this gratuitous practice, I was so inundated by visitors. All seemed eager to test phrenology by an examination of their own cranium. I frequently, when a more than ordinarily marked head presented itself, drew out a written analysis for the person's guidance and education. Of the different heads brought under my notice I do not remember one more strikingly characteristic and harmonious with phrenology than a youth of Dunfermline. At the time I first saw him he was in his fifteenth year. His head was very large, measuring at that early period upwards of 23 inches in circumference, and every part was fully and freely developed. The organs of Constructiveness, Form, Size, Coloring, Ideality, Imitation, Wit, and Language, were very large indeed, and there was not an organ in the entire brain that was deficient in power. The temperament was a compound of sanguine and nervous. I recom-

mended the father of this youth to allow him to cultivate
the arts, affirming that I was yet young enough to live
to see him at the head of his profession as an artist.　I
employed him to paint me several portrait illustrations
of eminent men, and I was amazed at the fidelity of
the likenesses, as well as the just form and proportion
of the different heads he executed; I was no less
astonished at the rapidity with which he executed the
work.　These portraits were painted in Indian ink to
imitate busts.　He also designed three illustrations for
my essay on 'Acquisitiveness,' and although only just
turned fourteen at the time, these illustrations were pronounced, by competent critics, perfect master-pieces of
composition.　With one of these I present my readers.
It illustrates a fact in the history of Henry viii., which
I had introduced into my essay on 'Acquisitiveness,'
from Spelman's 'History of Sacrilege.'　'When Henry
wanted his first act to be passed for confiscating the
property of the monasteries, the Commons rejected the
bill twice.　Henry then summoned them to attend him
in his hall, and after keeping them waiting for four or
five hours, he entered, and going up among them, looking
angrily on one side and on the other, "I hear" (said he)
"that you will not pass the bill—but I will have it, or
I will have some of your heads."　This did the work, and
the Commons passed the bill.'*　The design illustrates
Henry in his passionate display, telling the story most
faithfully.

During the great controversy between the Established
Church of Scotland and the Voluntary Church, he painted
three emblematical caricatures, placing the ministers of
the Established Church in the most ludicrous positions,
and illustrating his designs with the most pungent witticisms.　They are marvellous evidences of inventive
genius and mental power, and, were they published, would
inflict more mental suffering upon the Church party than
all the numerous lectures and speeches that emanated

* See 'Essay on Acquisitiveness,' p. 21.　Second Edition.

HENRY THE EIGHTH IN HIS GALLERY.

— By John Junr Decr 1836 —

from the Voluntary party. These caricatures were presented to me, and are now in my possession. I showed them to a connoisseur a short time since and he pronounced them worth a hundred guineas. It must be remembered that I am speaking of a youth, then only in his fifteenth year; but I am proud to say that that youth has fully justified my phrenological predictions, and is at the present time considered one of the most eminent artists Scotland has yet produced.

I had now studied phrenology for nearly twenty years, and at length I considered myself competent to become a lecturer on the science. I remembered my promise to the lady who had presented me with Spurzheim's works, and I determined to redeem it. In looking attentively at the marked bust I observed all the sentiments of morality and religion were situated in the coronal region; the intellectual faculties in the anterior, and the propensities in the posterior; and my own observations had confirmed me in the truth of the position of the several organs. In reading the writings of Swedenborg, particularly upon the human brain, which he designated a congeries of all the wonders in the universe, I was much struck with the harmony of his views with those of the best instructed phrenologists, and the following passage determined me to make it a kind of text for my first lecture :—
'The human mind is distinguished into three regions, from the highest of which [the coronal region] a man regards God; from the second or middle [the anterior] the world; and from the third, or lowest, [the posterior] himself; and in consequence of this, its true nature and constitution, the mind is capable of being raised and of raising itself, because it can look towards God and heaven. It is also capable of being diffused and of diffusing itself laterally in every direction, because it can look around into the world and its nature; and lastly it is capable of being sunk and of sinking itself, because it can look towards the earth and hell.' * In my examination of

* Swedenborg's 'Universal Theology,' section 395.

the different casts in the Phrenological Society's **Museum**, I found the above remarks most wonderfully confirmed, so, as I said before, I determined to make this **passage** a kind of text upon which to found my principal lecture.

It may be expedient here to say, that there may be passages in my lectures unmarked by inverted commas, which I have met with in the course of my reading, of which I do not know the authors' names; but these are so blended with my own ideas that I could hardly separate them. My authorities are Gall, Spurzheim, Combe, 'The Phrenological Journal,' and some other sources. I will also add, that for nearly fourteen years I read every work published on phrenology both in this country and the United States. I state these particulars that I may not be accused of borrowing the ideas of others without acknowledgment. But I have depended principally on my own observations. The following is,

MY FIRST LECTURE.

In calling the attention of our hearers to the science of phrenology, we are not insensible to the difficulties which present themselves at the outset; and we are aware of the odium which will attach itself to the individual who attempts to lift the veil of antiquity, and to show that the speculations of the schoolmen did not always evince superhuman wisdom. Time has thrown around the classic authors of antiquity the venerable robe of sanctity, and it is almost considered impious to propound any doctrine which carries not with it the stamp of their authority. A little reflection will, however, convince us, that even among the sages of antiquity, new doctrines have ever met with persevering hostility; and the propounders of them have, in some instances, suffered ignominious deaths, or been incarcerated in dungeons, or banished from their country, kindred, and friends. In all ages, the antipathy to what is termed NEW has displayed itself, and those who have labored the most disinterestedly and the most zealously to instruct mankind, have been those who have suffered most from ignorance. A few illustrations will suffice to prove this.

The intelligence and the virtue of Socrates was punished with death ! Anaxagoras, when he attempted to propagate a just notion of the Supreme Being, was dragged to prison ! Aristotle, after a long series of persecutions, swallowed poison ! Virgilius, bishop of Saltzburg, having asserted that there existed Antipodes, the Archbishop of Mentz declared him a heretic ! The Abbot Trithemius, who was fond of stenography, having published several curious works on that subject, they were condemned as full of diabolical mysteries : and Frederick II, Elector Palatine, ordered Trithemius's original work, which was in his library, to be publicly burnt. Galileo was condemned at Rome publicly to disavow his sentiments ! Cornelius Agrippa was compelled to fly his country, merely for having exhibited a few philosophical experiments which now every schoolboy can perform ! Des Cartes was cruelly prosecuted in Holland, where he first published his opinions ; while the great geometricians and chemists, Gerbert and Roger Bacon, were abhorred as magicians, and looked upon as objects of horror ! The persecution of that which is new has lost but very little of its virulence in our own time ; for, although phrenology is received with much more complacency now than formerly, yet the reader can form but a very imperfect estimate of the obloquy which attached itself to its first promulgation; [and the present lecturer can safely say, he has, perhaps, suffered as much as any.] Not only was it difficult to obtain an audience to lecture to, but even a room to lecture in ; and when the late Dr. Spurzheim, by great interest, procured a hall at the University of Cambridge, he found himself, at the commencement of his lecture, with but one solitary hearer. At present, no such difficulties present themselves to a man of average ability ; but still the advocates of t' science are often assailed with the epithets of ّ<name us

materialists ; and the staple objections now rest principally on these terms. It is contended that the science is hostile to religion ; that it is a system of materialism and fatalism ; and that the philosophical infidel is its most potent champion. We feel it necessary to examine each of these objections :—

OBJECTION I. *It is hostile to Religion*—It is true, clergymen have written against it ; but, it is presumed, they have done so from a misapprehension of its principles, and in consequence of such misapprehension, which has generally originated in hearsay, they have not gone into the investigation sufficiently single-minded ; and many have condemned it altogether without reading a single volume of the works of its great discoverers. But the objection of a clergyman against the science is no proof of its fallacy. Many clergymen have been warm advocates of its principles. The late Rev. Dr. Welch, professor of Church History in the University of Edinburgh, was the founder of the first Phrenological Society in Great Britain. That society, in the metropolis of Scotland (Edinburgh), still exists, has a large museum and library, and has produced some of the most eminent phrenologists, —the late lamented and amiable Dr. Combe, and his brother, the justly-celebrated George Combe, one of the most profound philosophers of the present day ; Robert Cox, Esq., the editor of the 'Phrenological Journal' ; James Simpson, Esq., the celebrated educationist ; Sir G. S. Mackenzie, Bart. ; and many others of equal note. Dr. Welch has left a valuable testimony in favor of the science ; his own words are :—' I think it right to declare that I have found the greatest benefit from the science, as a minister of the gospel. I have been led to study the evidence of Christianity anew, in connection with phrenology, and I feel my confidence in the truths of our religion increased by this new examination ; and, in dealing with my people, in the ordinary duties of my calling, the practical benefit I have derived from phrenology is incalitself, and further, the present Archbishop of Dublin, Dr.

Whateley, one of the most profound scholars, and the most eminent logicians of the present day, has declared that the objection brought against phrenology, on the ground of its opposition to religion, is utterly futile, and unworthy any rational mind. Thus, if clergymen have written against the science, eminent and dignified clergymen have written in its favor. But, if phrenology is opposed to religion, how does it happen that the bust describes special religious faculties?—and these are, by phrenologists, absolutely declared to be among the most important powers of the mind. If phrenologists were anxious to overthrow religion (a thing utterly impossible), would they take so much pains to cultivate those sentiments which by all are admitted equally indispensable to the well-being of society as well as to the individual man? Why take so much pains to prove that there is a sentiment of benevolence, or charity; of faith or marvellousness, which induces a belief in a Supreme Being; of hope of futurity; of veneration, or a reverence for the Great Supreme; of conscientiousness, or a love of integrity and truth; of ideality, or a love of excellence; and of firmness, or perseverance in well-doing?—They might at once blot out all these faculties from their authenticated and well-drawn map of the mind, if they were the opponents of religion. But it is well known that the contrary is the case; and phrenology has among its advocates clergymen of talent, and of all religious denominations.

OBJECTION II. *Phrenology leads to Materialism, nay, say its opponents, is Materialism.*—It cannot be denied that there are some phrenologists who so contend, but there are enow of us who protest against it. It is scarcely possibly to conceive how such a charge can be sustained. The mind may easily be proved to act by material organs, but this does not prove the mind itself to be material. Phrenologists do not deny that the mind communicates in some mysterious way with the brain; they only say they cannot tell how. Will our opponents enlighten our darkness by informing us; if they cannot, why do they blame us

for that for which they have no solution themselves ?
Matter, whether in its more gross or etherealised form, is
matter still ; and if it could possess any of the attributes
of spirit, it would cease to be matter. The brain itself
does not think, and phrenologists—at least the majority
of them—have never contended that it does. They have
never pretended to show in what manner spirit becomes
united with matter; nor is it necessary that they should. To
those who believe in Divine Revelation, it is quite easy to
prove that spirit can and does exist without matter ; but
as this is a question pertaining to theology, of course it
cannot be discussed here.

OBJECTION III. *Phrenology leads to Fatalism.*—Now,
fatalism literally implies that man is a passive being ; that
he has no will of his own, but is acted upon by a power
he is incapable of resisting.

Phrenology has no such tendency. If one organ is in
excess, there are others which may be brought to bear upon
it, to restrain it and keep it in order. If one organ is deficient, by commencing its cultivation at a proper period,
there is proof that its power can be increased ; and there
are also other powers which may be called in to aid, and,
in some degree, to compensate for, its weakness. But
this no more implies fatality, than the case of the servant
mentioned in the gospel, who received his Lord's money
to trade with. The man that had but one talent was not
condemned because he had but one, but because he did
not make use of that one. But we contend that it is
quite possible to alter and improve the organization, if
commenced at a proper period of life.*

Human responsibility is undoubted, and is fully admitted by phrenologists ; but, in cases of insanity, it is
impossible to hold a man responsible.

---

* Richard Beamish, Esq., F.R.S. in a lecture delivered some time
since, at the Town Hall, Buckingham, states, that his own head had so
much changed by two years' hard study, as to render the casts taken of
him at several previous periods scarcely recognisable as belonging to the
same individual ; and such is also the case with respect to the author of
this Biography.

It is urged further, as an insuperable objection to phrenology, that cases have been well authenticated, in which the brain has been injured, altered in structure, and even partially destroyed, while the mind has continued unimpaired, and carried on its operations with its accustomed regularity. It should, however, be borne in mind, that the organs of the brain, like the other organs of the animal economy, are double ; and therefore, as one eye may be lost, and the faculty of sight remain perfect in the other, so one organ, or one set of organs, may be diseased, or even destroyed, while the functions of the brain may still be performed with the other. A very interesting proof of the duality of the brain is given in the ' Phrenological Journal ' (vol. x.), which we will cite :—

' Mr. S. dreamed that he was in his parlor with a friend, and that a piece of *black cloth* was lying on the table, but which his friend happened to remark was flesh-colored. Hereupon arose a discussion as to the color of the cloth, Mr. S. maintaining that it was black, and his friend as strenuously insisting that it was flesh-colored. The dispute became warm, and Mr. S. offered to bet that it was black ; his friend also offering to bet that it was flesh-color. Mr. S. concluded the bet, when his friend immediately exclaimed, "And is not black the color of more than half the human race ? "—thus completely stealing a march upon Mr. S., and winning the bet. Mr. S. declares that the idea of black being flesh-color never occurred to him.—The extraordinary part of this dream is, that two operations were going on at the same time, and in the same mind—the workings of the one apparently quite concealed from the other. For instance, the part of the brain which personated himself had no knowledge whatever of the loop-hole which the part of the brain personating his friend had in reserve to close the argument. On the contrary, Mr. S. says he was utterly abashed by the remark, immediately thinking to himself how foolish he was not to have been in possession of the idea, and this very vexation caused him to awake.'

It is thus proved the brain is dual. But the brain, besides being dual, consists of a congeries of organs, and this is easily demonstrable. If the brain were a single organ, then the idea of the metaphysicians that the mind is a *tabula rasa* would be correct, and educators would have it in their power to form the statesman, the lawyer, the divine ; or the architect, the painter, the sculptor, as the wishes and the means of the parent might direct. But we every day see the reverse of this, and different individuals are biassed to various pursuits, as their organization seems to impel them. If we walk the streets of large towns as observers of others, we shall perceive the multitude attracted by different objects. While the tradesman is attracted by the stock of his brother in trade, and the taste with which it is displayed to attract the eye of the public, the student will be found at the bookseller's ; and while the mechanic is observing with attention tools and machinery, the artist will be attracted by the printseller.

But if all men were similarly organised, the same attractions would arrest the attention equally of all. It is true, that as all minds possess that in common which makes them human, they acquire, to a certain extent, the same *general* development ; but each mind possesses something peculiar to itself, which disposes it to a course of action distinctly different to that of any other ; and this, surely, is one of the most beneficent arrangements of the Supreme, endowing different individuals with different powers or faculties, that each may minister to the general good of the whole :—

> ' Some at the sounding anvil glow ;
> Some the swift-sliding shuttle throw ;
> Some, studious of the wind and tide,
> From pole to pole our commerce guide ;
> Some, taught by industry, impart
> With hands and feet the works of art ;
> While some, of genius more refined,
> With head and tongue assist mankind.
> *   *   *   *   *

The monarch, when his table's spread,
Is to the clown obliged for bread ;
And, when in all his glory dress'd,
Owes to the loom his royal vest.
Do not the mason's toil and care
Protect him from th' inclement air ?
Does not the cutler's art supply
The ornament that guards his thigh ? '

*　　*　　*　　*　　*

The same may be affirmed of everything connected
vith taste and art, and the bias displays itself almost
nvariably in infancy—at least, long before reflection leads
o what is called the choice of a profession. The first
levelopment of the musical genius is while yet an infant.
The harmony of sweet sounds not only catches the ear,
)ut excites the desire to produce similar sounds. The
:elebrated violinist, Paganini, began his career as soon as
ie was able to hold the instrument. Is there any incon-
;ruity in supposing that this desire should manifest itself
)y some external development ? Here is a portrait of
Handel :—

, Let the reader examine well the lateral parts of the

forehead, where the No. 32 is marked, and he will observe them much enlarged ; and as he passes the shop-window of the music-sellers, let him observe the lateral parts of the forehead of the portraits of those eminent composers, frequently exhibited, and he will find them all freely and fully rounded.

Handel's father was a physician at Halle, in Saxony, and destined his son for the profession of the law ; and, seeing his early predilection for music, determined to check it. He excluded from his house all musical society, nor would he permit music or musical instruments to be ever heard within its walls. The child, however, notwithstanding his parents' precautions, found means to hear somebody play on the harpsichord ; and the delight which he felt having prompted him to endeavor to gain an opportunity of practising what he heard, he contrived, through a servant, to procure a small clarichord or spinnet, which he secreted in a garret, and to which he repaired every night after the family had gone to rest.   Mr. Hogarth, in his popular ' History of Music,' has the following observations :—' A childish love for music or painting, even when accompanied with an aptitude to learn something of these arts, is not, in one case out of a hundred or a thousand, conjoined with that degree of genius, without which it would be a vain and idle pursuit.'   But as phrenology would enable us to judge of the capability by the organization, if we will but appeal to it, to abide by what Mr. Hogarth advises, is to hide under a bushel that light which might serve to illuminate the whole hemisphere of that particular department of art; and we say to parents, that where, as in the case of Handel and West (mentioned just below), music and painting develop themselves at nine years of age, and in defiance of all the difficulties opposed to them, cultivate respectively such talents : such children are public benefactors in embryo, and the parents may live to behold them arise to eminence.

It is the same with painting. The infant painter no

sooner sees the effect produced by the pencil, than the will impels him to grasp the tiny tool, that he may gratify his love of the art by attempting to sketch a picture for himself. Is it too much to say that this love will develop itself by some striking external development ? The late Benjamin West, the son of Quaker parents, who prohibit, by their discipline, the cultivation of the arts, yet gave indications of his talent for drawing in his ninth year. 'It is thus that the latent talents of the soul, as they expand under proper culture, and sometimes in defiance of it, acquire the gratification and delight after which they pant ; and it is not more difficult for the tree to return to the seed from whence it sprung, than for the person so endowed to cease to act. The soil which produces the vine, in its most healthy luxuriance, is not better adapted than the world we live in, to draw forth and mature the latent energies of the soul, and fill them with life and vigor. Is there aught in eloquence that warms the heart ? she draws her fire from natural imagery. Is there aught in poetry to enliven the imagination ? in natural imagery lies the secret of her power ; and he who possesses an expansive ideality, with faculties in combination to give scope to its sublimity, will throw the rays of his genius over the most apparently unseemly objects !'

It may be as well to remark here, that we are accused of having the head mapped out into too many and too minute portions. But, if the writings of the metaphysicians be consulted, it will be found that they enumerate quite as many. But we shall prove, as we proceed, that the phrenologists assign no more powers to the mind than experience demonstrates the absolute existence of. And if they assign to certain portions of the brain faculties, whose functions display various powers, it is because they are possessed of abundant facts to demonstrate what they assert.

We conclude this part of our lecture, by affirming that phrenology is a true science of mind ; that the brain, as

20

a whole, is the organ of the mind ; that the **brain is** dual ; and that there exist a congeries of organs.

We proceed now to show that the size of the brain, other conditions being equal, is an index of power. On dissecting the head of the late Baron Cuvier, the most remarkable feature was the great size of the brain.

'Semmering,' says M. Berard, 'computes the weight of the human brain to be from two to three pounds. I arrived at the same conclusion, by taking two **brains :** the one from a woman, aged thirty, weighed, with its membranes, 2lb. 11oz. 2drs. ; the other from a **man,** aged forty, weighed 2lb. 12oz. 6½drs. The **brain of** Cuvier weighed 3lb. 10oz. 4½drs., being nearly a pound heavier than the weight of the others. But that which is most interesting to the phrenological investigator, is, upon comparing the weight of the cerebellum with that **taken** from the man just mentioned, a difference of one **dram** and a half only was found in favor of Cuvier : hence it followed, that the excess of weight in his brain was distributed almost entirely to the cerebral lobes, as the seat of the intellectual faculties.'

The comparative estimate respecting the dimensions of the heads of the inhabitants in several counties in England is as follows :—The male head in England, at maturity, averages from 6¼ inches to 7⅔ in diameter ; the medium and most general size being 7. The female **head** is smaller, varying from 6¾ to 7 (or 7¼ the medium male size). Fixing the medium of the English head at 7, there can be no difficulty in distinguishing the portions of society above, from those below, that measurement. In London, the majority of the higher classes are above the medium ; while among the lower it is very rare to find a large head. The Spitalfields weavers have extremely small heads, 6⅔, 6½, and 6¾ being the prevailing admeasurement. In Coventry, almost exclusively peopled by weavers, the same facts are peculiarly observed. Hertfordshire, Essex, Suffolk, and Norfolk, contain a larger proportion of small heads than any part of the empire. Seven inches in diameter is here, as in Spitalfields and Coventry, quite unusual—6⅝ and 6¼ are more general ; and 6⅜, the usual size of a boy of six years of age, is frequently to be met with here in the full maturity of manhood. In Kent, Surrey, and Sussex, an increase of size of the usual average is observed, and the inland counties, in general, are nearly upon the same scale. In Devonshire and Cornwall the heads are of full size. Herefordshire is superior to the London averages. In Lancashire, Yorkshire, Cumberland, and Northumberland, there are more large heads in proportion than any part of the country. In Scotland, the full-sized head is known to be possessed by the inhabitants, their measurement ranging from between 7¾ to 7⅞, and even to 8 inches, of which the author has seen many. From this it may be safely inferred that the size of brain is an index of power. This fact extends to individual organs and regions, as well as to the whole brain.

We will now show how the brain exercises its power, and through what medium, by a simple analogy :—If we blow through the mouth-piece of a flute, we produce a certain sound. Putting the pieces of the flute together, and placing the fingers on the holes, we produce a different sound ; raising now one finger, and then another, by different combinations of stopping we produce a complete harmony. This, however, is not the result of different air or wind, but of the same wind issuing through different channels. So the mind, acting upon different regions of brain, according to the power or quantity of brain in the region on which it operates, produces different results. Acting on the upper or coronal surface of the head, it produces the religious and moral sentiments, as in the portrait of Oberlin. Acting on the posterior part of the head, it exhibits the power of the lower or animal propensities, as in the portrait of Pope Alexander vi. Acting on the fore-part of the head, it exhibits the power of the intellectual faculties, as in the portrait of Gall. But this is only a general view of the character of the

OBERLIN.

respective persons, from the predominance of brain in
each region. Besides this, it must be stated that every
organ has a power and functions peculiarly its own, subject, however, to the modifying influence of temperament.
This modifying influence, and the power and functions
of the respective organs, we shall illustrate as we proceed.

It now becomes necessary to say a few words on the
discovery of the principles on which this science is based ;
and in so doing, we will condense the account given by
Dr. Gall himself, observing, however, by the way, that
though he possessed eminent powers of reflection, he was

but moderately endowed with the perception of *form* and size, and hence almost all his discoveries were from extreme cases. Spurzheim, on the contrary, who became

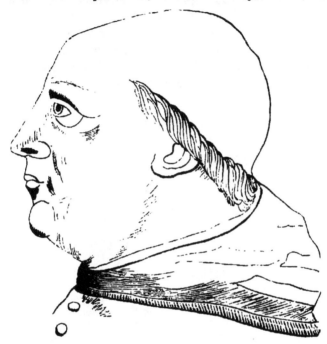

POPE ALEXANDER VI.

associated with him in 1804, in addition to excellent powers of reflection, had large form and size, a very large brain, and perhaps the keenest general perception of any phrenologist, either during or since his time, and his discrimination of character was amazingly quick and accurate. To predicate character is not so easy a matter as many have imagined ; for though the situation of the organs on the head must, on all occasions, be the same, still, as the size and formation of the head vary in almost every instance, of course the organs will be higher up or lower down than an unpractised person supposes. Then, again, the powers of the mind blend so closely with each other, and different shades of character, originating in

different portions of the brain arise, so that many errors
are likely to arise by an ignorant or careless manipulator :
—the functions of the organ of Secretiveness are liable to
be mistaken for those of Cautiousness ; Combativeness
for Destructiveness ; Adhesiveness for Benevolence ; and
vice versa.   But to return to the discovery of the science.*
Here are portraits of Gall and Spurzheim—two noble
heads, but still differently excellent :—

GALL.

From an early age Gall was given to observation, and

* This account is condensed from the 'Edinburgh Phrenological
Journal,' and the ' Journal de la Société Phrenologique de Paris.'

was struck with the fact, that each of his brothers and sisters, companions in play, and school-fellows, possessed some peculiarity of talent or disposition, which distinguished him from others. Some of his school-mates were distinguished by the beauty of their penmanship, some by their success in arithmetic, and others by their talent

SPURZHEIM.

for acquiring a knowledge of natural history, or of languages. The compositions of one were remarkable for elegance, while the style of another was stiff and dry; and a third connected his reasonings in the closest manner, and clothed his argument in the most forcible language.

Their dispositions were equally different, and this diversity appeared also to determine the direction of their partialities and aversions. Not a few of them manifested a capacity for employments which they were not taught ; they cut figures in wood, or delineated them on paper. Some devoted their leisure to painting, or the culture of a garden, while their comrades abandoned themselves to noisy games, or traversed the woods to gather flowers, seek for birds' nests, or catch butterflies. In this manner each individual presented a character peculiar to himself, and Gall never observed that the individual who had in one year displayed selfish or knavish dispositions, became in the next a good and faithful friend.

The scholars with whom young Gall had the greatest difficulty of competing were those who learned by heart with great facility, and such individuals frequently gained from him, by their repetitions, the places which he had obtained by the merit of his original compositions. Some years afterwards, having changed his place of residence, he still met individuals endowed with an equally great talent of learning to repeat. He then observed that his school-fellows so gifted possessed prominent eyes, and he recollected that his rivals in the first school had been distinguished by the first peculiarity. When he entered the university, he directed his attention from the first to the students whose eyes were of this description, and he soon found that they all excelled in getting rapidly by heart, and giving correct recitations, although many of them were by no means distinguished in point of general talent. This observation was recognised also by the other students in the classes ; and although the connection between the talent and the external sign was not at this time established upon such complete evidence as is requisite for a philosophical conclusion, yet Dr. Gall could not believe that the coincidence of the two circumstances thus observed was entirely accidental. He suspected, therefore, from this period, that they stood in an important relation to each other. After much reflection he conceived, that if memory for words was indicated by an external sign, the same might be the case with the other intellectual powers, and from that moment all individuals distinguished by any remarkable faculty became the objects of his attention. By degrees, he conceived himself to have found external characteristics which indicated a talent for painting, music, and mechanical arts. He became acquainted, also, with some individuals remarkable for the determination of their character, and he observed a particular part of their heads to be very largely developed. This fact first suggested to him the idea of looking to the head for signs of the moral sentiments. But in making these observations he never conceived, for a moment, that the *skull* was the cause of the different talents, as has been erroneously represented—he referred the influence, whatever it was, to the brain.

In following out, by observation, the principle which accident had thus suggested, he for some time encountered difficulties of the greatest magnitude. Hitherto he had been altogether ignorant of the opinions of physiologists touching the brain, and of metaphysicians respecting the mental faculties, and had simply observed nature. When, however, he began to enlarge his knowledge of books, he found the most extraordinary conflict of opinions everywhere prevailing, and this, for the moment, made him hesitate about the correctness of his own observations. He found that the moral sentiments had, by an almost general consent, been consigned to the thoracic and abdominal viscera ; and that, while Pythagoras, Plato, Galen, Haller, and some other physiologists, placed the sentient soul, or intellectual faculties, in the brain, Aristotle placed it in the heart, Van Helmont in the stomach, Des Cartes and his followers in the pineal gland, and Drelincourt and others in the cerebellum.

He observed, also, that a great number of philosophers and physiologists asserted, that all men are born with equal mental faculties, and that the differences observable among them are owing either to education, or to the accidental circumstances in which they are placed. If all differences are accidental, he inferred that there could be no natural signs of predominating faculties, and consequently, that the project of learning by observation to distinguish the functions of the different portions of the brain must be hopeless. This difficulty he combated by the reflection, that his brothers, sisters, and school-fellows had all received very nearly the same education, but that he had still observed each of them unfolding a distinct character, over which circumstances appeared to exert only a limited control. He observed, also, that not unfrequently they whose education had been conducted with the greatest care, and on whom the labors of teachers had been most freely lavished, remained far behind their companions in attainments. 'Often,' says Dr. Gall, 'we were accused of want of will, or deficiency in zeal; but many of us could not, even with the most ardent desire, followed out by the most obstinate efforts, attain, in some pursuits, even to mediocrity; while, in some other points, some of us surpassed our school-fellows without an effort, and almost, it might be said, without perceiving it ourselves. But, in point of fact, our masters did not appear to attach much faith to the system which taught the equality of the mental faculties, for they thought themselves entitled to exact more from one scholar, and less from another. They spoke frequently of natural gifts, or of the gifts of God, and consoled their pupils in the words of the gospel, by assuring them that each would be required to render an account only in proportion to the gifts which he had received.'*

Being convinced by these facts, that there is a natural and constitutional diversity of talents and dispositions, he encountered in books still other obstacles to his success in determining the external signs of the mental powers. He found that, instead of faculties for languages, drawing, memory for places, music, and mechanical arts, corres-

* Preface, by Dr. Gall to the 'Anatomie, etc., du Cerveau.'

ponding to the different talents which he had observed in his school-fellows, the metaphysicians spoke only of general powers, such as perception, conception, memory, imagination, and judgment. And when he endeavored to discover external signs in the head, corresponding to these general faculties, or to determine the correctness of the physiological doctrines regarding the seat of the mind, as taught by the authors already mentioned, he found perplexities without end, and difficulties innumerable.

Dr. Gall, therefore, abandoning every theory and pre-conceived opinion, gave himself up entirely to the observation of nature. Being physician to a lunatic asylum in Vienna, he had opportunities, of which he availed himself, of making observations on the insane. He visited prisons, and resorted to schools ; he was introduced to the courts of princes, to colleges and the seats of justice, and wherever he heard of an individual distinguished in any particular way, either by remarkable endowment or deficiency, he observed and studied the development of his head. In this manner, by an almost imperceptible induction, he conceived himself warranted in believing that particular mental powers are indicated by particular configurations of the head.

Hitherto he had resorted only to physiognomical indications, as a means of discovering the functions of the brain. On reflection, however, he was convinced that physiology was imperfect when separated from anatomy. Having observed a woman of fifty-four years of age, who had been afflicted with hydrocephalus from her youth, and, with a body a little shrunk, possessed as active and as intelligent a mind as that of other individuals of her class, Dr. Gall declared his conviction that the structure of the brain must be different from what was generally conceived—a remark which Tulpius also made on observing a hydrocephalus patient, who manifested the mental faculties. He therefore felt the necessity of making anatomical researches into the structure of the brain.

In every instance, when an individual whose head he had observed while alive happened to die, he used every means to be permitted to examine the brain, and frequently did so; and he found, as a general fact, that on removal of the skull, the brain covered by the *dura mater* presented a form corresponding to that which the skull had exhibited in life.

The successive steps by which Dr. Gall proceeded in his discoveries, are particularly deserving of attention. He did not, as many have imagined, first dissect the brain, and pretend by that means to have discovered the seats of the mental powers. Neither did he, as others have conceived, first map out the skull into various compartments, and assign a faculty to each according as his imagination led him to conceive the place appropriate to the power. On the contrary, he first observed a concomitance between particular talents and dispositions, and particular forms of the head; he next ascertained, by removal of the skull, that the figure and size of the brain are indicated by these external forms; and it was only after these facts were determined, and the brain was minutely dissected, that light was thrown upon its structure.

Although it is impossible to form a correct judgment of the particular character or disposition of a person from observing one organ, or one set of organs, yet a general idea may be formed by observing the contour of the whole head by attending to the following rules :—

1. A very small head is indicative of idiotcy, partial or general.

2. A small head, formed in good proportion, indicates capacity for discharging ordinary duties; but incapacity for filling any commanding situation, from deficiency of power.

3. A narrow or oval head, elongated at the occipital region, will be found to indicate a warm, friendly, and affectionate disposition, as in the female. (See page 317.)

4. A narrow head, elevated at the coronal surface, is

indicative of a moral and benevolent character. (See Oberlin, page 308.)

5. A head, round and narrow, is indicative of a quarrelsome and irascible disposition. (See Caracalla, p. 318.)

6. A head well developed in the forehead, is indicative of an intellectual character. (See Daniel Webster, p. 319.)

7. A large head, developed in all its parts, is indicative of a mind of the highest order of genius. (See Napoleon, p. 320.)

We have replied to the principal objections urged against the science of phrenology by ministers of the gospel, but there is an objection urged by anatomists (which we have in part anticipated,) which is to the following effect, namely : ' That there is no cognizable division of the brain into separate portions, corresponding to the so-called organs of phrenologists.' To this we reply, such a division is by no means necessary for the establishment of the truth of the science. It is quite possible that the blood, in passing through the different parts of the brain, may in one part excite, stimulate, or produce the faculty of Secretiveness, while in another it may excite, stimulate, or produce that of Conscientious-

CARRACALLA.

ness, while the brain may still appear homogeneous in structure, and apparently composed of one mass. This is no more than occurs in other parts of the body. The nerves of motion and sensation are enclosed in one common sheath, and there is no line of demarcation to mark where the one terminates and the other begins; and there is, besides, no perceptible difference in their structures, yet their functions are as widely different as the two faculties of Secretiveness and Conscientiousness just above named. Anatomists cannot discover the functions of the brain, nor are they capable of discovering the function of any organ. It is a general law of nature that each function must have a separate organ. This proves that the brain cannot be a single organ, but a congeries of organs. In accordance with this law, Dr. Spurzheim, long before the discovery was made, affirmed that there must be separate nerves for motion and sensation. Sir

DANIEL WEBSTER.

Charles Bell has demonstrated this to be the case, and by this has added another illustration to the law, that every function must have its own organ. The analo to be of the other parts of the body, therefore, are in entirely of the phrenological doctrine, that the brain, alòm home, apparently one homogeneous mass, is in reality a congeries of distinct organs, manifesting distinct and separate functions.

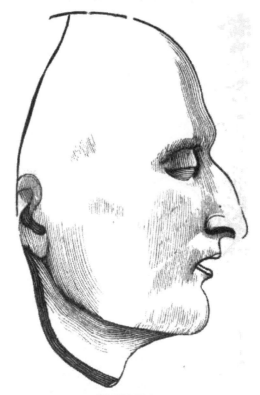

NAPOLEON.

We have already stated that size, other conditions being equal, is an index of power, This is one of the fundamental doctrines of phrenology ; and as several objections have been brought against it, we are anxious to establish its truth. In their objections, the qualification, *cæteris paribus*—that is, other things being equal —has been entirely overlooked by our opponents. It is affirmed that the largest or heaviest man is not always tion strongest ; but this arises from the difference of each ᵗerament or constitution, which we shall illustrate that thᵗly. A man may be large and bulky, but there may be more water and fat about him than muscular fibre. But of two men, of the same temperament, and equal in every other condition, the one who has got the larger muscles will be proportionally stronger than the other. This is saying nothing more than the established mathematical axiom, that the whole is greater than a part. The maniac often exerts more strength than another man of equal temperament and size of muscle, but the conditions are not equal. The nervous influence sent to the muscles in the time of furious madness, far exceeds what is sent to the muscles at other times, and this accounts for the greater degree of power manifested.

The principle that size is a measure of power, pervades the whole of nature, inorganic as well as organic. The bar of iron two inches square, is stronger than that which is but one inch square. The function of the liver is to secrete bile; the larger the liver is, the more bile will it secrete. A liver eight inches square will secrete more bile than one four inches square. The more capacious the lungs are, the better will they perform their function of aerating the blood. The left ventricle of the heart is much thicker and stronger than the right ventricle; for this reason, that the former has to send the blood through the whole of the body, from the very top of the head to the sole of the foot, while the latter has merely to propel the blood to the lungs.

In some structures of the body, the nerves of motion preponderate over those of sensation; while, in others, the nerves of sensation are much larger than those of motion, and the manifestations are invariably in accordance. Again, those parts of the body which are possessed of little sensation, are feebly supplied with the corresponding nerves, while in every sensitive part, such as the hand, the nerves of sensation are very large. The whole sum of sensitive nerves which go to the liver (an organ possessed of little feeling), is no greater than those sent to the *thumb*, which is not the fiftieth part of the size entirely liver. The analogy holds equally good, if we draw from home, the inferior animals. The mole has the olfactory nerves very largely developed, while the optic nerves are very feebly so : and this is strictly in accordance with its known character. In the eagle, however, the case is reversed, the optic nerve being very large, and the olfactory very small. The extreme power of vision possessed by the eagle is known to every one. The same holds good with regard to the auditory nerve ; and from all these cases it is reasonable to infer, that the brain forms no exception to what appears to be the universal law of creation.

But there are circumstances which modify the effects of size. These depend upon the constitution, or upon what physiologists denominate the temperament.

Phrenologists are agreed that there are four pure temperaments, which point out the quality of the brain, or degrees of mental activity, viz. :—1. Lymphatic ; 2. Sanguine ; 3. Bilious ; 4. Nervous.

1. The lymphatic constitution, or phlegmatic temperament, is indicated by a pale white skin, fair hair, roundness of form, and repletion of the cellular tissue. The flesh is soft, the vital actions are languid, the pulse is feeble ; all indicates slowness and weakness in the vegetative, affective, and intellectual functions.

2. The sanguine temperament is proclaimed by a tolerable consistency of flesh, moderate plumpness of parts, light or chestnut hair, blue eyes, great activity of the arterial system, a strong, full, and frequent pulse, and an animated countenance. Persons thus constituted are easily affected by external impressions, and possess greater energy than those of the former temperament.

3. The bilious temperament is characterised by black hair, a dark, yellowish, or brown skin, black eyes, moderately full but firm muscles, and harshly expressed ~rms. Those endowed with this constitution have a tion~ly marked and decided expression of countenance ; each manifest great general activity and functional that they.

4. The external signs of the nervous temperament are, fine thin hair, delicate health, general emaciation, smallness of the muscles, rapidity in the muscular actions, vivacity in the sensations. The nervous system of individuals so constituted, preponderates extremely, and they exhibit great sensibility.

Those four temperaments are seldom to be observed pure and unmixed; it is even difficult to meet them without modifications. They are mostly found conjoined, and occur as lymphatic-sanguine, lymphatic-bilious, sanguine-lymphatic, sanguine-bilious, sanguine-nervous, bilious-lymphatic, bilious-sanguine, bilious-nervous, etc. The individual temperaments which predominate may be determined; but it is difficult to point out every modification.

Besides the temperaments, there is a disturbing element in the estimation of character, which may be termed antagonistic, or the action of those faculties whose functions are in some measure opposed to each other.

Every faculty in the human mind acts in accordance with its specific functions, and its actions are regulated and limited only by the counteraction of other opposing faculties. Thus, Acquisitiveness simply gives the tendency to acquire; and, were it the only active organ in any person's brain, he would incessantly draw and grasp all objects indiscriminately to himself, without any restriction or limitation whatever, having no regard in his accumulations to his own use or convenience, or to the rights of others.

In like manner, were Destructiveness the only active organ, the individual would be nothing else than a mischievous machine; and so on with all the other faculties whatever be their nature or functions. But when two, three, or more organs are active, the act although still moving in its own specific some degree modified and restrained. when combined with Conscientiousness active in its tendency to acquire, but is limited, and a boundary is drawn. Conscientiousness says, ' Thou shalt not steal,' or, ' Thou shalt not covet,' and Acquisitiveness is made to obey either command ; and the result is, that the individual will be just and honest, although

> ' He'll gather gear by every wile
> That's justified by honor.'

Still he will be just and honest, and, if he possess well-developed Love of Approbation and Benevolence, he will expend his acquisitions as well for the public good as for his own. Individuals exemplifying the action of what may be termed antagonistic organs, are frequently to be met with. I know an elderly lady in whom Acquisitiveness and Benevolence are both very energetic, and, were it not for the former of these organs, the latter would certainly become irregular in its action. But constituted as she is, she is rather penurious in laying out her money. Yet she is kind, and has a strong inclination to relieve the wants of the needy ; but, instead of taking the money out of her own pocket, she almost always solicits the contributions of others, more wealthy than herself, to effect her benevolent purposes.

I am also acquainted with a mercantile gentleman in this city (Glasgow) whose actions betray powerful Acquisitiveness, Conscientiousness, and Love of Approbation ; and, to a person who has acquired a knowledge of the principles of phrenology, it is extremely interesting to observe the uniformity with which his conduct harmonises with his development. On paying an account, for instance —these three organs being called into play—he very generally uses words to this effect : 'Now, Mr. ——, you must, with your usual liberality, allow me off this odd hair, of nine shillings ; for really, at the present time, I moderat to buy as cheap as possible : however, if you say terms. Those are as cheap as you really can afford to sell tionally marked you in full, for I would not wish you to each manifest question. Let every man have his due ; that they.

The preceding shows the action of organs *partly* antagonistic ; but there are two organs whose functions are, we may say, almost completely opposed to each other, which we will now turn to the consideration of. We refer to the organs of Inhabitiveness and Locality. The former gives a love of home, and a desire for permanent residence. The latter, on the contrary, gives a disposition to travel, and to be continually moving from place to place. When they are equally developed, each, of course, pulls with equal force in its own particular direction. But then the question arises, whether will the individual travel or remain at home ? This must be settled by circumstances, and by the vote, as it were, of other faculties. If the faculties which would be gratified by his travelling preponderate over those which would prefer a permanent abode, then (circumstances allowable) he will travel. In thus gratifying Locality, however, his attachment to home will not be annihilated or remain quiescent. On the contrary, it will often annoy him in his rambles. The happiness he would experience in freely roving from place to place will be checked, or, at least, very much alloyed, by the constant desire of returning to his native land, and his heart language would be,

> ' Where'er I roam, whatever realms to see,
> My heart, untravell'd, fondly turns to thee.'

He therefore will not be entirely happy, and the probability is, he will be affected by *nostalgia*. He will enter into the spirit of the song, ' Home, sweet home !' and it will be with the warmest emotions he will return to his own country. His pleasure here, however, will often be dashed with sadness ; he will like to be roaming again, or, perhaps, compensate the gratification of his propensity by reading lives of eminent travellers, descriptions of foreign countries, voyages, etc. If we suppose the individual with large Inhabitiveness and Locality to be a denizen of our city, and so circumstanced as entirely to preclude him from travelling, or going far from home, we shall find that he will relish very much to walk into the country on a summer morning, and he will, in all probability, gratify himself in this way very frequently. He will visit, and become acquainted with, all the interesting spots round the city. He will be constantly in search of new tours. In the library, he will be found to ask most frequently for such books as give descriptions of countries, buildings, etc. It will from hence de seen that a man's conduct is frequently influenced by the action of what may be termed antagonistic forces or faculties. Each faculty, in proportion to its power, demands gratification, although the mode in which it will be gratified depends upon, or is determined by, the other powers of the mind.

The character of the human mind is either elevated and intellectual, as the brain is fully developed in the fore and upper parts of the head ; or it is low, animal, and sensual, as the brain is more fully developed behind the ear, and at the back part of the head. (See the quotation from Swedenborg.)

The brain may be divided into three great regions— highest, middle, and posterior. From the highest of these compartments, a man may be said to regard God, because in this resides the moral and religious sentiments. From the second of these divisions, a man may be said to regard the world and his neighbor, because in this the intellectual faculties have their seat. From the posterior, or lowest of these divisions, a man regards himself, because in this the animal propensities are located. As the various organs which are now considered established were discovered at different times, one organ being on the orbitar process of the frontal bone (Language), another just above the occipital bone (Philoprogenitiveness), a third at the posterior part of the vertex of the head (Self-esteem), now that the head presents to our view a pretty fully mapped delineation of the various powers of the human mind, we propose to conclude this lecture, by showing that this is in itself an argument in

favor of the truth of the science. As already observed,
Dr. Gall did not map out the skull into compartments,
and arbitrarily assign a position to each faculty. We
observe, by referring to the bust, that the posterior or
animal region is occupied by propensities (No. 1 to 9);
the sincipital region, by sentiments (10 to 21); and the
anterior region, by intellectual faculties (22 to 35).
We do not find an intellectual faculty in the animal
region, nor an animal propensity in the moral and religious
region. Again, we see each organ associated with others
best adapted, so to speak, to minister to the aid of the
group of which it appears to be a necessary member.
Thus, Causality (35) is the support of Comparison (34);
Time (32), of Tune (31); Number (28), of Order (29);
and so of the rest. Every organ in each division of the
brain seems to be confined to its own particular class, and
each class, or division, appears to be under the direction
of a superintendent. Self-esteem watches over the propensities, Veneration over the religious sentiments, Comparison and Causality over the intellectual faculties, and
Conscientiousness over the whole. In consequence of this,
the mind is capable of being raised, and of raising itself
upwards, and it can look towards the Great Supreme
and his kingdom of heaven. It is capable of being diffused,
and of diffusing itself, laterally in every direction, and can
thus look around into this world and its nature, and can
render itself useful to every class of the community. And
it is capable of degrading and sinking itself downwards,
seeking merely animal gratifications, and thus becoming
associated with sensuality. And here we may with propriety again ask, what can be a more satisfactory and
even beautiful exemplification of what we have just stated,
than the arrangement of the organs on the phrenological
bust, constituting, so far as discovery has proceeded, a
complete map of the mind? Veneration (14), which
disposes to the reverential worship of the Great Supreme.
Conscientiousness (16), which imposes integrity, uprightness, and love of truth, by which alone the moral and

religious duties can be faithfully exhibited before the
world.   On each side of Veneration, the organ of **Hope**
(17) developes itself—proper situation for so exhilarating
a faculty ; it seems to depend upon Conscientiousness and
Veneration for its blissful anticipations.   The object of its
reverence it one day hopes to behold, having an ambition
for living in a world which

> ' Honor, fame, and all this world calls great,
> Can never satisfy.'

The certainty of a future state of being, which Hope, aided by
Veneration, gives to the Christian phrenologist, enables him
with fortitude to bear ' the thousand ills to which the flesh is
heir.'   Below Veneration is Benevolence (13), that godlike
virtue, which can, even by sympathy, soothe and mitigate
the bitterest sufferings, but which, by its active charity, shows
its close connection with Veneration, by the love of the
brethren derived from the love of God.   Thus, the proper
situation of Benevolence or Charity is below Veneration.
Below Hope, on either side of Benevolence, with Imitation
(21) between the two, is situated Wonder or Marvellousness, or, as some have termed it, Inductive Faith (18).
Now, can Faith be better associated than in conjunction
with Charity or Benevolence, with Hope raised upward,
Imitation between Benevolence and Faith, and Conscientiousness overlooking the whole ?   Behold ! here
the religious group of faculties becomes established ; a
group which all but the sceptic will acknowledge to be of
the highest consequence, and occupying the supreme region
of the head.

  The second group of organs, those by which a man
is led to regard his neighbor, and do his duty in the
world, are a numerous family, but they are as necessary
as they are numerous.   It is quite impossible to observe
with accuracy, unless the faculty of Individuality (22)
is fully developed ; and as this faculty is the source of
minute observation, it is conspicuously placed in the
centre between the eyes, at the upper part of the nose.

'Everything we love and everything we hate, everything we desire and everything we fear, is an individual. It is by individuality, therefore, and by what is presented to the mind from individuality, that all our feelings are excited and brought into activity, and therefore Gall had no little reason to term it the organ of Educability. ('Phren. Journal,' vol. v. p. 249.) A little below Individuality are the organs of Form (23) and Size (24), both exceedingly necessary to accurate delineation.— Weight (25), Color (26), Order (29), and Number (28), belong to the group denominated knowing or perceptive faculties, forming a division of the Intellectual group. And here again we are struck with the beauty of the position. The knowing, or as they may be termed, the scientific organs, take cognizance of two classes of objects—existences and events—or of things as they now are, and things as they may hereafter be. For example, make a solution of carbonate of soda. This is an existence. Again, make a solution of tartaric acid. This is also an existence, though of a different body. Pour the two solutions together, and a violent effervescence takes place. This is an event. Thus, there is existence and event, perception and remembrance. To perceive and remember existences, the perceptive faculties are necessary; and to perceive and remember events, Eventuality (30), Locality (27), and Time (31), are necessary. Still, however, we are enabled to perceive that every individual does not possess these faculties with the same energy. Form and Size may be freely developed, while Coloring may be imperfectly so ; and thus a man may be an expert draughtsman, but be unable with accuracy to discriminate tints and shades in color. To keep these organs under proper control, to regulate their various functions, another division of this group is called into exercise, at the upper part of the forehead namely, Comparison (34), Causality (35), and Wit ('no or Discrimination. Here we may close our n/a him-the second class, with the assumption that that this

eminently useful, and their position shows how intimate
they are connected with that group which enables
to do our duty in the world and to our neighbo
But there is yet another group which we must brie
notice, and which leads the man chiefly to consider hi
self. And here we may observe, that there are no b
faculties, as some opponents of phrenology have terme
the lower propensities. No faculty in itself is hurtf
or useless, and still less criminal ; but if we regard only
ourselves, and take for our motto the detestable apothegm
'Every man has a right to do the best he can for himself'—(every man has not a right to do the best fo
himself, if that right interferes with the right of hi
neighbor)—then these organs, or rather the abuse o
them, are the sources of most of the evils which afflic
mankind. But our present purpose is to show that they
are all useful, or the Divine Being would not have bestowed them upon us.

The feelings of regard which are necessary to link
together so large a family as that which constitutes the
human species, must be exceedingly fervent ; and though
the feelings may differ in intensity, according to the difference of sex and constitution, still the effects will be
manifested in those portions of the brain where the
affective faculties have been proved to exist. Philosophers have long divided the mind into will and
understanding. We see no reason to question this. We
have hitherto treated of those faculties which relate to
the understanding, as well as to those feelings which
belong to what may be termed the higher affections of
the mind. We now come to treat upon the lower feelings
existing in the will. The cerebellum, or little brain, is
the situation of the strongest and the most absorbing of
the affections. The Supreme himself has affirmed, that
'it is not good for a man to be alone.' The Amative (1)
is propensity disposes to the peculiar affection existing
minute n the sexes. Above this organ is Philoprogeni-
entre be (2), which is cognizant of the affection subsisting

ween parents and children, and affor
sensations which parents in genera
particular, feel the full force of. A
n of Inhabitiveness (3), which indu
e and country. The home rendered h
bial affections and the recreations of Philo
as, is the chief solace of man's sublunary
n each side of Philoprogenitiveness is Comb
), and on each side of Inhabitiveness is Adhes
). Again, the harmony of the locality, in the
ation of home and friendship, strikes us as remarkab
nd when we have children, whose defenceless state no
ly requires care and watchfulness, but frequently the
otecting power of resolute courage, the locality of
hiloprogenitiveness and Combativeness is equally remark-
le. In a state of celibacy, the female is retiring and
assuming; but no sooner does she become a mother,
an a new feeling seems to put forth its power
d take possession of her. She guards her young
arge with the most tender and unwearied solici-
de. Her weakness seems all lost in the infant, and
hysical power becomes associated with parental love,
that, if any attack were made upon her infant charge,
ough the aggressor might be possessed of herculean
rength, she would resist even to the death. It is Com-
ativeness which enables the otherwise timid female to
and up in defence of the object of her love—preventing
e tyrannical, so far as her energy can reach, from
miting with the fist of wickedness. The superintending
ower of this group is Self-Esteem (10), supported on
ach side by Love of Approbation (11) and Cautiousness
12). Cautiousness again appears to superintend Secre-
iveness (7), Acquisitiveness (8), and Destructiveness (6),
hich are all beneath it. This closes the group of
he inferior propensities. Self-Esteem seems indispens
the government of this group; he who loses
ect has nothing to interpose in the regulati
petites. The Love of Approbation is well

It operates as a check against arro-
selfishness, while it at the same time
Acquisitiveness from becoming mercenary,
ness from becoming evasive. In the acquisi-
th, for the double purpose of obtaining our
now, and providing for it when old age im-
our physical and mental energies, Acquisitive-
comes eminently useful. Cautiousness shows its
application, Secretiveness imposes discriminative
dence, and teaches us the proper regulation of our
Acquisitiveness, and thus there is a check and a balance
throughout the whole system. Even Destructiveness
itself cannot be dispensed with. The path to excellence
is beset with difficulty and danger, and requires the
physical energy which this organ imparts, to rise superior
to and overcome it.

Phrenology being thus illustrated—the three regions of
the head thus exhibiting different powers—we may now
affirm that our proposition has been established, that all
the faculties are useful, and the position of the organs a
proof of the truth of the science. It is education which
must direct the whole organisation. It is education
which must train the noble powers with which God has
endowed us : the mode of education we shall refer to as we
proceed.

We must now conclude this introduction to our subject,
and we do so by exhorting the student to commence and
persevere, and observe for himself—and let him begin with
himself—let him not be deterred by the fear of ridicule.
Let him take the advice of the writer, who has for thirty-
one years, at much loss, and under much censure, pursued
his investigations—in a great measure trained himself by
its principles, and also trained and educated his family
successfully, seeking for them those employments which
suited their organisation. In his surviving family,
enumerate a skilful physician, an excellent practical
a good chemist, and a clever musician. Per-
ader may not have had the advantage of a

hrenological parent ; let him then commence the study
nd education of himself. In a 'Tour by a Lady through
the Upper Provinces of Hindostan,' is the following anecdote : ' The Hindoos never, if they can avoid it, forsake
the trade of their fathers, and are tenacious even in im-
roving it. I once asked a baker to make muffins, and
ffered to translate a receipt I had for them into Hindos-
tnee, promising him, at the same time, a recommendation
) all my acquaintance, which was large, being at the
rincipal military station. He listened very attentively
ill I had finished my speech, when, closing his hands
1 a supplicating posture, he said, "Pardon me,
ady, but my father never made them, my grand-
ather never made them, and how can I presume to do it ?
My grandfather brought up sixteen children, my father
ourteen, without baking *mufkeens*, and why should not
[? " ' The reader will not, surely, imitate this Hindoo,
ut having become his own master, remember that it is
eft to himself to complete his own education :—' For the
ormation of his character, while under the control of
thers, he is by no means accountable, but when he is freed
rom all restraint, deep responsibility is entailed upon him.
He has taken the guidance of a human being, and he is
tot the less accountable that this being is himself. The
igament is now cut asunder by which his mind was
ound to its earthly guardian, and he is placed on his own
ower, exposed alike to the bleak winds of persecution,
ind to the gentle breezes of perseverance, fully accountable
or his conduct to both God and man. Let him not be
nade dizzy from a sense of his own liberty, nor faint
mder the weight of his own responsibility ; but let him
emember, that while the eye of his Father is upon him,
iis words are, ' Occupy till I come.' Let him find out the
xtent of his own powers, and seek to direct them into
heir proper channels '; and to assist him in this important
work, let him take phrenology to his aid—there is no
icience better adapted to make him acquainted with him-
elf. He may by this science be brought to see, that this

natural world is one vast mine of wisdom, and this world
he may discover a miniature existence of within; in
observing which he will become soundly philosophical,
and in loving which he will become rationally religious.

I had a very numerous and a highly respectable
audience to my first course of lectures. The first, which
I have now inserted, and which, with slight modifications, I have continued to use till this day, gave universal satisfaction, and my room was crowded. I should,
however, observe, that in Scotland all introductory lectures are gratuitous, so that an audience is thus secured,
and an opportunity afforded for the hearers to judge
of the capability of the lecturer. It is also the custom
in Scotland to lecture on science, and even in times of
contested elections on politics, in churches. Although a
well-known Swedenborgian, I have several times been
granted the use of large churches to lecture in,
and some of my most intimate friendships have been
formed with clergymen of widely different religious views
to myself. In truth, the Swedenborgians are rather an
exclusive class of people; to use a Scottish phrase,
they are peculiarly clannish; they associate with but one
class of persons, and read in general but one set of
books; they canton out to themselves a little Goshen in
the intellectual world, where light shines and day blesses
them, but they seem careless of cordially mixing with
the great body of scientific and philosophic minds, although
they are quite aware that all science is vain and
sometimes mischievous unless religion sanctifies. I never
missed an opportunity of mingling freely with all classes,
and I can truly say that from the humblest I have
learned something. I was anxious to see life in all
its phases, more particularly with the view of observing
the configuration of the head, and of ascertaining how
far the general character harmonised therewith. I lectured to popular institutions gratuitously, and found
among the operatives men of enlarged and liberal minds,

d very many among them of highly cultivated intellect.
here was scarcely an institution within a circle of forty
iles round Glasgow to the members of which I had not
ctured, and received handsome testimonials from, so
at my name soon became known as an earnest and per-
vering lecturer on mental science.

About the year 1838 I had a most extensive corres-
ndence all over the country on matters pertaining to
e science of mind ; and I now began to notice the
culiarities of the different styles of writing. It occurred
me that there might be some truth in the supposition
at the handwriting gave an *inkling* of the mind of
e writer. I had somewhere read that men of genius
rote in a very obscure and eccentric character, and
f these I had seen autographs of Scott, Byron, Jeffery,
nd Chalmers. The writing of Dr. Chalmers was described
s if traced with the feather end of a pen, and was a most
nmeaning scrawl. Of Brougham's handwriting I possess
veral specimens—it is hasty, but bold. Washington
as described as writing a fair, even, straightforward
ne, every letter legible and distinct. Napoleon the
reat wrote a most detestable scrawl. Canning's pen-
anship had a chaste and classical appearance. Wash-
gton Irving is described as writing a perfect lawyer's
nd. Lord Jeffery wrote as if with a stick dipped in
k ; of his sentences scarcely a word was intelligible.
remy Bentham's hand was nearly as bad as Jeffery's,
nd the handwriting of the late Sir Harcourt Lees was
mpared to the leg of a spider dipped in ink, and dancing
a wall.

Many years since, but I cannot recall the precise date,
ere was an article in 'Chamberss Journal' on Auto-
raphy, in which the author classified the different styles
f writing, and which, to the best of my recollection, were
s follows :—

1. Vigorous, light-haired, excitable temperament,
hat is commonly called the Sanguine. The hand-
riting large, flowing, open, and irregular.

2. Dark-haired, excitable temperament, with brown florid complexion. The handwriting small, equal, and rather free and easy, with a firm and full stroke.

3. Light-haired, little excitable temperament, the complexion brown or sallow, the form spare. The writing less free and more methodical than No. 1, but less vigorous and less decided than No. 2.

4. Dark-haired, slowly excitable temperament, dark complexion, spare form, and melancholic habit. Small, cramped, upright writing, without ease or freedom, evidently slowly formed.

5. Feeble, light-haired, little excitable temperament, character timid and nervous. The writing small, unequal, or feebly traced, not written with decision.

6. Mixed temperament, combining two or more of the above.

I began to preserve my letters, and at the same time prepared a book which I carried with me, and into which I got my friends to favor me with their autographs.

But I made no progress in deciphering the character of people by their writing, though I continued to collect autographs. But a new impulse took hold of me. My deafness, though it did not appear to increase, still kept me for long periods in a state of comparative solitude, and threw me on my own resources for amusement. My position as a Dissenting minister required close study, but I did not write my sermons. I had a good library, still I had perused most of the books therein more than once or twice. But it occurred to me that I would now begin to re-read my books with the view of studying their authors' peculiarities and especial talents. I thought a minute describer would be a man with large Individuality and Locality—the former because of the number of small incidents he would crowd into his descriptions, and the latter that he might place them in such positions as to tell with most effect in his narratives. I concluded that those authors whose descriptions abounded with embellishments, and were highly colored, would have an enlarged ideality; that if these were descriptions humorous and witty, the writer would possess freely developed organs of Imitation, Wit, and Secretiveness; in short, I imagined that every author would delineate his own intellectual and moral character in his works, since he could hardly describe and illustrate efficiently the functions of justice and integrity without having a free development of Conscientiousness himself; or exhibit a glowing fancy in his work without a good deal of Ideality and Marvellousness; or give effect to the powers of morality, and virtue, and religion, unless he united in his own organisation the faculties or sentiments of Benevolence, Veneration, Hope, Marvellousness, and Ideality. To commence this study, my old books would become to me as new ones. I should now have real portraits before me of the authors of every book I read, though no trace of resemblance might be communicated to me by an engraved portrait.

No sooner had the idea presented itself to my mind than I entered upon it, and I abandoned my autographic studies that I might the more completely pursue this new branch of phrenological investigation. To assist me in this work I made an index of every book I read as I proceeded, and I resolved I would read no book without attempting an analysis of the author's organisation. I pursued this plan for some time, but I kept my observations to myself. I occasionally reviewed a book for a publisher, and concerned myself principally with the author's talents from what I conceived to be his organisation, and I felt satisfied, from experience, that my conjectures were really founded in fact; that such as was the organisation of a man, such was his book. At length I thought I would test my system by drawing the character of some public man, of whom I knew nothing otherwise than through his published works—an author of whom there should be no engraved portrait in existence. I had been much interested in the works of Mr. John

22

Kitto, afterwards Dr. Kitto, and I determined to make my
first experiment on him. I therefore procured his ' Pictorial Bible,' and his ' Pictorial Palestine,' in five large
imperial octavo volumes, and I patiently read every
word of his notes to the Bible three times over, until
I had mastered what I conceived his organisation ; but I
did not immediately draw an analysis of him. I read his
' Physical History of Palestine,' and compared the faculties
necessary for the production of such a work, with those
needed for the production of the notes in the ' Pictorial
Bible,' and I was satisfied in my own mind that I could
draw a mental portrait of him which should answer to his
physical organisation. I set to work, and I concluded
the following (from which I drew an analysis) to be his
probable organisation :—

Brain must be large and above the average (average
22½ inches in circumference). Temperament probably
bilious and nervous, the former having the predominance,
giving great endurance and average activity to the character. Back brain must be freely developed to account
for the power displayed in his writings.

Organisation of the moral sentiments must be large.
Firmness, Conscientiousness, Hope, Marvellousness, Ideality,
and Benevolence I should set down as decidedly large.
Concentrativeness, Individuality, Locality, and Language,
very large. I did not perceive much disposition to Music,
and I concluded that would be but moderately developed.
For, although much was written on the musical instruments of the Oriental nations, still these were but descriptions resulting from powerful Individuality, and did not
give any great indication of what has been termed an ear
for melody itself. There were no musical strains introduced. Of course I could not set down precisely and
definitely the size of the respective organs ; but from the
power displayed in his various works (and size being to
Phrenologists an index of power), I set down the predominating organs as decidedly large. The following is a
brief account of my analysis :—

I conclude this gentleman to have a very powerful brain, probably much above the average size, and I should expect, from the rapidity with which his works are issued, as well as their uniform regularity, that his temperament is equally active and enduring, probably a combination of Bilious and Nervous, and that he is orderly and methodical. He enters freely into the social manners and habits of the people whom he describes, and the evident pleasure and interest with which he describes the domestic habits of the people in the various countries through which he has travelled, induces me to believe that he has freely developed social affections—he will probably be married, and enter fondly into all the domestic relations. I should expect also that he will be energetic and possessed of great moral courage. There will in all probability be large Love of Approbation and equally large Benevolence. There is an absence of all sectarianism in the writings of Dr. Kitto, which I have read, and hence I conclude Benevolence, and Conscientiousness, and Love of Approbation to be well defined. The candid, but still careful manner in which he speaks of the various religious authorities whom he quotes, satisfies me of well defined and well balanced moral and religious sentiments, and while he discriminates with the utmost nicety all the peculiarities of divers religious bodies, he never expresses himself harshly of any, but observes a truly Catholic spirit. He is charitable and yet just—reverential but not superstitious—prudent, circumspect, and thoughtful. He does not exaggerate nor embellish, but gives a plain and unvarnished statement. I conclude that Benevolence, Veneration, Conscientiousness, and Cautiousness, are all largely developed; and that Hope, Marvellousness, and Ideality, will be comparatively moderate. I should expect the powers of Reflection, namely, Causality and Comparison, aided by Discrimination, or what some call Wit, to be very large. The severe logical induction which runs through the whole of his writings induces me to believe this. The extent of his travels convinces me that his Locality must be very large, and the minuteness of his descriptions, and the felicity with which he conveys them, affords evidence irresistible to me of his immense Individuality and great power of Language. I should also expect a well-defined superciliary ridge to account for the closeness of his observation. From the root of the nose upward I should expect the forehead to be prominent, though it will probably decline to the lateral parts. Upon the whole, this must be a very powerfully organised brain, and one much above the average in ability as well as power.

I did not, however, immediately send this analysis, but suffered it to remain in my desk for two or three years, but I at length made up a small parcel of books, principally phrenological, and sent them to Dr. Kitto through his publisher. I apologised for the liberty I had taken, stated my infirmity of deafness, and my consequent isolated and lonely condition. I mentioned to him my attachment to phrenological studies, and while I thanked him for the pleasure and instruction I had derived from his Biblical researches, I told him I had resolved to ascertain whether it was possible to predicate the character of a person from the perusal of his writings, and I made him my first experiment. I hoped he would excuse the liberty I had taken, and if I were not soliciting too much, I begged him to afford me the satisfaction of knowing whether there was any resemblance to his character in my predication. After waiting some weeks I received the following answer :—

Woking, Surrey, July 5, 18—.

'DEAR SIR—Your parcel has, after some delay, been forwarded to me at this place. I owe you many thanks for your kind consideration in presenting me with the books which it contained. I have examined them with some attention, as the subject of phrenology is by no means uninteresting to me. I have not, indeed, been led to study the science with that measure of attention which should authorise me to state that I have formed a distinct opinion on all its claims, but *my impressions are favorable to it : and it seems to me that its general principles are in entire agreement with what are called the laws of nature, and with all the revealed processes and objects of the divine government.* I hesitate chiefly with respect to the collocation and assigned influence of particular organs, and to some points in the system of mental philosophy which has become connected with, or has grown out of, this distinction.

'Your conjectures respecting my own developments *are, in general, remarkably correct.* The chief exception arises from a sort of flattening or sloping away of the forehead, at the place of the organs of tune and number, which detracts much from its apparent breadth. It is, however, so prominent, that I have never yet found a hat which did not press inconveniently upon it. The flattening over tune, I take to be a remarkable circumstance in connection with my deafness,* but I feel incompetent to draw any inference from the circumstance. The science of number, over the organ appropriated to which the flattening also extends, is very difficult to me, if not entirely beyond my grasp. As I see that the girth of the head is an important element in your calculation, I will just add, that mine measures, over thin hair and partial baldness, $23\frac{3}{4}$ inches.

'One feels some difficulty in stating these personal details, but I supply them in deference to your wish, and to the interest you take in such information.

'I am, dear Sir, very faithfully yours,
'*Rev. D. G. G.*'   (Signed)   'J. KITTO.'

I need not say how much pleased I was with this explanatory letter from Dr. Kitto. I returned my thanks in the following letter :—

'*Glasgow, July* 30, 18—.

'I am happy to learn, as I do from your letter,

---

* I knew nothing of Dr. Kitto's deafness, till I received this letter. He subsequently published two volumes on Blindness and Deafness, in 'Knight's Weekly Volume,' which I possess.

that my anticipation of your organisation is so far correct.

'If there were any truth in phrenology, I was sure your head must be very large to account for the power displayed in your writings, and I now learn it to be an inch and a quarter above the average size.

'I was satisfied your temperament must have been enduring, as well as active, and that your perseverance was equalled by your power of Concentrativeness, hence large Firmness. You could not have described with so much minuteness without large Individuality; while the facility with which you clothed your ideas satisfied me of your command of words, hence large Language. Then your extensive travels gave me an idea of powerfully developed Locality, and the high tone of moral and religious feeling displayed in your works, satisfied me of the great height of the head at the coronal region, while I anticipated also a good portion of back brain to give physical energy to the whole character.

'I thank you for the trouble you have taken in replying to my letter, and beg to assure you I will make no unworthy use of your confidence.*

'Your deeply obliged and faithful servant,
'D— G— G—.'

Although I had, as I have stated, abandoned my autographic studies, I still carried with me, wherever I went, my book for the collection of autographs, and whenever I saw any person in my audience more than usually striking in configuration, whether of Wit, Ideality, Form, Size, and Coloring, Language, or Music, I generally solicited the person to favor me with his autograph, and any observation he might think proper to add, and by this means I have had frequently further proofs of the truth of the science I was then so anxious to disseminate.

In 1838 I was invited to deliver a course of lectures at

* The decease of Dr. Kitto allows me to give his letter without any violation of etiquette.

Dunblane, to which I acceded, and delivered five lectures on five successive evenings, in the Rev. Mr. H——'s church. As usual, the church was crowded to hear the introductory lecture ; which was, of course, gratuitous, and nearly the same in substance as that already inserted.

Here I had an opportunity of again confirming the truth of the science, in the persons of the clergyman himself, and one of his congregation. The clergyman had a most powerful brain—the breadth at the front from Ideality to Ideality was very great, and the eye was prominent and piercing in its expression. I concluded he had large Ideality and Language, as well as powerfully developed observing faculties.

I requested him to write his name in my book of autographs, to which he kindly acceded, and besides wrote the following stanzas, confirming my observation of his powers of Ideality, Language, and descriptive faculties :—

'THE DESTRUCTION OF PHARAOH.

The Israelites rose, and to Canaan ascended,
  While Egypt bewail'd her first-born smote in ire ;
The angel, *Jehovah*, by day them defended,
  Pavilion'd in darkness, by night, in a fire.

'Twas midnight's high noon : floods of glory were streaming
  Around from Sechinah on ocean and steep,
The wing'd winds harp'd sweetly, the Red Sea waves gleaming,
  Rode, crested in silver, along the bright deep.

Before Baalzephon the tribes were encamping,
  Not dreaming that danger from Egypt was nigh,
Like a whirlwind a sound rose of war-horses tramping,
  And a deep prolong'd war-shout that burden'd the sky.

The tribes, looking round, saw the Chemin* come dashing
  With chariots and war-horse in fearful array ;
Each warrior his arms on his brazen shield clashing,
  Was frantic with rage, and was keen for the fray.

* Chemin—an ancient name of Egypt.

As the eagle's eye darts, when on wing in swift egress
 Away from his nest he sees quarry appear ;
As glare the red eyes of the dry-dugged tigress,
 When crouching she sees the mark'd victim draw near ;

So Pharaoh's eye-balls, as if burning, glared wildly,
 When first from the summit of Magdolum's height
He saw the white tents of the tribes gleaming mildly,
 Immers'd in the flood of Sechinah's soft light.

"On, havock!" his words were. As swells the wild ocean,
 And heavily rolls to the surf-beaten shore ;
So up rose the Chemin in wildest commotion,
 So roll'd they to combat ; their chief went before.

The Red Sea was parted, and Israel wond'ring,
 March'd through on its bed between two walls of waves,
Behind them the army of Egypt came thundering,
 To slaughter the tribes, or to lead them back slaves.

Jehovah looked down, from his burning cloud frowning;
 Proud Pharaoh's hosts shrunk from the bright glare of God,
Their chariot wheels brake, and their horses sunk drowning,
 Engulph'd in the sand which they erst safely trod.

The horses plung'd madly; the chariots sunk deeper ;
 The warriors in agony leap'd on the ground.
"Let us flee ! " they all shouted, " from Israel's Keeper ;
 Jehovah fights for them, the sea is around ! "

They fled : but the Red Sea, Jehovah obeying,
 With sullen roar burst its aërial dome,
They saw it approach, and from helpless flight staying,
 Look'd wildly on death, and thought sadly on home.

They died ! thus was punish'd the mystical Dragon,
 And thus was the mystical Israel sav'd :
Go, Christian ! Thou always shalt see honor put on
 The God whom *you* honor ; the God whom *they* brave.'
A— H—.

The other gentleman to whom I have alluded, and
who was a surgeon in good practice, was somewhat different in configuration. His brain swelled out at the
fontanel, and was particularly prominent at the outer
and upper part of the forehead. Now, thought I, here
is a man of wit and of eminent good nature, as well

as of fine intellect, I must get his name. So I told
him I was a collector of autographs, and should feel
obliged by his name in my book. He at once acceded
to my request, and seeing several poetic scraps, he wrote
almost impromptu the following stanzas :—

> ' To me was granted little time,
> And little skill in writing rhyme,
>   Yet up my pen in haste took,
> For love of approbation said,
> A friend's commands must be obey'd,
>   To write in G—'s waste book.
>
> I've sojourned in the desert long
> Ungifted with the pow'rs of song,
>   Or metrical endowment ;
> I never climb'd Parnassus' hill,
> Of Helicon I've got no skill,
>   You see this is a truement.
>
> Hence for the muse, though wondrous fair,
> To flirt on earth or fly in air,
>   Give me a succedaneum ;
> Since like the dove on watery waste,
> Her pretty feet can find no rest
>   In all my pericranium.
>
> Through Nature's walks I like to ramble,
> Though sometimes stuck in briers and bramble,
>   That sharply pierce and pain ;
> But never sigh for what I want,
> On what I have I feast and rant,
>   And all goes right again.
>
>   'C. S.'

This course of lectures was reported in the ' Stirling
Observer,' the clergyman himself, at whose church I had
lectured, furnishing the Editor with the particulars, and
appending the following handsome testimonial :—

' Characterised by novelty, as the science of Phrenology
is, it is no cause of surprise that many of those who
were privileged to listen to Mr. ——'s beautiful, lucid,
and powerful prelections, had, for the first time, the science
of phrenology presented to them as a whole. Presented,
however, as a whole, it was, amidst the advantages of

the expositions of a man of true genius. The exposition of the higher faculties of the mind, as evinced by the magnitude and connection of the local volumes of the brain on which they separately operate, was exceedingly beautiful. The extreme felicity of illustration which characterised these lectures was their least valuable quality. They were *convincing*. The facts adduced by the lecturer in support of the system which he advocates—the harmony of its principles with the divine principles of the Gospel— and the advantages which will result to society when Phrenology shall be brought into universal practice, were so ably, so convincingly enforced, as to produce a sensation which cannot fail of being highly favorable to the interests of the science in this town.'

I have inserted this testimonial as coming from a clergyman who is now a professor in the university of the denomination to which he belongs, to show that he, at least, saw no danger from the science to religion, and I could, were it needful, insert many more to the same purpose. I know many of the most eminent Swedenborgians admit its principles freely, at the same time I know many more who have censured, not to say persecuted me, because I have so openly advocated it on all occasions. But to return to my narrative. My usual course of lectures, explanatory of all the principles of Phrenology, extends to forty. In this work I give but a brief outline—such an outline as is usually given to Mechanics' and popular institutions. I proceed now to

MY SECOND LECTURE.

The class of feelings called propensities, are common to man and animals. They are not used to procure knowledge, or to generate ideas. It is to this class I shall now direct your attention.

In Dr. Gall's large work, the portion which treats of the Cerebellum, extending to 98 pages, is left untranslated, probably from delicacy to the non-professional reader, but it is impossible to unite a greater number of proofs in demonstration of any natural truth, than may be presented to determine the functions of the organ of Amativeness. It may be denominated the instinct of reproduction. Its functions give rise to the passion of love.

The situation of the organ is between the mastoid process behind the ear and the occipital spine in the middle of the lower and back part of the skull. In children the cerebellum is smaller than in adults; and in women and females generally, it is less than in men and males. It generally attains its full growth between sixteen and twenty-five years of age. In some adults it is exceedingly small, in others moderate, and in others again very large. Sometimes it is of great magnitude in children, and then its special function appears in early life. It is very large in the portrait of Caracalla (See p. 318). The influence of this feeling on society is immense, and there is no propensity requiring more care and watchfulness. Teachers, ministers of the gospel, physicians, and, in short, all who value the peace of society, and the happiness of the beings who compose it, are concerned in regulating the sexual propensity.

Dr. Spurzheim has earnestly exhorted parents on the necessity of instructing young persons in the fearful consequences of improper indulgence, and this advice they may be best enabled to attend to by making phrenology a family study. We shall in all our lectures blend the ethics of phrenology with its scientific details.

The social affections, Amativeness (No. 1), Philoprogenitiveness (No. 2), Inhabitiveness (No. 3), and Adhesiveness (No. 4), are often dignified by the names of household virtues: such they really are, when properly hallowed by those higher feelings, and guided by the intellectual faculties which the Creator has bestowed upon us.

They comprehend the duties of married partners towards each other, to their children, and to the community

of which they are members.   These duties do not occupy
the attention of the public so much as their importance
deserves, and the aim of the phrenologist is to call the
attention of parents to them, so as to direct their functions
into their proper and legitimate channel.   The neglect of
duty on the part of parents, in not properly training and
educating their children, is the cause of most of the
miseries which married partners endure.

It is impossible to speak in terms too impassioned of
the wisdom with which the Supreme has adapted the
sexes to each other—an adaptation in which wisdom
joins with affection, strength with weakness, firmness with
feeling, and dignity with beauty.   There is, indeed, an
admirable partition of qualities between the sexes, which
the great Author of our being has distributed to each with
a wisdom which calls for our admiration.   Man is strong,
woman is beautiful.   Man is daring and confident, woman
is diffident and unassuming.   Man shines abroad, woman
at home.   Man talks to convince, woman to persuade and
please.   Man has a rugged heart, woman a soft and tender
one.   Man is a being of science, woman of taste.   Man
has judgment, woman sensibility.   Man is rather a being
of justice, woman of mercy.   Indeed, each principle and
quality in the one sex is formed to unite with its similar,
and yet in some sense contradictory, correlative in the
other.   And it is this circumstance that causes everything
proceeding from the one sex to appear to the other as
unceasingly imbued with, and adorned by, the graces and
freshness of the other.   And inasmuch as the relation
between the sexes is thus a compendium of all the relations that can exist between human beings, whether
scientific, intellectual, moral, spiritual, and eternal, together with additional uses peculiar to marriage, it
thence results that the all-bounteous Creator has collated
into marriage all the happiness attainable by rational
creatures.   If these remarks be admitted as true, and if
to them be added the advice of a high authority ' *Be not
unequally yoked,*' then surely the very threshold of our

subject seems to present us with matter for the gravest
reflection ; and if phrenology presents parents with the
means of so training their children that unhappy and
ill-assorted unions may be prevented, then to neglect
applying its principles is to render themselves. doubly
culpable.

' It is well known that no method of discovering, with
reasonable success, the natural dispositions of human
beings has hitherto existed.   The general intercourse of
society, such as is permitted to young persons of different
sexes   before   marriage,   reveals,   in   the   most imperfect
manner, the real character ; and hence the bitter morti-
fication and lasting misery in which some prudent and
anxious persons find themselves involved, when the
blandishments of a first love have passed away, and when
the inherent qualities of the minds of their partners begin
to display themselves without restraint.   The very fact
that human affection continues in this most unhappy and
unsuccessful condition ought to lead us to the inference
that there is some great principle relative to our mental
condition undiscovered, in which a remedy for these evils
will be found.   The fact that man is a rational creature,
who must open up his own way to happiness by means of
knowledge, ought to lead us, when misery is found to
result from our conduct, to infer that we have been
ignorant or reckless, and that we ought to seek new
light, and take greater care in future.   Far from its
being incredible, therefore, that a method has been
provided by the   Creator whereby the mental qualities of human beings may be discovered, this supposition
appears to be directly warranted by every fact which
we perceive and experience connected with his government
of the world.   If God has placed within our reach the
means of avoiding unhappy marriages, and if we neglect to
avail ourselves of this gift, then are we ourselves to blame
for the evils we endure.   I cannot too frequently remind
you, that every fact, physical and moral, with which we
are acquainted, tends to show that man is comparatively a

recent inhabitant of this globe ; that, as a race, he is yet in his infancy, and that you ought no more to be astonished at new and valuable natural institutions, calculated to promote human enjoyment and virtue, evolving themselves from day to day to our understandings, than you are at the obviously increasing intelligence of an individual as he passes from childhood to youth, and from youth to manhood.' *

If we turn our attention to many of the marriages of the present day, we might be led to infer, that, instead of the union being a solemn and important contract, one involving happiness or misery, it was a mere agreement for temporary convenience, as well as for the necessary propagation of the species. How many young persons of both sexes are there, who have scarcely any other ideas of marriage than those just stated !   Tell them they ought to be well-assured of their suitability for each other, both morally and physically—that the contract is a most onerous engagement—and they smile at your primitive notions. But in how many thousand instances is it verified, that after a short period of married life, sensual indulgence was all they sought for ; in every other sense of the word, they have proved their ignorance of, and unsuitability for, each other ! It would have been otherwise had the moral and spiritual, as well as the physical, laws been obeyed.

'Upwards of ten years ago,' † says Mr. Combe, 'I had a short interview with an individual who was about to be married to a lady with whom I was acquainted. In writing this piece of news to a friend at a distance, I described the gentleman's development of brain, and expressed my regret that the lady had not made a more fortunate choice. My opinion was at variance with the estimate of the lover made by the lady's friends from their own knowledge of him. He was respectably connected, reputed rich, and regarded altogether as a desirable

* Combe's ' Moral Philosophy.'
† " Moral Philosophy." Edit. of 1841, consequently now 27 years ago.

match. The marriage took place. Time wheeled on in its ceaseless course, and, at the end of about seven years, circumstances occurred of the most painful nature, which recalled my letter to the memory of the gentleman to whom it had been written. He had preserved it, and after comparing it with the subsequent occurrences, he told me that the description of the natural disposition coincided so perfectly with those which the events had developed, that it might have been supposed to have been written after they had happened.'

It can easily be proved, that, among the wealthy, many marriages originate in covetousness ; the suitability as to physical conformation, temper, and disposition is rarely, if ever, consulted. A woman is often married, not merely at the suggestion, but at the command, of her parents, in order that estates belonging to different branches of the same family may be united in one. And even among the poor, there is too often a greater looking to dowries than to suitability of disposition and temper,* and station in life.

There is no greater evil in the sequel than marriages between blood relations. In Scotland, and indeed in some parts of England, the practice of full cousins marrying is not uncommon, and the results may be seen in the debilitated frames, or in the rapid deaths of the offspring or of the parents.†

* The Rev. Gilbert White used to say to neighbor Barboy—'Never marry for a fortune. There is Dame —— scolding her husband, as I passed the cottage, because she brought him a dowry. "You good-for-nothing fellow," she said, "what would you have been had I not married you? whose was the baking kiver, whose the pig trough, whose the frying-pan and iron-hooped bucket ; whose, but mine, when you married me, you good-for-nothing fellow !" O neighbor, neighbor!' repeated the old naturalist, 'never marry for wealth.'

† In 'Galignani's Messenger,' of 1846, was the following paragraph : 'The deaths of the Count and Countess de Noailles were attended by extraordinary and interesting circumstances. They were *cousins*, and both previous to their marriage bore the same name. Being brought up together, they became attached to each other from their infancy, but as the constitution of each was so feeble as to indicate premature death, their parents long opposed their union. At last, however, from their

' The children of healthy cousins are not so favorably organised as the children of the same parents, if married to equally healthy partners not at all related in blood, would have been.

' Another law relating to marriage is, that the parties should possess sound constitutions. The punishment for neglecting this law is, that the transgressors suffer pain and misery in their own persons from bad health ; perhaps become disagreeable companions to each other, feel themselves unfit to discharge the duties of their condition, and transmit feeble constitutions to their children. They are also exposed to premature death ; and hence their children are liable to all the melancholy consequences of being left unprotected and unguided by parental affection and experience, at a time when these are most needed. The natural law is, that a weak and imperfectly organised frame transmits one of a similar description to offspring, and the children inheriting weakness are prone to fall into disease and die. Indeed, the transmission of various diseases founded on physical imperfections from parents to children, is a matter of universal notoriety : thus, consumption, gout, scrofula, hydrocephalus, rheumatism, and insanity, are well-known to descend from generation to generation. Strictly speaking, it is not disease that is transmitted, but organs of such imperfect structure that they are unable to perform their functions properly, and so weak that they are easily put into a morbid condition by causes which sound organs could easily resist.'

own earnest entreaties, their marriage was consented to and solemnised. Their maladies rapidly increased. The countess could not bear the slightest degree of cold. Her physicians ordered that her apartments should always be kept at a certain height of temperature. The count, on the contrary, required to be in a fresh and cool atmosphere. They consequently seemed to be doomed to constant separation even in this life. That, however, they might at least see each other, they were placed in rooms adjoining, the partition between which was plate glass, through which they were able to communicate, but by looks and signs alone. Not more than one year elapsed between their wedding and their funeral.'

Another violation of the natural laws is, marriages contracted at too early an age—before the physical constitution of either of the parties is sufficiently developed, and certainly, as already hinted, before the parties are sufficiently acquainted with the deep responsibilities consequent upon the union.*

We recommend to the consideration of the reader, Mr. Combe's 'Moral Philosophy,' where the subject of marriage is treated of both scientifically and philosophically ; and to this advice we would add the study of the subject upon moral and spiritual grounds—that is, viewed from the moral and religious sentiments.

Swedenborg affirms that while the LOVE OF GOD and of OUR NEIGHBOR is representative of HEAVEN within the SOUL, the love of SELF, and of the WORLD, is a representation of HELL ; and Mr. Pope remarks, that nothing hinders the constant agreement of people who live together, but selfishness, or mere vanity—a secret insisting upon what they think their dignity and merit ; an inward expectation of such an over-measure of deference and regard as answers their own extravagant false scale, and which nobody can pay because none can tell readily what pitch it amounts to. Thousands of married people would be happy to-morrow, if they would but remember this, and if they would have the courage to apply it to themselves ; and this they would if they were to study first their own organisation, and then that of the parties to whom they are united.

When the duties of husband and wife respectively are performed under the principle of affection, guided by the higher sentiments of Justice and Benevolence, the married state will be found as perfect a state of happiness as can be found in this lower world. I will only add, that the statistics of matrimony prove that it is favorable to longevity. It has been computed that at the age of 60 there are but 22 unmarried men alive for 58 married : at 70, 11 bachelors for 28 married : and at 80 there

* 'Moral Philosophy'—Combe.

23

are for every three bachelors, nine married men. Very nearly the same proportion holds good in the female sex ; of whom, while 72 who have been married attain the age of 45, only 52 unmarried reach the same term of life. Perhaps one great cause of this difference is the circumstance of that tenderness of friendship, which we will hope does in most cases exist between those who are yoked together for life.

2. PHILOPROGENITIVENESS.—Nature, says Dr. Gall, by another organ, secures the existence and prosperity of beings procreated in consequence of the instinct of propagation. In all animated nature there is manifest an imperious propensity to preserve and cherish offspring. We admire it in the insect, and it commands our respect even in the tigress.

How happens it that neither philosophers nor physiologists have made any serious researches in relation to this propensity. No one has endeavored to discover the origin of this preserving instinct ! No one has examined why this propensity differs in manifestation in different species, in the two sexes, and in different individuals. Does it result from the organisation, taken collectively, or does it depend upon an isolated part ? These are questions which, prior to the time of Dr. Gall, were never asked. He gives the history of the discovery of the love of offspring as a fundamental quality, and of its origin, in the following language.

On comparing, with indefatigable perseverance, various forms of head, Dr. Gall observed that in most of the heads of females, the superior part of the occipital bone recedes more than in the heads and crania of men. In the portrait on page 355, Philoprogenitiveness is but moderately developed, and Self-esteem, marked 10, is very large, while in the portrait of the female, inserted on page 317, these developments are reversed.

As this prominence of the occipital bone is evidently produced by brain, it follows that the subjacent cerebral part is, in most instances, more developed in woman

ıan in man. What was, then, more natural than the
lea that this cerebral part might be the material cause

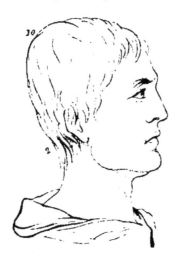

of a faculty, or quality, manifesting itself in a greater
degree in woman than in man? But then, the question
arose, what was that faculty or quality? In examining
and comparing the skulls in his numerous collection,
Dr. Gall at length discovered, that in the crania of
female animals, distinguished for their attachment to
their young, the back of the head towards the occipital
bone always presented an enlarged appearance; this
he found to be uniform, although, in other respects they
were very differently formed. He next observed the
crania of females of the human species, and the same
configuration presented itself. After this he commenced
a round of observations on the living. He visited schools,
carefully observing and discriminating the form of head
in the female children, and in the governesses who had
the superintendence of them; and though the configuration of the part we are describing varied in size—being
in some very elevated, and in others but moderately so,
yet in all it presented a difference to the configuration
at the same part to men and boys. Wherever any

person was distinguished for love of children he strove to gain a sight of their heads; and, at length, after a multitude of observations and facts connected with this cerebral part, he set down this portion of the brain as the organ of the love of offspring.

This is the organ which prompted the sentiment of the Roman mother, who, when presenting her children, exclaimed, 'These are my jewels!' Controlled by Firmness and Cautiousness, and assisted by Benevolence, it is one of the noblest feelings in the female character. 'It is,' says an amiable writer, 'a happy instinct which enables us to value these little pledges so highly, and a curious thing to reflect, that as we stumble through the parks, knee-deep in children, there is not one little unit in these diminutive millions that has not (God bless it) a circle of admiring relatives, to whom it is the prettiest, the dearest, the cleverest — in fact, the only child that ever was worth a thought.'

But if this affectionate principle be the source of so much happiness when controlled by Firmness and Cautiousness, and under the guidance of the intellect, it is calculated to be destructive of the little beings' future happiness if improperly exercised. The parent has no right to blame nature, but rather to blame her own negligence and bad customs. 'It is,' says Jeremy Taylor, 'the neglect of a field which causes fern and thistles to grow. It is not because the ground is accursed, but because it is neglected, that it bears thorns.' *

Parents! you are placed in this world as the representatives of the Most High to your children: and the first thing needful in the training of your children is

---

* 'Were it not a serious thing to contemplate, I might be excused for smiling at the self-opinionative turn of young ladies and gentlemen of the present generation. On religious and secular topics of every kind they are quite at home; the best divines, philosophers, and politicians are they; and as for medical qualifications, their opinions on this matter are infallible, and not to be questioned. Impatience, irritability, and disobedience, are the inevitable results, destroying all domestic peace.'—Dr SPURGEON.—*The Physician for All.*

to attend to your own conduct. One rule is worth a thousand volumes of speculation—Be yourselves what you would wish your children to be. Irascibility on your parts will not produce mildness or patience on theirs. If you are libidinous, they will not be chaste. If you are sensual, they will not be temperate. If you are extravagant, they will not be economical. You perceive, then, example is the first thing needful.

There are no beings so observant as children ; their senses are not more acute than their perception. Do not imagine, therefore, oh parents ! that your own conduct is overlooked by your children. From natural affection they look up to you as the most superior of human beings, and they think you honored, if they imitate all your actions. Hence, your power for good or for evil is immense, and the advice of Solomon was sound and practical, 'Train up a child in the way he should go, and when he is old he will not depart from it.' It is true, the impetuosity of passion in the young may for a time stifle the voice of parental exhortation, or even of parental example, but as age advances, reflection brings to mind the useful lesson, and the useful life, of the parent, and the prodigal returns and gives evidence of the value of the wise man's advice, and of the parents' attention to it.

Children are supposed to be, by some parents, amply provided for if they be clothed, fed, and sent to a school to be instructed in the ordinary branches of a worldly education. Or this is added to by taking them to church, teaching them to bend the knee in prayer, and acquiring a knowledge of the creed or faith of their parents. And having accomplished this, parents congratulate themselves that they have done their duty to their children. This is a part, and very small part, of the duty of parents. It is the regulation of the feelings and temper which should occupy the chief attention of the parent, and in early years this important duty is the duty of the mother. 'Deep and awful,' says a sensible writer, ' is the responsibility of those mothers, who voluntarily immerse themselves in maternal duties without first seriously and anxiously considering whether they be capable of discharging them.'   That eminent philosopher and good man, Locke, observes, 'We should always remember that the faculties of our souls are improved and made useful to us just after the same manner that our bodies are.'   But as well may we rest contented with saying to the hungry, the destitute, and the naked, ' Be ye clothed and fed,' as to say to the young, ' Be ye kind, compassionate, and generous,' or, ' Be ye just, true, and pious,' if we exercise them not in these Christian graces.   The first years of life ought to be devoted to the cultivation of the feelings, and no one can accomplish this so successfully as the mother.   A mother that will delegate this sacred duty to another, let her occupy what station she may, is unworthy the name of a mother.   Who, may we ask, can undertake a parent's duty ?   Have others a parent's feeling ?   Have they the devotedness of a real mother's love ?   When passion in the child kicks against authority, is there in the hireling the true charity that endureth, the true love that ' overcometh evil with good '?   No : either there is a want of patience and forbearance, or there is a display of unnecessary harshness ; or, from the turbulent display of the child, the 'hireling flees because she is an hireling.'   None but a father should exercise the influence of a father.   None but a mother can display the pure feelings of a mother ; and, where father and mother neglect their duty, there is great danger that the children will sink to 'eternal ruin.'   The necessity of parents becoming intimately acquainted with the dispositions of their children is obvious from the advice of the apostle, 'Fathers, provoke not your children to wrath, but bring them up in the nurture and admonition of the Lord.'   Children have widely different tempers and dispositions.   Some are so mild and docile that a single check, a word, or even a look is sufficient to

ensure their obedience. Others are fiery and headstrong, and on these it is necessary to enforce a mild
but firm discipline, that they may not be provoked
to anger, and so become obstinate and unmanageable.
Others are sullen and perverse, and harsh language,
or corporal chastisement, will only add fuel to fire.
The father is scarcely able, through his own asperity,
to deal with the affections of a child when they take
the opposite of good. He wants the forbearance of
the mother ; he wants also the patient *endurance* of the
mother ; he wants, above all, the affection, the love
of the mother ; and therefore to the mother should the
early education of the child be committed. But, oh,
mothers ! how responsible is your situation, how onerous
your duties. With the tempers and dispositions of your
children already alluded to, it may well be asked,
' Who is sufficient for these things ? ' and who would
enter upon such duties in a thoughtless or careless
manner, were they to be reflected on under the light of
true science and religion ?

We offer, then, the science of phrenology to aid the
Christian mother in her important work, and we feel
justified in affirming that by applying the principles of
this science to the proper regulation of the feelings and
cultivation of the intellect, she will most effectually train
her children for use in this world : while the due exercise
of the religious feelings which should hallow all the
others, will as assuredly train them for heaven.

' It is,' says a great authority, ' the highest privilege
of parents to be able to think that they have enriched
heaven with as many angels as they have had descendants,
and that they have furnished society with as many ministers to its happiness as they have had children.'

The feeling of love of offspring is sometimes inor-
dinately developed ; in other words, diseased ; and requires
the aid of a skilful physician to bring to its normal state.

The late Dr. Andrew Combe mentions an instance of
this kind in one of his patients, which is to the following

effect :—' While the fit lasted, which was for three days, her constant exclamation was for her children. Sometimes she imagined them carried away and murdered ; at other times they were suffering great distress, and exposed to unheard-of calamities. On her recovery, she complained of the greatest pain in the back part of her head. She knew nothing of phrenology. But she described the seat of pain as exactly residing in the cerebral part, where Philoprogenitiveness developes itself.'

There is a class of ladies, both unmarried and married, the latter without children, who indulge a fondness for animals of the small and delicate kind. This results, in all probability, from an enlarged development of the faculty, which, failing gratification in the natural way, turns its attention to the animals alluded to. These ladies are frequently made the subject of ridicule, but they rather deserve our forbearance and respect. They are merely following the bent of a strong natural propensity, implanted in them for the wisest of purposes, and which, in more favorable circumstances, would have rendered them affectionate mothers and excellent mistresses of families.*

Deficient as many of the savage tribes are in Benevolence, they yet have this propensity fully developed. In the savage tribe of the Charibs, the organ is decidedly marked. Of five casts in the Phrenological Society's collection, one has the organ very large, three large, and one rather full. Whenever the faculty is not developed in women in very fair proportion, it leads to carelessness of offspring, sometimes to infanticide. In proof of this, Dr. Gall relates the following facts :—

'I knew, at Vienna, a lady who loved her husband tenderly, who managed the affairs of her household with intelligent activity, but who sent from home, immediately after their birth, all the nine children of which she was successively delivered, and for years she never desired to see them. She was herself astonished at this indifference, and could not account for it. In order to acquit her con-

* ' Phrenological Journal,' vol. ii., p. 499, 500.

science, she required that her husband should daily see her children, and attend to their education.' *

' Of twenty-nine women who had committed infanticide, that we (Gall and Spurzheim) had occasion to examine, the organ of the love of offspring was very feebly developed in twenty-five.'†

3. INHABITIVENESS, CONCENTRATIVENESS.—The organ of Inhabitiveness is placed above that of Philoprogenitiveness, at the upper end of the occipital bone. On this organ, Dr. Spurzheim remarks :—

' In examining the manners of living of different animals, it is obvious that particular kinds are attached to different and determinate localities, regions, and countries. Some seek the water from the moment of their existence ; the turtle and duck, as soon as they are hatched, run towards it. Certain species, as the chamois, wild goat, ptarmigan, &c., select elevated regions for their haunts ; others prefer low countries and plains. Among the inhabitants of the air, some species hover principally in the upper regions : others, although their power of flying is great, live in lower strata, or on the banks of rivers. Some birds build their nests on the tops of trees, others at the middle branches, others again in the holes of their trunks, or on the earth.

' In conformity with all these considerations, I admit a primitive faculty and special organ which determines animals in their dwellings. This power, however, is modified in different animals. It varies in land and water animals, just as the senses of smell and taste vary in herbivorous and carnivorous animals.' ‡

' My attention has been directed to such individuals of the human kind, as show a particular disposition in regard to their dwelling-place. I have many facts in confirmation. I saw a clergyman in Manchester known

---

* Gall's Works, vol. iii., p. 282, Boston Edit.
† Gall's Works, vol. iii., p. 283, Boston Edit. We may here, once for all, state, that all our quotations from Gall and Spurzheim's works are from American Editions.
‡ Spurzheim's Outlines.

to his friends as particularly attached to his dwelling-place, so that he should be unhappy if obliged to sleep elsewhere. I examined his head in company with several gentlemen, some of whom were opponents, but every one was obliged to admit, that the spot of the head where No. 3 is situated was warmer than the rest of the head. I merely asked what part was the warmest, and all agreed at the same place. Some nations are extremely attached to their country, while others are readily induced to migrate. Some tribes of the American Indians and Tartars wander about without fixed habitations, while other savages have a settled home. Mountaineers are commonly much attached to their native soil, and those of them who visit capitals, or foreign countries, seem chiefly led by the hope of getting money enough to return home and buy a little property, even although the land should be dearer there than elsewhere.'*

The situation of this faculty—closely as it is in connection with Amativeness, Philoprogenitiveness, and Adhesiveness—is to me a proof that it is a purely affectionate feeling, and does not at all take cognizance of the intellect, although its connection with the intellectual faculties, like the other subjective feelings, is close and intimate. It appears that the real effect of this organ is to render a person mechanical in his habits and actions, to go through the same invariable routine. It will thus create a dislike of change of place and action, and so beget a love of staying at home, where the organs can be best gratified by its usual occupation.

But the love of home is but an individual part of the use of this organ. It extends its influence to the love of country, which may be considered as a man's home in a more extended sense of the word. Mrs. Opie, in her tale of the ' Welcome Home', makes Ronald Breadalbane thus apostrophize Scotland :—' O Scotland ! dear Scotland ! land of the mountain and the vale ! land of beautiful women and of brave men ! land of genius and of song !

* Spurzheim's System, 1832, p. 167.

land of kindness and hospitality ! I bring to thee an unchanged heart, my country, and a conviction that there is nought like thee upon the habitable globe.'

Sir Walter Scott, in Canto VI. of the 'Lay of the Last Minstrel,' has these thrilling stanzas on home :—

> ' Breathes there a man with soul so dead,
> Who never to himself hath said,
>   This is my own, my native land?
> Whose heart hath ne'er within him burn'd,
> As home his foosteps he hath turned,
>   From wandering on a foreign strand?
> If such there breathe, go, mark him well ;
> For him no minstrel raptures swell ;
> High though his titles, proud his name,
> Boundless his wealth as wish can claim ;
> Despite those titles, power, and pelf,
> The wretch, concentred all in self,
> Living, shall forfeit fair renown,
> And, doubly dying, shall go down
> To the vile dust from whence he sprung,
> Unwept, unhonored, and unsung.

> ' O Caledonia ! stern and wild,
> Meet nurse for a poetic child !
> Land of brown heath and shaggy wood,
> Land of the mountain and the flood,
> Land of my sires ! what mortal hand
> Can e'er untie the filial band
> That knits me to thy rugged strand?
> Still, as I view each well-known scene,
> Think what is now, and what hath been,
> Seems as, to me, of all bereft,
> Sole friends thy woods and streams were left ;
> And thus I love thee better still,
> Even in extremity of ill.'

While Scotland has thus eloquently been described, England has found a no less powerful illustrator in the person of the late Dr. Clarke. In the last volume of his Travels—and few men had seen more of the world —he thus apostrophizes England :—

' O England, decent abode of comfort, cleanliness, and decorum ! O blessed asylum of all that is worth having upon earth ! O sanctuary of religion and liberty for the

whole civilized world !   It is only in viewing the state of
other countries that thy advantages can be duly estimated.
May thy sons who have fought the good fight, but know
and guard what they possess in thee.   O land of happy
firesides and cleanly hearths ! of domestic peace, of filial
piety, and parental love, and connubial joy ! the cradle of
heroes, the school of sages, the temple of law, the altar of
faith, the asylum of innocence, the bulwark of private
security and of public honor—

> " Where'er I roam, whatever realms to see,
>   My heart untravell'd fondly turns to thee." '

Our own experience of the functions of this organ
harmonizes with that of Dr. Spurzheim, and we feel
satisfied that of the numerous individuals who have left
this country for America, the major part will be found
moderately developed in Inhabitiveness, and largely developed in Locality.   Where it is otherwise, the probability
is, that the organs of Inhabitiveness and Locality are
equal in power, and when the individuals have achieved
the objects of their journey, they will return with increased zest to their own country.

Emigration cannot be safely carried on where this organ
is large, and Locality moderate.   To be productive of all
the advantages which are so frequently held out to induce
persons to emigrate, the following seems to be the best
combination :—A bilious nervous temperament, moderate
Inhabitiveness, full Combativeness and Destructiveness,
rather large Secretiveness, Acquisitiveness, Firmness, and
Self-Esteem, with large Locality, and well-developed
powers of reflection and observation.   Even where the
organisation is so moderate, and the education so
limited, as to keep the emigrants to mere hewing of wood
and drawing of water, there would be misery and discontent and suffering, if Inhabitiveness were too freely
developed.

4. ADHESIVENESS.—Dr. Gall observes on the discovery
of this organ—' I was requested to take, for my col-

lection, a cast of the head of a lady, who was, as they told me, a model of friendship. I took her cast—more out of kindness than in the expectation of making any discovery—and I endeavored to get a correct one. On examining this head, I found two great prominences, constituting the segment of a sphere, by the side of the organ of love of offspring: (Philoprogenitiveness): as up to that time I had never seen these prominences, which, however, were evidently formed by the brain, and exceedingly symmetrical; I considered them as a cerebral organ. But what were the functions of this organ? In order to get some general view on this point, I inquired of all the friends of the lady, respecting her qualities and faculties. I attempted to learn of the lady herself what propensities and faculties she believed she possessed. All united in confirming what had been told me, that she had an invincible attachment to her friends. Although her fortune, at different periods, had experienced great changes, and, by degrees, she had passed from poverty to honor, her feelings for her old friends had never changed. This characteristic trait struck me. The idea occurred to me that the disposition to friendship might also be found in a particular cerebral organ. This opinion acquired with me a still greater degree of probability, as the prominences that I had observed on the head of the lady were placed immediately above the organ of physical love (Amativeness), and by the side of that of the love of offspring, and these three sentiments have some analogy with each other.'*

Subsequent observations have confirmed the existence of this organ, and it is now established.

Wherever the ardor of strong attachment distinguishes itself, the individual under its influence seems almost impelled to embrace its object. If there be any true friendship in man, it will manifest itself by the firm grasp of the hand and the sparkling lustre of the eye when it meets the object of its attachment.

* Gall's Works, vol. iii., p. 300.

Perhaps one of the most striking exemplifications of Adhesiveness, under any circumstances, is evidenced in David, king of Israel, for Saul and Jonathan. Hunted as David was by Saul, and subjected to every privation which his infuriated jealousy could devise, David ever distinguished himself by attachment to the exasperated but deluded monarch. Twice might he easily have rid himself from Saul's persecution, but he spares him each time, and, by the gentle expostulations of friendship, revives, for a time at least, all the better feelings which had slumbered in Saul. The beautiful elegy over Saul and Jonathan is a fine illustration of Adhesiveness :—' Saul and Jonathan were lovely and pleasant in their lives, and in their deaths they were not divided. They were swifter than eagles ; they were stronger than lions. How are the mighty fallen in the midst of the battle ! I am distressed for thee, my brother Jonathan ; very pleasant hast thou been unto me : thy love to me was wonderful, passing the love of women. How are the mighty fallen in the midst of the battle !' To say that the love of Jonathan surpassed the love of woman was to say much indeed, and perhaps, with the exception subsisting between Damon and Pythias, there never has been so striking an exemplification of pure Adhesiveness subsisting between men. But for all this, the faculty is more energetic in women than in men. ' Man is but a rough pebble without the attrition received from contact with the gentler sex. It is wonderful how the ladies pummice a man down into smoothness, which occasions him to roll over and over with the rest of his species, jostling, but not wounding, his neighbors, as the waves of circumstances bring him into collision with them.'*

Dr. Gall observes, women are generally more devoted to their friends than men, and display an indefatigable activity in serving them. Whoever has gained the affections of a woman, is sure to succeed in any enter-

* Captain Marryatt.

prise in which she assists him. Men draw back much sooner in such cases. Frequently in my life have I had occasion to admire in females the most generous zeal on behalf of their friends. Who is not astonished at the courage shown by a woman, when her husband—whose misconduct has, perhaps, a thousand times offended her—is threatened with imminent danger? Who does not know many instances of the most heroic devotedness on the part of the sex? A woman spares no effort to save her friend. When it is a question of saving her husband, her father, her brother, she penetrates prisons, she throws herself at the feet of sovereigns. Such are the women of our day, and such has history represented those of antiquity. Happy is the man who has a woman for his friend!

Nor are the sweets of friendship confined to any privileged class of mortals, in contradistinction to their brethren of mankind generally. Every upright, generous, social soul, will find a fellow-feeling glowing warmly in the congenial breast of some kindred spirit, where Adhesiveness is largely developed, whether the fleshly tabernacle thereof be arrayed in silk attire, or clad in a homely suit of russet grey—whether it stretch its weary limbs on a humble pallet of straw, or recline its pampered carnality on a gilded couch of downy softness. The same heavenly influence illumines the lowly cot of the peasant and the gaudy palace of the prince. Friendship is, indeed, the wine of human existence.

> ' It is no lingerer in a monarch's hall,
> A joy it is and a wealth to all,
> It breathes of bliss over land and sea—
> Friendship, what gift hath the world like thee!'

The natural language of Adhesiveness, in its most energetic action, inclines the body sideways and backwards, so that, as nearly as possible, the head may touch the organ which is situated on the outer side of Philoprogenitiveness. This posture has been very faithfully given by the ancients.

There is a beautiful group of Castor and Pollux, in which we see their arms resting on each other's shoulders, and these friends pressing together their organs of attachment.

In the Madonna of Raphael, Mary presses this region of her head against the corresponding region of the head of the child.

Notwithstanding all that has been said of the want of attachment of the cat, I affirm they are capable of the strongest attachment. They testify this by turning their heads laterally backward, and from above downward, rubbing gently the organ of attachment against him whom they caress.

The faculty is as much distinguished from Benevolence as from Amativeness. A man may be purely benevolent, but still be an anchorite with respect to friendship. The ballad of Edwin and Angelina may serve as an illustration of this. The most degraded of characters are frequently instances of this attachment. I should think the proverb, ' There is honor among thieves,' may be traced to it. When it is excessively developed it leads to despair at the loss of friends, and, if combined with large Inhabitiveness, extreme agony at being compelled to leave home and country.

5 COMBATIVENESS.—This organ is situated on either side of Philoprogenitiveness, and communicates the propensity of physical courage. Dr. Gall thus describes its discovery.* He collected a number of individuals of the lower ranks of society into his house. To gain their confidence he treated them with wine and money, and, by this means, drew from them a complete history of their various qualities, good and bad. He thus discovered many striking exemplifications of his system. During the narratives which the Doctor's wine was the means of freely drawing forth, he was much struck with the observations and epithets of contempt which the most quarrelsome bestowed upon the meek and unobtrusive. They were stigmatized as milksops, cowards, poltroons, etc.

* Gall's Works, vol. iv, page 14.

Upon an examination of their heads, he found invariably that the parts now under review were freely and fully developed in those who used the coarsest language and displayed the most irritable feelings, while, in those who were stigmatised as cowards, the parts were generally flat, and sometimes hollow. Continuing his observations, he discovered similar developments in the heads of quarrelsome students, valiant officers, and those who were in the habit of engaging in duels. He also discovered that the heads of courageous animals were wide between and behind the ears, while those which were shy and timid presented a narrow appearance.

13 Benevolence large.
5 Combativeness small.

13 Benevolence small.
5 Combativeness large.

24

The organ is more fully developed in men **than** in women, though we read in Tacitus of a lady, **named** Verulana Gracilia, who abandoned her children, her kindred, and her relations, and followed nothing **but** the war. Dr. Gall also mentions a young lady, in **whom** this propensity was so energetic, that she disguised herself repeatedly in male attire, that she might engage in combat with the other sex. Combativeness is **a** very distinguishing feature in all polemics. He in whom it *is* large will seek every opportunity of indulging it, whether in the forum, the pulpit, or even the convivial party Here is an illustration :—

> ‘ I knew two holy friars, as holy men
> As ever snor’d in sackcloth, after sinning.
> And they were learned. What now was the upshot ?
> I should have said, one’s crucifix was white,
> The other’s black. They plied mild arguments
> In disputation. Brother was the term
> At first ; then sir ; then nothing worse than devil.
> But those fair words, like all fair things, soon dropp’d :
> Fists were held up, grins in the face grew rife,
> Teeth (though in these one had the better of it
> By half a score) were closed like money-boxes
> Against the sinner damn’d for poverty.
> At last the learned and religious men
> Fell to it mainly, crucifix in hand,
> Until no splinter, ebony or linden,
> Was left, of bulk to make a toothpick of.’
>   WALTER SAVAGE LANDOR.

Such are often the effects in religious feuds : but Combativeness makes its way, too, into the convivial party. The late justly celebrated Dr. Barclay, who was a wit and a scholar, as well as an eminent physiologist, exposed very happily the tendency to debate, on one occasion, when he was at a large party, chiefly composed of medical men. As the wine-cup circulated, the conversation accidentally took a professional turn, and, from the excitation of the moment, two of the youngest individuals present were the most forward in delivering their opinions. Sir James Macintosh once told a political opponent, that, so far from following his example of using hard words and soft arguments, he would, if possible, pass into the opposite extremes of soft words and hard arguments. But our young M.D.s disregarded this salutary maxim, and made up in loudness what they wanted in learning and experience. At length one of them uttered something so emphatic — I mean as to manner—that a pointer dog started from his lair beneath the table, and *bow-wow-wowed* so fiercely that he fairly took the lead in the discussion. Dr. Barclay eyed the hairy dialectician, and, thinking it high time to close the debate, gave the animal a hasty push with his foot, at the same time exclaiming, in good broad Scotch, ' Lie still, ye brute ! I'm sure ye ken just as little about it as ony o' them.' This sally was followed by a hearty burst of laughter, in which the disputants good-humoredly joined.

There is, indeed, a great necessity to restrain this organ. It is Combativeness which gives flippancy to the tongue, which, as a high authority has observed, is a world of iniquity, and has destroyed more than the sword. The different styles of preaching, in ministers of the gospel, may be safely inferred from the moral or the animal region. Those in whom the animal region predominates, are perpetually engaged in theological strife and bitterness. Those in whom the moral region predominates, breathe the spirit of tenderness and charity to all, however much they may differ from them in doctrine. Calmness and command of temper are absolutely necessary in the investigation of any subject, but more especially of religion. It will be invariably found that persecution never answers the end of the powers that design it. Oppression naturally begets resistance. The oppression of one class of religionists rouses the Combativeness of another. But this is not altogether without its use. It makes men more careful for true religion, and thus it is that God out of evil still educes good, causing the wrath of man to praise him, while the remainder of wrath he restrains.

In all ages this faculty seems to have been stimulated
and industriously cultivated. The gladiatorial combats of
the Romans were got up to stimulate and gratify this
organ. They had gladiators from all countries, and these
men often fought with their native weapons, and after the
manner of their own country. The savage directors of
these brutal exhibitions frequently took advantage of the
national antipathies between the combatants, and found no
way so ready for exhibiting to the populace all the bloody
circumstances of a real battle, as to match together men
of different nations.

Among modern pugilists, the faculty of Combativeness
has been strongly exemplified; and though those brutal
exhibitions, prize-battles, are not so frequent now as
formerly, there are still not wanting persons—and those,
too, in the highest walks of life—who bestow both time
and money to obtain the gratification. It would, perhaps, be difficult to say in which of these classes, the
backers or the combatants themselves, the organ most
predominates. Probably Self-esteem is the only means of
preventing noblemen themselves (so called) from pursuing
this degrading amusement.

There is a highly interesting anecdote in Mr. Selby's
'History of British Ornithology,' in which the force of
parental affection is exhibited in birds, who were supposed
totally deficient in physical energy. 'A person engaged
in a field not far from my residence,' says Mr. Selby,
'had his attention arrested by some objects on the ground,
which, upon approaching, he found to be two partridges, a
male and a female, engaged in a battle with a carrion
crow, till it was seized and taken from them by the
spectator of the scene. Upon search, the young birds,
very lately hatched, were found concealed among the
grass. It would appear, therefore, that the crow, a mortal
enemy to all kinds of young game, in attempting to carry
off one of these, had been attacked by the parent birds,
and with the above singular success.'

Mr. Combe observes that this organ very differently

develops itself, as it respects energy, in various animals. Rabbits are more courageous than hares. The bull-dog forms a contrast, in this propensity, to the greyhound; and the head of the former is much larger, between and behind the ears than the latter. The same difference is also discoverable between game-cocks and game-hens, in comparison with domestic fowls. Horse-jockeys, and those who are fond of fighting-cocks, have long made this observation.

6. DESTRUCTIVENESS.—As this organ has excited more controversy than all the others put together, we feel it our duty to state the circumstances connected with its discovery, from both Drs. Gall and Spurzheim.

Dr. Gall thus states the discovery:* 'By carefully comparing the skulls of animals, I found a characteristic difference between those of the frugivorous and those of the carnivorous species. Placing the skulls of the frugivora in a horizontal position on a table, and raising a perpendicular from the external opening of the ear, I found that there remained, behind this perpendicular, only a small portion of the posterior lobes and cerebellum; consequently, the external opening of the ear, and the petrous portion of the temporal bone, mark the limits of the cerebellum in these species. Testing the skulls of the carnivorous species in the same manner, I saw that in the most of them, the perpendicular strikes the middle of the whole encephalic mass, or, at least, leaves behind it a very large portion of the cerebral mass. Ordinarily in the carnivora, the greatest prominence of the brain is exactly over the external opening of the ear.

'I saw, therefore, that in the carnivora there are cerebral parts above and behind the ear, not possessed by the frugivora, and the same difference I found in birds, as well as the mammifera. In all the birds of prey, this part of the brain swells out, while, in all other species of birds, it seems to retreat, and the whole

* Gall's Works, vol. iv, p. 50, 51.

brain is situated in front of the external opening of the ear. For a long while I contented myself with communicating this observation to my hearers, without making the slightest practical application of it to organology. I showed them only how, by inspection of the skull, even when the teeth were wanting, they might tell whether it belonged to a frugivorous or carnivorous animal.

'The skull of a parricide was once sent me, which I put aside, without ever thinking that the skulls of murderers would be of use to me in my researches. Shortly after, I received the skull of a highway robber, who, not satisfied with committing robbery, had murdered a number of persons. I placed these two skulls side by side, and examined them very frequently. Every time I was thus engaged I was struck with the fact, that, though very differently formed in other respects, there was in each a prominence strongly swelling out, immediately over the external opening of the ear. The same prominence I found also in some other skulls in my collection. It appeared to me not merely accidental, that in these two murderers the same cerebral parts should be so much developed, and the same region of the skull so strongly prominent. I then began to make use of my discovery on the different conformation of the brain and skull in the frugivorous and carnivorous animals, and, for the first time, understood the meaning of the difference. The brain of the latter, I said to myself, and of the murderers, is developed in the same region. Is there any connection between this conformation and the disposition to kill? At first the idea was revolting; but when the object is to observe, and to state the result of my observations, I know no law but that of truth. Here, too, then, let us endeavor to unveil the mysteries of nature. It is only when we have discovered the secret springs of our actions, that we can learn to guide the conduct of man.'

Dr. Spurzheim remarks ('Outlines of Phrenology,' p.

10); ' Observation shows that violent death is an institution of nature ; that the propensity to kill exists, beyond a doubt, in certain animals, and that this disposition is more or less active in particular kinds, and also in some individuals of the same species. Man, it must also be admitted, is endowed with the same propensity, for he kills almost every variety of animated beings, either to procure food or to supply his wants, while the carnivorous tribes of creation confine their destructive powers to a comparatively small number of kinds, and this merely to supply themselves with nourishment.— Moreover, in man, this propensity offers different degrees of activity, from a mere indifference to destruction, to pleasure in seeing animals killed, and even to the greatest desire to kill. The sight of public executions is insupportable to some individuals, and delightful to others. Some highwaymen are satisfied with stealing, others show the most sanguinary inclination to kill without necessity.

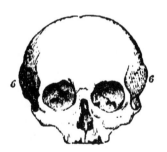

' Idiots, and the insane, sometimes feel an irresistible desire to destroy all they lay their hands on. Some of the insane thus affected manifest the strongest aversion to the deeds they would do, and even thank those who coerce and keep them from mischief.

' The primary nature of this propensity is a simple impulse to destroy ; it does not consider the object of its application, nor the manner of destroying. It uses indifferently pointed and cutting instruments, poison, water,

and fire, to accomplish its desires. It is indispensable
to animals which live upon flesh. I do not, however,
think that it determines the taste for this kind of aliment.
The faculty is commonly more active in children than in
adults, yet children generally prefer fruits and vegetables
to meat.

'Besides the necessity of this instinct to procure
animal food, its employment in self-defence is not only
permitted by justice, but is even rewarded as a virtue.
A sword is one of the emblems of state. If the faculty,
however, cause the destruction of aught that should not
be destroyed, it produces disorders, as when it punishes
trifling crimes with death, assassinates, murders, administers poison, or sets fire to houses.

'If we place two skulls, the one of a carnivorous, the
other of an herbivorous animal, horizontally, and trace
a vertical line through the opening of the external ear,
we shall observe that there is more brain over the ear
in the carnivorous than in the herbivorous animal.

'The organ of Destructiveness lies, in man and animals,
immediately above the ear, and is covered by the temporal
bone.'

The organ is now fully established. There is no
propensity in man which has more powerfully developed
itself. The field of blood and strife is too frequently
dignified by the term, 'field of glory,' and thousands upon
thousands have recklessly rushed to it and finished their
existence in literally seeking the bubble reputation, even
in the cannon's mouth. No organ is more stimulated, or
better paid for its desolating labor. 'It were well if
there were fewer heroes, for I scarcely ever heard of any
but did more mischief than good. These overgrown
mortals commonly use their will with their right hand,
and their reason with their left. Their pride is their
title, and their power puts them in possession. Their
pomp is furnished from rapine, and their scarlet is dyed
with human blood. If wrecks, and ruins, and desolation
of kingdoms are marks of greatness, why do we not

worship a tempest and erect a statue to the plague? A panegyric upon an earthquake would be every jot as reasonable as upon such conquests as these.'* Man is, in this respect, below the standard of the fiercest of the animal tribe. It seems reserved for the most intellectual beings to fall, in this respect, below the level of the most savage, and that he delights in carnage is too notorious to all who have read the history of the Peninsula war to be doubted. Man may be justly entitled the great destroyer and exterminater of life, without regard to time, place, or circumstance. By his power the strongest are overcome; by his ingenuity the most subtle are circumvented, and their energies of body and mind made subservient to his necessities or pleasures. He is superior to the whole animal kingdom in the noblest attributes, but he enjoys one pre-eminence for which even the lowest have no cause to envy him. All the destructive animals fulfil their dire offices upon creatures belonging to other kinds. When the lion leaps from his ambush, it is in the neck of the wild ox or antelope that he buries his claws. When the wolves howl in unison, it is the deer they are pursuing. When the scream of the eagle sounds shrillest, then let the wild duck beware. Even the insatiably ferocious tiger keeps aloof from his brethren of blood. But when the drums roll, and the trumpets clang, when the banner folds are shaken abroad upon the air, and the neigh of the charger re-echoes the deep notes of the bugle, then is man, with his boasted reason, preparing to spill the blood of his brother, to drive his desolating chariot over the faces of his kindred, spread havoc and despair before his path, and leave famine and pestilence to track his footsteps.

It has been computed that 82 per cent. of the whole public expenditure of Great Britain is offered at the shrine of war, and a member of parliament once stated in public, that every working man in this country labors, on an average, two hours a day for the support

* 'Pearls of Great Price,' edited by J. Elmes.

of our warlike establishments.*   While such a premium
is offered for the cultivation of this propensity, is it to be
wondered at that it so fearfully predominates?   If we go
through the length and breadth of the land we scarcely
find a testimonial raised in public to those who have spent
their lives in bettering the condition of their fellow-
creatures, and in devising means for saving life.   But
what large town will you visit where the warrior has not
his triumphal pillar, or his triumphal arch, or his eques-
trian statue?   How loud are the songs of glory, the
pæans of triumph for the victor chief, but alas! how sad
for the dying soldier!

SONG OF THE SWORD.

' Weary and wounded and worn,
    Wounded, and ready to die,
A soldier they left all alone and forlorn,
    On the field of the battle to lie.
The dead and the dying alone
    Could their presence and pity afford,
Whilst with a sad and terrible tone
    He sang the song of the sword.

    Fight—fight—fight!
Though a thousand fathers die;
    Fight—fight—fight!
Though thousands of children cry:
    Fight—fight—fight!
While mothers and wives lament!
    And fight—fight—fight!
Whilst millions of money are spent.

    Fight—fight—fight!
Should the cause be foul or fair;
Though all that's gain'd is an empty name,
    And a tax too great to bear:
An empty name, and a paltry fame,
    And thousands lying dead;
Whilst every glorious victory
    Must raise the price of bread.

    War—war—war!
Fire, and famine, and sword;
Desolate fields, and desolate towns,
    And thousands scattered abroad,

* Peace Advocate.

With never a home and never a shed,
  Whilst kingdoms perish and fall,
And hundreds of thousands are lying dead,
  And all for nothing at all.

        War—war—war!
  Musquet, and powder, and ball;
Ah! what do we fight for?
  Ah! why have we battles at all?
'Tis justice must be done, they say,
  The nation's honor to keep;
Alas! that justice is so dear,
  And human life so cheap.

        War—war—war!
  Misery, murder, and crime,
Are all the blessings I've seen in thee
  From my youth to the present time.
Misery, murder, and crime—
  Crime, misery, murder, and woe:
Ah! would I had known in my younger days
  A tenth of what now I know.

Ah! had I but known in my happier days,
  In the hours of my boyish glee,
A tenth of the horrors and crimes of war,
  A tithe of its misery;
I now had been joining a happy band
  Of wife and children dear,
And I had died in my native land,
  Instead of dying here.

And many a long, long day of woe,
  And sleepless nights untold,
And drenching rain, and drifting snow,
  And weariness, famine, and cold;
And worn out limbs and aching heart,
  And grief too great to tell,
And bleeding wound, and piercing smart,
  Had I escaped full well.

Weary, and wounded, and worn,
  Wounded and ready to die,
A soldier they left all alone and forlorn,
  On the field of the battle to lie.
The dead and the dying alone
  Could their presence and pity afford,
While thus with a sad and a terrible tone
(O would that these truths were more perfectly known)
  He sang the song of the sword.'

With these frightful examples before us, it is impossible to deny the existence of Destructiveness in excess. Not that God has implanted in man a propensity to destroy his fellow-creatures—that is not the case ; the propensity was given to assist him to subdue the earth ; to have dominion over the fish of the sea, over the fowl of the air, and over every living thing that moveth upon the earth. But man has unhappily abused the power he was entrusted with, and has achieved the bad eminence we have already described.

How then, let us now inquire, can this propensity be kept within its legitimate boundaries, and subjected to proper control ? We answer, and speaking phrenologically, the superior religious and moral sentiments, Conscientiousness, Veneration, Benevolence, Cautiousness, and Love of Approbation, must be cultivated. Here we see the necessity of a good education and proper training. To control the destructive propensity, and keep it within the sphere where its functions may be legitimately exercised, the Holy Scriptures must be the best guide. Here we are forewarned that we must not give the rein to our licentious appetites. The command, 'Thou shalt not kill,' is as imperative now as when first promulgated. But the same command, as illustrated by our Redeemer, 'I say unto you, whosoever is angry with his brother without a cause,' may well induce us to reflect upon the solemn truth, that whosoever 'hateth his brother is a murderer.' Anger, when in its malignant and unbridled exercise, is indeed the parent of many sorrows. Every one that is angry with his brother without a cause, stimulates to undue action Destructiveness, and if Self-Esteem did not rise up to protect the object of his hatred, he would certainly effect his destruction. We do not say it is possible for a man to be entirely exempt from the passion of anger ; he would not be a man if he were. Perfect love can only be associated with a perfect being ; that Being is God ; therefore God is Love ! A man may feel anger, but still not be revengeful, or harbor malignant feelings. A man may be a good man, and yet be strongly endowed with Destructiveness, in the phrenological sense of the word ; which implies physical energy, determined to overcome in a righteous cause :—

> ' E'en the good patient man, whose reason rules,
> Rous'd by bold insult and injurious rage,
> With a sharp and sudden check, th' astonish'd sons
> Of violence confounds. Firm as his cause,
> His bolder heart in awful justice clad,
> His eyes effulging a peculiar fire ;
> And as he charges through the prostrate war,
> His keen arm teaches faithless men, no more
> To dare the sacred vengeance of the just ! '

A man of this description is angry and sins not : he lets not the sun go down upon his wrath. In this sense only can anger be tolerated. In this sense the just man figuratively breaks the jaws of the wicked.

Anger has its origin in this organ, whatever the predisposing cause may be. One man, in whom Destructiveness is powerfully developed, and Cautiousness but moderate, feels an insult rush almost momentarily to the head. His countenance becomes flushed by the rushing of the blood upwards, his eyes emit an almost preternatural lustre, and the lightning glance which is darted upon the aggressor is frequently more powerfully felt than a torrent of harsh language. Another, in whom Cautiousness is large, presents a totally different appearance. An ashy paleness overspreads the countenance, the fists are clenched, the teeth become almost imbedded in the lips, and these are sometimes bitten to the effusion of blood. Cautiousness may prevent the violence of the ebullition, but the feelings are not the less seriously wounded.

Anger sometimes proves fatal, the severity of its shock at once suppressing the action of the heart, or, as occasionally has happened, causing an actual rupture of this organ, or some of the large blood-vessels. Apoplexy, hemorrhages, convulsions, or other grave

affections, may also succeed to it, speedily terminatin
existence.

'The celebrated John Hunter fell a sudden victim to
paroxysm of anger. Mr. Hunter, as is familiar t
medical readers, was a man of extraordinary genius, bu
the subject of violent passions, which, from defect e
early moral culture, he had not learned to contro
Suffering during his last years under a complaint of th
heart, his existence was in constant jeopardy from hi
ungovernable temper, and he had been heard to remark
that "his life was in the hands of any rascal who chos
to insult him." Engaged one day in an unpleasan
altercation with his colleagues, and being peremptoril;
contradicted, he at once ceased speaking, hurried int
an adjoining room, and instantly fell dead.'—*Menta
Hygiene.*

Destructiveness displays itself sometimes in a place
and through a medium, where, upon reflection, one woul
have thought it could never have entered : we allude t
the pulpit. 'The mild spirit of Christianity calls upo
us to hate nothing but evil, and he, among Christians
who is constantly terrifying his hearers into submissio
by the thunders of his own destructive energy, seldon:
fails to represent the Divine Being as altogether such s
one as himself. Much as the denunciations of certain
divines is to be reprobated, it is too unhappily true, that
where in clergymen this faculty is large, it indulges in
coarse and bitter invective, fierce and angry denunciation,
and sometimes cruel and insulting irony, totally at
variance with the pacific principles of the gospel, and
alike derogatory to the character of God, as it is justly
abhorred by all well-regulated minds.' 'How different'
(says Dr. Caldwell of America) 'is the temper and spirit
of Christ from that miserable substitute for Christianity,
that revolting caricature of piety—whining, coarse,
obstreperous, and denouncing—which so assails us in
some places of worship, and which has its source as
exclusively in the animal organs, as the uproar of the

bacchanalian, the shout of battle, or the howling of wolves ! This indecent storminess of instruction affects only the animal propensities of the brain, because, as just stated, it is itself grossly animal ; and we venture to assert that no teacher or minister ever practised it, who was himself largely developed in the moral and reflecting faculties—we mean, in whom those compartments fairly predominated, and gave character to the individual. On the truth of this we would be willing to peril the fate of Phrenology. It is a caste of pulpit pugilists alone, with heads of the true animal mould, or nearly approaching to it, that deal in nothing but discourses of terror, who, in sermonising or otherwise, exercise their combative and destructive faculties to draw their flocks into the pale of their religion, precisely as they would employ a whip or a goad to drive sheep into a fold, or black cattle into their stalls. Terror is their chief, if not their only instrument of reform, and a worse can scarcely be imagined. Their appeal is to Cautiousness, the organ of the craven passion of fear, whose influence never infused morality or religion into any one, and never can. Their plea of conversion and worship is not gratitude for existence and all its enjoyments, nor yet the love of moral purity and holiness, but the dread of punishment. They would frighten sinners into heaven, as a mere refuge from a place of torment.'

We hesitate not to say, that no such slavish inducements are necessary. We are persuaded, if ever a man enters into the heavenly kingdom, it must be because he loves God with all his heart and soul ; and loving Him, he loves peace, purity, and order, and, from these, desires to be an inhabitant of that kingdom where they can be enjoyed in all their fulness. A Christian doctrine should never be maintained with an anti-Christian spirit. In endeavoring to convince, we must be cautious not needlessly to irritate, lest the adversary's unfavorable opinion of religion be augmented by the faults of the champion, and lest be attribute to the former passions, sentiments, or feelings emanating only from the animal organs of the latter.

7. SECRETIVENESS.—The organ of Secretiveness is situated in the centre of the lateral portion of the brain just above Destructiveness and below Cautiousness. Dr.

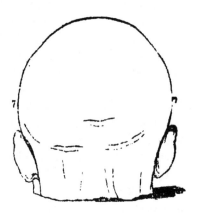

Gall gives the following account of its discovery. In early youth he was struck with the form of the head of one of his school-fellows, who, with amiable dispositions and good abilities, was nevertheless distinguished by peculiar traits of cunning and concealment. He observed the same in another school-fellow, but who, to look at and judge of from the physiognomical expression of his countenance, appeared all sincerity and open-heartedness. The doctor, nevertheless, observed that he was a great cheat — that he imposed on every person he came in contact with, whether school-fellows, teachers, or even his own parents. Continuing his observations, he next examined the head of one of his patients who had died, and during his life was supposed to be a very honest man, but was discovered afterwards to have cheated both his acquaintances and his relatives out of large sums of money. In all these persons, the portion of the brain we are now illustrating presented an extra large appearance.

'At Vienna,' observes Dr. Gall, 'I was often in company with a physician of uncommon attainments, whose character for cheating rendered him universally despised. Under pretence of dealing in objects of art, and of lending on pledges, he fleeced all who put any confidence in him. He carried his trickery and cheating so far, that the government warned the public, through the newspapers, to beware of him ; for he had practised his arts with so much dexterity, that he never could be legally condemned. He frequently told me, with an air of sincerity, that he knew no greater pleasure, no more exquisite enjoyment, than that of duping people, and especially those who distrusted him most. As this physician's head was also very large at the temples, I was naturally impressed with the idea, that the essential quality of this character, cunning, is a primitive one, and is manifested by a particular organ of the brain.'*

It must be remembered that almost all the discoveries of Gall were from organs in a state of excess or abuse; and the phrenological nomenclature, imperfect as it still is, was much more faithfully expressed by the observations and corrections of his colleague, Dr. Spurzheim. No one power of the mind ought to be considered as baneful or injurious. *There is no such thing as a bad organ.* Cunning is an abuse of the organ of Secretiveness. But Secretiveness, in the exercise of its legitimate functions, is the origin of prudence, tact, skill, and circumspection ; and it is indispensable for the regulation of our conduct towards each other. Of this we can produce the most unexceptionable authority. 'Behold, I send you forth as sheep among wolves ; be ye therefore prudent as serpents, and harmless as doves.' Our Saviour made use of this comparison, that we might not bring ourselves into difficulty from a want of that necessary precaution by which our success in life is so frequently determined. In giving his disciples this advice, it was the same as admonishing them that they would have many enemies to encounter, which would require the exercise of all their prudence to overcome, and he chose the serpent as an apt analogy of

* Gall's Works, vol. iv., pp. 119, 120.

25

this prudence. But there is another reason, which seems to have escaped the notice of most theologians. The perfection of the human character arises from the combined perfections of the animals referred to. Certain it is, that the life of man is a compound life, made up of an indefinite variety of affections and thoughts, and hence we may conclude that man will be more perfect as the variety is more extended ; we may, therefore, not only say, ' Be wise as serpents, and harmless as doves,' but ' Be strong as lions, playful as lambs, cheerful as larks,' etc., etc., and endeavor to unite in ourselves the distinct excellencies of all the inferior creatures, while we avoid their defects ; in other words, exercise all our propensities without abusing them.

Cardinal Perron says that the serpent is an excellent symbol of cunning, because it never carries its head directly before its body to the place it is desirous of reaching. In this it resembles a cunning man, who never betrays his intentions by his words or gestures.

But Secretiveness in excess manifests itself externally, or by a natural language, in a variety of ways. When you see an individual taking a side glance, and working his head round *a la Grimaldi*, you may be sure the possessor has very large Secretiveness.

Where Secretiveness predominates over. all the other powers, the individual's sole delight is in plotting. Dr. Johnson mentions that Pope took so great a delight in artifice, that he endeavored to attain all his purposes by indirect and unsuspected methods. He practised his arts on such small occasions, that Lady Bolingbroke used to say of him, in a French phrase, that he played the politician about cabbages and turnips.

Mr. Bulwer is most accurate in his definition of the character of Lord Vargrave, as a personification of Secretiveness in excess. ' He loved intrigue for intrigue's sake. Had it led to no end, it would still have been sweet to him as a means. He loved to surround himself with the most complicated webs, to sit in the centre of a million of plots. He cared not how wild some of them were.

He relied on his own ingenuity, promptitude, and habitual good fortune, to make everything he handled conducive to the purpose of the machine, self.' *

On this organ Dr. Spurzheim remarks, that it gives the propensity to conceal, without determining the object or the manner of concealing. It disposes to be secret in thoughts, words, and deeds. By its influence, the fox is careful not to be observed ; the dog hides the bone he cannot pick ; and the cunning man conceals his intentions, and sometimes professes opinions opposite to those he really entertains. It may be applied in an infinite number of ways, and employed under many varieties of circumstances and situation. If not directed by justice and the other moral feelings, it disposes to dissimulation, intrigue, duplicity, hypocrisy, and lying. It finds pleasure in all kind of underhand doings and clandestine manoeuvres. Whenever concealment interferes, be it for good or for evil purposes, this feeling dictates the course pursued.

8. ACQUISITIVENESS.—Acquisitiveness is situated at the anterior inferior angle of the parietal bone. In our description of the organ of Combativeness, we related the manner in which Dr. Gall discovered it. His discovery of this organ originated in the same circumstances. At these meetings, some of the company accused others of various acts of petty larceny, who seemed to exult at the adroit manner in which they plundered others. They invariably were very largely developed at the particular parts now under review. Others, in the same company, manifested the strongest abhorrence at such base conduct, and in them the same parts were sometimes flat and even hollow. Dr. Gall had also an opportunity of examining the head of a boy, 15 years of age, who was confined in the house of correction, and whose propensity to steal was so inordinate, that at that early period, he had been condemned to imprisonment for life. In his portrait, given in Dr. Gall's large work, the lateral region of the head is

* ' Alice, or the Mysteries.'

remarkably distinguished by a prominence, which is now established as the seat of the organ.

The following cases are extracted from Dr. Gall's Works, vol. iv., p. 131 :—

Victor Amadeus I., king of Sardinia, was in the constant habit of stealing trifles. Saurin, pastor at Geneva, though possessing the strongest principles of reason and religion, frequently yielded to the propensity to steal. Another individual was from early youth a victim to this inclination. He entered the military service, on purpose that he might be restrained by the severity of the discipline ; but having continued his practices, he was on the point of being condemned to be hanged. Ever seeking to combat his ruling passion, he studied theology, and became a Capuchin ; but his propensity followed him even to the cloister. Here, however, as he found only trifles to tempt him, he indulged himself in his strange fancy with less scruple. He seized scissors, candlesticks, snuffers, cups, goblets, and conveyed them to his cell. An agent of the government at Vienna had the singular mania for stealing nothing but kitchen utensils. He hired two rooms as a place of deposit : he did not sell, and made no use of them. The wife of the famous physician, Gaubius, had such a propensity to pilfer, that when she made a purchase, she always sought to take something. She was always accompanied by a servant, either to prevent or compensate for her thefts. Lavater* speaks of a physician, who never left the room of his patients without robbing them of something, and who never thought of the matter afterwards. In the evening his wife used to examine his pockets ; she there found keys, scissors, thimbles, knives, spoons, buckles, cases, and sent them to their respective owners. Moritz, in his experimental treatise on the soul, relates, with the greatest minuteness, the history of a robber, who had a propensity to theft in such a degree, that, being ' *in articulo mortis*,'

* 'Physiognomie,' edit. de la Haye, tom. ii., p. 169.

at the point of death), he stole the snuff-box of his con-
fessor.

In all these cases, there can be no doubt but the brain
was in a diseased state; for there was, at least, in most
of them, no apparent motive of appropriation. The
mode of treatment with such persons should have been
the same as that of lunatics. In the case of juvenile
thieves, they should not be sent to prison, but to an
establishment where the object should be to reform them,
and this on the commission of the first offence. When
prepared by moral and religious training to lead a regular
life, they might be restored to society, at first under strict
surveillance. At each relapse, however slight, the penalty
should be increased, and not until numerous relapses should
they be for ever excluded from society. Should they be
found incorrigible, they should be treated as lunatics, and
confined for life, under proper restraint, but yet with
such means of relaxation and exercise as might be proper
for the preservation of general health. Alas! how far
are we yet from such a mode of treatment in this country,
where, almost daily, they prevent the penitent offender
from returning to the paths of virtue! On discharge
from prison, who will receive him? What house of
refuge is open to him? None. He is forced to support
his existence by banding with criminals whom society
has rejected.

The necessity of adopting curative means in cases of
juvenile offenders, and the injustice of inflicting punishment
where this has been neglected, has been admirably illustrated in a work entitled 'Old Bailey Experiences,' from
which I extract the following letter; whether written in
irony or in sober truth from the supposed culprit, it is
equally deserving attention :—

'I was born in Dyott Street, in the city of London. I never
recollect my mother; but my father's companions sometimes spoke
of her as one who had been transported for passing bad money.
My father used to look gloomy and sorrowful when she was
mentioned, and never recovered without a glass of liquor; some
people said she died broken-hearted in gaol, but I never heard the

truth of it. In our street, he who thieved the most cleverly was the most admired, and the only disgrace that could be incurred was the shame of detection. I sometimes at the end of it, saw people ride past in fine coaches, and these, I supposed, had robbed still more successfully. I knew nothing, and was taught nothing but to steal; and I practised my art with an industry which I thought most laudable. I have heard of God, of hell, and the devil; and they once told me when the bell tolled at St. Giles', that people went there to pray that they might go to heaven, but I saw nobody who seemed to believe this, and I thought these words, like many others, were only useful to swear by. The only thing I was taught to fear was the thief-catcher, and though I eluded his vigilance for some time, he caught me at last. In prison the parson told me how I ought to have been brought up. He found that I had never been idle, that I had labored in my calling, that I had never robbed my father or cheated my landlady, and that to the best of my ability I had done what I was told to do, and yet I was put in gaol; and if I had not been a very little boy, the parson said, I should have been hanged. There are some hundreds of boys in London who are living as I lived; and when I was tried, a gentleman in a great wig talked very kindly to me, and if I knew what his name was, I would send this letter to him. He said he would have a school in Dyott Street, where boys might be told what was right; and I think, sir, before they are caught and hanged, it would just be honest to tell them they are in danger of it, and to tell them what is law and what is society, and not to let them hear of it, for the first time, when they are tried. I am going, they say, among savages, and I never desire to come back. The savages would have taken care of my education; have taught me to hunt, shoot, and fish, and would have told me how to be a great and good man; but the Christians have not done so, and if it was not that I am sorry for my companions that are left behind, and hope the gentleman in the large wig may see this letter, I would not give myself the trouble of asking my fellow-prisoner to write it.

'JACK WILD.'

There can be no question that the amount of juvenile delinquency is on the increase—nay, there are seminaries in which the art of pocket-picking is carried on most ingeniously, so that the description in 'Oliver Twist,' of the game between the Jew, Fagan, and his 'artful dodgers,' is not all fiction.

Mr. Richard Gregory, in his evidence before the police committee, says, 'I went the other day to a house in Wentworth Street, Whitechapel, which is kept by a very notorious character, and there were eighteen or twenty men and women, boys and girls, in bed together, in two rooms. The fellow who keeps the house had a sort of table for them. Some pay sixpence for their bed, some fourpence, and they all go out thieving. If they steal a handkerchief; the man says, " You had your dinner yesterday, that was *fourpence*, I will take this handkerchief for it "; and if they steal a watch which is worth £20 or £25, it will fetch twenty shillings in the thieves' market; then he says, " This will go on for next week."' There is, perhaps, with the single exception of Destructiveness, no organ that is more stimulated and cultivated than Acquisitiveness; we need not therefore wonder that it is grievously abused. Whether we look at the merchant, the manufacturer, or the shopkeeper, the cry is, ' Every one has a right to do the best he can for himself.'

To buy in the cheapest market, and sell in the dearest, is a rule, the justice of which is seldom called in question. It is, however, if fairly analysed, the rule of Acquisitiveness, and in absolute antagonism to the sentiment of justice. That rule is, ' Whatsoever things ye would that men should do to you, do ye even so to them.' With this rule before us, we say that every man has not a right to do the best he can for himself, if that right interferes with the right of his neighbor. How far the law of justice is observed by the keepers and customers of cheap shops, is a question worth considering. Such a rule has little sympathy with the spirit which grinds the faces of the poor, and strives to prosper by underselling the fair trader.

Mutual benefit is the soul of business. The announcement of '*ruinous prices*,' if true, is an injury to legitimate trade; if false, they are a fraud upon the .public: and fraud, in whatever way it is exercised, is an abuse of the organ of Acquisitiveness—a violation of the principle of justice. In either case, the customer's saving, whether real or supposed, cannot be honestly obtained; and those who prefer feeding the flames of voluntary martyrs, to providing fuel for honest men to cook their dinners with, are little or no better than receivers of stolen goods. On the other hand, they who mulct their customers by short weight or short measure, are as certainly thieves as those who put their hand into their neighbor's pocket, and rob him of his cash. Look again at the system of trade in too many shops, we had almost said all. The shopkeeper stands behind his counter like a spider in his web, and every customer he looks upon as his legitimate prey. In the exposure of his goods, lying and false affirmation are his legitimate weapons. If his customer is simply honest, and believes his affirmations, and listens to the praises bestowed upon his goods, and pays the prices asked, 'Ha! ha! ha! what a greenhorn! How far will a fortune go with him?' Want of Conscientiousness, on the one hand, and large Secretiveness and Acquisitiveness on the other, are the ruling powers of such a shopkeeper, yet how indignant would he be, if he were told what he really is, A THIEF! *

* 'The inordinate attachment to money, will, like every other passion, affect the bloods' constitution, and therefore the bodily health. Disorders of the digestive organs, as of the stomach and liver, and serious affections of the heart, spring from this passion. The functions of these organs concern more especially the well-being of the blood; consequently, when they are impaired, the blood suffers, and in this way a circulation of mischief is introduced, requiring much tact and skill on the part of the physician to counteract it.

'How does the painter portray the miser, or the victims of the other passions? The disorderly affections and appetites of human nature are deep-seated in their action, and therefore they fall upon brain and countenance, upon nerve and habit, upon muscle and gesture, conforming the body to their own ugliness; they are closely allied to the blood in all states and places, whether as a fluid in the nerves of subtle modifications; or as the purple streams in arteries and veins of slower undulations. And if here, a new constitution, or a perverted nature, is imparted to it, which propagates itself to descendants—an accumulating evil to many generations—spreading proportionately to the indulgence and the fashion; then the whole frame-work of the body, and eventually of society, becomes constituted by predilections, tendencies, and suscepti-bilities, quite foreign to the original intention of the Creator. In proof of all this, we have no greater instance than the sin of avarice, for it is one of the direst forms of selfishness, and vitiates the blood most deeply.'—Dr. SPURGIN.—'Physician for All.'

Or turn to the merchant. How foul have been his dealings *on change!* The words of good old Jeremy Taylor are as true now, as when first conveyed through the medium of a sermon in condemnation of covetousness and thievery. 'In this world, men thrive by villany! Lying and deceiving are counted just, and to be rich is to be wise ; and though little thefts and petty mischiefs are interrupted by the laws, yet if a mischief becomes public and great, and robberies be perpetrated by fleets and armies, it is virtue, and it is glory !' We say, such merchants, such warriors, are thieves, as much under the influence of Acquisitiveness in excess as the miserable wretch who steps on the tread-wheel ; though it may be, in the words of poor *Jack Wild*, they have eluded the vigilance of the thief-catcher. The system of spoliation by the great land-holders, called protection, was little else than a system of Acquisitiveness in excess. Sympathy for the poor, they had none—unless, indeed, by words. The condition of the agricultural laborer, until very recently—and it is not even yet very enviable—was one of misery and want. The 'Times' thus graphically describes the state of the poor in agricultural districts : 'We give the poor man every right and privilege under the sun—*upon paper*. He is the highest and loftiest of human beings—*in* " Blackstone's Commentaries," *and* " De Lolme on the Constitution." He is free, independent, and master of himself, and a lord of the creation ; in company with the squire, lawyer, and surgeon of the parish, as good as any of them. His house is his castle, and the air of heaven his birthright. He lifts up his hand and says, " *I'm a man and all that.*" The only drawback from this high state of existence is, that he has often no bread to eat, and that both the bodies and the souls of these favored beings are allowed to take their chance, as the saying is.'

But if further examples are needed of the effects of Acquisitiveness, look in the daily papers. How many poor wretches are there, whose only escape from suffering seems to be the Thames, or the nearest river !

Money seems to be the chief thing, at least in the estimation of many, for which we are called into existence. Boys are taught its value from the moment they enter the counting-room, nay, almost from the moment they begin to think at all.

A merchant, it has been said, has no faith but in his banker. The Exchange is his church, the desk is his altar, the ledger is his Bible, and his money is his God. With all these illustrations before us, have we said too much in affirming that Acquisitiveness is the most industriously cultivated organ in the whole brain—the organ which it is thought impossible to stimulate too highly ? While we set the example in the higher departments of society, of clutching at everything we can get, and doing the best we can for ourselves, is it to be wondered at that there are thousands, who, like *Jack Wild,* think they are doing no more than an industrious man should do to acquire money by any means which offers ? Assuredly not ! There remains then nothing but education, and a cultivation of the Christian precept, 'Thou shalt love thy neighbor as thyself,' to remedy this state of things, and to bring this organ down to the proper level it should occupy, namely, that of economy in providing for the period when strength fails, and when more comforts and conveniences are needed than in the heyday of youth and high health.

The proper exercise of Acquisitiveness under the influence of conscience and the moral powers, renders it one of the most useful of the animal propensities. It is then the spirit of economy, frugality, and forethought. It avoids all waste and squandering. It 'gathers up the fragments that nothing be lost.'

9. CONSTRUCTIVENESS.—The seat of the organ of Constructiveness is anterior to that of Acquisitiveness, and lies under the place where the frontal, parietal, and sphenoidal bones unite. Its appearance and situation

vary according to the development of the neighboring organs, according to the basis of the head, and the size of the zygomatic process. If the convolutions in the situation indicated project more than the external angle of the orbit, then the organ of Constructiveness may be admitted as large. If the basis of the skull be narrow, it lies a little higher than in heads which are very broad in the basilar region, and across the zygomatic processes. Moreover, it is covered with one of the masticatory muscles; this must, therefore, be examined by the touch, before the exact size of the organ in question can be distinguished.

Dr. Gall thus describes its discovery :* 'At Vienna, Dr. Scheele, of Copenhagen, had attended one of my courses of lectures; thence he went to Rome. One day he suddenly entered my house when I was surrounded by my pupils, and showed me a skull in plaster, on which he begged me to give him my opinion. I immediately exclaimed that I had never seen the organ of Constructiveness developed to the degree that it was in this cranium. Scheele continued to question me. I requested those present to observe a considerable development of the organ of physical love and that of imitation. How, continued he, do you find the organ of color ? I had not paid attention to it, for it was only moderately developed. M. Scheele then declared that it was the cast of the skull of Raphael which he had just sent me, and that during his residence in Italy, he had found my ideas confirmed by the study of the uniques.

'Many of my hearers spoke to me of a man endowed with an extraordinary genius for mechanics. I described to them, beforehand, the form which his head ought to have, and we went to find him. He was the skilful inventor of mathematical instruments at Vienna. His temples were swollen into two misshapen cushions. Before this, I had found nearly the same form in the head of the celebrated mechanician and astronomer, Daird, an Augustine friar.

* Gall's Works, vol. v., p. 108.

'At Paris, the Prince of Schwartzenberg, then minister of Austria, wished to put M. Spurzheim and myself to the test. At the moment when we arose from table, he led me into a neighboring apartment, and introduced to me a young man without saying a single word. I went to rejoin the company with the prince, and begged M. Spurzheim to examine the young man during his absence. I told the company what I thought of him. Spurzheim had hardly seen the individual, when he came to join us in the parlor, and likewise declared that he thought him a great mechanician, or a great artist in some similar department. In fact, the prince had induced him to come to Paris on account of his great talents for mechanics, and furnished him with the means to prosecute his studies there.

'At Vienna, and in the whole course of our travels, we found, among all the mechanicians, architects, draughts-men, and sculptors, this organ developed in proportion to their talent.'

When Dr. Spurzheim was in Edinburgh in 1817, he visited the workshop of Mr. James Mylne, brassfounder, and examined the heads of the workmen and apprentices.

'On the first boy presented to Dr. Spurzheim, on his entering the shop, he observed he would excel in anything he was put to. In this he was perfectly correct, as he was one of the cleverest boys I ever had. On proceeding further, Dr. Spurzheim observed of another boy that he would make a good workman. In this instance, also, the observation was well founded. An elder brother was working near him, whom he also said would turn out a good workman, but not equal to the other. I mentioned, said Mr. Mylne, that in point of fact the former was the best, but both were good. In the course of further observations, Dr. Spurzheim remarked of others that they ought to be ordinary tradesmen, and they were so. At last he pointed out one, who, he said ought to be of a different cast, and of whom I should never be able to make anything as a workman, and this turned out to be too correct. For though he had served seven years' apprenticeship, he was not able to do one-third of the work of other individuals. So much was I struck, observed Mr. Mylne, with Dr. Spurzheim's observations, and so correct have I found the indication presented by the organisation to be, that when workmen, or boys to serve as apprentices, apply to me, I at once give the preference to those possessing a large Constructiveness ; and if the deficiency be very great, I should be disposed to decline receiving them, convinced of their inability to succeed.'

The constructive faculty in the bee is singularly happy —in the formation of their cells, they are the most complete geometricians. Scarcely could a hexagon be more perfectly drawn by a skilful mathematician, than is presented in the cells of these insects. But this is not all ; it was said by Pappus, an ancient geometrician, that of all other figures, hexagons were the most convenient, for, when placed touching each other, the most convenient room would be given, and the smallest lost ; so the instinct of the bee has determined. The cells of the bees are perfect hexagons. These in every honeycomb are double, opening on either side, and closed at the bottom. The bottoms are composed of little triangular panes, which, when united together, terminate in a point, and lie exactly upon the extremities of other panes of the same shape in other cells. These lodgings have spaces like streets between them, sufficiently large to let the bees go in and out, but yet narrow enough to preserve the heat of the united hexagons. What the bee is among insects, the beaver appears to be among quadrupeds ; and the faculty of Constructiveness seems in them to approach as near to the same faculty in man, as is seen in human erections.

We shall notice some important particulars connected with this organ, when we come to treat of the organs of Form, Size, and Weight in combination. The organ of Constructiveness is fully established.

I now found the benefit of my medical studies, and

from being an authorised apothecary and chemist, I resolved to finish my medical education. It might be of
great use to me in after life ; at all events, it would
render me efficient aid in the prosecution of my phrenological investigations, and would, above all things,
enable me to acquire a knowledge of the brain from
nature, rather than from plates. So I entered myself a
student at the Glasgow University. I, however, only
attended one professor in the university, who was himself a Phrenologist. His department was the ' Institutions of Medicine.' He was a most admirable teacher,
but very delicate in health, and feeble in speech. My
great difficulty was now my deafness. I could not hear
the professor distinctly, though I was allowed to sit very
near the chair, right in front of the professor's table, in
fact. Many were the expedients I devised, with the
view of catching all the tones of the professor's voice.
I remembered that wood was a good conductor of sound,
and that a wooden rod, one end of which placed against
the teeth, and the other end rested on a table, conveyed sounds with accuracy from a considerable distance. So I constructed a rod of beech wood, cut with
a notch at one end, which I fixed to the edge of the
professor's table, and placed my teeth at the other end, and
I heard distinctly ; but, alas ! this experiment succeeded
too well, for any noise from the students—the scraping of
a pencil, for instance, the thrumming of the fingers on the
desk, or the shuffling of the feet on the floor, or even the
subdued conversation of the students—often rendered the
professor's voice confused and indistinct. I then changed
my wooden rod for a hollow tube of iron, and had it
deeply cut, with spiral lines on the surface, forming it, as
nearly as I could, to resemble the labyrinth of the ear,
and I found great relief from this, but still experienced
annoyance from the causes before mentioned. With the
view of deadening these sounds, and still preserving in-
tact the voice of the professor, I rested the posterior part
of the vertex of my head against the support at the back

of my seat, and I was amazed at the effect—I heard distinctly.*

In this way I listened to the various professors, and though I could not distinctly hear every word of the lecture, I, for the most part, was enabled to obtain the substance; and I attentively conned the subjects of each day's attendance at the University at my own home, and thus kept pace with the other students. As I have said, I attended but one professor in the University of Glasgow; for the principal medical school, and with an equally efficient staff of professors, was at the University founded by Dr. Anderson, and bearing the name of the Andersonian University. The fees here were much lower than at the principal University, and better accorded with my slender finances; though I may here with gratitude acknowledge, that after I had attended one session, many of the professors remitted my fees altogether, presenting me with perpetual tickets.

It has been the fashion—nay, I believe, still is—to decry medical education in Scotland, and to speak of those who have graduated at the Scotch Universities in terms very nearly allied to contempt. I can with truth affirm that the medical school in the Andersonian University of Glasgow possesses professors eminent in their respective departments, most indefatigable in their attention to the students, and affording facilities for completing medical education, which many of the schools in England are destitute of. I conscientiously believe, from several years' experience at this University, that it is one of the best medical schools in the world, and it is a pleasure to me to be able here to offer my tribute of admiration and gratitude for the instruction I have received from its able pro-

---

* I tried this experiment with the tones of the piano and organ, and heard well. I did further: passionately fond of music as I was (and am), I could not hear the tones of the musical box. I put the box close to my ear, but only caught a dull vibration; but when I placed the box on the top of my head, I heard every note distinctly. I now resort to this experiment frequently and always with the same result.

fessors, although, from my now almost total deafness, my medical education is of little value to me in a pecuniary point of view.

Well, pursuing my medical studies in this manner, my time was altogether taken up. My theological studies were mostly completed before breakfast, and well fixed in my memory ; for, as I have before remarked, I did not write my sermons. Besides my evening lectures at different institutions, I had also a class of ladies at my own house, whom I instructed in those parts of anatomy and physiology most suitable to the sex. I believe I was the only teacher of physiology who resorted to this plan ; and several ladies who attended my class had their sons educated under my direction.

My salary from the Swedenborgian Society was sixty pounds per annum ; but my large family, who were now growing up and educating, demanded double that sum, and to meet these expenses I was constantly in the lecture room or the study. My health, however, continued to be excellent, but my deafness certainly increased. Some of my Swedenborgian friends imagined that I devoted too much time to Phrenology, and too little to biblical studies. I recollect one person saying to me—'You can preach so good an extemporaneous sermon, that you give too little time for theological study. With your attendance at the University during the day, and your labors in the lecture room at night, how can you find time for study for the Sunday ? You have too many irons in the fire ; you cannot keep them all warm.'

To which I replied—'I get through my labor by system. I have finished my theological studies before you are out of bed. By varying my studies I give exercise to my various faculties, and while one class of faculties is in active labor, another class is reposing. As to my having too many irons in the fire, I have lived to realise the truth long ago uttered by Dr. Sir Edward Clarke, "The true secret of human happiness lies in the cultivation of all the faculties." I therefore, never suffer any of my energies to stagnate. The old adage which you have quoted of too many irons in the fire, is a libel and a falsehood. You cannot have too many ; when one iron cools, or when one faculty is wearied, I give it rest, and take up another ; thus, shovel, tongs, and poker, I keep them all a going. This is the principle upon which I act—so much time to one study, so much time to another. As to your remark, that I do not give sufficient time to theological studies, your observations that I can preach a good extemporaneous discourse refutes it.'

'Well,' replied he, 'how you manage to get through all this labor, I know not—you are fast wearing out that little body of yours ; you are working too hard, I tell you, and it cannot last long.'

'But,' continued I, 'what am I to do ? You cannot imagine that the sum the Swedenborgian Society allows me is sufficient to meet all my expenses. Here have I to keep up the appearance of a gentleman, with a house the rent and taxes of which amounts to upwards of £30 per annum, and with a large family to educate. I must do something else, not so much from choice, perhaps, as from necessity.'

I know this conversation was reported to some of the influential members of my little congregation, and my circumstances were a little improved thereby. I conscientiously believe that my Glasgow friends were among the most liberal of the Swedenborgians, that they supported me to the utmost of their ability, and though my salary was for many years not more than £60, yet there were a few who augmented it yearly by a new year's present. In truth, the Society of Swedenborgians in Glasgow are more liberal and attentive to the wants of their ministers than any other society in the whole connection.

But besides the pecuniary aid I derived from lecturing, I had now become known as a successful Manipulator, and my predications of character increased my resources. I was frequently tested by an eminent physician in the city, he measuring and manipulating the head, and sending

26

me the size and development of the respective organs, and
I drawing out an analysis from his numbers without
seeing or having any knowledge of the parties. In this
way, the Doctor procured me many fees. He has been one
of my warmest and best friends, and so continues to this
day.

In my predications of character, I never considered any
thing else than organisation ; however intimate an acquaintance I might have with the person who sat to me for a
mental portrait, I discarded all knowledge of him except
that derived from his organisation. From this, I inferred
his character, and from this spoke the plain truth ; very
often, it must be confessed, giving offence by my plain-
speaking, but frequently exciting wonder at the accuracy
with which I described the hidden causes of singular
traits of character. In my analysis of such persons whose
characters I drew from their printed works, I always
gave the why, and the wherefore, for my opinion ; but I
will now proceed to give, from close observation for many
years,

A CHAPTER OF PEN-AND-INK PORTRAITS.

'Some preachers thunder, but do not lighten; others lighten, but
do not thunder. The true preacher does both—the pretended neither.'
—CLOWES.

There are three ministers in the Swedenborgian connection, who have attracted my particular attention, and their
characters are so diverse and yet so strictly accord with
their organisation, that I cannot forbear first describing
them. As they are living, I will only say that they
minister in large churches and in large towns.

The organisation of the firsts presents a medium sized
head, large but languishing eye, a forehead moderately
deep, but less prominent at the upper part than over the
superciliary ridge. The anterior part of the coronal
region just below the fontanel is but moderate, behind the
fontanel it is better rounded, and at the vertex very
prominent. On each side of the vertex it slopes down

rather rapidly, but swells out as it reaches the centre of
ossification, that is, at the parietal bones. The temperament is a compound of Nervous, Sanguine, and Lymphatic,
the former two having the predominance.

The sermons of this gentleman are exceedingly beautiful, abounding in comparisons, and clothed in a respectable drapery of language ; but his appearance in the
pulpit is so impassive, that his sermons, beautiful though
they be, seem to make but feeble impression. You see
the lips gently move, and you hear a monotonous voice,
as from an automaton rather than a living throat ; but
the muscles of the face seldom relax, a finger is rarely
raised in action, not an emotion is manifested as he reads ;
cold intellectuality seems his distinguishing feature, and
but for the voice and the tremulous motion of the lips,
you would imagine the pulpit tenanted with a finely
carved bust of marble. He introduces dead facts, and
varies them by comparisons, but his appeals are chiefly to
the understanding, and even when he addresses the
imagination or the heart, he does not seem to feel what he
utters himself. The intellectual part of his congregation
are alone reached to edification, and he rarely raises
emotion.

The consequence is, that in a large church, there are
frequently more empty pews than hearers. He is a man
to keep an old or an intellectual congregation together,
but seems unable to raise a new one.

There is but small infusion of warm young blood, a
very limited addition to the members, and such as are
added are of the cold and intellectual class. 'He lightens,
but does not thunder.'

The second of this trio, is a man also with a medium-
sized head, of immense activity, easily excited, very
impulsive, the result of a temperament of Nervous and
Sanguine in nearly equal proportions. He has a well-
defined superciliary ridge ; and, from this, his observing
powers are quick, but the upper part of the forehead,

where are seated the reflecting faculties, is much less prominent. The coronal surface of the brain is high, particularly over the fontanel ; and those portions of the brain assigned by phrenologists to Benevolence, Veneration, Hope, Marvellousness, and Ideality, are strikingly developed. The eye is véry prominent, but restless, quick, and glancing. The muscles 'of the face are very flexible, and kept in constant play. The countenance is animated and expressive. The tones are uttered with considerable energy, but the voice is not well modulated ; sometimes, indeed, it degenerates into a scream.

This gentleman has more of theory than solidity—more of imagination than judgment. He is among the 'brilliant talkers and sparkling orators'; of the class of preachers who seem to attract the largest number of hearers, and his church is in general well filled. Abounding in words, and using them with energy, he seizes upon one idea, rolls it over and over in a multitude of words, like a small pearl tossed upon the Ægean, places his pearl in every point of view, so that its beauty is distinctly seen, and keeps his audience in an excited state, under the anticipation that something new will immediately be presented, and thus he proceeds till the expiration of his allotted time. 'He thunders, but does not lighten.' His audience departs. They ponder upon what they have heard. They wonder what it is that has so enthralled them during the delivery of the discourse—and at length they discover the small pearl, and are disappointed with the preacher and vexed with themselves. And yet they go again—again are entranced—again find the same pearl rolled over and over in the same ocean of words, presented, it is true, under varied aspects, but are able to distinguish it as the same pearl—again depart—and again are vexed with themselves ; but still the fascination draws them. 'He thunders, but does not lighten.'

I remember a very simple, and very plain speaker, once preached in this orator's church, and the people were delighted with the simplicity of the sermon, and the

multitude of truths and goods with which it abounded.
There were pearls and diamonds (not very skilfully
polished, it is true,) butter and honey, goodness and
truth, and all applied to the life ; homely, but good and
beautiful ; and the opinion passed upon the two preachers
was in favor of the plain one. 'Ah !' said one of those
who were discussing their merits, 'what is the chaff to
the wheat ?' I have recently read in a popular work a
passage which illustrates forcibly the opinion I have
offered on this gentleman, and which I will here
adduce :—

'The orator has an advantage over the writer. To
look at 2,000 people is itself an inspiration. No man of
feeling can be dumb then. The living mass before you
makes you live. Thoughts are borne to you—words
come to you. You stand up and find yourself possessed
of a power of passionate utterance ; and even, if you be
nervous, in a short while after you have made a beginning,
you will find that nervousness a source of fire and power.
Men may doubt whether the preacher have his inspiration
from above, but that he has inspiration—that that comes
to him from the crowded auditory that hang upon his
lips, there can be no doubt. They act and re-act upon
each other. An audience may thus be roused to an
enthusiasm, of which afterwards it may feel ashamed,
and the orator, in the excitement of the moment, may
thus utter words that will scarcely stand reason's cold
and unerring test. I believe few men of sensibility can
get up to speak to a crowded audience, without saying
more than they meant when they got upon their legs,
so unruly a member is the tongue : but the fact that
the orator does so is the secret of his success. The
audience warms as the speaker warms—fires and glows
as he glows and fires. The presence of the man helps
to complete the success. You see his flushed face and
flashing eye. It is a human tongue that thrills your
heart ; but wait awhile ; let that flood of eloquence
cease—let that crowd pass away—and the words you

deemed so winged and piercing shall seem to you cold and poor indeed.'*   Yes, yes : he thunders, but does not lighten.

The last of this trio presents a man with a large head, and with a temperament composed of Nervous and Bilious in about equal proportions.   The activity is very great, and the endurance is equal, so that it works uniformly and without fitfulness.   The perception is minute and quick, but accurate ; the sensations are very refined and tender.   The forehead is broad, and. deep, and massive, and as smooth and polished as ivory, showing that the brain is equally distributed beneath, and thus giving the whole of the Intellectual faculties equal power.   Before the fontanel the coronal arch is not so well defined as behind, but towards the vertex it is magnificent, exhibiting an equal development of Veneration, Hope, Firmness, and Conscientiousness, and well defined, though somewhat smaller, Imitation, Marvellousness, and Ideality ; and there is enough of back brain to give great physical energy to the whole character.   The face has a somewhat severe expression, but is often lit up with a smile which, for the time it lasts, is inexpressibly sweet.   The eye is large and expressive, and shines with a steady lustre.

I particularly noticed this gentleman about twelve years since, and though age has somewhat dimmed the lustre of his eye, it still retains much of its expression, and of its original power in arresting attention.   This is a real man of mark.   There are united in this gentleman vigorous powers of understanding, a strong will, with the ability to delineate to the life all the affections of the will, all the thoughts of the understanding, and all the beauties of the imagination with a force, and power, and severe logic, which are irresistible.   His discourses, which are principally extempore, are delivered in a calm and earnest tone, free from any of the affected displays of the would-be orator—there is no sawing the air, no

* 'The London Pulpit,' by J. E. Ritchie.

thumping the cushion, but every word tells. He lays
down his positions plainly—and he follows them, and
illustrates them calmly, and with an exact logic that wins
the attention of the man of science. He pursues his
theme and illustrates again, so that the highly intellectual are reached in their inmost recesses ; onward he
goes ; and moral science becomes blended with moral
truth, and the attention of another class is arrested.
Still higher he rises, and the Word of God is displayed
in its spirituality, and his illustrations are confirmed by
apt quotations from its sacred pages. Then he combines
the whole, descends by degrees as he ascended, and down
to the most simple in mind instructs them in their duties
from the high subject on which he has been discoursing.
He ascended from the scientific by a series of degrees,
and having reached the highest, he comes down again to
the most simple, and applies his subject to every class.
' The last becomes first, and the first last.'   There is not
a single hearer but that seems to feel the subject
especially addressed to himself. The discourse is ended.
You have something to carry home with you and reflect
upon. Something that becomes a part of your mental
pabulum—matter for a week's reflection ! Work for a
week's practice. Something by which you may do good
to or instruct your neighbor. A sermon, in short,
which has taken fast hold of you and of your affections.
You have had excellent moral instruction, sound ethics,
and spiritual philosophy—a philosophy which has made
you wiser, and will, by applying its precepts, make you
better. You have heard one who both ' *thunders and
lightens.*'

REV. ROBERT MONTGOMERY.

In 1840 I became a subscriber to the late Rev. Robert
Montgomery's Poems, which were published in Glasgow,
and printed at the office of Messrs. Bell and Bain. I
did this that I might study his character from his works,
which at that time extended to six volumes demy 18mo.

I read them carefully, but on one occasion, when at the printing-office of Bell and Bain, I had an opportunity of seeing the reverend gentleman himself. Never had I beheld a more truthful exemplification of Gall's organ of Pride (Self-esteem) than in this gentleman. The head was elevated and thrown backward, and there appeared an endeavor to raise himself upward, as if with the view of rendering himself taller. He was in earnest conversation with one of the firm relative to the printing of his poems, which were in course of re-publication. Having finished this topic, he entered upon another, and with a toss of the head, and still further elevating himself on his feet, he said in a kind of good humored contempt, ' By the way, I hear you are a disciple of Swedenborg. I should like to see some of his works ; perhaps I might get some poetical ideas from them.' This he said to one of the firm. I continued a silent, but close observer, and Gall's description, which I have already given in my notice of the pompous Mr. Larken was again acted to the letter. In the portrait prefixed to the edition of his works which I possess, the Rev. Robert Montgomery is the very impersonification of extravagant Self-esteem. He is endowed with well-defined perceptive faculties, the eyebrow being finely arched. The upper part of the forehead, where are seated the reflecting faculties, is comparatively feeble. The same may be said of Benevolence. Veneration, the portion of the brain behind the fontanel, is better defined, but by no means large ; but Firmness and Self-esteem tower up far above the other moral and religious sentiments. The upper and outer part of the forehead is fully developed, and the brain above and behind the ears is especially large ; there is also considerable breadth at the region of Ideality, but in consequence of the feebleness of the reflecting faculties, his application of this organ is loose and disjointed. He looks, as a witty author has described him, ' the very image of complacent self-conceit. He may not be on good terms with the world, but it is very clear that he is on excellent terms with himself.' But I will relate an anecdote of him which will best exhibit his inordinate self-esteem. He was first brought into notice in the city of Glasgow, where a few of his admirers fitted up a large room in a handsome style, with accommodation for about eight hundred sitters. It was situated in the principal street of the city (Buchanan Street,) but lay a little backward from the main street, and was approached by a rather narrow avenue. Mr. M. was speedily very popular, and his temporary church was always well filled. After one of his week-day evening lectures he requested the congregation to stop, for he had something to say to them. He then addressed them in the following supercilious terms :—

' I have had a call from Leeds, and I have had another call from Cheltenham, and if you think I am going to waste my talents in a back alley in Glasgow, you will find yourselves much mistaken; therefore, unless you build me a handsome church, and in a first-rate situation in the city, I'll leave you—that's all I have to say now.'

The result of this threat, was many presents the next morning, and many urgent requests to remain, with the promise of the erection at once of a handsome church ; and the promise was rapidly redeemed, a site fixed upon in Blytheswood Square, and the building carried up, completed, opened, and well filled. But the reverend gentleman panted for a still larger sphere of action, and in a few years he removed to the great metropolis, where he soon found his level, and where he finished his earthly career.

He was one of the bitterest opponents to phrenology that the city of Glasgow contained, but in no instance was its truthfulness more strikingly delineated than in his own person.

In an anonymous poem, entitled ' The Age Reviewed,' but which was afterwards acknowledged to have been written by him, he thus satirizes *Gall*, *Spurzheim*, and *Combe*.

' One night as Gall lay grunting on his bed,
  It chanc'd his night-cap fretted from his head ;
  With peevish yawn he grop'd his bristling hair,
  Loos'd his long jaws, and sniff'd the curtain'd air.
  Meanwhile the restless fingers felt some lumps ;—
  " 'Tis very odd," said he, " these boundless bumps
  Must be true organs of my inward brain ;
  I'll have some plaster heads* to show them plain."
  This said, he smooth'd his nob, and pleas'd resigned
  To cobweb dreams, his phrenologic mind,
  Soon spread the mapp'd out skulls through Scotia's towns,
  And Glasgow sawnies bump'd their dirty crowns ;
  Then foggy *Spurzheim* croak'd in bungling tones,
  Till gaping Scotland hugg'd the crack-brain'd mones.
  Last *Combe*, the printing Jabbernowl for all
  In half a thousand pages grubb'd for *Gall*,
  And found a deputy in smug Deville,
  With unwash'd hands to fumble and to feel.'

Macaulay in one of the severest articles he ever wrote
in the 'Edinburgh Review,' sums up the character of
Mr. Montgomery in the following language :

' We have no enmity to Mr. Robert Montgomery. We
know nothing whatever about him, except what we have
learned from his own works, and from the portrait prefixed to one of them, in which he appears to be doing his
very best to look like a man of genius and sensibility,
though with less success than his strenuous exertions
deserve. We select him because his works have received
more enthusiastic praise, and have deserved more unmixed
contempt, than any which, as far as our knowledge extends, have appeared within the last three or four years.
His writings bear the same relation to poetry which a
Turkey carpet bears to a picture. There are colors in
the Turkey carpet out of which a picture might be made.
There are words in Mr. Montgomery's writings, which,
when disposed in certain orders and combinations, have
made, and will again make good poetry. But as they now
stand, they seem put together on principle in such a manner
as to give no image of anything in the heavens above, or
in the earth beneath, or in the waters under the earth.'

* Gall never published a bust.

I do not unite with Macaulay in this sweeping censure. Many of Mr. Montgomery's poems abound with beautiful passages, which, were this the proper place, I could easily select. Moreover, his writings abound with beautiful moral illustrations, and in the cause of morality, virtue, and religion, he has ever raised his voice—while, as a pulpit orator, though by no means in the first class, he was certainly above mediocrity. But I have selected him as a proof of phrenological truth in the exemplification of Self-esteem, and I repeat that his whole organisation was one of the most complete illustrations of the truth of phrenology that I had ever seen.

While on the subject of Self-esteem, I cannot forbear quoting a striking instance of it in the person of the late celebrated comedian, Mr. Elliston, who, at the time I write, was held in high esteem, both by the members of his own profession as well as by the public, but by no means higher than he held himself. On one occasion, conversing with Mr. Moncrief, whom he had requested to become his biographer, he said, 'When you draw your parallels of great actors, you will not fail to recollect that Garrick could not sing : I can. That Lewis could not act tragedy : I can. That Kean never wrote a drama : I have. That Mossop could not play comedy : I can. Do not forget these things, Sir ; but in mentioning me, you cannot help associating with my name all that is memorable in the age in which I flourished.'—Those who have seen the portrait of Mr. Elliston, more especially those who have seen Mr. Elliston himself, will at once admit how truthfully he has drawn his own portrait in the above anecdote.

There are three other persons whose characters I wish briefly to illustrate before I leave this part of my narrative and I introduce them because they are universally read and admired, and the truthfulness of their organisation from their works may be the more readily perceived

and admitted.   I allude to Mr. Charles Dickens, the la
Thomas Hood, and the late Dr. McHale, Roman Cathol
Archbishop of Tuam, usually termed John of Tuam.

The brain of Mr. Charles Dickens I conceive to l
nearly balanced, so that he can and does freely discoun
upon all topics, and enter into all the feelings of tl
human mind, describing the peculiarities resulting fra
various organs, with their combinations, with an accura
and truth which has secured him readers from all class
of society.   Many of his readers imagine that he mu
have participated in every scene that he describes, ai
from this arises the universal popularity of his writing
while it accounts for the immense number of his reader
and for the delight which every class expresses as ead
successive work appears.   Now, when every organ of th
brain is fully and freely developed, the possessor of sud
an organisation is endowed with ability to describe al
classes without necessarily mingling with any.   But to do
this, he must, for the time being, suppress his own
natural character, so as to personate the character he is
desirous of delineating, and hence there must be certain
faculties in his brain, which, compared with others, are
unusually large.   This appears to me to be especiall
the case with Dickens.   I have read the whole of hi
works as they have successively appeared, most o
them twice over, some of them three times, but 1
have never seen him.   True, I have seen his portrai
and from this I am enabled to state, that he is endowed
with very large Individuality, equally large Language
and good perceptive organs.   But these observation
would not afford all the requisite materials for the delineation of his character.   From the portrait prefixed to his
work, ‘Nicholas Nickleby,’ the intellectual part of his
organisation is at once plainly depicted, and it is not
a mighty intellect.   It is, by no means, equal in power to
that of Thomas Hood.   Let any person attentively consider his portrait, observing the vast quantity of hair,
and remembering the number of organs which the hair

es, and which cannot be reached without a careful
nipulation, and he will at once admit, that all he can
rn of the character of Dickens from his portrait, is
t which principally pertains to the intellect, and to a
r of the organs on the coronal surface, which may be
erred from the comparative height of the sincipital
;ion. But my perusal of the works of Dickens con-
ices me, that the most powerfully developed organ in his
iin, is one which, in all probability, he would refuse his
ient to, namely, SECRETIVENESS. I have, from his
it appearance as an author, attentively studied Dickens
his works, and I find in every book he has published
stock character, and that character is a development of
cretiveness in one or other of its many phases; and
cretiveness developes itself in a greater or less degree
most of his characters. I have said that, as a whole,
s brain is exceedingly well balanced. But the most
iwerfully developed organs are Secretiveness, Indivi-
iality, Love of Approbation, Imitation, Ideality, Mar-
illousness, and Language. Of these, Secretiveness,
idividuality, and Language are the predominating
iwers. These organs, as it appears to me, give to
Iickens his leading points of character, and of these my
iaders will allow me to give an illustration. But, first
) make good my remark with regard to the stock charac-
ir of Dickens, and that character a personification of
lecretiveness, I will, before proceeding to the illustration,
numerate them. In 'Oliver Twist,' we have Fagan
he Jew and his 'Artful Dodgers.' In 'Pickwick,' we
iave Mr. Jingle and Sam Weller. 'Nickleby' presents
is with the immortal 'Squeers' and his friend the elder
Nickleby. 'Dombey and Son' introduces Mr. Carker
ind his teeth; 'Chuzzlewit,' Mr. Nadgett and Jonas.
'The Old Curiosity Shop,' Daniel Quilp, Sally Brass,
ind Codlin. 'Barnaby Rudge,' Mr. Gashford and Mr.
Chester. 'David Copperfield' displays the inimitably
humble Uriah Heap. 'Bleak House,' Skimpole and
Inspector Buckett; and even in his new work, 'Little

Dorritt,' the usual character, though not yet fully developed, appears in Mr. Flintwinch, and peeps out in Flora the widow, as well as in the Father of the Marshalsea.

The combination of Secretiveness, Imitation, Individuality, and Love of Approbation, are the organs most conducive to the production of humor, and all these are vividly depicted in the chapter devoted to the release of Smike from the cunning and cruelty of Squeers, by the noble-minded and benevolent, though eccentric, John Browdie. I refer my readers to this narrative, (Chapter xxxix of ' Nicholas Nickleby ') as an illustration of the humor of Dickens, as well as of the Secretiveness exhibited by John Browdie in the release of poor Smike.

Next I refer the reader to Mr. Dickens's Individuality. His minuteness of description can hardly have escaped the notice of the most cursory reader of his works. Perhaps one of the most striking, and certainly one of the most original illustrations of that organ, *Individuality*, is to be found in ' Martin Chuzzlewit.' It is an exemplification of ' the doings ' of the wind. I beg to call the especial attention of the reader to the number of objects introduced into this sketch, and to the play of the wind upon the leaves as they are rolled over and over in the description, as a confirmation of Dickens's very large Individuality.

' An evening wind uprose too, and the slighter branches cracked and rattled as they moved, in skeleton dances, to its moaning music. The withering leaves, no longer quiet, hurried to and fro in search of shelter from its chill pursuit ; the laborer unyoked his horses, and with head bent down, trudged briskly home beside them ; and from the cottage windows, lights began to glance and wink upon the darkened fields.

' Then the village forge came out in all its bright importance. The lusty bellows roared Ha ha! to the clear fire, which roared in turn, and bade the shining sparks dance gaily to the merry clinking of the hammers on the anvil. The gleaming iron in its emulation, sparkled too, and shed its red-hot gems around profusely. The strong smith and his men dealt such strokes upon their work, as made even the melancholy night rejoice ; and brought a glow into its dark face as it hovered about the door and

indows, peeping curiously in above the shoulders of a dozen
ungers. As to this idle company, there they stood, spellbound
y the place, and, casting now and then a glance upon the dark-
ss in their rear, settled their lazy elbows more at ease upon the
ll, and leaned a little further in : no more disposed to tear them-
lves away, than if they had been born to cluster round the
azing hearth like so many crickets.

'Out upon the angry wind! how from sighing, it began to
luster round the merry forge, banging at the wicket, and grum-
ling in the chimney, as if it bullied the jolly bellows for doing
nything to order. And what an impotent swagger it was too,
or all its noise : for if it had any influence on that hoarse
ompanion, it was but to make him roar his cheerful song the louder,
nd by consequence to make the fire burn the brighter, and the
parks to dance more gaily yet : at length, they wizzed so madly
ound and round, that it was too much for such a surly wind to
ear : so off it flew with a howl : giving the old sign before the
lehouse-door such a cuff as it went, that the Blue Dragon was
oore rampant than usual ever afterwards, and indeed, before
Christmas, reared clean out of his crazy frame.

'It was small tyranny for a respectable wind to go wreaking its
vengeance on such poor creatures as the fallen leaves, but this
rind happening to come up with a great heap of them just after
venting its humor on the insulted Dragon, did so disperse and
catter them that they fled away, pell-mell, some here, some there,
olling over each other, whirling round and round upon their
hin edges, taking frantic flights into the air, and playing all
nanner of extraordinary gambols in the extremity of their distress.
Nor was this enough for its malicious fury : for not content with
lriving them abroad, it charged small parties of them and hunted
hem into the wheelwright's saw-pit, and below the planks and
imbers in the yard, and scattering the saw-dust in the air, it
ooked for them underneath, and when it did meet with any,
whew! how it drove them on and followed at their heels!

'The scared leaves only flew the faster for all this : and a giddy
chase it was : for they got into unfrequented places, where there was
no outlet, and where their pursuer kept them eddying round and
round at his pleasure ; and they crept under the eaves of houses,
and clung tightly to the sides of hay-ricks, like bats ; and tore in at
open chamber windows, and cowered close to hedges ; and in short
went anywhere for safety. But the oddest feat they achieved was,
to take advantage of a sudden opening of Mr. Pecksniff's front-
door, to dash wildly into his passage ; whither the wind following
close upon them, and finding the back-door open, incontinently
blew out the lighted candle held by Miss Pecksniff, and slammed
the front-door against Mr. Pecksniff, who was at that moment
entering, with such violence, that in the twinkling of an eye

he lay on his back at the bottom of the steps. Being by this time weary of such trifling performances, the boisterous rover hurried away rejoicing, roaring over moor and meadow, hill and flat, until it got out to sea, where it met with other winds similarly disposed, and made a night of it.'

Lastly, as a further illustration of the Secretiveness of Mr. Dickens, I refer the reader to Chapter xxxviii of ' Martin Chuzzlewit,' which, by an attentive perusal, he will see, exhibits a battle of cunning between Tigg Montague, Mr. Nadgett, and Jonas Chuzzlewit. Now these circumventions, though they call many faculties into play, yet exhibits Secretiveness as the leading power.

To bear me out still further in my view of Mr. Dickens's extreme Secretiveness, I would refer the reader to the cunning of Daniel Quilp, not in one instance merely, but throughout the whole of the work, where Quilp figures as a character.

Of the many delineations of Benevolence, Ideality, and Conscientiousness with which the writings of Dickens abound, none have attracted greater notice and called forth more admiration than the character of Nelly in the 'Old Curiosity Shop.' The scene of the child with her grandfather after the latter, at the instigation of the gamblers, had resolved to rob his benefactress is inexpressibly touching as well as truthful.

I now turn to the organisation of Thomas Hood. In his portrait the forehead is much broader and deeper than that of Dickens, and the intellect is every way superior. But the whole of the Intellectual faculties and moral sentiments are controlled by two powerful organs, Wit and Language. Dickens may be described as an author of imagination. Hood is one of great intellect, combined with imagination. The coronal aspect of Hood is much higher than that of Dickens ; and the Benevolence of Hood is much more expansive. Hood's Benevolence is pure, and exercised towards those who need it. He seeks for no other reward than that of doing good for its own pure sake. Dickens, in the way of charity, does good, but it seems always to be influenced by Love of Approbation, hoping to receive as much again in public approval. Dickens excels in description, the result of his large Individuality. Hood, in matters of fact, the result of his powerful reflecting faculties, influenced by his Benevolence. Dickens is rather a humorist than a wit. Hood a wit rather than a humorist, though he is by no means deficient in imitation.

I have said that I had an extensive correspondence with persons of all ranks on the subject of mental science. To one of these I am indebted for the sketch which is now to follow of the late celebrated Dr. McHale, Roman Catholic Archbishop of Tuam, familiarly known in his day as 'John of Tuam.' At the time of which I write, there was a striking portrait of him in a Catholic bookseller's shop in Clyde Street, Glasgow, and I dare say his portrait is to be seen at most Catholic booksellers. My correspondent, a brother phrenologist, who died a martyr to the science, was Alexander Wilson, who resolved to pass through Ireland and lecture in every town, and who died in the prosecution of this design. Mr. Wilson was a man of a similar temperament to myself—Nervous and Sanguine—a head of medium size, very large per- ceptive faculties. Form and Size especially prominent, good reflecting faculties, well developed religious senti- ments, moderate Self-esteem, and very large Love of Approbation. He was an excellent practical phrenolo- gist; his descriptions were minute and truthful, and he was a warm and disinterested friend. At the conclusion of an animated lecture, he was struck with paralysis, and died in a few hours. I was a student in the Andersonian University School of Medicine at the time, the council of which granted me the use of their large lecture room to deliver a lecture on Benevolence, the proceeds being de- voted to his widow. But to return to Archbishop McHale. One of the most remarkable men in Ireland is Dr.

27

John McHale, Archbishop of Tuam, familiarly known as
'John of Tuam,' and 'The Lion of the tribe of Judah.'
The latter name he has acquired from the fierce and fearless
character of his politico-ecclesiastical fulminations. By
the might of his mind, and great perseverance, he rose to
his present elevated position from a very humble sphere
in life, his father (who is still living) having been an
operative village blacksmith, somewhere in the neighborhood of Castlebar, and he himself was 'a poor scholar,'
and - I believe, like Elihu Burritt, increased the vigor
of an originally good constitution, by working at the
anvil.   Next to O'Connell, his influence is felt and
dreaded in the Cabinet counsels of England.

My curiosity to see Dr. McHale induced me to visit
Tuam in November, 1835. I did not call upon him
at his episcopal residence, as I had been informed that
his grace had in strong terms denounced the phrenological
heresy, and as a 'defender of the faith,' warned his
people against it, but I was fortunate enough to see him
in his own magnificent cathedral while he was engaged in
celebrating high mass on All Soul's Day.   Having taken
my position at the railing of the altar, just behind where
he sat, and at which he kneeled, I had ample opportunity
of observing his cranial configuration.   His temperament
is a compound of the Bilious and Nervous, the former
predominating.   His hair and complexion are dark.
His eyes are small and deeply sunk, and being habitually
hid with downcast lids, I could not ascertain their precise
shade of color, but believe them to be dark.   His nose
belongs to neither of the classic orders—it is very
lengthened, and at the point has that curved droop
which distinguishes the Jewish nose, and which I
believe to be usually associated with a great development
of the organ of Secretiveness.   He has got a long thin
oval face, and the skin of it has a smoked appearance. His
brow is broad, deep, and massive ; the perceptive organs
particularly prominent. ·Individuality, Locality, Size,
Weight, Color, and Number, are very large ; Eventuality,

large ; Time full, and Tune moderate. Comparison is large and Causality full. Constructiveness rather large. All the organs of the religious sentiments are large. Veneration is prominent and seems to have been well exercised, as that part of the head, where its organs are located, has become divested of hair. *Benevolence* is large, but it has got pretty strong selfish feelings to contend against. Ideality and Wonder are very fully developed. His Self-esteem and Love of Approbation are very large, producing a love of power and distinction. His Concentrativeness and Firmness are very large, and he is quite remarkable for his powers of persevering application, while his great Combativeness, Destructiveness, and Self-esteem, his tough temperament and deficient Cautiousness, give him that fearless (I might almost say reckless) energy of character, which he is well-known to possess. His *Secretiveness* is very prominent, and its power is strongly manifested in his character. He is always subtle in his movements, but honest enough to declare his grand object to be to promote the supremacy of his church, while he is too cunning to disclose the fact of personal aggrandisement and distinction being one of the leading motive powers which inspires him to action. He excels as a scientific, classic, and Hebrew scholar ; is well acquainted with *Irish* or *Erse*, into which language he is at present engaged in translating a number of Moore's Melodies. His organ of *Language* is not more than full, but all the other organs necessary for acquiring language are largely developed. He is not a fluent speaker, for his ideas come more quickly than his words, producing hesitancy, but is a remarkably rapid writer. He is very retired in his habits, and while engaged in writing his political epistles, admits no one near him. I am informed that he has made considerable proficiency in chemistry, astronomy, and other sciences ; he is certainly very amply endowed with the organs necessary for their pursuit. He has taken the lead in the opposition raised against the provincial colleges of Ireland about to be established, and has not suffered a single school connected with the national system to exist in his diocese. Other prelates of his own church, such as Primate Croly, and Dr. Murray, of Dublin, have acted very differently.

Besides the numerous analyses of character drawn from the living head, I had many busts, and even crania, sent me to predicate upon, from distant parts of the country. I found at first much difficulty in estimating the character of a person from his bust, but by careful study of the busts in the Museum of the Phrenological Society, with their known peculiarities, I at length surmounted this difficulty. I always made allowance for the running of the plaster in taking the cast, and subtracted a little from the size of the head, and at length I became as much consulted by busts, as by the living head. I had several sent me from distant parts of the kingdom, some from the University of Cambridge, and I was successful in delineating all their more striking peculiarities, with the single exception of the organ of Language. I never could discern with accuracy the size of this organ in a plaster cast, and I always declined giving an opinion upon it.

But I was quite successful in predicating from crania. Whenever a skull was sent me, and that was very frequently, I withdrew to my museum, and shutting out all visitors, I first examined the crania in my collection, comparing them with the skull newly sent, and noted down the more striking points ; next I placed the skull over a strong light, observed carefully those parts which were thinnest, conjecturing that the brain had been most active at those peculiar points ; while the thick parts I concluded to have been less acted upon ; I then noted down the particular differences as to size, and judging of the activity of brain by the temperament, proceeded to indicate the character of the person to whom the skull had originally belonged ; and I was pleased to find that my indications were for the most part a correct exponent of the person's peculiarities.

In 1845, I was a candidate for the lectureship on Phrenology in the Andersonian University of Glasgow, and with the view of testing my knowledge of the science, a party of gentlemen procured a skull, and sent it to me to predicate upon, which I did. I extract the particulars from my printed testimonials :—

'We, whose names are hereunto subscribed, with the view of testing Mr. ——'s talents as a practical Phrenologist, procured a skull, the peculiarities of the person to whom it originally belonged being known to us. This skull we put into the hands of Mr. —— to predicate upon, only informing him that the person to whom it had belonged died at the age of fifty-one or fifty-two years, that the temperament was probably Bilious, and that the education the person had received was such as is usual to ordinary mechanics.

'Mr. ——, immediately after he saw the skull, pronounced it diseased.

'When it is known that the skull was that of M'Kean, who was executed at Glasgow some years since, but of which we took special care to keep Mr. —— in ignorance, the analysis of the character, of which a brief account is subjoined, will be found to be most remarkably correct.

Signed, { ANDREW GOW.
ROBERT WYLLIE, Jun.
H. RAILTON.
JAMES TAIT.
J. GRAEME, Surgeon.

' (COPY.)

' *Inferences from a Skull sent to* ——

'As the person to whom this skull belonged has "ceased from troubling," and as there is now no probability of his becoming better or worse, I shall waste no time in speculating upon what he *might have been*, had he been subjected to proper training, but state, as far as his cerebral organisation appears to me, *what he was.* The left side of the skull, particularly at the posterior part, is larger than the right, probably from injury or disease. The intellectual region is here comparatively large, the forehead being *broad*, and a large mass of brain before the ear. The moral region is flat, and conscientiousness is barely of average power. The animal region is strong, and gives evidence that he would delight in animal gratifications. He would be fond of the sex. If married, he would display some attachment to his wife, but more from animal feeling than real esteem, and he would not always treat her with that kindness which should ever characterise a husband. To his children, if he had any, he would be very affectionate, and this would be one of the redeeming points of his character; but this would not prevent him from occasionally displaying, even towards them, much violence of temper and of manners. He would be desultory in his habits, and would pass from one thing to another, as the whim of the moment would impel him. He was capable of friendship, but he would be indiscriminate in the formation of his friendships, except where his own interests were concerned; then he would attach himself like a leech to his object, and bleed him without mercy or remorse. He was well suited by animal courage for a soldier, and in the field of battle would have slain, without feeling or compunction. Probably he would be fond of field sports, as shooting and hunting. He had a great deal of low cunning about him, and would be skilful in plotting and manœuvring. He was very fond of money, and his Secretiveness was so large, that it would give him a good deal of tact in acquiring it. But it is probable he would spend as fast as he acquired, in gratifying his animal propensities. He would be of a planning and inventive turn, but he would design better than he would execute. He had not much regard to personal appearance, nor was he anxious about the respect in which he was held by others. Yet he would feel a kind of desire for reputation. He was not destitute of caution, but he had an immensity of cunning, and with many this passes for caution. He was not a person likely to bestow much in charity: if he gave, it was more from love of approbation than from real kindness; and he would show his benevolence off with the hope of receiving *as much again*. His character would be anomalous to different persons. He could be polite, affable, and agreeable whenever he chose, and he would do this to such persons as he wished to conciliate, and from whom he hoped to obtain favors. But he would be insolent to his equals, and a tyrant and a bully to his inferiors. He was not scrupulous in adhering to the truth; but he had so much cunning and adroitness that he would disguise his narratives, and "*lie like truth*." He was accessible to the marvellous, and might have been superstitious. If he was religious, the Roman Catholic religion might by him have been considered the most suitable, though his habitual love of concealment would prevent this from being easily seen. He was not insensible to the beautiful, which he could admire in nature as well as in art; he would not think meanly of his own personal attractions. He did not care much for literary display, nor was he an ardent student. Of his language I can say but little, not being able to estimate its size, but presume it was not always the most refined or chaste. He would have an inaptitude in estimating colors, and would find great difficulty in discriminating tints or shades to a nicety. In arithmetic he possessed some skill, and he knew how to increase the *bawbees*. I consider this a bad head. If he were uneducated, he would probably have been a reckless character; if not in some degree criminal.'

Many were the squibs let off at me, some of them good humored and amusing, others spiteful to a degree. One gentleman wrote an Epitaph for my tombstone, displaying a good deal of wit, and some discrimination of my real character, but withal so composed as to exhibit a good-humored contempt for the science, and a kind of compassionate regret for my weakness in so ardently prosecuting it. I studied this gentleman most attentively, though he never permitted me to examine him by measurement or manipulation. His Temperament was a pure Bilious; he had a large head, which was elevated at the region of Firmness, and he possessed a character inflexible and unyielding. He had great abilities, which he cultivated attentively, and raised himself from a comparatively humble origin to a position of great trust and emolument. He possessed a fund of quiet humor and wit, an inexhaustible fancy, great flow of words, which he used most felicitously, and a vein of quiet sarcasm; but with all this, he did not himself seem to enjoy what he uttered, and some of his smartest sayings came from him without the relaxation of a muscle. He was also a perfect illustration of the truth of phrenology, though he did not appear implicitly to credit its pretensions. He had very large Self-esteem, and persons of this description find great difficulty in bringing their pride to acknowledge the truths which phrenology has developed. But I must allow him to speak for himself by inserting his EPITAPH ON MYSELF.

' Here lies the Rev. —— —— ———— !
Of knotty points a great decider!
Of manners gentle—bearing hard,
A clear expounder of the Word;
On which he lectured by the hour,
Though not with Boanerges' power,
Yet had a power to reach the heart
Of sinners, with the gospel dart.

A great projector with small means,
And therein felt the want of teinds ;
A voluntary by the book,
Whate'er his flock could give he took.
He lectur'd too on bumps of skull,
Could tell whose parts were bright—whose dull ;
By closely looking at the head,
Not only those alive, but dead.

Could show the war bump of great Cæsar
(He handled skulls of king and kaiser),
The modern Cæsar, too, he knew,
Had this bump large, and others too.——
How some folks love a cheerful glass,
How others love a handsome lass.
Could tell how many a sturdy sinner,
Than work, would rather steal his dinner.

Sometimes he patronized the Fine Arts,
Of pictures well could show the fine parts ;
Where hidden beauties lie, and tell
Of Angelo, Titian, Raffaelle !
Could tell of old, who worked in marble,
Who carved the Med'cean Venus Fardle,
How high the Phidean Jupiter was,
Made up of iv'ry bound with brass.

Such was friend ——. Friends can say,
A gentler soul ne'er mix'd with clay ;
When these thou'st read, carv'd on his stone,
Sigh passenger ! and so be gone.'

Another of my satirists was a bookseller, who had a
rhyming propensity ; some called it poetical talent ; he
wrote a very amusing travestie on the science, and sent
a copy of it to me. I went to his shop, engaged him in
conversation on the merit of a book, and while so doing,
carefully noted his organisation.

He was endowed with respectable intellectual abilities,
with large Imitation, and a very prominent eye, indicative
of powerfully developed Language. His Self-esteem and
Love of Approbation were essentially large, while the
reflecting faculties were but moderately developed. I have
in the course of my experience observed, that where the

reflecting faculties are weak, and Self-esteem is large, all the facts which phrenology has disclosed seems to make but little impression on the mind.

The author of the travestie which I am about to quote, was a candidate for the Laureateship on the death of the poet Southey; he had written a flimsy poem on the Queen's progress to Scotland, from the publication of which he anticipated court favor, but was disappointed.

I admired the humor and good temper in which the travestie was penned, and I think my readers will be as much amused with it as I was. The very title is a curiosity in its way, and I resolved upon including it among the memorabilia of my memoirs.

The following is the satire. It is entitled

'SUTERMICROSCOPOGRAPHY;

BEING A SCIENCE LIKELY CALCULATED TO EXTINGUISH PHRE-
NOLOGY, MESMERISM, AND ALL OTHER OLOGIES AND ISMS.
BEING A GENTLE SATIRE.

' O this is the age of invention,
    The reign of large heads and what not,
So what I'm going to mention
    Is another discovery, red hot !
'Tis a wonderful time, eighteen hunder;
    Luc'fer matches and all I would quote ;
But certainly all must sink under
    My own most ingenious plot.

'Tis called Sutermicroscopography,
    A name that is perfectly new ;
A jaw-breaker in its orthography,
    But listen and learn what I'll do :
Instead of the person attending,
    Just send me his boot or his shoe ;
I'll tell ye to what he's pretending,
    And teach you his character true.

I know by the bumps on the leather
    Right well if he's fat or he's lean,
And whether in hot or cold weather
    He's likely to shoot at the Queen !

I know if he's single or married,
    And if he is young or is old;
I know if his hopes have miscarried
    And if he is poor or has gold.

I'll tell you the gist of his learning,
    And whether 'tis useful or not,
And every particular concerning
    The cut of his castor and coat,
His height and his manner of walking,
    If sober inclined or a sot;
The tone and the style of his talking,
    And whether he's brains or has not!

I'll tell you his temper completely—
    A thing every maiden should know!
If he dresses untasteful or neatly,
    And whether a clown or a beau;
If he's noisy or loves to be quiet,
    And whether his life is—so— so;
If a gourmand concerning his diet,
    If fond of retirement or show.

So, fair maids! attend to my science,
    And send me the boots and the shoes;
On me you may place great reliance
    Whatever you do on my muse!
No longer be troubled with sorrow,
    Nor know whom to take or refuse,
So send me some dozens to-morrow
    Enclosing the fees—if you choose.'

A copy of the above was, as I have said, sent to me, doubtless, under the anticipation that it would diminish my phrenological zeal: but I enjoyed its perusal amazingly, and as I said before, went to the author's shop that I might notice his peculiar organisation, and having satisfied myself that I had another proof of the truth of phrenology in its author, put his poem into my scrap book, and now present it for the amusement of my readers. The number of these curiosities which have come to me in my phrenological capacity would fill volumes, and amusing volumes too, if not instructive, but I must now hold my hand in this department of my narrative.

My scientific labors were confined to the winter season, between the months of November and May, and in the summer months I visited many of the towns in Scotland in the capacity of a Home Missionary. I am now about to present my readers with a narrative of one of my longest and most interesting journeys, with a summary of the different subjects I treated upon.

I commenced my labors in the village of Alloa, in Clackmannanshire, where at that time a controversy was carrying on between two classes of Presbyterians, one named Morrison contending for the Universality of the Atonement, the other taking the extreme Calvinistic view of limitation to the elect.

I thought this would be a good opportunity of declaring the Swedenborgian view of that great doctrine, and accordingly announced that I would deliver a lecture on the Apostolic Doctrine of the Atonement, showing that it was not God the Father who received the Atonement but MAN.

I proceeded first to examine the contending views of the two parties, and attempted to show that neither of them were in harmony with the Apostolic teaching ; and that the doctrine of a vicarious sacrifice and substitution did not appear to be in harmony with the Divine character and attributes. I then quoted the words, ' We joy in God through our Lord Jesus Christ, by whom WE have received the atonement.' A person in the congregation exclaimed, ' There is no such passage—give us chapter and verse, if you please.' I referred him to Romans v, 11. Upon which, turning to the place, he found it, and acknowledged he had never noticed it before.

I replied that might be probable, but that was the only passage in the New Testament where the word atonement occurred, and upon that passage I intended to found my argument for the great doctrine in dispute.

1. The word which in our English New Testament is translated *atonement*, properly signifies *reconciliation*—the *agreement* of two parties formerly at variance ; or the

means by which that agreement is brought about. I am
well aware that this argument has been used by the
Unitarians in their endeavors to deny the atonement
altogether : and that hence it will be looked upon by many
with *suspicion :* but as truth is no less truth even when
spoken by Satan ; so the observation I have just made is
really correct, though perverted by the enemies of our
Lord's divinity. The word *atonement* properly signifies
reconciliation, either in its *means* or its act ; and is so
translated in another passage. ' If when ye were
enemies ye were reconciled *(atoned)* to God by the death
of his Son,' etc. : and the *atonement* which we receive is
the ministry of *reconciliation.* In the Old Testament, the
word translated *atonement,* is Copher, *a covering,* or
closing over of something which is hidden or put away,
and gives the same idea of the *hiding* or *putting away* for
ever of former things, and their being *covered* by a *reconciliation,* free, complete, and eternal.

2. Having made these remarks, I would further observe, that in order to know in what the *atonement*
consists, we have only to consider the consequences which
arose out of the fall of man, and his subsequent
degradation : for as the atonement was intended to
remedy those consequences, and to raise man from that
degradation, the means employed will be such as the case
evidently calls for.

3.-When man was created, his mind was placed in an
equilibrium : with perfect freedom to weigh down either
scale, by throwing his will into it. Unfortunately, the
determination was in favor of evil ; and its effects soon
followed, in the instant separation of the soul from God,
and his immediate union with the infernal powers. Likeness of affection joins spirit with spirit, while difference
of love separates soul from soul. They who are of like
affections, are in the other life intimately united ; and,
even while in this life, are actually united as to their
spiritual nature. On the other hand, they who love
opposite things, are necessarily separated from each other ;

or opposite loves can never coalesce. While man was pure and holy, he was really *united* to God, because he loved good, even as God loves it : but when forsaking good he fell into the love of evil, he was then *separated* from God ; for he then loved what God hates. By the same law he became joined with the infernal spirits, for his love of evil was then like to theirs. From henceforth his mind was liable to be acted upon and bound by them ; for in his mind they found principles congenial to their own, and through which they could operate, and tempt, and govern. In corroboration of this, the apostle expressly tells us that man 'was led by the devil at his will' ; and that he was thus led by 'the chain of his sins' ; that is, the *sinful affections* existing in his mind formed a means by which hell could tempt and enslave him ; even as the chain by which a captive is bound, is that by which his captor leads him.

4. Nor did their state of degradation remain as at first it was. As the influence of hell predominated, the love of evil increased. That increasing love gave the devil still greater power, and that power again was used to stimulate and still increase the evil love, on which his dominion was founded. The evil in man, and the power of hell, mutually strengthened each other ; the one tempting to, and increasing evil, and evil adding to and increasing the power of hell. To such a height had this last attained, that at the period of our Lord's advent the evil spirits began actually to usurp the natural powers, and to act in the bodies of men. It was indeed the 'fulness of time,' or as we commonly say, 'it was full time' for the Redeemer's approach. Earth was on the point of becoming a mere province of hell, and the interference of Divine power to free man was absolutely required.

For, be it observed, no power in man could free himself. No one will voluntarily forsake what he loves, and turn to that he hates ; but man *loved evil*, and his will therefore prevented him from forsaking it. He *hated good* and would not therefore turn to it. Here lay the strength of the chain with which Satan had bound him: the very presence of his bonds induced him to embrace them; and that which was the greatest cause of his bondage was with him a reason for preferring it to the freedom of God. What was to be done in this case? Man, sinful as he was, could not approach to God, and if he *could* he *would* not. God in his infinite purity, and in his divine essence, could not approach to man; for such is the eternal opposition between good and evil that the approach of Infinite Good would have driven the evil before it. Man must have perished; for divine love is to every infernal affection, ' a consuming fire.'

What was then to be done? Here the wisdom of God found out a remedy; and by veiling his glory in flesh; by assuming humanity, and becoming as to his *flesh*, ' the Son of God,' and as to his *manifestation*, the divine truth or 'wisdom of God,' he approached to man. Hell was to be subdued: but God in his inmost nature could neither be tempted nor could he approach to combat with the infernal powers. The humanity however could be tempted, and in that humanity he stood forth as the champion of man. By a series of temptations and combats, continuing from the manger to the cross, he combatted for his falling creatures; and in the last contest on the cross he finally conquered 'him that had the power of death, even the devil.' 'It was finished.' Hell was conquered; ' and he spoiled principalities and powers; leading them openly, triumphing over them by the blood of his cross.'

5. By the self-same process of temptation and victory, he ' sanctified himself'; that is, he so purified his humanity that, on his final conquest, he united it to his essential divinity, and having made his humanity wholly divine, from thence the assertion of the Athanasian Creed was true; ' as the reasonable *soul and flesh* make one *man*; so, God and man,' the divinity and the glorified humanity, 'make one Christ.' One God the Redeemer, as before he was one God the Creator and Preserver of his people.

6. The *humanity*, thus exalted to full union with Deity, became thenceforth the mediator or medium of access to the Father, the indwelling Deity. ‘A wall of separation’ divided God from man—the wall of corrupt humanity : but in this, the humanity of the Lord became *a door*, through which God might approach to man, and by which man could come ‘with confidence to the throne of grace.’ Thus were the consequences of the fall removed. 1. Man was the bondslave of hell ; but ‘Jesus conquered hell,’ and the power of the oppressor was broken. 2. Man was separated from God by an impenetrable wall of corruption ; Jesus made a door in that wall, and opened an approach to the Deity. The broken chain—the golden chain which united heaven and earth—was once more united ; and thenceforth, man had free access to the throne of grace, to find mercy and grace to help in each time of need.

Nor was this the only benefit which resulted from the finished work of the Saviour. There is a remarkable expression used by the Apostle, viz., ‘He has united all things to himself, whether things in heaven or things on earth ’; and we shall take too narrow a review of the atonement if we consider it as applying to *this* earth alone. It was a work in which all creation had an interest, and in which (not our little planet merely) but every habitation of man had the deepest stake.

For what was the design of the atonement ? It was ‘to unite *all things* to himself’ :—to apply a remedy which should be applicable to every world throughout the universe, and to which every sinner, whether in this or on other earths, might come and be healed.

But ere I enter on this subject, let me lay down one axiom. That which includes all, includes every part : that which is sufficient to cleanse from the *grossest* sin, is sufficient to cleanse from all the lesser evils : that which encompasses within itself the *extreme* of evil, must encompass every thing of evil up to that extreme. Let this be granted, and the objection of the deist who tells us that this earth was too insignificant a portion of the universe for to call forth the death of a God, is fully answered. The design of the Saviour was to provide a medium, by which *every* sinner might approach the Deity and obtain forgiveness. For this purpose he chose to withstand the utmost temptations of the infernal powers. Supposing that there are other earths in which sin has appeared, he certainly chose the *worst and most sensual* when he chose our own. Let any one peruse the character which the Apostle Paul has given of the natural man of *this earth* in his Epistle to the Romans, and then let him say whether one degree lower would not make a fiend. However low, however degraded, the inhabitants of other worlds may now be, or may be hereafter, they cannot go lower in the scale of evil than those who lived when Paul wrote. And whoever fairly considers the subject must admit that, save and except hell itself, nothing could be more debased than the situation of this world.

To this world, then, as the extreme of unpunished evil, the Redeemer descended. Nor did he take upon him the most honorable degree, even in this sensualised planet; but he chose the most sensual nation and the lowest class of that nation, for his abode in nature. He went to the very extreme of evil and degradation; yet from that extreme he raised his humanity to omnipotent power. Here, then, applies our maxim. If he included in his plan of redemption the extreme of evil, he embraces in it all intermediate degrees! If his plan reached the *lowest and most sensual* world, it must reach every other! Having atoned for the utmost evil, he must have atoned every lesser degree! In this grand plan, therefore, he joined all things to himself, and provided a plan whereby *every* sinner throughout the universe may find redemption, and be healed of his disease.

If we turn to the Scriptures we have abundant proof of what I have asserted. If he united *all things* to himself, he must have provided a remedy for every degree of evil. Man was *captive*; he came to 'proclaim liberty to the captives.' Man was bound ; He came to ' unloose the prison doors.' Man was ' led captive by the devil,' and He came ' to destroy the work of the devil.' Man was separated from God, and the Saviour came ' to unite all things to himself.' This is an atonement worthy of God, and worthy of his goodness,—an atonement in which

> ' Justice and compassion join
> In their divinest forms.'

This lecture, with large additions, I afterwards published in the Glasgow Series of Christian Tracts, and it got introduced into Mr. Morrison's Congregation, where it excited much discussion, and led to the secession of four-teen members, who ultimately joined the society of Swe-denborgians in that city.

From Alloa I proceeded to Kinross, where I delivered three sermons, and as the cardinal doctrine of the Swedenborgians had never been proclaimed in this town [I was the first missionary who visited Kinross], I determined to make this my first subject. So I sent round the town drummer, and announced a lecture on the Supreme Divinity of the Saviour, in whom was the divine Trinity of Father, Son, and Holy Spirit. This lecture was substantially the same as that to which I have before alluded in my controversy with the Rev. Mr. Harris, of Glasgow. It was followed by a long discus-sion on the distinction existing between the Father and the Son. My observations, as nearly as I can remember, will be found in what follows :—

' In the New Testament, the terms Father, Son, and Holy Spirit, are of frequent occurrence, and wherever they occur they signify the same great and glorious God, though revealing himself through his different attributes. We will endeavor to illustrate this. We are informed at the commencement of Scripture, that *" God created man in his own image."* If any man cause an image of himself to be made, if that image be correct

28

we can form some opinion of the man from his image, though the man himself we may never have beheld. But "no man has seen God at any time": still, as saith the apostle, "the only begotten Son who is in the bosom of the Father, he hath declared him," that is, brought him forth to view: but if "Jesus Christ is the express image of the Father's person," and is "equal with God," yea, "is God over all, blessed for ever," and if Jesus Christ appeared on earth in the form of a man, we may very safely affirm, that we are created in the image of God.

'Some have asserted that the image of God, in which man was created was holiness. This, however, cannot for an instant be admitted, because it is not true. For the holiness in which man was originally created was not, and could not be, an image of the holiness of God. The holiness in which man was created was *negative;* the holiness of God is POSITIVE! The holiness of newly created man may be said to have consisted in freedom from sin—in the absence of evil, for as yet he had performed no active work of piety; his, therefore, was the holiness of an infant. But the holiness of God does not consist merely in the absence of all evil, but in the possession of ALL ABSOLUTE GOOD. Man, therefore, when first created, was not an image of the holiness of God. The image consisted in the constitution, or formation of the spirit, which, in its powers, its energies, and its operations was (and, though sullied and polluted), is, still an image of the ever active and almighty mind. By contemplating this image we may form a faint idea of its original. In the human mind there are two powers and a resulting operation. These two powers are the will with its innumerable affections: and the understanding with its multitudinous thoughts. The will may be pronounced as the interior, or essential part, of the spirit, the source of every desire and affection. The thought is an emanation from the will: it is the affection put forth into form—revealing itself by natural words and natural images. The will exists in itself; the thought proceeds forth from the will, nor can it exist without the will: and the will itself can operate only through, and by means of, the understanding.

'From this view of our own constitution we approach with humility the consideration of the Divine Trinity of Father, Son, and Holy Spirit. The Father is the divine centre, the very essential love. The Son is the manifested form of that love, the express image of it, "the Lord God merciful and gracious," who, "in his love, and in his pity, redeemed us," and became our Saviour; "God manifest in the flesh." Now the Son can do nothing of himself. "The Father judgeth no man, but hath committed all judgment unto the Son." As the will, understanding, and operation constitute one man, so the Father—the indwelling love; the Son—the reveal-ing Wisdom; and the Holy Spirit—the divine operation, constitute one God. The Father is God, in his infinite love. The Son is the same God in his infinite manifesting Wisdom; and the Holy Spirit is the same in his divine operation. And ALL—the *love*, the *wisdom*, and the *power*, are united in "the only wise God our Saviour, to whom be dominion and power." Such is the doctrine of the Divine Trinity, a doctrine of holy Scripture. In every object in nature, as well as in God, there is a Trinity in Unity, for all nature is an outbirth from God. Behold the glorious orb of day. Its essential property is *heat*, it is the source or manifestation of light, and the operation of both displays its use and power. A bright, though faint, resemblance is this of the divine Trinity, and con-firms, by analogy, what we have already advanced con-cerning the Lord, that he is a being of infinite love, wisdom, and power. God, it is declared, is a Spirit; and we may form an idea of his existence as the Sun of Righteousness, of which, as we have just stated, the sun of our world is a faint image. Of the great and immu-table Jehovah it is said, "Thou clothest thyself with light as with a garment." And *what is*, or rather, WHO *is, that light?* Jesus Christ is the true Light. With this true Light, then, the otherwise unapproachable Father is clothed as with a garment, and from this divine heat and light of the glorious Sun of Righteousness proceeds the energy, or operation, of the Holy Spirit. And thus the Father, the Son, and the Holy Spirit, dwell in one person, and that person is Jesus Christ our Lord. All men must, therefore, honor the Son, even as they honor the Father, for this is the *will of the Father.*'

My illustration of the terms Father and Son appeared to give much satisfaction. I had about three hundred hearers.

From Kinross I proceeded to *Perth*, where, by the kindness of a friend, I obtained the use of the Guild Hall, and as there was then going on a discussion on the Inspiration of the Scriptures, which a Socialist lecturer was warmly contending against, I issued placards for a lecture, in which I proposed to prove the absolute and plenary inspiration of the Holy Word, and offered to reply to any questions that might be put in writing after the lecture, but I declined discussion in consequence of my deafness.

At the hour appointed every part of the spacious hall was crowded, and a great many persons were unable to obtain admission. I opened my subject by quoting,

2 TIMOTHY iii, 16, 17.

'All Scripture is given by inspiration of God, and is profitable for doctrine, for reproof, for instruction in righteousness, that the man of God may be perfect, throughly furnished unto all good works.'

'The sacred word of the Most High, which is delivered unto us in the Holy Scriptures, is the basis and ground of pure Christianity. In proportion as the Bible is studied, and respected, will true religion extend itself; and as the doctrines of the gospel are made the rule of life, will real and experimental piety flourish and increase.

'It is a lamentable characteristic of the Church at the present day that few of its members appear to have

any clear ideas of what constitutes inspiration, or of
what it is which elevates the Word of God above the
ordinary class of human compositions. Hence, the Scriptures are read as any common book of history, and though
it is allowed that the writers were guided by a divine
influence, it is not believed that *that* influence has
produced any thing more than a history of the Jewish
nation, intermingled with moral reflections, and containing instructive lessons; yet still a mere history, and
no more. When, therefore, the historical relation has
been read, it is imagined that all that the WORD contains
has been acquired. It is not seen that there are any
other wonders in God's law than those wrought in
Egypt; and the historical portions of God's word, to a
multitude of readers, seems of very little more importance than the histories of France or England. This want
of a true knowledge of the Scripture has been the means of
ministering to the success of Infidelity, for, by pointing
out instances of *apparent* contradiction in the history,
the enemies of the Christian religion have exultingly
asked, Would the Almighty God so far demean himself
as to become the mere chronicler of assassinations,
adulteries, and other crimes equally detestable? —And
what answer has been returned? Have the advocates
of religion stood boldly up in defence of the pure divinity
of God's most Holy Word? No. They have endeavored
to palliate, to explain, and to reconcile. They have
treated the Bible as an ordinary relation of human affairs,
and have endeavored to explain it in the same manner.
Yet, surely there must be more in the Word of God than
a mere relation of Jewish crimes and Jewish obstinacy:
the Spirit of God surely intended something further than
to inform us of what the Jews did 2,000 years ago; of
the wars, quarrels, and miseries of their kings, and the
idolatry and stiff-neckedness of their people. The Scriptures are given as a means of salvation—but how is our
salvation forwarded by a knowledge of things like these?
As warnings they may be, indeed, considered as highly

useful ; but if this were all that was intended to be con- veyed, the warning events of English and European history would be equally useful. But it is certain that the events of Jewish history neither contain a reference to the Saviour, nor lead the soul to believe in his name, and profess and practise his doctrines. This is so much felt by many Christians that they scarcely ever read the historical portions of the Word, choosing the Prophets, the Psalms, and the Gospels, in preference, because in these they find mention of the Saviour which they cannot find in the history. Yet, if the Bible be true, nay, if our Saviour himself spake truth, "all scripture," the his- torical, as well as the prophetic, speaks of the salvation he came to offer unto men. As it is written : "And beginning at Moses and all the prophets, he expounded unto them (the disciples) in all the Scriptures the things concerning himself." Some information, then, must be wanting—something which can point out to the mind, how even the law of Moses itself refers to the Re- deemer.

'The divinity of the Scriptures does not consist in the truth of their history ; no, not though that history con- tains events which Revelation only could make known. The history of Josephus records the same events as the Bible, and in a more connected series ; but no one imagines that history to be inspired. The truth of a history does not make a history divine ; if it did, then the history of our own, as well as of various countries, would all be inspired volumes. But a history may be true, even to the letter, and yet be only a human composi- tion ; so the Bible is true, even to the letter, and yet the Bible, without some further evidence than what the letter discloses, may be no more than a human composition. It required no divine influence in a contemporary of Moses to record the events which came under his own observation. Moses might be inspired to declare the events of the creation and the fall ; but any one, whether inspired or not, after hearing them from him, might record them. The inspiration of Moses, and of the prophets mentioned in the Holy Word, does not necessarily infer the inspiration of the Word itself, since an uninspired person might write down what he had heard, and his writing would be no more than a common history. Had any of us lived in the time of Moses, or of Joshua, or David, or the Prophets, and been in the habit of seeing their actions, and hearing their discourses, we might have written down their sayings, and recorded their actions, without any special influence from the Lord, and our record, in consequence, would not have the smallest portion of inspiration in it. *The divinity of the Scriptures, therefore, arises neither from their truth as a history; nor from that history recording the actions and words of inspired men;* for all this may be true, and yet the Holy Word be no more divine than a volume of practical or experimental sermons.

'Nor does their divinity arise from the prophecies they contain, since the same observation holds as good here as in the remarks just made. Those who heard the prophets might write down their predictions without any supernatural influence. The history of the Jewish war contains a prophecy, delivered by Josephus to the Elder Vespasian—yet that history is not inspired. Dr. Jortin's Remarks on Ecclesiastical History contain a very remarkable prophecy delivered in our own country, but the volume which contains it has never been considered inspired. A book may, therefore, contain a relation of prophecies, and those prophecies may be shortly fulfilled, and yet that book may not be inspired. The Bible is full of prophecies, yet these prophecies do not in themselves prove the inspiration of the Holy Scriptures. *The divinity of the Scriptures, therefore, does not arise from their containing predictions which were afterwards fulfilled.*

'Nor does the inspiration of the Scriptures spring from the fact that they contain information of the primitive condition of man, his present state, and promised future happiness.—But if the divinity of the Scriptures arises neither from the truth of their history, the inspiration of the characters mentioned in them, the fulfilment of their prophecies, the events recorded, nor the excellence of the precepts which they taught, it will be asked, In what does their divinity consist? This question will be best answered by considering how far any work resembles its author.

'1. When a writer sits down to treat upon any subject he infuses into his writing the knowledge he himself possesses. His writing is, in fact, a transcript of his own mind at the time he makes it, and contains within it the wisdom of the writer upon the subject treated of. In reading such a treatise, we read the mind who indited it.

'2. Every human work must also resemble its author. If the author be ignorant, his work will be frivolous. If he be wise, his wisdom will be transmitted to his pages. If he be of a deep and thoughtful mind, his work will be fraught with profound and deep-thinking intelligence. And if his knowledge be but superficial, his treatise will be of no greater depth than his intellect.

'3. When an author commences a work he adapts his style to the persons for whom it is intended. If he be writing for the unlearned, his style will be plain, and his illustrations simple and easy of comprehension, while if he be writing for the learned, it will be less easy, and will abound in deeper arguments, and more intricate illustrations. Thus : Divinity has one style, earnest, solemn, and persuasive. The style of history is distinct from that of divinity, and is plain and open. In every case a reflecting writer or speaker will adapt his manner to his subject, and elevate or lower his reasoning according to the receptive powers of those whom he is called upon to address.

'4. If such be the case—if every work contains the wisdom of its author, is inspired by his knowledge, and resembles him in character—and if the style of every work is adapted to the subject and to the readers—then let us

nquire, what must be the character of a work which has
God for its author, the Church and Redemption for its
subject, and angels and men for its readers? An answer
o this question will at once place before us the peculiar
title of the Scriptures to the name of an INSPIRED
WORK.

'(1.) If any work contain the wisdom of its author, then
a work of which *God* is the author must contain the *wisdom
of God*, and as that wisdom is *infinite*, the wisdom contained
in the Scriptures MUST BE INFINITE ALSO : and that it is
so, nothing more unequivocally proves than the Scripture
itself. David speaks of *the wonderful things of God's
law*. Now the only Scripture which David had was the
Law or Books of Moses, containing a history from
Abraham to Joshua, and the books of Joshua and Judges,
carrying down the history until near his own time. It
will be difficult, however, to find any such wonders here,
if the books are nothing more than an historical record.
Yet there were such wonders, not merely the wonders
which were wrought in Egypt, but wonders which to
behold, drew forth the prayer, " OPEN THOU MINE EYES
that I may BEHOLD wondrous things out of thy law."

'(2.) If again every work resembles its author, then a
work by an author *infinite* in wisdom, goodness, and
power, must, like himself, contain, in its every portion, an
infinity of knowledge, beyond the power of the wisest
man, or the most exalted angel, fully to exhaust, or even to
fathom—in short, there must be portions *"past finding out."*
Thus the apostle says, " Oh the depths of the wisdom and
knowledge of God." " Into these things the angels desire
to look." It must be a part of the employment of angelic
beings to search out the depths of wisdom contained in
that Word which is declared to be " for ever settled in
heaven." " But as the heavens are higher than the earth,
so high are his thoughts above our thoughts, and his ways
above our ways " :—

> " In vain the highest seraph strives to sound
> Th' unfathomable, deep abyss of God."

The Scriptures, therefore, as they resemble their Author, must contain within them a wisdom as much above the comprehension of the highest angel, as God himself is incapable of being fully comprehended by angelic intelligence.

'(3.) Again, if every author adapts his style to his subject and his hearers, then, as the Scripture has for its subject Redemption and Salvation, the Church and the soul of man, and for its readers angels and men, then it must be adapted to the peculiar wants of angels in heaven and men upon earth. Heaven itself is governed by the Word of God as a transcript of His purity. Every part of it must then refer to the soul and to salvation, and must be applicable both to the state of man here, and to his consummation of glory hereafter.

'(4.) If then the Bible is the Word of God, written under his influence, and inspired by him, such must be its nature and quality. It must enclose within it the wisdom of its Author, and be like him in infinity, and must in every part be adapted, both to every state of man on earth, and the holy communion of angels in heaven ; the question then is—Can it be proved that the Bible is such a book as we have described ? We answer, it can ; and we shall briefly endeavor to prove what we assert. It is very certain, however, that the divine quality of infinite wisdom is not the letter of the Scriptures alone ; and as we fully admit this, we must search for that wisdom a little deeper than the surface. There must be an internal or spiritual meaning ; and the natural objects and events described are the symbols of spiritual and eternal things. To prove this, we must premise that there is a correspondence between everything on earth, and everything in the spiritual world, arising from the dependance which the former has upon the latter. For as the body is the visible form of the spirit, so are the things in the natural world, the visible forms of those in the spiritual. This is alluded to by the apostle where he says, "The invisible things of God are clearly seen in the things that are made."

' If, then, to use the apostolic simile, the *in*-visible things of the eternal world are made known to us by the visible, then the earth, with its natural and sensible objects, is a material representation of the things in heaven, and must depend upon heaven for its existence, as the shadow does on the substance. The earthly things, therefore, mentioned in the Word of God, must image forth the spiritual things, whose manifestation they are ; and consequently, these must be under the literal meaning, a spiritual sense of which the literal sense is but the symbol. If this be admitted, then can the Scripture be truly and properly called the Word of God ; then can the hundreds of passages which in the letter of the Bible seem to bear but feeble traces of wisdom and instruction, be proved to be replenished with a fulness of both. Then are the words of the apostle substantiated : " All Scripture is given by inspiration of God, and is profitable for reproof, for correction, and for instruction, that the man of God may be throughly furnished unto all good works." '

I then proceeded to illustrate the correspondence existing between things natural and spiritual, by a reference to various objects in nature, confirmed by numerous passages from Scripture. My space will allow me to adduce only one example. and as the most simple, I select the CLOUDS, which signify the *literal sense of the Holy Word*. And first I proceed to state their uses in a literal sense, from which it will be easy to deduce their meaning in a spiritual point of view.

' 1. The clouds veil and diversify the light of the sun, studding the atmosphere with a thousand beautiful forms. 2. They are the sources of rain. 3. They are the reservoirs of storms and tempests which, though desolating in their particular effects, serve to purify the atmosphere. 4. Though fulfilling these numerous offices, they are derived from the earth itself, being attracted thence through the influence of the sun.

In all these particulars they correspond to the literal

sense of the Word of God ; for :—1. As the clouds temper
and veil the solar rays, so *that* glory and wisdom
which is too bright for human apprehension, is tempered and
rendered available to the human mind, by being concèaled
beneath the letter of the Word of God, and while it thus
tempers the divine glory, it sets it forth in a thousand
graceful forms of natural wisdom, and of natural
truth.

' 2. From the letter of the Word of God, those natural
truths are derived, which, "like the former and the latter
rain," come down to refresh the natural, but simple mind,
and lead it from the first rudiments of knowledge to that
rest which remaineth for the people of God.

' 3. In the letter of the Word are found all those
elements of spiritual discord, those storms and tempests
which have agitated the church from its commencement
until now ; but which, nevertheless, have tended to the
elicitation of truth, and to the benefit of the church
and of the world.

' 4. Though the letter of the ˙Word of God thus
enshrines the divine glory—though it is the medium by
which truth is communicated—it is derived from the
mind of man himself ; it is composed of human ideas,
natural objects, and natural or human language, even
as the clouds are drawn from the earth, above which they
float, and which they appear to render fertile.

' Thus the correspondent figure, even in its minutest parts
and offices, agrees with its spiritual subject, and if we
apply it to those parts of the Holy Word where it occurs,
will always make a beautiful and consistent sense. Thus,
when the Divine Being by corresponding figures revealed
himself to the Jewish nation, a cloud always encompassed the divine glory. A cloud hung over the tabernacle and over the ark of the testimony. God said to
Moses when he gave the law on Mount Sinai, " Lo, I
come unto thee in a thick cloud," alluding to the multiplied figures of the ceremonial law ; the divine wisdom
being˙ thus hidden under the cloud of literal observances.

nd thus, too, when the incarnate Word was revealed to
man, and tabernacled with man, a voice out of the cloud
eclared, "This is my beloved Son IN whom I am well
leased" : the spiritual meaning revealed in the literal
manifestation. When the two heavenly witnesses men-
ioned in the Revelation, quitted the earth, they ascended
o heaven in a cloud : and the consummation of the age,
nd coming of *the new heaven and the new earth* is ushered
n by the sign of the "*Son of Man* coming in the clouds
f heaven." It is in this sense, that "the Lord makes
he clouds his chariot"; the truths of the letter are
he sources whence all doctrine must be drawn.'

From Perth I proceeded to Dundee : there a large hall,
apable of containing a thousand persons, had been
ngaged, and on entering it I found it completely
illed.

The subject announced was put forth in the following
question :—

IS THE RESURRECTION OF THE MATERIAL BODY
A DOCTRINE TAUGHT IN HOLY SCRIPTURE ?'

I introduced my subject by quoting the following text :

'Now this I say, brethren, that flesh and blood cannot inherit
the kingdom of God, neither doth corruption inherit incorruption.'
—1 Cor. xv, 50.

' The doctrine of the resurrection of the material body
has been so long received without examination, as a doctrine of Scripture, that to doubt, and especially to deny it,
is looked upon by many as an atrocity almost equal to
the denial of a God. Hence those who affirm that the
material body will never rise again, are generally classed
with Hymeneus and Philetus, of whom the apostle Paul
says that they taught "that the resurrection is past
already." But how unjust this classification is, will appear
from the fact stated by the ecclesiastical historians, that the
heresy of Hymeneus and Philetus did not consist in the

denial of the resurrection of flesh and blood, but in *denying the resurrection altogether*. They asserted that there was, and would be, no resurrection, except in a *figurative* sense—a resurrection from vice to virtue, through the preaching of the gospel ; and that when man died, he died both as to his soul and body, and thus ceased to be altogether. It seems to have been they, or some of their followers, who troubled the Corinthian churches, and to silence whom the apostle Paul wrote that remarkable, and, when rightly interpreted, beautiful piece of reasoning contained in the 15th chapter of his first epistle to the Corinthians. " How say some among you," he demands, " that there is no resurrection of the dead ? " And in opposition to these persons he proceeds to inform the church, that although the earthly body dies, yet God gives the real man or soul a *spiritual* body, and that it is in that body alone that man rises to eternal life. From these facts it may be seen that, to class those who hold the very doctrine which St. Paul taught with the heretics whom he opposed, is the grossest injustice. Yet under this injustice have the members of the New Church been made to suffer by their enemies, because they affirm, as will be clearly seen presently, that very doctrine which the apostle taught. Nothing, it will be seen, can be more clear from his writings than this, that he never taught, nor could possibly mean to teach, the resurrection of the material body. " Flesh and blood (says he) cannot inherit the kingdom of God." " Corruption cannot inherit incorruption." Words which at once destroy the too common idea, that at some future period the body of flesh will be rendered incorruptible, and will be raised to a state of spiritual glory ! To inherit anything, signifies to receive it from another at some future period ; and if the body is at some future period to enter the kingdom of heaven, then, whether changed or unchanged (for the supposed change will make no difference in the argument), it WILL inherit what the apostle expressly declares " it cannot inherit " ; consequently it follows that " flesh and

>lood," changed or unchanged, will never enter into, or inherit, the kingdom of God.

'Man in his present state of existence, as to his material body, " is of the earth, earthy " ; but man, as hereafter glorified and exalted, will possess a body like, although not the same as, his Redeemer's glorious body ; a body which the apostle calls a *"house"*—that is, a body— *"from heaven."*

'In order to take a comprehensive view of the apostle's argument, it will be necessary to go through the whole of his reasoning. He first proves the possibility of a resurrection from the fact that Christ has actually risen. Leaving his adversary the choice either to admit man's or to deny Christ's resurrection, he says, " If Christ be not risen, your faith is vain ; and if Christ be risen from the dead, how say some among you that there is no resurrection for the dead ? " But that he did not mean by the resurrection of man, a resurrection of the earthly body at some future period, is evident from the manner in which he follows up his reasoning by saying, " If the dead rise not : . . . . and if Christ be not raised : . . . . then they also who have fallen asleep in Christ are perished."

'Now, let the reader be at the pains to ascertain whether the apostle meant to declare, as he is *generally* understood to mean, that if " the dead rise not,"—that is, if there be no resurrection of DEAD BODIES—then they who have already fallen asleep in Christ have perished? Is this a fact, or is it not ? Why nothing can be farther removed from the truth ! On the apostle's own principles they cannot have " perished" ; for they are—where he expressed his own expectation of being as soon as he should become " absent from the body"—" present with the Lord ! " Can any one suppose the apostle guilty of such an absurdity as that of saying that the souls in glory " are perished " ?

'Most evident, then, it is, that the apostle *meant* to say, that if the dead rise not in their spiritual body imme-

diately after death, THEN they who are fallen asleep in
Christ are "perished." This statement is as true as the
other is untrue. The greater, then, the number of those
who understand the apostle to be speaking in this chapter
of a resurrection of *dead bodies*, the greater is the number
of those who bear false witness against him; and the
greater is the injustice done to him, and to his character
for truth. Nothing can be clearer than this, that
although there should be no resurrection of dead
bodies at all, the souls already safe in glory are not
"perished."

' The apostle, however, distinctly asserts, that "if the
dead rise not," they "*are* perished," evidently implying
that the converse is the real fact, namely, that the dead
do certainly rise in their spiritual bodies after death, and
therefore they are *not* perished. And since his argument
has no reference whatever to the resurrection of dead
bodies, it further implies, that if the dead have not
already experienced this immediate resurrection, and
which is the only resurrection he contends for, *they are
perished*, and consequently cannot at any future period—
such as the expected period for the rising of dead bodies,
enter into life eternal. If they *have not* already risen in
their " house," or body, " which is from heaven," they
are indeed perished ! They have ceased to be, and that
for ever, and therefore no resurrection of their dead bodies,
even *if it were to take place*, would be a resurrection
for them ; so says the apostle. They " are perished"
if they are not risen, and therefore never can rise.

' Supposing the apostle to mean, as generally supposed,
that if the *dead body* rises not, then those already dead
are perished, he must then, beyond question, be classed
with those who *deny the immortality of the soul ;* for these
persons understand him to say, " If the dead body rises
not, *since this is the only resurrection to be looked for*,
then those who have died are perished ; for they are not
in existence now, and will not be called into existence
again."

'Such, indeed, would be a *fair* interpretation of the apostle's words, *if they stood by themselves.* But *this* interpretation would have to be reconciled with his other words, "*absent* FROM *the body*—(not IN the body, when b shall be raised, observe, but *absent* FROM *the body*)— *present with the Lord."* Who, then, by obstinately adhering to the common belief, will dare to convict the apostle of not only denying the immortality of the soul, but of positively denying it in one place, and as positively affirming it in another? To say, as the apostle is generally made to say, "If the dead body rise not, they who have fallen asleep in Christ are perished," is to deny the immortality of the soul in language the most express and unqualified : to say that the dead are " present with the Lord," being "clothed upon with their house from heaven," their "spiritual body," is to affirm as positively the immortality of the soul ; and if it be added to the latter affirmation, that unless their dead bodies shall be raised, themselves " are perished," then the apostle is made to fall into a degree of inconsistency and absurdity without parallel. But happily the character of the apostle is in no such danger. It is plain that he must have regarded the *true* and *only* resurrection, as being that by which man passes at death, first to judgment, and then to his own place in the eternal world. He must have been looking to it as full of hope to himself, and to all those who "fall asleep in Christ," when he said, " If in THIS life only we have hope in Christ, we are of all men most miserable. . . . . If the dead rise not, let us eat and drink, for to-morrow we die ! " But if the immortal spirit still lives in a spiritual body, even although the material body *should never rise,* Christians cannot be said with any degree of truth to be *without hope !* Without the resuscitation of the dead body, equally as with it, there is a happiness unspeakable in store for the righteous immediately after death ; and for the righteous under such circumstances, and with such a "good hope through grace," (and consequently

29

for the apostle himself) to cry out, "Let us eat and drink, for *to-morrow we die*"—we have no hope! except this poor hope of a blessed immortality without our earthly body ; "we are of all men most miserable," for "to-morrow we die," and then we shall lose our mortal bodies for ever ; we shall never, never, get them again ;—this would be downright insanity !

True it is, indeed, that "if the dead rise not," we have no hope, for without rising out of the dead body, the spirit could not enter into heaven ; and therefore there would be no reward hereafter, as well as no punishment, for "flesh and blood cannot inherit the kingdom of God." Let us, we might well say in such a case, "Let us eat and drink, for to-morrow we die," and then there is an end of us for ever ! More plainly still does the apostle come to the point at issue, where he says, "But some will say, How are the dead raised up ? and with what body do they come (seeing that their earthly body is laid in the earth, or destroyed) ?" "Thou fool, (he replies) that which thou sowest is not quickened, except it die, and that which thou sowest, thou sowest not the body which shall be, but bare grain, but God giveth it a body as it hath pleased him, and to every seed its own body." The apostle here compares the death and resurrection of men to the sowing and rising up of a grain of wheat. Let us look for a moment at the beauty and exact propriety of the illustration. When a grain of wheat is cast into the ground, the outer part of it, or its visible form, dies, and sinks into decay, or corruption; and unless this took place, the essential principle of the wheat could not be quickened, or germinate. So it is with man : he dies, that is, his outward form is thrown off, or dies, decays, and entirely disappears ; but happily the body which is laid in the grave, "is NOT that body which shall be"; for just as from that corrupted and lost form of the grain of wheat, the internal grain springs up into a new form of beauty ; so also is the resurrection of the dead. From the ruins of the earthly frame, the spiritual and glorious body of those " who are fallen asleep in Christ," rises into the kingdom of God, there to exist for ever and ever.

' Further to prove the truth of this, the apostle goes on to show that " there is a spiritual body" perfectly distinct from the natural, by referring to the *different* kinds of bodies which already exist. " There is one body of men, another of beasts, another of fishes, another of birds. There are also terrestrial bodies, and bodies celestial, but the glory of the celestial is one, and the glory of the terrestrial is another. There is one glory of the sun, another glory of the moon, and another glory of the stars : moreover, one star differeth from another in glory : so, also, is (not will be, observe) the resurrection of the dead. It (the dead person as a bodily existence viewed in the abstract) is sown in dishonor, it is raised in glory : it is sown a natural body, it is raised (not, observe, it WILL BE raised, but it is raised in the case of every man who dies) a spiritual body. There is a natural body, and there is (not there shall be at some unknown period, but there actually now is) a spiritual body (within, but distinct from the natural). And thus it is written, The first man Adam (after whom is the natural body) was made a living man ; * the last Adam (from whom is the spiritual body) was made a life-giving man (or the giver of the holy spirit of life which he breathes on his disciples). Howbeit, that (body) was not first (either with Adam or with us) which is spiritual, but that which is natural, and afterwards (or after death) that which is spiritual. The first man (or the living natural body) is from the ground, earthy : the second man (or the living spiritual body)

* In the common translation it is 'a living soul'; but as Cruden's ' Concordance' shows, the word ' soul' sometimes means the whole man, according to the context, which it clearly does here. Some high authorities, indeed, render the words a 'living animal,' instead of a living soul, meaning a living material body. It will be observed, that in our quotations we deviate from the common translation sometimes, but we believe that our accuracy will not be questioned. We also add occasionally (in parentheses) such words as appear to be required to complete the sense.

is from heaven* (heavenly, and is called elsewhere ' our house which is from heaven'). As was the earthy (body with Adam), such are they also (his descendants after the flesh) who are earthy; and as was the heavenly (body with Adam after his death and resurrection) such will they also be that (after death) are heavenly. And as we (after Adam) have borne the image of the earthy, we shall also (like him) bear the image of the heavenly (body)."

'The whole scope of the apostle's argument plainly is to show that the natural and spiritual bodies, although co-existent in man in the world, are as distinct from each other as is the flesh of men from the flesh of beasts ; or as the glory of the celestial is from that of the terrestrial; and further, that as soon as the natural body dies, the spiritual body rises ; for that, says he, is not first which is spiritual, but that which is natural, and afterward that which is spiritual. He affirms also, that the material body is derived from Adam, and is from the ground, earthy, while the spiritual body is not from the earth, but "from heaven." He concludes with appropriately declaring, that the heavenly body will immediately succeed the earthly, by saying, "As we (like Adam) have borne the image of the earthy (body), we shall also (like him) bear the image of the heavenly."

'A still stronger assertion in proof of the non-resurrection of the material body next follows. "Now this I say, brethren, that flesh and blood cannot inherit the kingdom of God ; neither doth corruption inherit incorruption." A more clear and positive denial of the resurrection of the flesh cannot be expressed in words. Flesh and blood not only cannot enjoy the kingdom of heaven now, but never can inherit it at any future time. Corruption cannot

---

* In the common translation, we read, '*the Lord* from heaven',. but the words, *the Lord*, were added by the heretic Marcion, Tertullian tells us. (See Dr. Macknight.) They evidently interrupt the sense of the chapter. The Vulgate reads, Secundus homo de cœlo cœlestis.' See 2 Cor. v. 2.

become incorrupt now, nor can it inherit incorruption, as a future gift. Can any words more strongly express the doctrine we contend for ? or more strongly repudiate the common doctrine invented since the time of the apostle ? They at once, and for ever, put a bar to the resurrection of the material body of flesh and blood, for, agreeably to what he had already stated, the body sown in the grave is not the body that shall be—is not the body that "is raised," in the case of every man immediately after death. And mark the following words—"Behold, I show you a mystery (regarding our resurrection into the spiritual world), we shall not all sleep (as asserted by those who altogether deny a future state ; our undying spirits shall not lie insensible in the tomb), but we shall all be changed, (' we,' our identical selves, instead of these gross bodies, shall possess glorious spiritual bodies) in a moment, in the twinkling of an eye, at the last trumpet (alluding probably to the trumpets which were sounded to mark the watches of the night ; ' the last trumpet' being that sounded at daybreak. 'The last trumpet,' therefore, proclaims the opening of an eternal morn—an entrance into the promised rest in heaven) ; for the trumpet shall sound, and the dead (not the dead body, but the man who has died, and who transfers his consciousness from a natural to a spiritual state and body ;—the dead) shall be raised incorruptible, and we shall be changed."

' That the apostle did not in this change at the sound of a trumpet, refer to any remote general resurrection of dead bodies, clearly appears from his earnest and repeated declarations, that he expected his own resurrection to take place immediately after laying down his natural body. "Then," says he, "this corruptible (or ourselves in our present corruptible body) must put on incorruption (in a body not liable to decay) ; and this mortal (or we who are mortal) must put on immortality ; then shall be brought to pass the saying that is written, Death is swallowed up in victory." Death, even in the victory which he obtains over mortality, is himself swallowed up by life immortal !

Even while he triumphs over the mortal body, he is foiled by the resurrection from it of a body which is spiritual and everlasting.

'Well does the apostle say in another place,* that when we put off our mortal body, we nevertheless shall not " be unclothed, but shall be clothed upon with our house FROM HEAVEN, that mortality may be swallowed up in life ! " And so in the chapter before us, he speaks of putting off corruption, and " putting on incorruption," as of putting off one garment, and putting on another; the corruptible body, therefore, is not to be changed into incorruption, or into an incorruptible body, but is to be put off. The incorruptible is not the corruptible endued with new powers, but it is a new and glorious nature consciously "put on," when the latter is thrown aside. The same figure he uses (in 2 Cor. v.) when he describes the servants of God as groaning in their present gross bodies, with which they are clothed here, and as desiring to be clothed upon with their house, which is from heaven ; and further, to show that he considered this incorruptible body as something widely different from that of " flesh and blood," he calls the latter " an earthly house," " a tabernacle or tent" ; while the former he calls " a building" ; the one is " dissolved," pulled down,—taken away ;—the other is " eternal in the heavens."

'But let us recur to the question, *when* did he expect the resurrection to take place ? We have, indeed, completely anticipated the reply to this question already, especially by showing (and this will be still further shown presently) that, if the apostle looked upon the resurrection as a remote future event, his reasoning would be anything but conclusive. That, however, he did not do so, but believed the resurrection to mean, and consist in, the entrance of man's spirit into eternal life immediately after death, is plain from his saying, " We know that when this earthly house of our tabernacle is dissolved, we have

* 2 Cor. v.

a building of God, a house not made with hands, eternal
in the heavens"; that is, we know that when this earthly
house, our present body, shall be dissolved, we shall
immediately find ourselves in possession of a building
of God, a new and spiritual body, which shall be eternal
as the heavens. Indeed, the apostle deprecates the idea
that by putting off the material body we shall be "found
naked," or without any body, flitting about like an
unsubstantial vapor, which some strangely suppose the
"disembodied" spirit to be! He says—"not that
we would be unclothed, but be clothed upon, that (by
rising in this new clothing of a living immortal body
'from heaven,') mortality may be swallowed up in
life."

'What, pretence, then, can any one find for saying,
that a body whose origin is expressly said to be "from
heaven," is that same corruptible body which was "formed
of the dust of the ground"? If the atoms of the dead
material body are really, as is generally believed, to be
raised and transmuted into a heavenly body all at once,
there will still be no propriety in saying that that body is
"from heaven!" Even then it will be from the earth,
and therefore an "earthly body," and will still be
"earthy" in its substance, however sublimated it may, by
an extraordinary stretch of imagination, be supposed to
become! The "house from heaven," can be nothing
else than the "spiritual body"; it cannot be our present
"natural body," which he puts in contrast with it.

'We are bound, then, to conclude, that the resurrection
which the apostle contended for was not that of the
material body; and that he had no such resurrection as
this in his view; but that, on the contrary, the only
resurrection he meant was—a continuation of man's
existence in the spiritual world, commencing immediately
after the death of the body, by his resurrection into that
world in a spiritual body.

'We now refer to a higher authority than even that of
an apostle. Our Lord himself, in his dispute with the

Pharisees concerning the resurrection, says, "Have ye not read that God said, I am the God of Abraham, and the God of Isaac, and the God of Jacob ; He is not the God of the dead, but of the living." Not the God of the dead Abraham, but of the then living Abraham, observe. Now, if the only resurrection meant by the apostle Paul has not yet taken place, as generally supposed, then, though our Lord's words might teach the immortality of the soul, it would be difficult indeed to show that they proved the resurrection of the body. It is evident that the identical individuals named—Abraham, Isaac, and Jacob—must then have been living, although their bodies had certainly not been raised ; for our Lord declares, that God is the God of Abraham, etc., and that he is not the God of the dead, but of the living—not the God of dead bodies, but of living spirits. If we understand that the resurrection is an essential preliminary to the life hereafter, and that man must rise before he can enjoy eternal life, then do our Redeemer's words become irresistible in proving that there can be no life hereafter without a resurrection. Abraham, Isaac, and Jacob, are living; they must, therefore, have risen : then, as God is no respecter of persons, all mankind must rise, in like manner, immediately after death. This is further evident from the parable of Dives and Lazarus, whose immediate resurrection after death is there distinctly affirmed.

We need not dwell at any length upon the consolation which this doctrine imparts to the mind ; instead of looking through the long, dreary distance of an unknown period, for the fruition of our happiness, we have the consolation to know, that no sooner will the natural body be dissolved, than we shall at once rise in a spiritual body, and so be conducted by angels to our eternal home. Instead, then, of viewing the monuments of our friends as memorials of the power of death, we should view them as trophies of victory—as marks to point out from whence the servants of God ascended to the heavenly mansions. Death is indeed swallowed up, even at the moment of victory, and we can with truth exclaim—"O death, where is thy sting? O grave, where is thy victory? Thanks be to God, who giveth us the victory through our Lord Jesus Christ." Thanks be to God through his own divine humanity, by and from which cometh to us all power to triumph over death, both the death of the body and of the soul, the first and the second death!

'Having now cleared this famous chapter (1 Cor. xv) of the imputation of teaching the resurrection of dead bodies, we proceed to notice some passages principally relied on in support of the belief of this event, an event which, to the eye of reason, appears equally astounding and useless. One would think it were quite sufficient to overturn this belief, as being unscriptural, to quote the conclusion of the most sagacious and candid of human inquirers, the great Mr. Locke, who has these words in opposition to a statement of the then Bishop of Worcester :—"The resurrection of the dead I acknowledge to be an article of the Christian faith ; but I do not find in any place in Scripture any such expression as the resurrection of the body, meaning the dead body, or that that body shall rise, or be raised."

'Job xix, 25—27 :—When Job says, "In my flesh shall I see God," the context plainly shows that he only meant to express a conviction that God, who had hidden himself from him in his affliction, would restore the light of his countenance to him while he remained " in the flesh "; that is, before his death. This hope was actually verified in the last chapter, where Job exclaims, " I have heard of thee by the hearing of the ear, but now mine eye seeth thee."

'Isa. xxvi, 19 :—" Together with my dead body shall they arise." Bishop Lowth, though a believer in the doctrine we repudiate, shows that these words are a gross mistranslation, and after newly translating the passage, he says, " The deliverance of the people of God [the Jews, that is] from a state of the lowest description is explained by images taken from the resurrection of the dead."

'Daniel xii, 2 :—" They that sleep in the dust shall arise." It appears from the marginal notes to John v, that these words had their accomplishment at the Lord's first advent (see a passage referred to below), and that those who "sleep in the dust" (see Isa. lii, 2) are those of the Jewish church who then would be found living in the neglect of the law of God, some of whom, at the sound of the gospel trumpet, would wake up to the attainment of everlasting life ; while others, turning a deaf ear to it, would sink into everlasting shame and contempt.

'Matt. v, 29, 30 :—"The whole body be cast into hell." These words must be interpreted, not literally, but figuratively, like the rest of the passage. If the hand cut off be figurative, as every one sees, so must the body be to which it belonged.

'Matt. xxvii, 52, 53 :—"Many bodies of the saints which slept arose, and came out of the graves." All reason shows that this was a vision of a transaction in the spiritual world, not visible to the eyes of the body, but only to the opened spiritual sight of the few who witnessed it.

'John v, 25, 29 :—The words "now is," in ver. 25, plainly prove that a future resurrection of dead bodies is not meant ; to refer to this text, therefore, as having any bearing on that subject, is downright dishonesty or absurdity. Then was the fulfilment of Dan. xii, 2, above noticed.

'1 Thess. iv, 16, 17 :—" The dead in Christ shall rise first." The apostle states that he is referring to the "Word of the Lord," which we find in Matt. xxiv, 30, 31. If this passage in Thessalonians is to be referred to the resurrection of the body, those who think so, to be consistent, MUST conclude that NO dead bodies are to be raised but the bodies of "those who sleep in Jesus," for these are the only deceased persons referred to ; and, consequently, it is equally proved by this passage, that the bodies of neither the heathen, nor of wicked Christians, will ever be raised at all! The passage is very mysterious :

only one thing is clear, and that is, that it has no reference to the supposed resurrection of dead bodies !

We close with what is called the translation of Elijah. It appears from 2 Kings ii, 11, that " Elijah went up by a whirlwind into heaven." He who thinks that the way " up to heaven " is through the air, must remember, that, owing to the diurnal motion of the earth, what is " up " at noon is " down " at midnight ! Since, then, it is impossible to take the narrative literally, it is fair to conclude, that the passage only means that Elijah's body, by the force of a whirlwind, was separated from his spirit, and either rent to atoms, or carried away, while, by the opening of Elisha's spiritual sight as a favor (ver. 11), he was permitted to see the spiritual body of Elijah pass through the world of spirits into heaven. When Moses and Elijah were seen at our Lord's transfiguration, their persons or bodies were similar, and yet no one supposes that the material body of Moses had been translated !'

At the conclusion of this discourse a long and rather stormy discussion ensued, but, upon the whole, the subject was favorably received. One man, however, after the congregation was dismissed, approached me and said,

' Ye've gi'en us very strange doctrine the nicht, sir.'

' I believe I have given you the apostolic doctrine of the Resurrection.'

' I'm no gaun to controveart ye, but only to say that had ye preached such a searmon as yon at Sherrie Muir, or Forfar, they'd ha' stan'd ye oot o' the pu'pit.'

From Dundee I hastened on to Aberdeen, where I had engaged to assist a clergyman in the administration of the Holy Supper.

It may be proper to inform the English reader that in Scotland the Sacrament of the Holy Supper is only administered twice in the year, and on those occasions it is customary for the resident clergyman to invite some of his brother ministers to assist him in the duty.   I was a total stranger to the gentleman who invited me, but he had heard of my successful controversy with the Unitarians, and as he was himself then engaged in a controversy with that body of Christians, he was anxious to have my aid.

In Scotland the administration of the holy ordinance is usually preceded by a series of preparatory discourses. First, there is the fast day, which is usually held on a Thursday, on which day three sermons are delivered.   On Friday evening another discourse is delivered, and on Saturday, between the hours of twelve and two, a fifth discourse, which is called the preparation sermon.   These discourses are usually delivered by the visiting minister, or ministers, for often three, or even four, are invited. On Sunday morning the visiting minister again officiates, and in the afternoon the ordinance is administered.

At the church in which I officiated there were two hundred and fifty communicants ; and I must say I found the various exercises altogether too much for my strength, for though, during the excitement which prevailed, I was enabled to accomplish all that was required of me, I was quite prostrated when the stimulus was withdrawn.

The labor of administration was great, especially as the church was large, and required an extra exertion of the voice.   It kept the thinking powers, too, constantly on the stretch ; for, as I have said, all my discourses in Scotland were extempore.

The gentleman for whom I officiated. though somewhat eccentric, was a man of considerable ability, with a great flow of language,. and a stentorian voice.   He had a large head, excellent observing powers, good moral sentiments, rather large Self-esteem, and very large Love of Approbation.   The back brain was fully developed, and with an expansive chest his physical energies were great. He was a kind of independent minister ; he admitted the supreme divinity of our Saviour, and was favorable o the Swedenborgian doctrines generally, but he did not ally receive or acknowledge them. He had himself rected a large church, which was very numerously attended, but he was recognised by neither of the great Synods of Presbyterianism.

During my stay in Aberdeen I was entertained at this gentleman's house, but I was rendered miserable the whole time by the inveterate habit which he had contracted of smoking. I never saw him without a pipe n his mouth, except at the time of meals, and during the hours of worship. Before breakfast, there was the pipe ; after breakfast, pipe : a short suspension during the time of family worship, then pipe. Before dinner, pipe ; after dinner, pipe. Before tea, pipe ; after tea, pipe. Before going up into the pulpit, even in the vestry, pipe. Immediately after sermon, pipe ; and before and after supper, pipe ; the first thing in the morning, and the last thing at night, pipe. I even thought he had his pipe in bed, for the odor of tobacco saluted my olfactory nerves long before I was out of bed. I was in a continued state of nausea, and when I left Aberdeen, I was scarcely able to travel to the end of the first stage (a village called Stonehaven), when I was seized with vertigo and spitting of blood. I had a correspondent at Stonehaven to whom I made myself known. He received me very kindly and entertained me in his house three or four days, till I was able to resume my journey.

I have never been able to find a reason why so many clever men, and especially clergymen, are such slaves to tobacco. The late Rev. Robert Hall, of Bristol, I have been told, always had his pipe both before and after service, and I know several of the most able Swedenborgian ministers who are great smokers. To me tobacco is an utter abomination ; there are but three animals who can at all tolerate it. The first is the tobacco worm, one of the most disgusting reptiles that crawls on the face of the earth. The second is the rock-goat of America, whose foulness of odor, and filthiness of habit, render it an object of abhorrence and avoidance by all other animals. The third is, 'man—the glory, jest, and riddle of the world.' I should like to see a law enacted that all these living furnaces should be compelled to consume their own smoke.

One cannot now walk the streets without encountering the odor of this foul weed, and little boys, with short pipes, strutting up and down the pavement, obviously considering themselves as performing the manly part, by being able to smoke a pipe of tobacco without nausea.

If the sober part of the community are to be continually annoyed with this odious practice, I think the Chancellor of the Exchequer might turn it to account in improving the revenue. No one should be allowed to smoke in the streets, or in a railway carriage, without a license. I would divide smokers into three classes. Class 1 should wear a gold button in his hat or cap, with an excise mark stamped thereon, for this he should pay twenty shillings. Class 2 should wear a silver button, for which he should pay ten shillings. Class 3 should wear a steel button, for which he should pay two shillings and sixpence. These licenses should be renewable every year, and it should be lawful for any policeman to take into custody any person found smoking without his button, take him before a magistrate, and have him fined, say, first class, two shillings; second class, one shilling; third class, sixpence, for each offence. From the decision of the magistrate there should be no appeal. One-half of the fine to go to the poor, the other to the policeman. I calculate that these licenses would yield the government a clear revenue of at least a quarter of a million yearly. Of course I expect the Chancellor of the Exchequer will secure me a pension of thirty pounds a-year for my valuable suggestion : but to return to my narrative :—

Having, by the aid of the sea air, got myself purified from the tobacco weed, I took ship at Stonehaven and

proceeded to Kirkcaldy, in Fifeshire, where I obtained a
room, and delivered a lecture on the claims of Emanuel
Swedenborg on the Christian world as an Expositor of the
Holy Word. I had a small audience. From Kirkcaldy
I proceeded to Dunfermline, where I preached to a large
audience on the possibility of supernatural communication.
Both these discourses I afterwards published in the
Glasgow series of Christian tracts. From Dunfermline I
proceeded to Auchtermuchtie, where, through the influence
of a legal friend, I obtained the use of the Guild Hall,
and having found the town drummer, I sent him round
with an announcement that a Home Missionary minister
from Glasgow would deliver a discourse on Rev. xii, 1.

It was soon ascertained that I was a Swedenborgian
missionary, and as the subject announced was rather
singular in its phraseology, it was presumed that the
discourse would be mystical, if not fanatical. The clergyman declared that the Swedenborgians were a most dangerous class of men, and that their doctrines were not
only delusive, but devilish. These reports raised a very
uneasy feeling in the town against me, and as the hour of
meeting advanced, there were some who were desirous of
driving me out of the town. Others, however, thought
it was but fair that I should have a hearing, and the
voice of these last prevailed. At the hour announced I
repaired to the hall. It was a large upper room; it
was densely crowded, and I had to make my way
through a crowd of people who lined the staircase, and
who closed up as I ascended the stairs. From the top
of the staircase into the street a vast crowd had assembled, and it would have been utterly impossible for me to
escape had violence been offered. I saw the uneasy feeling
which pervaded the meeting, and I was not without
apprehension that I should be maltreated. I resolved
not to touch the religious prejudices of the people, but to
state fairly and candidly the view of the passage which,
as a Christian man, I had formed. I knew that the
Scottish people were deeply imbued with the truths of

science, and I also knew their deep reverence for the Scriptures, and I resolved to show them that I had an equal reverence for them. The passage I had selected would enable me to illustrate briefly the sublime science of astronomy, and, from the comparisons there used, I intended to unfold my subject. Having resolved upon this course, I proceeded to address the people previous to the commencement of the service. I stated myself to be a missionary connected with the New Jerusalem Church, a body of Christians, of which they had, perhaps, heard, but of whose doctrines and opinions of Scripture they were probably but imperfectly informed. I trusted they would favor me with an attentive and patient hearing, assuring them that I had the deepest reverence for Scripture ; every line, every word, yea, every letter of which I believed to be divinely inspired, and filled with the wisdom of the Most High God. I assured them of my belief in the sacred doctrine of the divine trinity of Father, Son, and Holy Spirit, whom I believed dwelt bodily in the person of the Lord Jesus Christ. I stated that I had selected the passage announced that I might show in what I considered the inspiration of the Scripture to consist, as well as to place before them, through the analogies which the passage presented, a figure of a true church. I then stated that it was our duty to pray for the divine assistance, and for the descent of the divine influence, that a blessing might attend our present inquiries.

I terminated this address with prayer, and then having, through the aid of one of the hearers, given out a short psalm, which the people united in singing, I proceeded with my subject, the substance of which is contained in what follows :—

REVELATION XII. 1.

'And there appeared a great wonder in heaven : a woman clothed with the sun, and the moon under her feet, and upon her head a crown of twelve stars.'

'I must beg my hearers to remember that the verse

which has now been read, is a portion of the divine word of God, and that the extraordinary appearances which are described were seen by John in heaven, and as nothing but that which is pure and good can exist in heaven, so we may feel assured that the subject before us has some reference to a future state of glory and beatitude analogous to the splendors represented in the appearances of the woman. But how are we to acquire a knowledge of what these appearances mean ? How are we to decipher this great wonder ?

'The apostle declares (Romans i, 20) that "the invisible things of God from the creation of the world, are clearly seen, being understood by the things that are made, even his eternal power and Godhead." Let us, then, try to ascertain the qualities of the sun, moon, and stars, and this will furnish us with a key to unlock the mystery of the woman's appearance. Although philosophers dispute about the substance of the sun, they are all agreed that he is the source of heat and light. They are further agreed that the moon is an opaque body, and shines only by reflection. And lastly, they are all agreed that the stars are themselves suns, the sources of heat and light to attendant worlds ; their immense distances from our earth presenting to us only the appearance of particles of shining dust.'

[I dwelt at some length on this part of my subject, illustrating it by the discoveries made by modern astronomers, until I saw that the uneasy feeling which pervaded the audience at the commencement of my lecture had greatly subsided, and a pleased attention existed in its place.]

'Now let us return to the apostolic quotation; the *visible things* of the creation being explanatory of the INVISIBLE things of God. Now our symbol of love is heat, answering to the sun. Our symbol of truth is light, answering to the moon, which derives all its light from the sun ; and our symbol of the stars are knowledges of both truth and goodness, which contain heat

30

and light in themselves, but which their great distance alone prevents us from feeling. Hence the woman, as seen in heaven, is clothed with the divine love ; the moon is under her feet, to symbolize the divine truth upon which she rests ; and the diadem of stars which encircle her head, are all the knowledges of truth and goodness. But of what is the woman herself a symbol ? She is a symbol of the future church, which in the last days would be established ; and her goodness, truth, and holiness are described by the glorious appearances which encircle her. Let us see if the Scriptures will bear us out in these assertions.

'Throughout the sacred Word, the woman, as a figure of the church, either in a good sense or its opposite, is repeatedly placed before us. When the church is described in its good or holy state, it is called in the prophets the wife of Jehovah ; as, "Thy Maker is thy husband, Jehovah of hosts is his name, the God of the whole earth shall he be called"; and in the New Testament, the church, under the figure of the bride, is called the Lamb's wife. But when the church in a state of corruption is alluded to, she is described as a harlot who has forsaken her husband, the Lord, and hath committed fornication with the kings of the earth, being intoxicated herself, and intoxicating her members with the wine of her fornication.

'But our subject presents us with the glorious appearance of the church as she will exist when Jesus Christ is her only head, and his divine perfections are her ornament and glory. And now, my hearers, behold the woman, as a figure of the church, clothed with the sun, and remember that the scene is in heaven, and symbolizes what the church on earth shall be in the last days.

'A WOMAN CLOTHED WITH THE SUN. What a glorious church must that be which is encompassed with so divine a garment ! For what is this sun with which the woman is clothed but Divine Love—the very essence of Deity ! He who is love itself, is to be as the garment of the church. The woman is to be encompassed with

, she is to be filled with pure affection for her Maker as her husband; and her children, or the members of the church, re to be clothed with the same heavenly garment. All the lessings, which, literally, the earth and the creatures who inhabit it receive from the sun of the natural world, will the hurch and every individual member of it receive from the Lord, when they make him the object of their supreme ffection. This love is so pure, and yet so tempered, that the hurch will be kept in perpetual health and happiness by it. Its divine rays will not be intercepted by fogs and exhalations from beneath, but will pour its kindly influence on all around; its light will be as uniform and undeviating as its heat. This sun, too, by which the church is to be encompassed, will never set; the dark clouds of error will never impede the progress of the rays of divine light which issue from the Sun of Righteousness. As the centre of the church, for "God will be in the midst of her," it shall bless all within its life-imparting influences, and as the circumference or garments of the church, it will encompass all with its pure and perfect love. It will diffuse around it joy and happiness; it will raise the dejected, remove all cause for affliction, dispel the mists of ignorance, and fill the soul with divine beatitudes. Such will be the woman clothed with the sun; such the church encircled with the divine love; and as a consequence the effects will be communicated to all who come within its sphere. How different will then be the feelings with which men will regard each other. The jealousies, heart-burnings, and theological rancor of hostile parties in religion will be superseded. Harsh and uncharitable judgment will find no place in the hearts of the Lord's servants; men will not then brand each other with the odious epithets of heretic, atheist, or infidel, merely because the light assumes the tint of a different hue, but they will regard each other as the sons of the same divine parent, as the members of the same pure church, as the offspring of the woman clothed with the sun.

'But the woman is described as having the moon under her feet. The moon, as we have seen, shines by reflection. In herself, her body is dark and opaque, and consequently, were there no sun, there could be no light from the moon. As then the light which the moon emits properly belongs to the sun, it is the light of the sun which is the cause of the moon's reflection. Now the sun, as we have seen, is pure divine heat or love, and the light of the sun is pure divine truth or wisdom. By the woman, therefore, having the moon under her feet is signified that the church of the Lord in the last days will be founded upon pure divine truth. The luminous parts of the moon are ever turned towards the sun, and truth must ever be in the same direction. But the reason why the woman has her feet upon the moon is to show that the church which is principled in love to the Lord must ever be founded upon divine truth, and without such a foundation it could not possibly stand. If we search the Scriptures we shall see that the true church is founded upon a rock, and that rock is Jesus Christ, he being pure Divine Truth itself. He is the light or truth, the garment with which the divine love, or Father, is clothed. How unequivocally does this prove, that the church symbolized by the woman clothed with the sun and the moon under her feet is the true church : for is not Jesus Christ declared to be the chief corner stone of the church ? Is he not declared to be the *foundation*, the only *sure, tried*, and *precious foundation?* that no other foundation can be laid than Jesus Christ ? What, then, can be more certain, than that the true church of the Lord must be built upon the truth that Jesus Christ is the chief corner stone ? What can be more certain than that Jesus Christ is the " way, the truth, and the life ? " And if the heat and light of the natural sun is, as we have shown, the source of natural life to all in the natural world, and if this glorious luminary itself owes its existence, as it does, to the Sun of Righteousness, or the sun of heaven, then the church owes its existence to the Lord, to the Divine Love as Father, and the Divine Wisdom as Son, and the resulting operation as Holy Spirit :—the chief essentials which constitute the true church are love to God and charity to man, and where these are, there the true church of the Lord is.

'The woman or church is described further as having upon her head a crown of twelve stars. We have seen that *stars* are *suns*, emitting heat and light, that they will therefore symbolize the knowledges of truth and goodness. A crown is a symbol of dominion and power ; and encircling the head, which is the seat of wisdom, implies the intelligence and wisdom of the church in which the Lord Jesus Christ is universally acknowledged, adored, and worshipped as THE ONLY "GOD, OVER ALL, BLESSED FOR EVERMORE."

'If, then, we now take a brief survey of this interesting passage, and bring the several particulars before us with the view of beholding their united signification, a most glorious and exalted church will be presented for our reflection. The wonder or sign of the church is seen in heaven ; and the true church on earth must be a close resemblance of it, and to become members of this church, we must acknowledge the Lord Jesus Christ as its supreme and only head ; we must believe in the sanctity and divinity of his word, and live a life in accordance with our belief.

'In the first place, the woman or church in heaven is a type or figure of what the true church upon earth is to be. Her being clothed or encompassed with the sun is to denote the sphere of holy love and charity with which, as with a garment, she is to be invested. Throughout her whole compass and extent, love or holy goodness is to be her distinguishing quality. Her members are to be principled in love to God as the supreme, and charity towards each other, and, in short, love to them is to be the fulfilling of the law.

'She is to have the moon under her feet, because, as the

moon in Scripture symbolizes that truth or faith which is derived from the sun of heavenly love, so such faith or truth is to be the foundation upon which the church shall rest.

'The woman is crowned with a diadem of twelve stars, to show that her wisdom, power, and dominion is derived from the truths of God's Holy Word, for these in their essence and their origin are himself, and these truths like the sparkling gems which bespangle the hemisphere of space, emit their different degrees of brilliance, and illustrate, by the words, " one star differeth from another star in glory," that one truth in the Holy Word differeth from another truth in glory, but all emit their divine light for the guidance, direction, and comfort of the creature. Wherever these principles are, there will the true church of the Lord be; wherever they are wanting, the church may have a name to live, but will be spiritually dead. Nevertheless, this spiritually dead church will claim the preëminence, she will persecute those who are described under the figure of the woman, but she will not prevail.'

Having finished the discourse, I concluded the meeting with the singing of a psalm and with prayer.

Many of the hearers came and shook hands with me. A sensation of pleased wonder seemed to pervade the body of the hearers, and the audience slowly dispersed, but continued in groups discussing the subject in the street.

As I was about to leave the hall, three of the hearers came to me, and, after saying they had heard a very different sermon from what they had been taught to expect, inquired if I had not a journey to make that night. I said I had, and one, too, of an intricate kind, which I had never travelled before; I had to proceed to Falkland, a distance of four or five miles, where a bed had been provided for me, and part of the way lay through a wood. They then inquired if it would be agreeable for them to accompany me a part of the way. I said I should be thankful if they would.

Having got clear of the town they stated that, prior to the commencement of the service, a number of men had resolved to stone me out of the town, and they were not quite sure that I was yet safe. This induced them to offer me their company, as their presence might deter the more violent from making any assault upon me, they being well known in the town. At the same time they thought the judicious manner in which the subject had been handled, would secure me from injury.

They accompanied me on my way nearly three miles, and under the protection of Providence I arrived safely at Falkland.

At Falkland I remained three days. One of them being the Sabbath I preached three times in the Guildhall, which had been granted me by the chief magistrate, who himself attended, and as the parish church was then closed, I had the hall well filled each time. I received the thanks of the magistrate for my labor, with the assurance that the hall should at any time be at my service, should I again visit Falkland.

This completed my labor, and I returned to Glasgow, after an absence of nearly four weeks, preaching almost every night, and three times on the Sabbath. I was accompanied during a great part of this journey by the late James Macara, Esq., of Edinburgh, through whose interest I was so often successful in obtaining the various Guild Halls, he being a member of the legal profession, a 'Writer to the Signet,' in Edinbro'. He was a most devoted Swedenborgian, a warm-hearted and benevolent man. His greatest delight appeared to be in circulating a knowledge of Swedenborg's writings. Whenever an opportunity presented itself of introducing them among professional men, he never neglected it. He edited and published by subscription four of the minor works of Swedenborg. He was a man of an intensely nervous temperament, a medium-sized brain, large anterior and sincipital region. His intellectual faculties were all freely developed, but the predominant power of his brain was Marvellousness, and he was frequently the subject of many eccentricities. To me he was a devoted friend, and in the journey above alluded to, rendered me much assistance. He has passed from this state of being.

While engaged in these duties, removing rapidly from place to place, studying as I journeyed, and expending the result of my cogitations every night at some new field of labor, my lost sense of hearing was but little regretted, though I invariably explained to whatever audience I addressed the infirmity under which I labored. But when my mission was accomplished, and I returned home, my deafness seemed to return with double force, and a sense of utter loneliness came upon me.

Whoever reflects upon the condition of a person in a state of deafness, will readily admit that there are few doors of labor open, which he can enter. In professions of buying and selling, he is, by his deprivation of hearing, utterly useless, and even in ordinary trades of handicraft, there is a *bar sinister* on his escutcheon. For few employers indeed will be encumbered with a deaf workman, when there are so many to choose from, with all their senses in a state of perfection.

As a lecturer on science, I was not called upon to hear, but to speak, and the same may be said of my office as a minister of the gospel. To these sources I resolved, so far as my ability would reach, to add literature, and upon lecturing and literature my means of existence have principally depended. For though I have constantly labored as a minister of the gospel, I have received comparatively little remuneration therefrom; and although I have qualified myself for the profession of medicine, my lost sense of hearing operates as a total bar to success in that department.

Books, then, to me were essential, they were my working tools, and I read to gain new ideas, that I might be in a condition to dispense those ideas to others. To me, conversation was, comparatively speaking, a blank. What others by the aid of the lecture room or the *converzatione* easily acquired, were by me only obtained by patient study and observation.

But I had read of persons disqualified by my infirmity from the intercourse of general society who had associated around them periodically men of ability, and who enjoyed society for one evening in a week or a month, why should not I do the same ? I was favorably known to many men of eminence in the city of Glasgow, to professors in the University, to painters, poets, and musicians ; why should I not invite these periodically to my house, throw myself upon their benevolence for one evening's social enjoyment as well as instruction ; when every one of my friends should address me through an acoustic tube, the only instrument by which I could hear distinctly, and my loneliness for a time be beguiled ? I resolved to act upon the idea suggested, and I at length gathered around me some of the choice spirits of Glasgow, and enjoyed the pleasures of social life at least once a month. My company consisted of twelve persons, among whom were three ladies. They were all persons who had patronised me in my phrenological capacity, and several of them, as I have said, were of eminence in the city ; one was a professor in the University ; another was professor of music in Queen's College. A third was an artist, who has since risen to eminence in his profession. One of the ladies was a teacher of singing, and a most brilliant singer herself. Three of the gentlemen were skilful instrumental musicians ; a fourth, a fine tenor singer. Two others were poets, and one of these was a most humorous descriptive writer of Scotch characters. They had all submitted themselves, as I have said, to my phrenological examination, and they were all striking proofs of the science. Of several of them I possess portraits, executed in crayons by the artist just alluded to. Besides the regular attendants at my monthly soirees, I frequently invited some of the senior medical students, and my friends were always privileged to introduce a stranger, so that these meetings were rarely fewer in number than twenty.

Every person considered himself or herself bound to contribute to the amusement of the evening. The articles read, or sung, or played, or narrated, were by their respective authors. Singing or instrumental music I could hear very well, and music has ever been with me a passion ; but poetry and descriptive sketches were always spoken through my acoustic tube. I generally invited one or two of my Swedenborgian friends, but very few availed themselves of the invitation.

'And a pretty sum they cost you, I dare say,' Mr. Careful will observe.

Well, I believe upon the whole they cost me five shillings per month, but not unfrequently I was a gainer even in a pecuniary point of view, for one would present me with a packet of tea, another with sugar, a third with a canister of biscuits, and so on; but besides this, I had the pleasure of hearing, for that night at least, everything that was read, or recited, or sung, or played, and that to me was priceless.

But I will now introduce the reader to one of my Soirees. And first allow me to introduce you to my writer of Scotch character. Here he is—mark the breadth of his forehead, and behold the twinkle of his humorous eye. How finely the coronal arch is developed. There is Imitation, Ideality, Wit, and Individuality so plainly depicted that you already begin to smile ; his benevolence makes you at home with him at once, and if you have studied Phrenology, you are prepared for a good deal of quaint and covert humor, for you can perceive there is no want of Secretiveness. But listen, he has raised my tube, and will now speak for himself.

A SOIREE.

JEAN DICKSON'S ACCOUNT OF DR. YELDELL'S VISIT TO COLDSTREAM.

A. M. F.

'Heard ye ever o' Dr. Yeldell ? Ah ! that Dr. Yeldell ! Adverteezements cam' to the toon, that ane Dr. Yeldell

had been sent out by a Humane Society to cure a' diseases
by the agency of MAGNATIC BELTS, and sic was to be the
efficacy o' them, that the blin' were to see, the deaf to
hear, an' the diseased o' a' classes in the twirl o'
a thoomb to be restored to perfect health. Them that
ail'd were recommended to purchase as a universal cure;
and them that were weel were also recommended to purchase ane as an antidote for a' diseases that afflict human
nature.

'The day cam,' and wi' it cam' Dr. Yeldell, and wi'
Dr. Yeldell cam' the MAGNATIC BELTS. He promised
advice gratis, but that only for a few hours, as the
Society had ordeen'd he was to travel post, an' dispense
the blessings of health to the world, in as short a time as
possible : wie nae time to pit aff. The stage was opened an'
hunders cam' to ask advice. This they got for naething,
but paid for the medicines ; a kin' o' red an' white powder
he gave them snuff. Had ye heard the sneezing ! for a'
body snuff'd, an' a' body sneez'd till their een water'd an'
their luggs rang again. Then cam' the application o' the
BELT to the person affected.

' " Do you feel a difference ? " said the Doctor.

' " A great difference, Sir ! "

' " You all hear how he attests the efficacy of the only
true MAGNETIC BELTS ! He feels better already."

'Happy the person who had a guinea to gi' for a BELT !
Meeserable they whose poverty wadna' reach ane.

' Uncle Robbie bowt a BELT for a sair *Lunnie.*[*]

'I bowt a BELT for a weak back. Bet Cranstoun
bowt a BELT for a dizziness o' the head. Tam the barber
bowt a BELT for what he did na' ken. Auld Mrs. Air
bowt a BELT, but let on to naebody. Hunders o' folks
bowt BELTS. I dare to say a' body bowt belts ; but Pate
Sharp, naething wad persuade him to buy ane ; he said,
fules needed belting.

'Hame gaed the folks to sit with their BELTS on : an' aff
gaed Dr. Yeldell to belt the folk o' Wooler.

* Lunnie, *Lots.*

'We were a' sittin' pleas'd wi' the thought o' the gude we were to getten' frae our BELTS, when Mrs. Air sent up word that she had open'd hers, an' there was naething in it but a bit of whalebone cover'd wi' a wee shambo leather. My back gaed weak in a moment ; and Bet Cranstoun turned sae dizzy that she thought the vera hoose closed like a perie.

'Uncle Robbie rode aff to Birgham and sell'd his ane to John Wood ; but the honest man might as weel have worn a forged note, or a bad guinea in his pocket, to cure his complaint, as the BELT about his waist. John wore it a week afore he found oot the cheat, and was very thankfu' it did him nae ill.

'But O, that Pate Sharp ! it was a gliff to meet wi' him ! he was aye BELTIN' !

'"Weel," says he to me, "what ha' ye made' o' your gran' MAGNATIC BELT ?"

'"O man," quo' I, "there's naebody minds them noo, but yoursel' !"

'"It is a pity, woman," says he, wi' ane o' his dry girns, "it is a pity, indeed, for they ance possess'd great attraction."'

The following poem is by the same writer and is entitled

THE CONFESSION.

Eastward the town, not far from Coldstream bridge,
A straggling hamlet crowns the neighboring ridge ;
Scarce picturesque. irregular in form,
The houses stand like relics of a storm.
Some front the road, others with gable ends,
But show a shoulder to their facing friends.
Height and materials own a common law,
Clay-built the walls, and crown'd with roofs of straw.
Some few there are that court the sunny ray,
With gardens sloping down the Well-park brae ;
Stock'd with potatoes, cabbages, and peas,
Nestling from sight 'mong pear and apple trees,

With hedge-rows trim along the bottom seen,
That skirt the margin fair of Lennel green,
Where, bound by rocky brae and verdant mead,
Stream past the waters of the silver Tweed.
Such is the scene, such the secluded place,
Where dwells an unsophisticated race ;
No habits vicious revelling in their haunts,
Few their desires, and few their simple wants ;
All equal seem, with no distinctive rank,—
Their dwellings thrown like shells upon a bank.
'Midst heartfelt sympathies entwin'd and curl'd,
Unsmoothed by friction from the busy world ;
Their occupation—hark !—the busy loom,
Is heard to bounce in every cottage room.
This, with the river fishing, forms a trade,
At which they labor for their daily bread ;
Most join both occupations—net and stream,
Eked with the toil of shuttle, lay, and beam,
Gives bread for labor, means to pay each rent,
And brings its blessings—joy and sweet content.
This is Newtown ; who owns distinction there,
Must be of single heart, devote, sincere,
Whose thoughts and actions point the heav'nward road,
Some pious elder in the Church of God—
A dignity of worth and high renown,
Of glory greater than an earthly crown.
Their education simple, chaste, and pure,
The Bible first each memory holds secure ;
Josephus next their wondering minds engage,
Whose writings verify the sacred page :
While all theology of modern date,
Was drawn from ' Boston on the Four-fold State.
Such the condition, morals, habits, tone,
That round the small community was thrown :
A state, society may reckon rude,
Where emulation strains at being good.
Here once there liv'd a man of honest fame
And guileless heart—JOHN BROWN his humble name ;
He liv'd unshackled, free from married cares,
His sister Nancy rul'd the house affairs.
The cottage old was all he deign'd to crave
As resting-place from cradle to the grave ;
But thoughts refin'd, and hours of happy bliss,
Are often spent in dwelling mean as this.
The white-washed walls, the solid mud-laid floor,
The latch and string that ope'd the outer door ;
Four panes of glass serv'd all they had for light ;
The string drawn in, secur'd the bolt at night ;—

A simple plan, security to win,
To bar out robbers,—honest folk keep in.
But slight precaution serves the bolt to bind
Where anxious dread ne'er stirr'd the virtuous mind.
Such were the features of this homely nook ;
And like the cottage was the master's look ;
His whole demeanor placid, calm, and mild,
With less of art, than any sportive child,
Though struck in years, his feelings fresh and warm,
Objects by other passed, his mind would charm.
The song of birds, the spring-day's sunny beam,
The May-flies dancing o'er the rippling stream,
The bursting buds, the furze, whose yellow bloom,
First lur'd the wild bee with its soft perfume ;
Such blessings to his heart would access find,
And open up the fountains of his mind.
When, 'midst the foliage of the summer glade,
He cool'd his brow, beneath the plane tree's shade,
It to his mind proclaimed the mighty plan
And mercies manifold bestowed on man.
When whistling breezes bent the yellow grain,
And mellow autumn held her golden reign,
His thrilling thoughts again would rise to heav'n,
For all the good to sinful mortals giv'n.
When wintry snow-blasts scourg'd the barren earth,
And a clear fire blaz'd on his homely hearth,
In thankful contrast, this he ne'er forgot—
Deserving millions shar'd a harder lot.
Each season brought with it a gladdening joy,
A fragrance fresh that never knew alloy.
John, like a grindstone, each revolving year,
Knew little change, except the change of wear.
Though imperceptible, yet still he found
Each swift revolving year came swifter round,
But blights with fall and sad reverses come ;
And sad reverses mov'd this happy home.
From unknown causes, trade had felt decay,
'Midst years of drought the fishing fell away ;
While penury with cold and horrid dream,
Stalked in where peace and plenty reign'd supreme.
Hands now were idle, once so well employed,
And hearts cast down with hopes almost destroy'd.
Still 'midst privations dire, thanks found a vent
To Providence for every mercy sent.
' I know,' said John, ' that wings are gi'en to wealth ;
But there's a blessing still—we have our health ;
And while that treasure's left to you and me,
Our thankfu' hearts should show the gratefu' ee.

One thought distracts my mind—my bosom yearns,
To think on Geordie's seven helpless bairns ;
Nance, dinna greet, though they and I be poor,
Before ye'll want, I'll beg frae door to door.
A thought has struck my mind, 'mang ither cares,
I've credit in the toon at William Air's.
Though this reverse has dung me sair of late,
I'll no sit brooding langer owre our fate ;
Tied in a table claith, brac'd on my back,
I'll face the road wi' yard-wand and wi' pack ;
Look to the bairns, Nancy, help them through,
I will do something baith for them and you.
But why repine ? though cluds and darkness lower,
The brightest sunshine aft succeeds the shower.'

John tried the chapman's calling for a while,
Though much, I fear, with lack of winning guile,
To lure the matron from her household cares,
With tempting art, to buy his simple wares.
Free from dissimulation from his youth,
His very features bore the stamp of truth ;
But mind, however fram'd, can scarce submit
To bear the odium of a lack of wit,
Or ordinary want of business tact ;
The sequel to our tale reveals the fact.
John, from his travels, once returning late,
Had met his pastor at the church-yard gate ;
He eased his load, at once the staple drew,
Undid the bar to let the Doctor through ;
Retreating backward, made his homely bow,
Lifted his hat, and smooth'd his locks and brow.

'John,' said the good man—in his manner bland—
'I'm glad to meet you'—shook his proffer'd hand.
'How fares your business, John ? Is Nancy well, ?'
'Baith bravely, sir ; I hope your weel yoursel' !'
'Yes, John, I'm free from bodily complaint,
Although at times, my spirit waxes faint ;
For I have witnessed with a heartfelt shock,
The changed condition of my humble flock :
And yet my visits always tend to show
Much of contentment amidst want and woe.
I've gaz'd on struggles that might well beguile
From host angelic an approving smile,
Where pressed by penury, the spirit meek,
Shines through the glistening eye and pallid cheek
But faith, their anchor, on a rock is set,
And the frail vessel holds together yet.

Lash'd by the tempest, frequently we find
More moral courage in the chasten'd mind,
Than with the prosperous thousands that may sail,
Ere struck and shatter'd by misfortune's gale;
Though doom'd to struggle on and labor hard,
They find this recompense a just reward.
But John, the evils met, we know its form—
You set th' example 'midst the lowering storm ;
My only fear was, trading with its lures,
Would scarcely suit an honest heart like yours.
Some said, with minds more tender than the rest,
'The chapman's conscience had a stretch at best ; '
And hinted broadly at the reason why,
They were a race both known to cheat and lie ;
At once I saw this was a false alarm,
To nickname traffic by so rude a term,
And found it both my duty and my trust
To smooth those scruples down, however just.
I met the argument, and rul'd it such—
They only little took by asking much ;
A kind of license, long by custom made,
Well understood in every part of trade.'

'Weel, sir,' said John, 'for that my thanks are due,
Though what they said, I only ken 'tis true.
Wha tries the packman-trade will find, like me,
Folk dinna like to buy unless ye lee;
Sae, step by step, to make it mair complete,
The lee itsel' is faither to the cheat.
I own, at first 'twas unco hard to learn—
Want was at hame, and I had bread to earn ;
I counsell'd Nance aboot it—lang was laith,
But thankfu' are we noo—I dae them baith ! '

One piece of prose and another of poetry introduces us
to music,* and I offer the reader my

---

* One of my peculiarities is a passion for music, and, singular to say,
I hear it better than anything else. If I can find a place against
which to rest my head, I hear the softest notes. There is one thing,
however, for which I am unable to furnish a reason—However close I
press a musical box against my ear, I cannot distinguish one note from
another; but if I slightly press the box on the vertex of my head, I
hear every note distinctly. In playing the flute, I also distinguish
the finest and softest notes.

SONG OF AFFECTION.

BY THE AUTHOR OF 'THE AUTOBIOGRAPHY.'

With - out af - fec - tion what is earth? A

spring by win - ter shrouded, A flow'ret wither'd

in its birth, A day by storms o'er - clouded.

With - out af - fec - tion wealth be - comes A

guide to nought but madness! And hope that gilds more

hap - py homes Breathes but the deep - est sad - ness.

SONG OF AFFECTION.

Without affection, what is earth ?
  A spring by winter shrouded ;
A flow'ret withered in its birth ;
  A day by storms o'erclouded.
Without affection wealth becomes
  A guide to nought but madness ;
And hope, that gilds more happy homes,
  Breathes but the deepest sadness.

Affection makes the wintry day
  Than summer more excelling ;
It cheers the wand'rer on his way,
  It gilds the humblest dwelling ;
It heaps the lap of poverty
  With joys that riches know not,
And cheers the waste of misery
  With flowers that elsewhere grow not.

Affection ! 'tis the air of heaven—
  A foretaste of its pleasure !
The highest boon to angels given,
  To man, the richest treasure.
With this he fears not what may come ;
  His hope is ever glowing ;
He finds his happiness in home,
  A bliss of heaven's bestowing.

Without affection, lost to all
  The hopes that others cherish,
The wretch, forsaken, sees his fall,
  And knows that he must perish ;
He sees his doom, yet lacks the pow'r
  By which he might avoid it,
And stolid views the fatal hour
  Approach, that must decide it.

Then grant me, heav'n, the humblest cot
  Where love hath heap'd its treasure ;
And leave to other men the lot
  Of riches, and of pleasure.
I would not give one happy hour
  That mutual love has gilded,
For all the joy that wealth and power,
  Apart from love, has yielded.

One of my poets had quite a marvellous development
of Philoprogenitiveness, and I thought him the most

suitable person to illustrate the organ. He responded to
my request, and produced the following. It has, it is
true, since been printed, but it will bear repeating.

THE WONNERFU' WEAN.

Our wean's the most wonnerfu' wean ere I saw,
It wad tak me a lang simmer day to tell a'
His pranks frae the mornin' till night shuts his ee,
When he sleeps, like a peerie, 'tween faither an' me.
For in his quiet turns siccan questions he'll spier—
How the mune can stick up in the sky that's sae clear?
What gars the wun blaw, an' where frae comes the rain?
He's a perfect divert—he's a wonnerfu' wean.

Or wha was the first body's, faither? an' wha
Made the vera first snaw-show'r that ever did fa'?
An' wha made the first bird that sang on a tree?
An' the water that sooms a' the ships on the sea?
But after I've telt him as weel as I ken,
Again he begins wi' his wha' and his when?
An' he looks aye so watchfu' the while I explain,
He's as auld as the hills—he's an auld-farrant wean.

And folks wha hae skill o' the lumps o' the head,
Hint there's mair ways than toiling o' winnin' ane's bread;
How he'll be a rich man, an' hae men to work for him,
Wi' a kyte like a baillie's, shug, shuggin afore him;
Wi' a face like the mune, sober, sonsy, an' douse,
An' a back for its breadth like the side o' a house;
'Tweel I'm unco ta'en up wi't, they mak' a' sae plain,
He's just a town's talk—O a bye-ordnar wean!

I ne'er can forget sic a laugh as I gat
To see him put on faither's waistcoat an' hat,
An' the lang-leggit boots gaed sae far ower his knees,
The tap loops wi' his fingers he gripped wi' ease,   [ben—
Then he march'd thro' the house—he march'd but—he marc'd
So like mony mair o' our great little men,
That I leuch clean outright, for I couldna' contain,
He was sic a conceit—sic an ancient-like wean.

But mid a' his daffin sic kindness he shows,
That he's dear to my heart as the dew to the rose;
An' the unclouded hinnie beam aye in his ee,
Mak's him every day dearer an' dearer to me.
Though fortune be saucy, an' dirty, an' dour,
An' glooms through her fingers like hills through a shower,
When a body has got a bit bairn o' their ain,
He can cheer up their hearts—he's the wonnerfu' wean.

Of course, I do not propose to give the musical illustrations of my professional musicians, I will only say they were of a very high order.

I conclude my Soiree with the following touching stanzas.

THE SCOTTISH WIDOW'S LAMENT.

Afore the Lammas tide,
  Had dun'd the birken tree,
On a' our waterside,
  Nae wife was blest like me.
A kind gudeman, and twa
  Sweet bairns were round me here,
But they're a' ta'en awa'
  Sin' the fa' o' the year.

Sair trouble cam' our gate,
  And made me, when it cam',
A bird without a mate,
  A ewe without a lamb.
Our hay was yet to maw,
  And our corn was to shear,
When they a' dwin'd awa'
  In the fa' o' the year.

I dinna' look afield,
  For aye I trou I see.
The form that was a bield
  To my wee bairns and me.
But wind, and weet, and snaw,
  They never mair can fear,
Sin' they a' got the ca'
  In the fa' o' the year.

Aft on the hill at e'ens
  I see him 'mang the ferns,
The lover o' my teens,
  And father of my bairns ;
For there his plaid I saw,
  As gloamin' aye drew near,
But my a's now awa'
  Sin' the fa' o' the year.

Our bonnie rigs theirsel',
  Reca' my waes to mind ;
Our puir dumb beasties tell
  O' a' that I hae tyned.

For whae our wheat shall saw,
  And whae our sheep will shear,
Sin' my a' gaed awa'
  In the fa' o' the year?

My hearth is grawing cauld,
  And will be caulder still,
And sair, sair in the fauld
  Will be the winter's chill;
For peats were yet to ca',
  Our sheep they were to smear,
When my a' dwin'd awa'
  In the fa' o' the year.

I ettled whiles to spin,
  But wee, wee patterin' feet
Come rinnin' out an' in,
  An' then I just maun greet.
I ken its fancy a'
  And faster rows the tear
That my a' dwin'd awa'
  In the fa' o' the year.

Be kind, O heav'n abune!
  To ane so wae and lane,
An' tak' her hamewards sune,
  In pity o' her mane;
Lang ere the March winds blaw
  May she, far—far frae here,
Meet them a' that's awa'
  Sin' the fa' o' the year.

A. Y.

Some of my friends to whom I have shown my memoirs have suggested the omission of portions of my narrative which appear to savor too much of Love of Approbation. In reply to this I will quote a passage from the memoirs of the late Dr. Kitto, to whom a similar objection was made. He was totally deaf.

'The desire to be honorably known among men—the craving for approbation—the wish to do something which might preserve one's memory from the oblivion of the grave—and the reluctance to hurry on through this short life and disappear along with the infinite multitudes who

"Grow up and perish as the summer fly,
    Herds without name—no more remembered" :—

these things savor seemingly of that "love of fame" of which so much has been said or sung. I cannot say that this, as a motive to exertion, and to perseverance in the course which I had taken, did not find a way to my mind. I should not think it necessary to say anything in excuse for this : but as it has been suggested to me, that objection may be taken on this point, I may just mention that I am dealing with my subject historically, describing things as they occurred, or existed as facts ; and do not hold myself responsible for the rightness of every feeling described, or of every measure taken. Woe to the man of forty and odd who holds himself bound to justify all the feelings and actions of his youth.'

That my Love of Approbation and desire for distinction is great, the analysis of my character given in a former part of this work will testify, and without this feeling, when my disqualification of deafness is considered, I could not have pushed my way at all. With it, and with large Hope, I have ever been borne onwards in my individual walk in life. It has stimulated me in my pulpit as in my platform duties, and though constitutionally timid and retiring, for my Self-esteem is not large, I have yet been enabled to meet and overcome difficulty and even danger where men of sterner stuff have quailed. It has also assisted me to curb my fiery temper, has pre-served me and kept me from falling amid many grievous temptations. I conclude, therefore, this part of my narrative with a circumstance peculiarly gratifying to my Love of Approbation, and which happened at a time when I especially needed that approval.

I had unfortunately rendered myself responsible for two persons—one a relative by marriage, the others men of business. The failure of both rendered me liable, and I had the whole liabilities, which to me were great, to make good. By the advice of a person who had misinformed me of the wishes of my Swedenborgian friends, I resigned my situation.

My phrenological friends immediately held a meeting, and the result is contained in the following paragraph :

' PRESENTATION.

' On Tuesday Evening, April 20th, 1847, a few of Mr. ———'s phrenological friends met in the Thistle Tavern in honor of this distinguished teacher of the doctrines of Gall and Spurzhéim. Dr. Hunter, Professor of Anatomy, occupied the chair. After a few preliminary and loyal toasts, the chairman rose and made some highly complimentary remarks upon Mr. ———'s abilities as a lecturer and teacher of Phrenology, and begged to present him, in the name of his friends assembled, with a purse of gold, as a small but substantial token of their esteem for him as a phrenologist, and as an acknowledgment for his valuable exertions in the propagation of this eminently useful science. Mr. ——— made a very feeling and appropriate reply, and said that he looked upon this as the brightest era of his phrenological career, when, as he had been informed, such talented and eminent men as the brothers Combe, and Mr. Cox, the editor of the Phrenological Journal, and others of high standing in literature and science, had contributed to the very handsome testimonial with which he was now presented, and had thus acknowledged his humble services in the diffusion of truths which he deemed to be of the highest importance to man. Then followed an able address by the Rev. A. J. D'Orsay, of the High School of Glasgow, upon the light which phrenology threw upon education ; and in proof of this he referred to the treatise published fourteen years ago[*] by Mr. Simpson, of Edinburgh, which is confessedly founded upon the phrenological doctrines, and which contains views which have been subsequently taken up by Drs. Hook and Vaughan, and more recently by Dr. Taylor of this city. He then gave a very lucid explanation of

[*] Now twenty-four years since.

the present government scheme, which, although not quite
as phrenologists would wish, yet he believed it was the
best that could be adopted in the present state of the
national mind.   Several toasts were proposed by Drs.
Hunter and Weir, and the other gentlemen present, and
the enjoyment of the evening was kept up with great
spirit till about half-past eleven, when the meeting
separated.'—*Glasgow Paper.*

Eighth and Concluding Period:

FROM FIFTY-TWO YEARS OF AGE TO THE PRESENT TIME.
1848 TO 1857.

'It was the duty of every rational creature to devote whatever talents God has given him to useful purposes; to aim at the largest usefulness of which he might be capable; and that as far as I did this—and abstained from rendering the good gifts of God ministrant to the idle vanities of life, so far might I expect His blessing upon the studious pursuits to which I seemed inclined, and which had hitherto done me much honor.'—*Quoted by Dr. Kitto in his 'Lost Sense of Deafness.'*

'And I may here say, what I have never said before in the pulpit, that the views of the human mind, as they are revealed by Phrenology, are those views which have underlaid my whole ministry: and if I have had any success in bringing the truths of the gospel to bear practically upon the minds of men, any success in the vigorous application of truths to the wants of the human soul, where they are most needed, I owe it to the clearness which I have gained from the science; and I could not ask for the members of a church any better preparation for religious instruction, than to put them in possession of such a practical knowledge of the human soul as is given by Phrenology.'—*Rev. W. H. Beecher, of the United States, cited from the Daily News, August 21st,* 1855.

HAVING resigned my situation in Glasgow, it became necessary for me to seek employment in some new locality. I determined upon visiting some of the societies of Swedenborgians in England, who were without a minister, and who might be able to allow me a small salary. Among the societies so visited were Melbourne, in Derbyshire, and Ipswich, in Suffolk. I fixed upon the latter place, and the Society agreed to allow me thirty pounds per annum, but, owing to the emigration of many members, and other causes not necessary to be here mentioned, this small salary was soon withdrawn. I then accepted a call for three years at Melbourne, in Derbyshire, but did not remove my family. In these services, and occasional lectures, I have since passed my time.

My small medical practice in Glasgow I left in the possession of my eldest son ; but, alas ! his health was exceedingly fragile, and he was obliged to relinquish it. He died in Ipswich at the early age of twenty-four. My second son, who had served an apprenticeship to an eminent engineering firm in Glasgow, emigrated to Australia, where he has since risen to eminence, and now occupies the responsible position of Deputy Surveyor General of South Australia. My third son was pursuing his medical studies at Glasgow University, and, besides, held the position of apothecary in the Royal Lunatic Asylum at Gartnavel, near Glasgow. He passed his examinations with honor, commenced practice at Spofforth, in Yorkshire, and was making respectable progress in his profession, when he was seized with inflammation of the lungs, and he, too, has passed away at the early age of twenty-nine. My fourth son was finishing his apprenticeship as a chemist and druggist at one of the Apothecary Halls of Glasgow, and my youngest daughter was travelling with an artist and his family on the continent ; so there was but myself and my wife comparatively unprovided for. The death of my eldest son, shortly after I had left Glasgow, put me again in possession of medical fixtures, and I resolved to attempt the establishment of a small business in Ipswich. My infirmity of deafness, of course, prevented my undertaking regular practice, so with the munificent assistance of my phrenological friends, and some other aid from a friend, of whom I shall shortly have occasion to make honorable mention, I fitted up a small shop, and with the profits of that shop, as a chemist and druggist, I have contrived to eke out a bare subsistence. I have occasionally lectured to the members of the Mechanics' Institutions in Suffolk, on Anatomy and Phrenology. When I speak of Anatomy, I, of course, mean that important science so popularised as to be apprehensible to members of such institutions. All my subjects have been imbued with Phrenology; and I may here add, all my children were educated in accordance with its principles, and all have been successful in their various pursuits. My surviving family consists of two sons and two daughters, the oldest a widow, at present superintending a school for young ladies at Adelaide, in South Australia. Thus much of my family.

I passed three years, as I have said, at Melbourne, in Derbyshire. There I became acquainted with a gentleman who, during my stay, treated me with uniform kindness and consideration. He was a gentleman with a large and powerful brain, very benevolent, and a most devoted Swedenborgian. He related to me the manner in which he was led to look into the writings of Swedenborg, and he was one of fifty whom I could name who received the testimony of Swedenborg through a somewhat similar medium. Indeed, the Swedenborgians are fully persuaded that if a man can be brought to read Swedenborg for himself, there is small doubt of his becoming an admirer of him. The majority of people have heard of Swedenborg through the voice of calumny, and I am sorry to say, though there are many clergymen who are constant readers of his writings, and constant preachers of them too, there are very many more who represent him to their hearers as a miserable enthusiast, if not something worse, and thus are the people prevented from reading books, which, were they to study, they would find of immense benefit to their souls.

It may be here stated, that although there is a distinct and separate body of Swedenborgians, existing under the name of the New Jerusalem Church, there are very many more who do not think it expedient to separate from the various communions in which they have been educated. The Swedenborgians are an eminently catholic people. Their creed is very short and simple: to love the Lord above all things, and their neighbor as themselves. 'The enlarged charity which thinketh no evil, is, as it were,

the Corinthian capital of the [New Church] Christia▓
fane, the last beautiful flowing ornament at the summit
the pillar ' ; and ' Let your charity be known of all me▓
is their frequent motto, and I know many who make it th▓
constant practice.

But to return to my Melbourne friend. While tran▓
acting business in London, he was in the habit of dinin▓
with a party of commercial gentlemen at a daily ordinary
one of which gentlemen attracted his attention by th▓
urbanity of his manners, and his uniform quiet cheerful▓
ness ; but he could not learn his peculiar religious senti▓
ments. His name was Jones. My friend was then in
connection with the Baptists. On one occasion he
requested Mr. Jones to inform him what were his religious
opinions, and Mr. Jones responded to his inquiry by
putting into his hand the late Mr. Noble's Missionary
Lecture, delivered at Dover. He read, and re-read it,
and endorsed every truth it contained, and from that time
he united himself to the Swedenborgians,* and at his death
or, I should rather say, a short time previous to his death,
he gave to his friends at Melbourne money to build a
small chapel, having previously presented them with a
freehold piece of land on which to build it, and he also
gave the interest of £400 towards the support of a
minister. Besides this gentleman, I had the good will and
the kind attentions of the whole of the members, and
spent three years in the quiet performance of my Sabbath-
day duties, devoting the whole week to study. Here I
again improved myself in Greek, and published a revised
edition of the text of the Gospel according to Matthew,
to which I appended many notes. I also prefixed to it an

---

* This gentleman, then resident in London, having been requested to
procure a writing desk for an eminent literary gentleman, then and now
residing in Leicester, took the opportunity of enclosing within it a copy
of the same sermon, which was eagerly read, and its truths most cordially received ; and he, too, has become a most ardent receiver, as well as
a successful commentator, on many portions of Swedenborg's writings.
He is the author of a work, entitled, ' The Latter Day Glory,' proving the
divinity of our Lord Jesus Christ.

troductory Essay on 'Swedenborg and His Mission.' is work has been very favorably spoken of by some of most eminent literary authorities, while the Essay on Mission of Swedenborg has been extensively read, and gely circulated, both in this country and the United ates, as well as at the antipodes.

In the year 1852 the Suffolk newspapers recorded a ost extraordinary case of abstinence from food for many eeks, the subject being a young girl, aged fourteen ars, her name Elizabeth Squirrell. The parents belonged to the Baptist denomination, her grandfather having been a minister in that persuasion for many years.

The interest I took in phrenology induced in me an intense desire to visit this young girl, and investigate the case for myself, and at length, on one of my periodical visits to my family, I gratified it. Her parents then resided in the village of Shottisham, about sixteen miles from Ipswich.

I found her to be a most interesting child, as it respected physiognomical expression. The forehead was deep and square, the hair long, and flowing about her shoulders and neck ; the face by no means emaciated, as any person might have imagined, by long abstinence from food, but, on the contrary, presenting the appearance of comparative health, with a delicate roseate tint on the cheeks.

I stated to her parents that I had studied medicine, that I felt great interest in the extraordinary state of their daughter, and should feel obliged if they would allow me to examine her person. My request was at once granted, and in the presence of the child's mother, I commenced my investigations. She was quite deaf, was deficient in the sense of smell, labored under amaurosis in one eye, while the pupil of the other was covered with a thick film, so that she could neither hear, see, nor smell. The abdominal muscles were contracted ; there was also weakness of the spine, and the extremities were completely paralysed. On examination of the mouth I found the œsophagus much contracted, indeed, so small as scarcely to admit of a drop of water without danger of suffocation ;

solid food was therefore quite out of the question. A more helpless condition I never witnessed.

I now requested permission to measure and manipulate the head, which was also acceded to with equal readiness, and I subjoin the analysis which I drew from the measurement, and which has appeared in the Autobiography of Miss Squirrell, only premising that the predominating powers of her brain were, in 1852, Philoprogenitiveness, Adhesiveness, Love of Approbation, Veneration, Benevolence, Conscientiousness, Hope, Marvellousness, Ideality, [the two last are the predominating powers of the whole brain] and Individuality.

'A BRIEF SKETCH AND ANALYSIS OF THE ORGANISATION AND PROBABLE CHARACTER OF ELIZABETH SQUIRRELL, DRAWN FROM CEREBRAL DEVELOPMENT, BY —— —— ——.

'This is a brain of nearly average size, although the person is yet little more than fourteen years old. I can only speak of the organisation as it appeared to me on the 7th July, 1852.

'I was informed that she had been two years ill; for the last twelve months had taken very little solid food, and for the last nine weeks neither solid or fluid nourishment of any kind; she could neither hear, see, or smell, but her speech was perfect, and her feeling also acute. She conversed with me through a gutta percha tube (I being very deaf), and I returned answers to her by the aid of the deaf and dumb manual, making the respective signs on her left hand, and in this way enjoyed (nearly or perhaps more than) four hours' conversation with her. Her countenance was during this time indescribably beautiful and animated; her smile very sweet; her complexion as the blending of delicate carnation and lily; her lips a pale ruby. Her disease seemed to me to be enlargement of the heart, but during my conversation with her, her pulse was regular, about seventy-five beats to the minute. I was told her education had been of the ordinary village kind.

'I will now proceed to infer her probable character.

'Her affection to her parents must be great, and her respect and reverence for them may be inferred from the combined power of Philoprogenitiveness and Veneration. She has well developed Inhabitiveness, and I should infer will feel strong attachment to home and country; but, in consequence of Locality possessing greater functional energy than Inhabitiveness, she would, did circumstances permit, like to visit new scenes and new society. Her attachments are likely to be very devoted when formed, and whatever power she might possess, she would use to serve her friend. There seems to me to be an entire absence of selfishness in her character; her disposition is likely to be very kind, amiable, and sincere; she does not want for courage and determination; for her Combativeness, and Destructiveness, and Firmness are all fully marked. But this part of her organisation is so powerfully controlled by the moral and religious region, that it will only tend to a noble moral dignity and uprightness, and abhorrence of all that is evil, with, at the same time, a desire mildly to rebuke and correct it. The most perfect candor and openness is depicted in the countenance, and may be safely inferred from her large Conscientiousness. Her Secretiveness, which, though well marked and indicative of great prudence and circumspection, will yet be hallowed (so to speak) by the strong power of conscience.

'As a Phrenologist, I must say I would take her word for anything. There is, as already hinted, a perfect negation of self; she is one who will spiritually defer to the poetic apophthegm:

> "Man wants but little here below,
> Nor wants that little long."

The Acquisitiveness, which is barely average, seeks not worldly accumulations; and did she possess property, her

desire would be to dispense it, and to dispense it to those
to whom it would be most useful, for her generosity
would always be guided by her justice.   Her powers
of invention are great, and were she blessed with health,
notwithstanding that her senses of hearing and seeing
are lost, I should expect her to devise many expedients,
by which her great apparent deprivations might be miti-
gated.   She has much self-respect and moral dignity of
purpose ; everything of a mean, sensual, or selfish nature
will be abhorrent to her ; yet I think she is much under
the influence of Love of Approbation, has a strong desire
to please, and feels acutely everything which has a tendency
to disparage her in the estimation of others.   Her disposition is essentially kind.   She would suffer pain herself
with comparative equanimity, rather than those she loves
should be subjected to it.   It would afford her the highest
possible delight to be of use to others, and she would use
her powers of persuasion to turn her friends into the paths
of virtue.   She has the deepest reverence for the Supreme
Being—Veneration being one of the most powerfully
developed organs in her head ; and this, combined
with the other religious sentiments, all of which are
large, will induce a reverence for sacred subjects, and
lead her with confidence to a belief in the wonders of the
unseen world.   What she sees to be just, she will maintain with steady determination.   I believe her to be
utterly incapable of uttering a wilful falsehood ;   and
nothing is likely to give her more pain than hearing that
her word is questioned.   Whatever view others may take
of her descriptions of the eternal world, I am persuaded
that she fully believes she beholds them.   Her imaginative powers of Ideality and Marvellousness are, indeed,
the most powerfully developed organs in her brain ;
but I will not go to the extreme length of saying they are
affected by disease, though they may be.   Still, I am
convinced she sees what she describes ; and I feel assured
that the eye of the soul is as bright and penetrative as
that of the body is dark.   Her blindness seems to me to

arise, in part, from nervous causes. One eye is covered with cataract, the other with that nervous blindness termed, by medical men, amaurosis. Her descriptions of celestial scenery are exceedingly beautiful, but she generally concludes with "They are indescribable, or ineffable." She has great poetic ability, and her language is likely to be very polished, chaste, and elegant. Altogether the combination of Hope, Marvellousness, Ideality. Individuality, Order, Time, and Tune, presents such extraordinary power, that, were her health restored, would render her a poetess of surpassing beauty. Her perception is exceedingly minute and accurate. In argument she will be calm but very observant; and she would detect and expose, though with great gentleness, any sophistry or attempt to mislead her: she would unmask the most plausible hypocrite. Her ideas of form and proportion are very minute and precise; and were an artist with her to take down in words the descriptions she gives of celestial scenery, he might produce a picture such as the world rarely saw. Her ideas of Order are great, and she would like everything around her to be neat and even elegant, and arranged in the best taste; and I should think that she would give instructions that they should be so. Her large Individuality, Form, Size, Color, and Order, will induce a love of flowers; but, in truth, she loves all beautiful things. She has ability for the acquisition of almost every kind of knowledge; but, of course, the loss of sight and hearing must prevent such acquisitions. Her musical powers are beautifully developed, and she will sing with taste, pathos, and tenderness. No language (could she hear) would be difficult of attainment; and her powers of reasoning are likely to be of a high order. I have never seen so much beauty and sweetness, blended with so much meekness of wisdom, as in the case of this young girl. I am in no wise disposed to discredit her assertion, that she is in communication with angels. I believe I have been made better by being permitted to hold conversation with her, and by the confidence

32

with which she speaks of the bright and glorious spirit-land.'*

From the time of writing the above analysis, up to the present moment (1857), I have enjoyed much of the society of this young person, and have also received many highly interesting communications from her. The following letter furnishes a concise statement of her case, which she has permitted me to publish.

---

* The following alleged confirmation of Phrenology is taken from Mr. Spencer's 'Sight and Sounds'; it will doubtless be acceptable to those students of the science who have not seen it.

'In a recent interview with Dr. Leger, I had the gratification of witnessing the perfect manner in which this instrument (the magnetoscope) is found to vindicate the once ridiculed truths of Phrenology.

'It will be remembered that Phrenologists recognise in the brain *thirty-six* distinct organs. The pendulum of the magnetoscope has seven distinct motions, viz.:

'Elliptical (or oval) motion, normal rotation, inverse rotation, and the four different oscillations, N. and S.; E. and W.; N. E. and S. W.; and S. E. and N. W.

'To every organ in the head, is found to belong *one* of these seven motions of the pendulum, and that one only. So undeviating is this law, that Dr. Leger has been enabled to furnish in his book a printed list of the peculiar motion appurtenant to each organ. In phrenological examinations with the magnetoscope, the operator places his right middle finger, as usual, on the immoveable disc; his left upon the organ to be examined; the pendulum instantly begins to move in the direction found to belong to the organ; and the *degree* of motion to which it ultimately attains (measured by a number of concentric circles drawn on a card below it, and numbered), furnishes the amount of development to which the organ in question has reached. Thus in a quarter of an hour, by means of this uncourtier-like machine, with whose fidelity it is absolutely beyond the power of man to tamper, *you*, my friend, may glean a few hints, which, properly acted upon, may prove not unserviceable hereafter.

'It is obviously impossible to limit the important uses to which the magnetoscope may be turned. In cases of lunacy, the true state of the brain, and the mental tendencies, are clearly discoverable. Simulated madness is detected on the instant. Dr. Leger has made repeated visits to prisons, lunatic asylums, etc., and tested the powers of the instrument with startling success. In one of the former, out of one hundred prisoners submitted to his examination, he is understood to have fixed, in *ninety* cases, upon the peculiar character of crime attaching of each individual.'

... in she speaks of the bright and glorious spirit ...

From the time of writing the above analysis, up to the present moment (1867), I have enjoyed much of ... ... of this young person, as I have also received ... ... communication ... from her. The following letter furnishes a concise statement of her case, which she has permitted me to publish.

* The following alleged confirmation of Phrenology is taken from Mr. ... 's 'Sights and Sounds'; it will ... ... acceptable to the students of the science who have not seen it.

In a recent interview with Dr. Leger, I had the gratification of witnessing the perfect manner in which this instrument (the magnetoscope) is used to vindicate the science and mind truths of Phrenology.

It ... remembered that Phrenologists recognise in the brain ... ... distinct organs. The pendulum of the magnetoscope has s ... different motions viz.:

'Elliptical (or oval) motion, normal rotation, inverse rotation, and the four different oscillations, N. and S.; E. and W.; N. E. and S. W.; S. E. and N. W.

'To every organ in the head, is found to belong one of these motions of the pendulum, and that one only. So undeviating is ... law, ... Leger has been enabled to furnish in his book a printed ... ... motion appropriate to each organ. In phrenologising ... with the magnetoscope, the operator places his right ... ... upon the nnmoveable disc; his left upon the ... to ... the pendulum instantly begins to move in the direction ... ... to the organ; and the degree of motion to which ... ultimately attains (measured by a number of concentric circles traced on a card below it, and numbered), furnishes the amount of development to which the organ in question has reached. Thus in a quarter of an hour, by means of this uncourtier-like machine, with whose fidelity it is absolutely beyond the power of man to tamper, you may form ... give a few hints, which, properly acted upon may prove ... ... serviceable hereafter.

'It is utterly impossible to limit the important uses to which ... magnetoscope may be turned. In cases of ..., the true state of the ..., and the mental tendencies, are clearly discoverable. ... ... madness is detected on the instant. Dr. Leger was made ... visits to prisons, lunatic asylums, etc., and test ... the powers of ... instrument with startling success. In one of the ..., out of ... hundred prisoners submitted to his examination, he is understood ... have fixed ... cases, upon the peculiar character of crime of each individual.'

MISS M. E. SQUIRRELL.

[PAGE 499

' *October* 26th, 1855.

'My Very Dear Sir,

  ' In availing myself of the privilege of communicating with you on the more remarkable conditions of my affliction, I have chosen to narrate a few particulars, illustrative of those states, in the form of a *Letter*—firstly, because I cannot bring myself to address one whom I greatly esteem and love in a formal or documentary manner, and lastly, because there is naturally a greater freedom and versatility of subject allowed in the dictation of an epistle than in that of a detailed and especial *narrative*. And, besides, holding, as I do, in loving and constant remembrance, those visits of yours to my sick couch, at a time when my physical being was in a perpetual hovering between life and death, and again, when I was almost riven with sharp *mental* pain, I could not give to you any statement without making in it some few *personal* and *friendly* allusions.

  ' It is the sorrow-stricken who are ever the best receivers and retainers of friendship, for grief clears away the grosser part of the understanding, and opens up in the heart of its child a higher, a better appreciation of *the* true friend—and the sorrow-tried are never unfaithful. And it seems to me as if all who reflect on it must acknowledge in their hearts that it is unspeakable, a not-to-be-enough esteemed privilege, that they are now and then permitted a lesson in the school of adversity and sorrow—for where else the discipline so heaven-tending, so wholly subversive of evil, or so essentially love ? There are evils within us which only He who made us can remove ; we have spiritual wants which only He can know and supply ; and He regenerates us most and oftenest by *trials, various* indeed, as His own natural creations, but all and each exquisitely adapted to our individual minds and necessities. There is not a single trial in which we might not, if we would listen, hear the still small voice, saying, "It is I, be not afraid,"—not one in which we are not carried in the arms of the "Good Shepherd," and not, as our foolish hearts would often have us believe, *frowned* upon and *driven* onward into the better path.

'Sorrow enlightens, purifies, raises up, and more than all subdues the soul. And all whom sorrow blesses in this wise are blessed indeed, and are true sheep of that Good Shepherd, of whom, through all his journeying onward to the perennially divine, it was truly said, " He was a man of sorrows and acquainted with grief." I have not been able in every suffering to recognise the hand of a good Providence, or to say, " The Lord's will be done," but I am satisfied that this want of submission has always arisen solely out of non-reflection on the condition of my mind and heart, and from the naturally selfish feeling which prompts us always to shun *pain*, of whatever nature. When, however, I have been able to see that my trial was needed, that it was not given for the mere purpose of making me suffer, but only as *one* needful medicine for my ultimate *cure*, only as another step by which I could obtain a nearer view of the " Better Land," then have I indeed been enabled to bring out the psaltery and the harp for rejoicing, as well as to set a more vigilant watch over my heart, thereby bringing up its secret motives before me for judgment, and determining what evil my trials had been intended to remove, and what good principle to supply in its stead.

'But I fear you must think me rambling from my original purpose, which was to give you some account of my states, from the period in which you first became acquainted with me and interested in my condition. I will therefore begin from your first *visit* to me, which occurred in the July of 1852. I had then abstained entirely from food and drink for upwards of ten weeks. I well remembered your being introduced to me—it was as a Phrenologist of many years standing and of great knowledge of the science, as well as one who would gladly listen to any communication I might wish to make regarding my most peculiar condition of body, or of my yet more peculiar spiritual experiences. And here let me add, that I did not then, nor do I now, consider these experiences as incidental to, or at all depending upon, my *physical* position. I regard them as coming (as in fact every blessing does) directly from the Lord, and solely for the purpose of doing myself and those around me good— for giving us greater knowledge of the heavenly kingdom and its divine Lord, that we may be purer seekers after its glories, and better worshippers of the Eternal. Neither has this preception of the *interior* been granted as any especial mark of God's favor towards me, either to exempt me from any trial or suffering, necessary to the regeneration of us all, or raise me to any high place of special distinction among my fellow-beings—on the contrary, it is to humble me in my own esteem, by showing to me the beauty and bliss of those who love to do well continually, and to incite in me the greater love for and sympathy with those, who, like myself, are *desirous* of entering in at the "strait gate," but who find the way thereof often tortuous and difficult, by reason of the bias of their own natural unregenerate hearts, which is ever, more or less, a downward one.

'So soon as ever I appropriate a spiritual blessing to myself, to the exclusion of any one of the equally loved children of God, I render myself entirely useless as a medium or disciple of the truth, and render wholly void the blessing itself. This is the true view I have always taken on the matter of my intercourse with spirits, and which will, I trust, remain unaltered. But to return to your first visit to me.

'On receiving the above-named introduction, I felt a sudden vivid delight, and soon afterwards, an inclining to you, wholly unaccountable upon any hypothesis, save that of *spiritual, intuitive*, sympathy. Long before you had conversed an hour with me, it seemed to me that I could read your whole mind and heart, and, as you will remember, I unburdened to you my whole condition, as freely and as fearlessly as if I had known and walked and talked with you for a hundred years. A sense of your superiority intellectually was ever with me, but, it did not shut my lips, for I felt, how—I know not, that on every subject of vital importance, we had an instant, onelike, and entire sympathy.

'Physiognomy is all that ever Lavater asserted it to be, and we are all as great physiognomists as himself. We learn physiognomy from our cradle. We have an intuitive knowledge of it to begin with, and we go on increasing in the knowledge and use of it, as naturally as we breathe. *Intuitive* physiognomy, by which we are all instinctively impelled onward to, or driven backwards from, an individual, as his mental and moral beauties and deformities are disclosed to us in the expression of his features, or the tone of his voice, is to me of a far higher and more unerring kind than that which we know scientifically, and which is laboriously delivered to us, line upon line, and precept upon precept, without end. I had no external physiognomy to guide me in my apprehension of your character at that time—but I had that *most* unerring talisman of the truth, spiritual intuition—and which in your case gave me a consciousness of *united* and not of opposed spheres. All human souls make around them an atmosphere peculiar to and corresponding with themselves—and this sphere being clearly visible to our inward perception, we receive it as an indication of the conditions of all with whom we associate. So that *analogically*, arguing from *outward* to *inward*, from *natural* to *spiritual*, from body to soul, we have two means by which we may enter that strange temple, the human heart, and see to what we can best liken the mystic brotherhood of its thoughts and feelings. I certainly knew what your mind and heart were like before you had spoken many sentences to me—and *mine* must have been wholly a spiritually intuitive knowledge. At the time of this first visit of yours to me I was in a wonderfully *ethe*realized condition—physical and psychical. My body was scarcely more than a semi-transparent garment to my soul, and no impediment. Being fed with a food essentially *atmo-*

spheric, imbibing momently its finest and most subtile combinations, and not with the coarser aliment common to its ruder state, my whole physical being was made intensely clear and susceptive, and a thoroughfare for the continual entrance of the most exquisite mental enjoyments.

' During all the " fasting " I was mentally and spiritually in a state of the highest felicity. My refined habits of body, however, contributed neither to the beauty or the number of the *spiritual* objects I beheld. Because *they* were realities, and not the hallucinations of a mind made fanatical, through absorbed devotion, nor of a brain morbid from disease. I had but very little suffering of any kind during my abstinence, and never a single pain in the *head*. My brain was never even casually clouded, never for a moment listless, but was unceasingly clear, calm, and active. I had not the opportunity to grow recluse or fanatical, or to fancy myself set apart for the subjugation of the world to the spiritual I was learning ; for all but a third of my time was spent in conversing with my friends—and for *this* fact I ought to be truly thankful, for it kept me faithful to the only *really legitimate* sources of happiness and improvement in *this* life, *i.e.*, human affections and sympathies, human endeavors and experiences. It is not well to be solicitous of holding *visible* intercourse with the spiritual world. It is here on earth, while we live earthily, that our true sphere of action lies—we are to find the sources of our happiness and improvement in the *hearts* and *works* of our *fellow beings*—and if it please the Divine Parent that we *shall* have *views* of his inner kingdom before we leave the outer natural one, we are to communicate them simply and lovingly to all about us, *feeling* that they are only as a handful of beautiful flowerets, given by the dear Heavenly Father into the hands of *one*, to be equally distributed to *all* his children.

' We are not to fancy that an etherealized body and a spiritually perceptive mind make a gulf of separation between us and the common mass of mankind—and so soon as in our hearts they *do* this, we are surely and sadly out of our proper sphere.

'Very many who saw me during my abstinence looked upon me as a young fanatic, a devotee to some wild spiritual illusion, *supposing* that I considered myself an altogether supernatural person—that is, sustained by miracle, receiving especial spiritual benefits, and beyond the interchange of human affections. Now, absurd as it may seem, with all my intimate communing with them, I could not disabuse those people of their impressions concerning me. My external appearance was with them, for my refined habit of body, together with my blindness and deafness, made me look white and appear peculiar— and so they persisted in making me out to be *what I was not*, and in imputing to me sayings and statements, of which I was so far guiltless as to have never even *dreamed* of. Many of the absurdities put in circulation concerning me at that time, could hardly have been surpassed by those that were rumored of the imputed witches and wizards of the fifteenth and sixteenth centuries, when one had only to have an epileptic fit, walk in one's sleep, or write and communicate the contents of a *moderately* intelligent book, to be regarded as the colleague and machine of Satan, and delivered over to the tender mercies of an *infuriate mob*, who in turn gave him or her over to the stake, rack, or river.

'And *now*, even when I have merged again into the usual substantial and evident method of eating and drinking, and have (God be thanked for it!) the use of the blessed senses of sight and hearing, I *fear* I am looked upon by the majority, if not as an imposter, yet as a something little better—a being with no heart except for notoriety and a mind vitiated by spiritual illusions, and spiritual *pride*. But to return. During my abstinence, of course, the great mooted question with all was—how was I *sustained?* but to the supposition offered by many that it was probably by a miracle, I always returned the most unequivocal negation—because I trembled for the consequence of admitting such an hypothesis as that, when science ought to have done and could have accounted for it to the satisfaction of *all*. To me it was clear that I was sustained by the atmosphere surrounding me—the air. In it was food exactly suited to my attenuated and delicate state of body—and I lived and thrived on this food, until my body again resumed its former habit. At the time of my abstinence, the atmosphere was redolent with the odors of *innumerable* flowers and herbs (for it was the height of summer time) and so far from being "*starved*," I was literally *feasted*, and no more abstained *really* than the plant does, because we do not feed it with *meat* and *bread and cheese*, or give it wine to drink. I could not live on air now, because I am not in a condition of body to do so. Many secret atmospheric exhalations pass by me unheeded *now*, whereas in my abstinence they were all noted, and not a breeze went by, but it brought with it—something for me to eat. I delighted much during the "fasting" in *water*, not to drink, but to bathe my face, neck, and arms in. I have made as many as twenty of these ablutions in a day.

'I did not begin to see spirits with the commencement of my *abstinence*. I had been in the habit of seeing spiritual objects (with my inner eye, of course) from almost the first few days of my attack—and I had been ill two years before I abstained. The first time I saw a spirit, or into the inner world, was on the afternoon of the third Sunday of my illness, when I had a vision—but of such glorious beauty and truth that I can render but a faint reflection. I was only twelve years old when this vision occurred, and of course could not have been warned of any impending illumination from any abstract theory existing in my mind, regarding the subject of "angelic ministrations," or any kind of spiritual intercourse. Indeed, an hour before the vision, I had as little conception of what was awaiting me, as if I had never even heard of existence beyond the natural one.

' In health, though timid, I had never been a superstitious child—and as for the indulgence of any "spritual
chimeras," however prone my unbiassed taste might have
been to lead that way, my religious education had been
too stern, and too unmistakeably *practical*, to admit of any
such indulgence *long*.   I had always considered, however,
intercourse with spiritual beings *possible*—but this was
wholly an intuitive conviction.   I will describe to you,
my dear friend, as well as I am able, my first vision, and
you will then have some idea of the nature of *all* my
spirit-seeings.   I have always looked upon that *first*
vision as the truest and most beautiful of all the spiritual
scenes I have witnessed.   It was the first and last, and it
came to me when I was in agony of mind, consequent
on a dread of death, which lay on me continually, for many
days, like a horrid *nightmare*.   I thought I was a great
sinner, and that because of it God could not love me—
and I saw, whenever I thought of *dying*, hell with all its
horrors yawning at my feet.   I had in my VERY young
days especially, a very powerful and sensitive imagination
—and what I suffered during those few days I have
named ought to head a record of the tortures of the
Inquisitions of *Rome*.   Thankful, indeed, I am that I look
upon death as no such enemy now, but only as the "white
robed keeper of the gates of the heavenly city."   To how
many aching, unresisting hearts does he hourly unseal the
fountain of everlasting felicity.   Death has his *errors*,
but they are reserved for those of the black heart and
foul mind, and not for the child of a few brief summers,
to whom sin is little more than a *name*—to *such* he is
only as a welcoming angel.

' It is to him whose whole life has been a negation of
good, who has lived but to add shadow on shadow to his
dark soul, until he believes everything beyond it a lie—it
is to such a one as this that death comes armed with
terrors. He comes to the infant, like a scarcely perceptible
shadow on the beauty of a midsummer night—laying a
hand gently on its heart and breathing tenderly for a

moment over its brow—and the little life has gone—while
a few tears fall like dew over its head, a few flowrets are
strewn here and there about the clay, consecrating that to
be grave, while they *symbolise* the higher life of the life
which has gone. To such as this, death has no *terrors*.
To those a little more advanced in their pilgrimage, who
are just in the bloom of their noonday, death comes, a
little darker shadow, a little more mysterious, a little more
unwelcome guest—because he has to break the spell of a
few golden visions, a few bright hopes—but he does his
work so speedily and so lovingly that the troubled one has
soon found rest and peace, and hails death as his best
friend. To the aged one, death is but as a necessary
pilot through the stream which divides him from that *new
life* for which he has long wished to exchange his poor
time-worn one, and he looks for his coming impatiently—
and when death comes to *him* there will be no struggle :
a sigh of relief, as he bears the soul away, is all that
will be heard by those who listen without the "vail" *it*
has just entered beyond. Such is death—to the one, the
mysterious and awful—to the other, the beautiful, the
"white robed keeper of the gates of the heavenly city."

'On the afternoon of the day of my *vision* I lay on my
sick bed in unusual weariness and listlessness of body, but
with the fullest and deepest tranquillity of mind. I was *so*
peaceful that I could have fancied myself on the eve of an
everlasting rest. There was no gloom of doubt hanging
over my soul — no fear brooding within it — nothing
came between it and its glorified Redeemer. Everything
about me was tending to *enhance* that pure, celestial like
joy I was having. It was early evening, and within my
room the sun shone—not with his most vivid glory, but
with a gentle fervor. The part of the sky visible to me
from where I lay was of a stainless and deep blue—while
in sweet relief to its thrilling clearness and deep hue,
stood ranged, as far as my eye could look, a long line of
tall green poplars. By my bedside were seated my father
and eldest brother. I had held a long conversation with

my dear relatives, which had exhausted me, and I had
laid quite calm and still for many minutes in order to
recover myself. As I lay thus, unmoving, and with my
eyes closed, my friends, thinking me asleep, suspended their
talking, and throughout the apartment there was a dead
silence. I was, however, thoroughly awake. I was so far
from being in a dreamy unconsciousness as to be almost
preternaturally wakeful—and very painfully cognizant of
all surrounding objects and motions.

'While lying in this still and thoughtful position, my
attention was suddenly arrested by distant sounds, as if
of human voices employed in singing. These voices were
indescribably sweet and mellifluous, but carried to such
ethereal heights as to induce in the listener a "*tremulous
felicity of fear.*" I listened with my whole soul and sense
absorbed in what I heard. The singing ceased not for
many minutes; but when it did cease, such an excessive
brightness of light so filled and illumined the whole room
that my friends were hidden from me, and I only saw one
unspotted space of colorless brightness. A moment it
remained, full and fixed, and then it was *parted*, and
dissolved on either side of me, while I felt as if rapidly
ascending upward. Higher and higher I seemed to ascend,
but with full consciousness about me, until I felt as if
finally leaving the earth and winging my way to God,
and, with a mortal's fear, I shook with amazement and
apprehension. As I faltered, my ascent was stopped, and
I stood in a small enclosed space, with nothing remarkable
about it save one very large window, which fronted the
part in which I stood, and through which was pouring a
flood of brilliancy utterly overwhelming. I seemed to
wait here a great while, and feeling that I was in his
hands, I prayed to God that, if it were his will to show me
further of his mysteries, he would enable me to endure
their presence without sinking. Before I had ended
praying, I was aware of a presence beside my own in the
place, and looking up, I beheld a person of majestic mien
and stature gazing on me with looks of anxious and

troubled *tenderness.* He did not speak, until I asked fearfully and humbly, "Where am I? Tell, I beseech you, sir, to *where* am I brought?"

' "Ah! poor distrustful child," replied the spirit, "can you not trust in Him, when your God is pleased for an instant to separate you from your earthly friends and habitations? But, come with me, for I have much to show you, but if you *fear*, you cannot receive *any truth aright.*"

'I answered, "*I would have courage,*" and, taking me by the hand, he led me up a long and narrow ascent, on the top of which stood a large mansion. A house it certainly was, though unlike those we inhabit here. It appeared reared of the choicest and fairest marble, was *vast*, but most exquisitely proportioned, and altogether lovely and pure in appearance. An extensive portico was supported on either side by four colossal looking pillars, each of which were thickly studded with what seemed diamonds; the entire top of the portico was wreathed about with white blossoms. As we neared this lovely palace, I grew too happy for containment, and cried out with rapture to my guide, "Surely this is the house called 'Beautiful'; it must be angels *alone* who could dwell *here!*"

'On entering this lovely palace, to which my spiritual guide had brought me, a scene burst on my bewildered gaze which could not be depicted, so as to be realisable by any, except with the pen and spiritual knowledge of an angel. Of its solemn grandeur, mighty vastness, and surpassing glory and beauty, I can give no adequate description whatever—did I make the attempt, I should only be wasting words in *vain* speech.

'We were ushered into what seemed a temple, for an immense concourse of persons was assembled around as if for worship. I can give you no idea of the space occupied by this assemblage, or of the number of the assembled. The former appeared to be illimitable, and yet to be travelled over at a glance, while the latter was so great that the mind could not calculate upon it. The *persons*

510 THE AUTOBIOGRAPHY OF

of the assembled were all so perfect, pure, and beautiful,
that I felt assured I was in the midst of a company of
that heavenly host we read of in Scripture as "encamping
around those that fear the Lord." Every individual of
this vast congregation was arrayed in a garment of purest
white, while girdles of gold encircled their waist, crowns
of gold their heads, and each held a book and a stringed
instrument. On the latter, they with one accord performed, accompanying the music with their voices. *I*, a
poor frail child of earth, introduced into such hitherto
unimagined glories and felicities, stood still, speechless
and afraid, not daring to utter a word. My guide saw
my amazement, and, taking me aside, spoke with me
as follows : "You are afraid," said he in tones of great
serenity.

'I dared not avoid a reply, and said : "Forgive me,
you are a *spirit*—perhaps, indeed, an angel—and such
scenes as these just witnessed are *your* daily meat and
drink. With me it is otherwise. *I* am a poor earth-child,
accustomed to grovel among things tainted and worthless,
until my soul has almost forfeited its birthright—immortality. Before the glories of the Lord's spiritual kingdom
I stand amazed and dumb, while all my imperfections
stare me in the face and overwhelm me with confusion."

'To this my guide replied : "You ought, as a
Christian, to possess unlimited confidence in the good
providence of God, knowing that all things *shall* work
together for good to those that fear him. Not even a
sparrow falls to the ground without our heavenly Father's
notice, and he has numbered the very hairs of our heads.
But," added he, "come with me, we must give you
spiritual *instruction*, and so help you to *gain* the necessary
confidence in our Lord."

'And again taking my hand, this spirit led me into an
apartment, small, but the perfection of beauty and order.
In this room a few persons were convened, bearing a close
resemblance to those of the larger congregation. In the
centre of this group, and in the attitude of one who teaches,

ood a man of most solemn and heavenly bearing. Before
im lay an open book, apparently the Word of God ; his
ght hand reverently grasped its leaves, while at intervals
e stooped and touched it affectionately with his lips. The
reacher (for such he evidently was) was descanting on
ıe love and wisdom of God, as seen in the creation and
reservation, and then in the redemption and regenera-
ıon of man.

' I listened breathlessly, for the words seemed as if spoken
xclusively to *me*. I listened, and presently my terror
ıad fled from me — my fears had departed — and my
ıssurance was full and unbroken. Presently the preacher
ınded his discourse, the assembly dispersed, and again
:aking my hand, my guide led me forth into a place or
state, even more grand and glorious than I had yet seen.
Here were mingled young and old, all uniting in perfect
peace and harmony, although variously employed. Some
were formed into groups where they sang and read together
from the Word of God ; some were dictating spiritual
exercises and lessons, while others were instructing in the
way and works of God, little children. Every individual
was *beautiful*, not one deformity of face or form was
distinguishable, of all the myriads that were here convened
together. Every face was a sure index of its possessor,
and reflected back nothing but the light of a pure,
holy, and loving soul. None were unemployed ; all
were in happy, joyous activity. There were no bick-
erings, no angry contentions ; *here* each acted towards
the other with perfect charity and love, and with
all meekness, patience, and gentleness. Wisdom and
intelligence, in their brightest arrays, beamed from every
eye, and sat on every brow. There was no subject of a
moral, spiritual, or celestial interest, of which they could
not converse, and with the fullest understanding of what
they uttered. I can still remember the *substance* of what
they spoke—but to reproduce it in their own language
would be beyond a mortal's power. While I waited in this
heavenly abode, a company of spirits came around me,

and conversing gently with me, gave me much spiritual counsel and even temporal advice. They told me the nature of my illness, and what would be the best treatment for me to receive. They assured me of many strange conditions of body into which I should relapse, and of much persecutions and contempt, of which I should become the subject. But added they, "*Be assured that everything will ultimately tend to the glory of God, and to the progress of your own regeneration.*"

' This, my dear friend, is the plainest reflection I am able to give you of a spiritual scene, which was in itself too beautiful for any description to do it justice, and too spiritually hidden in some of its parts to be revealed by any other than a dweller in the eternal world. This first vision was the type of all succeeding ones—each subsequent spiritual " view " has borne some correspondence to this *first*. This first vision formed a *centre-planet* for my spiritual experience, around which every diversity of it has revolved in order—reflecting back again in some degree the brightness of its truth and beauty. This *first* vision made an epoch in my little life, the greatest it has ever known. *From it* I date my love for spiritual and elevated things, and the light which makes *these clear*. Ever since it occurred, I have had a conscious love for God in my heart, which neither *pain*, nor *persecution*, nor *sorrow*, has ever been able to remove. If I have sometimes murmured at God's dispensations to me, I have never in my heart doubted him, nor ever ceased to love him, and when my madness has been past, my love has always shone out more fervently and bright. Since that vision I have always realised the whole spirit of that statement of the apostle's, " God is love." He has always been essentially love to me.

' And I have been enabled, since that period to appreciate *better* everything which God has made—seeing that nothing exists without *his* especial support, and that all he has created bears resemblance in some sense to *himself*. When the Lord in his mercy opened my eyes to a view of his spiritual kingdom, he opened my heart also to the reception of a few truths, which are to me so blessed that life—*mere being*—is in comparison to them as nothing. They are as the life-blood of my soul. They give me my hope of *immortality*, and tell me how to make myself meet for its inheritance. I find them in the blessed Word of life, and they are faintly reflected in my heart, and, in the hearts of all about me. Every soul thirsts for them—and they are to be found by any simple seeker after them—without the intervention of either creed or commentary. What a blessed thing it is that we can be good here, and happy hereafter, if we will. God has given us enough of love, and truth, and beauty *here* to make us blessed citizens of *this present life*—and in his word he has given us a key for the entrance into *both* worlds—and a sure guide through all the intricacies of each. And then, God loves us all, equally and ever-lastingly. He keeps us in existence by his love, and he never looks on us but in love.

'But, my dear friend, it is not good for me to continue to you a repetition of those truths with which your heart is so familiar, and of which I know too your life forms daily an illustration—and yet when the heart gets warmed with the thought of spiritual things, who can refrain?

'I *will* now, however, bid you a brief adieu. I need not particularize the events of the last two years of my life, you are in part familiar with them. It is sufficient to say that my bodily condition is not only ameliorated, but is made permanently better—that I am now able to see, hear, and take food, and am only wanting the ability to stand and walk to make me comparatively *well.* I am *altogether* physically better. Spiritually I am happy. Of *mental* food, I have, through the kindness of friends, if in no other way, a plentiful supply. I have, indeed, *much* to be thankful for; and, dear Sir, I hope I may with truth subscribe myself,

Your thankful and affectionate young friend,

E. M. SQUIRRELL.

33

I forbear to make any comments on this letter, further than to say that Miss Squirrell ·has taken the most correct view of her own case, and her statement is fully borne out by eminent medical authorities. Besides the numerous authentic cases quoted in her Autobiography, by 'One of the Watchers,' the following cases of *adipsia*, or those who have abstained from food for long periods of time, are taken from Martin Schurig, 'Chylologia Historico-Medica,' cap. iv. 'De Asitia et Adipsia,' p. 175—204 ; 4to., Dresdæ, 1725.

'Christopher Mich. Adolphus relates the case of a Silesian girl who took no food for nine months.* Alexander Benedictus, of a person at Venice who took no food for forty-six days.† Johannes Matthaeus Hessus mentions several similar cases from other authors ; for example, of a native of Almeria who neither ate nor drank for four months : of one Margareta Rhodia who took no sustenance for more than sixteen months: of a young female, a native of Germany, with whom this was the case for two years.‡ Johannes Wier gives an account of Henricus ab Hasselt, who abstained on two occasions for forty days.§ Paulus Lentulus has published a little treatise respecting one Apolonia Schreiera, who abstained for eighteen years ; ‖ and Josephus Quercetanus ¶ and Gregorius Horstius ** have also made mention of the same person. Another instance is that of a girl at Spire, Margareta Seyfritia by name, whom Ferdinand, king of the Romans, in 1542, consigned for the purpose of observation to the charge of his own physician and another person, both extremely trustworthy men ; and Gerardus Bucoldianus, physician to the king, and a witness difficult to deceive,

* 'Ephemerid. Acad. Nat. Curios., cent.' vii, and viii, obs. 34, p. 81,82; Norib, 1719.
† ' De Re Medicâ,' lib. xi., cap. X, p. 204; fol. Basil, 1649.
‡ ' Quæstion. Medic.,' quæst. v, p. 26 ; 12o. Franc., 1503.
§ ' De Comment Jejun.' oper., p. 761 ; 4to., Amstelod, 1660.
‖ ' Histor. Admirand. de prodigiosâ Apollon. Schreieræ Inediâ.
¶ ' Diætet. Polyhistor.,' sect. ii, cap. iv., p. 173-175 ; 8vo., Lips., 1607.
** ' Instit. Medic., disput. iii.. op., tom. i , p. 141; also tom. ii., lib. ii., obs. 29, p. 97 ; and lib. xi., obs. 1, p. 519; fol., Norimb., 1660.

declares that this girl took no food from 1530 to 1540, and [again] after this, not for three years.* Johannes Langius also mentions the case.† Guil. Fabricius, Hildanus, gives an account of a girl at Cologne who abstained for three years ; ‡ and of a girl at Meurs, named Eva von gen End, *alias* Eva Flegen, who abstained for sixteen years. § Johannes Wolffius, of a girl living near the town of Commercy, in the district of Toul, with whom this was the case for ten months ; ‖ and Petrus Gregorius relates that the asitia of this patient lasted for twelve years.¶ Franciscus Citesius relates the case of a girl (Johanna Balam) living at Confolent, who remained without food for fourteen years.** See also the account of brother Nicolas, a hermit, who did the like for nineteen years and six months.†† Of a boy in Brunswick, who lived in this way for four years, as mentioned by Gregorius Horstius.‡‡ Of a girl at Halberstadt, who lived for ten years without food, [although not without drink,] as stated by Daniel Sennertus.§§ Of a Norwegian girl who abstained for [nearly] a whole year [only eating and drinking when compelled to do so,] as stated by Caspar Bartholin. ‖‖ Of [one Esther Johanna], a Swedish maid, born in the village of Norre Oby, in Scania [Schonen], who abstained from food for ten years, and from drink for eight, and whose case was carefully watched by many ; and is treated of by Joh. Jac. Doebelius,¶¶ Professor of Medicine in the University of Lund, and by Jasper Swedberg, Doctor of Theology and Bishop of Scara.'

* 'De Puella quæ sine Cibo et Potu Vitam transigit.'
† 'Mediciu. Epistol.' lib. ii., epist. xxvii., p. 604 ; Hanov., 1605.
‡ 'Obs. Chirurg.' cent. ii, obs. 40, p. 116 ; Opera, Franc., 1646.
§ 'Ibid,' cent. v, obs. 33, p. 413.
‖ 'Lect. Memorabil.,' ceut. ix, p. 218 ; Lauingæ, 1600.
¶ 'Syntax. Art. mir., tom. i., lib. xxxv., c. x., p. 399 ; 8vo., Colon., 1610.
** 'Abstinens Confolentanea.'
†† 'Philosophia Mystica,' p. 100 ; 4to., Neustadt, 1618.
‡‡ 'Opera,' lib. xi., obs. 1, p. 519 ; fol., Norimb., 1660.
§§ 'Medicina Practica,' lib. iii., part i., sect. i., cap. ii., p. 385 ; op., tom. iv. ; Lugdun., 1676.
‖‖ 'Act. Med. et Philos. Hafn.,' vol. i., obs. 139, p. 292, 293 ; an. 1671, 1672.
¶¶ 'Historia Inediæ diuturnæ Estheræ.'

In August, 1853, I attended the funeral of the Rev. Samuel Noble, of Cross Street, Hatton Garden, London, of whom mention has been made in a former part of my memoirs.

In point of learning he was perhaps the most able minister the Swedenborgians have yet possessed. He was a good Hebraist and Grecian, as well as a respectable Latin scholar. In person he was of the middle height, his head was large, his forehead deep and square ; the superciliary ridge was well defined but not prominent ; his Individuality was decidedly large—and the other observing powers fully developed. His Language was rather large, although the eye, by the fulness of which Phrenologists' decide upon the power possessed by the organ of Language, was deeply imbedded in the socket. The upper part of the forehead also was prominent, giving excellent powers of reflection, moderate Wit, but large Causality, and extra large Comparison. The coronal arch was moderately high and well defined, Benevolence, Marvellousness, and Ideality were rather large ; Veneration was essentially large, and Hope on either side was equally prominent. The vertex of the head towered up, giving great power to Firmness, Conscientiousness, and Self-esteem ; towards the parietal bones there was a slight declination, and Cautiousness and Secretiveness, though fully developed, were not possessed of the same functional energy as the other sentiments. There was no deficiency in Combativeness ; but the rest of the posterior region was only moderately developed. The greatest amount of cerebral matter lay distributed in the anterior and sincipital regions. The constitutional temperament was a compound of Lymphatic, Bilious, and Nervous, the two former having the predominance.

As a preacher, Mr. Noble was not among the most attractive, but the excellence of the matter made ample amends for the attractive graces which distinguish more florid but less solid preachers. A celebrated Editor who attended the opening services of the Chapel in Cross Street, in 1828, after a little playful satire on the person and abilities of the reader of the Liturgy— thus alludes to the preacher (Mr. Noble)* :—

'At the conclusion of the service, the preacher, a different individual from the reader, ascended the pulpit ; dressed, like the other, in a white surplice ; for though the church "has not made the use of a particular dress obligatory on its ministers," it has "determined that white robes, especially of linen, are significant of genuine truths, grounded in goodness." His text was, "I am the Lord thy God," etc. His tones were not prepossessing, for he had either some peculiarity in the nasal organ, or an uncommon quantity of "the prest nostril, spectacle bestrid." But his manner was grave and calm ; which is sufficient for uttering the truth. The sermon was not *extempore* but read. The exordium was majestic, temperate, and firm—the best adapted that can be imagined for a man professing to stand between what he conceives to be the errors of a powerful Establishment on the one hand, and the equal errors of its opponents on the other. It is an extraordinary thing—the more the pity—to hear a man in a pulpit talk strong sense for a mortal hour, and to wile away that hour to minutes. The silence among the audience, was like nothing but the deep attention that used in some parts to wait on Mrs. Siddons. "A greater than Irving was there." '

Mr. Noble had his faults, as where is the man who has not ? One of these was an unbending obstinacy, the result, I believe, equally of large Firmness and Conscientiousness. Once convinced that the course he was pursuing was just, nothing could induce him to swerve from it ; and, in thus proceeding, some of his most attached friends were alienated from him.

After all, it is perhaps difficult to determine whether this obstinacy was more the result of large Firmness or Conscientiousness. His great Firmness was evidenced by

* I believe it was Fonblanque the Editor of the 'Examiner,' newspaper then one of the most caustic writers of the public press.

the unflinching fortitude with which he submitted to several painful operations on the eye for the removal of cataract, although upwards of *seventy years* of age at the time. All these operations proved unsuccessful.

Often have I wished that I could induce all my friends to study Phrenology. How differently would they then form their judgment. They would be enabled to see the cause of constitutional defect, and so judge more leniently, or at all events more righteously, of their brethren, and be able to make allowance for peculiarities of temper and habit. I believe that Mr. Noble's extreme and unbending Firmness was aided and increased by his Conscientiousness. He believed he was acting justly, and his high sense of integrity would not allow him, even at the solicitation of his most devoted and attached friends, to swerve from it. His was a mind that would say, 'Perish friendship, if truth is to be sacrificed; better be a thorn in the side of my friend than to be merely his echo. No. "Let justice be done though the heavens should fall." '

He departed this life in August, 1853. His remains were interred in the Cemetery of Highgate, where a marble monument, in the form of a Greek tomb, with a suitable inscription, was erected to his memory by the joint subscriptions of the great body of Swedenborgians.

Mr. Noble is principally known by his publications. Among these is his 'Plenary Inspiration of the Scriptures Asserted,' a most elaborate and magnificent work, which has completely taken the ground from beneath the feet of deists and sceptics in general, and established the inspiration of the Word of God on an impregnable basis. It abounds in examples and proofs of the most felicitous and irrefragable kind, and has served as a model for all succeeding writers on the inspiration of the Scriptures in the Swedenborgian Church.

Another work which has been even more attractive and popular, is his 'Appeal in Behalf of the Views of the Eternal World and State,' etc., with answers to the different objections which have been brought against the Swedenborgian views of doctrine. While the former work has served as a guide or assistant in deciphering some of the most intricate passages of Scripture, the latter has proved a complete armory of defensive weapons. It has never been successfully assailed. On the death of Mr. Noble it was suggested that the publication of this work at a nominal cost, would be the most suitable monument to his memory; accordingly the Swedenborgians generally subscribed, and the work has been stereotyped and published at a price which has caused it to sell by thousands. A more useful book has scarcely ever emanated from the press; it is equally interesting and instructive to the great body of Christians, as to the body in whose defence it was specially written: it proves most convincingly the existence of a future state, and meets with perfect candor and charity all objections brought against it. With this book of defence the Swedenborgians fear no opponents that may assail them.

In 1853, I concluded my temporary engagement at Melbourne, and returned to Ipswich, where I have continued to reside, rendering a gratuitous service to the small Society of Swedenborgians who meet for worship in that town.

In 1854, I lost by his removal to the spiritual world, my dearest friend, in the person of the late Mr. Joseph Senior, of whom I have made slight mention at the commencement of the Seventh period of my history (p. 271), reserving for the conclusion of my narrative a more extended notice of him. I have already alluded to the slight assistance I rendered him in the publication of his letter to the Rev. David James, of Aldmonbury church, near Huddersfield; but this assistance led to a more frequent and extended employment of my pen, and for which he always remunerated me. Connected

with the place of worship at Dalton, near Huddersfield,
of which he was the owner, there was a Sunday School
of between two and three hundred children, whom
he was anxious of having instructed in the principles
of religious truth, and for whose instruction he purchased
a large quantity of elementary works. There was at
that time no Sunday book which entirely accorded with
his views, or embraced the various subjects which he
thought necessary for aiding the pupil in acquiring and
understanding scriptural history. The Bible was at
all times near, but the pupils, who were mostly engaged
at the public works during the week, could not be supposed to understand all its allusions and comparisons,
and even many among the teachers were but ill-informed
respecting oriental customs and manners, with which the
parables and discourses of our Saviour abounded. My
friend, therefore, applied to me to write or compile a work
which should serve both teachers and pupils as a Biblical
Assistant. I at once entered upon the labor, and in
1841 produced a work, partly original, and partly
selected. It consisted of eight sections, which included
a treatise on Scriptural Analogies—a chapter on Scriptural Natural History — a section of Sacred Poetry—
another of Experimental Piety, a description of the
Human Body, and a short Dictionary of Correspondence.
Besides paying me for the composition of the work, he was
a subscriber for fifty copies. It was generally approved,
and was soon out of print. After this he employed me to
write a series of children's books, paying for the printing
of some, and always remunerating me for their composition. He next desired to see a series of tracts written
in popular and simple language, suitable for general
distribution among all classes of Christians. This originated the 'Glasgow Series of Christian Tracts'; many
of these were sermons, modified for general perusal,
which had been preached by me in various parts of
Scotland, and a few were by the Rev. W. Mason.
Among which latter were — Religious Instruction for

Youth—three Tracts on the Blood of Christ—one on the
Nature and Uses of Prayer—one in answer to the question, ' What is Conscience ?'—and one on the Will and the
Understanding. Mr Senior also paid for the printing
of the ' Young Christian's Earliest Friend ' ; (a series of
lectures to Children,) and the ' Manual of Piety for the
Young,' both prepared by the Rev. W. Mason, employing
me to see them through the press.

In the year 1844, my friend was very desirous of
seeing a book of family devotion, suitable for the great
body of the Swedenborgians, and to comprehend Morning
and Evening prayers for every day in the year—Illustrations of Scripture for the same period, and Psalms and
Hymns—in short, a complete book of Family Worship
for an entire year. He begged me to undertake this
work. I acceded to his request, and entered on its
composition, sending portions regularly every month.
These portions he at once adopted in the family worship
of his own house every morning and evening. The composition of this work, which extended to 730 prayers,
the same number of illustrations of Scripture, and Psalms
and Hymns, occupied nearly all my leisure time for a
period of seven years. At length, much to his satisfaction, I completed it, and he had the whole in his possession ; but anxious that it should be copied and bound
in volumes, he sent the whole to me for that purpose.
I had completed and sent to him the second volume,*
and had entered upon the third, when he was called to his
reward in the heavens : had he lived to see its completion,
I have no doubt he would have settled a small annuity
on me for my life ; of this I had his promise.

In person Mr. Senior was a tall and handsomely formed
man. His head was of medium size ; the temperament
was Nervous-Sanguine. The forehead was deep and
broad, and towards the lateral parts was well rounded.
His aspect in the coronal region was high and partially
bald. All the religious and moral sentiments were beau-

The work extended to seven volumes.

tifully and evenly developed. He was deficient in Firmness, and but moderately developed in Self-esteem, but his
Love of Approbation was decidedly large. His organs
of Time and Tune were developed in great proportion, and
to these he added a fine voice. He was one of the sweetest
singers I ever heard, and in his early life was an
excellent performer on the pianoforte and organ. In
my intercourse with the world I never met with a more
noble and princely-minded man. To me, he was the
'friend that stuck closer than a brother.' He was a
man of warm passions, and frequently expressed himself
severely, but he had scarcely given vent to a hasty
ebullition of temper, when he repented and made apology
to those whose feelings he had hurt. He was gentle and
condescending to his inferiors, ever ready to lend a
helping hand to the deserving. I feel sure that hundreds
of pounds have passed from his hands to the poor of the
neighborhood in which he lived, and when he did alms
after this manner he was careful not to let his left hand
know what the right accomplished. In his person and
in his house he was very orderly, neat, and precise. He
was modest and unassuming in his deportment, and
though possessed of good abilities, always preferred others
to himself. He was very tolerant in his religious principles, and provided good could be done, through whatever medium, his purse was always open to assist. A
more just and honorable man I do not think ever existed.
Towards the conclusion of his life he had two or three
attacks of paralysis, which impaired both his speech
and his memory. I did not see him during his last
illness, but his end was peaceful and happy.

He left a handsome property, consisting of a church,
schools, and two dwelling houses, to the Swedenborgian
Conference.

Farewell, my friend—my brother ! 'Would to God I
had died for thee.'

My narrative is now brought to a close. But, in taking leave of the reader, I cannot forbear recommending to his attention and perusal a work which has been a principal source of consolation to me through all my trials, and has supported me under the most severe afflictions : that work is a 'Treatise on the Divine Providence,' published by the Swedenborg Society. That work to me has been more than a worldly wealth could purchase. It has brought me to feel that 'God's providence is my inheritance' ; and I conclude my narrative by quoting from a tract on the Divine Providence published by me some fourteen years since :—

'It is a mark of divine wisdom, that it has differently constituted the human mind, and fitted it for the multifarious uses necessary to carry on the government of the world, and promote the true happiness of its inhabitants. As various medicines are required for the cure of various diseases in the human body, so are various dispensations required, as the medicines of the soul, to remove the diseases of sin. All men are not mentally constituted to possess wealth without injury to their own state ; for although some may employ it for the glory of God, and the benefit of their fellow creatures, it would in others be sure to engender pride only, and instead of softening the heart by the opportunity of assisting the needy, it might only serve to harden it the more, till it became " as hard as the nether mill-stone." Hence our Lord describes it to be HARD (no doubt, in consequence of the fallen principles of our nature) for those who have riches to enter into the kingdom of heaven ; the reason is, because it is hard for those who have riches to avoid TRUSTING in them, and being *proud* of them ; and he who trusts in riches makes mammon his God, for he is guilty of covetousness, and covetousness is idolatry. " If any man love the world, the love of the Father is not in him."

'Whatever is bestowed upon us here, is given to promote our fitness for eternity. It is not our enjoyment of a few years of comfort in this world to which our Heavenly

Father looks as an end ; but our attainment of the solid and lasting joys of eternity.

'There can be no preparation for eternal life unless the evil which is in man is subdued ; and, as a consequence, the affections of goodness be developed or implanted in their place ; while the perceptions of truth are rendered more clear, by deriving new vital energy from the union of truth and love : that course of Providence which would check evil in one man might foster it another ; that which might fill one man with gratitude to the Supreme, might tend in another to induce forgetfulness of God ; and hence it is that our Heavenly Father, knowing the heart of man, permits affliction and suffering to be the portion of one, while he bestows competence, or even wealth, upon another. The end in view we may safely presume is the same in both cases—namely, the subjugation of evil, and the implantation of good, that the mind or soul may be fitted for that kingdom, where the rich and the poor are equal, provided their attainments in holiness are equal.

'Dispositions vary. Some men may be subdued only by kindness and affection ; these will melt with gratitude whenever they think of the tenderness of the divine love. Others can only be conquered by the strong arm of power : these require "stripes," some few, some many ; but the hand of goodness invariably wields the rod! Among those who may be led by kindness, there are some, however, whose easiness and pliability of temper is such, that they would (were they possessed of wealth) become the victims of even the slightest temptations to depart from rectitude, provided only those temptations were glossed over with an appearance of friendship. Hence we may suppose that the Lord wisely withholds from such persons that wealth which would only prove injurious to them ; while, on the other hand, he permits them to be afflicted, still, however, sustaining and comforting them when they trust in him, that so he may perfect their dependence upon him, and teach them how much better it is to " trust in the Lord than to put any confidence in man."

'The sole design of the Almighty Governor of the universe in the exercise of his providence being not the comfort and happiness of man in this world merely, but his everlasting comfort and happiness in another; the means adapted to effect this are either spiritual or temporal. The spiritual means by which the Divine Providence operates, is the appointed agency of good, and the permitted agency of evil, spirits. For even evil spirits are made of use in the work of human regeneration, by exciting to activity the evil that lurks in the natural mind of man, and thus bringing it forth to be seen, hated, and removed.

'Spirit undoubtedly operates on spirit, even as matter operates on matter, and on this account angels are said to be ministering spirits, who minister to the heirs of salvation—happy mediums of communicating divine blessings to those who place themselves in the way of receiving them, by faith, love, and obedience. It requires no very strong exercise of faith in a sincere believer in the Scriptures to acknowledge that few things can happen, even in the outward circumstances of life, in which good angels are not employed as mediums, to guide, to guard, and to bless. "He shall give his angels charge over thee," is as true now as it was in the days of David. (See also Psa. xxxiv, 7; and 2 Kings vi, 17.) Hence we see that a part of the Divine Providence is carried on through the medium of spiritual agents, good and evil, and that the influence of good angels operates upon our minds for good, while the influence of evil spirits operates for evil, with the opportunity afforded to us constantly, however, of turning their intended evil to our eternal good. His enemies are at peace with him.

'If evil dispositions, or dispositions to any particular evils exist in our minds, and if those dispositions are cherished, the evil spirits who watch about man to do him injury, endeavor, so far as they are permitted, to stimulate and increase that disposition, that so the inward evil may be brought into outward act, and thus man becomes a captive to their will. On the other hand, where the man struggles with his evils, the good spirits who wait about him to lead him to good join in the combat, and assist him to overcome his spiritual adversaries. These operations of evil spirits, although invisible to man, are nevertheless as real as anything he sees around him, and they are permitted, by the Divine Providence, in order that man, seeing his evils, may fight against and overcome them, and thus it is that hereditary evil becomes actual, and man becomes chargeable with guilt.

'Where an evil disposition exists by inheritance in the soul, the evil spirits are permitted to act upon it, and to call it into *actual* existence, when the evil, thus becoming palpable, the man not only sees it, but feels it, and now, if he strive against it, attendant good spirits are ready with their assistance to enable him to conquer it ; but if, instead of fighting against it, he cherishes it, and clings to it, then the evil spirits obtain the victory, and the hereditary evil disposition ends in actual and confirmed evil over sin.

'But the influence of outward things acting mediately upon the mind are also means in the hands of Divine Providence for effecting the regeneration of those who keep the covenant of their God. One of the most important of these means or mediums is the ministry of the Holy Word, and, besides these, there are individual meditation and prayer, as well as the practice of those domestic and social duties which wait upon the domestic relations. All these, when duly performed, are so many powerful and blessed mediums, whereby strength is acquired from on high, and truth and goodness are received into the heart.

'The providence of the Lord has for its object the eternal happiness of man, and to this end he so regulates man's worldly affairs, as to produce to those who co-operate with him, by observing the laws of order, the greatest amount of good and the least amount of evil, yet it depends entirely upon the will of the man

whether he will use the means of improvement so boun-
teously provided, or not, for although the Lord provides all that is needful for man's beneficial exercise
of his free agency, he never forces him to adopt the
right course. It rests altogether with man himself
whether the providence of the Lord shall work towards
him for good, or whether it shall tend to increase his
condemnation by his resistance. If with a sincere desire
to obey the Lord, man endeavors to make everything
around him contributive to the great business of regeneration, then the end of God in his creation and redemption, and for which his grace and providence continually
operate, will be answered in him. But if, instead of
"working together with God," he refuses to work at
all ; or if he work at all, works against his Maker,
then the gospel of salvation will be to him the savour
of death unto death ; and the preaching of eternal life
will only prove an introduction to eternal death and
misery.

'How unspeakably profitable will it become to us,
when everything that we see around us, and all that
we feel of good within us, we regard as mercifully
intended to promote the great object of our regeneration
and future happiness ; when we see and feel that it is
not the transient interests of a few years that the
Almighty looks to in his dealings with man ; but that
it is to make everything, both within and without him,
assist in the conquest of evil and the implantation of good,
and so to prepare him for a life not of a few years, nor
even of a few centuries, but life everlasting—for ever
and ever.'

'This, then, is a work worthy of the providence of
the Supreme ; the constant provision of the best means
whereby his banished ones may be brought home again.
It is in this light we shall do well to view the great
doctrine of Divine Providence ; and instead of looking
upon the Lord as busied respecting our outward life
and its comforts only, we should view him as giving or

withholding temporal comforts for the sake of a more important, because an eternal existence. Instead of murmuring when certain things which we desire are denied, we should examine ourselves, to seek out the evil intended to be mortified by such denial, and to fight against it, not doubting that the evil in us would use them, if given, to our ruin, and therefore that they are mercifully withheld.

'It should be our endeavor, both as citizens and as Christians, to work together with the Lord, by keeping in view the ends which he alone keeps in view, that so evil being conquered, and good implanted, we may at length take our place in that happy kingdom, where there is no more sorrow and sighing, and where the tears of worldly distress are wiped from every eye. And although in this world, while bearing our cross, and following our Lord through his path of suffering, we may often be tempted to deplore the disappointment of our natural wishes, still let us try to remember, for our comfort, that success will *always* attend our desires *except when our merciful Father sees it better for us that it should not.* We shall always realise our wishes, or else what is *better for us*, better in view of that wisdom which cannot err, and that goodness which cannot be unkind. It is eternal happiness that our God wills us, *together with affliction*—can we hesitate to prefer *this* to the temporary gratification of worldly desire, where it would have the sad effect, in the view of our Father in heaven, of unfitting our spirits for endless and satisfying joys ?'

MY THIRD LECTURE.—MORAL AND RELIGIOUS SENTIMENTS.

My limits prevent otherwise than a very brief outline of the Moral and Religious Sentiments and Intellect. I have confined myself principally to the relation of Dr. Gall's discovery of the organs, with one or two illustrations.

FEELINGS.

10.—SELF-ESTEEM.—This feeling is generally considered as factitious, or as the result of social circumstances ; but Phrenology proves that it is fundamental. A vast opinion of their own persons is sometimes observed

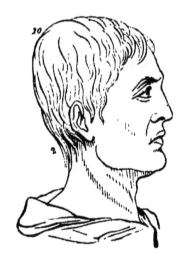

in individuals who have no claims to influence over others or to particular notice, either by birth, fortune, or personal talents. Pride is a sentiment that is commonly more active in men than in women. By the influence of its organ, the insane fancy themselves great geniuses, kings, emperors, ministers of state, and several even the Supreme Being. The horse, peacock, turkey-cock, etc., manifest feelings analogous to pride. Its great activity in society gives arrogance, self-conceit, pride, haughti-

34

ness, and an authoritative behaviour. Combined with superior sentiments and intellect, it contributes to true dignity and greatness of mind : its deficiency disposes to humility.

Dr. Gall thus relates the history of its discovery :—' A beggar attracted my attention by his extraordinary manners. I reflected on the causes which, independently of an absolutely vicious conformation, or of misfortunes, could reduce a man to mendicity, and believed I had found one of the chief of them in levity and want of forethought. The form of the head of the beggar in question confirmed me in my opinion. He was young, and of an agreeable exterior, and his head in the region of Circumspection was very narrow. I moulded his head, and on examining it with attention, remarked, on the upper and back part of the middle line, a prominence extending from above downwards, which could arise only from the development of the brain beneath. I had not previously observed this prominence in other heads, and for this reason I was very anxious to discover what it indicated. His head was small, and announced neither strong feelings nor much intellect. After many questions addressed to the beggar, with a view to discover the remarkable traits of his character, I requested him to relate his history. He said he was the son of a rich merchant, from whom he had inherited a considerable fortune : that he had always been too proud to condescend to labor, either for the preservation of his fortune, or the acquirement of a new one, and that this unhappy pride was the sole cause of his misery. This reminded me of persons who never cut their nails, in order to convey the idea that they are not obliged to work. I made several remarks to him, and let him know that I doubted his veracity. But he always reverted to his pride, and assured me that even now he could not resolve to follow any kind of labor. Although it was difficult to conceive how pride should cause a man to prefer begging to working, yet I was led, by this person's assurances, to reflect upon the sentiment of pride.' * The organ is now, by indisputable facts, established.

In adults this sentiment in too great activity, besides inducing a love of power, already alluded to, leads to contempt of the talents and capabilities of others. As Mr. Combe has aptly observed, it leads the individual to believe, that whatever he says or does is admirable, just because it proceeds from him.

This description of egotism, or inordinate Self-Esteem, is exceedingly prominent in the writings of the late Mr. Cobbett. There is a perpetual introduction of the pronoun *I.*

'With the pronoun *I*, the curl of the lip, the toss of the head, the raising of the superciliary ridge, is associated Self-Esteem in its most prominent exercise ; and then it is that the Alpha and Omega of selfishness and egotism are most graphically displayed. To *me* and *mine* is attached a great deal more consequentiality than to *thee* and *thine. My* views, *my* opinions, and *my* conclusions are altogether indisputable, and absolutely unexceptionable.' Here is an instance in point :—

Macdonald, the last of the Lords of the Isles, was on one occasion invited to dine with the Lord Lieutenant of Ireland. Happening to go in late, he sat himself down at the lower end of the table. His Lordship, who knew his pride, sent a servant to invite him to move to the head of the table. Macdonald asked in his own tongue what the carle said. He was told his Lordship requested that he would move to the head of the table. 'Tell the carle,' said he, 'that where Macdonald sits, THAT IS THE HEAD OF THE TABLE.'

11. LOVE OF APPROBATION.—'While engaged in the hospitals in establishing my discovery of the organ of Self-Esteem,' says Dr. Gall, (Works, vol iv, p. 184), 'I met with a woman who imagined herself to be the Queen of France. I expected to find the organ of Self-Esteem large, but instead of the long oval prominence on

* Gall's Works, vol. iv, p. 156.

the superior, posterior, and middle part of the **head**, found a very distinct hollow, and on each side of it a pretty large round prominence. At first, this circumstance embarrassed me. I soon perceived, however, that the character of this woman's insanity differed materially from that of men alienated by pride. The latter were serious, calm, impetuous, elevated, arrogant ; and they affected a masculine majesty. Even in the fury of their fits, all their motions and expressions bore the impress of the sentiment of domination, which they imagined themselves to exercise over others. In persons insane through vanity, on the other hand, the whole manner was different. There was then a restless frivolity, an incessant talkativeness, the most affected forwardness—eagerness to announce high birth and inexhaustible riches, promises of favor and honor—in a word, a mixture of affectation and absurdity. From that moment I corrected my ideas relative to pride and vanity.'

'The proud man is imbued with a sense of his own superior merit, and from the summit of his grandeur treats all other mortals with contempt or indifference. The vain man attaches the utmost importance to the opinions entertained of him by others, and eagerly seeks to obtain their approbation. The proud man expects that people will come to him, and find out his merit. The vain man knocks at every door to attract attention, and supplicates for the smallest portion of honor. The proud man despises those marks of distinction, which on the vain confer the most perfect delight. The proud man is disgusted by indiscreet eulogium. The vain man inhales with ecstacy the incense of flattery, however awkwardly offered. The proud man never descends from his grandeur, even in circumstances of the most urgent necessity. The vain man, to gain his ends, will humble himself even to crawling.' Pride and thirst of domination are the traits of a few individuals, while the domain of vanity extends at least in a certain degree to every member of the human family. This may be sufficient to show that pride and vanity, the former an excess of Self-Esteem, the latter an excess of Love of Approbation, are two very different fundamental qualities, and must admit a primitive organ for each. In its legitimate exercise, Love of Approbation makes us attentive to the opinion entertained of us by others, and in this sense it is eminently beneficial.

12. CAUTIOUSNESS.—The organ of Cautiousness is situated nearly in the middle of the parietal bones. The following is Dr. Gall's account of its discovery* :—'At Vienna I was acquainted with a prelate of excellent understanding, and considerable intellect. Some persons had an aversion to him, because, through fear of compromising himself, he infused into his discourses interminable reflections, and delivered them with insupportable slowness. In conversation, it was very difficult to bring him to a conclusion. He was continually pausing in the middle of his sentences, and repeating the beginning of them two or three times before proceeding farther. A thousand times he exhausted my patience. Never in his life did he happen, by any accident, to give way to the natural flow of his ideas, but would constantly recur to what he had already said, and consult with himself whether he could not amend it in some point. He acted just as he conversed. He prepared, with infinite precautions, for the most insignificant undertakings, and every connection was subjected to the most rigorous examination before forming it. This case alone, however, would not have arrested my attention ; but this prelate happened to be connected, in public affairs, with a counsellor of the Regency, whose external irresolution had procured for him the nickname of *Cacadubio*. At the examinations of the public schools, these two individuals sat by the side of each other, and my seat was directly behind them, so that I had an excellent opportunity of observing their heads. What particularly struck me was, that each head was very broad in the upper, lateral, and hind parts.

* Gall's Works, vol. iv, p. 195.

This extraordinary breadth, coinciding with the peculiar character of these two men, whose qualities and faculties were very different, and who resembled each other only in their circumspection, and in the conformation of their heads, suggested to me the idea that irresolution, indecision, and circumspection might be connected with a large development of certain parts of the brain. In a very short time my reflections on this quality, and the new facts that were presented, converted my presumptions into certainty.'

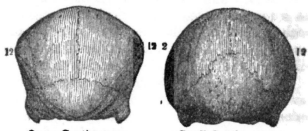

Large Cautiousness.   Small Cautiousness.

This sentiment prompts animals and man to take care. In due quantity, it makes us apprehend danger and consequences, and gives prudence; in large proportion, however, it occasions doubts, irresolutions, uncertainty, anxiety, and the host of hesitations and alarms expressed by the word *but ;* it also disposes to seriousness, melancholy, and sometimes to suicide from disease. It acts in those animals which place sentinels; and in those which, though they see by daylight, do not dare to seek their food except by night, it may be affected in a way called *fear*. Its deficiency disposes to levity and carelessness of behaviour; the other faculties, not being restrained by its presence, act according to their own natures and strength, without any shade of reserve or timidity to obscure their functions.

13. BENEVOLENCE.—The organ of Benevolence lies on the upper and middle part of the frontal bone. This part of the forehead is much higher in the bust of Oberlin, 'han in that of Pope Alexander VI., of whom portraits

are given at pp. 308, 309. The skulls of Caribs are flatter than those of Hindoos in the same situation.

This feeling differs widely both among children and adults. Some are complete egotists in all they do, and think of themselves alone ; others excel in goodness, and devote their lives to the relief of the poor and the afflicted. Whole tribes are mild and peaceable, whilst others are warlike and cruel.

The feeling of benevolence also exists among animals. Several species are naturally meek and good-natured, as the roe and sheep, whilst others are savage and mischievous, as the chamois and tiger. Some dogs, horses, monkeys, etc., are mild and familiar, whilst others of the same kind are bad tempered, fierce, and intractable.

In mankind, the feeling is greatly ennobled, and its sphere of activity augmented. It produces kindness, benignity, benevolence, clemency, equity, urbanity ; in short, it leads to the fulfilment of the great commandment, *Love thy neighbor as thyself.*

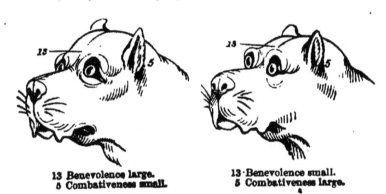

13 Benevolence large.   13 Benevolence small.
5 Combativeness small.   5 Combativeness large.

Dr. Gall thus relates the history of the discovery of this organ : *— 'One of my friends used often to say to me, " As you are engaged in the researches of the external marks which indicate the qualities and faculties, you ought to examine the head of my servant Joseph. It is

* Gall's Works, vol. v, p. 156.

impossible to find goodness in a higher degree than in this boy. For more than two years that he has been in my service, I have seen nothing in him but benevolence and gentleness." This is astonishing in a young man, who, without any education, has grown up in the midst of an ill-bred rabble of servants.

'Though at this period I was very far from placing what is called a good heart in the brain, and consequently from seeking a mark of it on the head, the repeated solicitions of my friend at length awakened my curiosity. I recalled to my recollection the constant conduct of a young man whom I had known from his tenderest childhood, and who distinguished himself from his numerous brothers and sisters by the goodness of his heart. Though he passionately loved the sports of his age, and his greatest pleasure was to scour the forest in pursuit of bird's nests; as soon as one of his brothers or sisters was sick, a more irresistible inclination kept him at home, and he bestowed on the patient the most assiduous attentions. When there were distributed to the children grapes, apples, cherries, he had always the smallest part, and rejoiced to see the others better provided for than himself, He was never better pleased than when anything agreeable happened to those he loved. In this case, he often shed tears of joy. He took care of sheep, dogs, rabbits, pigeons, birds, and when one of his birds died he wept bitterly, which never failed to draw on him the ridicule of his companions ; and even now, benevolence and goodness are the distinctive character of this individual. His character has certainly not taken this turn from education. On the contrary, others in regard to him have pursued a conduct which should have produced an opposite effect. I began to suspect, therefore, that what is called a good heart, is not an acquired quality, but innate.

'At the same time, I spoke of the goodness of heart, so highly extolled, of the domestic Joseph, in a numerous family. "Ah ! " interrupted the eldest daughter, " our brother Charles is precisely the same. You must really examine his head. I cannot tell you how good a boy he is!" etc., etc.

'I had, therefore, in sight three subjects, whose goodness of character was well acknowledged. I took casts of all three. I put their busts side by side, and examined them till I found the character common to these three heads, otherwise very differently formed. In the interval I had applied myself to similar subjects in schools, families, etc., in order to be prepared to multiply and rectify my observations. I also extended these observations to animals, and I collected, in a short time, so great a number of facts, that there is no quality, or fundamental faculty and organ, whose existence is better established than Benevolence, and the organ on which it depends.'

'Is man born really good or evil?' asks Dr. Gall, (Works, vol. v, p. 158.) This question has distracted and divided theologians and metaphysicians long enough, and has never been fairly and philosophically examined, until the phrenologists took it in hand.

Theologians have viewed it through the trammels of creed, and as there was a greater or less degree of the sentiment in themselves, so have their views been tinged with their own peculiarities. If they had studied it from the grand truth, *God is Love*, they must have been led to the conclusion, that the creature whom he made in his own image, after his likeness, and who, when first introduced to the beauteous earth, was pronounced to be VERY GOOD, could only have been originally as pronounced. If he fell (we stop not to inquire by what means), and indulged in the opposite disposition, his organisation would become more and more deteriorated, as he descended farther and farther from goodness, and evil would increase as it tainted its descendants—it being a philosophical as well as religious truth, that the sins of the parents descend to the children, to the third and fourth generations. And so must it ever be where there is nothing but evil and vicious example. The child will always emulate the sire, and hence the necessity of such an example, and of such a system of national education, as shall wipe off the foul evil which has so long degraded and debased the human character.

The Creator has stamped the image of his goodness on the creature he has made, and it requires only that man follow him, and learn of him, to be refilled with this godlike virtue. But neglected and oppressed as the great mass of the people have been by those who had the government—or rather misgovernment—of them ; degraded by serfdom, and rendered ferocious by sanguinary laws ; accustomed to see men hung up as dogs, and their fellow creatures butchered to gratify the insane ambition of kings and conquerors, why should it be wondered at, that goodness and benevolence have been almost suffocated, and cruelty, vengeance, and destructiveness encouraged, by the fearful examples so constantly before their eyes ? We ought not to expect to ' gather grapes of thorns, or figs of thistles.' ' The only marvel in the minds of the reflecting is, that in spite of all this hanging, fighting, burning, and wholesale destruction of men's lives, benevolence still asserts its influence, and that influence extends itself in every direction.'

But still Benevolence is sadly deficient in many, and until the moral feelings shall receive better training, we need hope but for small improvement. Let the theologian fume and fret as he may however, man is rather good, just, and benevolent, than the reverse. Our present purpose is to show the superiority of this sentiment over all coercive measures in the education of children, in the treatment of the insane, and in the treatment of criminals.

Upon the education of children, in a great measure, depends the future peace and well-being of the community. Until Phrenology pointed out the superiority of goodness and benevolence over all coercion, what was the usual means adopted by teachers to secure the improvement of their pupils ? The savage law of corporal punishment on the one hand, or appeals to the self-esteem and vanity of the pupils on the other. In everything else they were completely in the dark ; at sea without rudder, chart, or compass, working entirely upon these hap-hazard principles, and accompanying their ignorance of human nature with a pompous magisterial superiority, which terrified rather than conciliated the child. Nor was the conduct of many parents a whit better. When we were engaged in teaching, we recollect a mother coming to us—'My child makes very slow progress, sir.' 'He is rather dull and slow, ma'am,' said we. 'Whip it into him, then,' said the amiable parent. 'Don't you know that to spare the rod is to spoil the child ?'

Let us see what this whipping system is capable of accomplishing. At a common school convention in Hampden county, U.S., a clerical speaker related the following anecdote :—

'Many years ago, a man went into a district to keep school, and before he had been there a week, many persons came to see him, and kindly told him, that there was one boy in the school whom it would be necessary to whip every day, leading him to infer that such was the custom of the school, and that the inference of injustice towards the boy would be drawn whenever he should escape, *not* when he should suffer. The teacher, however, saw the matter in a different light. He treated the boy with signal kindness and attention. At first this novel course seemed to bewilder him. He could not divine its meaning ; but when the persevering kindness of the teacher begat a kindred sentiment in the pupil, his very nature seemed transformed. Old impulses died, and a new creation of motives supplied their place. Never was there a more diligent and successful pupil. Now,' continued the reverend gentleman, in concluding his narrative, ' that boy is the chief justice of a neighboring state.' The relater of the anecdote, though he modestly kept back the fact, was himself the actor.

We pass now to the superiority of Benevolence in the treatment of the insane. Although the faculty seem, as to the majority of its professors, determined to do all in their power to strangle Phrenology—although many of them are as violent, as abusive, and as dogmatical now, as were their predecessors when Harvey discovered and propagated the true doctrine of the circulation of the blood—yet there are professors, and able professors, too, of the healing art, who adopt and apply its principles to the great benefit of their patients. Among these may be mentioned Dr. Sir William Ellis, late physician to the Hanwell Lunatic Asylum, Middlesex. This asylum was formerly conducted on the old principle of violence, chains, whips, strait waistcoats, *et hoc genus omne.* Dr. Ellis, with his truly heroic and good wife, removed all this fiendish apparatus, and determined to govern only by benevolence, or not to rule at all. The result has changed the entire treatment of lunatic patients in this country.

In vol. i, p. 231, of Miss Martineau's Miscellanies, is the following narrative :—

'I have lately been backwards and forwards to the Hanwell Asylum for the reception of the pauper lunatics of the county of Middlesex. On entering the gate, I met a patient going to his garden work, with his tools in his hands, and passed three others breaking clods with their forks, and keeping near each other, for the sake of being sociable. Further on were three women rolling the grass in company, one of whom, a merry creature, who clapped her hands at the sight of visitors, had been chained to her bed for seven years before she was brought here, but is likely to give little further trouble henceforth than that of finding her enough to do. Further on is another, in a quieter state of content, always calling to mind the strawberries and cream Mrs. Ellis set before the inmates on the lawn last year, and persuading herself that the strawberries could not grow, nor the garden get on, without her, and fiddle-faddling in the sunshine, to her own satisfaction and that of her guardians. This woman had been in a strait waistcoat for ten years before she had been sent to Hanwell

'There is another place where the greater number of them go, with the greatest alacrity, to the chapel, where they may be seen on a Sunday evening, decked out in what they consider their best, equalling any other congregation whatever in the decorum of their deportment.

'Where are the chains, the straw, and the darkness? Where are the howls and the yells, without which the place cannot be supposed a madhouse? There is not a chain in the house, nor any intention that there shall be; and those who might in a moment be provoked to howl and yell, are lying quietly in bed, talking to themselves, as there is no one else present to talk to.

'I saw the worst patients in the establishment, and was far more delighted than surprised to see the effect of companionship on those who might be supposed the most likely to irritate each other. One poor creature in a paroxysm of misery could not be passed by; and while I was speaking to her as she sat, two of the most violent patients in the ward joined me. The one wiped away the scalding tears of the sufferer, while the other told me how genteel an education she had received, and how it grieved them all to see her there.'

And all this has been brought about by the enlightening power and influence of phrenology, which has gone to the origin of mania, and applied the proper means of remedy; taught the classification of the patients; shown the utility of constant employment, and above all, the humanising and softening power of benevolence.

And now we pass to the last division of our subject—benevolence in the treatment of criminals—and again the phrenologist will be found to occupy the vantage ground. Phrenologists have, from the first, contended that education alone can improve the organisation; and they have given the most incontrovertible evidence, that where the education has been attended to, even in cases where the organisation has been defective and inferior, the organisation has been gradually improved, and the happiest results have in the sequel ensued.

14. VENERATION.—This sentiment produces respect-fulness and reverence in general. In its supreme functions it induces worship and adoration. It is situated at the middle of the coronal aspect of the brain. Dr. Gall thus relates its discovery (Works, vol. v, p. 216):— 'There were ten of us in the house of my father—my brothers and sisters and myself. All received the same education, but our faculties and tendencies were very different. One of my brothers, from his infancy, had a strong tendency to devotion. His playthings were church

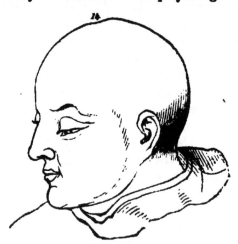

vases, which he sculptured himself, copes and surplices, which he made with paper. He prayed to God and said mass all day, and when he was obliged to miss service at church, he passed his time at the house in ornamenting and gilding a crucifix of wood. My father had destined him to commerce, but he had an invincible aversion to the business of a merchant, because, he said, it forced one to lie. At the age of twenty-three years, having lost all hope of pursuing his studies, he fled from the house and turned hermit; five years after he took orders, and till his death lived in the exercise of piety and devotion.'

The head of his brother, Dr. Gall declares, was very

elevated at the part we are now reviewing. After numerous observations, the organ has been fully established.

Among the numerous exemplifications of this organ, never, perhaps, was there a finer instance than in the justly celebrated John Frederick Oberlin. (See his portrait, pp. 308, 309.)

This model of the Christian religion—whose piety was cheerful, rational, and temperate—found the inhabitants of his parish, isolated in five different villages, poor, ignorant, agitated by heinous passions, and without the most necessary means of comfortable existence, but by laboring unremittingly, he by degrees succeeded in changing their wretched condition. He taught them to cultivate potatoes, flax, and such vegetables as succeeded best in light and sandy soils. He laid out a nursery in order to supply the peasants with trees of various kinds, and showed them the advantage they would reap by attending to their cultivation. He gave instruction to the children himself, teaching the younger to read, write, and calculate, while he lectured to the more advanced in age upon the cultivation of fruit trees, the principles of agriculture, and the useful and noxious qualities of the various plants which the country produced. He particularly accustomed them to cleanliness. The good pastor, with his parishioners at his back, actually worked at the formation of convenient ways from one village to another, and of a good and ready communication with the great road leading to Strasbourg. Besides his vast care of all his people's worldly concerns, he paid the greatest attention to moral and religious instruction. His sermons were simple, energetic, and affectionate, composed with great care, though plain and colloquial. His illustrations were drawn largely from objects in natural history, or in common life, with which the people were familiar. His discourses were often interspersed with anecdotes of persons distinguished for reverence of the Great Supreme. He cited largely from the Bible, for which he entertained the most devoted affection. He indulged in the common practice of the older divines, of drawing analogies between the natural and visible, and the spiritual world. But, above all, he loved to expatiate on the goodness of God, and the hopes, the promises, and the freeness of the gospel. For all denominations of Christians he had the widest toleration.

Such was Oberlin. Now look attentively at his portrait, and compare the height of the coronal region with those of Nero, Caracalla, and Pope Alexander VI.; then study the lives of the three last mentioned, as in history recorded, and then judge between them and Oberlin.

It is not possible for us to visit any country, whether civilised or savage, without being struck with the universal fact, that the inhabitants believe in and venerate a God. Pierre, in his 'Studies of Nature,' says—'Every nation has the sentiment of the existence of a God, not that they raise themselves to it as *Newton* or as *Socrates*, by the universal harmony of his works, but rather by fixing their attention on those blessings which interest them most. Thus, the Indians of Peru worship the sun ; the Indians of Bengal, the Ganges, which fertilizes their fields. The black Jolof worships the ocean, which cools his shores.' Plutarch also coincides in the sentiment, that there is neither town nor village in the world without a God, and consequently there can be no people entirely destitute of a faculty which tends to reverence and worship.

If we consult the writings of the ancients, the sentiment is assented to by Aristotle, Cicero, Plato, Seneca, and others. There is no sentiment for which we have such abundant evidence as that under review. The Saviour of mankind and his apostles, particularly the beloved apostle, are represented with this portion of the brain very elevated. Melancthon and Fenelon are instances of it in the Roman Catholic Church ; the late eminently learned and pious Bishop Heber in the English Church ; the late eloquent Robert Hall among Dissenters ; and the fervid and towering Chalmers in the

Scottish Church. These names are in themselves a tower
of strength; and if, where there is a similarity of organization, the same results are invariably perceived, who can
doubt that a particular portion of the brain disposes to
veneration and worship? The church has at all times
seen the necessity of exciting this organ to induce a feeling
of reverence in the mind of the worshipper. Whether we
admire the gorgeous splendor attendant upon the ceremonies of the Romish Church, or turn to the cathedral
services of the Episcopal Church, or even to the more
sober and quiet ceremonial of the Presbyterian Church,
they are all calculated to excite this organ, and intended
to excite it. Charity appeals to it when an oratorio is to
be performed, or when a sermon is to be preached by an
eminent prelate, and the organ presided at by an eminent
player. It is useful to stimulate it in an healthful manner;
and when we show our love to God by the love we bear to
each other, both Benevolence and Veneration are healthily
exercised.

Many persons have supposed that Veneration always
disposes to the worship of the Supreme Being; but experience has proved that though veneration always disposes
to worship and respect, still a man may be largely
endowed with the organ of Veneration, and yet be an
infidel. The truth is, and melancholy it is to state it,
there are as many, perhaps more, worshippers of self and
the world, than of the Supreme Being. A vast number
of persons worship the great—kings, for instance; among
the most devout worshippers of this class was Voltaire.
Some worship their wealth, their titles, their estates, their
pictures, their statues, their books, their horses, their
hounds, etc. Some worship their servants, as it is well
known many servants worship their masters. I am
acquainted with a strictly moral young man, a Deist,
who told me that the object of his worship was Lord
Brougham.

To those in whom the organ is strong, the word *old* is
synonymous with *venerable*, and, in their view, no institution

35

or doctrine, however hurtful or absurd, is, if sanctioned
by antiquity, to be at all meddled with. They obstinately
adhere to the religious tenets instilled into them in childhood, and will not listen to arguments to support doctrines
of a contrary kind. When, on the other hand, the organ
of Veneration is moderately developed, and the intellect
acute and enlightened, the individual regards only the
intrinsic merits of the doctrines and institutions which
prevail around him, and shapes his opinions accordingly.*

Mrs. Child observes that the mere circumstance of
antiquity is impressive to a character inclined to veneration. The Greek and Roman, when they became Christian,
still clung fondly to the reminiscences of their early faith.
The undying flame on Apollo's shrine re-appeared in ever-
lighted candles at the Roman Catholic altar; and the
same idea that demanded vestal virgins for the heathen
temple, set nuns apart for the Christian sanctuary. Tiara
and embroidered garments were sacred to the imagination
of the converted Jew, and conservatism, which in man's
dual nature ever keeps innovation in check, led him to
adopt them in his new worship. Thus did the spirituality
of Christ come to us loaded with forms not naturally and
spontaneously flowing therefrom. The very cathedrals,
with their clustering columns and intertwining arches,
were architectural models of the groves and high places
sacred to the minds of the pagans, who from infancy had
therein worshipped their strange gods. The days of the
Christian week took the names of heathen deities, and statues
of Venus were adored as Virgin mothers. The bronze
image of St. Peter at Rome, whose toe has been kissed
away by pious devotees, was once a statue of Jupiter.
An English traveller took off his hat to it as Jupiter, and
asked him, if he ever recovered his power, to reward the
only individual who had ever bowed to him in adversity.

The reverential habit of mind varies its forms according
to the temperament and character. The tendency betrays
itself in the rainbow mysticism of Coleridge, the patriarchal

* See Phrenological Journal, vol. viii.

tendencies of Wordsworth, and the divine aspirations of Beethoven.

In some minds it is shown by a strong affection for everything antique. They worship shadowy legends, architectural ruins, and ancient customs. This habit of thought enabled Sir Walter Scott to conjure up the guardian spirit of the house of Avenal, and re-people the regal halls of Kenilworth. The works of Sir Walter Scott were the final efflorescence of feudal grandeur—that system had passed away from political forms, and no longer had a home in human reason, but it lingered with a dim glory in the imagination.

Another kind of minds rise to a higher plane of reverence. Their passion for the past becomes mingled with earnest aspirations for the holy—such persons walk in a golden fog of mysticism. To such, Puseyism comes forward like a fine old cathedral made visible by a gush of moonlight.

But be not disturbed by POPE or PUSEY. They are but a part of the check and balance system of the universe, and in due time will yield to something better. Modes of faith last just as long as they are needed in the order of Providence, and not a day longer. *Truth* cannot be forced above its level, any more than its great prototype, *water.**

15. FIRMNESS.—The organ of Firmness is placed in the middle of the upper and posterior part of the sincipital region of the head, as in this portrait of M——

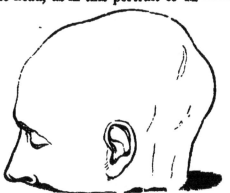

* See 'Letters from New York,' by Mrs. Child.

It is difficult to define this feeling. Its effects are often called *will*, and those who have it strong are prone to say, *I will;* but their will is not an act of reflection, a condition necessary to free-will and liberty. The meaning of their *I will* is—I desire, I command, I insist upon. This feeling contributes to maintain the activity of the other faculties, by giving perseverance and constancy. It also gives a love of independence; its too great activity produces stubbornness, obstinacy, and disobedience. Its deficiency renders man inconstant and changeable. Individuals so constituted have little determination, readily yield in their opinions, and are easily diverted from their pursuits or undertakings.

In the person of the celebrated Joseph Hume, firmness may be stated as his distinguishing peculiarity—without it he could never have achieved the eminence he reached. When he first went into Parliament, he stood almost alone as the advocate of economy and retrenchment. Hour after hour, when estimates were to be voted, he rose to propose reductions. He was assailed on all sides of the House by clamor. The members coughed, talked, crowed, and even, if report speaks truth, snored and brayed like asses, to put down Joseph Hume ; but all proved fruitless—he persevered. Opposition and insult were equally fruitless ; and the result was, his perseverance and honesty at length secured him the respect of the House, and in matters of finance, his sanction carried considerable weight with it. There were others equally ardent in their wishes for economy, quite as desirous of retrenchment as he was, but they wanted the power of brain which he possessed ; above all, they wanted the inflexible firmness by which he was distinguished. Joseph Hume is a fine study for a phrenologist.

16. CONSCIENTIOUSNESS.—Conscientiousness is situated on each side of Firmness, just before Love of Approbation, on the posterior and lateral parts of the coronal surface of the brain. To Dr. Spurzheim may be attributed the honor of its discovery. He says—' This faculty produces

the feeling of duty, the desire of being just, and the love · of truth. It looks for justice, and makes us wish to act justly, but it does not determine what is just or unjust. This determination depends on the combination of the sentiment with other affective and intellectual powers. He who unites Conscientiousness with active lower propensities, will call that just, which another, endowed with Conscientiousness, much Benevolence and Veneration, and little of the lower propensities, calls unjust. 'All the ways of a man,' says Solomon, 'are clean in his own eyes, but the Lord weigheth the spirits.'

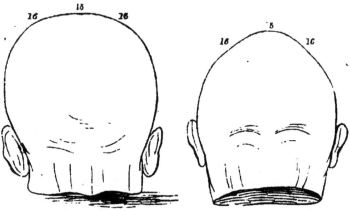

15.· Large Firmness. 15. Large Firmness.
16. Large Conscientiousness. 16. Small Conscientiousness.

'This primitive feeling may be disagreeably affected in a way called repentance or remorse. Its great and general deficiency among mankind is much to be lamented ; it is this that occasions, as it explains, the many unprincipled acts that are continually done.'

In illustrating the deficiency of this organ, I cannot help adverting to one common practice which unhappily distinguishes the present age.

While, in some places, more especially where ignorance gives scope to rapacity, it is the custom to do the best possible for *self*, by charging as much as possible for

articles of trade ; in others, especially where the buyer
knows as well as the seller the cost of production, it is
usual to charge the least possible price to conciltate his
favor. Hence ensues a sad contest. The laborer is
gradually pinched almost out of existence, to support the
bulky exterior of glittering poverty consequent upon this
system, which is found in the warehouse of the manufacturer.

" ' Let us," thus runs the short-sighted cant of the
counter—(the wholly deficient in Conscientiousness)—
" sell for next to nothing, or even really for nothing,
yea, at a dead loss for a time, that we may run off our
opponents, gain the confidence of customers, and establish
us a name." A name ! for what ? " *For* CHEAPNESS."
FOR CHEAPNESS ! Pray, what virtue does cheapness
represent ? Is it conscience ? Is it liberality ? Are we
desirous, by a cheapness which sacrifices living profit, and
which ruins the small capitalist dealing in similar goods,
to obtain the reputation of being spiritedly liberal ?
" Regardless of large gains !—above the love of amassing
a fortune ! " Is this our end ? There is somewhat of
life—true life, in such a disposition, but it belongs not to
the abettors of the system we are deprecating. A name
for liberality so acquired is in the mouths of some a
falsehood, and of others something worse, if that be possible.
The end is the all in all of the means, and that end is but
too clearly stated in the words, *to run off our opponents* :
in plain terms, defraud and starve their neighbors—keep
down the sentiment of conscience, in order that greater
gain may accrue to themselves. This spirit is the spirit of
covetousness, and the spirit of covetousness is the fountain
of theft. We think it would not require a lengthy
argument to prove, and yet it requires courage to write it
down, that every tradesman who, in a regular way, and
for the purpose of running off his opponents, sells his
goods, or peculiar portions of them, without profit, is
destitute of a real principle of conscience.'

Mr. Combe, in his ' Moral Philosophy,' gives us the

following case :—' I knew an individual in the situation of
a confidential clerk, who had a good intellect, with much
Benevolence, Veneration, and Love of Approbation, but in
whom a large organ of Secretiveness was combined with
deficient Conscientiousness. His life had been respectable
for many years in the situation of clerk, while his duty
was merely to write books and conduct correspondence.
But when he was promoted, and entrusted with buying
and selling, and paying and receiving cash, his moral
principles gave way. And the temptation to which he
yielded was not a selfish one. He was much devoted to
religion, and began by lending his master's money for a
few days to his religious friends, who did not always pay
him back. He then proceeded to assist the poorer
brethren with it. He next opened his house in great
hospitality to the members of the congregation to which
he belonged. These expenses speedily placed his cash so
extensively in arrear, that he had no hope of recovering
that deficiency by any ordinary means, and he then
purchased *lottery tickets* to a large amount, trusting to a
good prize for his restoration to honor and independence.
These prizes never came, and the result was disclosure,
disgrace, and misery.'

Covetousness results from the large development of
Acquisitiveness, unrestrained by the higher sentiments of
justice, benevolence, and the powers of reflection ; and
this covetousness, grasping at the gold which tends to
gratify its cupidity, has caused the most direful crimes ;
and, doubtless, it was the mainspring of the crime which
instigated the murderer Rush, and whose cupidity and
want of Conscientiousness has only been equalled by his
unbending obstinacy, and stimulated by his cunning and
duplicity. Indeed, unrestrained Acquisitiveness may be
said to be at the root of all, crime, as it is at the root of
all evil. War springs up from its unbridled exercise, and
pillage and blood follow in its train. It has banished
religion from the soul ; it has blunted and destroyed
parental feeling ; it has frozen the current of connubial

affection ; it has cut asunder the holiest ties of friendship ; it has served as an Upas, to shed its withering shade over the human family. It renders a once happy nation miserable, and transforms its rulers into a nest of stern exactors, who like the daughters of the horse leech, are continually crying—Give, give ! Nor is this bane of everything that is good confined to one class of the human family. It seems to have permeated all grades of society, and money has become the standard of respectability. It has surrounded the throne with its magic and corrupting circle. It has entered churches, and mitred heads have bowed before its debasing power. · It has become a moral pestilence, and has extended its baneful influence in every direction, and the golden calf is set up and worshipped as the universal god. From the throne to the coronet, from the coronet to the church, from the church to the man of the world, the railway speculator, and even to the poorest among us—the earnest plea is not for friendship, for virtuous love, for cultivated intellect, for conscience, for tenderness and benevolence of soul, but —FOR GOLD.

This covetousness and love of gold has supplanted in the breast of man the love of his Saviour. This mammon has usurped in men's hearts the throne of Deity himself. Foreign battle-fields, running with rivers of human blood, attest its desolating power. The perpetrators of which atrocities so stimulated are heroes, but the perpetrator, by a similar impulse, of one or more victims, is a murderer. Give honors, titles, decorations to the former, and suspend from the gallows-tree the latter. How great, then, is the need for the cultivation of Conscientiousness to restrain these evils.

17. HOPE.—Hope is situated on each side of Veneration. Dr. Gall considers hope as belonging to every faculty, but Dr. Spurzheim controverts this. Every faculty being active, produces desire. Acquisitiveness produces the desire for property ; Love of Approbation for praise. This is very different from Hope, which is a sentiment

necessary for every situation in life. Hope has been well considered as the sheet-anchor of the soul : what would existence be worth in this world without such a feeling or sentiment ? The man who is deficient in this sentiment, is always doubting of success in any of his enterprises. If success does crown his efforts, he feels surprise, and wonders at the accomplishment of an object, which the man with large Hope would scarcely have doubted. The man who is deficient in Hope, is prone to despond ; he can see but little, if anything, to cheer his progress through life. · If he has large Cautiousness, he is always fearing ; if to this is added large Destructiveness, he has the essential gloom which predisposes to solitude and suicide.

As a religious sentiment, associated with Benevolence, Veneration, and Conscientiousness, it is of the most exhilarating character. Connected with the ideas which man forms of a future state, it is hope which gives substance to faith. It is replete with bright imaginings. It rises superior to opposing difficulties ; it looks onward to the brightness of a future state, and anticipates the realization of its delights in a world where pain and sickness never comes. The man in whom this sentiment is suitably associated, and which predominates over Cautiousness, has no fear of the grave, because his desires never expect to receive full gratification until he reaches the world beyond it, and the glorious prospect of his future existence renders him patient under all the cares and the sufferings of this.

> ' O there are days when love and light,
>   Are to.our pathways given,
> When Hope takes her exulting flight
>   On eagle's wings to heaven !—
> Days when a thousand smiles unite
>   The peace-lit brow to bless,
> Chaste heralds of a new delight,
>   Bright harbingers of happiness.'

I consider Hope to be one of the most useful of the religious sentiments.

18. MARVELLOUSNESS.—Marvellousness is situated immediately below Hope, on each side of Benevolence and Imitation. This organ disposes to belief in the unseen world, and to the acknowledgment of the existence of a Divine Being. The great apostle of the Gentiles gives three distinguishing principles as essential to the formation of the Christian character—faith, hope, and charity. He describes charity as the greatest. If we look at the situation and connection of these three organs on the chart, we see that Marvellousness is in close connection with Hope. In fact, they run into each other. Charity, or Benevolence, is the centre. These three sentiments are also essentially connected with Veneration, or reverence for the Great Supreme, and Conscientiousness, or love of truth. These constitute the religious group of organs. That they are capable of abuse from disease or over-excitement, cannot be doubted. But, in the legitimate exercise of their functions, they are undoubtedly the foundation of the religious character, and are to be considered as the more spiritual powers of the mind.

19. IDEALITY.—Ideality is situated above the temples, in the course of the temporal ridge of the frontal bone. It is in the vicinity of Hope and Marvellousness, with Cautiousness behind, and Acquisitiveness just below it. It was a considerable time before Dr. Gall marked this organ as established; and when he did, he was still inaccurate in naming it. He distinguished it as the organ of poetry; Dr. Spurzheim has given to it the more just and elegant name of Ideality. He remarks on its functions, that it exalts the other powers, and makes us enthusiasts; gives warmth to our language, energy to our actions, and fires us with rapture and exultation, or poetic imagination, fancy, and inspiration, as it is termed.

Poetry, it is evident, neither consists in versification, nor in rhyming, since prose writings may be full of poetry, and verses show none of its glow or its coloring.

This feeling makes man aspire after perfection and look

for things as they ought to be. In the arts, it causes the taste for sublimity.

The want of this feeling leaves the mind to operate by the means of its other elements, and deprived of exaltation.

It was very largely developed in Tasso. It gifts its possessor, when suitably associated and aided by other powers, with that sublimity of description, that symmetry of form, that beauty of imagery, that grandeur of

description, that polish of language, which may be considered as the soul of eloquence. It imparts to Veneration a deep reverence and fervent adoration ; to Language, elegant and choice selection ; to Benevolence, refined tenderness and sensibility ; to Love of Approbation, a keener relish for approval. It aids the powers which delight in fiction : it adds and deepens the novelty inspired by Marvellousness : it etherealizes and elevates still higher Hope ; and, in short, it is the creator of a world of fancy, in which it loves to model every ideal excellence and perfection.

There is a space marked on the busts with a (?), to

denote that its functions are unascertained. The late Dr. Maxwell of Glasgow, who paid much attention to this portion of the brain, and to the manners and habits of those persons in whom it was largely developed, gave to it the name of Conservativeness. One very striking instance of it came under my own observation. Having predicated the character of a very beautiful poet, I marked this portion of the brain at 22, but without giving any idea of its functions or power, otherwise than stating to its possessor, that he was very largely endowed with what Dr. Maxwell termed Conservativeness (?). A few days after, I received the following letter :—

' *Glasgow*,———— ——

'DEAR SIR—That portion of my brain which lies between Ideality and Cautiousness, to which some have given the name of Conservativeness, is, according to your own measurement, so very large as to be marked 22, your average size being indicated by 14.

'According to my interior experience, there has been, as long as I can remember, one faculty at work in my mind more powerfully than any other, and which (whatever that faculty may be) has all along indicated itself to my own perceptions, by conferring on me certain peculiarities, of the principal of which the following is a concise statement :—I experience the most intense delight in the preservation of little things, especially, such as form a record of past states and circumstances, such as I perceive have no value attached to them by people in general. I have a copy of everything I ever wrote, however trifling. I have copies of my principal letters. I have a copy of every letter or card I ever received, with the exception only of those addressed to my firm when in business. I have innumerable scraps of paper, on which ideas were jotted down just as they occurred, and which I was fearful might not occur again in the same form or degree of intensity. I have begun scores of works, and written hundreds of title pages! I have a great many different places into which I thrust my papers, according to the subject, etc., and feel delighted when those various departments increase on my hands. Often I get harassed by anxiety, lest any small thing should be neglected or misplaced. I have kept a journal of my life, both as to feelings and events, without interruption, since the 12th year of my age. I am, besides, very careful of clothing, etc.; and it distresses me to see anything wasted, especially beautiful white writing paper: so I write as much as possible on useless fragments of bills, letters, etc. Though I should lose a thousand pounds, it would yield me pleasure the very same day to save a few sheets of writing paper, or note down a thought I considered worth preserving. I believe that, in reality, all things are equal in size, value, and the joy they give; that it is only comparatively they are different.

'These peculiarities may be produced by my organisation in general; but I think they are to be traced chiefly to the organ of Conservativeness. I leave you to judge in regard to this matter, and to make what use you please of these few hurried observations.

'Very sincerely,

'J. R. S.'

Shakespere was an individual in whose brain appeared every mental and ideal excellence. In English literature he reigns without a rival. As a sample of his general powers, in which, though he knew nothing of phrenology, its principles are most directly delineated, I will quote a passage from Richard II., act v., scene 4 :—

'I have been studying how I may compare
This prison where I live unto the world,
And for because the world is populous
And here is not a creature but myself
I cannot do it.   Yet I'll hammer it out;
My *brain* I'll prove the female to my soul,
My soul the father, and these two beget
A generation of still breeding thoughts,
And these same thoughts people this little world
In humors like the people of this world,
For no thought is contented.   The better sort,
As thoughts of things divine, are intermixt
With scruples; and do set the *Word* itself
Against the *Word*.
As thus; *Come, little ones;* and then again,
It is as hard to come as for a camel
To thread the postern of a needle's eye.
   Thoughts tending to ambition, they do plot
Unlikely wonders; how these vain weak nails
May tear a passage through the flinty ribs
Of this hard world, my rugged prison walls,
And for they cannot—*die* in their own pride.
   Thoughts tending to *content*, flatter themselves
That they are not the first of fortune's slaves,
Nor shall not be the last :—like silly beggars
Who, sitting in the stocks, refuge their shame
That many have and others must sit there ;
And in this thought they find a kind of ease,
Bearing their own misfortunes on the back

Of such as have before endured the like.
Thus play I in one person many people,
And none contented : Sometimes I am a king,
Then treason makes me wish myself a beggar,
And so I am : Then crushing penury
Persuades me I was *better* when a king,
Then am I king'd again : and by and by
Think that I am unking'd by Bolingbroke,
And straight am nothing.'

20. WIT.—The organ of Wit is situated on the upper
and outer part of the forehead, on the side of Causality, and
immediately before that of Ideality.   Of this faculty Dr.
Spurzheim remarks, that it diffuses over the mind a disposition to view objects and events in a ludicrous light,
in the same way as Ideality tends to exalt all its functions.   It may be combined with the affective as well as
the intellectual faculties.   If along with the higher powers

it be applied to ideas and conceptions of importance, its
agency is called *wit;* directed to common events and
lesser notions, it appears as *humor;* in union with Constructiveness and Configuration, it produces caricatures

and pictures, in the manner of Hogarth and of Callot ; acting unattended with Benevolence, particularly if Combativeness and Destructiveness be large at the same time, it originates satire and sarcasm. In short, jest, raillery, mockery, ridicule, irony, and every turn of mind or action that excites mirth, gaiety, and laughter, result from this sentiment. In the writings of Voltaire, Rabelais, Sterne, Prior, Boileau, Swift, etc., its activity is clearly perceived.

21. IMITATION.—The organ of Imitation lies on either side of Benevolence. If both of these organs be large, the superior anterior portion of the head is elevated in a hemispherical form ; but when the organ of Benevolence alone is large, and that of Imitation small, there is an elevation in the middle, and a declivity at the sides.

Of the discovery of this organ Dr. Gall remarks :—* ' When I was talking with one of my friends respecting the form of the head, he assured me that his own was a very peculiar one. He then directed my hand to the anterior superior part of the head. I found this region considerably bulging, and behind the protuberance, a depression, a cavity, which descended on each side towards the ear. Prior to this period, I had not observed this conformation. This man had a peculiar talent for imitation. He imitated, in so striking a manner, the gait, the gestures, the sound of the voice, etc., that the person was immediately recognised. I hastened to the Institution for the Deaf and Dumb to examine the head of the pupil Casteigner, who had been received into the establishment six weeks previous, and who, from the first, had fixed our attention by his prodigious talent for imitation. On Shrove Tuesday, when a little theatrical piece is usually represented in the establishment, he had imitated so perfectly the gesture, the gait, etc., of the director, inspector, physician, and surgeon of the establishment, and especially of some women, that it was impossible to mistake ; a scene which amused the more, as nothing like it was expected from a boy whose education had been absolutely neglected. To

* Works, vol. v, p. 201.

my great astonishment, I found in him the superior anterior part of the head as prominent as in my friend Annibal.

'Can the talent for imitation, I asked myself, be dependent on a particular organ ? And I sought opportunities for multiplying my observations. I visited families, schools, etc., and examined the heads of individuals who possessed the talent for imitation in an eminent degree. At this period, M. Maix, Secretary to the Minister of War, had gained great reputation by several parts which he played in a private theatre. I found in him the region of the frontal bone alluded to, as prominent as in Casteigner and Annibal. In all the other persons whom I examined I likewise found this region more or less prominent, according as they were endowed with the talent of imitation to a greater or less degree.

'They relate of Garrick, that he possessed a faculty of imitation so astonishing, that he forgot nothing of the retinue of the court composed of Louis xv, the Duke of Aumont, the Duke of Orleans, of Bussac, Richelieu, and others. All these personages, whom he saw once passing by, were fixed in his memory. He invited to supper the friends who had accompanied him, and, impatient to amuse them, said to them after supper—" I have seen the court only an instant, but I am going to prove to you the accuracy of my eye, and the excellence of my memory." He then arranged his friends in two lines, went out, and an instant after returned. All the spectators exclaimed—" There is the king ! there is Louis xv." He imitated, in succession, all the personages of the court ; they were all recognised. Not only had he imitated their gait, their walk, their figure, but even the lines and the character of their physiognomy. I soon considered that this faculty must constitute a considerable portion of the talent of the comedian. I therefore examined the heads of the best actors which we then had, and in all I found the region alluded to prominent.'

MY FOURTH LECTURE.—INTELLECTUAL FACULTIES.

By these faculties, the existence of external objects is known, and their physical qualities and relations are acquired.

GENUS I.—EXTERNAL SENSES.

Since the time of Locke, the greater number of philosophical systems rest upon the axiom of Aristotle. According to this hypothesis, the perfection of the mental functions depends on the perfection of the external senses. This, however, neither holds good in the case of animals nor men. Many animals have the senses more active and more perfect than men. No animal, however, can at all approach man in intellect. Many idiots have the external senses healthy and energetic, but this is no remedy against the deficiency of understanding. A most conclusive proof of the innate dispositions of the mind is found in the case of Laura Bridgman, who, deprived of sight, hearing, speech, and smell, yet displays great intellectual power and strong affective feeling. The external senses are merely the instruments by means of which the internal faculties, acted upon by external impressions, manifest their activity. They do not acquire any knowledge of external objects, or of their qualities and relations. The eyes do not judge of color. The ears do not appreciate or produce melody, neither do they invent any verbal language. The smell does not possess local memory, nor does the touch give rise to the instinctive labors of animals, or the mechanical arts of man.* It remains to specify some functions of the senses.

Since 1815 (continues Spurzheim), in my lectures and publications, I have maintained that the nerves of motion differ from those of feeling, and I have adduced anatomical, physiological, and pathological proofs in support of my position.

* See Spurzheim on the External Senses.

36

FEELING.—The sense of feeling is the most extensive of all the senses, being continued not only over the whole external surface of the body, but also over the intestinal canal. It produces the most general perceptions of pain and pleasure, of temperature, and of dryness and moisture. All its other functions are mediate, that is, internal faculties perceive the numerous impressions it propagates.

TASTE.—The sphere of activity of taste is confined to the perception of savors; it is particularly useful to nutrition.

SMELL.—The sense of smell procures the sensations of odor. All its other functions are mediate. By its means, the world begins to act upon man and animals from a distance, odorous particles being detached from external bodies, and affecting the olfactory nerves. This sense informs animals of the existence of their food, and of the approach of friends and enemies.

HEARING.—The immediate function of the sense of hearing is the perception of sound; but it assists many of the internal, more especially of the affective powers.

SIGHT.—The sense of sight perceives light and its different degrees of intensity; it also informs man and animals of remote objects by means of an intermedium. Sight and hearing appear commonly later after birth than the other senses. Some animals, however, come into the world with perfect ears and eyes. Others are said to learn to hear and see; that is to say, they come into the world with imperfect organs of sight and hearing.

GENUS II. PERCEPTIVE FACULTIES.

These faculties are destined to make man and animals acquainted with existences, with the physical qualities of external objects, and with their various relations.

22. INDIVIDUALITY.—The organ of Individuality is situated behind the root of the nose, between the eyebrows; where it is large, it is found in connexion with that beautiful form of nose denominated Grecian.

After Dr. Gall had discovered an external sign of the talent of learning by heart,* he was not long in perceiving that it by no means indicated every species of memory. He observed that among his schoolfellows some excelled in verbal memory, and remembered even words which they did not understand, while others were deficient in this qualification, but recollected with uncommon facility facts and events; that some were distinguished by a great memory of place; some were able to repeat, without

POPE MARTIN V.
22 Individuality.   27 Locality.

mistake, a piece of music which they had heard only once or twice, while others excelled in recollecting numbers and dates; but no individual possessed *all* these talents combined in himself. Subsequently to these observations, he learned that philosophers before him had arrived at similar conclusions, and had distinguished three varieties of memory—*memory of things, verbal memory,* and *memory of places.* In society, he observed persons who, though not always profound, were learned, had a

* Gall's Works, vol. iv, p. 233.

superficial knowledge of all the arts and sciences, and knew enough to be capable of speaking upon them with facility, and he found in them the middle of the lower part of the forehead very much developed. At first he regarded this as the organ of the ' memory of things,' but on further reflection, he perceived that the name ' memory of things ' did not include the whole sphere of activity of the organ now under consideration. He observed that persons who had this part of the brain large, possessed not only a great memory of facts, but were distinguished by prompt conception in general, and an express facility of apprehension, a strong desire for information and instruction, a disposition to study all branches of knowledge, and teach these to others ; and also, that if not restrained by the higher faculties, such persons were naturally prone to adopt the opinions of others, to embrace new doctrines, and to modify their own minds according to the manners, customs, and circumstances with which they were surrounded. He therefore rejected the name ' memory of things,' and used the appellation somewhat analogous to the ' sense of perfecting education.' Dr. Spurzheim distinguishes this faculty as that ' which recognizes the existence of individual beings, whose activity and presence are denoted by substances in language. I acknowledge,' says he, ' that no objects are inseparable from their qualities, and that these constitute objects, but I think it possible to conceive existence or entity without knowing its qualities — as GOD — the mind.' These views of Dr. Spurzheim have fixed the name of the organ.

23. FORM.—The organ of Form is situated in the internal angle of the orbit. If large, it pushes the eyeball outwards and downwards, towards the internal angle, and thus separates the eyes from the root of the nose, and from each other.

Dr. Gall was struck with the curious fact,* that certain persons and animals recognise, with the greatest ease,

* Works, vol. v, p. 1.

individuals whom they have once seen, though years may elapse before they meet them again.

Being desired to examine the head of a young girl who had an extreme facility in distinguishing and recollecting persons, he found her eyes pushed laterally outward, and a certain squinting look; after innumerable additional observations, he spoke of it as the organ of the 'knowledge of persons.'

Dr. Spurzheim's designation appears to us to be the more appropriate and correct, namely, Configuration. ' To me there seems to exist an essential and fundamental power,' says Dr. Spurzheim, 'taking cognizance of Configuration generally, and one of whose peculiar applications or offices is recollection of persons, for persons are only known by their forms. I separate the faculty which approaches Configuration from that of Individuality, since we may admit the existence of being, without taking the figure into consideration. Individuality may be excited

by every one of the external senses, by smell and hearing as well as by feeling and sight, while the two latter senses alone assist the organ of Configuration. It is this power which disposes us to give a figure to every being and conception of our minds—that of a venerable man to God —to death a skeleton, and so on. This organ varies in size in whole nations. Many of the Chinese have it much developed. It is commonly large in the French, whose skill in producing certain elegant articles of industry is well known; combined with Constructiveness, it invents the patterns of dressmakers and milliners. It leads poets to describe portraits and configurations, and induces those who make collections of pictures and engravings to prefer portraits, if they have it in a high degree.' In a work called 'Arts and Artists,' vol i, p. 118, it is related that ' a man of the name of Huber had acquired such a facility in *forming Voltaire's* countenance, that he could not only cut out most striking likenesses of him out of paper with scissors held behind his back, but could mould a little bust of him in half a minute out of a bit of bread; and, at last, used to make his dog manufacture most excellent profiles, by making him bite off the edge of a biscuit, which he held to him in three or four different positions.'

Immediately after the organ of Configuration is situated—

24. SIZE.—' The faculty of distinguishing form differs from the faculty of size,' says Mr. Combe. ' The size may be the same, and the form different. One of these kinds of knowledge may exist without the other, and there is no proportion between them.' Dr. Spurzheim, therefore, inferred by reasoning, that there would be a faculty, the function of which is to perceive size; and observation has proved the soundness of this conclusion, for the situation assigned by him to the organ has been found to be correct. A member of the Phrenological Society called on Dr. Spurzheim at Paris, and the doctor observed to him that he had the organ of Size largely developed. This proved to be a correct indication of the talent in his case, for he possesses the power of discriminating size with great nicety. He is able to draw a

circle without the aid of any instrument, and to point out the centre of it with mathematical accuracy. Being in the army, he found himself able to make his company fall from column into line with great exactness, estimating correctly by the eye the space to be occupied by the men, which many other officers could never learn to do.'* Among professors of the useful arts, we frequently give preference to particular individuals who have such exact ideas of proportion, that if they are but informed of the size of a building, they will have every article of furniture corresponding. Thus, a cabinet-maker who has this faculty large will never take an order until he has been either accurately informed of the size of the apartment or otherwise seen the room where it is to be placed. A joiner will fit up a shop with the strictest attention to every part receiving its just proportion; an architect will bring into use and beauty every inch of ground upon which he intends to build; and a geometrician and mathematician will measure, with the nicest accuracy, the heavenly bodies or terrestial objects. Of these organs of Configuration and Size, we have some striking illustrations in the erection of the temple of Solomon.

Adjoining Size, at the commencement of the eyebrow—

25. WEIGHT is situated.—This faculty is as yet involved in some degree of conjecture. Dr. Spurzheim dismisses it in half-a-dozen lines; but Mr. Combe notices some interesting particulars in connection with it. The faculty being in the vicinity of Form, Size, and Individuality, would lead us to conclude that it is a necessary adjunct to the whole; and if this be admitted, then such a faculty must be necessary to the formation of a good mechanic. In men whose minds dispose them to mechanical pursuits, I have often observed that the parts where Size and Weight develope themselves give a heavy lowering brow, so that a physiognomist would, in many instances, pronounce them as a crabbed and ill-natured set. I have known persons of whom I have formed a similar

* 'Combe's Phrenology,' p. 288.

opinion, but who have turned out upon acquaintance to be men of the best hearts, and of the utmost good-nature. A gentleman of our acquaintance in Newcastle, and an engineer in the same town, present a most remarkable configuration of this sort. They are both largely developed in Weight. The reason, therefore, why we see so many engineers with heavy brows, is owing to the large development of the organs of Size and Weight. In man as well as animals, a knowledge of gravity or weight is indispensable for the preservation of the equilibrium. This power is in some more distinctly and fully developed than in others. Two persons unexpectedly meeting, one perhaps hastily coming from an avenue or turning a corner, the other as hastily passing, are differently affected by the violence of the collision. One stands like a ton of iron, the other staggers beneath the force of the resistance, and would assuredly fall were it not for the support which the opposing power lends. I have observed, and considered it remarkable, that in those in whom this faculty is large, in coming in collision with those in whom it is deficient, they generally catch them in their arms to prevent their falling. Dr. Epps knew a founder, who, endowed with all the perceptive faculties, so large as to amount to a positive deformity, was perpetually complaining of his men, because, when working in iron, they used too much or too little force. Had the founder studied phrenology, he would not have expected from men who had not so full a development of the organ as himself, the same degree of tact. In animals the power of weight or gravity may be said to manifest itself strikingly. If a cat be thrown from ever so great a height, it will constantly alight on its feet, thus showing that it estimates the force of the air, and provides, by the disposition of its body, for the spot on which it expects to alght.

A bird estimates the force of the air, and expands or diminishes its tail and wings as it rises into or descends from the atmosphere. A fish estimates the weight of water, and exerts its fins and tail accordingly to overcome the resistance. The facility of recovering the balance by a sudden jerk of the hand, is no doubt familiar to all. All these instances prove, that whether the organ be yet fully established or not, there must be a faculty which cognizes weight. But the part now indicated seems to be the real spot where this function developes its powers.

26. COLORING.—This organ is immediately adjoining Weight, and in the centre of the eyebrow. The functions of the organ consist in the distinction of color in all its variety of tints and shades.

Though the eye is the organ by which we are presumed alone to be able to distinguish color accurately, it is well known that there have been, nay, now are in existence, persons who have been unable to distinguish color ; and

RUBENS.

that, too, though in other respects the organ of sight has been singularly acute. This, therefore, proves that the organ of Coloring is an independent faculty; and this accounts for the fact that many artists who are singularly correct in the construction of their pictures, are greatly deficient in coloring. Some artists have been known to produce the most exquisite sketches in pencil, who, when they have taken a brush in hand to color, have produced the vilest daubs. Dr. Spurzheim mentions a family, the whole of the individuals composing which could only distinguish black and white, which, technically speaking, are no colors at all : and Dr. Epps mentions a tailor, with whom he is acquainted, who is so deficient in the organ of Color, that he frequently puts the cloth which is for lining the inside of the collar outside : his wife is obliged to exercise a vigilant superintendence over him to prevent this. Mr. Combe mentions a case of Mr. Milne in Edinburgh, which is equally authentic :— 'Mr. Milne's grandfather, on the mother's side, had a deficiency in the power of perceiving colors, but could distinguish forms and distance easily. On one occasion this gentleman was desirous that his wife should purchase a beautiful green dress. She brought several patterns to him, but could never find one that came up to his views of the color in question. One day he observed a lady passing on the street, and pointed out her dress to his wife, as the color that he wished her to get; when she expressed her astonishment, and assured him that the color was a mixed brown, which he had all along mistaken for a green. It was not known till then that he was deficient in the power of perceiving colors.' All these instances concur in establishing the fact, that the organ of *Color* is an independent power. This organ is indispensable in a dyer, painter, or enameller; success in either of these branches would be hopeless without it.

In a memoir of the late Mr. Troughton, the well-known astronomical instrument maker, which appears in the Annual Report of the Astronomical Society, 1835, there is the following statement :—'The only astronomical instrument which is not greatly indebted to Mr. Troughton is the telescope; and he was deterred from any attempt in this branch of his art by a singular physical defect which existed in many of his family. He could not distinguish colors, and had little idea of them, except generally, as they conveyed the idea of greater or less light. The ripe cherry and its leaf were to him of one hue, only to be distinguished by their form; and he was in the habit of relating some curious mistakes committed by himself, and others of his relations, in confounding green and red. With this defect in his vision, he never attempted any experiments in which color was concerned, and it is difficult to see how he could have done so with success.'

27. LOCALITY.—This organ is situated immediately above Weight, and adjoining Eventuality. In the discovery of this organ, Dr. Gall relates, that being much attached to the study of natural history, he frequently went into the woods to snare small animals, and to catch birds, and to explore their nests; and though he was expert in this, yet he experienced great difficulty in returning to the spot, even though he might have marked the tree, and placed boughs of trees near to serve him as a guide. He had a schoolfellow named Schiedler, who, without any apparent effort, went directly to the tree where the nest was, or to the spot where the snare was set; and though they might set many snares in places where they never had been before, Schiedler never failed to find them out. As this boy was possessed of but very ordinary talents in other respects, Dr. Gall was much struck with his facility in remembering places. 'How is it,' said he one day to Schiedler, 'that you contrive to find your way so easily through intricate places, through which you have only once been? 'How is it,' replied his companion with the same feeling of surprise, 'that you contrive not to find yours?' Hoping to come to a knowledge of this peculiarity at a future day, Dr. Gall moulded his head, and closely observed the persons of others who had the same facility of remem-

brance. He was informed by the celebrated landscape
painter, Schoenberger, that in his travels he was accustomed to make only a general sketch of the objects that
interested him, and when he wished to make a picture
at any time afterwards, bushes, trees, and even stones,
rose spontaneously to his mind, and upon comparing
them with the original scenes were always found correct.

Dr. Gall next became acquainted with M. Meyer, who
wrote a romance called ' Diana Sore,' and who found no
pleasure so great as wandering from place to place.
Having also moulded his head, he placed the three side
by side, and though they were different in every other
respect, they all presented the same appearance at the spot
now indicated as the seat of the organ. He also met one
day with a woman who had such protuberances in this
spot that the forehead was quite deformed by it ; and on
discoursing with her, he found she had the greatest desire
to travel, that she never remained long in the same
country or in the same house, her greatest' delight being to
visit strange places. From all these observations, Dr.
Gall concluded that the faculty of remembering places
depended upon a primitive organ ; and experience has
since demonstrated this to be true. That this is absolutely
the case may be demonstrated from the fact, that even
where sight is deficient, and in some cases wholly extinct,
if Locality be large, the individual experiences no difficulty
in finding his way with the greatest apparent ease. The
celebrated blind traveller, Holman, is an instance of this
faculty, and with it, I should think, associated a pretty
large share of Benevolence. ' In all my travels,' says he,
' I cannot recall a single instance in which any person
attempted to take advantage of the confidence I reposed
in them, either in the receipt, exchange, or payment of
moneys. In making bargains, or estimating the quality of
articles by their prices, whenever I depended on my own
judgment, I do not remember that I ever had any reason
to be dissatisfied, nor do I think that in such matters I
was more imposed upon than I should have been had I

possessed my sight. Notwithstanding I have travelled so much in foreign countries, and had so extensive an intercourse with strangers, I think I can safely say that I have not been more deceived, or suffered greater losses in money transactions, than any of my countrymen. Thank God I have not found sufficient cause to arm myself with suspicion : for although there are despicable characters in all countries, who would not hesitate to take advantage of others, I am happy to think that human nature is not so bad as she is portrayed.' There is considerable benevolence in this description of mankind ; but the feeling of sympathy which the most callous sometimes may exemplify when viewing the deprivations of others, may not have been wholly without its influence in the treatment of the blind traveller. My principal object was, however, to bring forward Holman as an instance of the faculty of Locality. Again, the poet Rogers is an exemplification of this faculty, and in his portrait the organ is large; thus he observes :— ' Would he who sat in a corner of his library poring over books and maps learn more, or so much in the time, as he who, with his eyes and his heart open, is receiving impressions all the day-long from the objects themselves ? Assuredly not. Knowledge makes knowledge, as money makes money, nor never, perhaps, so fast as on a journey. How accurately do the *forms* arrange themselves in our memory—*towns, rivers, mountains ;* and in what *living colors* do we recall the *dresses, manners*, and customs of the people ! ' * All this is true in the case of an individual who, like Rogers, may have large knowing organs and a good Locality ; but it would be but little attractive to him in whom Inhabitiveness was large, and the organs of Form, Size, Color, and Locality deficient. In short, it will be found an invariable truth, that as the organs which develope themselves on the head predominate, so will the attachments of the individual tend, and nothing is more true in this respect than in Locality.

* Rogers' ' Italy,' pp. 172, 173.

28. NUMBER, OR CALCULATION. — The organ of Number is placed at the external angle of the orbit ; if it be large, this part projects and appears full. It embraces whatever concerns number ; hence, algebra, arithmetic, and logarithms belong to it.

A scholar of St. Poelton, near Vienna, being much spoken of on account of his arithmetical talent, Dr. Gall sent for him to Vienna. He was the son of a blacksmith, and had received no other education than is bestowed upon young persons in a similar walk of life. Dr. Gall observed in this boy a remarkable prominence in the external angle of the eye. 'I presented him,' says Dr. Gall,* 'to my audience : at this period he was nine years of age. When they gave him three numbers, each expressed by ten or twelve figures, asking him to add them, then to subtract them two by two, to multiply, and then divide them by numbers containing three figures ; he gave one look at the numbers, then raised his nose and eyes in the air, and announced the result of his mental calculation before my auditors had time to make the same calculation with their pens in their hands. He had created his method himself.'

An advocate of Vienna having stated his regret that a child of his had spent all his time, even to the exclusion of childish sports, in arithmetical calculations, Dr. Gall examined him, and found a similar prominence in the same situation. He next observed the head of Counsellor Mantelli, who was constantly occupying himself in the invention and solving of mathematical and arithmetical questions, and again the same prominence presented itself. Pondering on this, he visited several schools, and always found that those who excelled in arithmetical talent had this peculiar configuration. In Baron Vega, author of Tables of Logarithms, and at that time professor of Mathematics, he also discovered a similar configuration ; and he excelled in this particular department of science, although in everything else the doctor considered his

* Works, vol. v, p. 81.

talents as nothing above mediocrity. From all this evidence Dr. Gall concluded that this was a primitive faculty. Arithmetical talent has been often exemplified

JEDEDIAH BUXTON.

in children in this country, and has called forth much discussion among metaphysicians, as to whether the faculty is intuitive. Some teachers are of opinion, that boys of moderate talent, may, by diligent practice, be brought to equal, if not rival, the feats of the celebrated Zerah Colbourn, the American calculator. Mr. Hill, in his 'Plans for the Education and Liberal Instruction of Boys in large numbers,' says : — 'At one of our public exhibitions, a class of ten or twelve boys stood prepared to extract the cube roots (disregarding fractions) of any numbers, whether exact cubes or surds, which did not exceed two thousand millions. Many gentlemen present were furnished with tables of cubes and their roots : several questions were proposed, and answered with a rapidity which astonished the audience. This class had received very frequent practice, with the view of trying whether boys of tolerably good talents could not be educated to rival, or even to exceed the feats of this kind performed by the American youth, Zerah Colbourn.' There is no doubt but boys who have a good development of Number may, by training, be brought to exhibit the most astonishing arithmetical talent. But if Mr. Hill, or any other educator, were to take ten or twelve boys in whom this particular configuration was not to be found, all the drilling to which he might subject them would never enable them to exhibit powers above mediocrity.

In the portrait of Jedediah Buxton this organ is very prominent. He was unable to read or write, but his knowledge of Number and his facility of working intricate arithmetical questions was marvellous.

29. ORDER.—This organ lies between Coloring and Number, and Dr. Gall remarks respecting it, that from various observations which he has made, he has been enabled to elicit facts which prove that Order depends on a primitive power ; but on account of the difficulty of observing the organs placed in the superciliary ridge, and the small size of this organ in particular, as pointed out by Dr. Spurzheim, he has not been able to collect a sufficient number of determinate facts to authorise him to decide on its situation. Dr. Spurzheim, however, pronounces it established. The faculty itself gives the function of peculiar regularity and method in arrangement, and when well developed, there is great neatness and cleanliness in its possessor, as well in person as in the general order and arrangement of the house. There is nothing like bustle or confusion. The motto of such a person is, 'A place for everything, and everything in its place,' and with him all things are done decently and in order. In the portrait of Southey, the poet, this portion of the brain is prominently developed ; and Order was so predominant in him in his literary pursuits, that he absolutely wrote upon different subjects according to an arrangement previously made, which he was so exact in

adhering to that he wrote by a stop-watch. He was as orderly a mechanic in literature as can be well found; not only from day to day, from week to week, was this methodical arrangement persevered in, but absolutely from year to year.

Sir Walter Scott says, in a letter (1813) to Lord Byron, 'Southey is a real poet, such as we read of in former times, with every atom of his soul and every moment of his time dedicated to literary pursuits, in which he differs from almost all those who have divided public attention with him. His whole soul is dedicated to the pursuit of literature. In this respect, as well as in many others, he is a most striking and interesting character.' Surely, man of imagination was never so systematic, never so methodical as he. Rising at eight o'clock—never before eight, though his time for retiring to bed was the sober period of half-past ten; less than nine hours' sleep he found insufficient—he devoted the entire interspace between breakfast and dinner, that is to say, from nine A. M. to five P. M., or six P. M., to literary toil; after dinner, he attended to his private correspondence, which was unusually large; and so pointedly regular was he, that all letters were answered on the same evening which brought them. Well might he astonish less methodical people with the amount of elaborate business which he managed, by an unvarying system of arrangement in the distribution of his time. Southey was a student on principle; he pursued the muse with a chivalric devotion hat was no mere impulse of ebullient and transitory fervor, but a life-long passion, an all-pervading and ever-animating love. Hers he was, hers he would be, in evil report and good report, in season and out of season, whether she would or whether she would not. What name, in the whole cata-logue of authors, comes nearer the *beau ideal* of the man of letters? None was ever so perseveringly attached to his craft, none more uniformly loyal to the sovereignty of mind. He was a poet—some say of the very highest order; he was an antiquary—and had the true Oldbuck

37

gusto for matters archæological ; he was a critic—and received his hundred guineas (or thereabouts) per article for the reviews ; he was a biographer—and there are able men who prefer his lives of Nelson and Wesley to all his other productions ; he was an historian—and few more diligent in research, or lucid in style. In short, his industry was proverbial. Byron laughs savagely at it in his parody of the 'Vision of Judgment' :—

> ' He said (I only give the heads) he said,
> He meant no harm in scribbling 'twas his way
> Upon all topics; 'twas, besides, his bread,
> Of which he buttered both sides. 'Twould delay
> Too long the assembly (he was pleased to dread),
> And take up rather more time than a day,
> To name his works.'

The sarcasm does not stifle an underlying truth most honorable to the memory of this true working man. Southey was no idler upon earth ; his creed was exalted, and, as his creed was, so was his practice. His bitterest opponents must admire his conscientious industry.

When this organ is small, it leads to irregularity and slovenliness. The appearance of a slattern is but the proof of the want of order. Persons of this description have sat down with the utmost contentment in the midst of confusion, second only to Babel, and they seem to have an utter inability to rectify the abuse. The Esquimaux are instances of deficiency in this organ, and they are described on all hands as equally filthy and disgusting.

30. EVENTUALITY.—Dr. Gall admits both in man and animals a peculiar organ of Educability, or of the memory of things and events. Daily we meet with individuals possessing a general knowledge of the arts and sciences, and who, without being profound, know sufficient to be capable of speaking on them with facility; individuals who are deemed clever and brilliant in society. The middle part of their foreheads, Dr. Gall found was very regularly prominent. At first he called the cerebral part in the above situation, the organ of "the

memory of things," because those largely endowed with it were commonly well informed, and knew a great deal ; he afterwards named it "the sense of things." In comparing animals with man, and one species of animals with another, he found that tame have fuller foreheads than wild animals, and that animals are generally tameable, as the forehead is more largely developed ; he, therefore, afterwards, called it the organ of Educability. Dr. Spurzheim objects to this name, as every faculty may be educated; or, in other words, exercised and directed : consequently, he has named it Eventuality.* It enters into a large share of the business of actual life ; it takes cognizance of things past or present : it confers an aptitude for anecdote, and a general facility for the acquisition of the principles of science and philosophy. It is also powerful in aiding the memory, and bringing forth, at seasons most necessary, those felicitous illustrations, which carry, as it were, conviction with them. Memory is to the mind what a storehouse is for goods, preserving all kinds of merchandise, that it may meet every emergency of the market, and thus be able to compete with all. In the person of the celebrated Magliabechi, who was considered a prodigy of learning, this faculty was strikingly exemplified, as will be exemplified by the following anecdote : 'A gentleman of Florence, having written a piece, which he intended at a future time to publish, lent the manuscript to Magliabechi for his perusal, who returned it to the author with many thanks. Some time after, the writer with a melancholy countenance came to Magliabechi, and told him of some invented accident, by which he said he had lost his MS., and entreated Magliabechi—whose character for remembering what he read was already very great—to try and recollect as much of it as he possibly could, and write it down for him against his next visit. Magliabechi assured him that he would do so, and setting about it, wrote down the whole MS., without missing a word, or even varying, according to his

* Spurzheim's 'Phrenology.'

biographer, anywhere from the spelling.' In this case, there must have been great Locality and Form, as well as Eventuality and Language. Individuality must, likewise, have been largely developed. Of his Locality, it is stated that he could not only lay his hand on a book that he might want, momentarily, but could direct any other person, with such minuteness of detail, to the very spot where a book was to be found, that filled all persons with astonishment at the extent of his powers of memory. Of his Individuality, Form, and Language, we have an instance in the anecdote just narrated, that he wrote down the whole of the piece without varying from the spelling, etc. But Eventuality seemed to be the predominating power, and, it accordingly lent its aid to those other faculties that were fully developed. This person left his library to the public, the bare catalogue of which filled three volumes folio. He died in 1714.

Hazlitt, in his contemporary portraits, thus describes Sir James Mackintosh:—' There is scarcely an author that he has not read ; a period of history that he is not conversant with ; a celebrated name of which he has not a number of anecdotes to relate ; an intricate question that he is not prepared to enter upon in a popular or scientific manner. If an opinion in an abstruse metaphysical author is referred to, he is probably able to repeat the passage by heart ; can tell the side of the page on which it is to be met with ; can trace it back through various descents, from Locke, Hobbes, Lord Herbert of Cherbury, to a place in some obscure folio of the schoolmen, or a note in one of the commentators of Aristotle or Plato, and thus give you in a few moments' space, and without any effort or previous notice, a chronological table of the progress of the human mind in that particular branch of inquiry. This is the result of very large Causality, Eventuality, Locality, and Language.' Brougham is thus described by the same author :—' There are few intellectual accomplishments that he does not possess, and possess in a very high degree. He speaks French and several other modern languages fluently ; is a capital mathematician, and obtained an introduction to the celebrated Carnot in this latter character, when the conversation turned on squaring the circle, and not on the propriety of confining France within the natural boundary of the Rhine.'

31. TIME.—Above the centre of the eyebrow, directly over Color, is situated the organ of Time. This is a distinctly different organ from those of Order and Number, its functions being more properly to give the idea of duration, than strictly to take cognizance of exact numbers, or of orderly arrangement. It is essential to all persons. To the musician it is highly useful—it gives that just and accurate duration to the several parts of a piece of music, which so essentially contributes to the power of the harmony. We do not, however, find it unusual to meet with persons who have what is called a good musical ear—in phrenological language, a good organ of Tune—but, who, nevertheless, are so sadly deficient in Time, as to be totally unfit for performing in a concert.

This was the case with Paganini, who, though the most celebrated violinist that perhaps ever lived, was yet sadly deficient in Time.—Some persons judge with exceeding exactness in regard to time. In the phrenological analysis of Campbell (the murderer), Time was so large, that the individual who indicated his character assumed that he would probably be able to tell the hour without the aid of a clock or watch, and this has, to a degree, been proved correct. On the contrary, on a similar analysis by Mr. Simpson of the cast of a gentleman, he mentions a want of punctuality of appointments, owing to a deficient perception of the lapse of time. This the gentleman acknowledges to be true : observing—' Appointments I never on any occasion wilfully break, as I consider the thing dishonest ; but I sometimes, or rather frequently, do so from forgetting them, or from forming a wrong estimate of time. I can make nothing of time unless I have my watch. I have seen me, when my watch was mending, mistake three o'clock P.M. for noon, and *vice versa*.

To the poet, the faculty of Time imparts a knowledge of that harmonious duration, which gives what is technically termed the exact number of feet, *i. e.*, of syllables, in a line. This regularity is particularly observable in the compositions of Pope and Wharton. In blank verse poets, as Milton, there is a frequent closing of a stanza with a line which either contains one or two less, or one or two more, syllables, than the strict measure of time will allow. This, however, is only tolerated where the sense would be incomplete without it, or where the verse is acknowledged as irregular. Rogers is an instance of this innovation on the order of time. The organ is useful to the orator, and marks the necessary gradations for emphasis, pause, and cadence. To the Christian, the faculty is also indispensable. The duration of his existence in this world is but seventy years, and, as he believes in divine revelation, he should take due heed to the lapse of time ; as he knows that every hour brings him nearer to eternity, he should endeavor constantly to improve it. It should never be absent from his remembrance that time is but the germ of eternity.

3. MELODY OR TUNE is situate over the organs of Order and Number, towards the lateral part of the forehead, between Time and Construction.

Some persons are so instantly arrested by music played in the street, that they find it almost impossible to leave the spot whence the sounds emanate, until the whole of the piece is played through. Others will pass by during the performance of the most exquisite strains, and be not at all affected by what many would term the most *soul-subduing harmony*.

Some pupils who have been placed under the care of music masters learn almost intuitively : others, with the utmost labor and diligence, can never compass a single

tune. Music masters have evidenced the truth of this remark hundreds of times.

I once had under my care at Bristol a deaf and

HANDEL.

dumb pupil, who had a very large development of Tune, and manifested extreme anxiety when it was pursued in the regular business of the school. By the mere motion of the lips, as he perceived it in myself, he had acquired one tune perfectly, and gave utterance to it in low, plaintive, and not inaccurate sounds. He was considered as a prodigy amongst us, and many were the individuals that came to hear the dumb boy hum a tune: of course there was no articulation, and indeed at that time no knowledge of words. This shows that music is an independent and primitive power, and does not depend upon any of the other faculties; but this was never known until phrenology, as a science, was promulgated by Gall.

The functions of this organ produce a desire for melody or tune, and of all the delightful arts that tend to throw a charm over man's chequered state of being, music is certainly one of the most charming. It seems wonderful there should be any persons who object to it — such, for instance, as the Quakers ; but this could never be, unless there was a deficiency of the cerebral organisation ; and this, if persons will take the opportunity of observing the generality of Quakers, will be found the case ; the lateral parts of the forehead are in many of them quite flat, and in some absolutely hollow. This is not, however, the case with all. I knew a young Quakeress in Bristol in 1825, who was an excellent performer on the guitar, and another elderly one of Liverpool in 1827, who was one of the sweetest singers I had ever heard, and as she attended the girls in a large school that I superintended, I had the gratification of frequently hearing her sing. In both these ladies the organ of music was full, but they exercised it in direct violation of an express law of the Society of Friends. I have no doubt but this law originated in the founder, George Fox, through an excessive development of Conscientiousness, supposing that there was more gratification to the creature than real praise to the Creator, at least in most instances of the use of music. Should phrenology make way among the Society of Friends, as it is sure to make way everywhere in time, there is no doubt but that they will use the organ of music without abusing it, and thus gratify both Conscience and Order at the same time, while they give proper latitude to music.

At a meeting of the Phrenological Society at Paris, some years since, M. Follati, the president, made some curious demonstrations on the plaster cast of the head of Bellini, taken the morning after the death of that young and eminent composer. From the observations of the learned Doctor, it would appear that the strong feeling and expression which characterised the inspirations of the author of Norma, is to be attributed to the organ of Benevolence, which was largely developed. He ascribed the graceful *nonchalance* and sweet soft delicacy of his airs, to the smallness of his organs of Courage and Firm-

ness. If rhythm was generally the deficiency of all others
in the composer's works—if the melodious expression is
brief, and appears to want breadth, he considered it was
to be attributed to the organ of Time, or the faculty
of embracing many objects at once, which organ was
also very slightly developed. This deficiency was followed by another equally remarkable in the Doctor's
opinion, viz., the organ of Construction, which indicates
dexterity of fingers. And, in fact, it is well known
that Bellini was very *mal-adroit* at the piano, even when
playing his own compositions.

The organs of Time and Construction are, on the contrary, much more developed in Paer, Rossini, and generally in all geniuses possessing the powerful talent of
rhythm and harmony.

The bust of Paganini supplied M. Follati with facts
not less interesting than the foregoing. The organ of
Music, he stated, was developed to the fullest extent,
as well as the *tactivitie* or firmness of touch evinced
in his fingering the strings. The organ of Time is
deficient, which accords with the remark often made,
that this prince of fiddlers was very neglectful of the
strict rules of harmony.

33. LANGUAGE is situated about the middle of the
orbitar process of the frontal bone, and, when large, gives
fulness to the eyes. The scholars whom Dr. Gall had
the greatest difficulty of competing with, were those who
had the most prominent eyes. These ·learned their
several tasks with the utmost facility, and those who
possessed not this talent, among whom was Dr. Gall,
revenged themselves in a small way, by nick-naming
them *ox-eyed.* To the observation of Dr. Gall in this
respect, we primarily owe the establishment of this
science. Whatever seminary Dr. Gall studied at, he
invariably observed that the *ox-eyed* students always
learned by heart with the greatest ease ; and though they
were, in many instances, much inferior in real talents
to those whom they eclipsed in the learning of words,

yet this very circumstance drew upon the others very severe rebukes from the different teachers. This is also the case at the present day among teachers. When phrenology has made sufficient progress that teachers have

become acquainted with its principles, they will cease to exact from their pupils those long catalogues of words which are acquired with great pain, and forgotten with real pleasure. Dr. Gall continued to make his observations on this circumstance, and the organ is now fully established. The special function of this organ is explained in its name; and may be considered as the power by which language itself is acquired, whether the language be native or foreign, dead or living. Persons who have a large endowment of this faculty abound in words : there seems to be no lack ; like a copious stream, they pour forth words in a torrent of profusion, and appear never at a loss for an expression by which to give utterance to their ideas.

In the cultivation of the faculty of language, it is much to be lamented that children's memories are generally overloaded with an abundance of words, of the meaning of which they are almost wholly ignorant. Pestalozzi recommended to his disciples, that the best method of learning boys a language was to permit them to progress in the knowledge of words no further than they could comprehend them. Let them write down half a dozen words; then find out their derivation; then proceed to form them into sentences, and this will exercise all their faculties; whereas any child may be taught to repeat *words*, although of the true meaning of them he may continue in hopeless ignorance. 'Great linguists, (says the author of the Book of Aphorisms) are for the most part great blockheads.' I say nothing of Sir William Jones, the admirable Crichton, and other exceptions to the rule. But, generally speaking, what I say holds true. To master a variety of languages requires only one talent, and that by no means a high one, viz., a good verbal memory, which is sometimes possessed, in great perfection, even by simpletons and idiots. It is difficult for men of very strong and original minds to become good linguists. They are so much taken up with substantialities, that they think little about words. The knowledge of a number of languages does not communicate a single new idea. It only gives the power of expressing what we already know in a variety of ways. 'I would rather (says Dr. Spurzheim) acquire one new idea, than twenty ways of expressing an old one.' If men of great genius are occasionally formidable as linguists, they are so in spite of their genius, which rather stands in their way than assists them; and they would have been still greater linguists if they had possessed their powerful verbal memory unaccompanied with less original talent.—When a person is found deficient in words to express his ideas, although his ideas may be very distinct before him, he may, to a certain extent, remedy the defect by learning pieces by heart, or translating into his own, pieces from a foreign language.

GENUS III.—REFLECTING FACULTIES.

These powers constitute what is usually denominated reason. They are the supreme powers of the intellect, and contribute to direct and assist the respective faculties in their various duties.

34. COMPARISON.—This organ is situated in the upper part of the forehead, with Eventuality before and Benevolence behind. Of this organ Dr. Spurzheim remarks :— 'Each other intellectual faculty compares its own appropriate and peculiar notions. Melody, for instance, compares tones; Coloring, colors; Configuration, forms; Calculation, numbers, etc. ; but this special power compares the functions of a l the other primitive faculties, points out resemblances, analogies, identities, and differences. Its essential nature is to compare. It is therefore fond of analogies, in the same way as Melody likes the harmony of tones, and Coloring the harmony

of colors ; but it also appreciates differences, just as Melody and Coloring feel discords among their respective impressions. Differences, in fact, are the discords of the faculty of Comparison. This power produces discrimination, generalization, abstraction, and induces the mind, wishing to communicate unknown ideas, to refer and to illustrate by such as are known, or to speak in examples. It is destined to establish harmony among all mental phenomena. By the influence of this power, artificial signs become figurative. The nations, consequently, who have it active, have a metaphorical language.

The organ of Comparison is also large in myself, and I have frequently used particular associations to remember events in history, without the aid of which I am, through a deficiency in Individuality, unable to recollect dates. In a system of *Mnemonics*, which I compiled for my own and my children's use some years since, I associated in my mind the accession of Elizabeth with the color *yellow*. I did this because yellow is the frequent comparison of melancholy; and she was frequently in the melancholy mood. Mary I associated with a *bonfire*. And when the late king, William iv., ascended the throne, and there was a strife between the two great parties in the state [which should get the most power,] I pictured in my mind the state infested with *vermin*. But I took care, in all these instances, that whatever I associated in my mind should give me an answer to the question, what times the various sovereigns ascended the throne.

35. Causality is situated on each side of Comparison. It has very frequently been observed, that men who possess comprehensive minds—such as Socrates, Bacon, Galileo, and others—have the upper part of the forehead finely and fully prominent. At Vienna, Dr. Gall remarked, that in the most zealous disciples of Kant, men distinguished for profound, penetrating, metaphysical talent, the parts of the brain immediately outwards, and to the sides of the organ of Comparison, were distinctly enlarged. Drs. Gall and Spurzheim, after noticing this configuration in the disciples of Kant afterwards saw a mask of Kant himself, moulded after death, and perceived an extraordinary projection of these parts. At a later period they became personally

acquainted with Fichte, and found a development in
that region still larger than in Kant.   Innumerable
additional observations satisfied them of the functions
of this organ.   Dr. Gall named it ‘ *Esprit Metaphysique,*’
but Dr. Spurzheim calls it *Causality*.   ‘The ancient
artists,’ says Dr. Spurzheim, ‘have given to Jupiter a
head more prominent than any other of the antique
heads ; and hence it would appear that they had
observed that the development of the forehead has a
relation to a great understanding.’

Mr. Combe gives some highly interesting illustrations
of this faculty. ‘A gentleman in a boat,’ says he, ‘was
unexpectedly asked to steer.   He took hold of the
helm, hesitated a moment what to do, and then steered
with just effect.   Being asked why he hesitated, he
replied—“I was unacquainted with steering, and required
to think how the helm acts.”   He was requested to
explain how thinking led him to the point, and replied
that he knew, from study, the theory of the helm’s
action ; that he just run over in his mind the water’s
action upon it, and its action on the boat, and then he
saw the whole plainly before him.   He had a large
Causality, and not much Individuality.   A person with a
great Individuality and little Causality, placed in a similar
situation, would have tried the experiment of the helm’s
action to come to a knowledge of the mode of steering.
He would have turned it to the right hand and to the
left, and observed the effect, then acted accordingly ;
and he might have steered his whole life thereafter,
without knowing any more of the matter.’   In those
persons in whom Causality is large, there is a constant
endeavor to trace up things to their proper source.
They will not believe the effect, unless to a certain
degree they are acquainted with the cause, We should
certainly hold the apostle Paul to be an illustration of
this faculty, from the circumstance of his using the
precept—‘ Prove all things ; hold fast that which is
good.’   So, too, the apostle Peter must have recognised

its power, when he exhorted his converts to be always ready to give a reason of the hope that is in them, with meekness and fear.

In all great and original thinkers, this faculty is largely developed. In the portraits of Bacon and Locke it is eminently conspicuous, and in the bust of Gall it is strikingly large. When the organ is small, the mind is apt to be superficial, and the individual experiences great difficulty in reasoning after a logical manner. Such persons as these will find very great difficulty in receiving the truth of phrenology, because the power of evidence will make but small impression on their minds. This is also one reason why persons who have large Self-esteem will not admit the evidence of phrenology. They, generally speaking, have too high an opinion of their own discernment to listen to the evidence of others. Thus, then, if Self-esteem be large, and the reflecting faculties small, it will be almost hopeless to convince such an individual.

The organ of Causality, situated as it is on each side of Comparison, seems to act by necessary correspondency. It does not place implicit faith in analogies, and thus acts as a necessary check on the rapid, often plausible, but sometimes erroneous conclusions of Comparison. In searching out causes, it, of necessity, infers a great First Cause. The faculty of Individuality makes us acquainted with objects ; that of Eventuality with facts ; that of Comparison points out their analogy or difference ; and the faculty of Causality desires to know the causes of occurrences. Where all these faculties are fully developed, the truly philosophic understanding is formed.

CONCLUDING OBSERVATIONS ON THE ART OF PRACTICAL PHRENOLOGY.

Accurate knowledge in regard to the different regions of the brain gives facility in finding the locality of the different organs. There are several bony prominences on the skull, which do not indicate developments of the

brain : these are the mastoid prominences behind the
ears ; the crucial spine of the occiput, or bony projection
situate below Philoprogenitiveness ; the zygomatic process, extending from the cheek-bones to the temples ;
and the ridge in the middle of the coronal surface of the
skull, occasioned by the longitudinal sinus. The individual
organs extend from the medulla oblongata, or top of the
spinal marrow, to the surface of the cerebrum or cerebellum.
The line, or axis, passing through the head from one ear to
the other, connecting together the two *meatus auditorii,*
or openings of the ear, would nearly touch the medulla
oblongata, and hence is assumed as a convenient point
from which to estimate length. The distance from the
centre of the line to the peripheral surface of the brain,
measures the length of the organ there situated. A line,
for instance, drawn from that point to that part of the
surface of the brain where the organ of Comparison is
situated, measures the length of that organ.   But the
size of an organ depends upon its breadth, as well as
its length ; the breadth is estimated by its peripheral
expansion at the surface. Each organ has some resemblance to an inverted cone, having its apex at the centre
of the axis, and its base at the surface of the brain.
As a general rule, the size of the organ indicates its
power. The same general law, that, under like conditions, proportions the strength of a body to its size, and
is everywhere found coupling power with large dimensions, applies as infallibly to the cerebral organs as to
all other organs in the animal system, and all other
parts in the system of things ; the same rule that ascertains the contents of a cone, ascertains the contents of
the cerebral organs.   The size of an organ is therefore
essentially different from its prominence at the surface
of the brain. If an organ possesses an ample development, while its neighbors that bound it on every side are
defectively developed, then it will present a prominence ;
but if the organs surrounding it are equally well developed,
no prominence at the surface will be perceived, but a

general fulness, indicating an equal extent of development. It is precisely the same in regard to a defectively developed organ. Both the prominences and recessions presented at the surface speak only a relative, not an absolute language. The only true mode of ascertaining size, is to estimate, as near as possible, the dimensions of the organ at the surface of the brain, and the distance of that surface from the centre of the axis. In an equal development of the organs, a difficulty may occur in estimating the dimensions of an individual organ at the surface, as no prominence will then be presented ; and hence, as many would infer, no positive data upon which to ground an estimate. In a case of that kind, the superficial dimensions may be calculated from the general size of that region of the head where the organ is situated. In the equal development of a number of organs, their superficies will increase in proportion as they recede from the axis. The periphery of the whole head must obviously increase in the direct ratio to its size. The periphery of its several parts must follow the same general rule. It therefore follows, as a necessary consequence, that in equal developments of different organs, the breadth of each organ will increase in proportion to the increase of its length ; hence, in cases of that kind, the length of an organ affords the data from which its breadth may be estimated. In regarding size as indicative of power, care must be taken to distinguish between power and activity. The one has reference to the *energy*, the other to the *rapidity*, with which the faculties act. The one accomplishes by a slow but sure movement, the other by a quick and sudden turn. While the balance-wheel of a watch exhibits activity, the elements of power are manifested in the walking-beam of a steam-engine ; hence you *perceive* that a watch has a sanguine-nervous temperament, while a steam-engine has a *bilious-lymphatic*. The same quantum of power, other circumstances being equal, ought to be attended with the same degree of activity ; which is, in fact, nothing more than a facility

38

and quickness in the exercise of it by the individual. The general rule, that the size of an organ indicates its power, must of course be subject to the condition of other things being equal. The circumstances under which individuals have been placed, and their agency in calling forth the faculties into active manifestation, together with the different temperaments of individuals, ﹑ or the strong original tendencies of their constitutions, are disturbing elements in the application of the general rule. Their disturbing forces can to some extent be estimated, and the effects they produce be calculated upon in the modification of size. Exercise, in effect, varies power, by rendering it more available. The size of the organ gives the tendency to the proper exercise of its functions. The tendency to that exercise is also given by the presentment of external objects fitted by nature to excite to activity. Let those objects be wanting, and the power itself might slumber, and would possess less aptitude to exert itself in proportion to the paucity of objects that could call it into exercise. Men are variously situated in regard to the conditions under which they act, and the circumstances that surround them : hence, faculties of the same degree of strength in different individuals may have been exposed in different degrees to those objects that constitute their natural aliment. From this results the difference in the opportunities afforded for their exercise. To estimate properly the influence of this modifying cause, the circumstances in which the individual has been placed must be considered. That influence, under ordinary circumstances, seldom forms a large item in the estimate, because the kind of objects fitted to call into exercise the activities of the mind may be found in almost every sphere of human life. We all breathe the same atmosphere, tread the same earth, are overhung by the same heavens, and surrounded by the same kind of natural objects. Had the destiny of a Franklin penned him within the limits of a sheepfold, we might not, at this time, have seen the lightning of heaven controlled by human agency ; but his faculties would, nevertheless, within a limited sphere, have sought and found the objects they were framed to act upon. ' Orfila,' says the ' Medical Times,' ' the best known of living scientific men, doctor of medicine and surgery, professor of chemistry, and dean of the most distinguished medical faculty in the world, member of the academy of medicine, commander of the legion of honor, peer-elect of France in 1844, so illustrious alike in rank and deeds, was in 1804 a *poor pilot boy* in a miserable Spanish coaster.'

To estimate properly the disturbing force of exercise as a modification of size, it becomes necessary to be acquainted with individual history. The modification of size most important to be attended to, results from the original constitution or quality of the body. These are indicated by the *temperament* of the individual.

In the reduction of this science to practice, after ascertaining the general size of the head, the next point to be settled is—are the different regions of the brain and the organs that compose them equally developed ? If so, the tendencies to action will be every way alike ; the individual will exhibit the most opposite phases of character, and his actions will be called forth, not by the predominance of faculties, but by the predominating influence of the circumstances in which he may happen to be placed. If those circumstances are in their nature calculated to excite the propensities, the rein will be given to them. If to call into exercise the higher sentiments, they, for the time being, will exercise a controlling influence ; the one would lead to sin, the other to repentance, and these together would form no inconsiderable item in his biography. Such a person was Sheridan. In the estimate of such a character, or rather such an absence of all fixed character, the circumstances should be alone considered. But these are varying every hour. An individual of this description would, therefore, be a subject that would set calculation and estimate, and every kind of conclusion, at defiance ;

excepting always the conclusion that nothing could be
concluded upon. Possessing tendencies to action, and
capacities of acting, every way alike, he would be the
unresisting subject of circumstances ; a case of this kind,
however, is of rare occurrence.

The subject next to be ascertained would be, whether
any one organ was developed to any considerable extent
beyond others. If so, its controlling influence will pervade, in a greater or less degree, every department,
whether of feeling or of intellect. It would constitute
what is generally termed a leading feature, or prominent
trait, in his character. A large Love of Approbation
would seek its appropriate aliment, through all the means
that could be rendered available for that purpose by the
faculties that were combined with it.

In no instance is this more strikingly exemplified than
in the career of the late Sir Francis Burdett. I cannot
forbear quoting a newspaper sketch of him, published in
1837 :—'At one time we find him as the leader of the
radicals, standing almost alone in the Commons against
the ancient oligarchy, launching his thunder against the
boroughmongers, sent to the Tower for defence of a private citizen's rights, and encountering a government
prosecution and its consequences for his indignant denunciation of the magistracy and yeomanry who cut down a
peaceable and unarmed multitude met at Manchester for
the purpose of petitioning for Parliamentary Reform. At
another time we find him coldly supporting the Grey
administration in its forward movements, but giving it his
hearty support whenever the Stanley and Graham obstruc-
tive interests predominated ; and, when the Melbourne
administration came into power, with the promise, at least,
of carrying out nearly all the principles which he formerly
professed, we find him abandoning all those principles, and
regularly enlisting in the ranks of the men who had ever
been the enemies of that reform which it had been his
glory to advocate.

'Does the history of England present another such

instance of inconsistency and imbecility? And does the philosophy of Stewart and Reid, with their understanding and will, and judgment and imagination, and memory and common sense, afford any explanation of the extraordinary and pitiable changes which take place in the conduct of public men?

'The truth is, that in looking for the cause of Sir Francis Burdett's tergiversation, we must come to the science of Gall, and Spurzheim, and Combe. Sir Francis has always had an exceeding "Love of Approbation." When a very young man, his desire for applause took the direction of literary fame, and he was proud to figure as one of the interlocutors in John Horne Tooke's "Diversions of Purley." Subsequently, and still under the influence of Horne Tooke's more powerful mind, it was gratified with the shouts of the multitude, and the title of "England's Glory and Westminster's Pride." Even his palmiest days, when these misgoverned islands "rung from side to side" with his name, and he was the object of admiration, and almost idolatry, to every youthful reformer, it was understood that his Westminster committee could keep him to his professed principles only by administering strongly to his vanity, and by persuading him that at the head of the reformers he was indeed "England's glory." The firm-minded, right-principled, and venerable Major Cartwright early exposed the hollowness of his pretensions, the narrow grasp of his intellect, his slender hold of principles, and the low source of his ambition. The man is the same still, though his course of conduct has changed, as a stream is the same though it finds its way into another channel. The motive of Sir Francis—his spring of action —is the same. Applause has been his daily food. When he was young and ardent he sought it from the multitude, and now he is old and idle he seeks it from the ancient dowagers in trousers, who adorn the house of hereditary wisdom. His daily vocation was gone long before the Reform Bill was introduced. Better intellects had come into the field that had been his own exclusive possession

38 a

Reform principles were advocated with a power that he never possessed, even in his most energetic days. Instead of being at the head of the glorious army that was advancing with firm steps and well-pointed arms against the old strongholds of corruption, he had but a subaltern's command, and less than a subaltern's reputation. No shouts from admiring crowds burst upon his ear. He disliked the toil which brought him no "glory," and took the first opportunity of stealing away to the enemy's camp, and there found that flattery and deference which had become necessary to his existence.'

The next inquiry should be—Are any particular regions of the brain, or sets of organs, more extensively developed than other organs or sets in the same head? If so, their combined action will strongly influence the general course of conduct. Is the region *round, above,* and just *behind* the ear, better developed than any other? Secretiveness, Combativeness, and Destructiveness, may be presumed to predominate. Does the same occur in regard to the region in front of the ear? Acquisitiveness and Constructiveness predominate; the former seeking a gratification through the medium of the latter. Is the upper back part of the head more largely developed than other parts? Self-esteem, Love of Approbation, and Firmness may be expected to communicate their modified result to the whole character. Is the upper central part of the head similarly developed? Cautiousness, Conscientiousness, and Ideality may be expected to carry through the entire mental economy the sense of fear, of justice, and of beauty. Is a larger quantity of cerebral matter found in the upper frontal region of the brain, than in other parts of it?—we may calculate that Hope will clothe the future in brightness; that Veneration will look up with awe and reverence to a superior being; and that Benevolence will be ever ready to extend relief to the wretched. The character will thus exhibit goodness rather than greatness. In the large development of the frontal region of the brain, the strong operations of an ever-active intellect are to be found.

After acquiring a facility in estimating the influence of one predominating faculty, or of particular sets of faculties, the next object to acquire, is the modifying influence which one faculty or set of faculties will exercise over others. Veneration, for instance, when influenced by faith, hope, and charity, and aided by Conscientiousness, will regard the Supreme as all that man can desire or love, and all that he should adore and worship ; but large Veneration, where there is a deficiency of faith, hope, charity, and Conscientiousness, and an energetic development of Acquisitiveness, will make gold the object of its worship, and bow down at the shrine of wealth. The same combination, assisted by Self-esteem, will lead to the veneration of titles, of kings, and kingly state. A large Ideality, aided by large Hope, and with moderate Cautiousness and large reflecting faculties, constitutes the wild visionary projector. The same combination, with small Conscientiousness and Benevolence, and large Acquisitiveness, constitutes the gambler. A miser, in the money sense of the word, has large Self-esteem, large Acquisitiveness, moderate Benevolence, and deficient Love of Approbation. Destructiveness, Combativeness, Secretiveness, Firmness, Self-esteem, and Love of Approbation constitute the warrior ; death seeks his victims through all these organs largely developed. Cunning and stratagem result from large Secretiveness uncontrolled by Conscientiousness. Courage and perseverance result from Combativeness and Firmness ; honor, ambition, and a thirst for praise and greatness, from Self-esteem and Love of Approbation. The same combination existing in the virtuous and upright man, is hallowed and controlled by Conscientiousness, Veneration, faith, hope, and charity. The practical applications of the science are numerous and important. In mental derangement, in education, in jurisprudence, its principles and practice become interesting objects of inquiry. The phenomena of disease can only be understood by a reference to healthy action. This science, by investigating the action of the faculties in health, their relation with each other, and their connection with the organisation, with the view of arriving at the condition under which they act, is prepared to take enlarged views of medical ethics, and to suggest the proper remedy for every mental alienation. Education is, or should be, the cultivation of the mental faculties by supplying each with its proper aliment. What is the object and end of all jurisprudence, civil or criminal? It is the collection of general principles, and their application to human acts, so far as those acts affect the rights or privileges of others ; or, in other words, it is the ascertaining and embodying of the relations existing between man and man, arising from the familiarity of intercourse. But all these relations will be understood and acted upon when all the faculties are brought to act in harmonious concert with each other. Then man will have attained the ultimate perfection of his nature, and the same general principles that are now reposing in black letter, and slumbering beneath the lumber of ten thousand volumes, will bind together the framework of society, and will be constantly evolving in all their beautiful proportions of life, from the warehouse of the merchant, the shop of the mechanic, and the homestead of the agriculturist.

[These concluding remarks include the opinions of some of the most celebrated Phrenologists, as well as my own personal observation. Among other authorities may be named Dr. Spurzheim, the late Dr. Andrew Combe, Mr. George Combe, Dr. William Weir, late lecturer on Phrenology in the Andersonian University of Glasgow, Dr. Caldwell, and Mr. Amos Dean of the United States, and various articles in the Edinburgh 'Phrenological Journal,' the 'American Phrenological Journal,' and the French Phrenological Journal.']

INDEX.

A.

O.

Order, 576.

P.

Parents, advice to, 356—Parks, St. James's, in 1802, 6—Patriotic Songs for the Army and Navy, 11—Peace of 1802, 4—Pegg, Mr., poetic letter from, 227—Pitt, Rt. Hon. W., 15—Printer's chapel, a, 101—Technicalities of office, 102—Way Goose, 107—Pharaoh's Destruction, 343—Phrenology, confirmation of the truth of, 489— Motto, 498,(note)—Lecture iii, 529—Lecture iv, 561—Phrenologists' Testimonial to Author, 487—Phrenological Portraits, 402—Proud Rev. Mr., 67—Description of, 85—His ability as a preacher, 87— As a poet, 88—His proposal to the Swedenborgians to support their own poor, 178—Philoprogenitiveness, 354.

S.

Scottish Widow's Lament, 484—Secretiveness, 384—Senior, Mr. Joseph, his advice to propagate Swedenborgianism in Scotland, his assistance to the Author, 273—His death, 519—his character, 521—Servant's Hall, at the Ship Hotel, Brighton, 78, 9—Sermons, Curious, 45, 46—Sermons, Written, a villager's opinion of, 198— Soldiers, dress of, in 1802, 7—Spurzheim, Portrait of, 311—Stow, Mr. David, remarks on his Training System, 191—Squirrell, Mary Elizabeth, her case, 498—Analysis of her organisation, 494— Letter to the Author in illustration of her own case, 499—Story telling at Public Schools, its results to the Author, 44—Skull, inference of character from, 420—Skull, Swedenborg's, controversy respecting, 134—137 — Self Esteem, 129 — Size, 566—Senses External, 561.

T.

Tegg, the Publisher, early career of, 106—Temperaments, 322— Tobacco, a protest against, 461—Proposed License for street and railway carriage smokers, 462—How much the Revenue would gain from such Licenses, 462—Transubstantiation, controversy on, 244—Phrenological description of the challenger, 245—Time, 581 —Tune, 582.

V.

Veneration, 542.

W.

Wilson, Alexander, his description of Dr. Mc Hale, 417—Wit, 558— Weight, 567.

Y.

Yeldell, Dr., his visit to Coldstream, 474.

J. M. BURTON AND CO., PRINTERS, IPSWICH.

Lightning Source UK Ltd.
Milton Keynes UK
UKHW020306100223
416720UK00002B/381